Mazda RX-7 Owners Workshop Manual

by Scott Mauck
and John H Haynes Member of the Guild of Motoring Writers

Models covered:
Mazda RX-7 2 + 2 Sports Coupé

ISBN 1 85010 244 9

ABCDE
FGHIJ
K

Printed in England   *(2M2–460)*

Haynes Publishing Group
Sparkford Nr Yeovil
Somerset BA22 7JJ England

Haynes Publications, Inc
861 Lawrence Drive
Newbury Park
California 91320 USA

Acknowledgements

We are grateful for the help and co-operation of Mazda Motors of Compton, California, USA; Mazda Car Imports (GB) Ltd of Tunbridge Wells, England; and Toyo Kogyo Co Ltd of Japan. The Champion Sparking Plug Company supplied the illustrations showing the various spark plug conditions. The bodywork repair photographs used in this manual were provided by Holt/Lloyd Ltd who supply 'Turtle Wax', 'Dupli-color Holts', and other Holts range products.

Special thanks are due to White Oak Automotive of Thousand Oaks, California, USA for their invaluable assistance with the engine and transmission work.

About this manual

Its aims

The aim of this book is to help you get the best value from your car. It can do so in two ways. First it can help you decide what work must be done, even should you choose to get it done by a garage, the routine maintenance and the diagnosis and course of action when random faults occur. It is hoped that you will also use the book for the fuller and more satisfying purpose of tackling the job yourself. On the simpler jobs it may even be quicker than booking the car into a garage and going there twice, to leave and collect it. Perhaps most important, money can be saved by avoiding the costs a garage must charge to cover labor and overheads.

The book has drawings and descriptions to show the function of the various components so that their layout can be understood. Then the tasks are described and photographed in a step-by-step sequence so that even a novice can cope with complicated work.

The jobs are described assuming only normal tools are available, and not special tools. But a reasonable outfit of tools will be a worthwhile investment. Many special workshop tools produced by the makers merely speed the work, and in these cases guidance is given as to how to do the job without them. On a very few occasions when the special tool is essential to prevent damage to components, then their use is described. Though it might be possible to borrow the tool, such work may have to be entrusted to the official agent.

Using the manual

The book is divided into thirteen Chapters. Each Chapter is divided into numbered Sections which are headed in **bold type** between horizontal lines. Each Section consists of serially numbered paragraphs.

There are two types of illustration: (1) Figures which are numbered according to Chapter and sequence of occurrence in that Chapter. (2) Photographs which have a reference number in their caption. All photographs apply to the Chapter in which they occur so that the reference figure pinpoints the pertinent Section and paragraph number.

Procedures, once described in the text, are not normally repeated. If it is necessary to refer to another Chapter the reference will be given in Chapter number and Section number.

Cross-references given without use of the word 'Chapter' apply to Sections and/or paragraphs in the same Chapter (eg, 'see Section 8' means also 'in this Chapter').

When the left or right side of the car is mentioned it is as if looking forward from the rear of the car.

Great effort has been made to ensure that this book is complete and up-to-date. However, it should be realised that manufacturers continually modify their cars, even in retrospect.

Even though extreme care has been taken during the preparation of this manual, neither the publisher nor the author can accept responsibility for any errors in, or omissions from, the information given.

Introduction to the Mazda RX-7

The RX-7 represents a new breed in the line of cars from Mazda. This sports car has been designed exclusively for the now-proven rotary engine, indicating the high degree of confidence that the Toyo Kogyo Company has in this powerplant.

The progression of the novel rotary engine has not been without its drawbacks, most notably fuel economy and overall durability. New design and manufacturing techniques, including a re-shaped combustion recess, new iron alloy apex seals and a formed aluminium rotor housing, have overcome these shortfalls while still providing excellent performance and low emissions.

While some of the components which make up a rotary engine may sound foreign to a home mechanic more familiar with piston engines, the engine work is straightforward. The remainder of the car is conventional and should be no more difficult to work on than standard piston-engined automobiles.

As previously mentioned, the RX-7 has been designed for one, and only one, type of engine — the rotary. Transmission options, on the other hand, include a 4-speed manual, 5-speed manual and automatic, which are dealt with separately in this manual.

The Mazda engineers have chosen independent front suspension with MacPherson struts, coil springs and anti-roll bar up front and a coil-sprung live axle with four trailing arms at the rear. The steering is of the recirculating ball and nut type with a variable ratio. Brakes are ventilated discs up front and finned drums at the rear (standard) or disc brakes front and rear (optional on later models).

The RX-7 has gone through little in the way of changes through its production run, with principal updates in the area of emission systems. Changes and modifications are outlined in the appropriate sections, and for 1981-1985 models, in Chapter 13.

Contents

Mazda RX-7

Mazda RX-7

General dimensions and capacities

Refer to Chapter 13 for specifications and information related to 1981 through 1985 models

Dimensions

Overall length	169 in (4285 mm)
Overall width	66 in (1675 mm)
Overall height	50 in (1260 mm)
Wheelbase	95 in (2420 mm)

Gross weight

4-speed	2350 lb (1066 kg)
5-speed	2385 lb (1082 kg)
Automatic	2410 lb (1093 kg)

Capacities

Fuel tank	14·5 US gal (12.1 Imp gal, 55 liters)
Coolant	10·0 US qt (8·4 Imp qt, 9.5 liters)
Engine oil	4·4 US qt (3·7 Imp qt, 4·2 liters)
with filter change	5·5 US qt (4·6 Imp qt, 5.2 liters)
Manual transmission oil	
4-speed	1·8 US qt (1·5 Imp qt, 1·7 liters)
5-speed	1·8 US qt (1·5 Imp qt, 1·7 liters)
Automatic transmission fluid	6·6 US qt (5·5 Imp qt, 6·2 liters)
Rear axle oil	1·3 US qt (1·1 Imp qt, 1·2 liters)

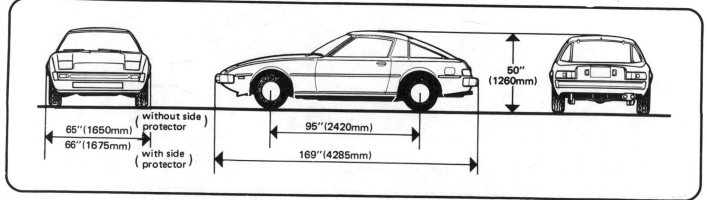

Buying spare parts and vehicle identification numbers

Buying spare parts

Spare parts are available from many sources, for example: Mazda garages, other garages and accessory shops, and motor factors. Our advice regarding spare parts is as follows:

Officially appointed Mazda garages – This is the best source of parts which are peculiar to your car and are otherwise not generally available (eg, complete engine cases, internal gearbox components, badges, interior trim etc). It is also the only place at which you should buy parts if your car is still under warranty; non-Mazda components may invalidate the warranty. To be sure of obtaining the correct parts it will always be necessary to give the storeman your car's engine and chassis number, and if possible, to take the old part along for positive identification. Remember that many parts are available on a factory exchange scheme – any parts returned should always be clean! It obviously makes good sense to go to the specialists on your car for this type of part for they are best equipped to supply you.

Other garages and accessory shops – These are often very good places to buy material and components needed for the maintenance of your car (eg, oil filters, spark plugs, bulbs, fan belts, oils and grease, touch-up paint, filler paste etc). They also sell general accessories, usually have convenient opening hours, charge lower prices and can often be found not far from home.

Imported autoparts store – Good parts stores will stock all of the more important components which wear out relatively quickly (eg, clutch components, exhaust systems, brake cylinder/pipes/hoses/seals/shoes and pads etc). Autopart stores will often provide new or reconditioned components on a part exchange basis – this can save a considerable amount of money.

Vehicle identification numbers

Whichever source of parts is used it will be essential to provide correct information concerning the model and year of manufacture, plus other pertinent information given in the vehicle identification numbers.

The vehicle identification plate is located on the dashboard on the left side. It can be seen through the windshield.

The chassis number is on the firewall of the engine compartment on the left side.

The engine serial number is stamped on the engine block on the left side of the engine.

The model plate is on the right side of the firewall.

The color codes and vehicle emission control information can be found on the underside of the hood on the left side.

The motor vehicle safety certificate and tire pressure chart are on the trailing edge of the driver's door.

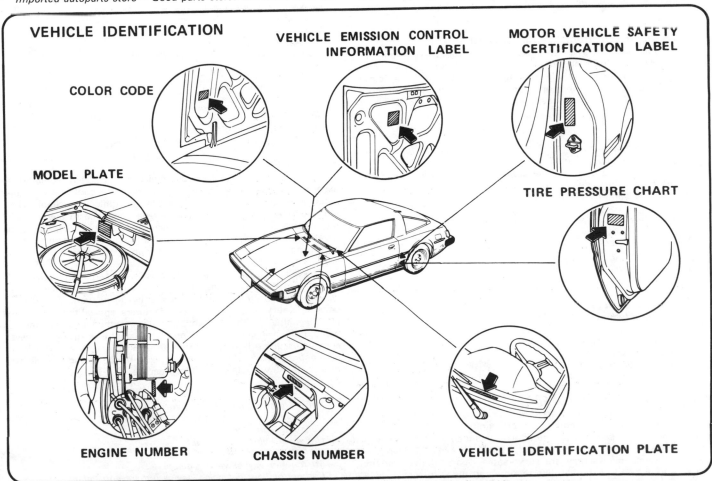

VEHICLE IDENTIFICATION

COLOR CODE

MODEL PLATE

VEHICLE EMISSION CONTROL INFORMATION LABEL

MOTOR VEHICLE SAFETY CERTIFICATION LABEL

TIRE PRESSURE CHART

ENGINE NUMBER

CHASSIS NUMBER

VEHICLE IDENTIFICATION PLATE

Tools and working facilities

Introduction

A selection of good tools is a fundamental requirement for anyone contemplating the maintenance and repair of a motor vehicle. For the owner who does not possess any, their purchase will prove a considerable expense, offsetting some of the savings made by doing-it-yourself. However, provided that the tools purchased are of good quality, they will last for many years and prove an extremely worthwhile investment.

To help the average owner to decide which tools are needed to carry out the various tasks detailed in this manual, we have compiled three lists of tools under the following headings: *Maintenance and minor repair*, *Repair and overhaul*, and *Special*. The newcomer to practical mechanics should start off with the *Maintenance and minor repair* tool kit and confine himself to the simpler jobs around the vehicle. Then, as his confidence and experience grows, he can undertake more difficult tasks, buying extra tools as, and when, they are needed. In this way, a *Maintenance and minor repair* tool kit can be built-up into a *Repair and overhaul* tool kit over a considerable period of time without any major cash outlays. The experienced do-it-yourselfer will have a tool kit good enough for most repair and overhaul procedures and will add tools from the *Special* category when he feels the expense is justified by the amount of use these tools will be put to.

It is obviously not possible to cover the subject of tools fully here. For those who wish to learn more about tools and their use there is a book entitled *How to Choose and Use Car Tools* available from the publishers of this manual.

Maintenance and minor repair tool kit

The tools given in this list should be considered as a minimum requirement if routine maintenance, servicing and minor repair operations are to be undertaken. We recommend the purchase of combination wrenches (ring one end, open-ended the other); although more expensive than open-ended ones, they do give the advantages of both types of wrench.

Combination wrenches - 6, 7, 8, 9, 10, 11, 12 & 14 mm
Adjustable wrench - 9 inch
Engine sump/gearbox/rear axle drain plug key (where applicable)
Spark plug wrench (with rubber insert)
Spark plug gap adjustment tool
Set of feeler gauges
Brake adjuster wrench (where applicable)
Brake bleed nipple wrench
Screwdriver - 4 in long x $\frac{1}{4}$ in dia (flat blade)
Screwdriver - 4 in long x $\frac{1}{4}$ in dia (cross blade)
Combination pliers - 6 inch
Hacksaw, junior
Tire pump
Tire pressure gauge
Grease gun (where applicable)
Oil can
Fine emery cloth (1 sheet)
Wire brush (small)
Funnel (medium size)

Repair and overhaul tool kit

These tools are virtually essential for anyone undertaking any major repairs to a motor vehicle, and are additional to those given in the *Maintenance and minor repair* list. Included in this list is a comprehensive set of sockets. Although these are expensive they will be found invaluable as they are so versatile - particularly if various drives are included in the set. We recommend the $\frac{1}{2}$ in square-drive type, as this can be used with most proprietary torque wrenches. If you cannot afford a socket set, even bought piecemeal, then inexpensive tubular box wrenches are a useful alternative.

The tools in this list will occasionally need to be supplemented by tools from the *Special* list.

Sockets (or box wrenches) to cover range in previous list
Reversible ratchet drive (for use with sockets)
Extension piece, 10 inch (for use with sockets)
Universal joint (for use with sockets)
Torque wrench (for use with sockets)
Vise grip - 8 inch
Ball pein hammer
Soft-faced hammer, plastic or rubber
Screwdriver - 6 in long x $\frac{15}{16}$ in dia (flat blade)
Screwdriver - 2 in long x $\frac{15}{16}$ in square (flat blade)
Screwdriver - 1$\frac{1}{2}$ in long x $\frac{1}{4}$ in dia (cross blade)
Screwdriver - 3 in long x $\frac{1}{4}$ in dia (electricians)
Pliers - electricians side cutters
Pliers - needle nosed
Pliers - circlip (internal and external)
Cold chisel - $\frac{1}{2}$ inch
Scriber (this can be made by grinding the end of a broken hacksaw blade)
Scraper (this can be made by flattening and sharpening one end of a piece of copper pipe)
Center punch
Pin punch
Hacksaw
Valve grinding tool (where applicable)
Steel rule/straight edge
Allen keys
Selection of files
Wire brush (large)
Jack stands
Jack (strong scissor or hydraulic type)

Special tools

The tools in this list are those which are not used regularly, are expensive to buy, or which need to be used in accordance with their manufacturers' instructions. Unless relatively difficult mechanical jobs are undertaken frequently, it will not be economic to buy many of these tools. Where this is the case, you could consider clubbing together with friends (or a motorists' club) to make a joint purchase, or borrowing the tools against a deposit from a local garage or tool hire specialist.

The following list contains only those tools and instruments freely available to the public, and not those special tools produced by the vehicle manufacturer specifically for its dealer network. You will find occasional references to these manufacturers' special tools in the text of this manual. Generally, an alternative method of doing the job without the vehicle manufacturers' special tool is given. However, sometimes, there is no alternative to using them. Where this is the case and the relevant tool cannot be bought or borrowed you will have to entrust the work to a franchised garage.

Valve spring compressor (where applicable)
Piston ring compressor (where applicable)
Balljoint separator
Universal hub/bearing puller
Impact screwdriver
Micrometer and/or vernier gauge
Carburetor flow balancing device (where applicable)

Dial gauge
Stroboscopic timing light
Dwell angle meter/tachometer
Universal electrical multi-meter
Cylinder compression gauge
Lifting tackle
Floor jack
Light with extension lead

Buying tools

For practically all tools, a tool dealer is the best source since he will have a very comprehensive range compared with the average garage or accessory shop. Having said that, accessory shops often offer excellent quality tools at discount prices, so it pays to shop around.

Remember, you don't have to buy the most expensive items on the shelf, but it is always advisable to steer clear of the very cheap tools. There are plenty of good tools around at reasonable prices, so ask the proprietor or manager of the shop for advice before making a purchase.

Care and maintenance of tools

Having purchased a reasonable tool kit, it is necessary to keep the tools in a clean serviceable condition. After use, always wipe off any dirt, grease and metal particles using a clean, dry cloth, before putting the tools away. Never leave them lying around after they have been used. A simple tool rack on the garage or workshop wall, for items such as screwdrivers and pliers is a good idea. Store all normal wrenches and sockets in a metal box. Any measuring instruments, gauges, meters, etc, must be carefully stored where they cannot be damaged or become rusty.

Take a little care when tools are used. Hammer heads inevitably become marked and screwdrivers lose the keen edge on their blades from time to time. A little timely attention with emery cloth or a file will soon restore items like this to a good serviceable finish.

Use of tools

Throughout this book various phrases describing techniques are used, such as:

'Drive out the bearing'.

'Undo the flange bolts evenly and diagonally'.

When two parts are held together by a number of bolts round their edge, these must be tightened to draw the parts down together flat. They must be slackened evenly to prevent the component warping. Initially the bolts should be put in finger-tight only. Then they should be tightened gradually, at first only a turn each; and diagonally, doing the one opposite that tightened first, then one to a side, followed by another opposite that, and so on. The second time each bolt is tightened, only half a turn should be given. The third time round, only quarter of a turn is given each, and this is kept up till tight. The reverse sequence is used to slacken them.

If any part has to be 'driven', such as a ball bearing out of its housing, without a proper press, it can be done with a hammer provided a few rules for use of a hammer are remembered. Always keep the component being driven straight so it will not jam. Shield whatever is being hit from damage by the hammer. Soft headed hammers are available. A drift can be used, or if the item being hit is soft, use wood. Aluminium is very easily damaged. Steel is a bit better. Hard steel, such as a bearing race, is very strong. Something threaded at the end must be protected by fitting a nut. But do not hammer the nut: the threads will tear.

If levering items with makeshift arrangement, such as screwdrivers, irretrievable damage can be done. Be sure the lever rests either on something that does not matter, or put in padding. Burrs can be filed off afterwards but indentations are there for good, and can cause leaks.

When holding something in a vise, the jaws must go on a part that is strong. If the indentation from the jaw teeth will matter, then lead or fibre jaw protectors must be used. Hollow sections are liable to be crushed.

Nuts that will not undo will sometimes move if the wrench handle is extended with another. But only extend a ring wrench, not an open jaw one. A hammer blow either to the wrench, or the bolt, may jump it out of its contact: the bolt locally welds itself in place. In extreme cases the nut will undo if driven off with drift and hammer. When reassembling such bolts, tighten them normally, not by the method needed to undo them.

For pressing things, such as a sleeve bearing into its housing, a vise, or an electric drill stand, make good presses. Pressing tools to hold each component can be arranged by using such things as socket wrenches, or short lengths of steel water pipe. Long bolts with washers can be used to draw things into place rather than pressing them.

There are often several ways of doing something. If stuck, stop and think. Special tools can readily be made out of odd bits of scrap. Accordingly, at the same time as building up a tool kit, collect useful bits of steel.

Normally all nuts or bolts have some locking arrangement. The most common is a spring washer. There are tab washers that are bent up. Castellated nuts have split pins. Self-locking nuts have special crowns that resist shaking loose. Self-locking nuts should not be reused, as the self-locking action is weakened as soon as they have been loosened at all. Tab washers should only be reused when they can be bent over in a new place. If you find a nut without any locking arrangement, check to see what it is meant to have.

Working facilities

Not to be forgotten when discussing tools, is the workshop itself. If anything more than routine maintenance is to be carried out, some form of suitable working area becomes essential.

It is appreciated that many an owner mechanic is forced by circumstances to remove an engine or similar item, without the benefit of a garage or workshop. Having done this, any repairs should always be done under the cover of a roof.

Wherever possible, any dismantling should be done on a clean flat workbench or table at a suitable working height.

Any workbench needs a vise: one with a jaw opening of 4 in (100 mm) is suitable for most jobs. As mentioned previously, some clean dry storage space is also required for tools, as well as the lubricants, cleaning fluids, touch-up paints and so on which become necessary.

Another item which may be required, and which has a much more general usage, is an electric drill with a chuck capacity of at least $\frac{5}{16}$ in (8 mm). This, together with a good range of twist drills, is virtually essential for fitting accessories such as wing mirrors and reversing lights.

Last, but not least, always keep a supply of old newspapers and clean, lint-free rags available, and try to keep any working area as clean as possible.

Wrench jaw gap comparison table

Jaw gap (in)	Wrench size
0.250	$\frac{1}{4}$ in AF
0.275	7 mm
0.313	$\frac{5}{16}$ in AF
0.315	8 mm
0.344	$\frac{11}{32}$ in AF; $\frac{1}{8}$ in Whitworth
0.354	9 mm
0.375	$\frac{3}{8}$ in AF
0.394	10 mm
0.433	11 mm
0.438	$\frac{7}{16}$ in AF
0.445	$\frac{3}{16}$ in Whitworth; $\frac{1}{4}$ in BSF
0.472	12 mm
0.500	$\frac{1}{2}$ in AF
0.512	13 mm
0.525	$\frac{1}{4}$ in Whitworth; $\frac{5}{16}$ in BSF
0.551	14 mm
0.562	$\frac{9}{16}$ in AF
0.590	15 mm
0.600	$\frac{5}{16}$ in Whitworth; $\frac{3}{8}$ in BSF
0.625	$\frac{5}{8}$ in AF
0.629	16 mm
0.669	17 mm
0.687	$\frac{11}{16}$ in AF
0.708	18 mm
0.710	$\frac{3}{8}$ in Whitworth, $\frac{7}{16}$ in BSF
0.748	19 mm
0.750	$\frac{3}{4}$ in AF
0.812	$\frac{13}{16}$ in AF
0.820	$\frac{7}{16}$ in Whitworth; $\frac{1}{2}$ in BSF

Jaw gap (in)	Wrench size	Jaw gap (in)	Wrench size
0.866	22 mm	1.417	36 mm
0.875	$\frac{7}{8}$ in AF	1.437	$1\frac{7}{16}$ in AF
0.920	$\frac{1}{2}$ in Whitworth; $\frac{9}{16}$ in BSF	1.480	$\frac{7}{8}$ in Whitworth; 1 in BSF
0.937	$\frac{15}{16}$ in AF	1.500	$1\frac{1}{2}$ in AF
0.944	24 mm	1.574	40 mm; $\frac{15}{16}$ in Whitworth
1.000	1 in AF	1.614	41 mm
1.010	$\frac{9}{16}$ in Whitworth; $\frac{5}{8}$ in BSF	1.625	$1\frac{5}{8}$ in AF
1.023	26 mm	1.670	1 in Whitworth; $1\frac{1}{8}$ in BSF
1.062	$1\frac{1}{16}$ in AF, 27 mm	1.687	$1\frac{11}{16}$ in AF
1.100	$\frac{5}{8}$ in Whitworth; $\frac{11}{16}$ in BSF	1.811	46 mm
1.125	$1\frac{1}{8}$ in AF	1.812	163 in AF
1.181	30 mm	1.860	$1\frac{1}{8}$ in Whitworth; $1\frac{1}{4}$ in BSF
1.200	$\frac{11}{16}$ in Whitworth; $\frac{3}{4}$ in BSF	1.875	$1\frac{7}{8}$ in AF
1.250	$1\frac{1}{4}$ in AF	1.968	50 mm
1.259	32 mm	2.000	2 in AF
1.300	$\frac{3}{4}$ in Whitworth; $\frac{7}{8}$ in BSF	2.050	$1\frac{1}{4}$ in Whitworth; $1\frac{3}{8}$ in BSF
1.312	$1\frac{5}{16}$ in AF	2.165	55 mm
1.390	$\frac{13}{16}$ in Whitworth; $\frac{15}{16}$ in BSF	2.362	60 mm

Jacking and towing

The jack, jack handle and spare tire are located in the rear compartment, under the glass hatch. The jack supplied from the manufacturer is intended for the use of changing a tire only, not for repair work. Raise the vehicle and use jack stands for repairs when it is necessary to get under the vehicle.

There are two jacking locations on each side of the car. These positions can be identified by indentations in the side sill, designed to mate with the top of the jack. Use the jack only in these locations.

To remove a wheel

Park on a level surface and set the parking brake firmly.

Use wheel blocks on the opposite side of the car to prevent the vehicle from rolling.

Automatic transmissions should be set in P (park), and manual transmissions in Reverse.

Remove the wheel ring and center cap with the flat end of the supplied wheel lug wrench.

With the wheel still on the ground, loosen the wheel bolts one turn

Location of jacking points

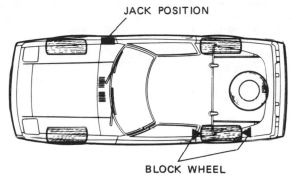

JACK POSITION

BLOCK WHEEL

Place blocks against wheel on opposite side to that being raised

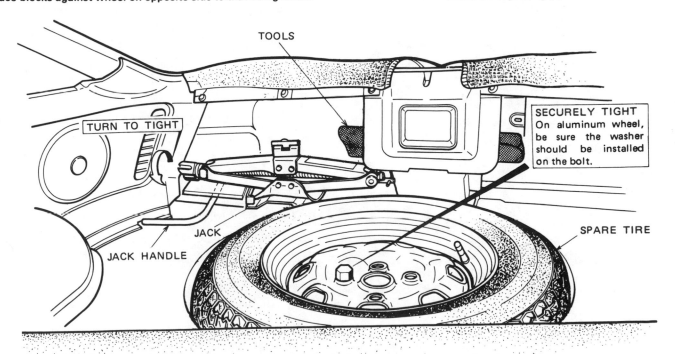

TOOLS

TURN TO TIGHT

JACK

JACK HANDLE

SECURELY TIGHT
On aluminum wheel, be sure the washer should be installed on the bolt.

SPARE TIRE

Positions of spare wheel, jack and tool bag

each. Do not remove any bolts until the wheel is off the ground.

Turn the handle of the jack clockwise until it is at the approximate height of the bottom sill. Place the jack into position at the jacking location closest to the wheel you are changing.

Insert the jack handle into the jack opening and turn it clockwise until the wheel and tire clear the ground. Before continuing make sure the vehicle is stable and there is no chance for it to slip or move.

Remove the lug bolts by turning them counter-clockwise and then remove the wheel.

Mount the spare wheel and tire in position and tighten the lug bolts by turning clockwise.

Turn the jack handle counter-clockwise and lower the vehicle to the ground. Tighten the lug bolts firmly in an 'X' pattern, and re-install the wheel ring and center cap.

Towing

Proper procedures must be followed to prevent damage to the vehicle during any towing operation. State and local laws applicable to vehicles in tow must be followed.

Vehicles with manual transmission may be towed on all four wheels if there is no damage to the transmission, rear axle or steering. If these components are damaged, a towing dolly must be used.

If your vehicle is equipped with an automatic transmission it can be towed with all four wheels on the ground for distances up to 10 miles. Vehicle speed must not be in excess of 30 mph (15 km/h). This is provided that there is no damage to the transmission, rear axle or steering systems. If there is damage to the transmission or rear axle, the vehicle should be towed with the rear wheels off the ground, or the propeller shaft disconnected.

When towing, the gearshift lever or selector lever must be in the

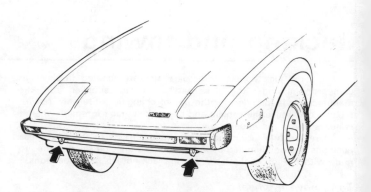

Towing hooks are located on either side of the front bumper for emergency situations

'Neutral' position and the ignition key in the 'ACC' position. The power brake assist will not be available when the engine is not running.

Towing hooks have been provided at each side of the car, just under the front bumper. These should be used only in an emergency. To pull the car out of snow, mud or some other situation, secure a cable or chain to one of the towing hooks. Make sure the towing material is strong enough for the job, as serious injury can occur from a broken or disconnected towing strap under load.

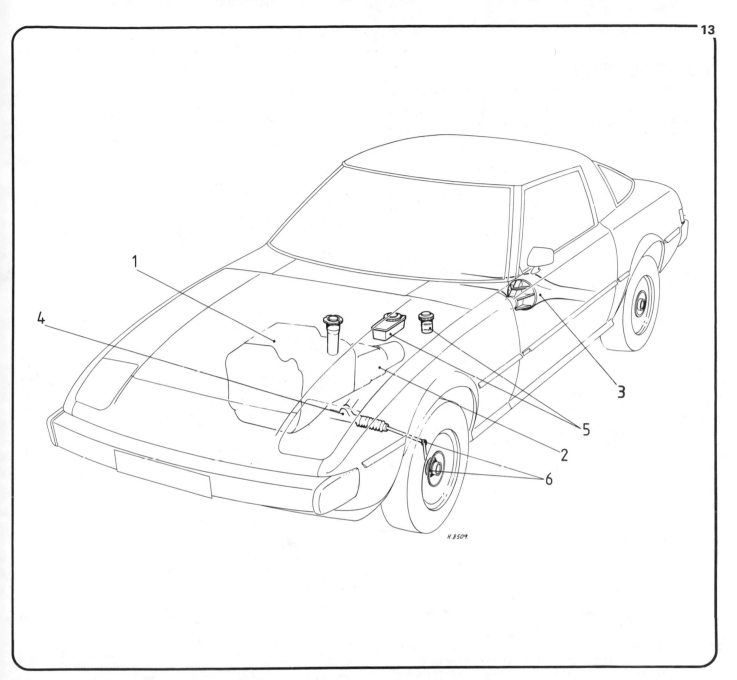

H.8509.

Recommended lubricants and fluids

Refer to Chapter 13 for specifications and information related to 1981 through 1985 models

Component or system	Grade or type
Engine (1):	
-10° to +50°C (15° to 120°F)..	20W/50
-10° to +40°C (15° to 100°F)..	20W/40
-18° to +50°C (0° to 120°F)...	10W/50
-18° to +40°C (0° to 100°F)...	10W/40
-18° to +30°C (0° to 85°F)..	10W/30
Below -18°C (0°F)	5W/20 or /30
Manual transmission (2):	
Above -18°C (0°F)	API Service GL4 or GL5 SAE 90
Below -18°C (0°F)	SAE 80
Auto transmission (2)..	M2C33F (Type F)
Rear axle (3):	
Above -18°C (0°F)	API Service GL5 SAE 90
Below -18°C (0°F)	API Service GL5 SAE 80
Steering box oil (4)...	API Service GL4 SAE 90
Brake and clutch fluid (5).......................................	FMVSS 116, DOT 3 or 4, SAE J1703C
Wheel bearings, steering balljoints, etc (6).....................	NLGI No2 multipurpose lithium-based grease

Safety first!

Professional motor mechanics are trained in safe working procedures. However enthusiastic you may be about getting on with the job in hand, do take the time to ensure that your safety is not put at risk. A moment's lack of attention can result in an accident, as can failure to observe certain elementary precautions.

There will always be new ways of having accidents, and the following points do not pretend to be a comprehensive list of all dangers; they are intended rather to make you aware of the risks and to encourage a safety-conscious approach to all work you carry out on your vehicle.

Essential DOs and DON'Ts

DON'T rely on a single jack when working underneath the vehicle. Always use reliable additional means of support, such as axle stands, securely placed under a part of the vehicle that you know will not give way.

DON'T attempt to loosen or tighten high-torque nuts (e.g. wheel hub nuts) while the vehicle is on a jack; it may be pulled off.

DON'T start the engine without first ascertaining that the transmission is in neutral (or 'Park' where applicable) and the parking brake applied.

DON'T suddenly remove the filler cap from a hot cooling system – cover it with a cloth and release the pressure gradually first, or you may get scalded by escaping coolant.

DON'T attempt to drain oil until you are sure it has cooled sufficiently to avoid scalding you.

DON'T grasp any part of the engine, exhaust or catalytic converter without first ascertaining that it is sufficiently cool to avoid burning you.

DON'T allow brake fluid or antifreeze to contact vehicle paintwork.

DON'T syphon toxic liquids such as fuel, brake fluid or antifreeze by mouth, or allow them to remain on your skin.

DON'T inhale dust – it may be injurious to health (see *Asbestos* below).

DON'T allow any spilt oil or grease to remain on the floor – wipe it up straight away, before someone slips on it.

DON'T use ill-fitting spanners or other tools which may slip and cause injury.

DON'T attempt to lift a heavy component which may be beyond your capability – get assistance.

DON'T rush to finish a job, or take unverified short cuts.

DON'T allow children or animals in or around an unattended vehicle.

DO wear eye protection when using power tools such as drill, sander, bench grinder etc, and when working under the vehicle.

DO use a barrier cream on your hands prior to undertaking dirty jobs – it will protect your skin from infection as well as making the dirt easier to remove afterwards; but make sure your hands aren't left slippery.

DO keep loose clothing (cuffs, tie etc) and long hair well out of the way of moving mechanical parts.

DO remove rings, wristwatch etc, before working on the vehicle – especially the electrical system.

DO ensure that any lifting tackle used has a safe working load rating adequate for the job.

DO keep your work area tidy – it is only too easy to fall over articles left lying around.

DO get someone to check periodically that all is well, when working alone on the vehicle.

DO carry out work in a logical sequence and check that everything is correctly assembled and tightened afterwards.

DO remember that your vehicle's safety affects that of yourself and others. If in doubt on any point, get specialist advice.

IF, in spite of following these precautions, you are unfortunate enough to injure yourself, seek medical attention as soon as possible.

Asbestos

Certain friction, insulating, sealing, and other products – such as brake linings, brake bands, clutch linings, torque converters, gaskets, etc – contain asbestos. *Extreme care must be taken to avoid inhalation of dust from such products since it is hazardous to health.* If in doubt, assume that they *do* contain asbestos.

Fire

Remember at all times that petrol (gasoline) is highly flammable. Never smoke, or have any kind of naked flame around, when working on the vehicle. But the risk does not end there – a spark caused by an electrical short-circuit, by two metal surfaces contacting each other, by careless use of tools, or even by static electricity built up in your body under certain conditions, can ignite petrol vapour, which in a confined space is highly explosive.

Always disconnect the battery earth (ground) terminal before working on any part of the fuel or electrical system, and never risk spilling fuel on to a hot engine or exhaust.

It is recommended that a fire extinguisher of a type suitable for fuel and electrical fires is kept handy in the garage or workplace at all times. Never try to extinguish a fuel or electrical fire with water.

Fumes

Certain fumes are highly toxic and can quickly cause unconsciousness and even death if inhaled to any extent. Petrol (gasoline) vapour comes into this category, as do the vapours from certain solvents such as trichloroethylene. Any draining or pouring of such volatile fluids should be done in a well ventilated area.

When using cleaning fluids and solvents, read the instructions carefully. Never use materials from unmarked containers – they may give off poisonous vapours.

Never run the engine of a motor vehicle in an enclosed space such as a garage. Exhaust fumes contain carbon monoxide which is extremely poisonous; if you need to run the engine, always do so in the open air or at least have the rear of the vehicle outside the workplace.

If you are fortunate enough to have the use of an inspection pit, never drain or pour petrol, and never run the engine, while the vehicle is standing over it; the fumes, being heavier than air, will concentrate in the pit with possibly lethal results.

The battery

Never cause a spark, or allow a naked light, near the vehicle's battery. It will normally be giving off a certain amount of hydrogen gas, which is highly explosive.

Always disconnect the battery earth (ground) terminal before working on the fuel or electrical systems.

If possible, loosen the filler plugs or cover when charging the battery from an external source. Do not charge at an excessive rate or the battery may burst.

Take care when topping up and when carrying the battery. The acid electrolyte, even when diluted, is very corrosive and should not be allowed to contact the eyes or skin.

If you ever need to prepare electrolyte yourself, always add the acid slowly to the water, and never the other way round. Protect against splashes by wearing rubber gloves and goggles.

When jump starting a car using a booster battery, for negative earth (ground) vehicles, connect the jump leads in the following sequence: First connect one jump lead between the positive (+) terminals of the two batteries. Then connect the other jump lead first to the negative (–) terminal of the booster battery, and then to a good earthing (ground) point on the vehicle to be started, at least 18 in (45 cm) from the battery if possible. Ensure that hands and jump leads are clear of any moving parts, and that the two vehicles do not touch. Disconnect the leads in the reverse order.

Mains electricity

When using an electric power tool, inspection light etc, which works from the mains, always ensure that the appliance is correctly connected to its plug and that, where necessary, it is properly earthed (grounded). Do not use such appliances in damp conditions and, again, beware of creating a spark or applying excessive heat in the vicinity of fuel or fuel vapour.

Ignition HT voltage

A severe electric shock can result from touching certain parts of the ignition system, such as the HT leads, when the engine is running or being cranked, particularly if components are damp or the insulation is defective. Where an electronic ignition system is fitted, the HT voltage is much higher and could prove fatal.

Routine maintenance

Refer to Chapter 13 for specifications and information related to 1981 through 1985 models

The following pages detail the routine servicing procedures which should be carried out on the car. These maintenance functions have the prime purpose of ensuring the least wear and optimum efficiency from the vehicle components.

But servicing your car at routine intervals serves another useful and important purpose. By looking the car over, top to bottom, you have the opportunity to spot trouble areas before they can become expensive repairs or, even worse, a danger to you and your passengers. Loose nuts or bolts, leaks and rusted areas can be relatively minor problems if caught early. Intervals should be calculated monthly or in miles, whichever comes first.

1   Weekly and/or whenever you refuel

Check the tire pressures. This should be done when the tires are cold, as heat is generated quickly inside the tire after running. The proper cold pressures for both front and rear tires are 26 psi (1.8 kg/cm² for Canadian vehicles).

Check the engine oil level. The car should be on level ground with the engine off for at least five minutes. Oil level should not fall below the 'L' mark on the dipstick, nor should the system be overfilled above the 'F' indicator. The distance between these marks on the dipstick

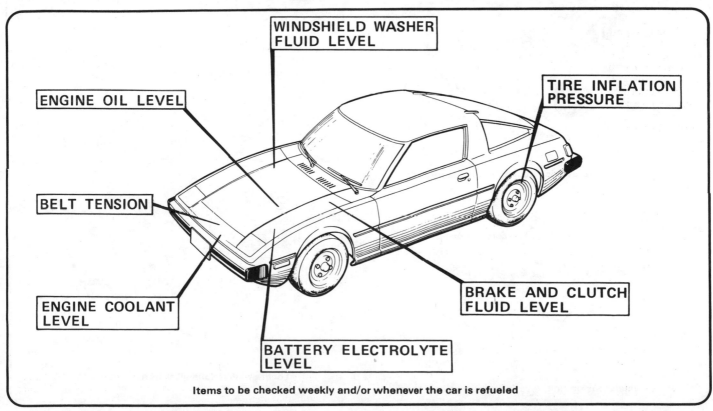

Items to be checked weekly and/or whenever the car is refueled

represents one US quart (one liter, 0.9 Imperial quart). Use only the recommended engine oil.

Check the engine coolant level. The radiator should be completely full and the coolant in the plastic reservoir between the 'Full' and 'Low' marks. If the level is at or near the 'Low' mark a mixture of ethylene glycol antifreeze and water at a 50/50 ratio should be added to bring the level up to the 'Full' mark. Should it be necessary to remove the radiator cap, do so only after the engine has cooled. Wrap a thick cloth around the cap and release the pressure slowly by turning the cap to the first stop. With all pressure gone, push down and remove the cap, still using the cloth for protection.

Check the brake and clutch fluid levels. Add fluid according to manufacturer's specifications.

Check and/or adjust the drive belts on the engine. The tension can be checked by applying pressure midway between the pulleys with your finger. The deflection should be approximately $\frac{1}{2}$ inch. The alternator and air pump belts are adjusted by loosening the mounting and adjusting bar bolts, moving the air pump or alternator to obtain the correct belt tension, and then tightening the bolts. The air conditioner belt is adjusted by turning the adjusting bolt on the idler pulley until the correct tension is obtained.

Check the electrolyte level in the battery. If it is low, add distilled water to a point approximately 0.4 to 0.8 inches above the cell plates. Check to make sure the battery is securely mounted and that it is clean and dry.

Check the windshield washer fluid level. Do not fill with radiator antifreeze.

After first 2000 miles (3000 km) — new cars

Change the engine oil, replacing with the specified grade for your

area. Change while the engine oil is hot and allow it to drain for about ten minutes. See Chapter 2.

Inspect the engine oil level warning system for proper operation. Refer to Chapter 2 for this.

Adjust the idle speed and idle mixture on the carburetor. Refer to Chapter 3 for this adjustment.

Adjust the ignition timing as detailed in Chapter 4.

Inspect the distributor breaker points. If they are not badly pitted or worn, they can be cleaned with a fine stone like those used for sharpening knives. Refer to Chapter 4 for more information on this operation.

Inspect the engine coolant level warning system as detailed in Chapter 2.

Change the oil in manual transmissions, replacing with gear oil of the proper viscosity. Add lubricant until the level reaches the bottom of the filler plug hole.

Every 7.5 months or 7500 miles (12,000 km)

Change the engine oil.

Inspect the battery electrolyte level. Check the specific gravity by using a hydrometer; if the reading is low the battery must be recharged.

Inspect the clutch fluid level in the reservoir.

Inspect the manual transmission oil level.

Inspect the automatic transmission fluid level. This should be done with the vehicle on level ground and with the engine operating at idle for about two minutes. Move the selector lever through all the gear positions and set it to the 'P' (Park) position. Remove the dipstick located at the rear of the engine and wipe it clean. Replace it fully, remove it once again and check that the level is between the 'L' and 'F' on the dipstick. If required, add fluid through the filler tube.

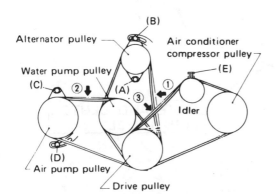

Engine coolant level is checked at the reservoir

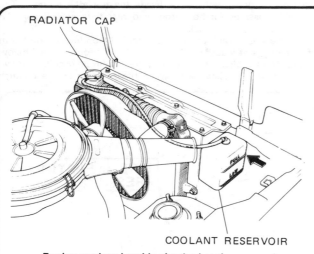

Points at which tension on the various drive belts is checked

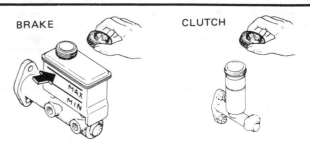

Checking brake and clutch fluid levels

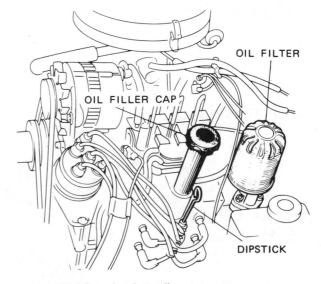

Location of various oil system components

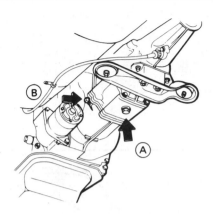

Drain plug (A) and filler plug (B) for transmission

Inspect the axle oil level.

On new cars, replace the rear axle oil at this stage. This is done by removing both the drain and filler plugs while the oil is still warm. After draining completely, wipe off the surfaces and fill with fresh oil until the level reaches the bottom of the filler plug hole.

Inspect the steering wheel for free play (Chapter 11).

Check the brake fluid level in the reservoir.

Inspect the brake pedal, clutch pedal and parking brake.

Inspect the disc brake pads for wear.

On new cars, inspect and tighten any loose nuts or bolts on the chassis or bodywork.

Every 15 months or 15,000 miles (24,000 km)

Replace the oil filter.

Inspect the cooling system fluid level, and check all hoses and connections for wear and leaks.

Check the seat belt warning system (Chapter 12).

Check the engine oil level warning system (Chapter 2).

Visually inspect all brake lines, hoses and connections (Chapter 9).

Check the level of oil in the steering box.

Examine the rear brake linings for wear.

Inspect brake servo and hoses.

Examine and tighten any loose nuts and bolts on the chassis or bodywork.

Every 30 months or 30,000 miles (48,000 km)

Adjust drive belts other than the air pump drive belt (if fitted).

Replace the air cleaner element.

Replace the spark plugs, ensuring that the replacements are recommended for use with the RX-7 engine.

Drain the cooling system and refill with a 50/50 mixture of ethylene glycol antifreeze *for aluminium engine parts* and water.

Inspect the engine coolant level warning system (Chapter 2).

Change the manual transmission oil.

Change the rear axle oil.

Evacuate the brake fluid from the hydraulic system and replace with fresh fluid, bleeding the system carefully (Chapter 9).

Grease the front wheel bearings.

Inspect the steering linkages and ball joints.

Inspect the exhaust system heat shields.

Appearance care

It is important to care for your car's components, both appearance-wise and mechanically, to keep up its value as well as prevent corrosive action which would lead to major replacements.

Use a mild detergent and soft sponge to wash the exterior of the car and rinse immediately with clear water. Owners who live in coastal regions and where salt or chemicals are used on the roads should wash the finish religiously to prevent damage to the finish. Do not wash the car in direct sunlight or when the metal is warm. To remove road tar, insects or tree sap use a tar remover rather than a knife or sharp objects which could scratch the surface.

A good coat of wax or polish may be your best protection against the elements. Use a good grade of polish or wax suitable for a high-quality synthetic finish. Do not use a wax or polish which contains large amounts of abrasives as these will scratch the finish.

Bright metal parts can be protected with wax or a chrome preservative. During winter months or in coastal regions apply a heavier coating or, if necessary, use a non-corrosive compound like petroleum jelly for protection. Do not use abrasive cleaners, strong detergents or materials like steel wool on chrome or anodized aluminium parts as these may damage the protective coating and cause discoloration or deterioration.

Interior surfaces can be wiped clean with a damp cloth or with cleaners specifically designed for car interior fabrics. Carefully read the manufacturer's instructions and test any commercial cleaners on an inconspicuous area first. The carpet should be vacuumed regularly and can be covered with mats.

Cleaning the mechanical parts of the car serves two useful functions. First, it focuses your attention on parts which may be starting to fail, allowing you to fix or replace them before they cause problems. Second, it is much more pleasant to work on parts which are relatively clean. You will still get dirty on major repair jobs, but it will be less extreme. Large areas like the firewall and inner fender panels should be brushed with detergent, allowed to soak for about 15 minutes, and then carefully rinsed clean. Cover ignition and carburetor parts with plastic to prevent moisture from penetrating these critical components.

Fault diagnosis

This section provides an easy-reference guide to the more common faults which may occur during the operation of your Mazda RX-7. These faults and their probable causes are grouped under their respective systems, eg. 'Engine', 'Cooling system', etc, and then cross-referred to the chapter, section and paragraph which deals with the problem. For example, the reference '1/5:2' applies to Chapter 1, section 5, paragraph 2.

Remember that successful fault diagnosis is not a mysterious 'black art' practiced only by professional mechanics, it's simply the result of a bit of knowledge combined with an intelligent, systematic approach to the problem. Always work by a process of elimination, starting with the simplest solution and working through to the most complex — and never overlook the obvious. Even the most thorough and organised motorists have been known to forget to fill the gas tank or have left the car lights on overnight, so don't assume that you are above such oversights.

Finally, always get clear in your own mind why a fault has occurred and take steps to ensure that it doesn't happen again. If the electrical system fails owing to a poor connection, check all other connections in the system to make sure that they don't fail as well; if a particular fuse continues to blow, find out why — don't just go on replacing fuses. Remember, failure of a small component can often be indicative of potential failure or incorrect functioning of a more important component or system.

Engine

1   Engine will not crank or cranks sluggishly

1   Turn the ignition key to the 'ON' position and switch on some of the electrical systems such as windshield wipers, headlights, etc. If these fail to function, battery failure is indicated. Check the battery itself (10/2:1) and the main connections to the battery (10/2:5).
2   If the headlights work normally, turn the ignition key to the 'START' position with the headlights switched on. If the lights and the ignition warning light dim, this again indicates that the battery is discharged or the connections are poor.
3   If the headlights stay bright and the warning light doesn't dim when the ignition key is turned, this suggests a fault in the wiring between the ignition switch and the starter motor. First, check all electrical connections in this system, then check the ignition switch by using a short length of wire to short out between the white/red and black/yellow wires at the back of the switch. If this causes the starter to crank the engine, then the ignition switch is at fault and must be replaced.
4   If the switch works correctly, check the solenoid (4/13:2) then the starter motor itself (4/11:1). In cars with automatic transmission the inhibitor switch should be checked for correct adjustment and operation (6/7:1).

2   Engine cranks but fails to start

1   First check for obvious causes such as lack of fuel or incorrect operation of choke.
2   Check that the plugs are sparking. To do this, remove one of the leading plugs (4/3:1) and connect it to its plug cap. Holding the plug cap with a pair of insulated pliers, touch the threaded metal part of the plug body to ground (*not* to part of the alloy engine casing), crank the engine and look for a spark jumping between the three outer plug electrodes and the central electrode.

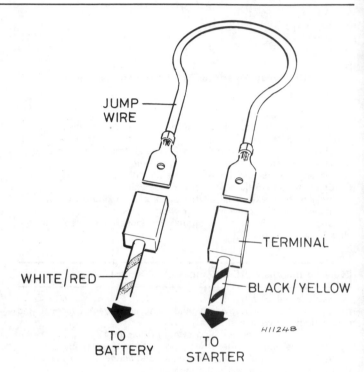

JUMP WIRE

TERMINAL

WHITE/RED

BLACK/YELLOW

H11248

TO BATTERY

TO STARTER

Checking ignition switch

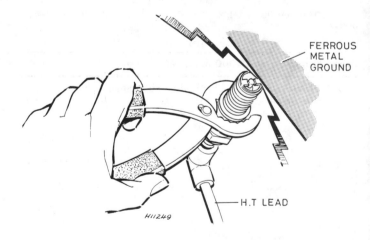

FERROUS METAL GROUND

H.T LEAD

H11249

Checking for proper spark at plug

3   If no spark can be seen jumping the plug electrode cap then current is not reaching the plugs. First ensure that the distributor cap is free from cracks and moisture and that electrical connections are sound, then check back through the ignition system (4/1:1).
4   If there is a strong spark at the plug, the fuel system must be examined. To locate the area of the possible fault, first switch on the ignition and check that the fuel pump is clicking. The pump is located

at the rear of the car. If there is no clicking, check the fuel pump wiring (3/3:1) and if no fault can be found in the wiring the pump must be checked (3/3:1), and replaced if faulty (3/4:1).

5 If the fuel pump is operating normally, remove the carburetor air cleaner and check the carburetor sight glass to see if the fuel level is maintained with the fuel pump operating. If not, then fuel is not reaching the carburetor and the fuel system between the tank and carburetor must be checked (3/3:1).

6 If fuel is reaching the carburetor, check for blocked or improperly seated jets or air bleeds, and check the operation of the air vent solenoid valve (3/37:10).

3 Engine difficult to start when cold

1 Check all electrical and fuel systems as detailed in Section 2 of this chapter.

2 Check the choke valve to ensure that it is closing fully when choke knob is pulled out (3/17:1).

3 Check for faulty operation of the anti-afterburn valve (3/34:1).

4 Check for air leaks in the carburetor or inlet manifold. A useful trick here is to use a length of flexible tube as a stethoscope; hold one end to your ear and move the free end to areas of possible leakage and listen for hissing sounds while the engine is running or is being cranked over.

5 Check for defects in the sub-zero starting assist system (if installed) (3/12:1).

6 Examine fuses and fusible links for possible failure or faulty connection (10/5:1).

7 Check ignition timing (4/9:1).

8 Have your Mazda dealer check the engine for low compression ratio; note that conventional compression test equipment cannot be used on the rotary engine.

4 Engine difficult to start when hot

1 Check through electrical and fuel systems as detailed in Section 2 of this chapter.

2 Check for incorrect adjustment of the idle screw (3/15:1).

3 Examine the operation of the anti-afterburn valve (3/34:1).

4 Check for defects in the hot start assist system (3/14:1).

5 Examine fuses and fusible links for possible failure or faulty connection (10/5:1).

6 Check ignition timing (4/9:1).

7 Have your Mazda dealer check the engine for low compression; note that conventional compression test equipment cannot be used on the rotary engine.

5 Poor performance during warm-up, with fast engine idle and poor engine response with choke pulled out

1 Check for a defect in the choke system, ensuring that the choke valve is closing fully when choke knob is pulled out (3/22:1).

2 Check the throttle valve opening angle when the choke knob is pulled out (3/27:1).

3 Check the carburetor for blocked or improperly seated jets or air bleeds (3/25:1).

4 Check for improper operation of ignition control system (if fitted), (3/32:1).

5 Check for defects in the air inlet temperature control valve (3/8:1), the idle compensator (3/10:1), the anti-afterburn valve (3/34:1) and the coasting valve (manual transmission only), (3/34:1).

6 Check that the automatic choke release system is working correctly (3/17:1).

7 Check that the coolant thermostat is operating correctly (2/8:1) and that there are no restrictions to the cooling system and underhood ventilation (2/1:1).

6 Engine idles erratically and often stalls at idling

1 Check adjustment of the carburetor idle screw (3/15:1).

2 Check the carburetor for correct float level (3/26:1), and examine for blocked or incorrectly seated jets or air bleeds (3/25:1).

3 Check for improper initial opening angle of primary throttle valve (3/26:1) and for poorly seated secondary throttle valve (3/26:1).

4 In vehicles with manual transmission, check the richer solenoid (3/25:8).

5 Examine the ignition system for poor or loose connections, and the spark plugs for fouling or incorrect electrode gaps (4/3:1).

6 Check for water in the fuel. Drain the fuel tank if necessary (3/5:1) and refill with fresh fuel.

7 Check for air leaks in the carburetor and inlet manifold (see 3:4, this chapter) and look for faults in the inlet air temperature control valve (3/8:1).

8 Check for defects or improper operation of the idle compensator (3/10:1), and altitude compensator (3/11:1).

9 Check the anti-afterburn valve (3/34:1), the coasting valve (if fitted) (3/34:1) and the operation of the dash pot (if fitted), (3/34:10).

10 Check the air control valve in the emission control system (3/31:22).

11 Check ignition timing (4/9:1).

12 Have a Mazda dealer check engine compression; note that conventional compression testing equipment cannot be used on the rotary engine.

7 Lack of power, poor acceleration

1 Check through fuel and electrical systems to ensure that they are functioning correctly (Section 2). In particular examine the spark plugs for evidence of poor combustion or incorrect fuel/air mixture.

2 Examine the air cleaner filter for signs of blockage and replace it if in doubt (3/8:1).

3 Examine the crankcase and evaporative emission control systems and in particular check for defects in the check and cut valve (3/37:13) and for clogged hoses in the evaporative line (3/37:1).

4 Check the automatic transmission, particularly for faults in the kickdown control (3/35:1).

5 With manual transmission, check for clutch slip by starting the engine, putting the transmission into top gear and gently raising the clutch with the foot brake firmly applied. Clutch slip is apparent when the engine continues to run without stalling.

6 Check ignition timing (4/9:1).

7 Have a Mazda dealer check engine compression; note that conventional compression testing equipment cannot be used on the rotary engine.

8 Erratic performance during cruising

1 Check the fuel system for faulty fuel pump (3/3:1) and dirty or clogged fuel filter (3/2:1).

2 Check for faults in the ignition advance system (4/5:1).

3 Ensure that the air cleaner element is clean (3/8:1).

9 Car surges while decelerating

1 Check for faults in the anti-afterburn valve (3/34:8). In cars with manual transmission also check the coasting valve (3/34:1) and the dash pot adjustment (3/34:1).

2 Examine the exhaust emission control system for faults in the air control valve (3/30:22) or the check valve (3/30:1).

3 Check idle screw adjustment (3/15:1).

4 Check the ignition system for incorrect timing (4/9:1).

5 In cars with manual transmission check the operation of the richer solenoid (3/25:8).

6 Check the operation of the ignition control system (if fitted), (3/32:1).

10 Poor engine braking

1 Check for delayed return of secondary throttle valve (3/34:1).

2 Check for faults in the anti-afterburn valve (3/34:8). In cars with manual transmission also check the dash pot adjustment (3/34:10).

Cooling system

1   Coolant overheating

1   Examine the level of coolant in the reservoir. If this is below the 'LOW' mark and the coolant level warning light on the dash panel has not lit up, top up the coolant (2/1:1) and remove and check the coolant level sensor (2/10:1).
2   If there is evidence that the system is losing fluid – indicated by the frequent need to top up the reservoir – examine all hoses and fitting for signs of leaks. Tighten hose clips and replace hoses as necessary.
3   Examine the fan drive belt for correct tension (2/11:1).
4   Check the engine fan drive (2/11:1) and if the fan revolves at less than the recommended rate of 1400 ± 200 rpm the fan drive clutch must be replaced (2/12:1).
5   If the engine overheats rapidly but the lower part of the radiator remains cool, remove and check the thermostat (2/8:1), replacing it with a new unit if necessary.
6   Check for weak fuel/air mixture by removing one of the leading spark plugs and examine the condition of the electrodes. A weak mixture may cause engine overheating.
7   Check that the ignition timing is correct (4/9:1).
8   If the thermostat is operating correctly but there is an apparent lack of flow through the cooling system, drain the system (2/3:1) and flush through with a proprietary flushing product. CAUTION: before using any such product first ensure that it is suitable for use in alloy engines.

2   Coolant too cool

1   Remove the thermostat and check to see if it is jammed open (2/8:1). Replace if necessary.

Electrical system

1   Battery rapidly discharges

1   Examine the alternator drive belt for slipping or wear and adjust or replace as necessary (10/7:1).
2   Check electrolyte (fluid) level in battery and top up if required (10/2:1).
3   Check lighting circuit for short causing continual battery drain (see wiring diagrams, Chapter 10).
4   Clean and check settings of regulator unit (10/10:1). Replace regulator if faulty.
5   Check to see if the alternator is working correctly (10/7:1). If not, check the brushes and clean or replace as necessary (10/9:1). Check the stator coils and rotor windings (10/9:1) and if either is faulty the alternator must be replaced (10/8:1).

2   Wiper motor fails to work

1   Check fuse and replace if necessary (10/5:1).
2   Check motor wiring for loose, disconnected or broken connections (10/21:1).
3   Check motor brushes and armature, and replace if necessary (10/21:1).
4   Check the field coils, and if faulty replace complete motor unit (10/21:1).

3   Wiper motor works very slowly and draws excess current

1   Check the commutator for dirt, grease or burning and replace if necessary (10/21:1).
2   Check the drive linkage for bending or lack of lubrication (10/21:1).
3   Examine the wiper arm spindle. If it is binding or damaged, overhaul or replace (10/21:1).
4   Check for lubrication or incorrect alignment of the armature bearings (10/21:1).
5   Examine the armature and if it is badly worn or faulty, replace it with a new armature (10/21:1).

4   Wiper motor works very slowly but draws little current

1   Check brushes for wear and replace if necessary (10/21:1).
2   Check commutator for dirt, grease or burning and clean if necessary (10/21:1).
3   Check the armature for wear or damage and overhaul or replace as necessary (10/21:1).

5   Wiper motor works but blades remain static

1   Check drive linkage and replace if faulty (10/21:1).
2   Examine wiper motor gearbox parts and replace the wiper motor if they are badly worn (10/21:1).

6   Headlights do not come on

1   Check bulbs and replace if necessary (10/16:1).
2   Test appropriate fuse and replace if necessary (10/5:1).
3   Check all wiring connection; check wiring for breaks or damage.

7   Headlights come on but fade out

1   If the engine is not running when symptom occurs, recharge battery.

8   Lights give poor illumination

1   If lamp glasses are dirty, clean them thoroughly.
2   Check the reflectors for dirt or corrosion and replace if necessary (10/16:1).
3   Check adjustment of lights (10/14:1).
4   If headlight unit is old and badly discolored, replace (10/16:1).
5   Check the electrical circuit for poor connections or worn wiring.

9   Lights flash on and off intermittently, especially over bumps

1   Examine the wiring for faulty connections or broken wires and check that there is good ground return through the mountings (10/16:1).

10 Headlights do not raise when retractor switch is turned to 'raise' position

1   Raise the headlight manually (10/15:1) and check retractor wiring and fuse (10/15:1).

11 Horn does not work

1   Check fuse and replace if necessary (10/5:1).
2   Examine horn button (11/20:1) and check for loose connections.
3   Remove the horn and readjust (10/22:1).

12 Horn remains on

1   Remove the appropriate fuse (10/5:1) to stop the horn, then check button and relay for jamming (11/20:1).

13 Horn tone poor

1   Check wiring for loose connections (10/22:1).
2   Disconnect each horn in turn and check (10/22:1).

14 Temp/fuel gauge always reads maximum

1   Check for defects in wiring, sender unit or gauge (10/24:1).

15 Temp/fuel gauge gives no reading

1   Check for loose or broken wiring (10/24:1).
2   Check fuse and replace if necessary (10/5:1).

16 No reading on tachometer

1   Check for leading ignition defect by testing ignition at plug (2:2, this chapter).
2   Remove panel (10/24:1) and check wiring for circuit or tachometer defect (10/24:1).

17 Tachometer reading wildly inaccurate

1   Tachometer faulty – replace (10/25:1).

Clutch – manual transmission

1   Clutch judders when taking up drive

1   Check engine and gearbox mounts for loose bolts or worn mountings (1/24:1) and tighten or replace as necessary.
2   Examine clutch for worn or oily friction surfaces (5/3:1). Replace parts as required and, if necessary, rectify any oil leaks.
3   Check the pilot bearing in the flywheel center and replace if rough, loose or damaged (1/19:1).
4   Examine propeller shaft for looseness or wear in the universal joints (7/4:1).

2   Clutch drag, ie, failure to disengage so that gears cannot be meshed

1   The clutch friction plate may be jammed on the splines. This is usually apparent if the car has been left standing for some time. Engage top gear, apply the parking brake, depress the clutch pedal and crank the engine; this may free the clutch plate. If the friction plate is badly jammed the engine will not turn – in any case, a solution of this kind is only temporary and the friction plate should be examined and, if necessary, renewed at the earliest opportunity (5/2:1).
2   Examine the pressure plate assembly for damage or misalignment and replace if necessary (5/3:1).

3   Clutch slip, ie, increase in engine speed does not result in increased car speed, especially on hills

1   Adjust clutch clearance to give full engagement of clutch (5/5:1).
2   Examine clutch friction surfaces for wear (beyond further adjustment) and for oil on the clutch surfaces. Replace friction plate and cure source of oil leak (5/3:1).

Manual transmission

1   Transmission baulks on downshifts. Gear shift slow

1   Synchromesh cones worn, split or damaged. If not too severe, double declutching on downshifts will overcome this problem. If severe, the transmission will require stripping and synchro-rings replaced (6/5:1).

2   Gears jump out of mesh

1   This is caused by either worn shift forks or synchro grooves; worn detent grooves in the selector rod; excessive gear end-float. In all cases the transmission will have to be stripped and repairs made (6/5:1).

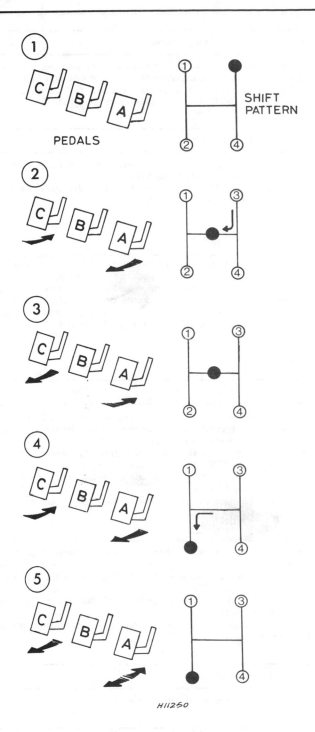

H11250

Double de-clutching

A - accelerator
B - brake;
C - clutch.
  Black spot represents gearshift lever position.
1   Transmission in 3rd gear
2   Raise accelerator, depress clutch and shift to neutral
3   With shift in neutral, raise clutch and 'blip' accelerator to synchronize gearbox revs with engine revs
4   Raise accelerator, depress clutch and shift to 2nd gear
5   Raise clutch and set accelerator according to requirements - if engine braking is required for deceleration, keep accelerator raised; if downshift has been made to achieve better acceleration depress accelerator. These actions should be practiced until they can be fused together in one fluid, consecutive series of motions

3   Excessive transmission noise

1   Check oil level and top up if necessary (6/3:30).
2   Noise may be caused by worn needle roller bearings, bushings or gear teeth. Shaft snap rings may be too thin. In all cases, strip the gearbox, examine, and replace parts as necessary (6/5:1).

4   Difficulty in engaging gears

1   Check shift linkage for damage or excessive wear (6 Part II/5:1).
2   Check adjustment of clutch (5/5:1).
3   Examine the shift rods and interlock pins for damage or excessive wear and replace if necessary (6/5:1).

Automatic transmission

For all problems related to the automatic transmission it is recommended that you consult your nearest Mazda dealer. The complexity of this kind of transmission and the requirement for many special tools makes it unsuitable for the do-it-yourself mechanic to tackle. However, do ensure that the automatic transmission fluid is kept topped up to the recommended level (6 Part II/4:1).

Drive train

1   Excessive vibration

1   Check rear wheel bearings for looseness or wear (8/2:1).
2   Check for loose securing bolts at the flange where the propeller shaft joins with the differential housing (7/2:1).
3   Examine the propeller shaft universal joints for bearing wear and replace if necessary (7/4:1).
4   Check differential bearings and axle shaft bearings for wear and replace if necessary (8/2:1).
5   Have the complete propeller shaft dynamically checked for balance and distortion (7/3:1).

2   Knock or 'clonk' when taking up drive or changing gear

1   Check for loose securing bolts where the propeller shaft joins with the differential housing (7/2:1).
2   Examine universal joint in propeller shaft for bearing wear and replace if necessary (7/6:1).
3   Check for looseness and wear in rear axle locating mounts and shock absorber mounts (11/15:1).

3   Rear axle noisy on turns

1   Check differential gear for wear (8/4:1).

4   Rear axle noisy under all driving conditions

1   Examine differential for worn or incorrectly adjusted ring and pinion gear (8/4:1).

Braking system

1   Brake pedal travels almost to floor before brakes operate

1   Check master cylinder reservoir for fluid level; top up if necessary.
2   Check brake pads and linings for excessive wear and replace if necessary (9/2:1 and 9/8:1).
3   Examine all brake lines and hoses for fractures or leaking and replace immediately if necessary (9/1:1).
4   Remove master cylinder and inspect seals, piston cups, etc (9/13:1).

2   Brake pedal feels springy

1   New pads or linings not yet bedded in.
2   Examine the brake discs and drums for excessive wear. If scoring is light the surfaces can be skimmed at a machine shop, otherwise the disc or drum will have to be replaced (9/6:1).
3   Examine the master cylinder bolts for looseness and tighten if necessary (9/13:1).

3   Brake pedal feels spongy and soggy

1   Bleed the system to remove any possible air in the hydraulic lines (9/17:1).
2   Examine the calipers and wheel cylinders for leaking and repair or renew as necessary (9/5:1 and 9/12:1).
3   Check for leaks in the master cylinder by examining the fluid for bubbles. Overhaul or replace master cylinder as necessary (9/14:1).
4   Examine brake lines and hoses for leakage and replace immediately if necessary (9/1:1).
5   Examine all unions in the hydraulic system, and tighten or replace as necessary (9/1:1).

4   Excessive brake pedal pressure required to slow car

1   Check the servo unit for faulty connections and tighten or replace as necessary (9/16:1).
2   Examine brake pads and linings for excessive wear and replace if necessary (9/2:1 and 9/8:1).
3   Have you changed the pads or linings to ones of harder specification? If so, revert to standard items.
4   Check friction surfaces for contamination by oil, grease, etc, and if necessary replace friction material and clean metal friction surfaces (9/9:1).

5   Brakes pulling to one side

1   Check friction surfaces for contamination by oil, grease, etc and rectify if necessary (9/9:1).
2   Check tire pressure (11/25:1).
3   Examine pads or linings for excessive wear and replace if necessary (9/2:1 and 9/8:1).
4   Have front suspension checked for correct alignment (11/26:1).

6   Brakes tend to bind, drag or lock on

1   Check that the rear brakes are not overadjusted, and slacken off if necessary (9/10:1).
2   Check handbrake adjustment and slacken off if necessary (9/19:1).
3   Examine the master cylinder for incorrect operation (9/13:1).
4   Bleed the hydraulic system to eliminate any air which may be present (9/17:1).

Suspension and steering

1   Steering vague, car wanders and 'floats' at speed

1   Check that tires are inflated to recommended pressures (11/15:1).
2   Examine shock absorbers and replace if worn (11/2:1).
3   Check the steering balljoints for wear and replace if necessary (11/2:1).
4   Check suspension geometry and have it realigned if necessary (11/26:1).
5   Check steering box for excessive free-play and adjust or overhaul if required (11/22:1).
6   Tires mixed between radial and crossply - ensure all tires are of one type only and are of equal rolling radius.

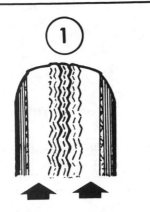

Common tire wear patterns

1 Wear at outer edges - tire underinflated
2 Wear at center - tire overinflated
*3 Wear at one side - incorrect wheel alignment. Check camber and
toe-in*

2 Steering heavy and stiff

1 Check tire pressures and inflate to recommended figures (11/25:1).
2 Check oil level in steering box and top up if required (11/21:1).
3 Examine front suspension for correct toe-in, and have it realigned if necessary (11/26:1).
4 Check steering gear for over-tight adjustment and rectify if necessary (11/21:1).

3 Wheel wobble and vibration

1 Check that wheel nuts are correctly tightened (11/24:1).
2 Check that the wheels are correctly balanced (11/24:1).
3 Examine the balljoints for excessive wear and replace if necessary (11/2:1).

4 Examine the wheel hub bearings for wear and replace if necessary (9/7:1).
5 Check through the steering gear for excessive free play and adjust as required (11/2:1).
6 Examine tire side-walls for bulges or distortion and replace tire(s) if necessary.

4 General rattling from steering and suspension

1 Examine suspension bushings for wear and replace if necessary (11/2:1).
2 Examine steering balljoints for wear and replace if necessary (11/2:1).
3 Examine the steering box for excessive free play, and adjust the sector shaft endfloat if necessary (11/22:13).
4 Examine all suspension and shock absorber mounts for wear in bushings or loose fixings (11/15:1).

Chapter 1 Engine

Refer to Chapter 13 for specifications and information related to 1981 through 1985 models

Contents

Specifications

Type
Displacement	573 cc (35.0 cu-in) x 2 rotors
Compression ratio	9.4 : 1
Compression pressure	
Limit	6.0 kg/cm² (85 lb/in²) at 250 rpm
Max. permissible difference between chambers	1.5 kg/cm² (21 lb/in²)

Port timing
Intake opens	32° ATDC
Intake closes	40° ABDC
Exhaust opens	75° BBDC
Exhaust closes	38° ATDC

Side housings (Front, intermediate and rear)
Width standard	
Front	40 mm (1.575 in)
Intermediate	50 mm (1.969 in)
Rear	60 mm (2.362 in)
Limit of distortion	0.04 mm (0.0016 in)
Limit of wear	
Sliding surface	0.10 mm (0.0039 in)

Rotor housing
Width	70 mm (2.756 in)
Max. permissible difference in width	0.06 mm (0.0024 in)

Rotor
Width	69.85 mm (2.750 in)
Clearance of side housing and rotor	
Standard	0.12 to 0.18 mm (0.0047 to 0.0071 in)
Limit	0.10 mm (0.004 in)

Apex seal
Length	69.85 mm (2.750 in)
Width	3.0 mm (0.118 in)
Height	
Standard	8.5 mm (0.335 in)
Limit	7.0 mm (0.276 in)
Clearance of apex seal and side housing	
Standard	0.13 to 0.17 mm (0.0051 to 0.0067 in)

Clearance of apex seal and rotor groove
    Standard .... 0.05 to 0.09 mm (0.0020 to 0.0035 in)
    Limit .... 0.15 mm (0.0060 in)

Apex seal spring
Free height
    Standard .... 6.9 mm (0.272 in) or more
    Limit .... 5.5 mm (0.22 in)

Side seal
Thickness .... 1.0 mm (0.039 in)
Height .... 3.5 mm (0.138 in)
Clearance of side seal and rotor groove
    Standard .... 0.03 to 0.08 mm (0.0012 to 0.0031 in)
    Limit .... 0.10 mm (0.0039 in)
Clearance of side seal and corner seal
    Standard .... 0.05 to 0.15 mm (0.0020 to 0.0060 in)
    Limit .... 0.40 mm (0.016 in)
Side seal protrusion .... More than 0.5 mm (0.0197 in)

Oil seal
Height .... 5.6 mm (0.220 in)
Contact width of oil seal lip .... Less than 0.5 mm (0.020 in)
Oil seal protrusion .... More than 0.5 mm (0.020 in)

Corner seal
Outer diameter .... 11.0 mm (0.433 in)
Height .... 7.0 mm (0.276 in)
Corner seal protrusion .... More than 0.5 mm (0.020 in)

Main bearing clearance
Standard .... 0.04 to 0.08 mm (0.0016 to 0.0031 in)
Wear limit .... 0.10 mm (0.0039 in)

Rotor bearing clearance
Standard .... 0.04 to 0.08 mm (0.0016 to 0.0031 in)
Wear limit .... 0.10 mm (0.0039 in)

Eccentric shaft
Eccentricity of rotor journal .... 15.0 mm (0.591 in)
Main journal diameter .... 43 mm (1.693 in)
Rotor journal diameter .... 74 mm (2.913 in)
Max. permissible run-out .... 0.06 mm (0.0024 in)
    End play:
        Standard .... 0.04 to 0.07 mm (0.0016 to 0.0028 in)
        Limit .... 0.09 mm (0.0035 in)

Alternator belt tension (slack)
Between alternator and eccentric shaft pulleys
    Belt deflection .... 15 $\pm$ 2 mm (0.59 $\pm$ 0.08 in)

Air pump belt tension (slack)
Between air pump and water pump pulleys
    Belt deflection .... 12 $\pm$ 1 mm (0.47 $\pm$ 0.04 in)

Torque wrench settings

	m-kg	ft-lb
Oil pump sprocket	3.0 to 3.5	22 to 25
Oil pan	0.7 to 1.0	5 to 7
Inlet manifold	1.9 to 2.6	14 to 19
Thermal reactor	4.5 to 5.5	33 to 40
Spark plugs	1.2 to 1.8	9 to 13
Eccentric shaft pulley	10 to 12	72 to 87
Temperature gauge unit	0.7 to 0.8	5 to 6
Tension bolts	3.2 to 3.8	23 to 27
Water temperature switch	1.0 to 1.8	7 to 13

1 General description

The engine used in the RX-7 is the latest in the line of rotary engines.

The engine used in the RX-7 is the latest version of the Wankel rotary. Although very similar in design and concept to those incorporated in the RX-2 and RX-3, there have been fundamental changes in the RX-7 engine to overcome previous shortcomings.

Home mechanics well versed in the operation of piston-type engines will have no problem in slanting their way of thinking towards the rotary concept. However, because of the novelty of the Wankel, novice mechanics will not have the advice and experience of others readily available to them, as they would with a conventional engine. But if care is taken the engine can be successfully stripped and reassembled at home. In many respects it is actually easier to work on than a conventional piston engine.

Basically, the Wankel engine used in the RX-7 features two rotors which could be compared to pistons in a conventional engine. The rotors revolve around, and turn, a crankshaft known as an eccentric shaft in the rotary engine. Each rotor does one revolution to every three of the eccentric shaft. The eccentric shaft turns a flywheel at the rear of the engine and in turn powers the car in the conventional manner via transmission propeller shaft and rear differential.

It is the manner in which the rotary propels the eccentric shaft that makes it unique. Each rotor rotates within a chamber. Since the rotor is shaped similar to a triangle, it divides the chamber into three sections: one for bringing in the air/fuel mixture, one for igniting this mixture with the spark plugs and one for expelling the spent exhaust gases. It is this sequence, obviously happening very quickly, which provides power.

The related pieces of equipment found on the rotary, like the carburetor and induction system, ignition and exhaust are conventional in design and function. While there may be slight differences to adapt them to the rotary, mechanics who have had experience with these parts will find them virtually the same.

2 Planning work on the engine

1   With the engine in place accessibility is good for removing or adjusting most of the external components. The engine should only need removal if the housings or internal rotors and seals need attention.

2   Access at the front of the engine is greatly improved by removing the radiator and cowling, a job which is fairly easy to do. This may prove useful for servicing the water pump, fan or front cover.

3   For checking engine components micrometers measuring 0 to 1 in and 2 to 3 in will be needed. Without these precision measuring devices, parts may have to be scrapped to ensure a good job.

4   In anticipation of engine work parts which will be necessary should be obtained beforehand. Since basic engine parts like gaskets, O-rings and seals are not as readily available as parts for piston engines. It is advisable to purchase these parts first to eliminate any delays in the work sequence.

5   Read through the entire section of this book which pertains to the repair work being done before work begins. This will give you an idea of the tools and spare parts which will be necessary, as well as the ease or difficulty of the job at hand.

3 Engine removal – without transmission

1   There are three basically accepted methods of removing this or any other engine: with the transmission intact, with the transmission removed separately; with the transmission left behind still secured under the car. All three of these methods can be used with the RX-7. If the transmission needs major work at the same time as the engine refer to the removal sequence detailed in Chapter 6 or the Section in this chapter devoted to removing the engine with the transmission. If the transmission does not need work leave it in the car and remove just the engine following the sequence outlined in this Section.

2   No matter which method is chosen some suitable lifting tackle must be used. Ideally a small crane mounted on wheels (commonly called a "cherry picker") should be rented. These are readily available and easy to use. An alternative method is to suspend lifting tackle from a roof beam or lengths of timber. The beam should be strong enough to support the full weight of the engine and the work area large enough (and level) in order to manoeuver the car from under the

suspended engine.

3   Drain the oil from the engine. After all oil has drained, clean and replace the drain plug.

4   Remove the seven bolts securing the engine undercover. Lower the front of the undercover slightly and then slide it forward to free it from the crossmember. Lay the undercover and bolts out of the way.

5   Disconnect the negative battery cable at its post on the top of the battery.

6   Use a felt pen or pencil to outline each hinge on the hood. This will allow you to replace the hood in the exact same location.

7   With the outline of each hinge on the hood, have a helper support the hood while the four bolts are removed. Carefully lay the hood and its bolts in a safe place where they cannot be damaged or lost.

8   Disconnect the two high tension leads running from the center of the coils to the distributor. Disconnect them at the coils, noting their color and position. Identify them further with tape and numbers if in doubt.

9   Disconnect the primary wire and condensor leads next to the distributor cap. These are snap-in connectors and are color-coded. If not fully coded, identify them in a suitable fashion.

10   Disconnect the oil level sensor connector located just behind the oil filter. It is a plastic snap-in connector for easy re-installation.

11   Remove the two bolts securing the clutch release cylinder. Tuck the cylinder out of the way (photo).

12   Disconnect the vacuum sensing tube running from the switch on the firewall to the evaporative control system located on the top of the engine (California models only).

13   Disconnect the couplers for the oil thermo-sensor (except California) and water temperature gauge unit. These snap-in connectors are located just behind the oil filter assembly.

14   Disconnect the oil hoses from the radiator located on the left-hand side of the engine. Use a container to catch any fluid which may leak from these lines (photo).

15   Disconnect the bullet-type coolant level sensor connector at the top of the radiator.

16   Disconnect the reservoir hose running from the radiator cap to the coolant reservoir.

17   Remove the four bolts attaching the fan and fan assembly to the pulley. Place the fan and fan assembly inside the radiator shroud for now.

18   Remove the air cleaner assembly. To do this first remove the top plate by loosening the three spring clips. Next remove the wing nut inside the housing, at the center of the carburetor. There is also a bolt which must be removed, located near the top radiator hose inlet to the engine. Before removing the assembly carefully disconnect and identify all hoses leading to the air cleaner. Remove and set aside with wing nut, support bolt and all tagged hoses (photo).

19   Drain the cooling system by disconnecting the lower radiator hose. Allow the coolant to drain into a suitable container. Do not re-use this coolant mixture.

20   Disconnect and remove the upper radiator hose from the radiator and the engine.

21   On vehicles equipped with automatic transmission, disconnect the oil pipes from the radiator.

22   Disconnect the heater hose from the lower right-hand side of the radiator.

23   Remove the four bolts and one nut securing the radiator and

3.11 Two bolts hold the clutch release cylinder to the top of the transmission. The flexible hose can remain intact and the cylinder placed aside

3.14 The two oil cooler hoses are located at the left side of the oil cooler

3.18 Removing the air cleaner assembly from the top of the engine

shroud assembly. Lift the radiator, shroud and fan assembly (previously unbolted) from the engine compartment. Lay all pieces, including bolts and nut aside (photo).

24 From the right rear of the rear of the engine, behind the carburetor, remove the rubber hose for the power brake assist, the two nuts securing the air pipe to the inlet manifold and the two top bolts attaching the transmission to the engine.

25 Also on the right-hand side of the engine, remove the two bolts and two nuts attaching the thermal reactor cover. Only the smaller, rear portion of the three-piece cover should be completely removed at this time, gaining access to the exhaust flange beneath it (photo).

26 Of the three nuts mating the main exhaust pipe to the thermal reactor, remove the top one now.

27 The main wiring loom for the engine runs from the left side, at the firewall, across the engine to just above the thermal reactor. The only wires to this loom which are not on color-coded quick-disconnect connectors are the two wires which connect to the back of the alternator and a ground wire at the rearmost solenoid of the emissions control device at the top of the engine. Disconnect all wires from the main loom making sure you understand the color coding system. If there are any doubts, you should tag each wire with a coding system of your own before continuing. The loom with its disconnected wires can then be placed out of the way of the engine.

28 Disconnect the heater hose from the left side of the engine.

29 Disconnect the main and return fuel hoses at the top of the carburetor. Note that one is a larger diameter than the other to prevent mix-ups. Push an appropriately sized spare bolt in the ends of the hoses to prevent leakage (photo).

30 Disconnect the accelerator, choke and hot-start assist cables from the carburetor. The outer cable housings are locked in place with lock nuts at a bracket on the carburetor. The small inner cables then run through the bracket and are connected with rollers which must be carefully turned and removed from the carburetor linkage system. After disconnecting the inner cables, loosen the lock nuts slightly and remove the cable from the bracket. Position the cables out of the way of the engine (photo).

31 On cars equipped with air conditioning, it is important that none of the hoses is removed without first de-pressurizing the system. Serious injury can result. If care is taken, the engine on the RX-7 can be removed without disconnecting or damaging the air conditioning system.

32 Remove the air conditioning pump from its bracket by removing the long pivot bolt and shorter adjusting bolt. Use wire to secure the pump against the inner fender panel.

33 Remove the large bracket from the engine block, unbolting the three bolts and one nut. Don't lose the two spacers used. Make sure the pump and two hoses connected to it will be clear of the engine as it is removed.

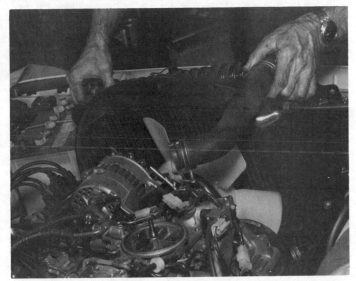

3.23 Removing the radiator with the fan assembly inside the shroud

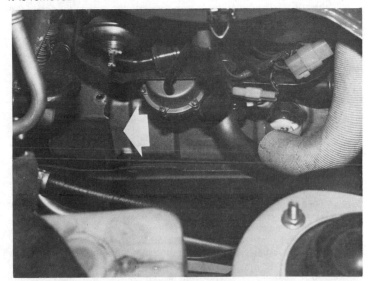

3.25 Remove the small, rearmost thermal reactor cover to gain access to the exhaust pipe nuts

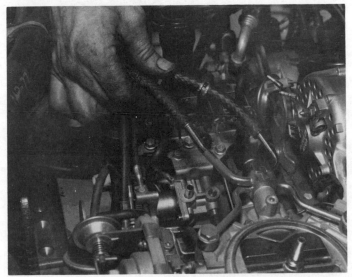

3.29 Disconnecting the fuel main and return hoses from the carburetor

3.30 Disconnecting the throttle, hot-start and choke cables from the carburetor and bracket

34 Jack up the vehicle and support it with stands to gain access underneath for the remaining component removal steps.

35 Disconnect all wiring to the starter. Mark each wire for easy reinstallation. Remove the starter from under the vehicle (Chapter 10).

36 Remove the remaining three bolts attaching the transmission. Two are at the lower part of the transmission and one on the upper left-hand side.

37 Remove the two remaining nuts securing the main exhaust pipe to the rear of the thermal reactor (photo).

38 Remove the two nuts holding the rubber air pipe to the bottom of the thermal reactor.

39 Towards the rear of the transmission, on the right side, is a hanger bracket for the exhaust system. Remove the two bolts going through the bracket and into the transmission housing and the single bolt on the lower portion of the hanger.

40 Disconnect the main exhaust pipe and heat exchanger pipe from the pre-silencer.

41 If equipped with automatic transmission the torque converter must be removed from the flywheel (see Chapter 6).

42 Support the front end of the transmission with a suitable jack. A block of wood may be used to spread the load.

43 Attach the lifting chain or sling to the hanger brackets bolted to the engine. The two brackets are located one at the rear of the engine and one on the left-hand side at the front (photo).

44 With the engine hoist hooked up, remove the nuts at the top of the left and right engine mounts located on each side of the engine towards the front (photo).

45 Lift the engine slightly to clear the engine mount bolts. Check that all wires, hoses, cables and the air conditioning system (if equipped) are clear of the engine (photo).

46 Check that the jack is still supporting the transmission.

47 Pull the engine forward (or push the car rearwards, depending on your lifting apparatus) until the engine clears the clutch shaft. Then lift the engine straight up out of the engine compartment (photo).

4 Engine removal – with transmission

1 To remove the engine with the transmission still attached to it, most of the previous steps for removing the engine without the transmission can be followed. There are, however, some differences in the removal procedure which should be followed.

2 Follow all steps of Section 3 on removing the engine without the transmission up until paragraph 33, noting these two changes: A. In addition to the radiator and shroud being removed, the support section forward of the radiator should be removed as well. This will give you more room to pull the longer engine/transmission assembly forward before lifting it clear (photo). B. Do not remove the two top bolts attaching the transmission to the engine.

3 On the inside of the car, unscrew and remove the gearshift lever knob by turning in a counter-clockwise direction.

4 Remove the two screws securing the shift boot and boot plate to the center console. Lift up on the plate and slide it forward to disengage it from the clips at the rear.

5 Remove the five screws now exposed which secure the gearshift lever and retaining plate.

6 Pry back the rubber boot and remove the three bolts securing the gearshift lever mechanism to the top of the transmission. Remove the gearshift assembly.

7 Raise the vehicle as high as possible while still allowing it to be firmly supported on stands.

8 Drain the lubricant from the transmission by removing the drain plug. Allow the fluid to drain. Clean and replace the plug after all fluid has drained.

9 Refer to Chapter 7 for the proper procedure of removing the propeller shaft.

10 Disconnect the wiring to the starter, duly marking each wire for easy re-installation.

11 Remove the two bolts securing the starter motor to the transmission bellhousing. One long bolt runs through the engine, bellhousing and then into the starter flange. The other bolt is smaller and runs through the flange and into the bellhousing. Remove the starter.

12 Disconnect the plug-in couplers to the back-up lamp switch, top switch (California with manual transmission), and over-drive switch (California with manual transmission). These couplers are located on the left side of the transmission and are color-coded.

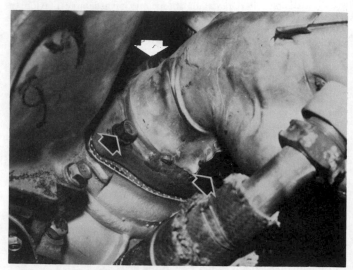

3.37 The main exhaust pipe is held to the thermal reactor with three nuts. The top one is accessible from the engine compartment and the others should be removed from below

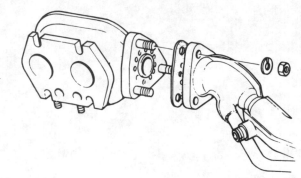

Fig. 1.1 Disconnecting main exhaust pipe from thermal reactor (Sec 3)

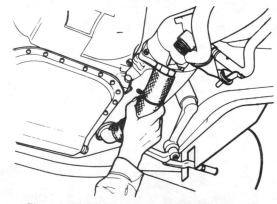

Fig. 1.2 Disconnecting rubber air pipe (Sec 3)

13 Remove the two remaining nuts securing the main exhaust pipe to the rear of the thermal reactor.

14 Remove the two nuts holding the rubber air pipe to the bottom of the thermal reactor.

15 Towards the rear of the transmission, on the right side, is a hanger bracket for the exhaust system. Remove the two bolts going through the bracket and into the transmission housing, and the single bolt on the lower portion of the hanger.

16 Disconnect the main exhaust pipe and heat exchanger pipe from the pre-silencer.

17 Support the transmission with a suitable jack which can be raised or lowered. Use a block of wood between the transmission and jack to

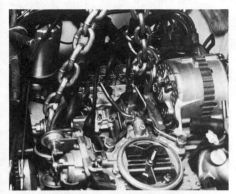

3.43 Lifting brackets are provided at the front and rear of the engine

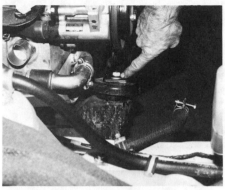

3.44 The locknut and washer for the engine mount

3.45 Lift the engine slightly and check for any obstructions

3.47 After the engine is clear of the clutch shaft it can be lifted clear of the engine compartment

4.2 This support section and air conditioning matrix (if equipped) should be removed for extra forward room

4.25 The longer engine/transmission assembly will require manipulation of the hoist to remove

spread the load.

18 Remove the two nuts at the center portion of the transmission crossmember mount.

19 Remove the two bolts mounting the transmission crossmember to the body. Remove the transmission mount from under the vehicle.

20 Disconnect the speedometer cable at the transmission using pliers to loosen the collar.

21 Attach the lifting tackle to the engine. The engine/transmission assembly will have to be raised in the front and lowered at the rear to properly clear the engine compartment. To do this hook the front chain tight and leave the rear one with some slack.

22 Make a final check that all wires, hoses, cables and the air conditioner (if equipped) are out of the way.

23 Place rags or newspaper on the floor behind the transmission, as fluid will probably leak as it is tipped up.

24 You will need an assistant to help control the transmission assembly as it is removed.

25 Slowly raise the engine with the hoist and at the same time lower the transmission. In gradual movements, continue to raise the engine and lower the transmission until clearance allows you to pull the assembly forward and over the front nosepiece of the body. Be careful that the unit does not damage the body surfaces as it is lifted free (photo).

5 Removing components from the outside of the engine

1   If the transmission was removed with the engine, it must now be separated. Lower the unit to the ground and support the engine separately with jacks or blocks. On manual transmissions, remove the five bolts and carefully separate the two components. With automatic transmissions, remove the sheet metal inspection covers (top and bottom) and unbolt the torque converter from the flywheel. Then pull the transmission from the engine.

2   The engine will be much easier to work on if placed on an engine stand. Mazda recommends a special hanger to secure the engine to a stand. This hanger uses a bracket which bolts into the front housing, allowing you to systematically strip the engine leaving only the front housing attached to the stand. Many standard automotive engine stands and their support systems can be used on the rotary engine, so long as the supports will mate to the front housing bolts (photos).

3   Remove the spark plugs and plug wires. Use stick-on numbers, or tape with numbers, to mark each wire for re-installation.

4   Remove the two nuts securing the oil filter and oil filter housing to the engine block. The filter can be left intact on the housing; however it is advisable to replace the cartridge when the engine is overhauled to this point. Don't lose the O-rings on the bottom of the housing flange (photo).

5   Two bolts hold the alternator in place. Remove the small bolt on the adjusting bracket, and the long pivot bolt with the nut on the backside. There is also a spacer used with the long bolt. Place the alternator, bolts, spacer and drive belt aside (photo).

6   To remove the air pump, first disconnect the rubber air outlet hose, then the short adjusting bolt and long pivot bolt. Place the pump, outlet hose, bolts and drive belt aside (photo).

7   To prevent damage to the delicate emissions system components, remove them from the top of the engine at this stage. The valve and piping can be removed as a complete assembly by removing the three bolts into the engine housing and the one nut at the water outlet at the front of the engine. The vacuum lines which must be removed should be duly tagged in order to replace them in their proper locations. Place the assembly with bolts, nut and vacuum lines in a safe place where the plastic solenoids cannot be damaged (photo).

8   Completely remove the thermal reactor air pipe. Disconnect it at the front of the thermal reactor and remove the two bolts on the flange at the top of the thermal reactor (photo).

9   The two remaining thermal reactor covers can now be removed.

10 Disconnect the connecting rod at the metering oil pump located at the front of the engine. Pay close attention to which hole in the rod the cotter pin was installed in, as it must be placed in the same hole upon reassembly.

11 Disconnect the two oil hoses at the metering oil pump.

12 Disconnect all vacuum hoses leading to the carburetor, and inlet manifold. Identify each hose and its relative connection in some

5.2a The engine can be bolted to a stand by provisions on the front housing. One bolt into the rear housing can be used for initial support

5.2b For greater accessibility to the engine an adjustable engine stand may be used

5.4 The oil filter and pedestal can be removed as a unit after removing the two attaching nuts

5.5 The long pivot bolt and smaller strap bolt securing the alternator to the engine

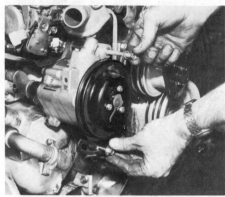

5.6 The air pump also has a long pivot bolt and strap bolt which need to be removed

5.7 The emission system solenoids being removed from the top of the engine as a complete unit

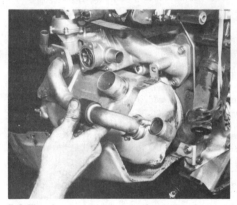

5.8 The thermal reactor air pipe being removed

5.13 The carburetor and intake manifold can be removed as an assembly

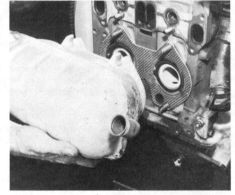

5.14a Four nuts secure the thermal reactor to the engine

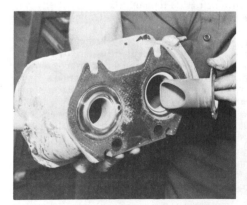

5.14b Note that there are two small pipes inside the thermal reactor. Their positions should not be changed

5.15 Four attaching nuts secure the engine mount

5.16 After making the necessary indicator marks the distributor locknut can be removed, followed by the distributor

fashion to ease re-assembly.

13 The inlet manifold and carburetor can be removed as an assembly by removing the four bolts and two nuts securing the manifold to the engine block. Place the assembly aside, along with bolts and hoses. Cover it to keep dirt and foreign mater out of the carburetor (photo).

14 Remove the four nuts attaching the thermal reactor to the engine block. Remove the thermal reactor and accompanying gasket (photos).

15 Remove the engine mount running across the front of the engine (photo).

16 Before removing the distributor it should be properly marked for easy re-installation. Align the yellow painted leading timing marks on the eccentric shaft pulley with the indicator pin located on the front cover. Pop off the distributor cap; make a mark on the rotor and a corresponding mark on the distributor cap. With the leading marks aligned, your indicators on the rotor and cap should be towards the forward leading plug wire. Remove the distributor lock bolt and then remove the distributor. Completely cover the distributor to keep it clean and set if aside where it cannot be damaged (photo).

17 If equipped with air conditioning remove the four bolts securing the air conditioning compressor pulley.

18 The water pump is secured to the front of the engine with four bolts. Remove these four bolts and lift off the water pump (photo).

19 Remove the metering oil pump assembly (photo).

20 Remove all bolts securing the oil pan to the bottom of the engine. Use a scraper or putty knife to very gently pry the pan away from the housing, being very careful not to gouge or damage the housing surface. Remove the oil pan (photo).

21 Remove the two bolts attaching the oil pickup and strainer to the engine. Lift off the pickup, strainer and accompanying gasket (photo).

22 Remove the front eccentric shaft pulley bolt and pulley. It may be necessary to attach a brake to the flywheel or use vise grips on the pulley to keep it from turning as the bolt is loosened (photo).

23 Six bolts secure the front housing to the engine block. Remove these bolts and then gently tap the rear of the cover with a rubber mallet to break the seal. Lift off the front cover and the O-ring on the oil passage (photo).

24 Slide the distributor drivegear off the eccentric shaft (photo).

25 Before removing the oil pump assembly, check the tension of the

5.18 The water pump and water housing can be removed from the engine as a unit

5.19 Removing the oil metering pump assembly

5.20a After removing the securing bolts, care is required when breaking the sealant bond

5.20b The oil pan is then lifted away

5.21 Two bolts secure the oil pickup tube to the engine housing

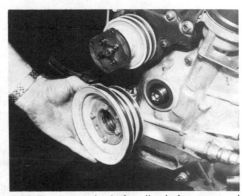
5.22 The eccentric shaft pulley being removed

5.23 A rubber mallet may be required to break the seal between the front cover and the engine

5.24 Slide the distributor drivegear off the eccentric shaft

5.25 Checking the tension of the oil pump chain

5.27 The oil pump assembly and drive chain can be removed together from the two shafts

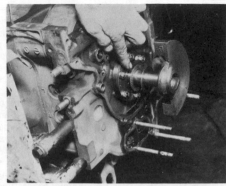

5.29 Showing the positions of the balance weight, thrust washer and roller bearing on the eccentric shaft

5.30a The large locknut and washer securing the flywheel

5.30b A puller is used to remove the flywheel from the engine

chain to ascertain if a new one is needed. At an equal distance between the two pulleys, push in on the chain with your finger. The slack in the chain should not be more than 0.47 in (12 mm) (photo).

26 Straighten the lockwasher tab on the oil pump sprocket. Remove the nut and lock washer.

27 Slide the oil pump sprocket, eccentric shaft sprocket and chain simultaneously off the shafts. Keep these together as a unit (photo).

28 Remove the four bolts securing the oil pump to the engine block. Remove the oil pump.

29 From the eccentric shaft, remove the balance weight, thrust-washer, roller bearing and key. Then remove the six bolts retaining the bearing housing. Remove the housing and the roller bearing, spacer and thrustwasher behind it. Lay these parts aside in the order in which they were removed (photo).

30 On vehicles equipped with manual transmissions the clutch and flywheel must now be removed. Before removing the clutch assembly it is advisable to make an identifying mark in order for the clutch and flywheel to be properly aligned upon re-installation. These is one small hole in the clutch mounting flange, next to one of the bolts. Use a dab of paint or a sharp scribe to make a mark on the flywheel through this hole. Then gradually, and in a diagonal fashion, remove the six bolts securing the clutch to the flywheel. Remove the pressure plate and clutch disc, being careful not to get grease or oil on the surfaces. Use a chisel and hammer to straighten the locking tab on the flywheel nut. A large $2\frac{1}{8}$ in (54 mm) wrench is needed for removing the nut. It is secured with tremendous torque, thus a box wrench with a length of pipe for leverage may be needed to break it loose. A suitable puller with bolts threaded into the holes provided in the flywheel should then be used to pull the flywheel off the shaft. Alternately turn the puller handle and strike the head of the puller until the flywheel is free. Be careful not to drop the flywheel (photos).

31 On vehicles equipped with automatic transmissions, remove the six bolts retaining the driveplate (comparable to the flywheel). Remove the drive plate. Straighten the locking tab on the counter weight nut. Use a $2\frac{1}{8}$ in (54 mm) wrench to loosen the counter weight nut. A suitable puller with bolts threaded into the counter weight holes is then used to pull the counter weight off the shaft. Alternately turn the

puller handle and tap the head of the puller until free. Be careful not to drop the counter weight.

6 Engine – disassembly

1 Remove the 18 tension bolts securing the rear housing. It is important that these bolts be loosened a little at a time and in the sequence illustrated in the photo (photo).

2 Carefully lift the rear housing off the rotor housing. If there are any seals stuck to the inside surfaces of the rear housing refit them in their respective positions (photo).

3 Remove the sealing rubbers from the housing and the O-ring on one of the dowel pins now exposed.

4 The two dowel pins must now be removed from the rotor housing. These pins go through the rotor housing and into the intermediate housing. To remove them, thread a bolt into the dowel and then use a slide hammer puller to pull the dowel upwards. Hold onto the housing to prevent movement as the dowel is forced up and out. As the dowel pins are not in very tight, it may be possible to use vise-grips on the threaded bolt to pull the pins free (photo).

5 The rear rotor housing can now be lifted off the eccentric shaft and rotor. If any of the rotor seals fall off during this operation replace them on the rotor in their original positions (photo).

6 Remove the sealing rubber gaskets and the O-ring on the other side of the rotor housing and set the housing aside. Apply an identifying mark to the housing so you will know that it is the rear rotor housing.

7 At this point it is imperative that a system be set up to identify each of the many seals for the rotors. You can use dividers inside a cardboard box to form compartments for each seal, or you can draw a rough sketch of each rotor on a large piece of cardboard or paper and place each seal on the drawing. Make sure the box or sketch includes both sides of each rotor.

8 Clean the face of the rotor and take note of the numbers located about two inches from each of the three apexes. Use these numbers to identify each seal as it is removed from the rotor (photo).

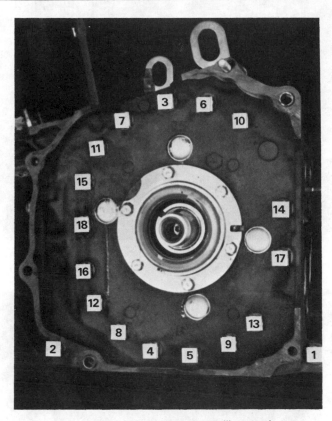

6.1 Loosen the tension bolts in sequence as illustrated

9 Remove the side pieces and each apex seal and spring, and place them in your compartment box or on the sketch.

10 Remove all corner seals, corner seal springs, side seals and side seal springs. Place them in the proper location in the box or on the sketch (photo).

11 The rear rotor can now be lifted off the eccentric shaft. Place it gear side down on a clean surface and remove the side seals and springs from this side of the rotor. Again, place them in the proper location in the box or on the sketch of the rotor.

12 Using a small screwdriver or pick, pry the inner and outer oil seals out of their grooves on the rotor faces. Pry the seals out a little at a time, working completely around their circumference. Place each seal and its respective O-ring and spring together in the box or on the sketch.

13 Remove the oil seals. O-rings and springs from the other side of the rotor following the same procedures.

14 The stripped rotor can now be placed with its corresponding components.

15 Using the pulley or vise-grips, pull the tubular dowels off the intermediate housing. Hold the housing in place as the dowels are forced out (photo).

16 To remove the intermediate housing it is necessary to slightly lift the eccentric shaft (about an inch) and then lift the housing clear of the rear rotor journal. Set the intermediate housing aside (photo).

17 The eccentric shaft can now be carefully lifted out of the remaining components and set aside (photo).

18 The front rotor housing and front rotor are removed in the same manner as the rear rotor and housing. Be sure that each seal and spring is properly identified and placed in the proper identifying box or sketch (photo).

7 Engine – cleaning

1 Rather than cleaning all of the components together, the rotors, housings, seals and springs should be cleaned individually to prevent mix-ups in the identifying process. Remove each part from your compartmented box or sketch, clean it and then replace it immediately

6.2 Lifting the housing off the rear rotor housing

6.4 Using a puller and a bolt to pull out the dowel pins

6.5 Lifting the rear rotor housing over the rotor and eccentric shaft

6.8 Identifying numbers are stamped onto each rotor about two inches from the apexes. Use these to identify the many rotor seals

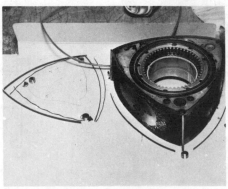

6.10 It is imperative that each seal and spring on the rotor be clearly identified using a sketch or compartment box

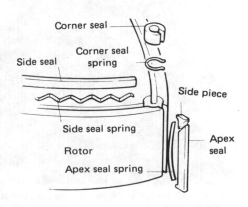

Fig. 1.3 Various rotor components (Sec 6)

Corner seal

Corner seal spring

Side seal

Side piece

Side seal spring

Apex seal

Rotor

Apex seal spring

6.15 A puller and bolt are used to pull the dowel pins out of the intermediate housing

6.16 The eccentric shaft must be lifted slightly and the intermediate housing tilted before removal

6.17 The eccentric shaft can now be carefully lifted up and out of the front rotor

6.18 The front rotor housing and rotor are removed in the same manner as the rear components previously disassembled

8.1 A straight edge and feeler gauge are used to check the housings for warping

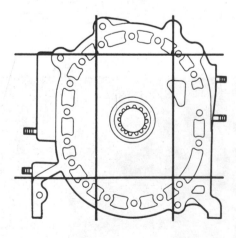

Fig. 1.4 Checking the housings for warpage (Sec 8)

before the next part is done.

2   Remove all carbon from the surfaces of the rotors using a carbon remover or emery paper. Wash the rotors in cleaning solution and dry with compressed air if available. Pay close attention to the recessed grooves where the oil seals and apex seals seat. The apex seal grooves should be perfectly clean with no sharp burrs which could prevent the seals from expanding against the housings.

3   The front, rear and intermediate housings have a finished surface which can be damaged if not cleaned properly. Use a soft cloth with a solution of ketone or thinner to remove any carbon on the machined surfaces. The leftover sealing agent used to mate the housings can be removed with a brush soaked in ketone or thinner.

4   Before cleaning the rotor housings check for traces of gas or water leakage along the inner margin of each side face. This will indicate a failure in the rubber sealing gaskets. Carbon should be removed from the inner surfaces with a soft cloth soaked in ketone or thinner. Remove all deposits and rust from the cooling water passages. Remove any excess sealing agent with a brush soaked in ketone or thinner.

5   Clean each seal and spring one at a time using ketone or thinner. Never use emery paper or a wire brush as these will damage the delicate surfaces.

6   Wash all parts in cleaning solution to remove all traces of grit and then lightly oil them with a solution of 1 part engine oil to 8 parts gasoline to prevent rust from forming while the parts await re-assembly.

7   Cover all parts to keep away any dust and make sure that all parts are located in a place where they cannot be accidentally jostled and mixed-up.

8 Housings – inspection and overhaul

1   The front, intermediate and rear housings should be checked for warpage by placing a straight edge along the surfaces and using a feeler gauge. Place the straight edge in four positions across the machined surface, measuring the distance between the straight edge and the housing surface. The warpage limit is 0.0016 in (0.04 mm). If any of the housings are warped more than this amount they should be resurfaced by a competent machine shop or replaced (photo).

2   A dial indicator mounted to a gauge body must be used to check for stepped wear on the front, intermediate and rear housings. The stepped wear measurements indicate the amount of material which has been worn off the housings from the rotors as they turn on the eccentric shaft. If the necessary tools are not available the housings should be taken to a competent machine shop or a Mazda dealer. There are three critical areas to be checked for stepped wear. The limit is 0.0039 in (0.10 mm) where the side seal of the rotor contacts the housing. Moving the dial indicator across the surface inside the oil seal tracing mark, the limit is 0.01 mm (0.0004 in). Outside the oil seal tracing mark on the housing the limit is 0.10 mm (0.0039 in). Wear caused by the oil seals themselves should not exceed 0.0008 in (0.02 mm). Again, a highly competent machine shop can resurface the housings although it may prove to be more economical to replace them if the limits are exceeded (photo).

3   Check the stationary gears in the front and rear housings for cracked, scored or worn teeth. Replace as necessary following the procedures outlined later in this Chapter (photo).

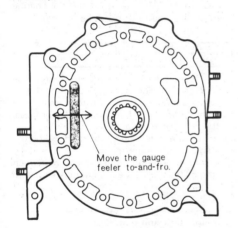

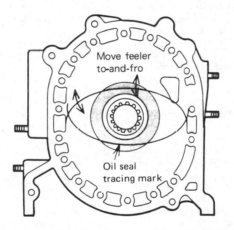

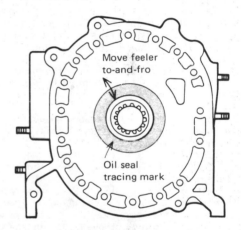

Fig. 1.5 Checking for stepped wear by side seal (Sec 8)

Fig. 1.6 Checking for stepped wear inside and outside of oil seal tracing mark (Sec 8)

Fig. 1.7 Checking for stepped wear by oil seal (Sec 8)

8.2 A dial indicator can be used to check for stepped wear on the housings

8.3 There are stationary gears on the front and rear housings. If excessively worn or damaged, they should be replaced

4   Check the main bearings in the front and rear housing for wear, scratching, flaking or damage. Replace as necessary following the procedures outlined later in this Chapter.

5   The clearance of the main bearings is checked by first measuring the inner diameter of the bearing with an inside micrometer and then the outside diameter of the eccentric shaft journal on which it rides. The difference between these two measurements gives the clearance, which has a limit of 0.0039 in (0.10 mm). If the bearing clearance exceeds this limit, the bearing should be replaced following the procedures outlined later in this Chapter (photos).

6   It may be wise at this time to replace the soft plugs (freeze plugs) located in the front and rear housings. They may not be bad now, but due to their inaccessibility after the engine is assembled and replaced they should be replaced with the engine torn down. Press the old ones out and replace with new ones using a sealant.

7   Check the chromium plated surface on the rotor housings for scoring, flaking or any damage. If any of these conditions exists, replace the rotor housing(s).

8   Check the width of each rotor housing with micrometers. Measure the width a number of times around the circumference of the housing and write down each measurement. Place the micrometers at a point close to the inner, running surface of the housings. The difference between the largest measurement and the smallest should not exceed 0.0024 in (0.06 mm). If it does, the rotor housing(s) should be replaced as they cannot be repaired (photo).

9   Stationary gears and main bearings – replacement

1   The main bearings to the engine are pressed into the stationary gears located on the front and rear housings. The removal and installation process is the same for the front and rear except that the rear main bearing has an O-ring which must be replaced into a groove in the stationary gear.

2   Remove the stationary gear attaching bolts and then remove the gear and bearing assembly from the housing. The assembly is removed from the housing by using a press, or by pounding it free with a piece of hardwood and a hammer.

3   Apiece of tubing or hardwood should then be used to remove the bearing from the stationary gear. A press is advisable, although a large vise will also do the job.

4   Clean the inside of the stationary gear, where the bearing rides, and the outside of the new bearing. Smooth any rough spots with emery paper.

5   Press the new bearing into the stationary gear, aligning the lug of the bearing and the slot of the stationary gear.

6   On the rear housing, apply a thin coat of Vaseline to the new O-ring and place it in he groove of the stationary gear.

7   Apply sealing agent onto the stationary gear flange and install the assembly into the housing, aligning the slot of the stationary gear

flange and the dowel pin on the housing.

8   Tighten the attaching bolts.

10 Rotor – inspection and repair

1   Carefully inspect the rotor and replace if it is severely worn or damaged.

2   Check the internal gear for cracked, scored, worn or chipped teeth.

3   To arrive at the clearance between the side housing and the rotor, measure the width of the rotor and compare with the measurements written down previously for the width of the rotor housing (8.8). The rotor width should be checked at three points between each apex with the micrometers on the internal gear. The difference between rotor width and the side housing width gives you the clearance. Standard clearance should be 0.0047 to 0.0071 in (0.12 to 0.18 mm) with a limit of less than 0.004 in (0.10 mm). If the clearance is more than the specification, replace the rotor assembly. If the clearance is less than the specification, it indicates that the internal gear has come out slightly and can be lightly tapped further into the rotor with a plastic hammer. Recheck the rotor width to make certain that it now falls into specifications (photo).

4   Check the rotor bearing for wear, flaking, scoring or any damage. If any of these conditions is found, replace the bearing as outlined later in this Chapter.

5   Check the rotor bearing clearance by measuring the inside diameter of the rotor bearing with inside micrometers, and comparing this measurement with the outer diameter of the eccentric shaft journal. The standard rotor bearing clearance is 0.0016 to 0.0031 in (0.04 to 0.08 mm) with a limit of 0.0039 in (0.10 mm).If the bearing clearance exceeds this limit, replace the rotor bearings (photo).

11 Rotor bearing – replacement

1   The rotor bearing is essentially a sleeve pressed into the rotor. A press, large vise or other suitable device must be used to firmly support the rotor as the bearing is pressed out. The rotor should have its internal gear facing downward during the bearing removal process. Be careful not to damage the rotor or internal gear.

2   Clean the inner surfaces of the rotor and outer surface of the bearing. Smooth any rough spots with emery paper.

3   Place the rotor with its gear side up and press the new bearing into place making sure that the oil hole in the bearing matches up with the slot in the rotor bore.

12 Oil seal and spring – inspection and overhaul

1   Check the oil seal for wear or any damage. Replace if necessary.

8.5a Inside micrometers are used to check the diameter of the bearing

8.5b The diameter of the eccentric shaft journal is then checked to determine main bearing clearance

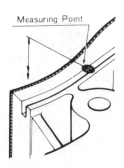

Fig. 1.8 Measuring width of the rotor housing (Sec 8)

8.8 Measuring the width of a rotor housing

10.3 Measuring the width of a rotor

10.5a Measuring the inside diameter of the rotor bearing

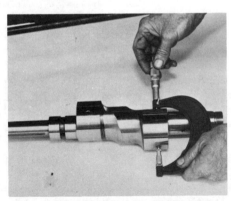

10.5b Measuring the outside diameter of the rotor journal on the eccentric shaft

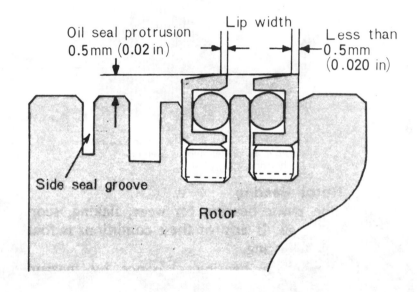

Fig. 1.9 Checking protrusion of rotor oil seal (Sec 12)

2   Check the width of the oil seal with a micrometer to ensure that the seal has not been widened through use. Width should not exceed 0.020 in (0.5 mm).
3   Replace the oil seal springs into their respective grooves and assemble the oil seals using new neoprene O-rings. Additional information on installing the oil seals can be found in Section 18.
4   Check for free movement of the oil seals by pressing with a finger. The seals should move freely in their grooves. If they don't, check that the seals and grooves are perfectly clean.
5   Check that the oil seals protrude from the rotor 0.020 in (0.5 mm). If the protrusion is less than specified, this indicates a failure in the oil seal spring. Replace the oil seal spring(s).

13 Apex seal and spring – inspection

1   Check the apex seals and accompanying side pieces for wear, cracking or any damage; replace if any is found.

2   Measure the height of the apex seals with a micrometer. The standard height of the seal should be 0.335 in (8.5 mm). The wear limit is 0.276 in (7.0 mm). Replace the apex seals if the height is less than the limit (photo).
3   To check the apex seals for warping, take the seals from one rotor at a time and measure them one against the other. Measure the clearance between the top surfaces of the seals by placing them top-to-top. The gap should not exceed 0.0024 in (0.06 mm); if it does, replace all three seals (Fig. 1.10). Take care not to mix any of the seals from one rotor with those of the other when measuring.
4   Place each apex seal into its respective groove and use feeler gauges to check the clearance between the seal and the rotor groove. Insert the feeler gauge until it touches the bottom of the groove. Standard clearance between apex seal and rotor groove is 0.002 to 0.0035 in (0.05 to 0.09 mm) with a limit of 0.006 in (0.15 mm). If the clearance exceeds the limit, replace the apex seals (photo).
5   If new apex seals are being used, check the clearance between the apex seals and the side housing. Do this by measuring the overall

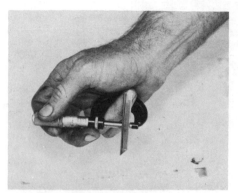

13.2 Measuring the height of an apex seal

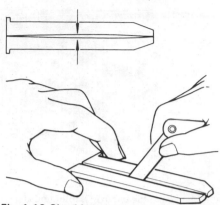

Fig. 1.10 Checking apex seals for warpage (Sec 13)

13.4 With an apex seal installed in its corresponding rotor groove, the clearance can be checked with a feeler gauge

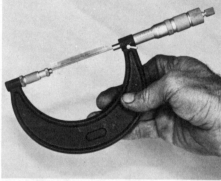

13.5 Measuring the overall length of an apex seal to arrive at the clearance between the seal and the housing

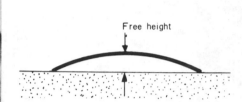

Fig. 1.11 Measuring free height of apex seal spring (Sec 13)

14.2 Measuring the protrusion of the rotor side seal

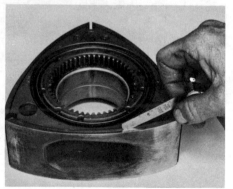

14.3 Checking side seal clearance

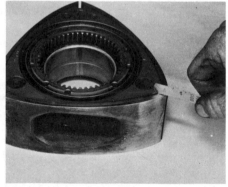

14.4 Measuring the clearance between a side seal and a corner seal

length of each apex seal with micrometers and comparing this with the rotor housing width. If necessary, the apex seals can be shortened with emery paper. Clearance between apex seal and side housing should be 0.0051 to 0.0067 in (0.13 to 0.17 mm) (photo).

6   Lay each apex seal spring onto a flat surface and check for free height. If the free height of the spring is less than 0.22 in (5.5 mm), replace the spring.

14 Side seal and spring – inspection

1   Place each side seal and side seal spring into its respective groove in the rotor and check for free movement by pressng with a finger. If there is no free movement, make sure the seal, spring and groove are perfectly clean.
2   Check the protrusion of each side seal by measuring with a depth gauge or feeler gauge. If the protrusion is not 0.02 in (0.5 mm) or more, replace the side seal ring (photo).

3   Check the clearance between the side seal and the groove in the rotor with a feeler gauge. If the clearance exceeds 0.0039 in (0.10 mm) replace the side seal (photo).
4   With the side seals and corner seals in their proper locations in the rotor, check the clearance between the side seals and the corner seals with a feeler gauge. The clearance limit between the side seals and the corner seals is 0.016 in (0.4 mm). If less than the limit, replace the side seals (photo).
5   If the side seals have been replaced, the gap between the side seals and the corner seals may have to be adjusted. A small amount can be ground off the round end of the side seal to arrive at a clearance of 0.002 to 0.006 in (0.05 to 0.016 mm).

15 Corner seal and spring – inspection

1   Replace each corner seal and its accompanying spring into the rotor.

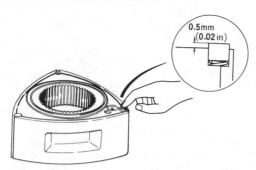

Fig. 1.12 Measuring protrusion of corner seal (Sec 15)

2   Check for free movement by pressing with a finger.
3   Check the protrusion of the corner seal from the rotor surface with a depth gauge or feeler gauge. The protrusion limit is 0.02 in (0.5 mm). Replace the corner seal spring if the protrusion is less than specified.

16 Eccentric shaft – inspection

1   Check the shaft for cracks, scratches, wear or damage.
2   Check that the oil passages are open.

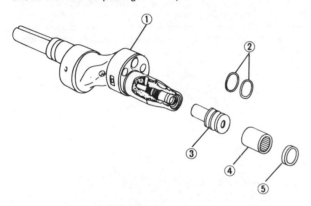

Fig. 1.13 Checking the eccentric shaft blind plug (Sec 16)

1	Eccentric shaft	4	Bearing
2	'O' rings	5	Oil seal
3	Blind plug		

3   The eccentric shaft can be checked for run-out by mounting it in V-blocks and using a dial indicator. Turn the shaft and take one-half the largest difference shown by the dial indicator. If this run-out is more than 0.0024 in (0.06 mm), replace the shaft with a new one.
4   Check the blind plug in the end of the shaft for oil leakage or looseness. If it is suspect, remove the plug with a hexagonal key and replace the O-ring inside.
5   Check the oil jet in the side of the eccentric shaft. Remove the plug with a thin-bladed screwdriver and check the spring for weakness, stick or damage to the steel ball just behind the spring. Before reassembly clean all parts and make sure the shaft cavity is open (photo).

17 Front and rear oil seals – replacement

1   The front oil seal fitted to the front cover and the rear oil seal fitted into the rear staionary gear should be changed as a matter of course during an engine rebuild.
2   Pry the seals out of their bores using a curved seal remover or screwdriver.
3   Clean the inside the bores and the outside of the new seals.
4   Position the new seals into place and use a hammer and a piece of hardwood to pound until flush with the surface. Do not hammer directly onto the seal, or use lubricant or sealing agent on the seal.

18 Engine – reassembly

1   The O-rings located inside the oil seals of the rotors should be replaced as a matter of course while performing an engine overhaul. In addition, any components found defective during the inspection process should be replaced with new ones (photo).
2   With the rotor resting on a clean surface, install the oil seals spring into their respective grooves. If these parts were properly identified and stored during disassembly this will be an easy task. If the springs have become mixed up or are being replaced, the cream-painted springs should be fitted on the front faces of both the front and rear rotors. The blue-painted springs go on the rear faces. The round end of the spring fits Into the stopper hole inside the groove and the squared-off end will fit inside a notch in the oil seal (Fig. 1.14).
3   Install a new O-ring into each oil seal, being careful not to stretch the O-ring out of shape.
4   Align the inner oil seal in the groove so that the notch in the seal will be pressed onto the square edge of the oil seal spring which is sticking up.
5   Press the seal into the groove using an old oil seal or your fingers. Press even around the circumference of the seal, until it is firmly seated. Be careful not to deform the lip of the oil seal (photo).
6   Install the outer oil seal in the same fashion.
7   Install the oil seals on the opposite side of the rotor and the oil

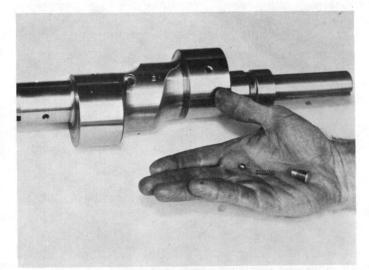

16.5 The oil jet, spring and steel ball removed from the side of the eccentric shaft

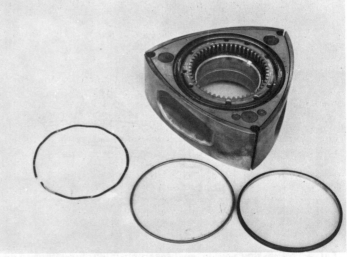

18.1 A rotor with one oil seal assembly. From the left, the oil seal spring, O-ring and the oil seal itself

On the front face of rotor

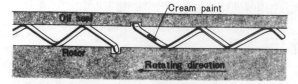

On the rear face of rotor

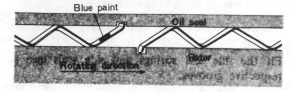

Fig. 1.14 Proper positioning of rotor oil seal springs (Sec 18)

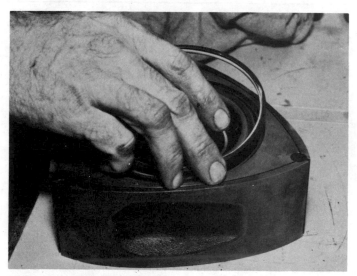

18.5 Installing an oil seal assembly

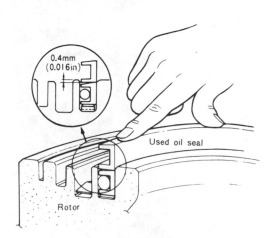

Fig. 1.15 Pressing new oil seal assembly into rotor with used oil seal (Sec 18)

seals on the other rotor.

8   Confirm the smooth movement of all oil seals by pressing lightly with your fingers. They should move freely inside the rotor grooves.

9   In order for the apex seals and side pieces to seal properly without gouging the rotor housing on initial start-up, Mazda has introduced a part called an assist piece which must be used when overhauling a rotary. The assist piece is made of a carbon material which disintegrates inside the engine after start-up. Its function is to relieve some of the spring tension of the apex seal spring during initial running after an overhaul.

10   Using a sharp knife or single-edged razor blade, cut the assist piece to a length of 0.08 to 0.10 in (2.0 to 2.8 mm).

11   Peel off the paper stuck to the assist piece and stick the small piece of the apex seal as shown in Fig. 1.16. Do this, one at a time, to all apex seals and return each seal to its proper location in your identifying box or sketch (photo).

12   Working on the front rotor, install the three apex seals without their respective springs.

13   On the front face of the front rotor (the side with the internal gear), place the corner seal springs and corner seals into their proper bores.

14   Still on the front of the rotor, fit the side seal springs and side seals into their grooves.

15   Confirm the smooth movement of all seals by pressing with your finger.

16   Mount the front housing on the engine stand.

17   Place the front rotor assembly on the front housing, being careful that none of the seals are dislodged from their positions (photo).

18   Mesh the internal gear and stationary gear so that the rotor is in the same location as when disassembled. The rotor is easiest to install with one apex pointed towards the top of the engine and the other two

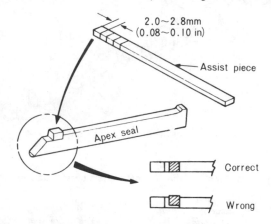

Fig. 1.16 Installation of assist piece to apex seal (Sec 18)

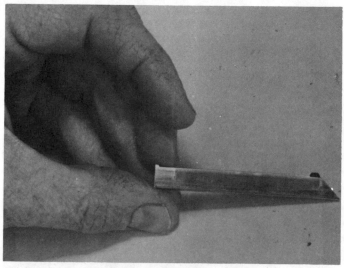

18.11 The small assist piece stuck to an apex seal

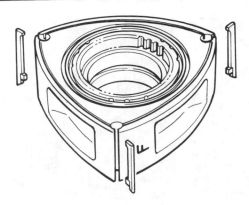

Fig. 1.17 Installation of apex seals to rotor (Sec 18)

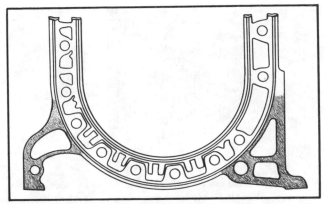

**Fig. 1.18 The area (shaded) to which gasket sealant is applied
(Sec 18)**

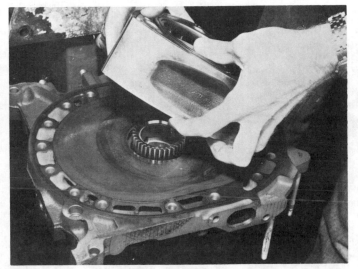

18.17 Placing the assembled rotor onto the front housing and meshing the internal gear

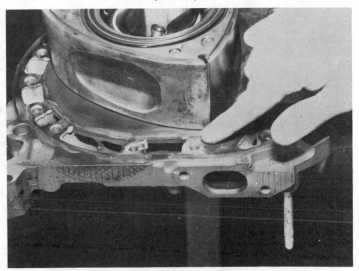

18.23 Applying a light, even coat of sealant to the front housing

symmetrically on either side.

19 Lubricate the front rotor journal and main journal on the eccentric shaft with engine oil.

20 Insert the eccentric shaft carefully, not damaging the rotor bearing or main bearing.

21 At this point it will be necessary to apply sealing agent onto the front rotor housing where it will mate to the front housing. Due to the fact that the housings are not really cinched into place until the torsion bolts are tightened later on, check the setting time of the silicone rubber-based sealant being used.

22 In order to have the entire engine assembly cinched before the sealant sets, it's a good idea to assemble the remaining rotor before any sealant is applied. Double-check that all components are clean and ready to install and that all necessary tools are at your disposal.

23 Apply sealant to the front side of the front rotor housing, working on around with your fingers to get a smooth, even coat (photo).

24 Also on the front side of the front rotor housing, install new sealing rubbers and a new O-ring in the recessed area where the dowel pin goes. The wider white line of the inner sealing rubber should face the combustion chamber and the seam of the rubber should be positioned in the area between the top point of the engine and the water port. Use Vaseline to hold the O-ring and sealing rubbers into place, as the housing will be inverted. Do not use grease for this.

25 Invert the front rotor housing and carefully place it onto the front housing. Make sure that the sealing rubber and O-ring do not come out of place.

26 Put some engine oil onto the two tubular dowels and push them through the rotor housing and into the front housing. You can use a rubber mallet to pound these into place (photo).

27 The apex seal springs can then be pushed into position at each apex of the front rotor (photo).

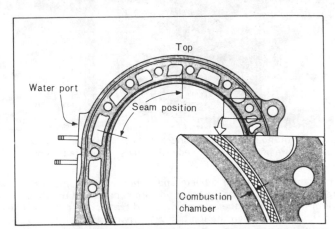

Fig. 1.19 Proper position for the sealing rubber seam (Sec 18)

28 Install the corner seal springs, corner seals, side seal springs and side seals into their proper locations on the rear side of the front rotor previously installed.

29 Fit each triangular shaped side piece in its original position. Confirm that the apex seal spring and assist piece are working properly and that the side piece is not resting against the rotor housing surface (photo).

30 Check that all seals are properly installed on the rotor and that there is smooth movement by pressing with your finger. If so, the eccentric shaft can be dropped into place.

31 Apply sealing agent to the rear side of the front rotor housing and

18.26 Use a rubber mallet to force the tubular dowel pins through the rotor housing and into the front housing

18.27 An apex seal spring being pushed into position behind an apex seal

18.29 Placing the small triangular side piece into position

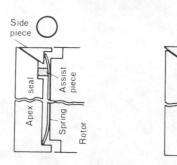

Fig. 1.20 Proper action of assist piece on triangular side piece (Sec 18)

18.33 Carefully lower the intermediate housing over the eccentric shaft and onto the dowel pins

18.34a Lifting the rear rotor into position, with one apex opposite the front rotor

18.34b With the rotor in place, check that all apex seals are properly positioned inside the grooves

18.37 The rear rotor housing in position over the rear rotor

18.42 Pushing a new sealing rubber into place on the rear rotor housing

install the new sealing rubbers and O-ring in the same fashion as previously described for the other side. Remember that the wide white line of the sealing rubber goes inward and that the seam in the rubber is positioned between the top and water port.

32 Apply engine oil or engine overhaul grease to each of the rotor seals and the inside surface of the rotor housing. Make sure that there is no foreign matter in the front rotor housing.

33 With an assistant pulling slightly up on the eccentric shaft (no more than an inch), install the intermediate housing through the eccentric shaft and onto the front rotor housing. Align the dowel pins and use a rubber mallet to fully seal the intermediate housing against the front rotor housing (photo).

34 The rear rotor with its apex seals and front side components installed is then lifted over the eccentric shaft and into position on the intermediate housing. One of its apexes should be towards the bottom of the engine, exactly opposite from the front rotor. Do not drop any of the seals into the openings at the sides of the housing (photos).

35 Apply sealing agent to the front side of the rear rotor housing,

smoothing it with your fingers.

36 As with the front rotor housing, use Vaseline to hold the sealing rubbers and O-rings into place on the front of the housing as it is inverted into place. The same rules apply to the wider white line and seam on the sealing rubber.

37 Invert the rear rotor housing and place it into position over the rear rotor. Check that the sealing rubber and O-ring remain in position (photo).

38 Apply engine oil to the two dowel pins and hammer them through the rear rotor housing and into the intermediate housing using a rubber mallet.

39 Insert each apex seal spring into its proper bore.

40 Install each corner seal spring, corner seal, side seal spring and side seal on the rear side of the rotor. Check for free movement.

41 Install each triangular side piece and check for free movement.

42 Apply sealant agent to the rear side of the rear rotor housing and then place a new O-ring and sealing rubber to this side following the same cautions about the wide white line and seam (photo).

43 Apply engine oil to the rotor seals and the sliding inside surface of the rear rotor housing. Check that no dirt or foreign mater has entered the rotor or rotor housing.

44 Coat the stationary gear and main bearing with engine oil and install the rear housing on the rear rotor housing. Tap with a rubber mallet to properly seat the two housings.

45 Install a new O-ring to each of the tension bolts and lightly coat the threads with oil

46 Install the tension bolts and tighten only finger tight. Note that one bolt is longer than the rest. This goes on the bottom left (photo).

47 Tighten the bolts in the proper order and a little at a time. The tightening should be done in about three steps to prevent any warping of the housings. Once all the bolts are tightened to the proper torque (23 to 27 ft lb, 3.2 to 3.8 m-kg), go around in a circular order to make sure that none of the bolts has been forgotten (photo).

48 Turn the eccentric shaft and confirm that the rotation is light and smooth.

19 Flywheel – installing

1 Apply engine oil to the oil seal in the rear housing.

2 Fit the key onto the eccentric shaft.

3 Install the flywheel to the eccentric shaft (photo).

4 Aply sealing agent to both sides of the flywheel lockwasher and place it in position over the end of the eccentric shaft.

5 Apply a thread locking agent such as 'Loctite' to the threads to the eccentric shaft and install the nut. It must be tightened to a torque of 289 to 362 ft-lb (40 to 50 m-kg). Assuming that most home mechanics will not have a torque wrench which will read this high, you can achieve this figure by using a length of pipe over your torque wrench. 100 pounds of torque applied 3½ feet from the nut will give a torque equal to 350 pounds. So depending on the type of torque wrench you have, cut a piece of pipe to slip over the torque wrench giving you a total length of 3½ feet. Then set the wrench to 100 pounds and tighten. A flywheel brake of some kind may have to be bought or fabricated to stop the flywheel from turning during this operation.

6 Use a chisel or screwdriver to bend up the lockwasher against one of the flat spots on the nut to prevent it from coming loose (photo). For automatic transmissions the counterweight is installed in the same manner, with the same torque specifications. Install the drive plate so that the hole of the drive plate lines up with the hole in the counterweight. To give you an idea of this position, the key for the counter weight should be in a straight line towards the bottom of the engine with the 'ears' of the counter weight towards the top. Then position the drive plate so that the drive plate hole lines up with the top mounting hole.

20 Front bearing and oil pump assemblies – installation

1 Slide the thrust plate, spacer and needle bearing onto the front of the eccentric shaft (Fig. 1.21). Apply sufficient engine oil or assembly lube to these components.

2 Place the bearing housing on the front housing and tighten the attaching bolts (photo).

3 Then slide the needle bearing, thrust washer and balance weight over the end of the shaft, oiling the needle bearing (photo).

4 Install the oil pump assembly onto the front housing. Tighten the four securing bolts.

5 Fit the key on the oil pump shaft.

6 Install the drive chain to the eccentric shaft sprocket and oil pump shaft sprocket and install together as a unit, aligning the keyways on each shaft.

7 Install the tab washer and nut of the oil pump sprocket and tighten to a torque of 22 to 25 ft-lb (3.0 to 3.5 m-kg). Use pliers to bend up the tab washer against one of the nut flats to prevent it from coming loose.

8 Align the keyways of the eccentric shaft sprocket and balance weight and install the key.

9 Slide the distributor drive gear onto the eccentric shaft with the 'F' mark towards the front of the engine.

18.47 The correct tightening sequence for the tension bolts

18.46 Tighten the tension bolts only slightly at first

19.3 Installing the flywheel over the eccentric shaft

19.6 Use a hammer and chisel to bend up the locking washer against one of the flats on the nut

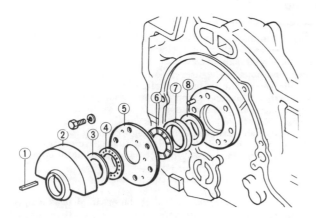

Fig. 1.21 Exploded view of front bearing and balance weight assemblies (Sec 20)

1	Key	5	Bearing housing
2	Balance weight	6	Needle bearing
3	Thrustwasher	7	Spacer
4	Needle bearing	8	Thrust plate

20.2 Tightening the bearing housing attaching bolts

20.3 Sliding the balance weight over the end of the eccentric shaft

21.4 Measuring the eccentric shaft endplay by prying the flywheel back and forth and measuring the movement with a feeler gauge

22.4 Place the front cover, with a new gasket and O-ring, into position

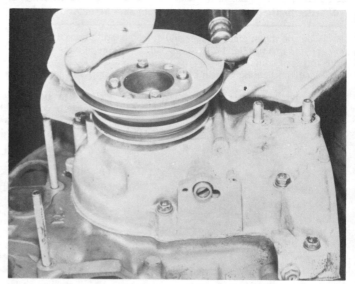

22.7 Installing the front eccentric shaft pulley

21 Eccentric shaft end play – adjustment

1   It is important to check the eccentric shaft end play after any major work is performed on the engine. The front cover need not be in place, but the front pulley must be temporarily installed.

2   Install the eccentric shaft pulley onto the shaft and tighten the attaching bolt to a torque of 72 to 87 ft-lb (10 to 12 m-kg). It may be necessary to use a flywheel brake of some kind to prevent the engine from turning as this is done.

3   The best way to measure end play is with a dial indicator mounted to the rear housing with its feeler contacting the flywheel. The flywheel is then moved back and forth by hand and a reading taking.

4   A cruder method can be used if a dial indicator is not available. Use the steel 'eye' bolted to the rear housing designed for lifting the engine out of the car. Turn the lifting eye and bolt around and thread a nut onto the bolt so that the steel just touches the flywheel when it is pried all the way out from the engine. Then push in the flywheel and measure the gap that the flywheel has moved with a feeler gauge (photo).

5   Standard eccentric shaft end play is 0.0016 to 0.0028 in (0.04 to 0.07 mm). The limit on end play is 0.0035 in (0.09 mm).

6   If the end play does not fall within tolerances, the oil pump and bearing assemblies must be removed and the spacer replaced with a thinner or thicker one.

22.10 Applying silicone sealant to the new oil pan gasket

22.12 Tightening each of the oil pan mounting bolts to the proper torque specifications

22 Front cover and oil pan – installation

1   Remove the front pulley previously installed to check the eccentric shaft end play.

2   Install a new O-ring on the oil passage of the front housing.

3   Make sure the gasket surface of the front housing is clean and smooth and then install a new gasket to the housing.

4   Place the front cover into position on the front housing and tighten the attaching bolts (photo).

5   If a new oil seal has not already been installed in the front cover, install one now by prying the old one out and tapping a new one into place with a hammer and wood block.

6   Apply a little engine oil to the front cover oil seal.

7   Install the eccentric shaft front pulley and tighten to specifications (photo).

8   Turn the engine over and install the oil pickup tube and strainer to the front housing with a new gasket.

9   Use a knife to trim off the excess gasket material location on the oil pan mounting flange where the front cover meets the front housing. The area where the oil pan mounts should be perfectly smooth and free of any dirt or old sealer.

10 Apply a bead of silicone sealant to the oil pan mounting flange as illustrated in Fig. 1.22. The sealant should be just inside the bolt holes (photo).

11 Apply more sealant to the oil pan gasket and then place the gasket onto the oil pan.

12 Install the oil pan and attaching bolts. Tighten the bolts to a torque of 5 to 7 ft-lb (0.7 to 1.0 m-kg). Tighten the bolts a little at a time, working around the oil pan (photo).

23 Minor engine components – installation

1   Install the water pump and tighten the nuts in the sequence as shown in Fig. 1.23. Torque the bolts to 13 to 20 ft-lb (1.8 to 2.7 m-kg) (photos).

2   Install the oil metering pump and its hoses to the front cover.

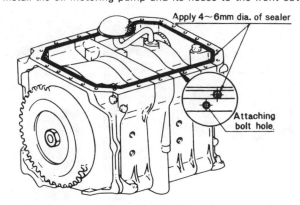

Fig. 1.22 Silicone sealant applied to the oil pan mounting flange (Sec 22)

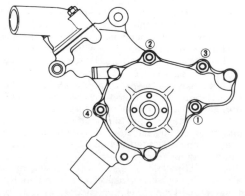

Fig. 1.23 Water pump tightening torque sequence (Sec 23)

23.1a The water pump housing being installed separately due to replacement of the water pump

23.1b The water pump is now installed to the housing with the attaching nuts tightened to the correct torque

23.3 Installing the oil filter pedestal with new O-rings

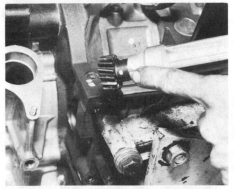

23.6 The tally marks painted on the distributor drivegear and distributor housing

23.10 The thermal reactor gasket with the metal sealers positioned towards the engine

23.11 Tightening the four thermal reactor attaching nuts

23.12a Use a new intake manifold gasket and O-rings

23.12b The carburetor and inlet manifold can now be installed

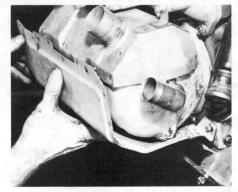

23.13 Installing the main thermal reactor shrouds

3   Install new O-rings onto the oil filter pedestal and tighten the oil filter assembly into place on the rear housing (photo).

4   Align the yellow-painted leading timing mark on the eccentric shaft pulley with the indicator pin on the front cover.

5   If you marked the distributor yourself upon disassembly, align your marks and install the distributor.

6   If you did not make your own indicator marks, align the small tally marks on the distributor housing and the drive gear at the bottom of the distributor, and install the distributor (photo).

7   For 1979 models, turn the distributor housing first counter-clockwise and then clockwise, stopping when the leading contact points just start to open. Tighten the distributor lock nut.

8   Install the distributor rotor and cap.

9   Noting the directional arrow, install the front engine mount.

10 Install a new thermal reactor gasket to the engine. Note that the wider metal area around the circular openings goes toward the engine (photo).

11 Check that the two short pieces of pipe inside the thermal reactor are correctly positioned and then install the thermal reactor. Torque should be 33 to 40 ft-lb (4.5 to 5.5 m-kg) (photo).

12 Replace the carburetor and inlet manifold as an assembly using new O-rings and gasket. Tighten the inlet manifold bolts to 14 to 19 ft-lb (1.9 to 2.6 m-kg) (photos).

13 Install the thermal reactor shrouds (photo).

14 Install the alternator with the spacer and adjusting shim located behind the water pump housing. Loosely install the long pivot bolt. Install the adjusting bracket and the drive belt and then tighten the alternator with the correct belt tension. Tension should be 0.59 plus or minus 0.08 in (15 plus or minus 2 mm) when pressed with a finger between the alternator pulley and the eccentric shaft pulley.

15 Install the air pump with its adjusting bracket and pivot bolt. Adjust the belt tension to 0.47 plus or minus 0.04 in (12 plus or minus 1 mm) when pressed between the pump pulley and water pump pulley.

16 Mount the anti-pollution solenoids and valves to the top of the engine as an entire unit.

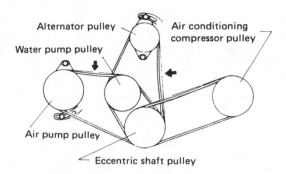

Fig. 1.24 Check points for drive belt tension (Sec 23)

17 Install the air valve and piping to its mounting location just above the thermal reactor (photo).
18 Place the clutch disc against the flywheel and fit the clutch cover over the disc. Note that two of the clutch bolts do not have threads all the way to the head. These fit into holes in the flywheel which do not have threads all the way to the top. Install all bolts finger-tight.
19 Centralize the clutch disc using a clutch centering tool or spare

input shaft. Then tighten all clutch bolts to 13 to 20 ft-lb (1.8 to 2.7 m-kg). Do this in many steps, working around the clutch to evenly compress the clutch spring (photos).

24 Installing the engine without the transmission

1 Thoroughly wipe clean the input shaft of the transmission.
2 Place a little lithium-based grease to the spigot bearing in the rear of the eccentric shaft.
3 Using the two lifting eyes, lift the engine slightly and remove the engine stand. The chains on the hoist should be positioned so that the engine will hang upright and straight.
4 Carefully lower the engine into position in the engine compartment, taking care not to damage the hoses or wiring in the engine compartment.
5 With the help of an assistant, line up the clutch opening with the transmission input shaft. Make sure the engine and transmission are in a straight line and not at angles to each other.
6 Slide the engine rearward onto the shaft. To engage the splines it may be necessary to turn the engine over by the crankshaft pulley. Take care that no strain is put on the clutch. If the two do not slide together easily, either the splines are not lined up or the transmission and engine are not in a straight line.
7 Keeping the weight of the engine on the hoist, install the bolts

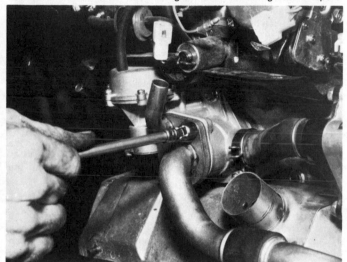

23.17 Installing the air valve and air pipe

23.19a Installing the clutch disc and clutch cover to the flywheel

23.19b Centralizing the clutch assembly

23.19c Tightening the attaching bolts to the proper torque

securing the engine to the transmission. Do not be tempted to use the bolts to draw the two components together; they should mate evenly without forcing.

8   Lower the engine into place on the front motor mounts and secure with the washer and nuts.

9   Refer to Sections 26 and 27 for reconnecting the engine components and the starting up sequence.

25 Installing the engine with the transmission

1   Thoroughly wipe clean the input shaft of the transmission.

2   Place a little lithium-grease on the spigot bearing in the rear of the eccentric shaft.

3   Using the two lifting eyes, lift the engine slightly and remove the engine stand. Lower the engine to the ground, using wood blocks between the floor and the engine.

4   Check that the release bearing and release fork are installed inside the transmission.

5   Slide the transmission into place behind the engine and line up the clutch opening with the transmission input shaft. Make sure that the transmission and engine are in a straight line and not at angles to each other.

6   Push the transmission and engine together, making sure that the weight of the transmission does not rest on the shaft alone. If necessary, turn the engine over with the eccentric shaft pulley to align the splines. The two should slide together easily without force (photo).

7   Bolt the transmission and engine together with the appropriate bolts.

8   Position the chains on the lifting hoist so that the engine/transmission unit hangs at an angle, with the transmission lower than the engine (photo).

9   It is preferable to have two jacks positioned under the vehicle; one to raise and lower the front of the car and one to raise the transmission once in place.

10 Raise the engine/transmission high enough to clear the front of the car and then carefully move the two components into place in the engine compartment (photo). At this point you will be able to judge if your angle is sufficient enough for installation. If not, remove the power unit and readjust the chains with the components resting on the ground.

11 Lower the transmission enough to clear the firewall and have an assistant position the transmission on the movable floor jack as the assembly is carefully lowered into position.

12 With the engine in the approximate location, raise the transmission and jockey the engine onto its front mounts.

13 Install the transmission crossmember to the body and remove the jack under the transmission.

14 Tighten the engine to its mounts using the appropriate washers and nuts.

15 Refer to the following Sections in this Chapter for reconnecting the engine components and the starting up sequence.

26 Reconnecting engine components after installation

1   Install the spark plugs using a little engine oil on the threads and tightening them to the proper torque (9 to 13 ft-lb or 1.2 to 1.8 m-kg).

2   Install each of the spark plug wires from the distributor cap to the appropriate spark plug.

3   Run the wiring harness across the engine, securing it with the original clips. Plug in all wiring connectors and install the two single wires from the harness at the rear of the alternator and on the emmissions control bracket.

4   Reinstall the clutch release cylinder to the top of the transmission with the two bolts, fitting its plunger into the release fork.

5   Connect the heater hose on the left side of the engine.

6   Install the two fuel lines to the carburetor, noting that one is of a large diameter than the other. The fuel hoses should be pushed onto the carburetor pipes 1.2 to 1.4 inches (30 to 35 mm) and secured with the clamps.

7   On the right side of the engine install the vacuum lines for the power brake assist. This hose is located at the rear of the engine. Tighten the screw clamp securely.

8   Connect the throttle, hot start assist and choke cables to the engine. The hot start assist cable is attached to the bracket on the bottom, the throttle cable attaches to the bracket in the center and the choke mounts near the top of the bracket. Have an assistant operate the choke and throttle from inside the car to check for proper operation. These two cables can be adjusted at their mounting bracket by loosening or tightening the locknuts.

9   If equipped with air conditioning, mount the condensor bracket, condensor and drivebelt.

10 If the front radiator shroud and support bracing was removed for greater clearance, this should be reinstalled on the nosepiece of the car.

11 Lift the radiator with the plastic shroud and fan attached in position and secure to the support bracing with the four bolts and one nut.

12 Connect the wire for the coolant level sensor at the top of the radiator.

13 Connect the hose leading from the top of the radiator to the coolant recovery tank.

14 Install the top radiator hose, securing it to the radiator and the thermostat housing with screw clamps.

15 Install the heater hose at the bottom right-hand side of the radiator. Tighten securely with clamp.

16 Install the lower radiator hose to the radiator and the engine just above the right-hand engine mount. Tighten securely with clamp.

17 Connect the fan assembly to the front pulley with the four bolts passing through the flange.

18 Raise the vehicle and place firmly on stands for access to components under the car.

19 Working under the car, install the starter and connect its wires.

20 Connect the wiring to the transmission switches and to the oil level sensor on the oil pan.

21 Slide the exhaust system forward into position and attach the main pipe to the thermal reactor flange with the three nuts.

25.6 Installing the transmission to the engine

25.8 The lifting chains should be positioned so that the engine/transmission assembly hangs at an angle

25.10 Lower the assembly into the engine compartment and check for any obstructions

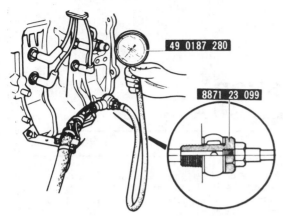

Fig. 1.25 Oil pressure gauge installation (Sec 27)

22 Connect the air pipe with the rubber pipe to the bottom of the thermal reactor with the two nuts. The thermal reactor cover is also secured with these two nuts.

23 Connect the remaining air pipe to the rear of the engine with two nuts.

24 Install the exhaust system hanger bracket to the transmission tailhousing with the two bolts. The remaining bolt at the top of this bracket goes into the exhaust support.

25 Install the two hoses for the oil system to the oil cooler located at the bottom left side of the radiator. Use one wrench to hold the fitting while the lock nut is tightened. Do not exert undue force in this area as the cooler can be damaged.

26 Install the metal cover under the radiator by first sliding the tabs into the front crossmember and then securing it with the five bolts, across the front and two bolts on the sides going into the frame.

If the transmission was removed with the engine, perform the following:

27 Reinstall the propeller shaft using the alignment marks you make upon disassembly. Tighten the flange bolts to a torque of 25 to 27 ft-lb (3.5 to 3.8 m-kg).

28 Connect the speedometer cable to the transmission, tightening the collar nut with a pair of pliers.

29 Remove the transmission fill plug on the side of the transmission and fill with the proper amount and grade of fluid. Allow the fluid time to drain to the rear of the transmission. This will take some time, so go on to other components and then come back and check the fluid level periodically.

30 Install the gearshift lever retaining housing, rubber boot and retaining plate. Install the gearshift lever faceplate and shift knob.

31 Make a final check that all wiring is firmly connected, all bolts are tight and connections secure before lowering the car to the ground.

27 Engine starting up sequence

1 As the Mazda is not equipped with an oil pressure gauge or warning light, it is highly advisable to take the time to make or buy a fitting which will enable you to install a temporary oil pressure gauge upon initial start-up. Mazda makes a connector (part number 88/1 23 099) which installs at the rear engine housing where the oil hose enters the engine. This can be purchased and installed, or the oil hose fitting can be drilled and tapped to accept a common screw-in oil pressure gauge.

2 Reinstall the air cleaner assembly and its various hoses, and reinstall the wing nut and securing bolt.

27.9 An external hand-held oil pressure gauge should be used to check for sufficient oil pressure after an engine overhaul

3 Fill the engine with the correct grade of engine oil of the specified amount.

4 Fill the radiator with water and anti-freeze (See Chapter 2).

5 Connect the negative cable to the battery. Check that there is no spark, as this will indicate some current flow. If sparking does occur, check that all switches are off and the doors are closed, preventing the interior lights from coming on. Continued flow means a short circuit, which should be traced before proceeding.

6 Make one more final check that everything is connected and looks in order. Check for any spare parts laying around.

7 Disconnect the two high tension leads to the coils and, by use of the ignition key, crank the engine over for about 30 seconds. This will ensure adequate lubrication by the fuel/oil mixture and expel excess oil from the sides of the apex seals.

8 Connect the two high tension leads to the coils.

9 Connect a hand-held oil pressure gauge to the fitting you have installed in the rear engine housing (photo).

10 Start the engine and check for oil pressure and that the alternator is charging. If, after a few seconds, the oil pressure gauge shows no pressure or the alternator light does not go off, turn the engine off. Trace the problem(s) before continuing.

11 If the warning lights go out correctly and the gauge indicates proper oil pressure, set the engine to run on the fast idle setting and check the engine for leaks. Run only for a few minutes and then shut off.

12 Check the coolant level; in the first few moments it is likely to go down as air locks are filled and the thermostat opens.

13 If the carburetor has been dismantled, temporarily adjust the idle.

14 Remove the temporary oil pressure gauge from the engine and plug the connector.

15 Reinstall the hood and go for a short test ride. Drive very gently, and for only about three miles.

16 Recheck for leaks.

17 With the engine fully warmed up, adjust the carburetor again if necessary.

18 Check the water, oil and transmission fluid levels for a final time.

19 It is important during the first 500 or so miles after an overhaul to keep a close eye on the oil level in the engine. A relatively high oil consumption during the break-in period is not abnormal so check frequently.

Chapter 2 Cooling and lubrication

Refer to Chapter 13 for specifications and information related to 1981 through 1985 models

Contents

Specifications

Water pump
Type	Centrifugal impeller
Feeding capacity at 6,500 rpm of engine	(150 to 160 liters/min. 39.6 to 42.3 U.S. gal/min. 33.0 to 35.2 Imp gal/min.)
Pump driven by	"V" belt
Pulley ratio of eccentric shaft and pump	1 : 1.18

Fan
Fan diameter	410 mm (16.1 in)
Number of fan blades	7
Fan drive	
Standard revolution of fan	1,400 ± 200 rpm at 4,200 rpm of engine

Thermostat
Type	Wax pellet
Starts to open	82 ± 1.5°C (180 ± 2.7°F)
Fully opens at	95°C (203°F)
Lift	8 to 10 mm (0.3 to 0.4 in)

Radiator
Type	Corrugated fin, with expansion tank
Pressure cap opens at	0.9 ± 0.1 kg/cm² (13.0 ± 1 lb/in²)

Cooling capacity
With heater	9.5 liters (10 U.S. quarts, 8.4 Imp. quarts)
Without heater	8.5 liters (9.0 U.S. quarts, 7.5 Imp. quarts)

Oil pump
Type	Rotor
Feeding capacity at 1,000 rpm of engine	5.0 liters/min. (5.3 U.S. quarts/min., 4.4 Imp quarts/min.)
Oil pump driven by	Chain and sprockets
Limit of chain slack	12 mm (0.47 in)
Outer rotor and body clearance	
Standard	0.20 to 0.25 mm (0.008 to 0.010 in)
Wear limit	0.30 mm (0.0118 in)
Clearance between rotor lobes	
Standard	0.01 to 0.09 mm (0.0004 to 0.0035 in)
Wear limit	0.15 mm (0.0059 in)
Rotor endfloat	
Standard	0.03 to 0.13 mm (0.0012 to 0.0051 in)
Wear limit	0.15 mm (0.0059 in)
Oil pressure at 3,000 rpm of engine	4.5 to 5.5 kg/cm² (64 to 78 lb/in²)
Oil pressure at idle speed of engine	0.9 to 2.7 kg/cm² (13 to 38 lb/in²)

Pressure regulator valve (Rear housing)
Operating pressure .... 5.0 kg/cm^2 (71.1 lb/in^2) at 3,000 rpm of engine
Free length of spring .... 46.4 mm (1.830 in)

Pressure control valve (Front cover)
Operating pressure .... 11.0 kg/cm^2 (156 lb/in^2)
Free length of spring .... 73.0 mm (2.874 in)

By-pass valve (Oil cooler)
Starts to close .... 50 to 55°C (122 to 131°F)
Fully closes .... 60 to 65°C (140 to 149°F)
Opening pressure .... 3.56 kg/cm^2 at 60°C (50.6 lb/in^2 at 140°F)

Oil filter
Type .... Full flow, cartridge
Relief valve opens at .... 0.8 to 1.2 kg/cm^2 (11 to 17 lb/in^2)

Oil metering pump
Feeding capacity at 2,000 rpm of engine .... 2.0 to 2.5cc/6 min. (0.068 to 0.085 U.S. oz/6 min.)

Lubricant
Classification .... A.P.I. Service SD or SE
-10°C to 40°C (15°F to 100°F) .... SAE 20W-40
-10°C to 50°C (15°F to 120°F) .... SAE 20W-50
-18°C to 30°C (0°F to 85°F) .... SAE 10W-30
-18°C to 40°C (0°F to 100°F) .... SAF 10W-40
-18°C to 50°C (0°F to 120°F) .... SAE 10W-50
Below -18°C (0°F) .... SAE 5W-20 or 5W-30

Oil capacity
Full capacity .... 5.2 liters (5.5 U.S. quarts, 4.6 Imp. quarts)
Oil pan capacity .... 4.2 liters (4.4 U.S. quarts, 3.7 Imp. quarts)

Torque wrench settings

	m-kg	ft-lb
Oil pump sprocket	3.0 to 3.5	22 to 25
Oil pan	0.7 to 1.0	5 to 7
Temperature gauge unit	0.7 to 0.8	5 to 6
Water temperature switch	1.0 to 1.8	7 to 13

1 General description

1   The water cooling system of the Mazda RX-7 is much the same as for a piston engine, but it takes away a smaller proportion of the heat. The cooling water is regulated by a thermostat, as in conventional engines.

2   The water pump is located high on the front of the engine and is driven by a belt from a pulley mounted on the front of the crankshaft. The fan used to cool the water in the radiator is also connected to the front of the crankshaft. The fan is a clutch type which allows for full cooling at low engine speeds and then cuts down its rotating speed at higher engine revolutions where maximum cooling from the engine is not needed.

3   Where the rotary engine differs from conventional piston engines is that some of the oil is used for cooling as well as lubricating. Because it would be nearly impossible to cool the rotors themselves with water, oil is sprayed onto the inside surface of the rotors by jets in the crankshaft. Because of this function the system is equipped with an oil cooler at the bottom of the radiator which plays an important role in keeping oil temperatures to a minimum.

4   The oil pump is located at the front of the engine and is driven by a chain from the crankshaft.

5   Also designed into the system is an oil metering pump which feeds oil directly into the carburetor to lubricate the internal seals during the combustion process. This oil is not retrieved, thus contributing to the higher-than-normal oil consumption of the rotary engine.

2 Water level and pressure

1   The cooling system should not normally need additional water. The coolant level in the radiator should be full, and between the 'Full' and 'Low' marks on the coolant reservoir when the engine is cool.

2   Do not under any circumstances attempt to remove the radiator cap while the engine is operating. To do so might lead to damage of the cooling system and the engine, and could result in serious injury

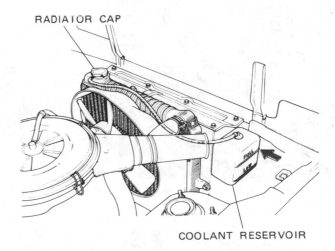

RADIATOR CAP

COOLANT RESERVOIR

Fig. 2.1 The cooling system fluid level is checked at the reservoir at the side of the radiator (Sec 2)

from hot coolant or steam blow-out.

3   Switch off the engine and wait until it has cooled. Even then, use extreme care when removing the cap from a warm radiator. Wrap a thick cloth around the cap and turn it slowly to the first stop.

4   Step back while the pressure is released from the cooling system. When you are sure all the pressure has been released, press down on the cap - still using a cloth - turn and remove it.

5   Normal routine inspection of the engine compartment should spot a coolant leak. If this is the case, rectify the problem immediately. Leaks are commonly caused by deteriorated water hoses and are easy to replace.

6   Because of the aluminium engine components in the RX-7 overheating can cause serious damage in a relatively short time. Due to this unforgiving nature, the driver has two dash-mounted system checks to warn of impending danger to the cooling system, and thus the engine. The temperature gauge should be watched closely to prevent overheating of the engine. The warning light which reads 'Add coolant' should be strictly adhered to. If the light comes on while driving, pull safely off the road and stop the engine. Allow the system to cool and check the coolant reservoir and the radiator.

3   Flushing and filling: antifreeze and inhibitors

1   The coolant used in the Mazda rotary engine has an ethylene glycol base for aluminium engine protection as well as anti-corrosive and anti-freezing ingredients. This coolant is mixed in the 50/50 ratio with water and protects against temperatures ranging from -20 degrees Fahrenheit (-29 degrees Centigrade) to boiling.
2   Alcohol or methanol based coolants should not be used in the Mazda rotary. Only soft (demineralized) water should be used in the coolant mixture (photo).
3   Before draining the coolant run the engine for about ten minutes to stir up any sludge, but not hard enough to get the system very hot.
4   Remove the radiator cap very carefully using a thick cloth. Turn it to the first stop to allow the pressure to be released, then remove it completely.
5   Remove the cap from the coolant recovery tank.
6   Disconnect the lower radiator hose on the right side of the engine to allow the coolant to drain out of the radiator.
7   Remove the drain plug on the left side of the engine. This is located just below the spark plugs. Water will drain from the engine at this point.
8   Disconnect the heater hose on the left side of the engine. Couple it to a supply of water, such as a garden hose.
9   Turn on the water from the hose and move the temperature control of the heater to the 'Hot' position. Flush the system with water so water pours out through the engine drain hole and radiator. Do this

until all traces of rust are gone, then let the system drain completely.
10 When completely drained, install the drain plug in the engine and connect the heater hose and the lower radiator hose. Install the cap on the coolant recovery tank.
11 Add a 50/50 mixture of ethylene glycol antifreeze and water to the radiator until full.
12 Run the engine at idle with the radiator cap removed and slowly add coolant in accordance with the drop of coolant level.
13 When the engine reaches normal operating temperature, pump the accelerator pedal 2 or 3 times and add coolant as required.
14 Install the radiator cap and inspect all connections for leaks.
15 Recheck the coolant level after a few miles of driving to make sure that no air pockets in the engine have caused the level to go down.

4   Water pump – removal and installation

1   The water pump is at the front of the engine, driven by a belt from the fan pulley. It can cause problems in one of two ways: either the bearings can fail or the water gland leak.
2   The most common problem with water pumps is that the water gland will break. This is readily identified by leakage from behind the pulley. A 'weep' hole in the water pump is where the water will exit the pump (photo).
3   Bearing failure may appear as a squealing noise, or too much free movement. Noises can be pinpointed with a length of hose held to the ear, while moving the other end around the water pump itself. If this is done, be careful of the fan and moving components of the engine which can cause serious injury. Free play can be felt by pulling the pulley back and forth.
4   Although access to the water pump is rather tight, it can be removed without dismantling many of the major engine components.
5   Cover the front fenders to protect the paint.
6   Disconnect the negative cable to the battery.
7   If air conditioning is fitted, loosen the two adjusting bolts at the top of the compressor mounting bracket and the one long pivot bolt under the compressor. Move the compressor and disconnect the drive

3.2 It is important to use the specified antifreeze mixture in the aluminum engine

4.2 Water pump gland leakage will appear out of a 'weep' hole in the pump body

4.7 Loosening the adjusting bolts at the top of the air conditioning compressor

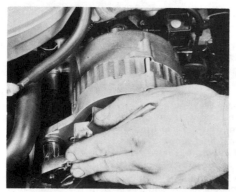
4.10 Loosening the long pivot bolt to disengage the alternator drivebelt

4.11 Removing the fan assembly retaining bolts using a large pair of pliers to prevent the assembly from turning

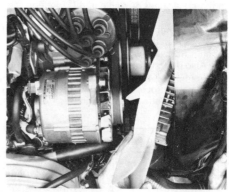
4.12 The fan assembly being removed from inside the radiator shroud

belt from the compressor (photo).

8 Loosen the long pivot bolt on the top of the air pump and the smaller adjusting bolt beneath the air pump to relieve tension on the drive belt. Swing the air pump inward and disconnect the air pump drive belt.

9 Disconnect the lower radiator hose on the right side of the engine to drain the coolant. Once drained, re-connect the hose.

10 Loosen the long pivot bolt and a smaller adjusting bolt on the alternator. Relieve tension on the alternator drive belt and remove the alternator drive belt (photo).

11 Remove the four bolts which secure the fan assembly to the pulley. It may be necessary to hold the fan flange with a pair of large pliers to keep the fan assembly from moving while the bolts are loosened (photo).

12 Pull the fan assembly out of the radiator shroud and set aside with the four mounting bolts (photo).

13 At this time completely remove the alternator adjustment arm where it bolts to the alternator at the top and to the water pump at the bottom. Set it aside with the two bolts.

14 Completely remove the air pump adjustment bracket where it bolts to the air pump and to the water pump. Set it aside with the two bolts and identify it in some way so as not to get it confused with the alternator adjustment bracket.

15 If air conditioning is fitted, remove the air conditioning pulley from the eccentric shaft.

16 Remove the four nuts and two bolts which secure the water pump to the water housing.

17 Remove the water pump by pulling it straight of the studs and then up and out of the engine compartment (photo).

18 The fan flange and water pump pulley can now be separated from the water pump by removing the four bolts. Before doing so, mark the front of the fan flange for easier reassembly.

19 Use a gasket scraper or putty knife to completely remove any traces of sealer or gasket material from the water pump housing still on the engine.

20 Install the fan flange and water pump pulley onto the water pump with the four bolts. Use your identifying mark to install the flange correctly.

21 Smear a light coat of silicone sealer around the gasket surface of the water pump and on the water pump housing. Press the new gasket into place on the water pump, aligning all of the bolt holes.

22 Place the water pump into position on the studs, being careful not to move or damage the gasket. Thread on the four nuts and two bolts against the pump but do not tighten at this time.

23 Install the alternator adjustment bracket and install the two bolts finger-tight.

24 Tighten the four water pump securing nuts to a torque of 13 to 20 ft-lb (1.8 to 2.7 m-kg). Looking straight on at the pump, tighten the lower right nut first, followed by the top center nut, top right nut and last, the lower left nut.

25 Tighten the remaining water pump bolts to the same torque.

26 Install the alternator drive belt so that it fits into the rear grooves of the water pump and crankshaft pulleys.

27 Adjust the belt tension to a point where approximately 0.60 in (16 mm) of deflection cable can be felt by pushing the belt with your finger half way between the alternator pulley and the crankshaft pulley. Tighten the alternator adjusting and pivot bolts.

28 Install the air pump adjustment bracket. Do not tighten the bolts yet.

29 Install the air pump drive belt into the forward groove of the water pump pulley and second groove of the crankshaft pulley. Adjust the tension until about $\frac{1}{2}$ in (12 mm) of deflection cable can be felt by pushing the belt with your finger half way between the air pump pulley and the water pump pulley. Tighten the pivot and adjustment bolts, and the bracket bolt at the water pump housing.

30 If air conditioning is fitted, install the pulley onto the eccentric shaft pulley with the four mounting bolts.

31 Make sure the raised lug on the compressor pulley goes into the larger hole in the eccentric pulley.

32 Install the air conditioning drive belt and adjust to a tension of approximately 0.35 in (9 mm) with finger pressure applied half way between the eccentric shaft and compressor pulley. Tighten the two adjustment bolts at the top of the compressor and the one pivot bolt underneath the compressor.

33 Install the fan assembly onto the water pump pulley flange with the four bolts. Keep the fan from turning by holding the flange with a

4.17 Pull the water pump off the studs, then out of the radiator shroud

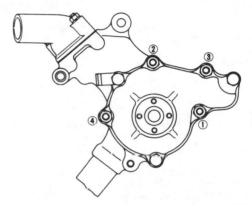

Fig. 2.2 Water pump tightening torque sequence (Sec 4)

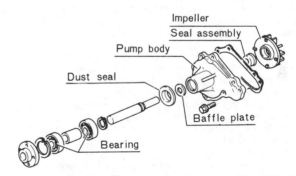

Fig. 2.3 Exploded view of water pump (Sec 5)

large pair of pliers or channel-locks.

34 Make sure the lower radiator hose clamp is securely tightened and then fill the radiator with a 50/50 mixture of soft (demineralized) water and ethylene glycol based antifreeze.

35 Connect the negative battery cable.

36 Start the engine and check for leaks.

5 Water pump – overhaul and inspection

1 Due to the fact that a press and special adapters are needed to disassemble the water pump, it may be advisable for the home mechanic to purchase a rebuilt water pump and install it following the sequence detailed in Section 4.

2 Purchase a water pump overhaul kit which will include all gaskets and seals necessary to replace if the water pump is disassembled.

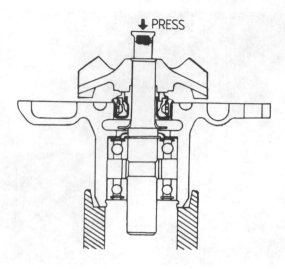

Fig. 2.4 Pressing out the water pump shaft (Sec 5)

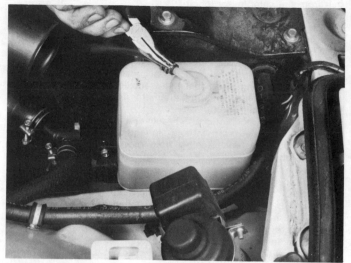

6.2 Removing the reservoir hose from the recovery tank

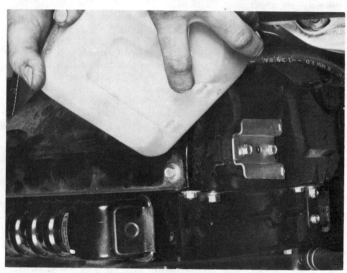

6.4 A metal clip attached to the radiator secures the tank

3   Support the water pump pulley and slowly press the pump shaft to remove the pulley boss.
4   With suitable pliers, remove the snap ring from the front of the shaft.
5   Support the pump body and apply pressure to the rear end of the shaft to press the shaft, spacer and bearing assembly out through the front of the water pump body.
6   Remove the impeller from the rear of the pump body.
7   Remove the seal assembly from the pump body.
8   Remove the bearing and spacer from the shaft with a puller or by using a hammer and drift.
9   Inspect the bearing for roughness or excessive play.
10   Remove any rust or scale from the bearing shaft with emery cloth.
11   Inspect the seat for seal on the impeller. It should not have pits, marks or scoring. If the seat for the seal is marked or damaged the impeller should be replaced.
12   Inspect the water pump body and the impeller for cracks and wear. Replace as necessary.
13   Ensure that the stop ring is correctly seated in the groove on the shaft.
14   Place the dust seal plate on the shaft.
15   Drive the baffle plate onto the taper of the shaft.
16   Press in the rear bearing, with the sealed side rearward, to the shaft until it contacts with the stop ring.
17   Press the shaft and bearing assembly into the pump body.
18   Place the spacer on the shaft and apply lithium based grease.
19   Install the front bearing with sealed side forward until the snap ring can be installed.
20   Install the snap ring.
21   Press the water pump pulley and pulley boss onto the shaft.
22   Install the seal assembly into the pump body.
23   Press the impeller onto the end of the shaft until it is flush with the end of the shaft.
24   Rotate the shaft by hand to see whether it rotates smoothly.
25   Install the water pump as described in Section 4.

6   Coolant reservoir – removal and installation

1   The coolant reservoir is located at the right side of the radiator and should periodically be checked for cracks, damage and leakage.
2   To remove the reservoir, first use a pair of pliers to open the hose clip. Move the clip back on the hose about two inches (photo).
3   Pull the water hose off its connection on the top of the reservoir.
4   The reservoir is then disconnected from its clips on the radiator by pulling outward on the bottom of the reservoir and at the same time pulling the reservoir straight up (photo).
5   To install, push the reservoir onto its mounting clips until it seats properly and then reconnect the water hose with the clip.

7   Thermostat – removal and installation

1   The thermostat is located at the front of the engine, inside a housing just to the right of the alternator. It prevents the cooling system from running the engine too cold at the beginning of a trip or in cold weather, and prevents the engine from overheating during normal driving conditions.
2   If the thermostat is functioning properly, the temperature gauge on the dashboard should rise to the normal driving position quickly and then stay there, only rising above the normal mark occasionally when the engine is unusually hot. If the engine does not rise to normal operating temperatures quickly, or if it overheats, the thermostat should be removed and checked, or replaced.
3   Disconnect the negative battery cable at the battery.
4   Remove the air cleaner assembly with its various hoses. There is a lock nut at the front of the air cleaner and a wing nut on the inside of the air cleaner.
5   Disconnect the lower radiator hose to drain the cooling system. After it has drained, reconnect the lower radiator hose and tighten the clamp.
6   Unclip the main engine wiring loom from the rear of the alternator and move towards the rear of the engine to gain access to the thermostat housing.
7   Remove the bolt which secures the metal vacuum line to the air cleaner mounting bracket. This adjoins the thermostat housing (photo).

7.7 The bolt which secures the vacuum line to the water inlet housing

7.8 Removing the top radiator hose

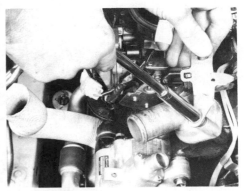

7.9 Remove the metal bracket from the housing

7.11 Pull the water housing off the stud

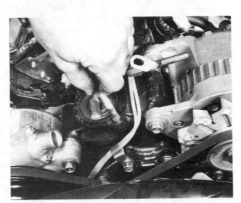

7.12 Note the position of the thermostat before removing it from the recess

Fig. 2.5 Testing thermostat operation (Sec 8)

8   Disconnect the upper radiator hose from the thermostat housing and the radiator. Remove the radiator hose (photo).
9   Remove the nut which secures the air cleaner bracket to the thermostat housing (photo).
10 Remove the nut, lockwasher and flat washer from the front of the thermostat housing and the bolt, lock washer and flat washer from the rear side of the thermostat housing.
11 Pull the thermostat housing straight off its mounting stud (photo).
12 Note the position of the thermostat in the water pump housing and then lift it out (photo).
13 When the thermostat is installed make sure the mating surfaces of the thermostat housing and the water pump housing are clean and free of excess gasket material and sealer. Use a gasket scraper or putty knife to clean the surfaces.
14 Install the thermostat in the water pump housing with the jiggle pin pointed upwards.
15 Install a new gasket to the housing using silicone sealer on both sides of the gasket. Smear the sealer around with your finger to get a light, even coat.
16 Place the thermostat housing over the stud and thermostat.
17 Tighten the mounting nut and bolt. Be sure to install the flat washers and lock washers with the nut and bolt.
18 Install the air cleaner bracket loosely to the thermostat housing. Do not tighten at this time.
19 Loosely install the securing bolt for the metal vacuum hose.
20 Install the upper radiator hose and securely tighten the clamps at either end of the hose.
21 Pull the wiring loom back into its clip at the rear end of the alternator.
22 Install the air cleaner assembly and its various hoses. Move the front bracket and metal vacuum hose to the correct position, as they are still loose on the thermostat housing.
23 Tighten the front air cleaner bracket bolt and metal vacuum hose bracket.
24 Check that both radiator hoses are in position and all clamps are tight. Then fill the radiator with 50/50 mixture of soft (demineralized) water and ethylene glycol base antifreeze.
25 Connect the negative battery cable and start the engine. Check for

leaks at the upper and lower radiator hoses and around the thermostat housing.

8   Thermostat – checking

1   Submerge the thermostat in a container with some water. Also place a thermometer into the water.
2   Gradually heat the container on a hot place or stove and check the temperature when the thermostat first starts to open.
3   Continue heating the container and check the temperature when the thermostat fully opens.
4   Using a bent coat hanger or similar device, lift the fully-opened thermostat out of the hot water and measure the lift height.
5   The thermostat should start to open at 180° plus or minus 2.7°F (82° plus or minus 1.5°C).
6   The thermostat should be fully opened at 203°F (95°C)
7   The thermostat lift should be 0.3 to 0.4 in (8 to 10 mm).
8   If any of these specifications are not met, replace the thermostat with a new one.
9   If, when removed from the car, the thermostat is fully open it must be replaced.

9   Radiator – removal and installation

1   The radiator is located at the extreme front of the engine compartment. Unlike many convenient piston-engine designs, the RX-7 incorporates a separate oil cooler at the bottom of the radiator.
2   The radiator can be removed separately from the oil cooler, or the two can be removed together as a unit. If it is desirable to remove the oil cooler with the radiator, the two oil hoses running from the engine to the lower left corner of the cooler should be disconnected and plugged to prevent fluid loss.
3   Disconnect the bullet connector for the coolant level sensor located at the top of the radiator. Route the wiring away from the radiator.

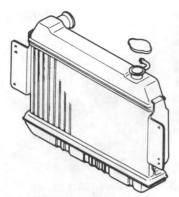

Fig. 2.6 Radiator with separate oil cooler attached at the bottom (Sec 9)

4   From the radiator cap, disconnect the water hose leading to the coolant reservoir. Move the hose out of the way of the radiator.

5   Remove the four bolts which secure the fan assembly to the water pump pulley. It may be necessary to hold the flange to prevent the fan from turning as the bolts are loosened.

6   Remove the fan assembly, or if this proves too difficult, it can be placed inside the radiator cowling and removed with the radiator.

7   Remove the engine under-cover for better access.

8   Disconnect the lower radiator hose and allow the coolant to drain. Bend the hose back out of the way of the radiator flange.

9   Loosen the clamp and disconnect the heater hose from the lower radiator hose nipple at the lower right side of the engine.

10 Disconnect the upper radiator hose from the radiator and push the hose out of the way of the radiator.

11 On vehicles equipped with automatic transmissions, remove the oil hoses from the bottom of the radiator.

12 Remove the four bolts and one nut which secures the radiator and shroud assemblies to the support system (photo).

13 If removing the radiator without the oil cooler, remove the bolts which join the cooler to the radiator. The joining brackets are on both sides of the radiator and are held by two bolts on each bracket.

14 The radiator, shroud and fan assembly inside should now be free to be lifted straight up and out of the engine compartment (photo).

15 Examine the radiator for signs of leakage. Any leaks should be repaired by soldering or, if too excessive, the radiator should be replaced.

16 Thoroughly clean the exterior of the radiator by blowing out with compressed air if available.

17 Install the radiator with the shroud attached and the fan assembly inside the shroud.

18 Loosely install the bolts at the oil cooler brackets and at the support system on either side of the radiator. Do not tighten any of the bolts until all securing bolts are started. Then tighten each of the attaching bolts.

19 On vehicles with automatic transmissions, install the fluid hoses.

20 Connect the upper and lower radiator hoses. Tighten the clamps securely.

21 Connect the heater hose at the lower right side of the radiator,

next to the lower radiator hose.

22 Use the four bolts to attach the fan assembly to the water pump pulley.

23 Connect the hose from the coolant recovery tank to the radiator.

24 Connect the coolant level sensor lead at the top of the radiator.

25 Install the engine under-cover by first placing it into the crossmember and then bolting across the front and sides.

26 Fill the radiator with a 50/50 mixture of soft (demineralized) water and ethylene glycol base antifreeze.

27 Install the radiator cap.

28 Run the engine and check for leaks. Recheck the coolant level after a few miles of driving.

10 Coolant level sensor – removal and installation

1   Disconnect the bullet connector to the sensor at the top of the radiator.

2   Remove the radiator cap once all pressure has been relieved from the system. Do this with a thick cloth wrapped around the cap.

3   Using a wrench, remove the sensor from the top of the radiator (photo).

4   When installing, the sensor should be tightened to the radiator to a torque of 13 to 21 in-lb (15 to 25 cm-kg). Further tightening may damage the top of the radiator.

5   Connect the wiring connector to the sensor, install radiator cap and start the engine.

6   Warm the engine up to normal operating temperatures and check for leaks around the sensor.

11 Fan belt – checking

1   The viscous coupling of the fan can fail in one or two ways. Either there can be excessive slip, which would prevent the fan from cooling the engine sufficiently at low engine speeds, or the drive could seize, creating noise and wasting engine power because the fan is turning with the engine no matter what the engine speed.

2   The fan can be checked using a stroboscope. Make a mark on one of the fan blades which will be plainly visible as the fan turns. Brightly colored tape works well.

3   Connect a tachometer to the engine, or use the dashboard mounted tachometer.

4   Warm up the engine until it reaches normal operating temperature.

5   Adjust the engine speed to 4200 rpm.

6   Using a stroboscope in accordance with the manufacturer's instructions, read the fan speed. With the engine operating at 4200 rpm, the fan should be revolving at 1400 plus or minus 200 rpm.

7   If the fan speed is not within the specifications, replace the fan drive clutch with a new one and perform the test again.

12 Fan drive – removal and installation

1   The fan assembly is attached to the water pump pulley at the front of the engine.

9.12 Four bolts and one nut secure the radiator to the support frame

9.14 Lift the radiator with the shroud and fan assembly out of the engine compartment

10.3 Removing the coolant level sensor from the top of the radiator

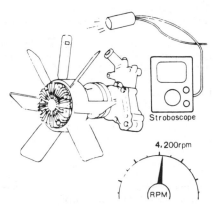

Fig. 2.7 Checking fan drive with a stroboscope (Sec 11)

2   Remove the four bolts securing the fan assembly to the flange at the water pump pulley.
3   Remove the assembly from out of the radiator cowling and the engine compartment. If this proves too difficult, the cowling will have to be unbolted from the sides of the radiator and lifted up slightly for more clearance.
4   Remove the four bolts which attach the fan to the drive clutch. Separate the two components.
5   For reassembly, bolt the fan drive to the fan and install the assembly to the flange on the water pump pulley.

13 Oil pump – removal and installation

1   It is unlikely that the oil pump will need servicing before the engine itself needs a major overhaul. If this is the case, the oil pump can be much more readily removed and overhauled with the engine out of the vehicle. However, the oil pump can be removed with the engine in place. Access and working conditions are less than ideal, but it can be done.
2   The oil pump is located at the front of the engine, inside the front housing. This means that most of the engine components at the front must be removed, in addition to dropping the oil pan.
3   Remove the radiator as detailed in Section 9.
4   Drain the engine oil and remove all the bolts securing the oil pan to the bottom of the engine. Remove the oil pan (Section 18). Extra clearance for this can be achieved by unbolting the engine at its front mounts and carefully jacking up the engine, with blocks of wood used as cushioners between the jack and the engine housings.
5   Remove the alternator. This is done by removing the small strap bolt on the adjusting bracket, the long pivot bolt and the wiring at the rear. Be sure to mark the wires disconnected for reassembly. Place the alternator and its related components aside.
6   To remove the air pump, first disconnect the rubber air outlet hose, then the short adjusting bolt and long pivot bolt. Place the pump and its related components aside.
7   Disconnect the two oil hoses at the metering oil pump located at the front, right side of the engine (Section 23).
8   Disconnect the connecting rod at the metering oil pump. Note which hole in the rod the cotter pin was positioned in for reassembly.
9   Align the yellow painted leading timing mark on the eccentric shaft pulley with the indicator pin on the front cover.
10   Remove the distributor cap, leaving the plug wires intact.
11   Remove the distributor lock bolt and then lift the distributor out of the front housing. Cover the distributor and set aside.
12   If air conditioning is fitted, remove the air conditioning pulley from the eccentric shaft pulley.
13   Remove the water pump (Section 4).
14   Remove the metering oil pump assembly.
15   Remove the eccentric shaft pulley bolt and pulley. It may be necessary to attach a brake to the flywheel or use vise grips on the pulley to keep it from turning as the bolt is loosened.
16   The front housing can now be removed from the engine block. Remove the attaching bolts and then tap the housing lightly with a rubber mallet to break the seal.
17   Slide the distributor drive gear off the eccentric shaft.
18   Before removing the oil pump assembly, check the tension of the

13.18 Checking the tension of the oil pump chain

chain to ascertain if a new one is needed. At an equal distance between the two pulleys, push in on the chain with your finger. The slack in the chain should not be more than 0.47 in (12 mm) (photo).
19   Straighten the lock washer tab on the oil pump sprocket. Remove the nut and lock washer.
20   Slide the oil pump sprocket, eccentric shaft and chain simultaneously off the two pulleys. Keep these together as a unit.
21   Remove the four bolts securing the oil pump to the engine block. Remove the oil pump.
22   To re-install, mount the oil pump on the engine and secure with the four attaching nuts.
23   Turn the pump by hand to make sure that it rotates freely.
24   Fit the key onto the oil pump shaft.
25   Install the drive chain, eccentric shaft sprocket and oil pump sprocket together as a unit, aligning the keyways on the oil pump shaft and eccentric shaft.
26   Install the tab washer and nut on the oil pump sprocket and tighten the nut to a torque of 22 to 25 ft-lb (3.0 to 3.5 m-kg). Use pliers to bend up the tab washer against one of the nut flats to prevent it from coming loose.
27   Slide the distributor drivegear onto the eccentric shaft with the 'F' mark towards the front of the engine.
28   Install a new O-ring on the oil pasage of the front housing.
29   Make sure the gasket surface of the front housing is clean and smooth and then install a new gasket to the housing.
30   Place the front cover into position on the engine and tighten the attaching bolts.
31   If a new oil seal has not already been installed in the front cover, install one now by prying out the old one and tapping a new one into place with a hammer and wood block.
32   Apply a little engine oil to the front cover oil seal.
33   Install the eccentric shaft front pulley and tighten to a torque of 72 to 87 ft-lb (10 to 12 m-kg).
34   Use a gasket scraper or putty knife to carefully remove all traces of sealer on the oil pan and bottom of engine. A small amount of the front cover gasket previously installed will have to be trimmed away to make a perfectly smooth mounting surface for the oil pan.
35   Apply a bead of silicone sealant to the oil pan mounting flange as illustrated (Fig. 2.8). The sealant should be just inside the bolt holes.
36   Apply more sealant to the oil pan gasket and then place the gasket onto the oil pan.
37   Re-install the oil pan (Section 18).
38   Install the water pump and tighten the nuts in the sequence shown in Fig. 2.9. Torque the bolts to 13 to 20 ft-lb (1.8 to 2.7 m-kg).
39   Install the oil metering pump and its hose and connecting rod to the front cover. Make sure the cotter pin on the connecting rod is in its original position.
40   Check that the eccentric shaft pulley is in the original position, with the yellow painted mark on the indicator pin. If so, align the tally marks on the bottom of the distributor and install the distributor.

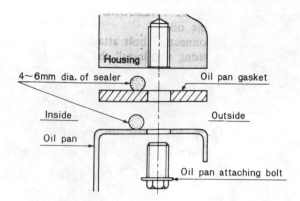

Fig. 2.8 Applying sealant to the oil pan surfaces (Sec 13)

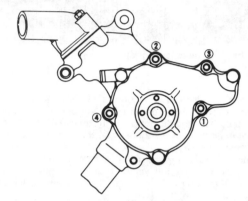

Fig. 2.9 Water pump tightening torque sequence (Sec 13)

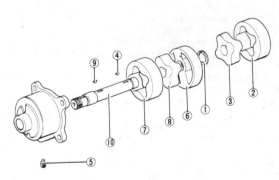

Fig. 2.10 Exploded view of oil pump assembly (Sec 14)

1	Snap-ring	6	Middle plate
2	Rear outer rotor	7	Front outer rotor
3	Rear inner rotor	8	Front inner rotor
4	Key	9	Key
5	Screw	10	Shaft

41 Turn the distributor housing first counter-clockwise and then clockwise, stopping when the leading contact points just start to open. Tighten the distributor lock nut (1979 models only).

42 Install the distributor cap and plug wires.

43 Install the alternator with the spacer and adjusting shim located behind the water pump housing. Loosely install the long pivot bolt and the adjusting bracket and strap bolt.

44 Put the alternator drive belt into place and adjust the belt tension until there is 0.59 in (15 mm) of deflection when pressed between the pulleys. Tighten the pivot and adjusting bolts. Connect the wires to the rear of the alternator.

45 Install the air pump with its adjusting bracket and pivot bolt. Adjust the belt tension to 0.47 in (12 mm) when pressure is applied to the belt between the pump pulley and water pump pulley. Tighten the pivot and adjusting bolts. Install the rubber air hose to the air pump.

46 Install the radiator as detailed in Section 9.

47 Fill the engine with the proper mixture of ethylene glycol antifreeze and soft (demineralized) water.

48 If a connector for an external oil pressure gauge has not already been purchased or made, do so at this time. See Section 27 of Chapter 1 for more details on this.

49 Fill the engine with oil.

50 Connect the negative battery cable.

51 Disconnect the two high tension leads to the coils to prevent the engine from starting, yet allowing it to be turned over.

52 With the key, turn the engine over for about 15 seconds to prime the oil pump and to lubricate the engine components.

53 Connect the high tension leads to the coils and start the engine. Allow it to run for a few seconds and check the gauge for proper oil pressure.

54 Disconnect the external gauge and plug the connector.

55 Run the car and check for water or oil leaks.

14 Oil pump – overhaul

1   The oil pump can either be removed and replaced with a rebuilt unit, or the original pump can be overhauled with new parts and reinstalled on the engine.

2   The oil pump for the RX-7 uses two sets of rotors which are not interchangeable. Because of this all the parts should be kept separate during the disassembly process.

3   Remove the snap ring on the shaft at the rear of the oil pump.

4   Invert the pump and the rear rotor assembly (inner and outer rotors) should fall out.

5   With needle nose pliers, remove the small keys on the oil pump shaft which is now exposed.

6   Using a screwdriver, remove the small set screw which runs through the pump housing and into the middle plate.

7   With the set screw out, the middle plate and front rotor assembly should fall off the end of the shaft.

8   Press the shaft out of the pump body and remove the key.

9   Clean all parts thoroughly, being careful not to mix-up their order for reassembly.

10 Install the rotor assemblies, one at a time, onto the shaft and place into the pump body. Check the clearance between the lobes of the inner and outer rotors of each assembly with a feeler gauge. If the clearance exceeds 0.006 in (0.15 mm), replace the rotors (photo).

11 Check the clearance between the outer rotor and the pump body with a feeler gauge. If the clearance exceeds 0.0118 in (0.30 mm), replace the rotor or body as necessary (photo).

12 To fully assemble the pump after checking for clearances, first install the front rotor assembly to the keyed shaft, aligning the tally marks on the inner and outer rotors. The tally marks should face the rear of the pump, or the engine.

13 Install the middle plate into the pump body so that the set screw will align with the recess portion of the middle plate.

14 Install the set screw and caulk it with hammer and chisel to prevent it from loosening.

15 Install the key to the shaft.

16 Install the rear side rotor assembly, again aligning the tally marks on the inner and outer rotors. The tally marks should be facing the rear of the oil pump.

17 Fit the snap ring to the end of the shaft.

18 Fill the pump with engine oil and install, referring to Section 13.

15 Oil pressure – checking

1   Drain the engine oil.

2   Remove the connecting bolt attaching the oil hose to the rear housing. At this point, either install a Mazda connector (part number 8871 23 099) which will adapt the Mazda oil pressure gauge (part number 49 0187 280), or drill and tap the end of the oil hose to mate to an external oil pressure gauge of your choosing.

3   Fill the engine with oil.

4   Start the engine and warm up the engine to the normal operating temperature.

5   Take a reading of the oil pressure gauge with the engine idling or in the 'D' range for automatic transmissions. Oil pressure should be within specifications.

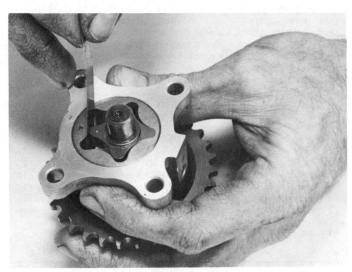

14.10 Checking the clearance between the inner and outer oil pump lobes

14.11 Checking the clearance between the outer lobe and the oil pump body

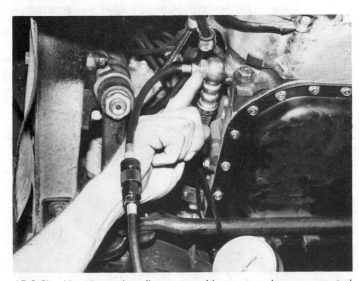

15.6 Checking the engine oil pressure with an external gauge mounted to the oil hose inlet fitting

6   Take another reading of oil pressure with the engine operating at 3000 rpm. The oil pressure should be within specifications for this rpm (photo).
7   If the oil pressure is not within these specifications, check the following:

    a)   Ensure that the oil level is within the 'F' and 'L' marks on the dipstick.
    b)   Check the pressure control valve as described in Section 19.
    c)   Check the oil pump as described in Section 14.

16 Oil filter – removal and installation

1   The oil filter is mounted on the top of the engine, on the left side. It is a throw-away type which cannot be cleaned and re-used.
2   Use an oil filter wrench to remove the filter, grabbing it at the top where the filter is less likely to collapse. If difficulty is experienced in removing the filter, a metal bar or long screwdriver can be driven through the filter near the top and used as a 'T' handle.
3   When installing a new filter cartridge, a thin film of clean engine oil should be spread on the oil seal at the base of the filter.
4   Clean the area where the filter attaches to the pedestal base.
5   Screw the new filter onto the pedestal and tighten only hand tight. Do not use a wrench to tighten the filter.
6   Add engine oil to the sump as necessary and start the engine, checking for leaks around the base of the filter. If leaks exist, try tightening the filter a little more, still by hand only.

17 Engine oil – changing

1   Due to the fact that the oil in the rotary engine not only lubricates engine components, but also is used for cooling, frequent oil changes are required. In any engine clean oil will help to provide longevity of engine parts.
2   In addition, vehicles operated under the following conditions should have the engine oil and oil filter changed more frequently.

    a)   Dusty conditions where excessive dust and dirt can enter the system.
    b)   Extended periods of idling or low speed condition.
    c)   Driving for a long time in cold temperatures or driving short distances.

3   Start the engine and allow it to get warm, which will stir up any sludge build-up.
4   Raise the front of the vehicle and place firmly on jack stands too gain access to the drain plug.
5   Move a suitable pan which will hold at least 6 US quarts (4.6 Imp. quarts, 5.2 liters) into position under the oil pan drain plug. Also have clean rags and newspapers handy to wipe up any spills.
6   Being careful not to touch any of the hot exhaust components, remove the drain plug which is located on the right side of the oil pan. Allow the warm engine oil to drain into the container.
7   Clean the magnetic drain plug thoroughly with a clean rag.

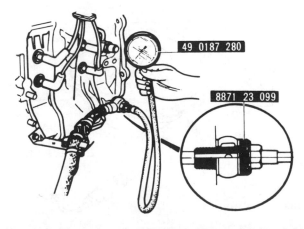

Fig. 2.11 Testing oil pressure with external gauge (Sec 15)

8   Replace the drain plug after the engine oil has thoroughly drained. Tighten the plug securely.
9   Clean the area around the plug of any drips.
10 Remove the pan, newspapers and rags from under the vehicle and lower to the ground.
11 Replace the oil filter with a new one if required (see Section 16).
12 Remove the filler cap located on the left side of the engine and fill with the proper grade of oil (see Recommended Lubricants). Add 4 US quarts (3.7 Imp quarts, 4.2 liters) and then check the oil level on the dipstick located just to the left of the filler.
13 Allow the oil time to drain into the oil pan and add more oil to reach the 'F' mark on the dipstick. Do not overfill the system.
14 Install the dipstick and filler cap and run the engine, checking for leaks at the drain plug and around the base of the oil filter.
15 Shut off the engine, wait a few minutes to allow the oil to drain back into the oil pan and then recheck the oil level on the dipstick. Add more oil as necessary.
16 The old engine oil cannot be reused in its present state and should be disposed of. Oil reclamation centers, auto repair shops and gas stations will normally accept the oil which can be refined and used again. After the oil has cooled, the old oil can be drained into a suitable container and taken to one of these places for disposal.

18 Oil pan – removal and installation

1   The oil pan, located at the bottom of the engine, is obviously much more accessible with the engine removed from the vehicle. The pan should not need removal except to remove the front cover or when damaged.

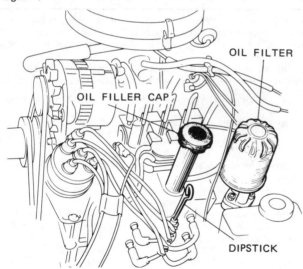

Fig. 2.12 Location of filler cap and dipstick (Sec 17)

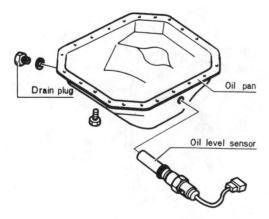

Fig. 2.13 The engine oil pan and various components (Sec 18)

2   Access for removing the pan can be attained by either removing the steering components to drop the pan straight down, or by unbolting the engine from its mount and jacking the engine up slightly.
3   Drain the engine oil and remove the engine under-cover.
4   Disconnect the bullet connector of the oil level sensor and the coupler from the oil thermo unit (except for California).
5   Remove the oil pan attaching bolts and remove the oil pan.
6   Check the oil pan for cracks or damaged plug threads.
7   When installing the oil pan, apply a continuous bead of silicone sealer to the mounting surface of the oil pan and place the gasket on it. The oil pan surface should be clean of all excess sealer and gasket material.
8   Apply sealer to the other side of the gasket, which mates to the engine.
9   Lift the pan into place and tighten the attaching bolts to a torque of 5 to 7 ft-lb (0.7 to 1.0 m-kg). Work around the pan, tightening the bolts a little at a time.
10 Connect the electrical couplers for the wiring and fill the engine with fresh oil.
11 Run the engine and check for leaks.

19 Oil pressure control valve – checking

1   The oil pressure control valve is located in the front cover. It should be checked whenever the front cover is removed or the engine is overhauled.
2   Remove the front cover of the engine referring to Section 13.
3   Use a suitable wrench to remove the valve from the front of the cover (photo).
4   Examine the spring and the plunger for corrosion or any damage. If it is severe replace the control valve with a new one.
5   Measure the free length of the spring and if it is not 2.874 in (73 mm), replace the valve.
6   Tighten the valve into the front cover and install the front cover, again referring to Section 13.

20 Oil cooler – removal and installation

1   The oil cooler is located at the bottom of the radiator and is separate from the radiator. It can be removed without removing the entire radiator.
2   Remove the engine under-cover.
3   Drain the engine oil.
4   Disconnect the two oil hoses at the bottom left side of the cooler. It will be necessary to use two wrenches to disconnect these pipes. Be careful not to damage the cooler with too much force in this area (photo).

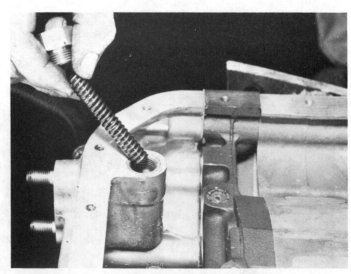

19.3 The oil pressure control valve located inside the front engine cover

20.4 Two wrenches are necessary to remove the oil lines from the oil cooler

21.3 The oil by-pass valve located at the bottom of the oil cooler

5   Remove the bolts which secure the cooler to the radiator on either side of the radiator. There are two bolts on each of these brackets.
6   Lower the cooler straight down and out from under the vehicle.
7   Visually inspect the cooler for damage, cracking and signs of leakage.
8   If repair is in order, either repair it with aluminium welding or replace the entire unit with a new one.
9   Position the cooler into place and secure loosely with the brackets to the radiator.
10   Connect the oil hoses and tighten the connections securely.
11   Tighten the bracket bolts securely.
12   Replace the engine under-cover.
13   Fill the engine with oil. Run the engine and check for leaks.

21 Oil by-pass valve – removal and installation

1   Drain the engine oil.
2   Remove the engine under-cover.
3   Remove the cap nut and pull out the by-pass valve. The cap nut and valve are located on the bottom of the oil cooler, adjoining the oil hose inlets (photo).
4   Install the valve and cap nut.
5   Install the engine under-cover.
6   Fill the engine with oil. Run the engine and check for leaks around

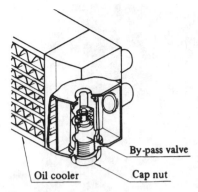

Fig. 2.14 Location of oil by-pass valve in oil cooler (Sec 21)

Fig. 2.15 Checking the protrusion of oil by-pass valve (Sec 22)

the cap nut. Tighten as necessary.

22 Oil by-pass valve – checking

1   Remove the by-pass valve as described in Section 21.
2   Soak the by-pass valve in clean engine oil and gradually heat up the oil on a hot place or stove.
3   With a thermometer submerged in the oil, check the temperature and the protrusion of the by-pass valve.
4   The valve should have a protrusion of more than 0.2 in (more than 5 mm) when the oil temperature is 158°F (70°C).
5   If not within specifications, replace the by-pass valve referring to Section 21.

23 Metering oil pump – measuring discharge

1   The metering oil pump injects a small amount of engine oil directly into the carburetor to lubricate the internal seals of the engine. The seals need this lubrication at all times, and in the proper amounts (photo).
2   Check the metering oil pump and oil hoses leading to the carburetor for leaks.
3   Make sure that the clearance between the metering oil pump lever and washer is 0 to 0.04 in (0 to 1.0 mm).
4   Connect a tachometer to the engine following the manufacturer's instructions, or use the dashboard mounted tachometer.
5   Warm up the engine to normal operating temperature.
6   Disconnect the two metering oil hoses at the carburetor. These are located on the left side of the carburetor.
7   At this time fill a small squirt can with clean engine oil to inject directly into the carburetor primary barrels. This means the air cleaner assembly should be removed and the idle compensator hose plugged for proper engine operations.
8   Place a graduated beaker or measuring cup under the disconnected oil metering hoses to check the discharge.
9   Start the engine and set the engine speed to 2000 rpm.

23.1 The oil metering pump located at the front of the engine

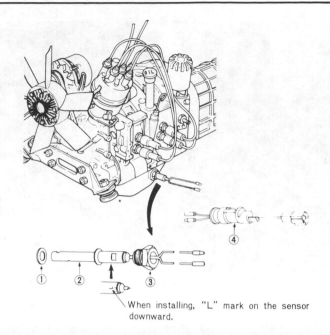

When installing, "L" mark on the sensor downward.

Fig. 2.18 Location and exploded view of oil level sensor (Sec 25)

1   Gasket   3   Attaching nut
2   Oil level sensor   4   Reed switch

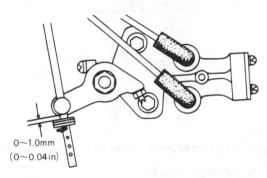

0~1.0mm
(0~0.04in)

Fig. 2.16 Checking clearance of metering oil pump lever (Sec 23)

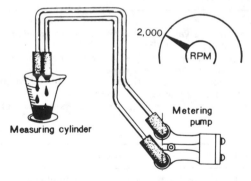

2,000
RPM

Measuring cylinder

Metering pump

Fig. 2.17 Measuring discharge of metering oil pump (Sec 23)

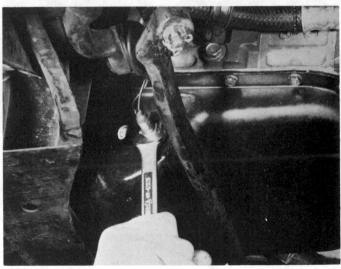

25.5 The oil level sensor is located on the left side of the oil pan

10 Run the engine for 6 minutes and check the amount of oil discharged into the graduated container. Do not forget that engine oil must be squirted into the carburetor primary barrels in the same proportion to the discharge into the container.

11 After running for 6 minutes, the oil discharge in the container should be 2.0 to 2.5 cc. If not within specifications, adjust the metering oil pump referring to Section 24.

24 Metering oil pump – adjusting

1   Adjustments made to the metering oil pump are made at the oil pump linkage located at the front of the engine adjoining the lower radiator hose.
2   Loosen the lock nut of the adjusting screw.
3   Turn the adjusting screw until the proper oil discharge is obtained

following the procedure in Section 23.
4   When the adjusting screw is screwed in, the amount of discharge increases, while the discharge decreases when the adjusting screw is turned out. The amount of oil discharge alters by approximately 0.2 to 0.3 cc per 6 minutes of engine operation at 2000 rpm.
5   Tighten the adjusting lock nut securely.
6   After adjusting is complete, check the clearance between the pump lever and the washer. The clearance should be 0 to 0.04 in (0 to 1.0 mm). If necessary, adjust it by using a suitable washer.

25 Oil level sensor – removal and installation

1   Drain the engine oil.
2   Disconnect the coupler to the sensor.
3   Remove the sensor attaching nut and remove the sensor from the oil pan.

4   To re-install, place the gasket onto the sensor and install the sensor to the oil pan with the 'L' mark on the sensor pointed downward.

5   Install the lock nut onto the sensor and tighten the nut to a torque of 18 to 22 ft-lb (2.5 to 3.0 m-kg) (photo).

6   Connect the coupler of the sensor.

7   Fill the engine with oil and start the engine, checking for leaks around the sensor.

26 Oil level sensor – checking

1   The oil level sensor is located on the left side of the oil pan and warns the driver of impending danger when the level of lubricant gets low.

2   Turn the ignition switch on. The oil level warning light on the dashboard should come on.

3   Start the engine and the warning light should go off.

4   Disconnect the coupler from the oil level sensor from under the vehicle. Ground the disconnected coupler and check to see the warning light comes on with the engine at idle.

5   To check further, drain the engine oil and remove the sensor from the oil pan (Section 25).

6   Check the oil holes of the sensor to make sure they are not clogged. Clean with solvent as necessary.

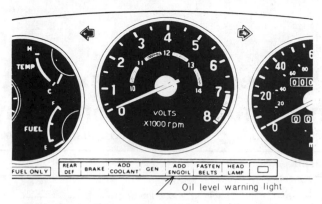

Fig. 2.19 The dashboard warning light for low engine oil level (Sec 26)

7   Check the resistance of the sensor with an ohmmeter. The specified resistance is 2 to 4 kilo ohm at 50 to 86°F (10 to 30°C).

8   Install the sensor into the oil pan and tighten securely (Section 25).

9   Connect the electrical coupler.

10 Fill the engine with oil and start the engine, checking for leaks.

Chapter 3 Fuel, exhaust and emissions control systems

Refer to Chapter 13 for specifications and information related to 1981 through 1985 models

Contents

Specifications

Fuel system

Fuel tank capacity.. 55 liters (14.5 U.S. gal, 12.1 Imp. gal)

Fuel pump

Type	Electrical plunger
Fuel pressure	0.26 to 0.33 kg/cm^2 (3.70 to 4.70 lb/in^2)
Feeding capacity	More than 1,100 cc/min. (1.16 US quarts/min. 0.97 Imp. quart/min.)

Fuel filter.. Cartridge, paper element

Carburetor

Type	Down draft, 2 stage 4 barrel

Throat diameter

Primary	28 mm (1.10 in)
Secondary	34 mm (1.34 in)

Venturi diameter

Primary	20 x 13 x 6.5 mm (0.79 x 0.51 x 0.26 in)
Secondary	28 x 10 mm (1.0 x 0.39 in)

	Manual transmission	Automatic transmission
Main jet		
Primary Calif.	93	94
Except Calif.	93	93
Secondary	160	160
Main air bleed		
Primary	90	90
Secondary	140	140
Slow jet		
Primary	46	46
Secondary	120	120
Slow air bleed		
Primary No. 1	70	70
No. 2	150	150
Secondary No. 1	160	160
No. 2	60	60

	Manual transmission	Automatic transmission
Richer jet..	40	—
Richer air bleed..	140	—
Power jet		
California...	50	50
Except for California...	—	50
Vacuum jet		
Primary..	1.8 mm (0.0709 in)	1.8 mm (0.0709 in)
Secondary...	1.0 mm (0.0394 in)	1.0 mm (0.0394 in)

Fast idle adjustment
(Clearance between primary throttle valve and bore...................... California 1.30 to 1.50 mm (0.051 to 0.059 in)
when choke is fully pulled)... Except for California 0.90 to 1.10 mm (0.035 to 0.04 in)
Float level (from surface of gasket).. 16.0 $\pm$ 0.5 mm (0.63 $\pm$ 0.020 in)
Float drop (from surface of gasket)... 51 $\pm$ 0.5 mm (2.0 $\pm$ 0.02 in)
Idle speed
   Manual transmission.. 750 $\pm$ 25 rpm
   Automatic transmission... 750 $\pm$ 25 rpm
   ("D" range)
CO. concentration at idle... Less than 0.1%
Sub-zero starting assist fluid.. Antifreeze 90%
Water 10%

Torque wrench settings

	m-kg	ft-lb
Inlet manifold..	1.9 to 2.6	14 to 19
Thermal reactor..	4.5 to 5.5	33 to 40

1 General description

1   The fuel system is fundamentally conventional. The carburetor is fed by an electric pump near the tank, the flow being through a filter, also at the back of the car. The carburetor is a two-stage, 4-barrel type.
2   Superimposed on this system is the complication of the fuel vapour and exhaust emissions control equipment. An engine driven pump supplies air into the exhaust to burn carbon monoxide to carbon dioxide, and complete the combustion of hydro-carbons. This is done in the 'thermal reactor', a chamber where the exhaust manifold normally is. To prevent the reactor getting too hot it is double skinned, and has a cooling air supply. For conditions when there are insufficient unburned products coming from the engine to sustain combustion in the reactor, the trailing spark plugs are cut, so that more unburned gases will be available.
3   Because of the long thin shape of the combustion chamber, there is a large surface area in relation to its volume. So combustion is cool, giving few oxides of nitrogen (NO_x). However the combustion is also incomplete, so there are large amounts of partly burned hydrocarbons (HC) and carbon monoxide (CO). The exhaust is hot enough for the combustion of these to continue after exhaust in the thermal reactor, supplied by air from the air pump.
4   Because of the combustion characteristics, the octane requirements of the engine are very low. Therefore lead free fuel should be used.

2 Fuel filter – replacement

1   The in-line fuel filter is located at the rear of the car, near the fuel tank. It is of the canister, throw-away type and cannot be cleaned for re-use (photo).
2   The filter should be changed at regular intervals. Refer to the Routine Maintenance schedules for replacement. The filter should be visually inspected whenever the vehicle is raised for other repair work. Check for leaks or small cracks in the filter housing.
3   Raise the rear end of the vehicle and support firmly with jack stands.
4   Have a container handy to catch excess fuel as the hoses are disconnected.
5   With a pair of pliers, open the spring clips on the end of each hose at the filter. With the clips opened, they can be slid back on the hoses about two inches.
6   Carefully note which hose leads into the fuel filter and which hose leads out of it. Identify with tape so as not to confuse the flow upon reassembly.
7   Disconnect the hoses from the filter by pulling and twisting the hoses.

2.1 The fuel filter is located under the car, in front of the gas tank

8   Use pliers or a screwdriver to loosen the retaining clip which holds the filter to the body (photo).
9   Remove the filter.
10 Install the new filter into the retainer noting the directional arrow printed on the filter. The arrow should point to the hose leading from the filter to the fuel pump, and ultimately the carburetor. Visually follow this hose to make sure it is the proper one.
11 Push the hoses fully onto the filter ends, and slip the spring clamps back into position near the end of each hose.
12 Lower the car and start the engine. Check for leaks at the hose connections of the filter.

3 Fuel pump – testing

1   There are two tests of the fuel pump; a pressure test which requires the use of a pressure gauge, and a volume test to measure the discharge of fuel at the carburetor.
2   Before either of the tests is performed, make sure the fuel filter is not clogged and has been replaced within the recommended interval.
3   To check for pressure, first remove the air cleaner assembly (See Section 9) and disconnect the main fuel hose at the carburetor. The fuel main hose is the larger diameter of the two hoses at the carburetor. Have a small container and some rags handy to catch

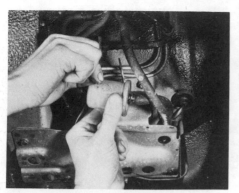
2.8 A retaining clip secures the filter

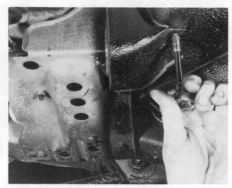
4.4 There is a small access cover in front of the main fuel pump cover

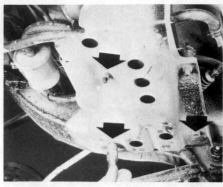
4.5 Two bolts and one nut secure the main fuel pump cover to the body

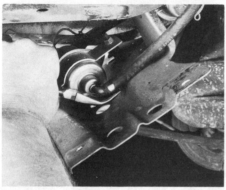
4.8 Pliers are used to loosen the hose clamps

4.10 Two attaching nuts hold the fuel pump to the cover

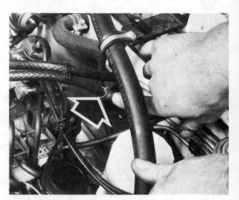
7.2 The check valve is located in the fuel return line, near the firewall

excess fuel as the hose is disconnected. The engine should be cool.

4   Connect a pressure gauge, a hose restrictor and flexible hoses so that the fuel can be discharged into a suitable container.

5   Turn the ignition switch to the 'on' position and vent the system into the container by opening the hose restrictor.

6   Close the restrictor and allow the pressure to stabilize. Note the reading on the pressure gauge. Fuel pressure should be 3.7 to 4.7 lb/in^2 (0.26 to 0.33 Kg/cm^2).

7   If the pump is not within specifications, replace the fuel pump with a new one. If it is within specifications, proceed to the volume test.

8   To test for volume, place the disconnected main fuel hose in a graduated container.

9   Turn the ignition switch to the 'on' position.

10   Open the hose restrictor and expel the fuel into the container. After exactly one minute, 1100 cc (1.16 US quarts, 0.97 Imp quarts) or more should have been discharged into the container. If this is not the case, replace the fuel filter with a new one.

4   Fuel pump – removal and installation

1   The fuel pump is electric, meaning that whenever the ignition key is positioned 'on', the pump is functioning. It is located under the vehicle, at the rear. There are two sheet metal covers underneath the pump for protection against the elements.

2   The wiring to the fuel pump runs through the floorboard and into the driver's compartment just behind the seat. Remove the rear floor mat and the sheet metal floor plate. With the floorcovering pulled back and the plate removed, the electrical coupler is visible. Disconnect the coupler and feed the wires through the floorboard.

3   Raise the vehicle and support firmly with stands.

4   Remove the front cover by removing the two small bolts going into the floorboard (photo).

5   Remove the two bolts and one nut which secure the main fuel pump cover. Lower this cover slightly, gaining access to the fuel pump which is attached to the top of the cover. Be careful not to disturb the hose connections as the unit is lowered (photo).

6   Carefully note which hose leads to the fuel filter and which hose leads to the fuel cut valve. Identify with strips of tape so as not to change the direction of flow upon reassembly.

7   Have a container and rags handy to catch excess fuel as the hoses are disconnected.

8   Use pliers to pinch and open the hose connectors and then slide the connectors about two inches up the hoses (photo).

9   Disconnect the hoses from the fuel pump by pulling and twisting the hose ends. Plug the ends of the hose to prevent further fuel loss.

10   Remove the two nuts on the fuel pump bracket and remove the fuel pump from under the vehicle (photo).

11   To install, place the fuel pump into position, noting any directional indicators on the fuel pump body. Secure with the two attaching nuts.

12   Connect the inlet and outlet hoses to the pump and slide the hose connectors back down the hoses to their original positions near the ends of the hoses.

13   Route the wiring through the body grommet and into the passenger's compartment.

14   Lift the assembly upward and install the two bolts and one nut which secure the main fuel pump cover. Tighten these securely.

15   Install the smaller front cover and secure with the two bolts.

16   Lower the vehicle to the ground and connect the electrical coupler inside the car.

17   Install the floor plate and place the floorcovering in its original position.

18   Start the engine and check for leaks at the fuel pump area.

5   Fuel tank – removal and installation

1   The fuel tank is at the rear of the car, protected by covers at the sides and front. The tank would have to be removed to make repairs or to flush out should some foreign material be entered into the fuel system.

2   When removing the fuel tank keep sparks, cigarettes and open flame away from the fuel tank.

3   The fuel tank should be as empty as possible for removal. This is

for obvious reasons. As there is no drain plug on the bottom of the tank, the only alternative is to pump the fuel out as described in Section 3 on volume-testing the fuel pump.

4   Raise the rear end of the vehicle and support firmly with stands.
5   Remove the sheet metal protector covers by using a socket wrench and a long extension.
6   At the front side of the tank, near the top, are all the hose connections. Carefully note their positions and mark each with strips of tape describing their location. Do not rely on your memory for this. There is the main fuel hose, fuel return hose and evaporation hoses.
7   On the left side of the tank, near the top, is the fuel gauge unit. Disconnect the wiring coupler leading to this.
8   Disconnect the fuel filler hose adjoining the gauge unit.
9   If available, position an adjustable jack (floor jack, scissors jack, etc) with a block of wood for cushioning, under the fuel tank.
10 Support the tank with the jack as the two attaching bands are removed. These attaching bands run under the tank and are secured by bolts at the front and rear of the tank.
11 Carefully, and slowly, lower the tank. As it is lowered, check for any hoses or wiring connections which were not previously disconnected.
12 Before installing the fuel tank, make sure that all traces of dirt and corrosion are cleaned. A coat of rust preventative paint is recommended.
13 Raise the fuel tank into position with a jack.
14 With the jack supporting the weight of the fuel tank, place the attaching bands into position and install their securing bolts at the front and rear of the tank. Do not tighten these bolts at this time. This will allow the tank to be moved slightly for easier hook-up of the connections.
15 Connect the fuel filler hose to the fuel tank. The hose should be pushed over the fuel tank pipe at least 1.6 in (40 mm).
16 Connect the electrical coupler to the fuel gauge unit.
17 Connect all hoses at the front of the fuel tank. The fuel main hose, fuel return hose and the evaporative hoses should be pushed onto the fuel tank fittings at least 1.0 in (25 mm). Attach the various hose connections securely.
18 Fully tighten the attaching band bolts at the front and rear of the tank.
19 Install the three side and front protector covers to their original positions.
20 Lower the vehicle and fill the tank, checking for any leaks in the tank or hoses.
21 Road test the vehicle and check for leaks in the first few miles of driving.

6   Fuel tank – repairs

1   Repairs to a fuel tank which require welding or any application of heat are jobs for a professional. Fumes present inside the tank are easily ignited, causing the tank to explode. A professional welder will thoroughly purge the tank with water and then steam to remove all traces of explosive gas fumes.
2   If the tank has rusted inside, there is little hope that it can be re-used. The corrosion will continually be drawn into the fuel system, clogging the filter and eventually the carburetor components.

7   Fuel check valve – checking and replacing

1   There is a fuel check valve located in the engine compartment spliced into the fuel return hose. It can be seen about two inches forward of the firewall, as a part of the hose. After a time it can become blocked, and thus should be periodically removed and checked.
2   To remove the check valve, use pliers to pinch the hose connector on either end of the valve and slide the connectors up the hoses about two inches (photo).
3   Have a container and rags handy to catch any excess fuel as the hoses are disconnected.
4   Disconnect the hoses from each end of the valve.
5   Note that there is an arrow on the body of the check valve. Blow through the valve in the opposite direction of the arrow. The air should flow freely through the valve. If not, replace the check valve with a new one.

8.2 Checking the bimetal control valve

6   Install the check valve with the arrow pointing towards the carburetor, away from the firewall.
7   Connect each hose with the clamps securely.

8   Air cleaner assembly – general information

1   The air filter is of the paper element type. It can be cleaned by blowing compressed air through it. However, in most cases the filter should be replaced with a new one. If the car is used continually in dusty road conditions, the element should be changed more frequently than is called for.
2   The intake of fresh air (from the horn of the air cleaner) and hot air (from the manifold shield) is automatically controlled by means of a bimetal control valve located inside the air cleaner. This operation can be checked by removing the top cover and air filter element and then pushing on the control valve plate. This is located at the entrance of the horn to the circular air cleaner body. If the control is easy to move up and down, and tension is felt, it is in proper working order (photo).
3   The air cleaner assembly will frequently need to be removed for better access to engine components and to check the filter element. There are a number of hoses connected to the air cleaner assembly and each must be installed properly and in its correct location for optimum engine performance.
4   Also incorporated into the air cleaner assembly is an idle compensator and a charcoal filter canister. More information on the idle compensator can be found in Section 10. The charcoal canister is a part of the emissions system and is detailed in Section 37.

9   Air cleaner – removal and installation

1   The air cleaner assembly will need to be removed for many engine repairs and to replace the paper filter element inside. It is important that it be properly disassembled and reassembled.
2   Remove the top plate by prying away the three spring clips.
3   Lift out the air filter element (photo).
4   Remove the wing nut inside the housing, at the center of the carburetor. This wing nut threads onto a stud coming up through the carburetor (photo).
5   At the front of the air cleaner is a support bracket, near the top radiator hose inlet to the engine. Remove the bolt which goes through this bracket and into the air cleaner (photo).
6   Pull the hot air hose off the bottom of the air cleaner. The hot air hose is the flexible hose which runs to the thermal reactor cover. It feeds warmed air into the carburetor.
7   Also near the top of the thermal reactor is a smaller air hose which must be disconnected from the air cleaner (photo).
8   At the front of the air cleaner is the air pump inlet hose which must be disconnected from the air cleaner (photo).

9.3 After prying the three spring clips away from the top cover, the cover and air filter element can be removed

9.4 Removing the wing nut at the center of the carburetor

9.5 The one attaching nut on a bracket at the front of the air cleaner must be loosened slightly

9.7 The hot air hose at the right side of the air cleaner

9.8 Disconnecting the air pump inlet hose at the front of the air cleaner

9.9 The hose leading from the coasting valve to the air cleaner assembly

9.10 This hose should be plugged if the engine is run without the air cleaner

9.11 Lifting the air cleaner assembly away from the engine

10.2 Checking the operation of the idle compensator

9   On the left side of the air cleaner is the coasting valve hose on manual transmission equipped cars. It should be pulled free of the air cleaner assembly (photo).

10   Finally, the idle compensator tube is located at the bottom of the air cleaner. It is best disconnected by lifting up on the whole air cleaner assembly slightly to gain access (photo).

11   Remove the air cleaner assembly and set aside with all mounting fasteners and hoses (photo).

12   Whenever work is done on the engine which does not require the engine to be started and run, cover the top of the carburetor to prevent anything from accidentally falling into the bores.

13   Any time the engine needs to be started and run with the air cleaner assembly removed, the idle compensator tube (the small one at the bottom of the air cleaner) must be plugged with a hose cap or a suitable bolt.

14   Installation of the air cleaner assembly is the reverse of the removal procedure.

10 Idle compensator – checking

1   An idle compensator is incorporated into the air cleaner body. This is a simple valve with a bimetal spring which reacts to temperatures. When the engine is cold, the valve is closed, allowing normal operation. When the engine has warmed to operating temperature, the valve opens and draws air through the valve.

2   Visually inspect the idle compensator. It should be fully closed when the temperature inside the air cleaner is less than 149° plus or minus 8°F (65° plus or minus 4°C). The valve can be further checked for proper closing by sucking into the hose. If excessive air leakage is found, replace the idle compensator as a unit (photo).

3   When the temperature inside the air cleaner is more than approximately 159°F (69°C) the valve should be open. Check again by sucking on the hose. A free flow of air should be sensed. If not, replace the idle compensator as a unit.

4   Since there is a constant vacuum running through this line, being controlled by the valve on the air cleaner body, if the air cleaner is removed for engine testing the idle compensator hose must be suitably plugged.

11 Altitude compensator – checking

1   There is an altitude compensator which affects the operation of the carburetor at varying altitudes. It is important that this function be peridically checked, especially if trips are planned to different geographical locations.
2   Disconnect the altitude compensator hose from its fitting on the carburetor. This is located at the base of the carburetor, on the left side. It is almost directly below the main fuel inlet hose. Access is greater if the air cleaner assembly is removed. Be sure to plug the idle compensator hose which runs to the bottom of the air cleaner.
3   Start the engine and run at the specified idle speed. On vehicles with automatic transmission, place the selector lever to 'N' or 'P' positions.
4   Plug the compensator hose opening on the carburetor with your finger. The engine speed should immediately drop.
5   If the idle does not drop, replace the idle compensator which is threaded into the carburetor body.

12 Sub-zero starting assist

1   In all areas except California, there is a device which automatically injects a starting fluid into the carburetor when the temperature is below zero.
2   The fluid level in the reservoir should be checked once a month, especially during the cold months of the year. The starting fluid is a 90/10 mixture of high-quality ethylene glycol antifreeze (for aluminium engine parts) and water.
3   To check for proper operation, first make sure there is sufficient starting assist fluid in the tank. Top up if necessary.
4   Disconnect the coupler from the starting motor switch marked 'S'.
5   Remove the air cleaner top cover to enable you to see down inside the carburetor.
6   Turn the ignition key to the 'Start' position and make sure that fluid does not squirt into the carburetor. Ambient temperature should not be below 0°F (-18°C).
7   Disconnect the coupler from the oil thermo unit on the oil pan and ground the coupler to the body.
8   Turn the ignition switch to the 'Start' position with the air bleeding button at the top of the tank depressed. Starting assist fluid should spout into the carburetor.
9   If these conditions are not met, replace the sub-zero starting assist motor switch.
10 If the oil thermo unit is suspect, it can be checked with an ohmmeter. It should show a flow of power only if the temperature is below 0°F (-18°C).

13 Accelerator cable – checking and adjusting

1   If the accelerator cable or linkage is not functioning properly, the carburetor will not be able to operate at its optimum performance level. This will most notably be evident by a lack of power with the accelerator fully depressed.
2   Remove the air cleaner assembly (Section 9) and, with the accelerator pedal fully depressed, check that the carburetor throttle valves are fully opened. They should be in the vertical position.
3   Check that there is no binding of the cable, and that the throttle valves fully return once the pedal is released.
4   If the accelerator cable needs adjusting, first measure the distance between the accelerator pedal and the brake pedal. The accelerator pedal should be approximately 1.8 inches (44 mm) lower than the brake pedal. This can be adjusted by turning the lock nut at the top of the pedal linkage.
5   Check the free play of the cable at the carburetor. The free play before the throttle bores are operated should be 1 to 3 mm. If this is not the case, adjust the lock nut at the cable attaching bracket adjacent to the carburetor.
6   If, after these checks, the throttle valves are still not opening completely with the pedal depressed, adjust the stopper bolt at the forward side of the accelerator linkage.

14 Hot start assist system – checking and adjusting

1   The RX-7 engine is equipped with an automatic system which injects fuel into the carburetor by opening the throttle valves when the engine is hot. The system is operated by a motor and a cable, located on the left fender panel.
2   Remove the top cover of the air cleaner so that you can see the throttle valves operating.
3   Warm up the engine to normal operating temperatures, then stop the engine.
4   Disconnect the electrical couplers for the leading and trailing primary wires from the distributor.
5   Have an assistant crank the engine by turning the key. Check to see that the hot start lever operates properly and the throttle valves inside the carburetor open.
6   To adjust the hot air assist, visually follow the cable from the motor until you locate the cable bracket adjacent to the carburetor. Remove the lock spring from the cable bracket (Fig. 3.3).
7   Slowly pull the outer cable until the hot start lever just touches the

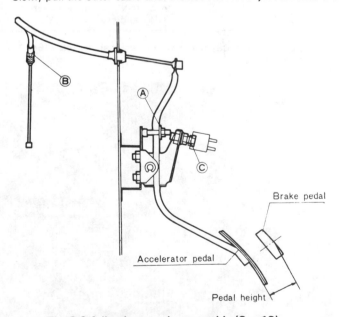

Fig. 3.2 Adjusting accelerator cable (Sec 13)

A   Adjusting nut for pedal position
B   Adjustment nut for free play
C   Stopper bolt for full opening

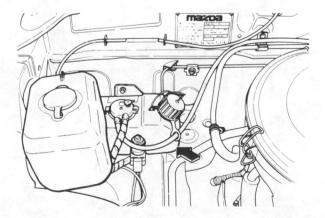

Fig. 3.1 The sub-zero starting assist fluid reservoir (Sec 12)

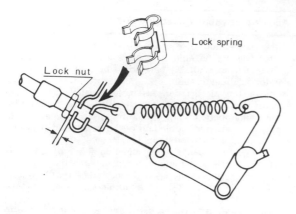

Fig. 3.3 Removing lock spring for hot start assist cable (Sec 14)

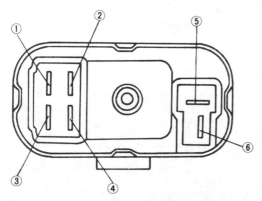

Numbers-continuity	Numbers-No continuity	Remarks
① to ④	③ to ④	Without power applied
③ to ④	① to ④	Connect the battery : positive to terminal ② and negative to ⑥ and or, connect the battery : positive to terminal ⑤ and negative to ⑥.

Fig. 3.4 Continuity check for hot start assist relay (Sec 14)

stopper lever. Hold the cable in this position and check the clearance between the cable bracket and the lock nut on the cable. This clearance should be 0.05 plus or minus 0.03 in (1.25 plus or minus 0.75 mm). Adjust the lock nut until this clearance is obtained, and install the lock spring.

8   There is one more component in the hot start assist system which can cause a failure of the unit. The hot start assist relay is located adjacent to the voltage regulator, under a small fender covering on the left side of the engine compartment.

9   To check the relay, remove it from the fender and disconnect the electrical coupler. Check for proper continuity using an ohmmeter between the specified terminals of the coupler coming from the relay. Refer to Fig. 3.4 for the proper specifications under the varying conditions.

15 Idle speed – adjusting

1   Adjusting the carburetor idle may require extended periods of engine running. Make sure there is sufficient fuel in the tank, and there is plenty of ventilation in the work area. If being done inside a garage, a cooling fan to blow out exhaust is advisable.

2   Set the parking brake and securely block the front wheels.

3   Switch off all accessories.

4   Remove the fuel filler cap.

5   Reach under the air cleaner on the left side and disconnect the idle compensator tube. Plug this tube with a hose plug or suitable bolt. No air must leak from this tube.

6   It is preferable to monitor the engine speed with an accurate hand-held tachometer, connected following the manufacturer's instructions.

7   Warm up the engine to normal operating temperature and then run for three minutes at 2000 rpm in neutral.

8   If available, connect an exhaust gas analyzer to the vehicle following the manufacturer's instructions.

9   On cars equipped with an automatic transmission, place the selector lever to the 'D' position. An assistant applying pressure to the brakes will give the highest degree of safety.

10 Check the idle speed on the tachometer. It should be 750 rpm. If not, turn the air adjust screw to obtain the proper idle speed. The air adjust screw is located at the base of the carburetor, on the left side. It is directly above the mixture adjusting screw and is the larger of the two screws. Do not accidentally turn the idle mixture screw. On all models, the air adjust screw will be open, and not covered by a plastic cap as is the case with the mixture screw (photos).

11 If an exhaust gas analyzer is used, the CO concentration should be less than 0.1% with the idle speed properly set.

12 If the engine hunts, dies or is unstable at this setting, this is an indication that the idle mixture screw needs adjusting.

15.10a A long standard screwdriver positioned as shown facilitates carburetor adjustments

15.10b The idle speed adjusting screw is on top, the mixture screw on the bottom

16 Idle mixture – adjusting

1   Adjusting the idle mixture screw greatly affects the operation of the carburetor and the output of emissions. It is highly recommended that an exhaust gas analyzer be used during this adjustment so that the emissions can be monitored properly.

2   Due to the critical nature of this adjustment, an idle limiter cap is incorporated over the top of the mixture screw. This can be readily removed to adjust the mixture on all USA models except those manufactured for California. California vehicles in the model year 1980 have a special Mas cap over the mixture screw to hamper the home mechanic from adjusting the mixture himself. A special anti-tampering tool is required to adjust the mixture on these models.

3   Remove the idle limiter cap (all models except 1980 California) from the mixture screw.

4   Turn the mixture screw clockwise until the engine 'hunts' severely.

5   Then, before the engine actually dies, turn the mixture screw counter-clockwise in small steps until CO decreases to the 0.1%. The mixture screw should not be over-turned to get CO concentrations less than 0.1%.

6   From the position above, turn the mixture screw counter-clockwise one half turn more and check that the CO concentration is still less than 0.1%.

7   If, during these steps, the idle speed changes from the specified rpm, adjust the engine speed with the air adjust screw and repeat the mixture adjusting steps.

8   Once correct idle is attained, install the limiter cap to fix the mixture adjust screw position.

17 Automatic choke release – checking

1   The RX-7 is equipped with an automatic choke which reacts to engine temperature and retracts on its own (Figs. 3.7 thru 3.11).

2   When the engine is cold, pull the choke knob out fully with the ignition switch in the 'off' position. The choke knob should return automatically.

3   On all California vehicles and US Federal models in model year 1980, start the engine with the choke knob fully pulled out and note the time it takes the knob to return halfway. On California models, this time should be between 20 and 70 seconds after engine starting, US Federal models of 1980 should have a time span of 48 to 72 seconds for the knob to retract halfway.

4   For all models, set the engine speed to 2000 rpm with the choke knob and check that the choke knob automatically returns completely when the temperature gauge indicates normal operating temperature.

5   On all California and US Federal models (1980), stop the engine and pull the choke knob fully with the ignition switch on. The choke knob should hold in the pulled out position.

18 Choke magnet – checking

1   If the choke knob is not functioning properly, one of your first checks should be the choke magnet. It is located above and inboard of the fuse box, under the dashboard (Fig. 3.12).

2   Disconnect the electrical coupler from the choke switch.

3   Use an ohmmeter to check continuity between the numbered terminals in the coupler. Using Fig. 3.13 as a reference, continuity should exist between the terminals numbered 8 and 6. If this is not the case, replace the choke magnet with a new one.

19 Choke return diaphragm (all models) and return delay valve (California only) – checking

1   Warm up the engine to normal operating temperature.

2   Stop the engine and remove the air cleaner assembly (Section 9).

3   Disconnect the vacuum sensing tube from the choke return diaphragm. This is the circular component on the right side of the carburetor, at the rear. Start the engine and run it at idle. Automatic transmissions should be set in the 'N' position.

4   Connect the vacuum sensing tube and check the time it takes for the diaphragm shaft to retract fully into the diaphragm. For all models, this time should not exceed 72 seconds.

5   If the above test proves a failure, the choke return delay valve should be replaced. This valve is incorporated on all California vehicles only. It is spliced into the vacuum sensing tube. For all other models (except 1980 US Federal) the above test indicates a failure of the choke return diaphragm.

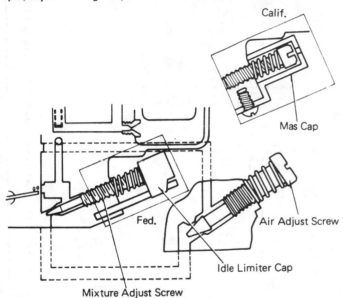

Fig. 3.5 Special anti-tampering Mas cap used on 1980 California vehicles (Sec 15)

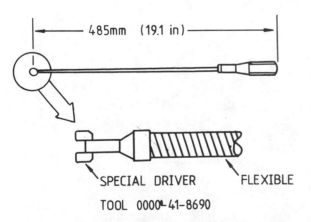

Fig. 3.6 Special anti-tampering tool needed to adjust idle mixture on 1980 California vehicles (Sec 16)

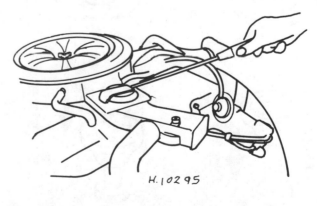

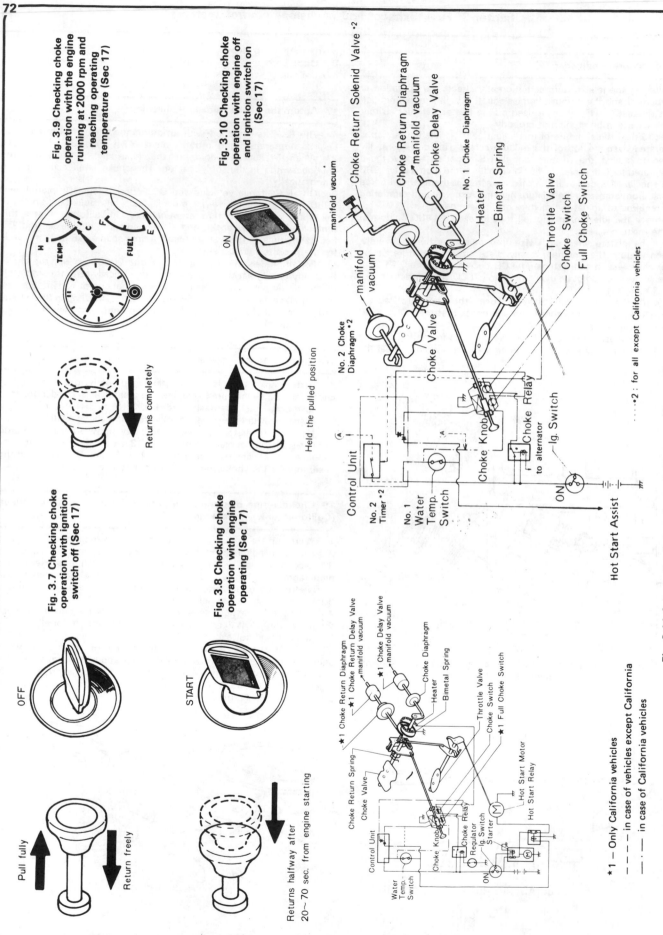

Fig. 3.7 Checking choke operation with ignition switch off (Sec 17)

Fig. 3.8 Checking choke operation with engine operating (Sec 17)

Fig. 3.9 Checking choke operation with the engine running at 2000 rpm and reaching operating temperature (Sec 17)

Fig. 3.10 Checking choke operation with engine off and ignition switch on (Sec 17)

Fig. 3.11 Automatic choke release systems for 1979 and 1980 vehicles (Sec 17)

* 1 — Only California vehicles
— — — in case of vehicles except California
— · — in case of California vehicles

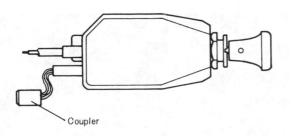

Fig. 3.12 The choke knob, magnet and electrical coupler (Sec 18)

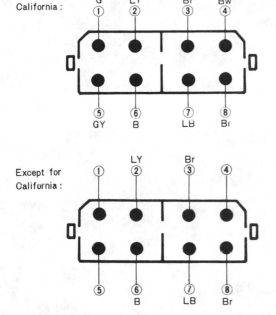

Fig. 3.13 Continuity check of choke switch (Sec 18)

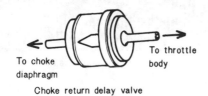

Fig. 3.14 Choke return delay valve used on some models (Sec 19)

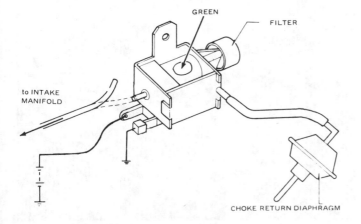

Fig. 3.15 Checking operation of choke return solenoid valve
(Sec 20)

6   On 1980 US Federal models, check the choke return solenoid valve as described in Section 20.

20 Choke return solenoid valve – checking (1980 US Federal models only)

1   In place of the choke return delay valve some models are equipped with a solenoid valve which does basically the same thing. This valve is located on the top of the engine, and can be identified by a green-colored dot.
2   To check, disconnect the vacuum sensing tubes from the solenoid valve and the diaphragm located on the right side of the carburetor, at the rear.
3   Blow air through the solenoid valve from the vacuum sensing tube (the one leading to the carburetor). Make sure that the air comes out at the disconnected port on the other side of the valve, and not through the round filter port.
4   Disconnect the electrical coupler from the solenoid valve and connect battery power to the terminal on the valve. Power can be picked up from running a jumper wire from the alternator terminal marked 'B'.
5   Blow through the valve from the vacuum sensing tube, as before, and make sure that the air comes out through the round filter port.

21 Choke delay valve – checking (California and 1980 US Federal models)

1   The choke delay valve incorporated on some models should not be confused with the choke return delay valve or the choke return solenoid valve: however, all of these components are closely related in the choke system.
2   To check the operation of the choke delay valve, first warm up the engine to normal operating temperature.
3   Stop the engine and remove the air cleaner assembly. Plug the idle compensator hose.
4   Disconnect the vacuum sensing tube from the choke diaphragm. The choke diaphragm is located at the rear of the carburetor, at the top.
5   Start the engine and run at idle. Connect the sensing tube and check the time it takes for the shaft to fully pull itself into a diaphragm. This time should be no more than 20 seconds.
6   If this is not the case, replace the choke delay valve with a new one. The delay valve is located in the vacuum sensing line, on the right side of the carburetor. It is just above the choke return delay valve.

22 Choke diaphragm – checking

1   All models are equipped with a choke diaphragm; however, the 1980 US Federal models are equipped with two. They are all checked in the same manner.
2   Remove the air cleaner assembly (See Section 9).
3   Plug the idle compensator hose.
4   Start the engine and run at idle. Automatic transmissions should be placed in the 'N' position.
5   Disconnect the vacuum sensing tube from the choke diaphragm. The diaphragm shaft should come out from the choke diaphragm.

23 Carburetor – removal

1   If the carburetor is to be rebuilt by a professional repair shop, much money can be saved if it is first removed at home.
2   If the carburetor is being overhauled, check on the availability of a rebuild kit which will contain all the necessary parts for the job. Do this before the carburetor is removed to prevent the car from being disabled as the parts are received.
3   Allow the engine to completely cool, as you will be working on areas which can cause serious burns to the skin if touched when hot. Also, fuel will more than likely be spilled and should not come into contact with hot parts.
4   Disconnect the negative battery cable at the battery.
5   Remove the air cleaner assembly as discussed in Section 9.
6   On the right side of the carburetor, towards the front, disconnect

the electrical couplers. As they are disconnected, check that they are clearly color-coded. If you are in doubt, make your own identification tags with pieces of adhesive tape (photo).

7 Disconnect the anti-afterburn solenoid tube. This is the tube leading to the anti-afterburn solenoid mounted at the front, right side of the carburetor (photo).

8 Open up the wiring harness clamp and place all wires clear of the carburetor.

9 Disconnect the metering oil pump connecting rod. This is located at the front of the carburetor, near the bottom. Disconnect by removing the cotter pin and washer, then push the rod through the arm of the carburetor.

10 Disconnect the vacuum sensing tube leading to the throttle opener. The throttle opener is the large round sensor at the rear of the carburetor, on the left side (photo).

11 The choke cable is disconnected by first removing the securing clip, then sliding the housing out of the mounting bracket. Release the inside cable from the carburetor by rotating it and then sliding it out of the lever (photo).

12 Working on the left side of the carburetor, disconnect the various hoses attached to the carburetor. It may be wise to make a rough sketch of your own showing the positions of these hoses for easier reassembly. Identification tags can be placed on the hoses. When disconnecting the main fuel line and the fuel return line, have a container and rags ready to catch any excess fuel (photo).

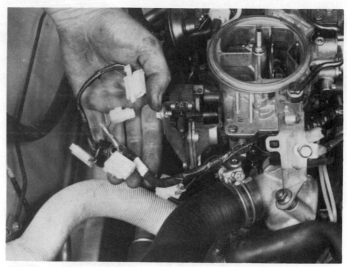

23.6 The various color-coded electrical couplers on the right side of the carburetor

23.7 The anti-afterburn solenoid located on a bracket at the front of the carburetor

23.10 Disconnecting the vacuum sensing tube at the throttle opener at the rear of the carburetor

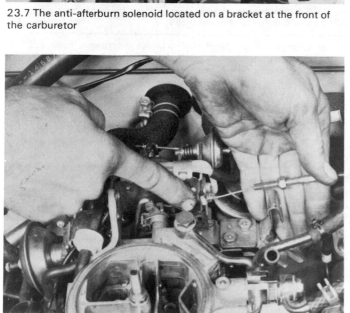

23.11 Of the three cables on the right side of the carburetor the choke cable is readily disconnected when the carburetor is in place

23.12 Disconnecting the fuel main and return lines

13 Disconnect the air vent solenoid electrical coupler on the left side of the carburetor.

14 To disconnect the two metering oil pump tubes where they meet the bottom of the carburetor, it is necessary to first open the spring clips. Note the position of each metering oil pump hose (photo).

15 Disconnect the altitude compensator hose next to the idle mixture screw.

16 Remove the four carburetor attaching nuts and lock washers. The nut on the left side, at the rear, will require a certain degree of patience.

17 Remove the hot-start assist cable and the throttle cable from the mounting bracket. Do this by loosening the lock nut while the cables are held firmly in place (photo).

18 Lift the carburetor slightly and tilt it forward for better access at the rear. Held in this position, the hot-start assist and throttle cables can be disconnected from their respective linkages on the carburetor (photo).

19 Remove the carburetor and cover the hole in the manifold to prevent anything from accidentally falling into the manifold bores, and to keep dirt out of the system.

24 Carburetor – disassembly

1 With a carburetor rebuild kit in hand, the disassembly can begin. The steps involved with disassembling the carburetor are illustrated in a step-by-step fashion with photos. Follow these photos in the proper sequence.

2 It will be necessary to have a relatively large and clean workspace to lay out all the parts as they are removed from the carburetor. Many of the parts are very small and thus can be lost easily if the work space is cluttered.

3 Work slowly through the disassembly process, and if at any point you feel the reassembly of a certain component may prove confusing, stop and make a rough sketch or apply identification marks. The time to think about reassembling the carburetor is when it is being taken apart. Now follow the photo sequence starting with photo 24.3/1.

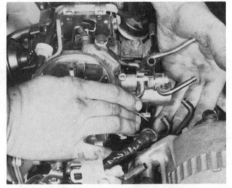

23.14 The two metering oil pump hoses are held to the carburetor with small spring clips

23.17 The throttle and hot-start assist cables being disengaged at their securing bracket

23.18 With the carburetor tilted in this position the throttle and hot-start assist cables are easier to disconnect

24.3/1 Suspend the carburetor with a center punch tool which is secured in a vise. With the wires unclipped, remove the three screws securing the bimetal spring housing

24.3/2 Remove the bimetal spring housing assembly after first compressing the spring on the adjacent diaphragm

24.3/3 The spring, and the washer can now be removed from the diaphragm shaft

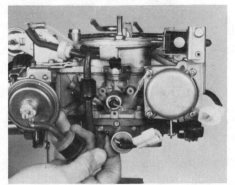

24.3/4 Disconnecting the choke return delay valve (if equpped)

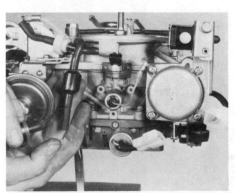

24.3/5 Disconnecting the choke delay valve (if equipped)

24.3/6 Disconnect the dashpot delay valve (manual transmission)

24.3/7 Disconnect the throttle return spring at the throttle lever

24.3/8 Disconnect the throttle sub-return spring from the throttle linkage by removing the cotter key and two flat washers

24.3/9 The rear throttle and choke mechanism can be removed after unscrewing five bracket screws. Shown is one bracket attaching screw on the left side

24.3/10 There are also two bracket attaching screws on the right side of the carburetor

24.3/11 This is the assembly being removed from the carburetor body. It includes the cable bracket, choke diaphragm, throttle opener and delay valves

24.3/12 Remove the small hot-start assist lever spring

24.3/13 Remove the clip which retains the choke cable lever and choke diaphragm lever. Note that the cable lever goes towards the outside

24.3/14 Remove the choke return diaphragm along with the throttle sub-return spring and bracket as an entire assembly

24.3/15 At the rear of the carburetor disconnect the fast idle rod by removing the split pin and two washers

24.3/16 To remove the fuel inlet and return assembly, first remove the bolt just above the air vent solenoid ...

24.3/17 ... then remove the two bolts on the top of the carburetor body

24.3/18 After removing the fuel return line, a thru-bolt above the air vent solenoid must be removed. Note any flat washers which are used on this assembly

24.3/19 The fuel main piping being removed from the carburetor

24.3/20 Six different length screws secure the top air horn assembly to the main carburetor body. As these are removed, note their proper positions for reassembly. One of the right-hand attaching screws incorporates an electrical clip

24.3/21 Three screws secure the air vent solenoid to the air horn assembly

24.3/22 Remove the air vent solenoid with its wiring coupler and plunger assembly

24.3/23 Before the top air horn assembly can be removed, the center stud to which the air cleaner attaches must be removed

24.3/24 The center stud goes all the way through the carburetor body

24.3/25 Lifting the air horn assembly with its gasket off the main body

24.3/26 The floats are easily removed from the air horn. Remove the float pin, float, needle valve, spring and retainer

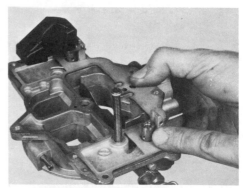

24.3/27 From the air horn, remove the needle seat with a screwdriver

24.3/28 Disconnect the accelerator pump rod at the throttle linkage by removing the split pin and two flat washers

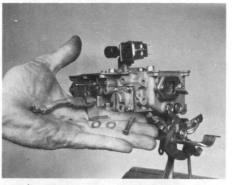

24.3/29 The accelerator pump rod can then be disconnected at the accelerator pump by removing the shaft which runs through the pump. This is held in place with a snap-ring and washers

24.3/30 Four screws secure the accelerator pump to the carburetor body

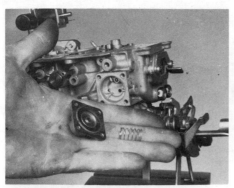

24.3/31 The accelerator pump cover (with diaphragm inside) and the return spring removed from the carburetor body

24.3/32 Remove the sub-zero starting assist inlet (or plug if not equipped with sub-zero system)

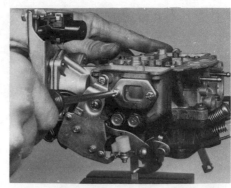

24.3/33 The fuel level windows, front and rear, can be removed from the main body

24.3/34 There are two blind plugs with washers which should be removed to gain access to the main jets (arrows). Also, disconnect the small idle switch spring

24.3/35 Two screws secure the idle switch to the main body

24.3/36 Remove the idle switch with its electrical coupler

24.3/37 Disconnect the secondary throttle valve rod at the diaphragm lever by removing the split pin

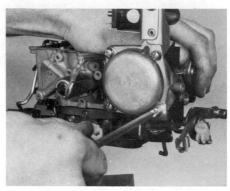

24.3/38 Remove the two screws which attach the anti-afterburn solenoid bracket (arrowed)

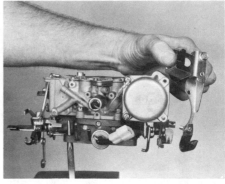

24.3/39 The anti-afterburn solenoid and bracket being removed from the carburetor body

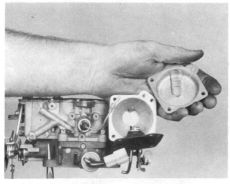

24.3/40 Remove the two remaining screws on the face of the diaphragm. The cover and return spring can then be removed

24.3/41 Remove the three screws towards the inside of the diaphragm

24.3/42 The diaphragm housing and diaphragm can then be removed

24.3/43 Unscrewing the coasting richer solenoid valve from the main body

24.3/44 The coasting richer solenoid valve is then removed together with the plunger

24.3/45 With a screwdriver, remove the inlet check valve seat, with the weight and inlet check valve beneath

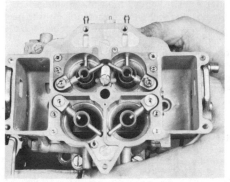

24.3/46 Before removing jets and air bleeds make a sketch and/or use a compartmental box to identify and separate components. They must be reassembled in their original positions

24.3/47 Once the blind plugs have been removed both the primary and secondary main jets are accessible

24.3.48 Remove the four bolts which attach the main body to the throttle body

24.3/49 Lift the main body, with its gasket, away from the throttle body

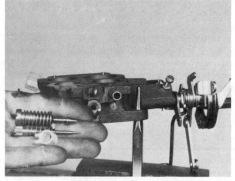

24.3/50 As the idle speed and mixture screws are unscrewed from the throttle housing note the number of turns. When reinstalling use the same number of turns

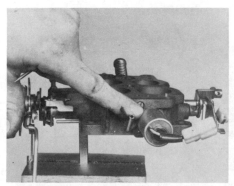

24.3/51 A thin wrench is necessary to remove the power valve solenoid

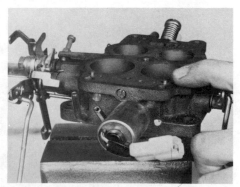

24.3/52 When installing the main carburetor body to the throttle body, use a new gasket and make sure the two small guide pins are seated properly

25 Carburetor – inspection

1   Before inspecting, wash the air horn, carburetor main body and related components in clean solvent and blow with compressed air if available. Do not clean the solenoids, choke etc. with solvent. Do not use a wire for cleaning the jets.
2   Inspect the air horn, main body and throttle body for cracks and breakage.
3   Inspect the choke shaft and throttle shaft for wear.
4   Check the linkage, connecting rod and return springs for damage.
5   All the jets and air bleeds should not be clogged.
6   Check the diaphragms for damage. These are ordinarily included in a rebuild kit.
7   Check the float for rupture or leakage. No fuel should be present in the float. The float and its related components should not have signs of rust or corrosion.
8   Apply battery power to the air vent solenoid valve and the richer solenoid valve (manual transmissions). The valve stem should be pulled into the valve body when power is applied.
9   When battery power is applied to the power valve solenoid (automatic transmission and California with manual transmission) the valve stem should come out from the valve body.

26 Carburetor – reassembly

1   Do not reuse any of the old gaskets. Use new ones supplied in the kit.
2   Make sure all the parts are in good condition and are clean.
3   The reassembly process can be followed by using the sequenced photos in reverse. However, before the air horn is installed to the main body of the carburetor the float level should be checked.
4   To check the float level, invert the air horn and allow the float to lower by its own weight. Measure the distance between the air horn gasket and the lowest point of the float. The distance should be 0.63 plus or minus 0.02 in (16 plus or minus 0.5 mm). If the clearance is not within specifications, bend the float seat lip until the proper clearance is obtained (photo).
5   Now turn the air horn to its normal position and allow the float to lower by its own weight. Measure the distance between the air horn gasket and the lowermost point on the float. The distance should be 2.0 plus or minus 0.02 in (51 plus or minus 0.5 mm). If not within specifications, bend the float stopper until the proper distance is obtained (photo).
6   Before installing the carburetor onto the engine, make the fast idle adjustment as described in Section 27.

27 Fast idle adjustment

1   After reassembling the carburetor, but before it is installed on the engine, the fast idle adjustment should be made. This cannot be done once the carburetor is installed.
2   To check the fast idle opening angle, close the choke valve fully

and measure the clearance between the primary throttle valve and the wall of the throttle bore. This is done through the bottom of the carburetor. California vehicles should have a clearance of 0.051 to 0.059 in (1.30 to 1.50 mm). All other vehicles should have a clearance of 0.035 to 0.04 in (0.90 to 1.10 mm). If necessary, bend the fast idle rod until this clearance is obtained.

28 Carburetor – installation

1   Before installing the carburetor, check that the four studs are in good shape and their threads are not damaged. Rn the carburetor attaching nuts over the studs to make sure they can be installed easily. This is especially true of the left, rear nut. It is difficult to tighten and thus should be in good condition.
2   Install a new base gasket onto the intake manifold. Make sure that any excess gasket material is first removed from the manifold.
3   Lift the carburetor into position and tilt it towards the front to gain access to the rear. Connect the throttle cable and hot-start cable to the operating levers on the carburetor.
4   Drop the carburetor over the four studs. Make sure it sits flat across the intake manifold, with no binding from components.
5   Install the left rear lockwasher and attaching nut to the stud. Access can be improved by lifting up on the carburetor as the nut is threaded onto the stud.
6   Install the three remaining lockwashers and attaching nuts. Tighten securely.
7   Place the hot start assist and throttle cables into the mounting bracket. Tighten the lock nuts while holding the outer cable.
8   Connect the two metering oil pump tubes to their nozzles at the bottom of the carburetor. Slide the spring clips into position near the ends of the tubes.
9   Connect the altitude compensator hose next to the idle mixture screw.
10   Connect the air vent solenoid coupler and all hoses on the left side of the carburetor. The main fuel hose and the return hose should be pushed onto their connectors 1.2 to 1.4 in (30 to 35 mm). Slide the clamps near the ends of these hoses.
11   Connect the choke cable to the operating lever and then into its mounting bracket.
12   Connect the sensing tube to the throttle opener at the rear of the carburetor.
13   Connect the oil metering pump rod. Push the rod through the carburetor arm and then secure with a washer and cotter pin.
14   Place the wiring harness back into the mounting clamp, and connect all the electrical couplers disconnected on the right side of the carburetor.
15   Connect the anti-afterburn tube to the afterburn valve.
16   Plug the idle compensator hose and start the engine. Check for fuel leakage and for vacuum leaks indicated by a hissing sound.
17   With the engine operating, check the fuel level in the sight glasses. The level should be at the specified mark.
18   Unplug the idle compensator hose and install the air cleaner assembly. Adjust the idle speed and idle mixture as described in Sections 15 and 16.

26.4 Checking the float level with the air horn inverted. Measure from the air horn gasket to the lowest point of the float

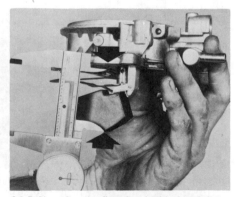

26.5 Checking the float level with the air horn in its proper position. Measure from the air horn gasket to the lowest point of the float

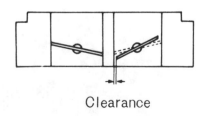

Clearance

Fig. 3.16 Measuring throttle valve clearance fast idle adjustment (Sec 27)

29 Emissions controls – general description

1   The emissions system on the RX-7 is actually seven different systems, each with a different function. However, they all interact with each other. Electrical solenoids, valves and relays can make trouble-shooting and repair work difficult for the home mechanic. But this should not be a deterrent for trying to isolate and rectify the problem components.

2   The seven systems, which are dealt with separately, are: the air injection and thermal reactor; secondary air control system; ignition control system; deceleration control; kick-down control; auxiliary emission devices; crankcase and evaporative controls.

3   As regulations governing emissions are constantly being changed,

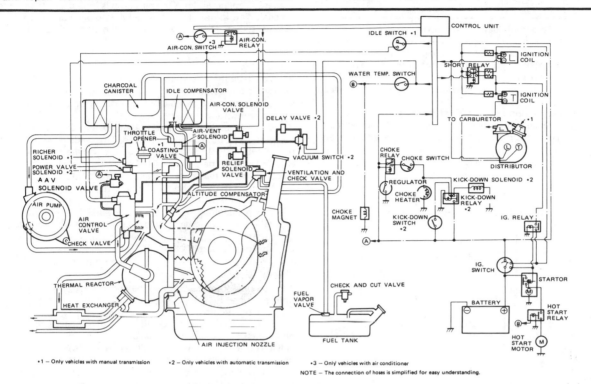

Fig. 3.17 1979 emission system for all vehicles except California (Sec 29)

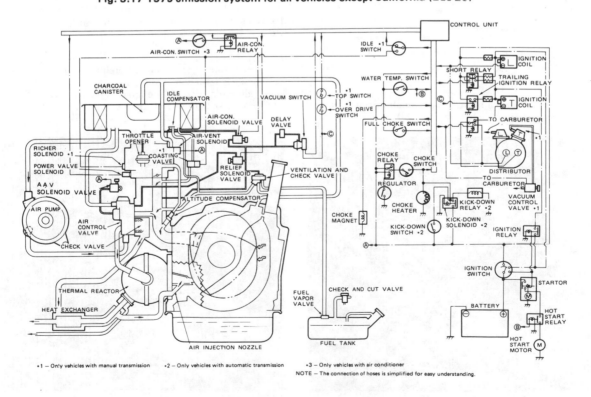

Fig. 3.18 1979 emission system for all California vehicles (Sec 29)

updates in these systems for the 1980 models years have been included as appropriate.

4   When reading through the emissions Sections, make certain that the tests and components are applicable to your specific vehicle. There are differences in relation to geographic areas where the vehicle will be operated, the transmission the car is equipped with and the model year.

30 Air injection and thermal reactor system

1   The air injection system consists of an air pump and check valve. The thermal reactor is incorporated in place of the more conventional exhaust manifold and works in conjunction with a heat exchanger. This system works very closely with the secondary control system, dealt with later.

2   Under certain engine conditions the system injects air into the thermal reactor and at other times air is pumped through injectors into the exhaust ports. This fresh air is needed for more efficient and cleaner burning of the air/fuel mixture.

3   The air pump is of the vane type and is driven by a drive belt off the eccentric shaft. The check valve is mounted in the intake manifold, behind the air control valve. This check valve is incorporated to prevent exhaust gas from flowing back into the fresh air system.

4   The function of the thermal reactor is not only to extract exhaust gases from the engine, but also to fully complete the combustion process. Cooling air from the air pump is forced into the reactor for this process. The larger of the two exhaust pipes carries the actual spent exhaust gases. The smaller pipe running alongside the main pipe vents cooling air.

Air pump

5   To check the operation of the air pump, warm up the car to normal operating temperature.

6   Disconnect the air hose which leads from the rear of the pump to the air control valve (photo).

7   Connect an air gauge to the air hose and measure the output of the pump at 800 rpm engine speed. The reading on the gauge should be 1.64 lb/in^2 (0.115 kg/cm^2). If not, replace the pump with a new one.

8   To replace the pump, first remove the air cleaner assembly, then disconnect the two hoses leading to the pump.

9   Remove the strap bolt and long pivot bolt and then disconnect the drive belt. Remove the pump.

10   When installing the pump make sure the drive belt is tightened properly. You should be able to press the belt with your finger halfway between the pump and the eccentric shaft pulley and have the belt deflect approximately $\frac{1}{2}$ inch (12 mm).

Check valve

11   To check the operation of the check valve, warm up the engine to normal operating temperature and disconnect the hose leading from the rear of the air pump to the control valve.

12   Have an assistant slowly increase the engine speed to 1500 rpm and watch for exhaust gas leakage at the air inlet fitting to the control valve. It may help to put your finger over this opening to actually feel any leakage. If there is leakage, replace the check valve.

13   To replace the check valve, the control valve must first be removed. See Section 31.22 for this operation.

14   With the control valve out of the way, the check valve can be merely lifted out of the intake manifold (photo).

15   When reinstalling make sure a new gasket is used and the hoses are properly installed.

Thermal reactor

16   The thermal reactor will not ordinarily wear out; however, cracks can appear after a number of miles. This is especially true if it has not been tightened properly. Periodically check for exhaust gas leakage and for proper tightness of the four securing nuts.

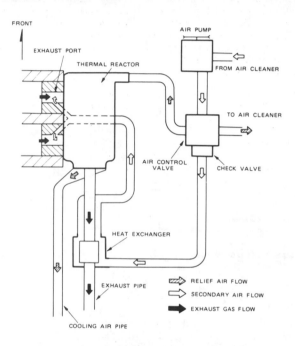

Fig. 3.19 Components and operations of the air injection and thermal reactor system (Sec 30)

30.6 Removing the rubber air hose which leads from the rear of the air pump to the air control valve

30.14 The check valve is located in the inlet manifold, behind the air control valve

17 To replace the thermal reactor, first remove the air cleaner assembly and the hot air duct hose leading from the top of the reactor to the air cleaner.

18 Disconnect the air pipe which runs from the thermal reactor to the air control valve.

19 Remove the three covers surrounding the thermal reactor. To remove the large main cover it is necessary to remove the two nuts on the lower side of the reactor.

20 From the engine compartment, remove the two upper nuts securing the thermal reactor to the engine.

21 Disconnect the air pipe which leads from the intake manifold to the heat exchange.

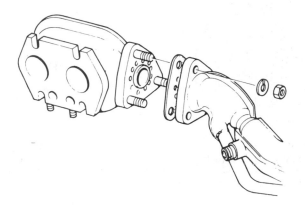

Fig. 3.20 Removing the locknuts for main exhaust pipe to thermal reactor (Sec 30)

22 Disconnect the air pipe which leads from the thermal reactor to the air duct.

23 Disconnect the air duct hanger bracket at the rear of the transmission. This is necessary to enable you to slide the exhaust system rearward slightly.

24 Remove the three nuts securing the main exhaust pipe to the rear of the thermal reactor. These nuts may be tight on the studs due to the heat. Try using a penetrating lubricant like WD-40 to break them loose, or as a last resort the nuts will have to be split off the studs.

25 Remove the two lower attaching nuts for the thermal reactor, and remove the thermal reactor. Be careful, as it is fairly heavy.

26 The installation is the reverse process: however, be sure to use a new gasket where the reactor meets the engine.

Exhaust gas recirculation – 1980 California only

27 Added to the California models in 1980 is an exhaust gas recirculation system, commonly called an EGR. The system operates under specific conditions when emissions are most likely to be created. The primary control components are the acceleration sensor, EGR relay and solenoid and the EGR control valve. A modified thermal reactor is also incorporated. This has a small additional passage to supply exhaust gas to the system (photos) (Fig. 3.22).

28 To check the operation of the solenoid valve, warm up the engine to normal operating temperature.

29 Connect a test light to the brown/yellow lead wire for the solenoid valve (gray-colored dot).

30 Start the engine and rapidly increase the engine speed to 2500 rpm. The test light should illuminate momentarily and then shut off after a few seconds.

31 The control valve is checked by disconnecting the vacuum hose to the EGR valve and then running the engine at idle.

32 When vacuum (hand pump) is applied to the vacuum port of the EGR control valve the engine should run rough or stall.

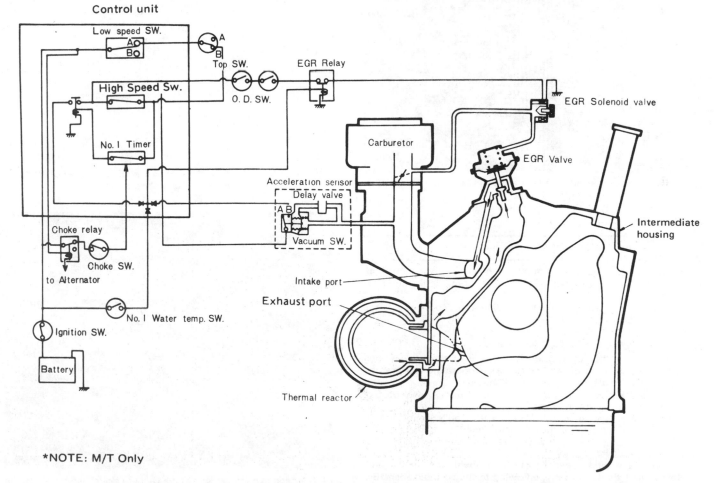

Fig. 3.21 Components and operations of the exhaust gas recirculation system added to California vehicles in 1980 (Sec 30)

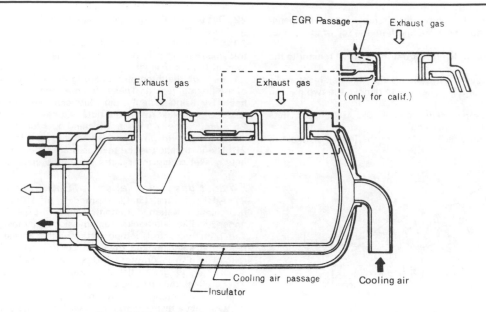

Fig. 3.22 Thermal reactor fitted to 1980 California vehicles (Sec 30)

30.27 An EGR valve was added to the emissions system in 1980. It is located on the top of the engine

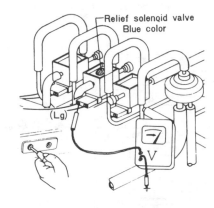

Fig. 3.23 Connecting voltmeter to electrical coupler of relief solenoid valve (Sec 31)

31 Secondary air control system

1   The secondary control system monitors engine operation, and controls where, and at which times, the air from the air pump is delivered.
2   This system consists of a relief solenoid valve and an air control valve.

Relief solenoid valve – California only

3   To check that the relief solenoid valve is getting the proper electrical signal, warm up the engine to normal operating temperature and connect a voltmeter to the electrical coupler.
4   Disconnect the electrical coupler from the vacuum switch, located on the firewall, next to the oil filter.
5   Start the engine with the choke knob fully pulled out. Current should flow to the terminal at the solenoid. Push in the choke.
6   Connect a small jumper wire to both terminals in the disconnected vacuum switch coupler (photo).
7   Increase the engine speed to 3500 rpm with the throttle and check to see that the current stops flowing to the solenoid after 130 seconds plus or minus 26 seconds. This is measured from the time the engine is first started.

31.6 Connecting a jumper wire at the vacuum switch electrical coupler

After 130 sec. from engine starting

Fig. 3.24 Checking current stoppage at relief solenoid valve (Sec 31)

Fig. 3.25 Checking current flow with engine more than 3000 rpm (Sec 31)

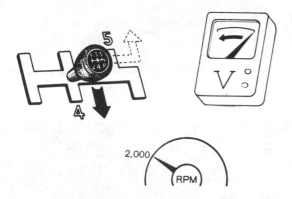

Fig. 3.27 Checking current flow on acceleration and deceleration (Sec 31)

Fig. 3.26 Checking for current stoppage with transmission in 4th or 5th gears (Sec 31)

8   Increase the engine speed again and check to see that the current stops flowing to the solenoid when the engine speed is more than 3000 rpm plus or minus 300 rpm.

9   On vehicles equipped with a manual transmission, set the engine speed to 2000 with the throttle and place the gearshift into 4th and/or 5th gears. The current should stop flowing when placed in these gears.

10 Remove the jumper wire from the vacuum switch coupler.

11 Increase the engine speed to 2000 rpm with the throttle and then decrase the engine speed, recording at what rpm the current begins flowing to the solenoid. Flow should begin at 1150 rpm plus or minus 100 rpm. Now increase the engine speed from idle and record when the current stops flowing. The difference between current flow on deceleration and current stoppage on acceleration should not be more than 150 rpm plus or minus 70 rpm.

12 To check the relief solenoid itself, disconnect the vacuum sensing tubes from the solenoid valve and vacuum pipe.

13 Blow through the valve from the vacuum sensing tube and make sure the air passes through the valve and comes out from the port of the disconnected vacuum pipe.

14 Disconnect the electrical coupler at the relief solenoid valve and connect battery power to the terminal. This can be done with a jumper wire from the alternator 'B' terminal.

15 Blow through the vacuum sensing tube and make sure the air comes out through the filter and not the vacuum pipe terminal as in the previous test.

16 To replace the solenoid valve, merely disconnect the vacuum hoses and the electrical coupler, then unbolt the solenoid from the top of the engine.

Relief solenoid valve – except California

17 To check for a proper signal at the relief solenoid valve, warm up the engine to normal operating temperature and connect a voltmeter to the terminal of the coupler.

18 Operate the engine at idle and make sure the current flows to the terminal.

19 Increase the engine speed to 2000 rpm with the throttle. Slowly decrease the engine speed and record at what rpm the current begins flowing at the terminal. This should be at 1150 rpm plus or minus 100 rpm (Fig. 3.30).

20 Now slowly increase the engine speed from idle and note at what

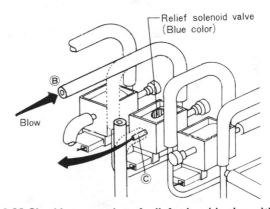

Fig. 3.28 Checking operation of relief solenoid valve without battery power (Sec 31)

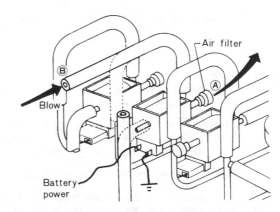

Fig. 3.29 Checking operation of relief solenoid valve with battery power applied (Sec 31)

rpm the current stops flowing. The difference between current flow on deceleration and current stoppage on acceleration should be 150 rpm plus or minus 70 rpm.

21 The relief solenoid valve itself is checked in the same manner as described in the steps for California vehicles (steps 3-16).

Fig. 3.30 Checking current flow with engine accelerating and decelerating (Sec 31)

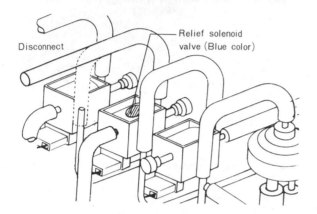

Fig. 3.31 Using relief solenoid valve to check operation of air control valve (Sec 31)

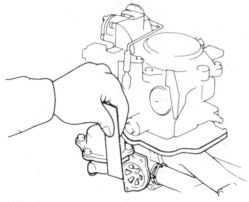

Fig. 3.32 Checking for air flow with thin paper at the air control valve (Sec 31)

31.36a Remove the three nuts securing the air control valve to the inlet manifold

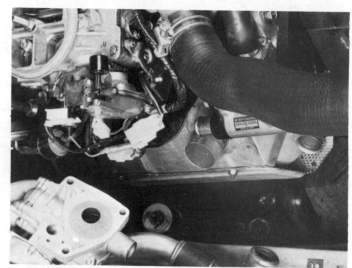

31.36b The air control valve being lifted away from the engine

30 Increase the engine speed to 4500 rpm and check to see that air does flow from the valve.

Air control valve

22 Before checking the air control valve for proper operation, inspect all the hoses and vacuum sensing tubes for good connection and damage.

23 Check the carburetor and air control valve attaching nuts for proper torque. Insure there is no leakage around these components.

24 Disconnect the vacuum sensing tube from the relief solenoid valve.

25 Disconnect the air hose at the air cleaner which runs to the air control valve.

26 Start the engine and run it at idle. Place a finger over the air hose opening and check to see the air does not flow out through the air hose.

27 Connect the disconnected vacuum sensing tube at the relief solenoid valve and slowly increase the engine speed. Air should flow out of the air pipe at about 1300 rpm.

28 Stop the engine and remove the air pipe. This is done by removing the two bolts at the flange.

29 Start the engine and run at idle. Check to see that air does not flow out of the control valve by holding some thin paper near the valve and check for movement of the paper.

Air control valve – removal and installation

31 Remove the flexible hot air duct which leads to the air cleaner.

32 Disconnect the air hose which leads to the air cleaner.

33 Disconnect the vacuum sensing tube.

34 Disconnect the air pipe which leads to the air pump. This is held in place by a metal clamp.

35 Disconnect the rubber hose leading to the rear of the pump.

36 There are three nuts which secure the air control valve. Remove these, and the control valve can be removed (photos).

37 When installing, use new gaskets and install the three nuts loosely until the solid metal air pipe is connected. Then tighten the attaching nuts and connect the various hoses.

32 Ignition control system – California

1   The ignition system on the RX-7 is actually two separate systems called leading and trailing. The leading system is the primary one, handling most of the conventional duties. The trailing ignition system is used for a number of purposes, interacting with many of the emission control devices. As the following tests will indicate, the

trailing ignition system does not operate all the time, but rather at times when a more complete burn is necessary or a warm-up of certain components is required.

Trailing ignition – checks

2 Disconnect the vacuum sensing tube from the dash pot diaphragm. This is located at the extreme rear of the carburetor.
3 Warm up the engine to normal operating temperature.
4 Connect a timing light to the high tension cord for the trailing spark plug on the front rotor housing.
5 Start the engine and run at idle. The timing light should flash.
6 Gradually increase the engine speed with the throttle, and check to see that the timing light flashes when the engine speed is more than 3000 rpm plus or minus 300 rpm.
7 Now increase the engine speed to 2000 rpm with the throttle and

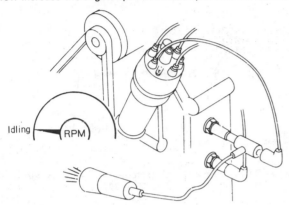

Fig. 3.33 Checking for spark with engine idling (Sec 32)

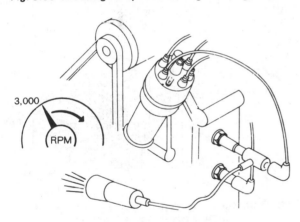

Fig. 3.34 Checking for spark with the engine operating at more than 3000 rpm (Sec 32)

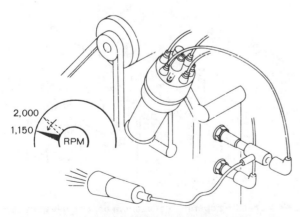

Fig. 3.35 Checking for spark with engine accelerating and decelerating (Sec 32)

slowly decrease the engine speed, recording at what rpm the timing light starts to flash. This should be approximately 1150 rpm. Increase the engine speed and record at what speed the light stops flashing. This speed should correspond closely (150 rpm plus or minus 70 rpm) with the speed previously attained.
8 On manual transmissions, set the engine speed to 2000 rpm and shift the gearshift lever into 4th and/or 5th gear positions. The timing light should flash when this is done.
9 On vehicles with manual transmission, raise the engine speed to 3000 rpm and quickly release the throttle. The timing light should immediately start to flash and continue flashing during deceleration and at idle.

Leading ignition – checks

10 Warm up the engine to normal operating temperature.
11 Connect a timing light to the leading spark plug of the front rotor housing.
12 Start the engine and check that the timing light flashes at idle and at any engine speed.
13 Stop the engine and disconnect the electrical coupler of the water

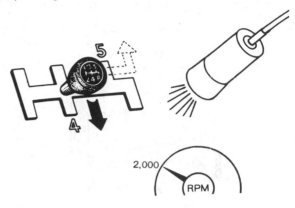

Fig. 3.36 Checking for spark with transmission placed in 4th or 5th gear (Sec 32)

Fig. 3.37 Checking for spark with engine decelerated quickly from 3000 rpm (Sec 32)

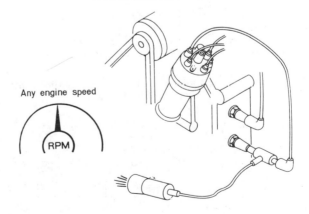

Fig. 3.38 Checking for leading ignition spark with engine at any speed (Sec 32)

temperature switch located near the top radiator hose inlet to the engine.

14 Connect a jumper wire to both terminals inside the coupler half which leads to the control box (not the coupler half attached to the water temperature switch).

15 Start the engine and set the engine speed to 2000 rpm with the choke knob (not the throttle). Observe the timing marks on the eccentric shaft pulley with the timing light. The indicator pin should be between the Yellow and Red marks on the pully.

16 Increase the engine speed with the throttle (not the choke) and check to see that the timing mark (yellow-painted) advances as shown in Fig. 3.41 with the engine speed more than 4500 plus or minus 400 rpm.

17 The yellow-painted timing mark should also quickly advance after 130 seconds plus or minus 26 seconds from the time the choke knob is pulled out.

Vacuum control valve (manual transmission)

18 Cars equipped with a manual transmission have a vacuum control valve that works in coordination with the ignition control system. This vacuum control valve is located at the top of the engine and can be identified by an orange dot.

19 Disconnect the vacuum sensing tubes from the vacuum control valve and vacuum pipe.

20 Disconnect the electrical coupler.

21 Blow through the vacuum control valve from the vacuum sensing

tube. Air should flow through the valve and come out of the port where the vacuum pipe was disconnected.

22 Apply battery power to the vacuum control valve. This can be done by running a jumper wire from the alternator terminal marked 'B'. Blow through the sensing tube again and make sure that the air comes out through the filter, not from the vacuum pipe outlet as before.

Retard relay and trailing ignition relay

23 This relay is located at the front of the engine compartment, just in front of the battery. It may be necessary to remove the battery for access. The location for 1980 models may differ.

24 Disconnect the electrical coupler from the relay.

25 Check for continuity by using an ohmmeter. Continuity should exist between the specified terminals under the varying conditions shown in Fig. 3.45.

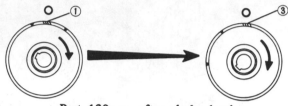

Past 130 sec. after choke knob has been pulled

Fig. 3.42 Checking advancing characteristics with choke knob pulled (Sec 32)

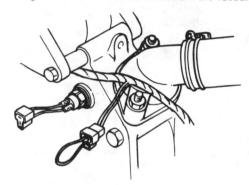

Fig. 3.39 Connecting jumper wire to water temperature switch coupler (Sec 32)

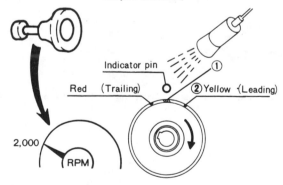

Fig. 3.40 Using the timing marks to check ignition control characteristics (Sec 32)

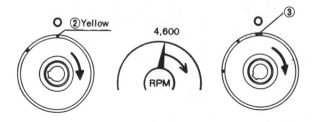

Fig. 3.41 Checking for proper advancing of the timing mark (Sec 32)

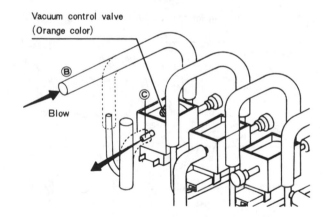

Fig. 3.43 Checking operation of vacuum control valve with no battery power applied (Sec 32)

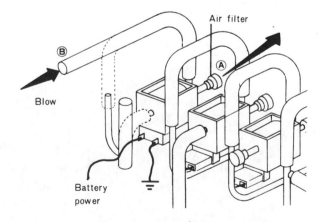

Fig. 3.44 Checking operation of vacuum control valve with battery power applied (Sec 32)

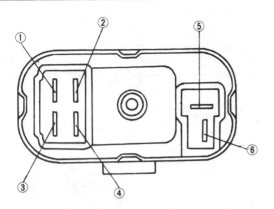

Numbers-continuity	Numbers-No continuity	Remarks
① to ② ④ to ② ④ to ①	③ to ② ① to ④	Without power applied
③ to ② ④ to ①	① to ② ④ to ② ① to ④	Connect the battery: positive to terminal ⑥ and negative to ⑤

Fig. 3.45 Checking for proper continuity at retard relay (Sec 32)

33 Ignition control system – 1980 models (except California)

1   In the model year 1980, the ignition control system was incorporated on vehicles other than those for California operation. Components unique to 1980 are an altitude switch and a second water temperature switch. The remainder of the system is basically the same as the California system of 1979.

Trailing ignition – checks

2   Warm up the engine to normal operating temperature.
3   Connect a timing light to the high tension cord for the trailing spark plug on the front rotor housing.
4   Disconnect the electrical coupler for the number 1 water temperature switch locate near the thermostat housing. Connect a jumper wire between the two terminals on the wiring harness side of the coupler.
5   Except for California vehicles, disconnect the coupler for the number 2 water temperature switch and run a jumper between the terminals.
6   On vehicles equipped with a manual transmission (except California) disconnect the coupler to the altitude switch and connect a jumper in the same fashion as with the water temperature switches.
7   Start the engine and set the engine speed to 2000 rpm with the choke knob. Slowly increase the engine speed using the throttle and check to see that the timing light flashes when the engine speed is more than 4600 rpm plus or minus 400 rpm. Push the choke knob back in completely and check to see that the timing light continues to flash.
8   On vehicles equipped with manual transmssion, the timing light will flash at 3000 rpm plus 300 rpm only after the choke knob has been fully returned for approximately 130 seconds.
9   On vehicles with an automatic transmission, the timing light will flash at any engine speed after the choke knob has been returned for approximately 130 seconds.
10 If the car is equipped with a manual transmission, increase the engine speed to 2000 rpm with the throttle and slowly decrease the engine speed. The timing light should start to flash at an engine speed of 1150 rpm. Now slowly increase the engine speed from an idle and note at what rpm the light stops flashing. This engine speed should be approximately the same as in the previous test (within 150 rpm plus or minus 70 rpm).
11 With the engine set at 2000 rpm with the throttle, the timing light should flash when the shift lever is placed in the 4th or 5th gear positions.

Leading ignition – checks

12 Warm up the engine to normal operating temperatures.
13 Connect a timing light to the high tension cord for the leading spark plug on the front rotor housing.
14 Except for California-equipped vehicles, disconnect the electrical

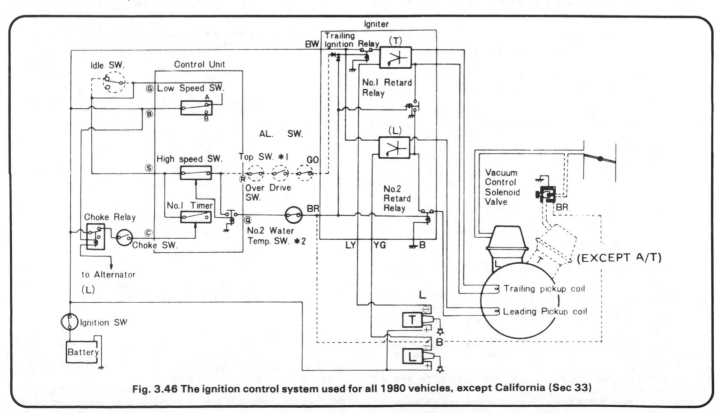

Fig. 3.46 The ignition control system used for all 1980 vehicles, except California (Sec 33)

couplers to the number 2 water temperature switch and the altitude compensator switch. Connect a jumper wire between the terminals at these connectors (as was done for the trailing ignition).

15 Start the engine and check that the timing light flashes at any engine speed.

16 Stop the engine and disconnect the coupler of the number 1 water temperature switch. Connect a jumper wire to the terminals.

17 Start the engine and set the engine speed to 2000 rpm with the choke knob. Observe the timing marks on the eccentric shaft pulley, using the timing light. The indicator pin should point between the yellow and red timing marks on the pulley.

18 Increase the engine speed with the throttle and check that the timing mark advances when the engine speed is more than approximately 4600 rpm.

Altitude switch

19 In order to prevent damage to the thermal reactor that could result from an overrich fuel mixture when driving at high altitude, an altitude switch is used to turn on the trailing ignition when it would not otherwise operate. The altitude switch is located on the left side of the firewall. This is used on manual transmission vehicles, except in California.

Number 2 water temperature switch

20 When the engine coolant is below 5°F (-15°C), the number 2 water temperature switch cuts off the leading retard signal, allowing normal operation to prevent overheating of the thermal reactor. It is located on the left rear facing side of the top radiator tank.

21 To check the water temperature switch, check for continuity between both terminals when the temperature is above 5°F (-15°C). Continuity should not exist below these temperatures.

34 Deceleration control system

1 The deceleration control system is operated by solenoids and valves, and its main function is to prevent backfiring when the engine is decelerated and immediately after the car is shut off. This system comprises an anti-afterburn solenoid valve, a dash pot and dash pot delay valve, and a coasting valve.

Anti-afterburn solenoid valve

2 The anti-afterburn solenoid is located away from the other solenoids. It is mounted on the right side of the carburetor, near the front.

3 To check for proper operation, remove the air filter from the solenoid and connect a suitable tube in its place.

4 Disconnect the tube from the other side of the solenoid.

5 Blow through the connected hose at the air filter port and check that air passes through the valve and comes out at the disconnected vacuum port.

6 Disconnect the electrical coupler for the solenoid and apply battery power (from the 'B' terminal of the alternator) to the coupler. Blow through the tube at the air filter port and air should come out of the port covered by a blind plug at the front of the solenoid.

7 To check the operation of the anti-afterburn valve itself, disconnect the hose leading from the air control valve to the air cleaner.

8 Disconnect the vacuum sensing hose from the relief solenoid valve.

9 Start the engine and run at idle. Check with your finger that air is not drawn into the hose coming from the air control valve. Air should, however, be drawn into this hose when the electrical coupler is disconnected to the anti-afterburn solenoid.

Dash pot and dash pot delay valve (Manual transmissions 1979)

10 The dash pot is located at the extreme rear of the carburetor. It is a circular device with a vacuum sensing tube coming out the top of it. The function of the dash pot is to maintain a balanced air/fuel mixture during deceleration.

11 To check the operation of the dash pot, first remove the air cleaner assembly (Section 9), and while doing so inspect all vacuum sensing tubes for damage.

12 Check that the dash pot rod does not keep the throttle lever from returning to the idle stop.

13 With your finger at the rear of the carburetor, quickly operate the

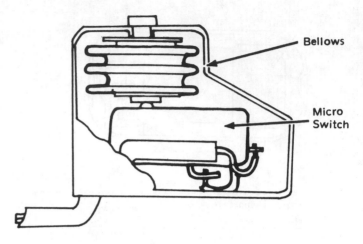

Fig. 3.47 Altitude switch used with 1980 ignition control systems (except California) (Sec 33)

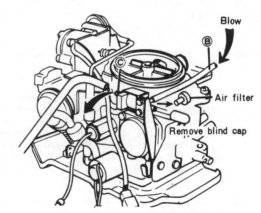

Fig. 3.48 Checking the anti-afterburn solenoid valve without battery supply (Sec 34)

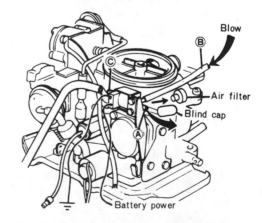

Fig. 3.49 Checking the anti-afterburn solenoid valve with battery power applied (Sec 34)

throttle lever and make sure the dash pot rod extends quickly. Release the throttle and make sure the throttle lever returns slowly to the idle position after it has touched the dash pot rod.

14 Plug the idle compensator hose and start the engine, allowing it to reach normal operating temperature.

15 Disconnect the vacuum sensing tube from the top of the dash pot diaphragm and operate the throttle lever until it is away from the dash

34.15 The dashpot with its vacuum sensing tube disconnected

34.17 The dashpot delay valve is located in the vacuum tube leading to the dashpot

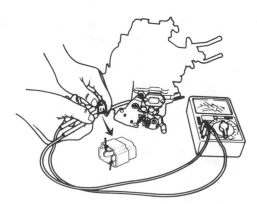

Fig. 3.50 Connecting ohmmeter to idle switch to check dashpot delay valve (Sec 34)

pot rod. Close the vacuum inlet with your finger (photo).

16 Release the throttle lever and note at which engine speed the dash pot rod stops moving after it has been pushed in by the throttle lever. This engine speed should be 1650 rpm to 1850 rpm. If this is not the case, loosen the lock nut at the vacuum inlet tube and turn the dash pot diaphragm until the proper rpm range can be attained upon deceleration.

17 To check the dash pot delay valve, located in the vacuum sensing tube on the right side of the carburettor, first disconnect the electrical coupler for the idle switch. The idle switch is on the left side of the carburetor, at the bottom (photo).

18 Connect an ohmmeter to the terminals inside the coupler coming from the switch.

19 Start the engine and operate the throttle lever until it is away from the dash pot rod. Keep the lever in this position for two to three seconds.

20 Release the throttle lever and check to see that continuity exists between the terminals of the idle switch after one to two seconds.

Dash pot (Manual transmission, 1980)

21 In the 1980 models a new dash pot design was produced. It is controlled by a liquid silicone material to improve its effectiveness. When the rod is pushed upwards, silicone oil will transfer from one chamber to the next through an orifice.

22 To check the operation of this dash pot, open the throttle beyond the contact point of the dash pot rod (with the engine off). The dash pot rod should extend quickly.

23 Now start the engine and slowly open the throttle. The dash pot rod should lose contact from the throttle lever at approximately 3500 to 3900 rpm.

24 If not within specifications, loosen the lock nut and turn the dash pot until the rpm range is attained.

25 The dash pot delay valve is checked in the same manner as with the 1979 models.

Coasting valve (manual transmission)

26 The coasting valve is another component of the deceleration system and its function is to feed fresh air into the intake manifold at certain engine speeds to prevent backfiring. The coasting valve is located on the top of the engine, between the carburetor and the emissions solenoids.

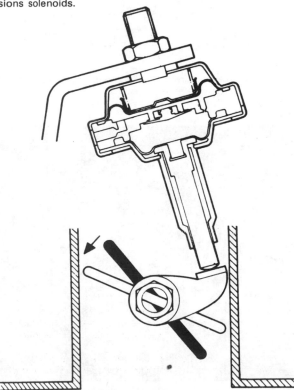

Fig. 3.51 Dashpot design used for 1980 models (Sec 34)

27 To check for a proper signal to the valve, warm up the engine to normal operating temperature and disconnect the electrical coupler from the coasting valve.

28 Connect a voltmeter to the terminals of the coupler leading away from the valve.

29 Disconnect the vacuum sensing tube from the dash pot diaphragm and increase the engine speed to 3000 rpm with the throttle.

30 Quickly release the throttle lever and check to see that current stops flowing to the terminal at an engine speed of approximately 1150 rpm plus or minus 100 rpm.

31 To check the coasting valve itself, run the engine at idle and disconnect the electrical coupler solenoid.

32 Disconnect the air hose leading from the coasting valve to the air cleaner (photo).

33 Place a finger over the air hose opening and check that air is not sucked into the air hose.

34 Apply battery power to the terminal of the coasting valve solenoid (power can be drawn from the 'B' terminal of the alternator). Air should be sucked into the air hose when power is applied to the terminal.

35 Kick-down control system (automatic transmission 1979)

1 To check the operation of the kick-down system, move under the car and disconnect the kick-down solenoid lead at the electrical coupler.

2 Connect a voltmeter to the solenoid lead coupler.

3 Start the engine and set at 2000 rpm with the choke knob. Current should flow at the solenoid lead.

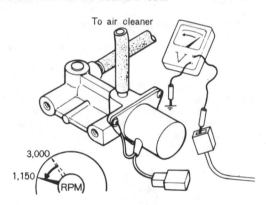

Fig. 3.52 Checking current flow to coasting valve (Sec 34)

34.32 The coasting valve with its vacuum line leading to the air cleaner disconnected

Kick-down relay

4 The kick-down relay is located on the left fender panel, inside the engine compartment.

5 To check the relay, disconnect the coupler from the relay and check for continuity according to the table.

Kick-down control system (automatic transmission, 1980)

6 Very small changes were made in 1980 models to the electrical circuits of the kick-down switch and kick-down relay to improve the operation and reliability of this system.

7 To check for proper operation, disconnect the coupler to the kick-down switch, located near the top of the accelerator pedal. Connect an ohmmeter to the coupler.

8 Depress the accelerator slowly and observe the ohmmeter as the switch makes contact to ensure that current is being passed.

9 The checks for the kick-down relay are the same as for the 1979 models.

36 Auxiliary emission control devices

1 The system incorporates the peripheral devices necessary to trigger and monitor the main components.

Control unit (California)

2 To check the control unit, a voltmeter is necessary to monitor the various terminals under different conditions. The control unit is located under the dashboard, adjacent to the fuse box.

3 Check the control unit fuse for burn-out. A 5 ampere fuse is used.

4 Disconnect the electrical connector to the control unit and check that current flows to the B terminal when the engine is operating at idle.

5 Check to see that current flows to the A terminal when the engine is operating at idle.

6 Check each of the terminals by connecting the negative probe of

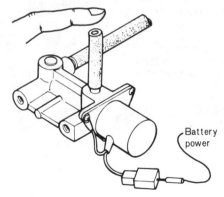

Fig. 3.53 Checking for vacuum at coasting valve with battery power applied (Sec 34)

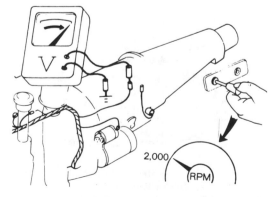

Fig. 3.54 Checking current flow to kick-down solenoid (Sec 35)

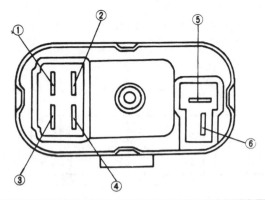

Numbers-continuity	Numbers-No continuity	Remarks
① to ④	③ to ④	Without power applied
③ to ④	① to ④	Connect the battery:positive to terminal ② and negative to ⑥ and or, connect the battery: positive to terminal ⑤ and negative to ⑥

Fig. 3.55 Checking for proper continuity of kick-down relay (Sec 35)

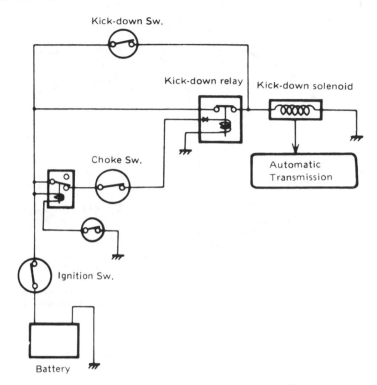

Fig. 3.56 The 1980 kick-down control system (Sec 35)

the voltmeter to the terminal P, and the positive probe to the remaining terminals, then use the accompanying table to check operation (Figs. 3.57 and 3.58).

Control unit (except for California)
7　Check that the control unit fuse has not burned-out. A 5 ampere fuse is used.
8　Disconnect the electrical coupler to the control unit and check to see that current flows to the B terminal with the engine idling.
9　Check to see that current flows to the A terminal with the engine idling.
10　Connect the negative probe of the voltmeter to the P terminal, and the positive probe of the voltmeter to each of the remaining terminals. Use the accompanying table to check for proper operation under the varying engine conditions (Figs. 3.59 and 3.60).

Idle switch (manual transmission)
11　The idle switch is located on the front side of the carburetor, near the bottom (photo). To check its operation, disconnect its electrical coupler and check for proper continuity by using an ohmmeter, referring to the accompanying table (Fig. 3.61).
12　To adjust the idle switch, remove the plastic limiter cap from the adjusting screw.
13　Disconnect the coupler and connect an ohmmeter to terminals one and three of the coupler leading to the switch.
14　Start the engine and slowly increase the engine speed with the throttle. Turn the adjusting screw so that the continuity between these terminals does not exist when the engine speed is approximately 1000 rpm.
15　Install the limiter cap to its original position.

Choke switch and full choke switch
16　These switches are at the rear of the choke knob.
17　To check, disconnect the electrical coupler from the choke switch.
18　Check the continuity of the terminals using an ohmmeter. Refer to the accompanying tables and check the continuity under the various conditions of the choke knob (Figs. 3.62 and 3.63).

Acceleration sensor (automatic transmission and California)
19　The acceleration sensor is located on the firewall, near the power

brake booster.
20　Disconnect the vacuum switch electrical coupler and connect an ohmmeter to the terminals A and B (Fig. 3.64).
21　Start the engine and run at idle. Continuity should not exist at these terminals.
22　Disconnect the vacuum sensing tube and continuity should exist between these two terminals.
23　To check the delay valve of the acceleration sensor, connect an ohmmeter to the same terminals as above.
24　Start the engine and increase the engine speed to 3000 rpm with the throttle. Keep it in this position for two to three seconds. Then quickly decrease the engine speed and check the continuity between these terminals. Continuity should exist for 3 to 25 seconds.

Water temperature switch
25　The main water temperature switch is located on the water pump housing, near the upper radiator hose inlet to the engine.
26　Remove the switch and place it in water, along with a thermometer. Heat the water gradually and check the temperature at which continuity ceases to exist at the terminals of the water switch coupler. This temperature should be 140°F plus or minus 11.7°F (60°C plus or minus 6.5°C) (Fig. 3.65).

Top switch and over-drive switch (California with manual transmission)
27　These switches are located on the transmission casing.
28　Raise the vehicle and support it with stands to gain access to the switches.
29　Disconnect the bullet connectors for the top switch, located near the clutch release fork. Connect an ohmmeter to the connecting (top switch side) and check to see that continuity does not exist when shifting the gearshift lever to the 4th gear position.
30　The over-drive switch is checked in the same way. It is located on the transmission extension housing, on the left side. Continuity should not exist as the shift lever is placed in the 5th gear position.

Choke relay
31　The choke relay is located under the dashboard, just to the right of the fuse box. An ohmmeter is used to check for proper continuity between the various terminals. Use the accompanying table and illustration for reference. (Fig. 3.66).

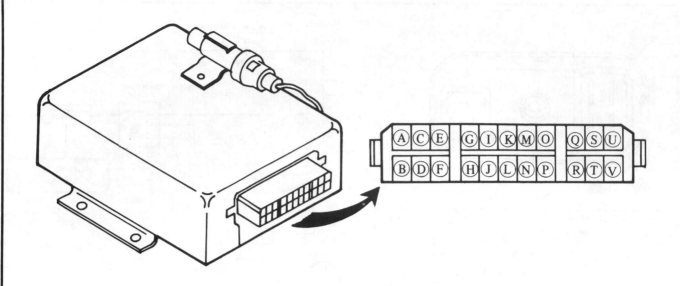

Fig. 3.57 Control unit and connector for California vehicles (Sec 36)

Terminal	12 V exists under the following condition	Engine condition
J	• Less than 1,150 ± 100 rpm of engine speed • When applying battery power to Ⓔ or Ⓣ terminals.	Decreasing engine speed Engine operating
K	• When applying battery power to Ⓞ or Ⓣ terminals.	Engine operating
L	• Less than 1,150 ± 100 rpm of engine speed	Decreasing engine speed
M	• Apply battery power to Ⓢ terminal. Less than 4,600 ± 400 rpm of engine speed within 130 ± 26 seconds after starting engine with choke knob fully pulled. • When applying battery power to Ⓔ terminal.	Increasing engine speed Engine operating
D	• Any time	Engine operating
H	• More than 4,000 ± 400 rpm of engine speed	Increasing engine speed
Q	• Apply battery power to Ⓢ terminal. Less than 4,600 ± 400 rpm of engine speed within 130 ± 26 seconds after starting engine with choke knob fully pulled.	Increasing engine speed
R	• Apply battery power to Ⓢ terminal. Less than 3,000 ± 300 rpm of engine speed • Apply battery power to Ⓢ terminal. Any engine speed within 130 ± 26 seconds after starting engine with choke knob fully pulled.	Increasing engine speed Engine operating
G	• More than 1,150 ± 100 rpm of engine speed	Decreasing engine speed

Fig. 3.58 Continuity checks for control unit on California vehicles (Sec 36)

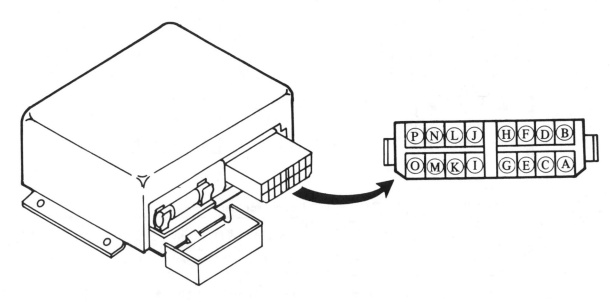

Fig. 3.59 The control unit and connector for non-California vehicles (Sec 36)

Terminal	12 V exists under the following condition	Engine condition
J, L	• Less than 1,150 ± 100 rpm of engine speed	Decreasing engine speed
D	• Any engine speed	Engine operating
H	• More than 4,000 ± 400 rpm of engine speed	Increasing engine speed
G	• More than 1,150 ± 100 rpm of engine speed	Decreasing engine speed

Fig. 3.60 Continuity checks for control unit on non-California vehicles (Sec 36)

36.11 The idle switch is located at the front of the carburetor

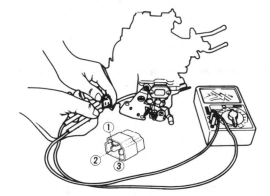

Numbers-continuity	Numbers-No continuity	Remarks
① – ③	① – ②	Run the engine at idle.
① – ②	① – ③	Increase the engine speed up to 1,000 ± 50 rpm with throttle.

Fig. 3.61 Checking for proper continuity at idle switch (Sec 36)

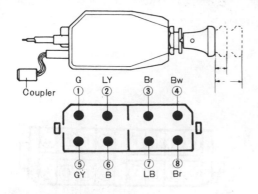

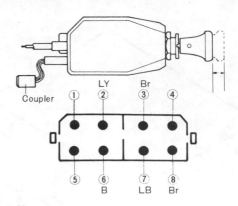

California

Choke knob pulled at	Numbers-continuity	
	Choke switch	Full choke switch
10 ± 2mm (0.4 ± 0.08in)	③ – ⑦	—
25.5 ± 1.5mm (1.0 ± 0.06in)	—	④ – ⑤

Fig. 3.62 Checking for proper continuity of choke switch (California vehicles) (Sec 36)

Except for California

Choke knob pulled at	Numbers-continuity	
	Choke switch	Full choke switch
10 ± 2mm (0.4 ± 0.08in)	③ – ⑦	None

Fig. 3.63 Checking for proper continuity of choke switch (non-California vehicles) (Sec 36)

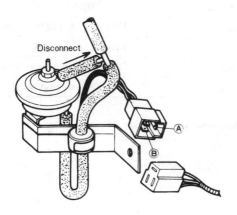

Fig. 3.64 The acceleration sensor and electrical coupler (Sec 36)

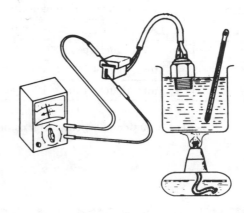

Fig. 3.65 Checking operation of water temperature switch (Sec 36)

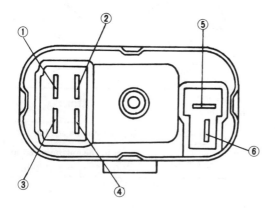

Numbers-continuity	Numbers-No continuity	Remarks
① to ② ④ to ② ④ to ①	③ to ② ① to ④	Without power applied
③ to ② ④ to ①	① to ② ④ to ② ① to ④	Connect the battery: positive to terminal ⑥ and negative to ⑤

Fig. 3.66 Checking for proper continuity at choke relay (Sec 36)

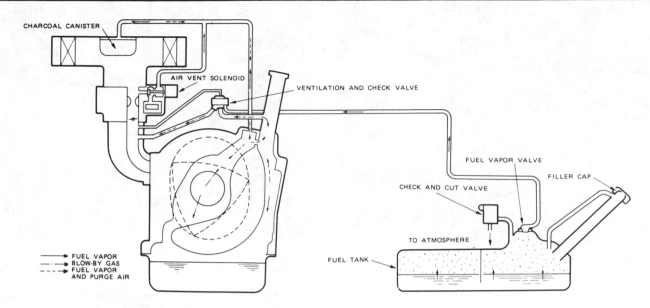

Fig. 3.67 The components and operations of the crankcase and evaporative emission control system (Sec 37)

37.3 Inspecting the charcoal cannister on the underside of the air cleaner top piece

37 Crankcase and evaporative emission control system

1   This system is designed to limit the escape of evaporative gasoline into the atmosphere.

Charcoal canister

2   The charcoal canister acts as a filter of sorts, and is located on the underside of the air cleaner top plate. It is permanently attached, meaning that if a fault is found the top plate must be replaced as a unit.

3   Visually inspect the canister for signs of leakage (photo).

4   To check to see if the canister is clogged, connect a vacuum gauge as shown in Fig. 3.68. The reading on the gauge should be -2.36 to 0 in-Hg (-60 to 0 mm-Hg) with the engine operating at 2500 rpm.

Ventilation and check valve

5   The ventilation and check valve is located on top of the engine, to the rear of the various emissions solenoids (photo).

6   To check, disconnect the hoses as shown in Fig. 3.69 and start the engine, running it at idle. Air should be sucked into the port marked A.

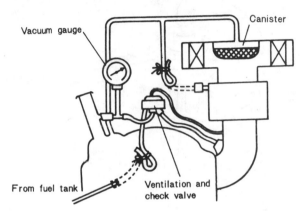

Fig. 3.68 Checking for a clogged charcoal cannister (Sec 37)

7   Plug port A with your finger and check that air is sucked into port B.

8   Now plug port A and disconnect the hose at the top (C). Air should not be sucked into port B.

9   Stop the engine and disconnect hose D and attach another suitable hose which can be used to blow through the valve. When blowing through this hose no air should pass through the valve.

Air vent solenoid valve

10   The air vent solenoid valve is located on the left side of the carburetor, near the top.

11   To check it, blow through the air vent hose and the air should go through the solenoid valve.

12   With the ignition switch on, air should not pass through this solenoid valve.

Check and cut valve

13   The check and cut valve is located near the gas tank, under the vehicle.

14   To check it, remove the valve from the car (put identificatin tags on each hose for easier reinstallation) (photo).

15   Connect a pressure gauge to the passage which goes to the fuel tank.

16   Blow through the valve and it should open with a pressure of 0.78 to 1.0 lb/in² (0.055 to 0.07 kg/cm²) (Fig. 3.70).

17   Remove the gauge and connect it to the passage which leads to the atmosphere. Blow through the valve from this point and the valve should open at 0.14 to 0.71 lb/in² (0.01 to 0.05 kg/cm²).

18   These tests should be performed with the valve in the horizontal position to prevent the weight of the valve from altering the tests.

37.5 The ventilation and check valve

37.14 The check and cut valve located near the gas tank. Identify each of the hoses before removing

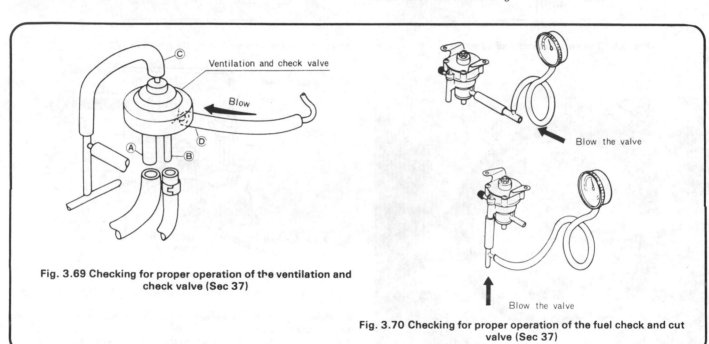

Ventilation and check valve

Blow

Fig. 3.69 Checking for proper operation of the ventilation and check valve (Sec 37)

Blow the valve

Blow the valve

Fig. 3.70 Checking for proper operation of the fuel check and cut valve (Sec 37)

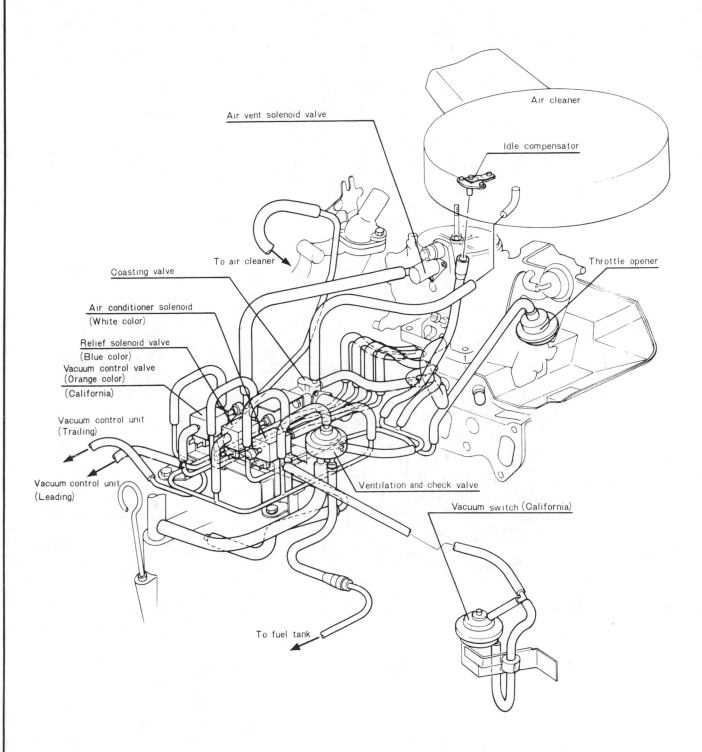

Air vent solenoid valve

Air cleaner

Idle compensator

To air cleaner

Throttle opener

Coasting valve

Air conditioner solenoid
(White color)

Relief solenoid valve
(Blue color)

Vacuum control valve
(Orange color)
(California)

Vacuum control unit
(Trailing)

Vacuum control unit
(Leading)

Ventilation and check valve

Vacuum switch (California)

To fuel tank

Fig. 3.71 Basic emission system pipings for 1979 vehicles with manual transmission

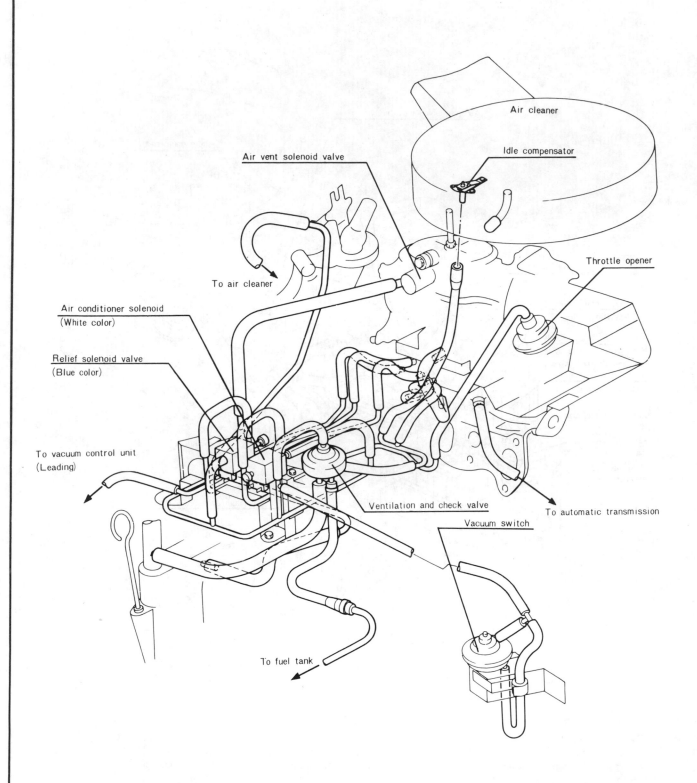

Fig. 3.72 Basic emission system pipings for 1979 vehicles with automatic transmission

101

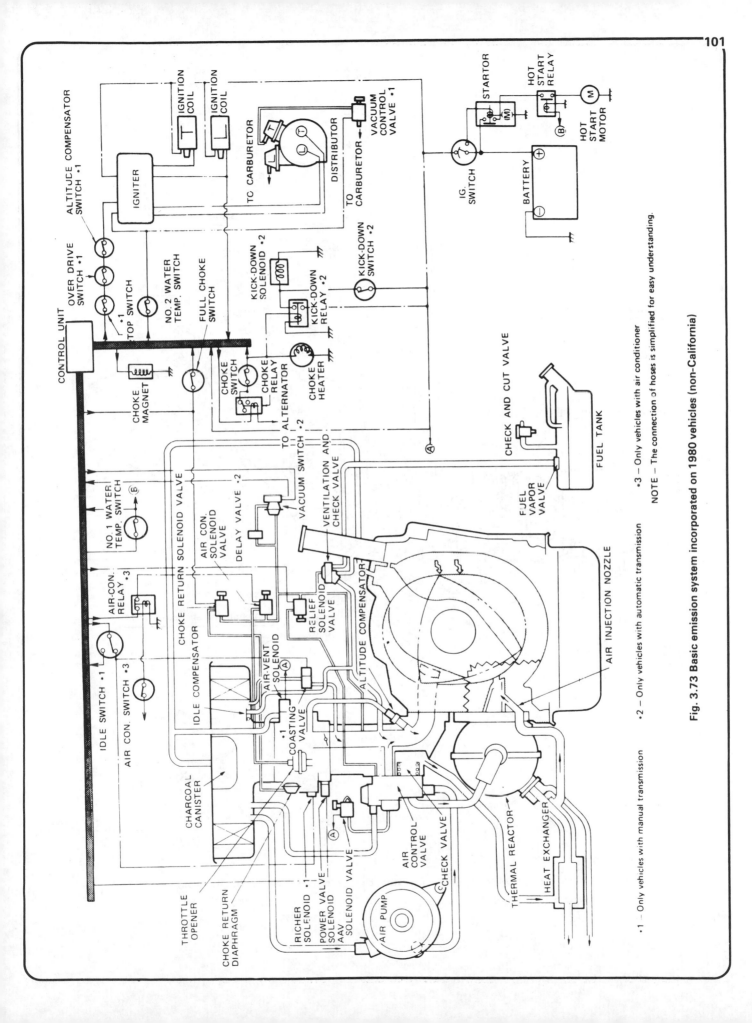

Fig. 3.73 Basic emission system incorporated on 1980 vehicles (non-California)

*1 – Only vehicles with manual transmission

*2 – Only vehicles with automatic transmission

*3 – Only vehicles with air conditioner

NOTE – The connection of hoses is simplified for easy understanding.

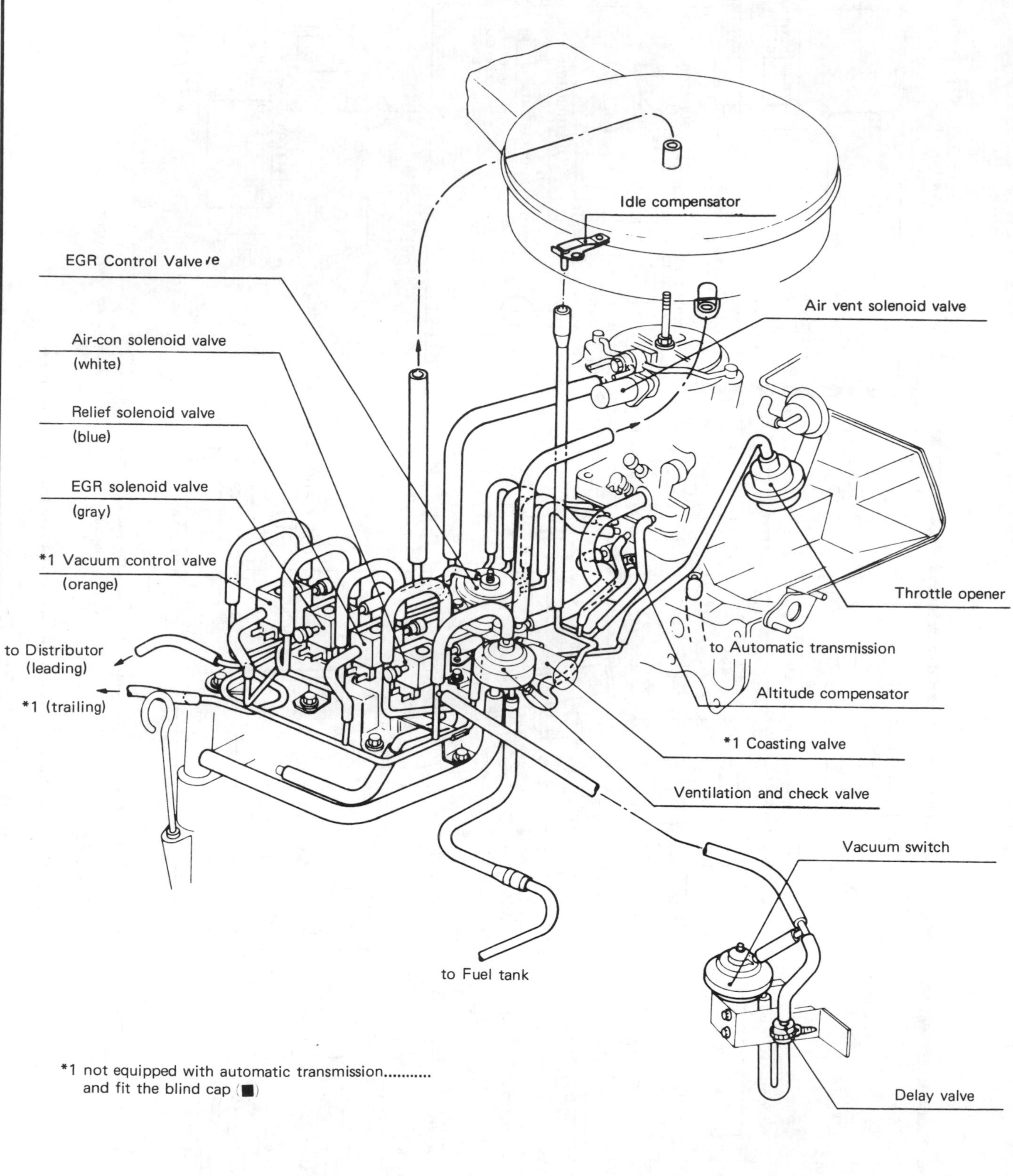

Idle compensator

EGR Control Valve *e*

Air-con solenoid valve
(white)

Relief solenoid valve
(blue)

EGR solenoid valve
(gray)

*1 Vacuum control valve
(orange)

to Distributor
(leading)

*1 (trailing)

Air vent solenoid valve

Throttle opener

to Automatic transmission

Altitude compensator

*1 Coasting valve

Ventilation and check valve

Vacuum switch

to Fuel tank

Delay valve

*1 not equipped with automatic transmission...........
and fit the blind cap (■)

Fig. 3.74 Basic emission system pipings for 1980 vehicles (California)

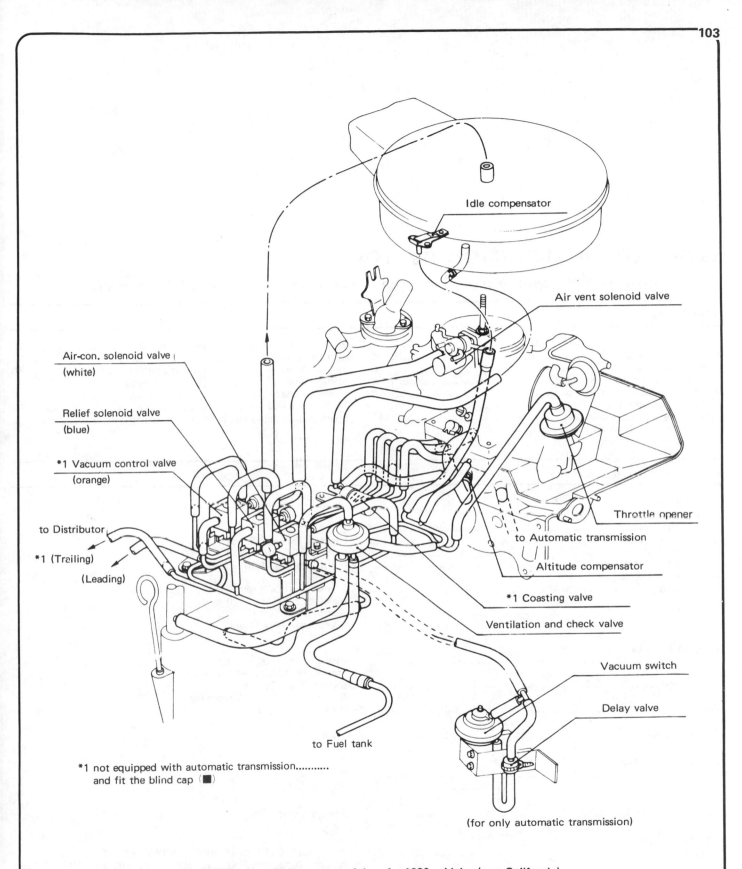

Idle compensator

Air vent solenoid valve

Air-con. solenoid valve (white)

Relief solenoid valve (blue)

*1 Vacuum control valve (orange)

to Distributor

*1 (Trailing)

(Leading)

Throttle opener

to Automatic transmission

Altitude compensator

*1 Coasting valve

Ventilation and check valve

Vacuum switch

Delay valve

to Fuel tank

*1 not equipped with automatic transmission...........
and fit the blind cap (■)

(for only automatic transmission)

Fig. 3.75 Basic emission system pipings for 1980 vehicles (non-California)

Chapter 4 Ignition system

Refer to Chapter 13 for specifications and information related to 1981 through 1985 models

Contents

Specifications

Distributor
Breaker point
    Number 2
    Dwell angle .... Leading, Trailing 58 $\pm$ 3°
    Point gap .... 0.45 $\pm$ 0.05 mm (0.018 $\pm$ 0.002 in)
    Arm spring tension .... 0.5 to 0.65 kg (1.10 to 1.4 lb)
Centrifugal advance
    Leading .... Starts: 0° at 500 rpm
        Maximum: 10° at 1,500 rpm
    Trailing .... Starts: 0° at 500 rpm
        Maximum: 10° at 1,500 rpm

Vacuum advance
    Leading .... Starts: 0° at -100 mm-Hg
        Maximum: 7.5° at -400 mm-Hg
    Trailing .... Starts: 0° at -200 mm-Hg
        Maximum: 15° at -400 mm-Hg
Condenser capacity .... 0.24 — 0.30 μF

Firing order .... 1 - 2

Ignition timing
Leading .... 0 $\pm$ 1° ATDC
Trailing .... 20 $\pm$ 2° ATDC

Timing mark location .... Eccentric shaft pulley

Spark plugs
Type .... NGK: B6ET, B7ET, B8ET, BR6ET, BR7ET, BR8ET
Nippon Denso: W20EB, W20EBR, W22EB, W22EBR, W25EB, W25EBR, W25EB
Champion: N-278B, RN-278B, N-280B, RN-280B, N-282B, RN-282B, RN-282B
Initial gap .... 1.05 $\pm$ 0.05 mm (0.041 $\pm$ 0.002 in)

Ignition coils
Type .... LB-84 or FTC-3
Primary resistance .... 0.9 $\pm$0.09 Ω at 20ºC (68ºF)

1 General description

1 The Wankel rotary is a fuel burning internal combustion engine, using spark plugs, coils and a distributor, in basic terms, these components function in the same manner as in a conventional piston-engine car.

2 The major difference is the need for two spark plugs for each of the rotary's 'cylinders'. Two plugs are needed because of the long thin shape of the combustion space at the moment of ignition. One spark plug alone would not be able to fully ignite the area, thus there is a 'leading' and 'trailing' plug. The leading plug has the greatest effect, as the combustion spreading from its spark can burn in a space ever-growing in size as the rotor sweeps by.

3 In a piston engine, each piston has its own plug, and that plug is cooled on each induction stroke by a great waft of incoming mixture with fuel still evaporating. On the rotary, the plug serves each rotor space in turn, and is always at combustion temperature, as the induction and compression phases are carried out in another part of the chamber. Because of this, the spark plugs have a more demanding duty and are constructed in a more exotic way than ordinary spark plugs.

4 Two separate coils are used, one each for the trailing and leading systems. Although only one distributor is incorporated, it is equipped with two sets of contact points (or pickups in the case of 1980 models), one each for the leading and trailing systems.

5 In place of a more common exhaust manifold, the rotary has a terminal reactor which is used to complete combustion so that the exhaust emissions do not contain unwanted products.

6 Many of the components in the ignition system are directly related to systems of the emissions control. Thus, much of the material covered in this Chapter can, and should, be cross-referenced with material covered in Chapter 3 on the emissions systems.

2 Spark plugs - choice

1 In the specifications it will be seen that a large variety of spark plug is available for the RX-7. The different plugs available meet specific driving conditions and the plug choice is critical to the overall performance of the engine and the longevity of the spark plug.

2 Cold type spark plugs are recommended for continuous high-speed and heavy-load driving conditions. A cold plug is constructed in such a way that the points will be burned away more slowly and features a better cooling path to lead heat away from it.

3 Hot type spark plugs, on the other hand, should be used in cold weather conditions or if the vehicle is driven mainly in low speed operation such as prolonged city driving. Under these circumstances, a standard plug or a cold plug would 'foul', indicated by rough running, poor driveability, or in extreme cases, difficult starting. These conditions can usually be temporarily cured by driving the car hard for about two miles.

4 In most cases, however, the standard spark plugs can be used. These have been carefully designed and tested to cover the widest driving conditions.

5 It should also be noted that spark plugs in all three of the heat ranges are available with built-in radio interference suppression. These radio suppression plugs should be used in areas which have regulations requiring their use.

	Hot type	Standard	Cold type
NGK	B 6 ET *BR6ET	B 7 ET *BR7ET	B 8 ET *BR8ET
NIPPON DENSO	W 20 EB *W 20 EBR	W 22 EB *W22 EBR	W 25 EB *W25 EBR
CHAMPION	N-282 B *RN-282B	N-280 B *RN-280 B	N-278 B *RN-278 B

Fig. 4.1 Recommended spark plugs

indicates radio interference suppression type (Sec 2)

3 Spark plugs – replacing, cleaning, inspecting

1 There is a total of four spark plugs for the RX-7 engine, two for each of the rotor housings. The high tension leads from the distributor to the spark plugs are clearly marked for 'leading' and 'trailing' by a blue and black color-coding.

2 To remove a spark plug, first disconnect the high tension cord from the end of the plug. Do this by pulling it off the plug at the rubber boot. Do not pull on the cord itself as this may separate the wiring connection. If it is necessary to remove all the plugs at the same time, use tape or some other identification process to further mark which plug wire goes to which spark plug.

3 Remove the spark plug with a suitable spark plug wrench. These are available as deep socket wrenches with cushioning inside to prevent damage to the porcelain insulator.

4 Check the plug for burned and eroded electrodes, black deposits, fouling or cracks of the porcelain.

5 If the plugs are to be cleaned and reinstalled, clean the electrodes with a fine wire brush and carefully scrape carbon off the insulator with a small file. The plugs should then be blown clean, with compressed air if available.

6 Measure the electrode gap with a wire gauge. This should be 0.041 plus or minus 0.002 in (1.05 plus or minus 0.05 mm). If the gap is incorrect, the spark plug must be replaced, as these special plugs cannot be properly gapped.

7 When installing the cleaned or new spark plugs, apply a little Moly-paste thread sealer to the threads of the plug. This will help to seal the metal threads against the aluminium engine housing.

8 Tighten the plug first by hand to ensure that the threads are properly matched. Then tighten the spark plug to a torque of 9 to 13 ft-lb (1.3 to 1.8 m-kg). Although torquing spark plugs is not that critical in normal piston-engined cars, it is very important with the Mazda due to the fact that the aluminium engine housings are not that strong, and too much pressure can easily damage them.

9 With the spark plug tightened to torque specifications, push the boot of the high tension wire onto the end of the plug. Make sure it is firmly seated; however, be careful not to damage the porcelain insulator of the plug.

4 Distributor – removal and installation

1 The distributor is quite easily removed from the engine. However, since it has a gear on the bottom care should be taken that it is replaced in the original location.

2 Using a remote starter or an assistant inside the car, turn the engine over until the leading timing mark (yellow painted) on the eccentric shaft pulley aligns with the indicator pin on the front cover (photo).

4.2 Aligning the leading timing mark with the indicator pin

3 Remove the distributor cap from the top of the distributor, with the high tension leads still attached. There are two spring clips which are pried out of their seats on the cap. Set the cap away from the distributor.

4 Disconnect the electrical couplers for the primary wires and condenser leads.

5 Disconnect the two vacuum sensing tubes coming from the vacuum control units. Use a strip of tape to help identify which hose goes to which vacuum unit. There is only one vacuum unit on automatic transmission vehicles.

6 Make note of which direction the rotor is pointed. Since the rotor has several contacts make a small identification mark on one side of the rotor and a corresponding mark on the distributor body. The distributor must be installed with the rotor pointing in the same direction.

7 Remove the lock nut which rides in the elongated adjustment slow on the side of the distributor (photo).

8 Pull the distributor straight up and out of the engine (photo).

9 To install a new distributor, to the original one after work is performed on it, first check that the yellow-painted leading timing mark on the eccentric shaft pulley is still aligned with the indicator pin on the front cover. If not, align the two by turning the engine over by the eccentric shaft pulley bolt.

10 If marks were made upon disassembly, align the indicator mark on the rotor with your corresponding mark on the distributor body. The distributor can then be slipped into place in the engine, with the distributor body and rotor (photo).

11 If the identification marks made upon disassembly have been lost or you are unsure about your identification, there is an alternative method. At the bottom of the distributor shaft housing is a raised tally mark. Turn the distributor shaft until this raised mark aligns with the circular tally mark on the distributor gear shaft. Alignment of these two tally marks serves the same purpose as making marks of your own at the distributor body and rotor (photo).

12 With the distributor in the engine, loosely install the locknut. Do not tighten at this time.

13 For 1979 models, turn the distributor housing counter-clockwise, and then turn clockwise until the leading contact points just start to separate. At this point, tighten the lock nut.

14 Connect the two vacuum hoses to their original positions. Automatic transmission cars have only one hose.

15 Connect the electrical couplers.

16 Press the distributor cap into position on the top of the distributor and secure with the spring clips.

17 Start the engine and check the ignition timing as described in Sections 9 and 10.

5 Distributor – overhaul

1 The distributor should only need servicing after many miles. The indication of wear will be that the cam wobbles slightly, spoiling the contact breaker (or pickup) gap setting and so the timing.

2 In the 1980 models an electronic ignition system was introduced. The overhaul of the distributor is much the same, the most notable differences being that 'pickups' are used instead of the conventional contact breaker points. Also the distributor cap and rotor were changed somewhat to go along with the electronic ignition system.

3 Before starting the disassembly of the distributor, check with local auto parts stores or Mazda dealers for the availability of the small parts necessary for this overhaul. You may find it more expedient or economical to simply replace the entire distributor with a new or rebuilt one.

4 Remove the distributor from the engine as described in Section 4.

5 Disconnect the primary wires from the leading and trailing contact points, or pickups in the case of 1980 models (photo).

6 Disconnect the couplers from the condenser leads.

7 The primary wires can now be removed from the distributor body by lifting out the rubber block which these wires pass through.

8 Inside the distributor, remove the clips holding the vacuum diaphragm links to the breaker base plate assembly.

9 On 1980 models, remove the interrupter from the distributor shaft.

10 Remove the screws attaching the vacuum control unit(s) to the distributor body. There are two screws for each unit.

11 Remove the two screws securing the breaker base plate to the inside of the distributor housing. Lift out the breaker base plate and bearing assembly.

12 On vehicles equipped with automatic transmission (after chassis number 522505), remove the breaker plate attaching screws and remove the breaker plate assembly.

13 Remove the cam attaching screw at the center of the distributor. Remove the cam.

14 Remove the springs attached to the governors, then remove the governors.

15 Remove the condensers from the outside of the housing.

16 At the bottom of the distributor shaft, use a hammer and small drift to drive out the gear lock pin.

17 Remove the gear and washers from the bottom of the shaft.

18 Pull the shaft out through the top of the distributor housing.

19 Inspect the distributor cap (still attached to the high tension leads on the car) for cracks, carbon tracks, burnt or corroded terminals. If in need of replacing, disconnect each high tension wire one at a time and transfer to the new cap. This will prevent mixing of the wires.

20 Check the rotor for cracks and evidence of excessive burning at the ends of the metal strips.

21 On 1979 models, inspect the points for wear, burning, transferred metal and pitting. If this is slight, the points can be cleaned with a stiff bristled brush or oil stone.

22 Inspect the bearing for roughness by turning the outer race by hand. When disassembled, the bearing should probably be replaced as a matter of course.

23 If a condenser tester is available, check the capacity to the condensers. It should be 0.24 to 0.30 uF.

24 Check the shaft, housing and gear for signs of fatigue, cracking and excessive wear. Replace the parts as necessary.

25 Install the shaft through the top of the distributor body and install the washers and gear. Drive the lock pin into position. Make sure the pin is fully inside the gear shaft.

26 Install the condensers to the outside of the distributor housing with the attaching screws. If the points or pickups are replaced with new ones, and the car has many miles, it is advisable to change the

4.7 The distributor locknut

4.8 Pulling the distributor straight up and out of the engine

4.11 The tally marks on the distributor housing and drivegear

5.5 Disconnecting the primary wires from the contact points

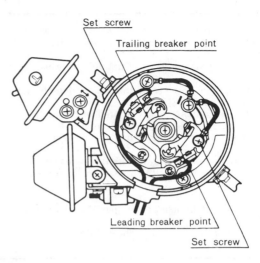

Set screw

Trailing breaker point

Leading breaker point

Set screw

Fig. 4.2 Basic layout of 1979 breaker point ignition system (Sec 6)

6.2 Removing the distributor cap and rotor

6.4 Pliers are used to pull the primary wires off the points

6.5 Carefully remove the contact points set screw

6.6 Lifting the points set off the plate

condensers with new ones during the overhaul process. Check the numbers on the old ones against the new ones, as different condensers are available.

27 Install the governors into the distributor body and secure with the springs.

28 Install the cam over the shaft and secure with the attaching screw at the top of the shaft.

29 Place the bearing assembly and breaker base plate over the shaft and secure with the two stopper set screws.

30 Install the vacuum control unit(s) and the clips holding the diaphragm links.

31 Push the rubber block with the primary wires into the recess in the distributor body and connect the primary leads to the contact breaker points.

32 Connect the condenser leads.

33 Set the contact breaker point gap (1979 models) referring to Section 6.

34 Install the distributor as described in Section 4.

6 Contact breaker points (1979 models) – replacement

1 Replacing, or at least checking, the contact points should be included in any normal tune-up of the 1979 specification engine. The fact that the Mazda distributor contains two sets of points should not be a deterrent in servicing them. The procedures involved with replacing the points on the rotary engine are basically the same as those of a piston engine.

2 Pry the spring clips off the distributor cap with a screwdriver or your fingers and place the cap, with the high tension leads attached, aside (photo).

3 Pull the rotor straight off the shaft and set it aside.

4 Using a pair of pliers, pull the primary wires off their mounts on the points. The primary wires are those which travel through the rubber insulating block (photo).

5 If available, use a magnetized screwdriver to remove the set screw on each of the point sets. The leading breaker point set screw has a ground wire under its head. Be careful not to drop the set screws down into the distributor body (photo).

6 The points sets can now be lifted free of the breaker plate (photo).

7 Examine the contacts of the points. Once the engine has run a few thousand miles the contact breaker burns, getting a lump on one contact, and a hole on the other. If this is not too extreme, the contacts can be cleaned with an oil stone or contact point file. The contact area should be completely flat. If you are in doubt as to the condition of the points, simply replace them with new ones.

8 Place the new point set into position on the breaker plate, aligning the hole in the breaker plate with the elongated hole in the point set.

9 Install the set screw until snug, but not tight. Make sure that the ground connector is attached under the leading point set screw. Again, be careful not to drop the set screws.

10 Using pliers, slide the primary wire leads onto the points sets.

11 To set the point gap, the rubbing block of the point must be resting against one of the high points of the distributor shaft. The shaft has four high points. The shaft can be turned by rocking the car in first gear (if manual transmission) or by turning the engine over by the use of the key (required for automatic transmission).

12 With the rubbing block of the points you are checking resting against the high point of the shaft, loosen the set screw enough to enable you to move the stationary contact.

13 Move the stationary contact point until there is a visible gap between the contact points.

14 Insert a feeler gauge of 0.018 plus or minus 0.002 in (0.45 plus or minus 0.05 mm) thickness between the two contact points. Move the stationary contact until the feeler gauge just slides between the two contact points (photo).

15 Tighten the set screw and check with the feeler gauge again to see if the gap has been altered while tightening the set screw. If the gap is still correct, fully tighten the set screw.

16 The same procedure is used to set the other set of contact points in the distributor. Make sure the rubbing block is contacting a high point on the shaft. The point gap is the same.

17 Inspect the rotor before reinstalling. If the metal strip across the top is damaged, excessively worn or burnt, replace the rotor with a new one. Push the rotor onto the top of the shaft. It will only go on one way. Make sure it is fully seated on the shaft.

6.14 Using a feeler gauge to check point gap

18 Inspect the inside of the distributor cap. The metal terminals for each high tension lead should not be excessively burnt, scored, corroded or damaged. The cap itself should not have any cracks or damage. If the cap is replaced with a new one, change the high tension leads one at a time so they cannot be mixed up. Place the cap onto the distributor body until it is fully seated all around, then push the two spring clips into position.

19 Connect the negative battery cable and start the engine.

20 Check the ignition timing as described in Sections 9 and 10.

7 Contact breaker points (1979 models) – dwell angle

1 The dwell angle of the contact points is a more refined way of checking the point gap. It is extremely difficult to get an exact point gap by using feeler gauges alone. Variables such as distributor shaft wear and play, and rubbing-block-to-shaft-high-point contact add to the problems of point gap setting.

2 To measure the dwell angle of the contact points, a dwell angle meter will be required. Due to the different methods by which these meters are connected to the ignition system, it is advisable to follow the manufacturer's instructions for the particular meter being used.

3 The dwell angle for the Mazda rotary engine is checked in the same manner as any conventional piston engine; however, both the leading and trailing contact point sets must be checked and adjusted separately.

4 The correct dwell angle for both the leading and trailing contact points is 58 degrees, plus or minus 3 degrees.

8 Electronic ignition (1980 models) – checking

1 In the 1980 model year Mazda introduced a high energy electronic ignition system to improve driveability while reducing maintenance costs and meeting emissions standards.

2 This system is closely related to the conventional breaker point system used in 1979. The electronic system incorporates what is known as an 'Igniter' (or 'brain box') and 'pickups' instead of breaker points.

3 Unlike the conventional points system, the electronic system is designed to function for a long time without periodic maintenance of its components. The pickups and interrupter inside the distributor should last almost indefinitely, as there is not a constant movement as with contact breaker points (photos).

4 In most cases of a failure in the electronic ignition system, the problem will lie in the igniter box rather than the peripheral components. This box is located on the left fender inside the engine compartment. It has a group of three wiring systems leading to it, with quick-disconnect couplers (photo).

5 To check the operation of the igniter, disconnect the two electrical

8.3a 1980 models use a different rotor in conjunction with electronic ignition

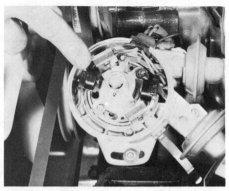
8.3b Pickups are used in place of conventional contact points

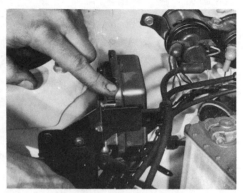
8.4 The igniter box on 1980 models is located on the left fender panel, by the coils

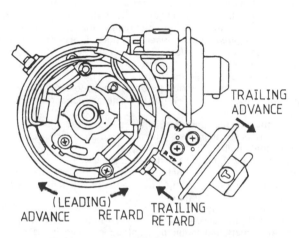

TRAILING
ADVANCE

(LEADING)
ADVANCE RETARD TRAILING
RETARD

Fig. 4.3 Basic layout of 1980 high energy ignition system distributor (Sec 8)

Fig. 4.4 Connection of timing light to spark plug and approximate angle for timing marks (Sec 9)

couplers leading away from the box, but do not disconnect the wires leading from the box to the distributor. Using an ohmmeter, check for continuity between the two disconnected couplers. With the probes attached one way, there will be no continuity. Testing the other terminals should give continuity with a reading of less than 1000 ohms. If there is no reading at all, or more than 1000 ohms, the igniter should be replaced with a new one. At this time it is not practical to try to rebuild the igniter box.

9 Ignition timing – all manual transmissions and automatic transmissions up to chassis number 522504

1 Ignition timing is the function by which the contact points open and close – or the pickups are interrupted (1980) – at a specific time during the engine revolution process. This is checked with a timing light and is adjusted at the distributor housing.

2 If equipped with an automatic transmission, the chassis number should be checked by looking on the engine compartment firewall, just above and to the left of the power brake booster.

3 As the ignition timing and ignition control system of the emissions system are closely related and checked similarly, it may be advisable to check both systems at the same time. The ignition control checks can be found in Chapter 3.

4 Warm up the engine to normal operating temperature. The choke should be fully released.

5 Connect a timing light to the engine following the manufacturer's instructions for the specific unit being used. The spark plug connection should be made between the high tension cord of the leading spark plug of the front engine housing and the plug itself.

6 Start the engine and run it at the specified idle speed. A hand-held remote tachometer is superior to the dash-mounted tachometer for

this. Adjust the idle speed as described in Chapter 3. Vehicles with automatic tranmission should have the selector level placed in the 'D' position with the front wheels firmly blocked to prevent the car from moving. The parking brake should be firmly set, and an assistant with his foot on the brakes is a sensible precaution.

7 Aim the timing light at the timing indicator pin on the front cover. The pin should be in alignment with the yellow painted notch on the eccentric shaft pulley. This is the first notch in the rotation cycle. If the leading timing notch is difficult to see with the timing light, stop the engine at a point where the notch is accessible and clean the area around the notch. Then use a fine brush and some white paint or white soapstone to clearly mark this location on the pulley. Be careful not to touch any of the moving engine components.

8 If the leading timing mark is not in alignment with the indicator pin, stop the engine and slightly loosen the lock nut on the distributor. This lock nut is on the side of the distributor housing, inside an elongated adjustable channel.

9 Start the engine and, with the timing light aimed at the indicator pin, slowly turn the distributor housing until the pin aligns with the leading timing mark on the pulley.

10 Tighten the lock nut and recheck that the pin and notches are still in alignment.

11 To check the trailing ignition timing, hook up the timing light to the trailing spark on the front engine housing.

12 Check that the second notch in the rotation cycle (red painted) on the front pulley is in alignment with the indicator pin. Again, clean the area and apply an identification mark on the notch if necessary.

13 If the trailing timing is not correct, slightly loosen the two vacuum unit attaching screws on the trailing vacuum unit. Vehicles with automatic transmission do not have a trailing vacuum unit, but rather an external adjusting lever with two attaching screws which must be loosened slightly (photo).

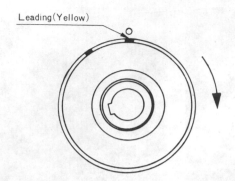

Fig. 4.5 Aligning leading timing mark with indicator pin (Sec 9)

9.13 The two adjustment screws which must be loosened to adjust the trailing ignition

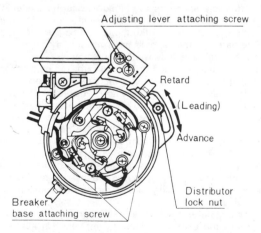

Fig. 4.6 Location of lockscrews for timing adjustment (Sec 10)

14 Start the engine and move the vacuum unit (manual trans) or adjusting lever (auto trans) until the trailing timing notch on the eccentric shaft pulley is in alignment with the indicator pin on the front cover. It will be noticed that a very slight movement of the vacuum unit or adjusting lever makes a big difference in the timing. Make just a little at a time.
15 Tighten the attaching screws and check that the timing is still correct.

10 Ignition timing – automatic transmission after chassis number 522504

1 Check the chassis number by looking on the engine compartment firewall, just above and to the left of the power brake booster.
2 Warm up the engine to normal operating temperature. The choke should be fully closed.
3 Connect a timing light to the engine following the manufacturer's instructions for the particular light being used. The spark plug connection should be made between the high tension lead of the leading spark plug on the front engine housing and the spark plug itself.
4 Set the parking brake, and block the front wheels firmly. If an assistant is available, have him apply pressure to the brakes to keep the car from moving.
5 Start the engine and place the selector lever in the 'D' position.
6 Check that the engine is running at the specified engine speed at idle. A hand-held external tachometer is superior to the dash-mounted tachometer for this. Adjust the idle speed as necessary, referring to Chapter 3.
7 Aim the timing light at the indicator pin on the front cover of the engine. The pin should be in alignment with the leading timing notch (yellow painted) on the eccentric shaft pulley. If this notch is difficult to see, stop the engine at a point where the notch is accessible and clean the notch area thoroughly. Use a fine brush and some white paint, or a soapstone, to clearly mark the notch. Be careful not to touch any moving engine parts while using the timing light.
8 If the leading timing is not correct, slightly loosen the lock nut on the distributor body. This lock nut is inside an elongated adjustment channel.
9 Start the engine again and rotate the distributor body until the indicator pin is in alignment with the leading timing notch in the eccentric shaft pulley.
10 Tighten the lock nut on the distributor and recheck to see that the two marks are still in alignment.
11 To check the trailing timing, hook up the timing light to the trailing spark plug of the front engine housing.
12 Aim the timing light at the indicator pin. The pin should be in alignment with the second notch of the rotation cycle. This is the trailing timing mark and should be painted red. Again, if it is difficult to see, clean the area and use paint or soapstone to mark the notch.
13 If the trailing timing is not correct, stop the engine and remove the distributor cap and rotor. Slightly loosen the two breaker base attaching screws. Install the rotor and cap.
14 Start the engine and run at the specified idle speed with the transmission in the 'D' position.
15 Loosen the two external adjusting lever attaching screws slightly and move the adjusting lever until the correct trailing timing is obtained. It will be noted that just a little movement makes a big difference, so move just a little at a time. If the adjusting lever seems to be binding, and the timing is difficult to alter, loosen the breaker base attaching screws a bit more.
16 Once the indicator pin is in alignment with the trailing notch of the pulley, tighten the two adjusting lever attaching screws securely and recheck the timing.
17 Remove the distributor cap and rotor. Tighten the two breaker base attaching screws securely.
18 Install the rotor and cap. Recheck the trailing timing one more time to make sure nothing has changed.

11 Ignition coils – checking

1 Before testing, run the engine until it reaches normal operating temperature.
2 Using an ohmmeter, check the resistance at the coils. Do this by touching the probes of the ohmmeter to both the positive and negative terminals of the coils. Check each coil separately. The primary resistance should be 1.35 plus or minus 10% ohms for both coils (photo).
3 Check the resistance of the external resistors (ballast resistors) in the same manner. The resistance should be 1.4 plus or minus 10% ohms for both (photo).

11.2 Using an ohmmeter to test the ignition coils

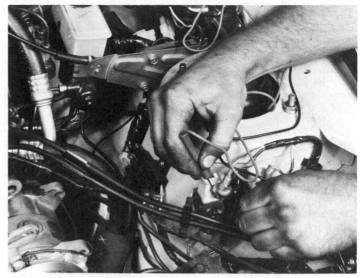

11.3 Checking the external resistors with an ohmmeter

12.3 Disconnecting the wires from the coils

12.5 Loosening the mounting bolt which secures both coils to the bracket

12.6 Removing a coil from the mounting bracket

14.1 The condensors are located on the out side of the distributor housing, towards the rear

12   Ignition coils – removal and installation

1   The two ignition coils are mounted on the left fender panel, just behind the battery. They appear to be rather shallow in depth, but are recessed into the panel and are longer than they appear.
2   Disconnect the negative cable from the battery.
3   Disconnect the wires from the positive and negative terminals on each coil. The negative terminals have wiring couplers which are merely disconnected. The wires on the positive terminals have lock nuts which must be loosened to remove the wiring connectors. Before removing, it is advisable that the wires be marked with a code on small pieces of tape in order to reinstall them in their proper locations (photo).
4   Remove the high tension leads from the center of each coil.
5   Loosen the bracket attaching bolt located in the center of the bracket, between the coils (photo).
6   Pull the coils straight out of the fender panel and the bracket (photo).
7   Inspect the coils for any cracks, especially near the high tension lead towers and the wire terminals.
8   To install, place the coils into the bracket and push into the fenderwell. Tighten the bracket bolt and then connect the high tension leads and other wires using the identification tape used on disassembly for the proper locations.

13   High tension cords – checking

1   The high tension cords running between the distributor and the spark plugs and between the distributor and the coils can be checked using an ohmmeter.
2   Remove the high tension cords, one at a time, from each spark plug and then from the distributor. Do not pull on the cord itself, but rather on the rubber boot.
3   Check the resistance of each cord by placing the probes of an ohmmeter on either end of the cord.
4   Do not puncture the cords with the probe. Place the probes on the metal connectors at each end of the cord.
5   The resistance should not exceed 16,000 ohms plus or minus 40% per 39.37 in (1 meter).
6   If it does, replace the cords with new ones.

14   Ignition condensers

1   The condensers, one for each contact point set or pickup, are located on the side of the distributor housing, adjacent to the vacuum control units (photo).
2   The condenser is put across the contact breaker points (electronic pickups) to help them quickly cut the current in the low tension circuit. The current flowing at the instant of opening the points (pickups) carries on into the condenser, rather than jumping across the gap. This reduction in arcing makes the contacts last longer.
3   Indications of a failure in the condensers are: hard engine starting, quick component wear, and an increased spark visible at the points.
4   High-quality radio test equipment is necessary to test the condensers, so if they are suspect it is more economical to try a new one.
5   The condensers are held to the distributor body by two screws. Remove these and then disconnect the electrical bullet connectors and remove the condenser.
6   Access at this point is difficult due to the close proximity of related engine components. The best tool to use is a very short screwdriver with a right-angled ratchet wrench. You may find it easier to remove the distributor from the engine to do this work. See Section 4 for the procedures necessary to remove the distributor.

Chapter 5 Clutch

Contents

Specifications

Clutch pedal
Free play (at pedal pad) .... 0.6 to 3.1 mm (0.024 to 0.122 in)
Engagement height (from floor) .... More than 75 mm (2.95 in)

Master cylinder
Bore .... 15.87 mm (0.625 in)
Clearance between piston and bore
    Standard .... 0.032 to 0.102 mm (0.0013 to 0.0040 in)
    Limit .. .. 0.15 mm (0.006 in)

Release cylinder
Bore .... 19.05 mm (0.750 in)
Clearance between piston and bore
    Standard .... 0.040 to 0.125 mm (0.0016 to 0.0049 in)
    Limit .... 0.15 mm (0.006 in)

Clutch disc
Thickness limit .... 7.0 mm (0.276 in)
Rivet depth limit .... 0.3 mm (0.012 in)
Lateral run-out limit .... 1.0 mm (0.039 in)

Diaphragm
Finger out of alignment limit .... 1.0 mm (0.039 in)
Finger groove wear depth limit .... 1.0 mm (0.039 in)

Torque wrench settings

	m-kg	ft-lb
Flywheel	40.0 to 50.0	289 to 362
Clutch cover	1.8 to 2.7	13 to 20

1 General description

1 A common diaphragm spring-type clutch is utilized in the RX-7. It is actuated by hydraulic pressure.
2 Because access to the clutch components is difficult, there are certain components which should be inspected carefully or replaced whenever either the engine or transmission is removed. The clutch disc, pressure plate assembly and release bearing are examples of this.

2 Clutch – removal

1 The clutch parts are located between the engine and transmission, and thus cannot be worked on without removing either the engine or transmission. If repairs which would require the removal of the engine are not needed, the quickest way to gain access to the clutch is by removing the transmission. The transmission removal description is outlined in Chapter 6.
2 From the inside of the transmission, remove the clutch release bearing and release fork. The bearing merely slides off the transmission shaft and the fork pulls through its rubber boot to be removed (photo).
3 Before removing the pressure plate and clutch disc from the flywheel, check to be sure that none of the metal fingers is distorted or bent. If there is evidence of damage in this area, the pressure plate will need to be replaced (photo).
4 In order to replace the pressure plate in the same location on the flywheel an alignment mark must be made. There is one small hole in the pressure plate mounting flange which can be used to mark the flywheel (Fig. 5.1). Use a dab of paint or a sharp scribe.
5 Remove the six bolts which secure the pressure plate and clutch disc to the flywheel. Loosen these a little at a time, and diagonally, to prevent distorting the pressure plate assembly. Note that two of the bolts are not threaded all the way to the head. These two fit into larger, reamed holes in the mounting flange, one next to the small marking hole previously mentioned and the other diametrically opposite (photo).
6 Remove the pressure plate and clutch disc, being careful not to get oil or grease on the disc linings or surface of the pressure plate or flywheel.

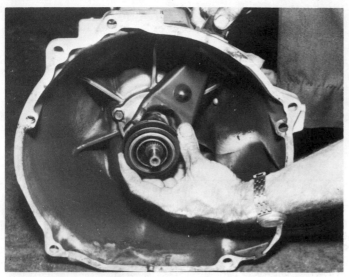
2.2 The release bearing and fork inside the transmission housing

2.3 Check the metal fingers of the pressure plate

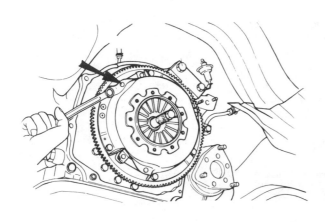
Fig. 5.1 Location of small alignment hole in the pressure plate flange (Sec 2)

2.5 Note that two of the bolts are dowelled

3.1a Check the surface of the pressure plate

3.1b The pressure plate fingers should be checked on both sides

3 Clutch – inspection and overhaul

1   Examine the pressure plate surface where it contacts the clutch disc. This surface should be smooth, with no scoring, gouging or warping. Check the pressure plate cover and fingers for damage. If any fault is found with the pressure plate assembly it must be replaced as an entire unit (photos).

2   Inspect the clutch disc for lining wear. There should be at least 0.012 in (0.3 mm) of lining above the rivet heads. Check for loose or broken rivets or springs. If there are any doubts about the quality of the clutch disc it should be replaced as a matter of course (photos).

3   Inspect the surface of the flywheel for rivet grooves, burnt areas or scoring. If the damage is slight the flywheel can be removed and reconditioned using a lathe. If the damage is deep, the flywheel should be replaced. Check that the ring gear teeth are not broken, cracked or seriously burned. Refer to Chapter 1 for the flywheel removal process (photo).

4   Check that the release fork has not been cracked or bent. Slowly turn the front face of the release bearing making sure it turns freely and without any noise. The release bearing is pre-lubricated and should not be washed in gasoline or any other solvent. Whenever a new clutch is installed a new release bearing should automatically be used.

5   If any traces of oil are detected on the clutch components the source should be found and eliminated. If oil is coming from the center of the flywheel, this indicates a failure of the eccentric shaft rear oil seal (Chapter 1). Oil at the rear of the clutch assembly may indicate the need to replace the transmission input shaft seal (Chapter 6).

4 Clutch – installation

1   Find the locator mark and two reamed holes in the flywheel surface.

2   Hold the clutch disc and pressure plate in position, lining up the indicator hole and the two shanked bolts. Use the two shanked bolts to locate the pressure plate accurately on the flywheel. Install all bolts finger tight.

3   Use a centering tool or a spare transmission input shaft to centralize the clutch disc. Since the transmission shaft must pass through the disc, it must be centered properly to ease the transmission installation (photo).

4   Recheck that the clutch disc is properly mounted with the larger boss and retaining plate away from the flywheel.

5   Tighten all the cover bolts gradually and in a diagonal pattern until the proper torque of 13 to 20 ft-lb (1.8 to 2.7 m-kg) is achieved.

3.2a Checking the depth of the lining above the rivets

3.2b Checking the disc springs

3.3 Inspecting the surface of the flywheel

4.3 Using a tool to centralize the clutch components

5 Clutch pedal adjustment

1   There are two adjustments to be made at the clutch pedal which affect the operation of the clutch components.
2   The height of the clutch pedal is fixed by an adjustable stopper bolt located at the forward side of the top of the pedal. Loosen the lock nut and then adjust the stopper bolt either in or out to arrive at the proper pedal height. This distance is measured from the center of the pedal foot pad to the firewall. The pedal height distance between these two points should be approximately 7.5 inches (190 mm).
3   The free travel of the clutch pedal is the distance that the pedal is moved before actuating the push rod, master cylinder and related components. This adjustment is made at the top of the pedal, on the rear side. There is a lock nut on the push rod going through the firewall and into the master cylinder. Loosen this lock nut and then turn the push rod to achieve the proper free travel. This free movement before the push rod actually contacts the piston inside the master cylinder can be felt. It should be 0.02 to 0.12 in (0.6 to 3.1 mm).

6 Bleeding the clutch hydraulic system

1   Although bleeding the clutch system to remove air may not be as critical as in the brakes, it is nonetheless a necessary procedure if the clutch components are dismantled or if the fluid level in the master cylinder gets too low.
2   Air in the hydraulic lines (indicated by a spongy feeling in the clutch pedal) is an indication of a fault in either the master cylinder or operating release cylinder.
3   To bleed the clutch hydraulic system a supply of fresh fluid, a clean see-through jar, a length of tubing and an assistant will be needed.
4   Clean the master cylinder reservoir cap and the area around it to prevent dirt from entering the system.
5   Cover the fender and cowling area completely. Hydraulic fluid will damage painted areas.
6   Fill the clutch master cylinder reservoir to a point just above the normal mark. Put about an inch of hydraulic fluid into the clean jar (photo).
7   Remove the rubber cap from the bleed nipple on the clutch release cylinder located at the top of the engine, just behind the oil filter.
8   Attach one end of the plastic or vinyl tube to the bleed nipple outlet and submerge the other end in the fluid at the bottom of the jar (photo).
9   Loosen the bleed nipple slightly to break it loose.
10   Have an assistant depress the clutch pedal a couple of times and then hold the pedal to the floor. With the pedal held to the floor, slacken the nipple about ¾ turn, until air bubbles or fluid are released into the jar. Tighten the nipple and raise the clutch pedal. Have the assistant continue the pumping and holding action from inside the car while the bleed nipple is alternately opened and closed. Do this until no air bubbles appear in the jar.
11   During the bleeding operation the master cylinder fluid should not be allowed to go down to a point where air may be sucked back into the system. Check the fluid level often.
12   Tighten the bleed nipple securely and remove the tube and jar. Refit the rubber cap to the bleed nipple.
13   Fill the reservoir to the normal mark and replace the filler cap.
14   Do not under any circumstances re-use the old hydraulic fluid as it may corrode the clutch components.

7 Clutch master cylinder – removal and installation

1   The clutch master cylinder is located on the left side of the firewall, adjacent to the brake servo. It should be serviced if leaks occur, if air is entering the hydraulic system, or if the wrong type of fluid has been used in it.
2   The master cylinder can either be removed and replaced with a rebuilt unit, available at most auto supply stores and Mazda dealers, or it can be removed, overhauled and reinstalled.
3   Completely cover the fender and cowling areas of the car, as hydraulic fluid will ruin painted surfaces.
4   Place some rags or newspaper under the master cylinder to soak up the fluid which will leak from the pipes as they are disconnected.
5   Disconnect the fluid pipe on the master cylinder and use a suitable

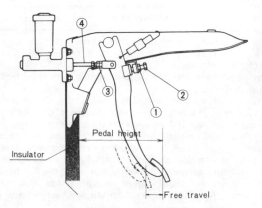

Fig. 5.2 Clutch pedal adjustment points (Sec 5)

1	*Locknut*	3	*Push rod locknut*
2	*Stopper bolt*	4	*Pushrod*

plug on the end of the pipe to prevent leakage and dirt from entering the system (photo).
6   Move to the inside of the car and remove the two nuts which secure the master cylinder to the firewall. These two nuts are located near the top of the clutch pedal.
7   Back in the engine compartment, pull the master cylinder out of the firewall and remove from the engine compartment. Do not allow excess fluid to drip on any painted surfaces (photo).
8   Before re-installation, the cylinder should be primed, so to speak. Do this by filling the reservoir with fresh hydraulic fluid and operating the piston with a screwdriver or the push rod until fluid is ejected at the outlet (photo).
9   Apply some silicone sealer to the master cylinder flange where it meets the firewall. This will create an air-tight seal.
10   As the master cylinder is placed into position the plunger which is attached to the clutch pedal must be centered in the cylinder. With the cylinder slightly away from the firewall, reach behind it with a curved wire or other suitable tool to lift the plunger into position. Then push the master cylinder against the firewall (photo).
11   Install the two nuts on the inside of the vehicle but leave them loose to enable you to move the cylinder slightly to engage the threads on the fluid pipe more easily.
12   Connect the fluid pipe to the cylinder. Make sure that the connection is not cross-threaded and will tighten easily.
13   Fully tighten the two attaching nuts on the inside.
14   Check that the fluid pipe is securely tightened.
15   Bleed the clutch hydraulic system, referring to Section 6.

8 Clutch master cylinder – disassembly and inspection

1   If the master cylinder is disassembled, some components should be replaced as a matter of course. Clutch master cylinder overhaul kits which contain the necessary replacement parts are readily available at auto parts stores and through Mazda dealers. This kit should be purchased before the disassembly process begins.
2   After completely draining all fluid from the cylinder at the reservoir, remove the connector bolt which secures the reservoir to the cylinder.
3   Remove the reservoir, bolt and related components.
4   From the rear end of the cylinder, remove the piston stop ring using needle-nose pliers or a small screwdriver.
5   Remove the washer following the stop ring.
6   The piston and secondary cup assembly should then fall out through the rear of the cylinder.
7   Remove the primary piston cup and spacer and return spring.
8   Wash all the parts in clean alcohol or brake fluid. Never use gasoline or any petroleum products. Blow the parts dry with compressed air if available.
9   Examine the cylinder bore and the piston for wear, roughness or scoring. If any of these conditions exist the parts should be replaced.
10   Check that the compensating port on the cylinder is open by

6.6 The master cylinder fluid should remain at the normal level during the bleeding operation

6.8 Bleeding the clutch release cylinder

7.5 Disconnecting the fluid pipe at the master cylinder

7.7 Removing the master cylinder

7.8 Priming the master cylinder before reinstallation

7.10 The plunger must be centered in order that the cylinder will seat properly against the firewall

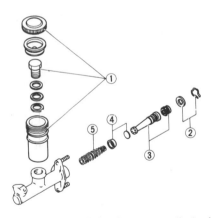

Fig. 5.3 Exploded view of clutch master cylinder (Sec 8)

1   *Connector bolt and reservoir*
2   *Piston stop ring and washer*
3   *Piston and secondary cup assembly*
4   *Primary piston cup and spacer*
5   *Return spring*

inserting a thin wire.
11 Check the clearance between the cylinder bore and the piston with a feeler gauge. The clearance limit is 0.006 in (0.15 mm). If the clearance exceeds the limit replace the piston or cylinder as required.
12 Reassemble the master cylinder using the new components in the overhaul kit. Dip the piston and cups in clean brake fluid during reassembly.

9   Clutch release cylinder – removal and installation

1   The clutch release cylinder is located at the rear of the engine,

adjacent to the oil filter. The release cylinder should be serviced if leakage is occurring or if air is entering the clutch hydraulic system. The release cylinder should also be serviced whenever the master cylinder is serviced, as it is usually the case that if one is bad the other is too.
2   The release cylinder can either be removed and replaced with a rebuilt unit, or it can be removed, overhauled and reinstalled.
3   Completely cover the fenders and cowling areas of the car as hydraulic fluid will damage any painted surface that it comes into contact with.
4   Remove the two attaching bolts which secure the release cylinder to the top of the transmission.
5   Move the wiring harness clear of the release cylinder.
6   Pull the cylinder forward until it disengages with the release fork (photo).
7   Released from its mounting, the flexible hose is now in an easier position to be disconnected from the release cylinder. Have a jar or plenty of rags handy to catch the excess fluid as the flexible hose is disconnected. Be careful not to lose the crush water at the flexible hose connector. Do not spill fluid on any painted surfaces (photo).
8   Plug the end of the flexible hose to prevent leakage and stop dirt entering the system.
9   Remove the release cylinder from the engine compartment.
10 When installing the release cylinder, first connect the flexible fluid hose to the cylinder and tighten the connector securely. Ensure that the crush washer is in place.
11 Place the cylinder into position and engage the release rod in the release fork.
12 Install the two attaching bolts and tighten securely.
13 Route the wiring harness back to its original position.
14 Bleed the clutch hydraulic system as outlined in Section 6.

10 Clutch release cylinder – disassembly and inspection

1   If the release cylinder is disassembled, some components should be replaced as a matter of course. Clutch release cylinder overhaul kits

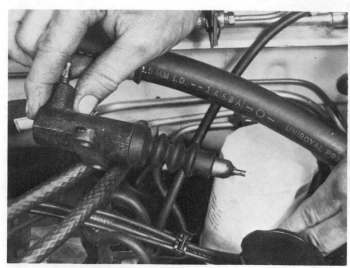

9.6 The clutch release cylinder pulled away from the transmission so that ...

9.7 ... in this position, the flexible hose will be easier to disconnect

which contain the necessary replacement parts are readily available at auto parts stores and through Mazda dealers. This kit should be purchased before the disassembly process begins.
2   Drain all fluid from the cylinder and clean the outside in clean alcohol or brake fluid. Do not use gasoline or kerosene.
3   With your fingers, pull off the dust boot and the release rod protruding from it.
4   Invert the cylinder and remove the piston and cup assembly.
5   The spring will follow these components.
6   With a suitable wrench, remove the bleed nipple and rubber cap.
7   Clean all parts in clean alcohol or brake fluid.

8   Examine the cylinder bore and the piston for wear, roughness or scoring. If any of these conditions exist, the parts should be replaced.
9   Check that the bleed nipple port is clear and free from any obstructions.
10 Check the clearance between the cylinder bore and the piston with a feeler gauge. The clearance limit is 0.006 in (0.15 mm). If the clearance exceeds the limit replace the piston or the cylinder as required.
11 Reassemble the release cylinder components using new parts which come in the overhaul kit. Dip the piston and cups in clean brake fluid during reassembly.

Chapter 6 Part 1: Manual transmission

Refer to Chapter 13 for specifications and information related to 1981 through 1985 models

Contents

Specifications

Gear ratios

	4-speed	5-speed
First	3.674	3.674
Second	2.217	2.217
Third	1.432	1.432
Fourth	1.000	1.000
Reverse	3.542	3.542
Fifth		0.825

Oil capacity

1.7 liters (1.8 U.S. quarts, 1.5 Imp quarts)

Mainshaft

Max. permissible run-out	0.03 mm (0.0012 in)
Clearance between mainshaft and gear (or bush)	
Wear limit	0.15 mm (0.006 in)

Reverse idle gear

Clearance between reverse idler gear and shaft	
Wear limit	0.15 mm (0.006 in)

Shift fork and rod

Clearance between shift fork and clutch sleeve	
Wear limit	0.5 mm (0.020 in)
Clearance between shift rod gate and control lever	
Wear limit	0.8 mm (0.031 in)

Synchronizer ring

Clearance between synchronizer ring and side of gear when fitted	
Standard	1.5 mm (0.059 in)
Wear limit	0.8 mm (0.031 in)

Lubricant

Above -18°C (0°F)	A.P.I. Service GL-4 or GL-5 SAE90
Below -18°C (0° F)	A.P.I. Service GL-4 or GL-5 SAE80

Torque wrench settings

	m-kg	ft-lb
Plug for interlock pin hole	1.0 to 1.5	7 to 11
Control lever to control rod end	0.8 to 1.2	6 to 9
Shift fork set bolts	0.8 to 1.2	6 to 9
Shift rod end	0.8 to 1.2	6 to 9
Mainshaft lock nut	13.0 to 21.0	94 to 152
Top switch	2.5 to 3.5	18 to 25
Overdrive switch	2.5 to 3.5	18 to 25
Back-up light switch	2.5 to 3.5	18 to 25
Speedometer driven gear	0.8 to 1.1	6 to 8

1 General description

The Maxda RX-7 can be purchased with either a 4-speed or 5-speed manual transmission. Both are conventional in design and thus quite straightforward to work on.

Both manual transmissions are very similar in makeup and are therefore combined in the various sections of this chapter. Where differences between the two arise, these are duly noted in the sequential text.

2 Planning major transmission work

1   The majority of the overhaul process can be done at home with common tools. There are, however, two areas of the process which could prove troublesome for the home mechanic. The first is the removal and installation of a lock nut on the mainshaft of the transmission. The $2\frac{1}{8}$ in (54 mm) nut is recessed into a clutch hub, thus requiring a special tool either to be purchased or made at home. Secondly, the clutch hub assemblies may need to be pressed off the mainshaft with a hydraulic press. These two procedures are detailed more fully in the text.

2   One of the biggest problems with doing transmission work for a beginner is trying to remember exactly where each part came from. To help alleviate this it may be helpful to draw your own simple diagram or take instant Polaroid photos during certain disassembly stages. Laying each part out in the order in which it was removed and tagging parts may also prove useful.

3   Although internal transmission parts for the Mazda are not as difficult to find as rotary engine parts, it is still advisable to look into replacements before work begins. Regardless of broken or badly worn components, there are parts which should be replaced as a matter of course when tearing down the transmission. These include: all transmission gaskets, snap rings, front oil seal and all bearings. Upon re-assembly you will need some multi-purpose lithium-based grease for all moving parts and silicone rubber-based sealant which is used in place of gaskets between the housings.

4   Cleanliness is important when performing a transmission overhaul, so the workshop should be kept as free of dirt and dust as possible. Adequate space should be available to lay out the various parts as they are removed.

3 Removal and installation

1   The manual transmission is fairly easy to remove from under the vehicle, especially when a pit or hoist is utilized to provide extra working space. If neither of these is available, or if engine work is to be carried out at the same time, see Chapter 1 for information on removing the transmission with the engine.

2   Open the hood and cover the front fenders to protect the paint while work is done in the engine compartment.

3   Disconnect the negative battery cable at its post on the top of the battery.

4   Remove the two bolts securing the clutch release cylinder to the top of the transmission housing. Tuck the cylinder up out of the way next to the oil filter (photo).

5   Remove the two top bolts which mate the transmission to the rear of the engine.

6   Remove the two nuts and disconnect the air pipe located at the rear of the engine, on the right side.

7   The thermal reactor on the right-hand side of the engine has a three-place cover with two nuts and two bolts holding the covers intact. Remove the nuts and bolts and then completely remove the small rear section of the thermal reactor cover. The other two cover pieces can remain intact.

8   Move to the inside of the car and unscrew and remove the gearshift lever knob by turning in a counter-clockwise direction.

9   There are two screws and clips which secure the shift boot and boot plate to the center console. Remove the two screws and then lift up and slide forward to remove the plate with the leather boot attached (photo).

10 Remove the five screws now exposed which secure the gearshift lever and retaining plate.

11 Pry back the rubber boot and remove the three bolts securing the gearshift lever mechanism to the top of the transmission. Remove the gearshift assembly.

12 At this point you must gain access to the underside of the vehicle for the remaining steps. You can use a hoist, a pit or raise the vehicle by supporting it with jack stands. Make sure the car is firmly supported before continuing.

13 Drain the lubricant from the transmission by removing the drain plug at the bottom of the transmission pan. Clean the plug and replace after fluid has drained (photo).

3.4 The clutch release cylinder is located on top of the transmission housing

3.9 Removing the gearshift boot and plate

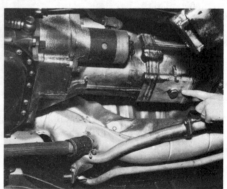

3.13 The transmission drain plug

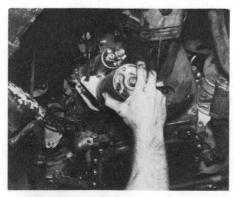

3.16 Removing the starter motor

3.17 Disconnecting the various electrical connections which run to the transmission switches

14 Refer to Chapter 7 for the proper procedure of removing the propeller shaft.

15 Disconnect the wiring to the starter. Remove the two wires with nuts at the starter solenoid and the one plug-in wiring connector. These should be plainly color-coded, but if there is any doubt mark them with tape and numbers, or by some other suitable means.

16 Remove the two bolts securing the starting motor to the transmission bellhousing. One long bolt runs through the engine, bellhousing and into the starter flange. The other bolt is smaller and goes through the flange, into the bellhousing. Remove the starter (see Chapter 10) (photo).

17 Disconnect the plug-in couplers to the back-up lamp switch, top switch (California with manual transmission only) and over-drive switch (California with manual transmission only). These plug-in couplers are located on the left side of the transmission and are colour-coded (photo).

18 Loosen the large (1½-in) nut mating the rubber air pipe to the exhaust system. Free the rubber pipe and move it out of the way of the transmission.

19 Disconnect the three nuts which secure the main exhaust pipe to the rear of the thermal reactor.

20 Towards the rear of the transmission, on the right side, is a hanger bracket for the exhaust system. Remove the two bolts going through the bracket into the transmission housing, and the single bolt on the lower portion of the hanger (photo).

21 By pushing the entire exhaust system rearward as far as it will go (two to four inches) you will gain enough clearance for the transmission to be removed. Use some wire to hold the exhaust to the rear.

22 Remove the three remaining transmission-to-engine bolts. Two of them are at the lower portion of the transmission and the other one on the upper left-hand side (photo).

23 The rear of the engine must now be supported to prevent it from dropping and thus exerting undue pressure on the front motor mounts. Use a jack and a block of wood under the oil pan.

24 Place a transmission or floor jack under the transmission. Make sure the transmission is firmly supported and that the jack will not damage the transmission oil pan.

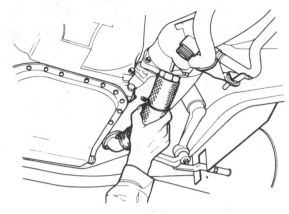

Fig. 6.1 Disconnecting the rubber air pipe for the exhaust system (Sec 3)

25 Remove the two nuts at the center position of the transmission crossmember mount (photo).

26 Remove the two bolts mounting the transmission crossmember to the bottom of the vehicle body. Remove the transmission crossmember mount (photo).

27 Disconnect the speedometer cable at the transmission using pliers to loosen the collar (photo).

28 With the transmission level with the engine, slide the transmission to the rear until the main shaft clears the clutch assembly. The transmission can then be lowered and removed from under the vehicle.

29 Installation is the reverse of removal but check that the clutch components are centralized (see Chapter 5) and apply some lithium-based grease to the input shaft splines of the transmission.

30 Check the clutch free-movement and adjust if necessary referring to Chapter 5 for this procedure. Be sure to fill the transmission with the correct grade and quantity of oil.

3.20 This hanger bracket must be disconnected from the exhaust system and the transmission

3.22 One of the remaining engine-to-transmission bolts accessible from under the car

3.25 Removing the two bolts which run through the mount and into the transmission

3.26 One of the two bolts which attaches the transmission mount to the body

3.27 Disconnecting the speedometer cable from the transmission

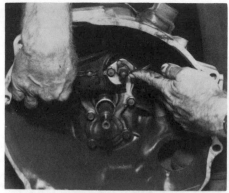
4.3 The release fork is held in place by a spring clip

4.5a Six bolts secure the front cover to the transmission body

4.5b There is an adjusting shim located behind the cover

4.5c Check the front oil seal in the cover. If it appears in good shape do not remove it

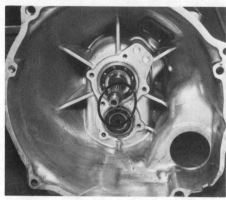
4.6 Remove the snap-ring located on the main shaft

4.7 Removing the gearshift lever retaining housing

4.8 Removing the rear extension housing bolts (left), and positioning the gearshift control rod forward and to the left

4.10 The rear extension housing and its various components

4.12a Using a hammer and drift on the two shafts to separate the housings

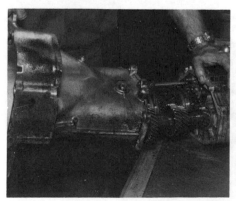
4.12b The front housing can then be lifted away

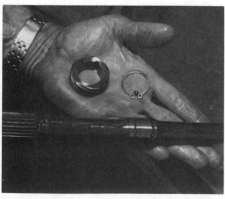
4.13 The speedometer gear, snap-ring and steel ball

4.14 The shift rod ends should be marked before removing

4 Dismantling

1   Clear an area in your workshop which can be kept relatively clean and is large enough to lay out the various transmission components as they are removed.

2   Clean the outside housings on the transmission and the inner surface of the clutch bellhousing, but do not get the clutch-withdrawal bearing wet as it is pre-lubricated and cannot properly be dried or regreased.

3   Remove the withdrawal bearing from the shaft by unclipping it from the fork (photo).

4   Remove the release fork by unclipping it from its pivot ball. Slide it towards the inside of the housing, through the rubber boot.

5   Remove the six bolts securing the front cover and remove the front cover and the adjusting shim(s) behind it. Leave the oil seal intact in the front cover unless there are signs of leakage, requiring the oil seal replacement (photos).

6   Remove the snap ring located on the mainshaft just ahead of the exposed bearing (photo).

7   The gearshift lever retainer is held in place with four bolts. Remove these and then lift off the retainer and accompanying gasket (photo).

8   Remove the bolts which secure the rear extension housing to the middle housing (photo).

9   To remove the extension housing, the control rod end (which the gearshift lever fits into) must be as far forward as possible and laid down to the left side. Tap the attaching flanges of the two housings with a rubber mallet to break the seal, and remove the extension housing. Never use a screwdriver or chisel to pry the housings apart, as this may damage the machined surfaces.

10 From the rear extension housing remove the control rod end, control rod, back-up light switch, speedometer gear assembly and over-drive switch (California with 5-speed only) (photo).

11 From the front housing, remove the top switch (California with manual transmission only).

12 The bearing housing and gear assembly is separated from the front housing by tapping the front of the main seal with a plastic hammer. Once the seal has been broken between the two housings, the bearing housing and gear assembly can be removed from the front housing. Again, do not pry the two apart with a screwdriver or chisel (photos).

13 There are two snap rings and a steel ball locating the speedometer gear onto the mainshaft. Remove the forward snap ring, then slide the gear off the shaft being careful not to lose the steel ball. Lastly, remove the rear snap ring (photo).

14 Before removing the shift rod and attaching bolts and shift rod ends, use a centrepunch or similar scribing tool to mark each rod and rod end for re-assembly. Remove the shift rod ends (photo).

15 Separate the bearing housing from the intermediate housing by lightly tapping around the area where they are joined with a plastic hammer. Slide off the intermediate housing leaving the thin bearing housing and gear assembly (photo).

16 Remove the three cap bolts with the springs and the check balls beneath them from the bearing housing. It may be necessary to use a magnet or magnetized screwdriver to lift out the check balls (photo).

17 Remove the snap rings on the shift rods. On 4-speed transmissions there is also a spacer located just beneath the snap ring on the reverse shift rod. Remove the spacer.

18 Remove the bolts attaching the shift forks to the shift rods.

19 Note and mark the position of each shift rod on its accompanying rod and then slide the rods clear of the housing. As the rods pass through the housing be sure not to lose the lock balls, springs and interlock pins. Be especially careful with the 5th and reverse rod as the check ball is under spring tension. Remove the rods and shift forks (photo).

20 At this point in the disassembly process you will need to remove the bearings from the mainshaft and countershaft and the large (2⅛-in, 55 mm) lock nut from the other end of the mainshaft. It is your option to either fashion tools at home for these procedures or to take the assembly to a Mazda dealer for removal (photo).

21 On 5-speed transmissions, following the removal of the main and countershaft bearings remove the spacer with its check ball, 5th gear, synchronizer ring and needle bearing from the mainshaft. From the countershaft, remove the counter 5th gear and spacer.

22 Following the removal of the large lock nut on the mainshaft, remove the clutch hub assembly, reverse gear, needle bearing, inner race and thrust washer (photo).

23 From the countershaft remove the snap ring (4-speed transmissions only) and the counter reverse gear.

24 From the small shaft between the mainshaft and countershaft remove the snap ring, thrust washers and reverse idle gear (photo).

25 Alternatively tap the ends of the mainshaft and countershaft to remove the two shafts from the bearing housing.

26 Carefully note the position of each component remaining in the mainshaft. It may be helpful for you to draw your own sketch at this time to ease the re-assembly procedure (photo).

27 In order; remove the snap ring, clutch hub assembly, synchronizer ring and 3rd gear, synchronizer ring and 2nd gear, clutch hub assembly, needle bearing and inner race, synchronizer gear and 1st gear, and the thrust washer. It may be necessary to use a press for the clutch hub assemblies.

28 Disassemble the clutch hub assemblies being careful to keep the parts separated.

29 Remove the five bolts securing the bearing cover to the housing and then remove the bearing using a press or a brass drift (photo).

5 Inspection and general checks

1   Clean all parts in suitable cleaner and dry with compressed air if available. If the ball bearings appear to be re-usable, they should be cleaned in gasoline while turning with the fingers. Do not allow them to spin if drying them with compressed air. Be certain there are no open flames in the general area where the cleaning is being done and that plenty of fresh air is available.

2   Inspect the transmission housings for any cracks or damage to the machined mating surfaces. Small nicks and burrs can be dressed out using a fine file.

3   Check the bushing and oil seal in the rear extension housing for wear and damage. If there have been signs of leakage at the rear of the transmission, or the seal appears suspect, replace it with a new one.

4   Slowly turn the outer race of each bearing by hand, noting any roughness or noise. If there is any doubt at all, the bearing should be replaced.

4.15 Separating the bearing housing from the intermediate housing

4.16 One of the cap bolts with its spring and check ball removed from the bearing housing

4.19 Marking each of the shift forks before removal

4.20 This large locknut on the main shaft is recessed into the clutch hub, and therefore, difficult to remove without a special socket wrench

4.22 The components which will follow the locknut off the mainshaft

4.24 Removing the reverse idler gear

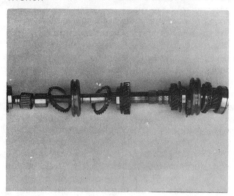

4.26 The components of the main shaft

4.29 After removing the bearing cover, the bearings can be pressed out of the housing

5.8 Checking the clearance between the synchronizer ring and gear with a feeler gauge

5   Inspect all gear surfaces for damage or excessive wear. Replace as necessary.
6   The mainshaft can be checked for run-out by placing it in V-blocks and using a dial indicator. If these parts are not available, a machine shop can do this for you.
7   Inspect the splines and gear teeth surfaces of the countershaft for damage or excessive wear. If any portion of the countershaft is defective it must be replaced as an entire unit.
8   The synchronizer mechanisms should be checked for wear and for damage to the teeth. Check the clearance between the side faces of the synchronizer ring and gear with a feeler gauge (photo). The standard clearance should be 0.059 in (1.5mm). The wear limit is 0.031 in (0.8mm).
9   Check the contact between the synchronizer ring and gear cone surface by using 'red lead' or 'engineer's blue'. If the contact pattern between the two surfaces is poor it can be corrected by lapping with a fine lapping paste.
10   Check that the clutch sleeve slides easily on the clutch hub.
11   Check the synchronizer key, the inner surface of the clutch sleeve and the key groove on the clutch hub for wear.
12   Check the synchronizer key spring for tension.
13   Check the clearance between the shift fork and sides of the clutch sleeve groove. It should be 0.02 in (0.5 mm).
14   Check to make sure the clearance between the control lever and the gate of the shift rod is no more than 0.031 in (0.8 mm).

6   Reassembly

1   All parts should be clean and free of any dirt or grease before reassembling.
2   During the reassembly process all sliding portions, gears and bearings should be liberally coated with a multi-purpose lithium-based grease.
3   Using a press or a brass drift and hammer install the bearings into the bearing housing. Place a straight edge across the housing and measure the clearance between the straight edge and each bearing

with a feeler gauge. Clearance should be 0 to 0.002 in (0 to 0.05 mm). If not within specs, shims are available to properly space the bearing.
4   Install the bearing cover and 5 bolts.
5   Assemble the clutch hub assemblies. If the old 'C' springs and keys are being used they must go back in their original hub. The open ends of the springs should be kept 120 degrees apart for uniform spring tension.
6   In the proper order, install the clutch hub assemblies, gears and synchronizers onto the mainshaft. A press may be needed to install the clutch hubs. If not available, use a brass drift and hammer. Note that the 1st and 2nd clutch hub has an oil groove which must be installed towards the front.
7   Install the mainshaft and countershaft through the bearings in the bearing housing.
8   Install the reverse idle gear, thrust washer and snap ring. Check the end play of the reverse idle gear by measuring the clearance between the snap ring and thrust washer. If not within specifications, adjust with auxiliary thrust washers available through Mazda dealers.

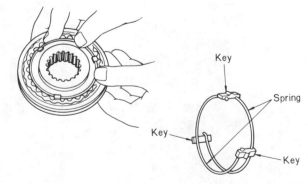

Fig. 6.2 Proper location of 'C' springs and keys in the clutch hub assembly (Sec 6)

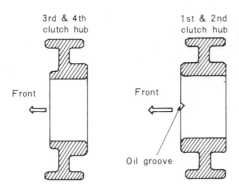

Fig. 6.3 Location of oil groove in clutch hub which must be installed towards the front (Sec 6)

9   On four-speed transmissions install the counter reverse gear and snap ring on the countershaft.

10 Onto the mainshaft, install the thrust washer, inner race, reverse gear, needle bearing and clutch hub assembly.

11 At this point the large mainshaft lock nut must be tightened to the specified torque. After the nut is tightened it should be caulked with a chisel to prevent it from coming loose.

12 On the 5-speed transmission install the spacer and counter 5th gear onto the countershaft. The synchronizer 5th gear, needle bearing, lock ball, spacer and snap ring are then installed on the mainshaft. Check the 5th gear end play by measuring the clearance between the spacer and snap ring. If not within specifications, thrust washers of varying thicknesses are available from Mazda dealers.

13 Install the bearing onto the mainshaft and countershaft. A press, large socket, or brass drift, can be used for this procedure. Just make sure that pressure is evenly applied around the outer race of the bearing. After installation, check mainshaft rear bearing end play and countershaft rear bearing end play by inserting a feeler gauge between the adjusting washer and snap ring. If it is more than 0.004 in (0.1 mm) use adjusting washers available at Mazda.

14 Slide the shift rods through the bearing housing in the same locations from which they were removed. The oblong-shaped interlock balls go in the holes between the shift rods just before each rod is installed. As the shift rods are slid into position the shift forks should be placed into the groove of each clutch hub assembly. If the shift rods and forks were properly marked on disassembly this will be an easy task.

15 Use a thread locking agent on the bolts attaching each shift fork to the shift rod. Tighten to the proper torque.

16 Install the snap rings on the shift rods. On 4-speed transmissions don't forget the spacer located on the reverse shift rod.

17 Through the cap bolt holes in the bearing housing install the check balls and springs for each shift rod. Note that the springs are in varying lengths, corresponding to the depth of the hole. Apply a thread locking agent to the threads of each cap bolt and tighten to torque specifications.

'18 Apply a bead of silicone rubber-based sealant on the bearing housing surface and smear it around with your fingers. Make sure any nicks or gouges have been filed smooth and that the sealant forms a solid, even layer. Slide the intermediate housing into place with the bearing housing (photo).

19 Using the scribing marks you made on disassembly, slide the shift rod ends onto their corresponding shift rods. Torque the rod end attaching bolts to the proper torque specifications (photo).

20 Install the speedometer drive gear, its steel locating ball and two snap rings on the mainshaft.

21 Apply rubber-based silicone to the mounting flange of the front housing and slide it into place over the main and counter shafts.

22 On the front housing, install the top switch (California with manual transmission only).

23 On the rear extension housing, install the over-drive switch (California with manual transmission only), speedometer gear assembly, back-up light switch, control rod and control rod end.

24 Apply the silicone sealant to the mounting flange of the rear extension housing. With the control rod end as far forward as it will go, and laid down to the side, install the rear extension housing. Apply thread locking agent to the extension housing bolts and tighten to a

6.18 Sliding the intermediate housing into position over the shift rods

6.19 Attaching the shift rod ends using the identification marks made upon disassembly

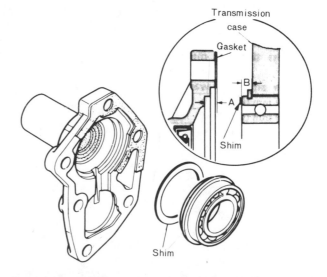

Fig. 6.4 Measuring main driveshaft bearing endplay (Sec 6)

torque of 15 ft-lb (2.1 m-kg). Do the tightening in several steps and in a diagonal pattern across the housing to prevent warpage.

25 Install the gearshift lever retainer with its gasket. Tighten the four bolts.

26 Using a brass drift or large socket, press the front bearings into the front housing. Install the snap rings in front of each of the bearings.

27 To measure the main drive shaft bearing end play, measure the depth of the bearing bore in the front cover end play, measure the bearing with a depth gauge. The difference between the two should fall between 0 to 0.004 in (0 to 0.1 mm). Additional shims are available through Mazda dealers (Fig. 6.4).

28 Install the shim(s), front cover gasket and front cover (preferably with a new oil seal pressed into place).

29 Slide the release bearing and shift fork into position. The spring on the rear of the fork snaps into place on a pivot ball.

30 As a final check before installation into the car, install the shifter and accompanying mechanism and test that the transmission goes into each gear properly.

31 See Section 3 of this chapter for the proper sequence to follow when replacing the transmission.

Chapter 6 Part 2: Automatic transmission

Contents

Specifications

Gear ratios
Low 2.458
Second 1.458
Top 1.000
Reverse 2.181

Fluid type .... M2C33F (Type F)

Fluid capacity .... 6.2 liters (6.6 U.S. quarts, 5.5 Imp quarts)

Drive plate run-out
Limit .... 0.5 mm (0.020 in)

Oil pump
Side play of inner gear and outer gear
Limit .... 0.08 mm (0.003 in)
Clearance between outer gear and crescent
Limit .... 0.25 mm (0.010 in)
Clearance between outer gear and housing
Limit .... 0.25 mm (0.010 in)
Side clearance between oil seal ring and groove on oil pump cover .. 0.04 to 0.16 mm (0.002 to 0.006 in)

Front clutch
Thickness of drive plate
Limit .... 1.4 mm (0.055 in)
Total clearance measured between retaining plate and snap ring .... 1.6 to 1.8 mm (0.063 to 0.071 in)
End play of front clutch drum .... 0.5 to 0.8 mm (0.020 to 0.031 in)

Rear clutch
Thickness of drive plate
Limit .... 1.4 mm (0.055 in)
Total clearance measured between retaining plate and snap ring .... 0.8 to 1.5 mm (0.031 to 0.059 in)

Low and reverse brake
Thickness of friction plate
Limit .... 1.8 mm (0.071 in)
Total clearance measured between retaining plate and snap ring .... 0.8 to 1.05 mm (0.031 to 0.041 in)

Gear assembly
Total end play .... 0.25 to 0.50 mm (0.010 to 0.020 in)
Planetary gear side play
Limit .... 0.8 mm (0.031 in)

Engine stall speed
In break-in period .... 2,250 to 2,500 rpm
After break-in period .... 2,300 to 2,550 rpm

Valve body springs

	Wire diameter	Free length
Pressure regulator valve	1.20 ± 0.03 mm (0.047 ± 0.001 in)	43.0 ± 1.0 mm (1.69 ± 0.039 in)
1st – 2nd shift valve	0.55 ± 0.015 mm (0.022 ± 0.0006 in)	32.0 ± 2.0 mm (1.260 ± 0.079 in)
2nd – 3rd shift valve	0.70 ± 0.015 mm (0.028 ± 0.0006 in)	41.0 ± 1.0 mm (1.61 ± 0.039 in)
Pressure modifier valve	0.40 ± 0.01 mm (0.016 ± 0.0004 in)	18.5 ± 1.0 mm (0.73 ± 0.039 in)
Throttle back-up valve	0.80 ± 0.015 mm (0.031 ± 0.0006 in)	36.0 ± 1.0 mm (1.42 ± 0.039 in)
Solenoid down shift valve	0.55 ± 0.015 mm (0.022 ± 0.0006 in)	21.9 ± 1.0 mm (0.86 ± 0.039 in)
2nd lock valve	0.55 ± 0.015 mm (0.022 ± 0.0006 in)	33.5 ± 1.0 mm (1.32 ± 0.039 in)
Throttle relief valve	0.90 ± 0.03 mm (0.035 ± 0.001 in)	26.8 ± 1.0 mm (1.06 ± 0.039 in)
Orifice check valve	0.23 ± 0.01 mm (0.009 to 0.0004 in)	15.5 ± 2.0 mm (0.61 ± 0.079 in)

Shift speeds

Throttle condition (Manifold vacuum)

	shift	mph
	D$_1$ to D$_2$	32 to 45
	D$_2$ to D$_3$	59 to 77
	D$_3$ to D$_2$	51 to 65
Kick-down (0 to 100 mm-Hg, 0 to 3.94 in-Hg)	D$_2$ to D$_1$	14 to 30
Half throttle (200 ± 10 mm-Hg, 7.87 ± 0.39 in-Hg)	D$_1$ to D$_2$	9 to 21
	D$_2$ to D$_3$	18 to 40
Fully closed throttle	D$_3$ to D$_1$	6 to 12
Manual 1	1$_2$ to 1$_1$	24 to 33

Governor pressure

Driving speed mph	Output shaft speed rpm	Governor pressure kg/cm^2	lb/in^2
20	1,070 to 1,170	0.8 to 1.3	11 to 18
35	1,900 to 2,030	1.6 to 2.3	23 to 33
55	3,000 to 3,170	3.1 to 4.2	44 to 60

Line pressure

Manual range

	Engine idling condition kg/cm^2	lb/in^2	Engine stall condition kg/cm^2	lb/in^2
R	4.0 to 7.0	57 to 100	16.0 to 19.0	228 to 270
D	3.0 to 4.0	43 to 57	9.0 to 11.0	128 to 156
2	8.0 to 12.0	114 to 171	8.0 to 12.0	114 to 171
1	3.0 to 4.0	43 to 57	9.0 to 11.0	128 to 156

Torque wrench settings

	m-kg	ft-lb
Drive plate to converter weight	4.2 to 6.3	30 to 46
Drive plate to torque converter	3.5 to 5.0	25 to 36
Converter housing to engine	3.2 to 4.7	23 to 34
Converter housing to transmission case	4.5 to 5.5	33 to 40
Extension housing to transmission case	2.0 to 2.5	14 to 18
Oil pan	0.5 to 0.7	3.6 to 5.1
Piston stem (when adjusting band brake)	1.2 to 1.5	9 to 11
Piston stem lock nut	1.5 to 4.0	11 to 29
Servo piston retainer	1.0 to 1.5	7.2 to 11
Servo cover	0.5 to 0.7	3.6 to 5.1
One-way clutch inner race	1.3 to 1.8	9 to 13
Control valve body to transmission case	0.55 to 0.75	4.0 to 5.4
Lower valve body to upper valve body......................................	0.25 to 0.35	1.8 to 2.5
Side plate to control valve body	0.25 to 0.35	1.8 to 2.5
Reamer bolt of control valve body	0.5 to 0.7	3.6 to 5.1
Oil strainer	0.3 to 0.4	2.2 to 2.9
Governor valve body to oil distributor......................................	0.5 to 0.7	3.6 to 5.1
Oil pump cover	0.6 to 0.8	4.3 to 5.8
Inhibitor switch	0.5 to 0.7	3.6 to 5.1
Manual shaft lock nut	3.0 to 4.0	22 to 29
Oil cooler pipe set bolt	1.6 to 2.4	12 to 17
Oil pressure test plug	0.5 to 1.0	3.6 to 7.2
Actuator for parking rod to extension housing	0.8 to 1.1	5.8 to 8.0

1 General description

1 The automatic transmission fitted to the RX-7 is conventional in that it has a torque converter and three forward gears. The gears are epicyclic, and they are engaged by hydraulically actuated clutches and brake bands.

2 The transmission is manufactured by the Japanese Automatic Transmission Company (JATCO). The only basic difference between this transmission and conventional automatics is that the converter has been designed to suit the rotary engine's liking for high rpm usage. There is no oil pump on the output shaft, so tow starting is not possible with the automatic. If the vehicle needs towing in the event of a breakdown, the propeller shaft should be disconnected at the rear axle and removed.

2 Removal and installation

1 As with the manual transmission, the automatic can be either removed intact with the engine or separately from under the car. If major engine work is required at the same time, refer to Chapter 1 for removing the transmission with the engine. A hoist or pit will greatly ease the removal and installation processes under the car.

2 In the sequential process of removing and installing the automatic transmission many of the steps are the same as with the manual transmission. Because of this it may be advisable to quickly thumb through the section on the manual transmission before work begins on the automatic. Where processes are the same or similar, references have been made to the appropriate illustrations in Chapter 6 Part 1 (Manual transmission).

3 Open the hood and cover the front fenders to protect the paint while work is being done in the engine compartment.

4 Disconnect the negative battery cable from the battery post.

5 At the rear of the engine, near the oil filter, disconnect the plug-in connector for the inhibitor switch. Also remove the converter housing upper cover and the vacuum sensing tub of the vacuum diaphragm located in this area.

6 Remove the two nuts and disconnect the air pipe located at the rear of the engine, on the right side.

7 Remove the two nuts and two bolts securing the thermal reactor cover pieces. Completely remove the small cover at the rear of the thermal reactor, gaining access to the three exhaust flange bolts.

8 Remove the bolts at the top of the engine attaching the transmission to the engine.

9 Of the three exhaust flange nuts at the rear of the thermal reactor, remove the top one at this time.

10 The remainder of the removal process will be under the vehicle. The most conventional method is to use a hoist or pit; however, jack stands will raise the car sufficiently. Make sure the car is firmly supported before continuing.

11 Remove the propeller shaft, referring to Chapter 7.

12 Remove the rubber pipe running from the bottom of the thermal reactor to the air pipe.

13 Remove the two remaining nuts at the exhaust pipe-to-thermal reactor connection.

14 Towards the rear of the transmission, on the right side, is a hanger bracket for the exhaust system. Remove the three bolts on this bracket.

15 Disconnect the two nuts mating the exhaust pipe to the silencer just below the bracket previously removed. The exhaust system should now be free to be moved out of the way of the transmission.

16 Disconnect the wiring to the starter motor. The wires are color-coded for easy re-installation, but if there is any doubt mark them yourself with tape and numbers, or some other suitable method.

17 Remove the bracket holding the starting motor intact and then the starter itself.

18 Remove the three bolts securing the converter housing lower cover.

19 Access to the drive plate and torque converter is now available through the bottom of the converter housing. Make a mark on the drive plate and torque converter for correct realignment during re-installation.

20 Reaching inside the access hole in the converter housing, remove the bolts attaching the torque converter to the drive plate with a wrench.

21 Remove the remaining transmission-to-engine bolts.

22 The rear of the engine must now be supported in some fashion to prevent it from hingeing on the front motor mounts, thus exerting undue pressure on the mounts. A jack with a block of wood to spread the load positioned under the oil pan will work fine.

23 Place a floor jack or transmission jack under the transmission and support it. Again, use a block of wood to prevent damage to the transmission oil pan.

24 Disconnect the speedometer cable using pliers to loosen the collar.

25 Just above the speedometer cable mounting is the select rod and lever. Disconnect the rod at the lever.

26 Remove the two nuts at the center portion of the transmission crossmember mount.

27 Remove the two nuts mounting the transmission crossmember to the bottom of the body. Remove the mount.

28 The fluid pipes must now be disconnected at the transmission housing. If access to these connectors proves too difficult, the engine and transmission can be carefully lowered for more room. Do this with care as pressure will be exerted on the transmission input shaft and the motor mounts.

29 With the transmission parallel to the engine, carefully slide the transmission rearward until the input shaft clears the rear end of the eccentric shaft. Remove the transmission and torque converter assembly from under the vehicle.

30 Re-installation of the automatic transmission is basically the reverse process of removal. Be sure to use the locator marks on the drive plate and torque converter, and to torque each bolt to the proper specification. Don't forget to fill the transmission to the proper level with the specified fluid.

3 General overhaul

If there has been internal failure inside the automatic transmission then a number of components will have been worn out as well as those which are bad enough to provoke symptoms. Such an overhaul needs expertise and facilities beyond the scope of most home mechanics, and should not be undertaken by a beginner.

If you are competent to deal with such a job and have the proper working tools and facilities then you will be able to understand the JATCO special book for this transmission, and should work from that. If not, the job should be left to a Mazda dealer or competent transmission specialist. Alternatively, a reconditioned transmission can be purchased and installed at this time.

4 Checking transmission fluid level

1 With the car on level ground, firmly apply the parking brake.

2 Warm up the engine to normal operating temperature.

3 Apply the brake and shift the selector lever through all of the drive positions (1, 2, D, N and R). Place the lever in the 'P' position. Do not stop the engine during the fluid level checks.

4 Wipe any dirt from the dipstick cap, pull out the dipstick, wipe clean and reinsert fully.

5 Pull the dipstick out again and check the level. The fluid level should be maintained between 'L' and 'F' marks on the gauge.

6 When any fluid is added this should be done through the dipstick filler tube. Under no circumstances should the transmission be overfilled, as foaming will occur which could cause serious transmission damage.

7 The fluid in the transmission should be a transparent red. If the fluid is dark in color or sticky in feel, this may indicate malfunctions in the internal parts.

5 Adjusting shift control linkage

1 Shift the selector lever to the 'N' position.

2 Raise the vehicle and firmly support with jack stands.

3 Disconnect the T-joint from the lower end of the selector lever operating rod located at the rear of the transmission.

4 By hand, move the selector range lever to the 'N' position (the third detent position from the rear of the transmission).

5 Loosen the T-joint attaching nuts and adjust the T-joint so that it

enters the hole in the selector lever arm.
6   Tighten the attaching nuts.
7   Connect the T-joint to the selector lever arm and secure the T-joint.
8   Lower the vehicle and check for proper operation in each selector lever position.

6   Adjusting kick-down switch

1   Disconnect the wiring connectors from the kick-down switch located on the inside of the firewall, behind the accelerator pedal.
2   Loosen the lock nut behind the switch and screw out the switch a few turns.
3   Fully depress the accelerator pedal.
4   Slowly screw the switch back down until the clicking sound is heard. Then screw it in one-half turn further.
5   Tighten the lock nut and connect the wiring connectors.

6   Electrical testing can be found in Chapter 10.

7   Adjusting inhibitor swtich

1   Put the selector lever in the 'N' position.
2   Raise the vehicle and support with jack stands.
3   The inhibitor switch is located on the left side of the transmission, just forward of the downshift solenoid and vacuum diaphragm. Loosen, but do not remove, the switch attaching bolts.
4   Remove the small screw on the switch body.
5   Rotate the switch and insert an alignment pin of 0.078 in (0.2 mm) through the alignment hole and into the hole of the internal rotor.
6   Tighten the switch attaching bolts and remove the alignment pin.
7   Replace the screw into the switch housing.
8   Lower the vehicle and check to be sure the car will start only in the 'P' or 'N' positions.
9   Electrical testing can be found in Chapter 10.

Chapter 7 Propeller shaft

Contents

Specifications

Max. permissible run-out	0.4 mm (0.016 in)

Max. permissible unbalance
At 4000 rpm:

At front	15 cm-gr (0.21 in-oz)
At rear	15 cm-gr (0.21 in-oz)

Universal joint

Spider diameter .... $25 \,^{+\,0.021}_{+\,0.008}$ mm $(0.9843 \,^{+\,0.0008}_{+\,0.0003}$ in)

Spider wear limit .... 24.908 mm (0.9806 in)

Journal swinging torque .... 3 to 8 cm-kg (2.6 to 6.9 in-lb)

Torque wrench settings

	m-kg	ft-lb
Yoke to rear axle companion flange	3.5 to 3.8	25 to 27

1 General description

1 Power is transmitted from the rear of the transmission to the rear axle by a tubular propeller shaft.

2 Universal joints are located at the front and rear of the shaft and allow for vertical movement of the rear axle and slight movement of the engine/transmission assembly. A four-legged 'spider' with needle bearings on each leg connects the propeller shaft to the front yoke and rear flange.

3 The front yoke features a sliding spline which is fitted to the rear housing of the transmission. This spline allows for slight movement of the drivetrain in a fore/aft direction.

4 The propeller shaft is connected to the rear axle assembly with four bolts passing through the rear propeller shaft flange and into the differential pinion flange.

2 Propeller shaft – removal and installation

1 Raise the rear of the vehicle and firmly support on jack stands. An alternative method is to position the car on ramps to gain access underneath. Chock the front wheels so the vehicle cannot move forward.

2 To maintain proper driveline balance make a mark across all mating surfaces at the rear of the propeller shaft (photo).

3 Remove the four bolts securing the propeller shaft to the rear end pinion flange. A large screwdriver positioned through the rear flange will prevent the propeller shaft from turning as the bolts are broken loose (photo).

4 Lower the rear of the shaft slightly and then slide it rearward until the front spine is clear of the transmission. Remove the shaft assembly from under the vehicle (photos).

5 The installation of the propeller shaft is the reverse procedure. Make sure the alignment marks on the mating surfaces are lined up. Torque the four bolts to 25 to 27 ft-lb (3.5 to 3.8 m-kg).

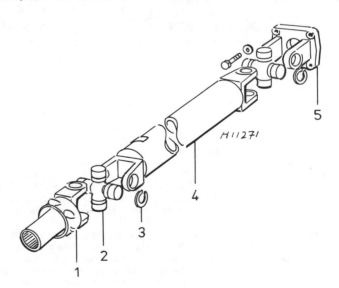

H11271

Fig. 7.1 The components of the propeller shaft

1	Front yoke	3	Circlips
2	Spider and bearing cup assembly	4	Shaft
		5	Rear yoke with flange

2.2 Mating marks should be made across the propeller shaft, universal joint components and axle flange before removing the shaft

2.3 Remove the four propeller shaft retaining bolts

2.4a Lower the propeller shaft to clear the rear axle housing while supporting the middle of the shaft

2.4b The propeller shaft can then be slid rearward clear of the transmission tailshaft

3   Propeller shaft – inspection

1   It is somewhat difficult for the home mechanic to make the proper tests of the propeller shaft due to the necessity for special measuring devices and machinery. It would be advisable to take the shaft to a competent machine shop or Mazda dealer equipped to make these checks.

2   The run-out of the propeller shaft is checked by placing the shaft in V-blocks and attaching a dial indicator so that its point just touches the shaft surface. The shaft is then slowly turned and the run-out duly recorded on the dial indicator. The run-out limit for the propeller shaft is 0.016 in (0.4 mm). If the run-out exceeds this limit, replace the entire propeller shaft.

3   The propeller shaft can also be checked for dynamic unbalance. This is done using special machinery with which the shaft can be spun at varying rpm. The maximum unbalance at both the front and the rear of the shaft is 0.21 in-oz (15 cm-gr) at 4000 rpm. If not within these specifications, the propeller shaft should be properly balanced or replaced as an assembly.

4   Universal joint – inspection on car

1   Wear in the needle roller bearings is characterised by vibration in the transmission, 'clonks' on taking up the drive, and in extreme cases of lack of lubrication, metallic squeaking, and ultimately grating and shrieking sounds as the bearings break up.

2   It is easy to check if the needle bearings are worn with the propeller shaft in position. To check the rear universal, turn the shaft with one hand and hold the rear axle flange with the other. Any movement between the propeller shaft and the rear half coupling is indicative of considerable wear. The front is checked in the same manner except that the shaft is turned while holding the front half coupling.

3   Lifting up on the shaft will also indicate movement in the universal joints.

4   If worn, the old bearings and spiders will have to be discarded and a repair kit, comprising new universal joint spiders, bearings, oil seals and retainers, purchased.

5   Read over the Sections on disassembling and reassembling the universal joints before purchasing parts or beginning work.

5 Universal joints – disassembly

1 Due to the critical nature of the propeller shaft balance, Mazda recommends that the universal joints should not be disassembled, but rather the engine propeller shaft should be replaced as a unit. However, if the imbalance of the propeller shaft assembly can be checked and corrected within the specifications, the universal joint may be replaced.

2 Before disassembling it should be noted that Mazda has snap rings available in nine different thicknesses as shown in the accompanying chart. These snap rings, with their very small thickness variations, must be used to place the spider at the exact center of the yoke. This is critical.

1.22 mm (0.0480 in)	1.32 mm (0.0520 in)
1.24 mm (0.0488 in)	1.34 mm (0.0528 in)
1.26 mm (0.0496 in)	1.36 mm (0.0535 in)
1.28 mm (0.0504 in)	1.38 mm (0.0543 in)
1.30 mm (0.0512 in)	

Fig. 7.2 Various snap-rings available to correctly space the spider (Sec 5)

3 Clean the outside of the universal joint with a suitable solvent.

4 Place the propeller shaft in a vise with wood blocks so as not to damage the shaft.

5 Remove the snap rings by pressing them out with a screwdriver. NOTE: If they are difficult to remove, tap the bearing cup face on top of the spider with a mallet which will ease the pressure on the circlip.

6 Tap the spider bearing in the yoke with a suitable tool until the opposite side bearing comes out sufficiently.

7 Remove the forced-out spider bearing by lightly tapping the base of the yoke with a hammer.

8 Remove the bearing at the opposite side by using the same procedure, and separate the flange yoke from the propeller shaft.

9 Remove the two remaining bearings in the same manner and separate the spider from the yoke.

6 Universal joint – inspection when disassembled

1 Examine the bearing surfaces of the spider. They should be smooth and free from pits.

2 Measure the diameter of the spider. If it is less than 0.9806 in (24.908 mm) replace with a new universal joint assembly.

7 Universal joint – reassembly

1 Apply grease on the bearing rollers and cup inner surface and then

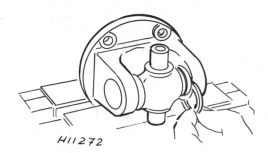

Fig. 7.3 The snap-ring must be pushed out from the inside of the yoke (Sec 5)

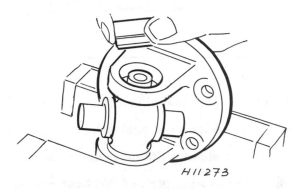

Fig. 7.4 The cup is pushed out by pressing the whole joint across till it can be lifted out (Sec 5)

assemble them.

2 Position the spider and one bearing on the flange yoke.

3 Use a suitable pusher, or a vise, to press the bearing until the snap ring groove is visible on the inside.

4 Install a suitable snap ring

5 Place the bearing in the bore at the other side of the yoke and press in the bearing until the spider is at the center of the yoke.

6 Install a suitable snap ring.

7 The sliding yoke and spider assembly is installed in the same manner.

8 Avoid re-using the old snap rings and use snap rings of the same thickness at both sides of the yoke.

9 Select snap rings of the proper thickness to place the spider at the center of the yoke and give a slight drag fit (not binding).

10 Have the propeller shaft checked for proper run-out and dynamic unbalance as described in Section 3.

Chapter 8 Rear axle

Refer to Chapter 13 for information related to 1981 through 1985 models

Contents

Specifications

Reduction ratio	3.909
Backlash of ring gear and pinion	0.09 to 0.11 mm (0.0035 to 0.0043 in)
Max. allowable variation of backlash	0.05 to 0.07 mm (0.0020 to 0.0028 in)
Pinion bearing preload (Without pinion oil seal)	9 to 14 cm-kg (7.8 to 12.2 in-lb)
Differential side bearing preload (Without pinion)	6 to 16 cm-kg (5.2 to 13.9 in-lb)
Backlash of side gear and pinion gear	0 to 0.1 mm (0 to 0.004 in)
Rear wheel bearing end play	0 to 0.01 mm (0 to 0.004 in)

Lubricant

Above – 18°C (0°F)	A.P.I. Service GL-5 SAE 90
Below – 18°C (0°F)	A.P.I. Service GL-5 SAE 80
Oil capacity	1.2 liters (1.3 U.S. Quarts, 1.1 Imp quarts)
'L' (Case spread)	185.428 to 185.500 mm (7.3004 to 7.3033 in)

Torque wrench settings

	m-kg	ft-lb
Ring gear	6.5 to 7.5	47 to 54
Differential side bearing caps	3.8 to 5.3	27 to 38
Companion flange to pinion	13 to 18	94 to 130

1 General description

1   The rear axle is conventional in design, thus mechanics who have previous experience on rear axle servicing will find the RX-7 assembly to hold no surprises.

2   The rear axle assembly consists of a solid housing with a differential gear assembly in the center and two half shafts leading to the wheels. This system is known as 'semi-floating'.

3   The most common faults in the rear axle assembly will present themselves as noises. There may be a constant whining sound which may or may not intensify with engine speed and gear selection, or there may be clunking or grunting noises on turns. Noises which grow gradually over many thousands of miles indicate a wearing condition, while sounds which come on quickly are an indication of a failure which must be remedied quickly.

4   Nearly all work on the rear end assembly requires a certain degree of experience and expertise. Usually, the necessity for special tools and measuring devices plays an important role. However, by talking with professional mechanics and by adopting an intelligent approach to the work, the home mechanic can save money by carrying out several overhaul and inspection procedures on his own axle.

2 Axle shaft – removal and installation

1   Axle shafts are commonly removed to replace bearings and seals which will, after a time, fail. An axle puller, sometimes called a slide hammer puller, will probably be necessary to remove the shaft from the axle housing. A press will definitely be necessary to remove the bearing and collar from the shaft.

2   Raise the rear end of the vehicle and support firmly with jack stands under the rear axle housing.

3   Remove the rear wheel.

4   Remove the two brake drum attaching screws and then the brake drum.

5   The axle bearing side play can be checked by pulling and pushing on the axle hub. A dial indicator mounted to the axle hub will give a precise measurement of this play. Standard side play is 0.012 to 0.018 in (0.3 to 0.45 mm). The side play limit is 0.028 in (0.7 mm). If not within specifications, the bearing will have to be replaced (photo).

6   Remove the brake shoe assembly referring to Chapter 9.

7   On the inboard side of the brake backing plate remove the parking brake cable clip and disconnect the parking brake cable. Do this by pulling back the rubber boot and working the cable back and forth until

2.5 A dial indicator can be mounted to the backing plate and the axle pushed back and forth to measure side play

2.10 Removing the backing plate attaching nuts

2.7 Removing the parking brake cable retaining clip

2.14 Using a puller to force the axleshaft assembly out of the housing

through the plate (photo).

8   Have newspapers or rags handy to soak up any fluid loss from the brake fluid pipes.

9   Loosen, but do not remove, the brake fluid pipe(s) at the inboard side of the backing plate.

10   Remove the four backing plate attaching nuts on the inboard side of the back plate (photo).

11   Completely disconnect the fluid pipe(s).

12   The axle shaft and backing plate assemblies will be removed from the axle housing together.

13   With your hands positioned behind the axle shaft hub, try to pull the assembly out of the axle housing. Depending on the mileage and tolerances, it may or may not come out with hand pressure.

14   Chances are that a puller mounted to the axle hub will be necessary. These are available at auto dealers and auto parts stores, or can be rented on a daily basis at rental dealers carrying automotive supplies (photo).

15   Once the bearing and collar are pulled free of the end of the axle housing, the shaft and backing plate assembly can be slid carefully out of the housing. Support the shaft as it is removed, and be careful not to damage the oil seal at the end of the housing (photo).

16   Inspect the oil seal located just inside the axle housing. If it shows signs of wear or damage, replace it with a new one. If there is any evidence of leakage, replace the seal. Pry it out of the housing with a

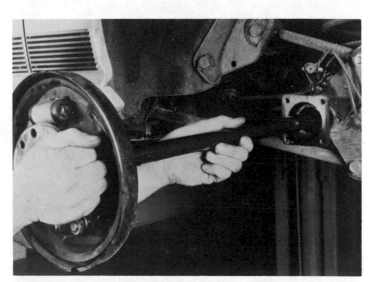

2.15 Support the axleshaft as it is removed from the housing to prevent damage to the oil seal

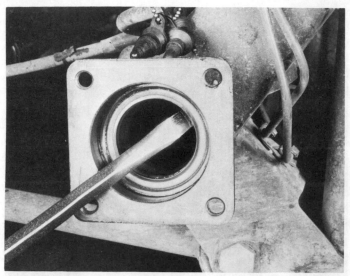
2.16 The oil seal can be pried out with a screwdriver

2.19 The axle bearing and retaining collar

3.6 Removing the drain plug from the differential housing

3.9 Removing one of the eight nuts which secure the differential assembly

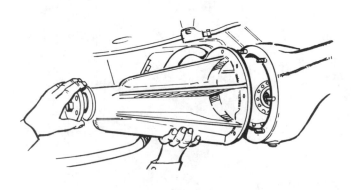
Fig. 8.1 Removing the differential assembly from the axle housing (Sec 3)

3.17 The filler plug is located at the rear of the housing. Use your finger to check the fluid level

seal puller or screwdriver (photo).

17 Cover the end of the housing to prevent dirt from entering the axle housing.

18 If the side play measurements taken before disassembly showed that the bearing was in need of replacement, or if the bearing is rough when turned or looks damaged, it should be replaced (photo).

19 It is recommended at this point to take the axle shaft assembly to a Mazda dealer or competent machine shop to have the bearing and retaining collar pressed off the shaft (photo). A press with approximately 5 tons of weight will be necessary for this operation. Special separators and spacers will also be necessary. If this equipment is absolutely not available, the retaining collar will have to be cut off the shaft with a cold chisel, being very careful not to mark the axle shaft. The bearing can then be removed from the shaft with a long bearing puller.

20 Inspect the axle shaft splines where the shaft meets with the differential inside the axle housing. If these splines are damaged or show signs of excessive wear, the axle shaft should be replaced.

21 Install the backing plate and spacer into the axle shaft with the chamfer of the spacer toward the axle shaft flange. Position the bearing on the axle shaft and press it until it comes in contact with the shoulder of the shaft.

22 Press the retaining collar onto the axle shaft until it is in firm contact with the bearing race. Do not use oil or grease on the collar or axle shaft. If the retaining collar can be fitted with less than 2.7 tons (5900 lbs) of force, it is not tight enough and should be replaced with another one.

23 Install the oil seal into the axle housing with a hammer and block of wood, tapping carefully around the circumference of the seal. Make sure the seal is firmly seated.

24 Apply a small amount of lithium based grease to the oil seal lip.

25 Thoroughly clean the end of the axle housing.

26 Carefully install the axle shaft and backing plate assembly. Do not damage the oil seal. It may be necessary to turn the axle slightly to engage its inner splines with the differential. If difficulty is found in pushing the bearing retainer collar into the end of the housing, tap the axle hub lightly with a mallet until it is seated properly.

27 Loosely install the four attaching nuts to the backing plate. Do not tighten at this time.

28 Connect the fluid lines, making sure that the connectors are not cross-threaded. Move the backing plate slightly to line up the threads properly.

29 Tighten the four attaching nuts securely and then fully tighten the brake fluid pipe connectors.

30 Connect the parking brake cable with its securing clip.

31 Install the brake shoe assembly referring to Section 9 of Chapter 9.

32 Install the brake drum with its attaching screws.

33 Install the wheel.

34 Lower the vehicle to the ground.

3 Differential assembly – removal and installation

1 Noises emanating from the rear end assembly cannot be properly diagnosed or repaired without removing the differential assembly.

2 Although overhauling the differential is a time consuming and exacting process, the home mechanic in most instances can remove the differential and carry out certain tests on the assembled differential. A visual inspection of the components can also be made to ascertain which parts it will be necessary to replace. Armed with these facts, you can effectively deal with the Mazda dealer or auto repair shop which will ultimately perform the overhaul work.

3 Raise the rear of the vehicle and support firmly with stands.

4 Raise the rear of the vehicle and support firmly with stands.

5 Move a container into position under the rear axle housing to catch the drained fluid. Also have newspapers and rags handy to mop up any spills. The container should be of sufficient size to hold at least 2 US quarts (1.1 Imp qts, 1.2 liters).

6 Remove the drain plug at the bottom of the axle housing. Allow the fluid to fully drain, then replace the plug (photo).

7 Remove both rear axle shafts, referring to Section 2.

8 Remove the propeller shaft as detailed in Chapter 7.

9 Remove the eight nuts which secure the differential to the axle housing (photo).

10 If necessary, tap around the housing lightly to break seal. Pull the differential assembly straight off the studs and then lift free from under the vehicle. It is somewhat heavy, so get a firm grip before pulling it off the studs. Don't drop it.

11 Place a clean rag over the opening in the axle housing to prevent dirt from entering.

12 Before installing, thoroughly clean the inside of the axle housing with a clean rag. Also remove all traces of gasket or sealer from the mounting flanges of the differential and axle housing. Install a new gasket, with a light coat of sealer to both sides, onto the axle housing.

13 Lift the differential assembly into position over the studs, temporarily holding it in place with one of the top nuts.

14 Now install all the nuts and tighten them a little at a time, working around the differential

15 Install the propeller shaft and tighten its four bolts.

16 Install the axle shafts as described in Section 2.

17 Fill with the proper grade of lubricant (see Recommended Lubricants section) through the inspection and fill plug located at the rear of the axle housing (photo).

18 Lower the vehicle to the ground.

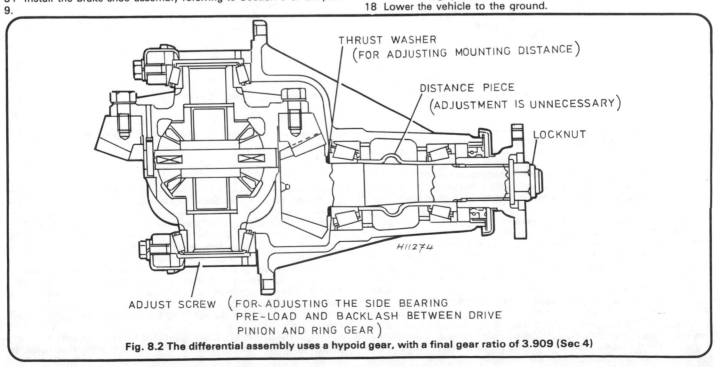

Fig. 8.2 The differential assembly uses a hypoid gear, with a final gear ratio of 3.909 (Sec 4)

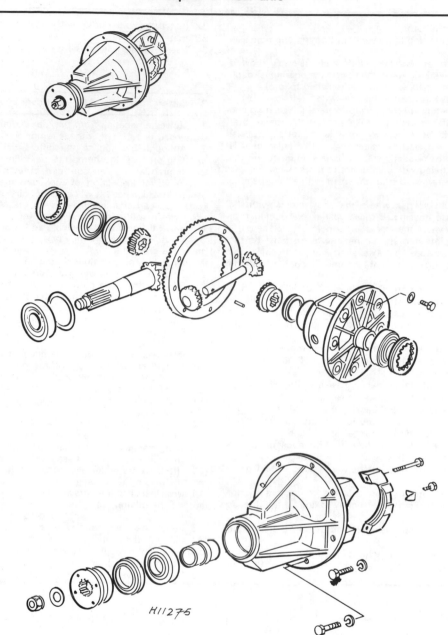

H11275

Fig. 8.3 Exploded view of rear axle differential assembly (Sec 4)

4 Differential assembly – inspection

1   Allow all fluid to drain from the differential and then clean the parts thoroughly. Cleaning will be somewhat difficult with the differential still assembled, but the gears especially must be clean and dry.
2   Look for visibly damaged parts, like broken or chipped teeth on the gears.
3   Inspect the bearings for roughness of travel, wear or damage.
4   Check for oil leakage at the front oil seal where it mates to the propeller shaft. This will indicate a failure of the pinion oil seal.
5   The tooth contact between the ring gear and pinion gear can be checked using red lead, or engineer's blue available at most auto supply stores. Apply a thin coat of red lead or engineer's blue to both sides of about six or eight ring gear teeth. Rotate the ring gear a few times both forward and backward. Check the pattern on the teeth using the illustrations as a guide (Figs. 8.4 thru 8.8).
6   Owing to the complexity of procedures, the need for special tools and the difficulty in obtaining appropriate spare parts, it is advisable at this point for the home mechanic to take the differential assembly and the information obtained through the inspection processes to a Mazda

dealership or competent auto repair shop specializing in jobs of this nature.

5 Pinion oil seal – removal and installation

1   It is possible that an oil leak may develop at the pinion shaft oil seal. This will be indicated by fluid leakage at the rear flange of the propeller shaft. This is fairly easy to replace, without removing or disassembling the differential assembly.
2   Raise the rear of the car and support firmly with jack stands.
3   Drain the lubricant from the differential assembly by removing the drain plug at the bottom of the axle housing. After all fluid has drained, install the plug and tighten.
4   Refer to Chapter 7 for removing the propeller shaft from the axle drive flange.
5   Apply the handbrake firmly to prevent the rear wheel from turning.
6   Remove the nut on the end of the pinion shaft that holds the flange in place.

7 Pull off the flange by using a conventional hub puller.

8 Pry out the old seal with a seal remover or a screwdriver.

9 Use a clean rag to clean the pinion bore and the outside diameter of the new oil seal.

10 Tap the new seal into the bore by using a plastic hammer or a hammer and a block of hard wood. The seal lips go inward. Tap a little at a time, working around the seal to keep it square.

11 Lubricate the running surface for the oil seal on the flange, and then slide the flange into place.

12 Release the parking brake.

13 Fit the washer and nut to the pinion shaft, and tighten it gradually, turning the flange so that the bearings can roll into position as the end load comes onto them.

14 Finally tighten the nut to a torque of 94 ft-lb (13 m-kg). This torque is important as it sets the bearing preload. While tightening this nut the pinion can be held in place by using your foot to prevent the wheels from turning.

15 Connect the propeller shaft as described in Chapter 7.

16 Fill the differential housing with the specified lubricant (see Recommended Lubricants).

17 Lower the vehicle to the ground and, after a test drive, check around the rear flange for any further leakage.

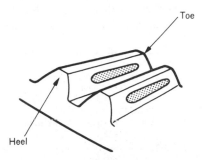

Fig. 8.4 This is the correct pattern for pinion position and backlash (Sec 4)

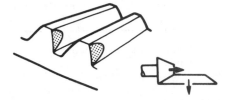

Fig. 8.5 Heel contact
Drive pinion is too far away from ring gear. A spacer will need to be added to bring pinion closer to ring gear (Sec 4)

Fig. 8.6 Toe contact
The drive pinion is too close to the ring gear. Pinion spacers will need to be added to move pinion away from the ring gear (Sec 4)

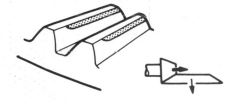

Fig. 8.7 Face contact
Adjustments will be necessary as described for Fig. 8.5 (Sec 4)

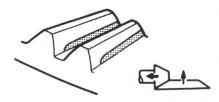

Fig. 8.8 Flank contact
Adjustments will be necessary as described for Fig. 8.6 (Sec 4)

Fig. 8.9 Tapping a new pinion oil seal into place (Sec 5)

Chapter 9 Braking system

Refer to Chapter 13 for specifications and information related to 1981 through 1985 models

Contents

Specifications

Brake pedal free travel
Before power brake piston operates .... 7 to 9 mm (0.28 to 0.35 in)

Brake pedal height (from floor) .... $190 ^{+5}_{-0}$ mm ($7.48 ^{+0.20}_{-0}$ in)

Master cylinder
Bore .... 20.64 mm (0.813 in)
Clearance between piston and bore
   Standard .... 0.040 to 0.125 mm (0.0016 to 0.0049 in)
   Wear limit .... 0.15 mm (0.006 in)

Power brake unit
Clearance between piston and push rod .... 0.1 to 0.5 mm (0.004 to 0.020 in)

Front disc brake
Thickness of brake disc
   Standard .... 18 mm (0.7087 in)
   Limit .... 17 mm (0.6693 in)
Max. allowable lateral run-out of brake disc .... 0.1 mm (0.004 in)
Thickness of lining
   Standard .... 9.0 mm (0.35 in)
   Wear limit .... 1.0 mm (0.04 in)
Wheel cylinder bore .... 50.80 mm (2.0 in)

Rear drum brake
Drum diameter
   Standard .... 200 mm (7.874 in)
   Limit .... 201 mm (7.914 in)
Thickness of lining
   Standard .... 4.0 mm (0.16 in)
   Wear limit .... 1.0 mm (0.04 in)
Wheel cylinder bore .... 19.05 mm (0.750 in)
Clearance between piston and bore
   Standard .... 0.040 to 0.125 mm (0.0016 to 0.0049 in)
   Limit .... 0.15 mm (0.006 in)
Remaining pressure .... 0.5 to 1.0 kg/cm² (7.1 to 14.2 lb/in²)
Clearance between drum and lining .... 0.1 to 0.15 mm (0.004 to 0.006 in)

Parking brake

Drum diameter	
Standard	200 mm (7.874 in)
Limit	201 mm (7.914 in)
Thickness of lining	
Standard	4.0 mm (0.016 in)
Limit	1.0 mm (0.04 in)
Lever travel	3 to 7 notches at 10kg (22lb)

Torque wrench settings

	m-kg	ft-lb
Master cylinder union	1 to 1.6	7 to 12
Master cylinder outlet plug	6 to 7	43 to 50
Brake tube union nut	1.3 to 2.2	9 to 16
Flexible hose union	2.2 to 2.7	16 to 20
Wheel cylinder union bolt	0.7 to 1.0	5 to 7

1   General description

1   The brakes are disc at the front and drum at the rear. Each disc caliper is mounted on slides, and is worked by a hydraulic piston on the inside.
2   Driver effort is assisted by a servo unit, mounted on the firewall of the engine compartment. This is vacuum operated.

2   Checking the front disc pads

1   The thickness of the lining on the front disc pads should be checked on a regular basis, as excessive damage can occur if the linings are worn to a point where they can harm the rotor. The thickness of the metal shoe and the lining together should be no less than 0.236 in (6 mm).
2   To check the front brake pads, raise the car and remove the front wheels. Looking down from above the caliper, the pads can be seen on either side of the disc.
3   The disc pad on the outside of the caliper is easier to see and

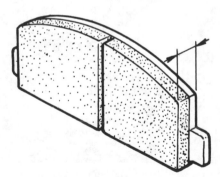

Fig. 9.1 The thickness of the metal shoe and lining material together should be no less than 0.236 in (6 mm) (Sec 2)

measure than the one on the inside; however, both should be inspected. Also, the pads may not necessarily wear evenly across the surface, so inspect and measure at different spots (photo).
4   At the same time the pads are checked the rotor surface itself should be inspected for signs of wear, most notably scoring marks or 'hot spots' indicated by small blemishes tinted a different color on the surface. If excessive damage is found on the rotor surface, the pads should be changed and the rotor either re-surfaced or replaced.

3   Front disc brake pads – removal and installation

1   Raise the front end of the vehicle and support firmly with stands.
2   Remove the front wheel.
3   Remove the four small locking clips which secure the locking plates to the caliper. Use pliers to pull these out.
4   Pull the two stopper plates outward with a pair of pliers. If they cannot be slid out easily, use a hammer and drift from the inboard side, forcing the plates out. Be careful not to strike the caliper (photo).
5   The caliper can now be removed and placed out of the way. The caliper should be suspended from the suspension using wire. Do not allow the caliper to hang freely from the flexible hose as damage to the hose and fittings may occur (photo).
6   Remove the anti-rattle spring, noting how it connects to the brake assembly (photo).
7   Lift off the brake pads on either side of the rotor (photo).
8   When replacing front disc pads all four pads (two on each front wheel) should be replaced at the same time. Also, do not mix different types of pad when replacing; purchase only pads manufactured from the same materials.
9   Before installing the disc brake pads apply a thin coat of lithium based grease to the spring metal located on the caliper bracket where the front of the pad meets the bracket. This is to prevent squeaks and rattles in this area (photo).
10 Install the pads by first pushing them tightly against this spring metal towards the inside of the rotor and then pushing them in position towards the outside edge of the rotor. When installing note that the disc brake pad with a small hole in it for the anti-rattle spring is located on the inward facing side of the rotor.
11 Reinstall the anti-rattle spring with the curved end fitting into the

2.3 Measuring a disc pad thickness

3.4 The stopper plates and the four locking clips

3.5 Pushing the caliper out of the way

3.6 Removing the anti-rattle spring

3.7 Lifting the brake pads away from the rotor

3.9 Applying grease to the caliper bracket where the front edge of the pad makes contact

3.11 Installing the anti-rattle spring in the inboard brake pad

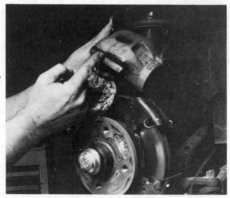

3.13a Apply a thin coat of grease to the caliper recessed areas

3.13b Apply some grease to the stopper plates

3.13c Some grease is also applied to the caliper mounting bracket where it contacts the caliper

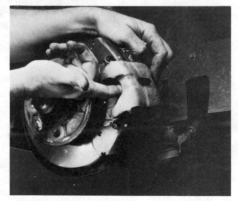

3.14 Checking that the anti-rattle spring is properly positioned before final assembly

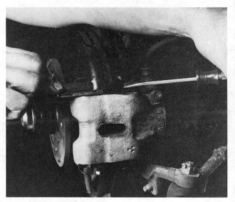

3.16 Installing the top stopper plate by prying downward on the caliper with a screwdriver

3.17 Installing the four locking clips into the stopper plates

4.3 Loosening the flexible brake hose to the caliper

small hole on the inboard disc brake pad (photo).

12 Check the caliper for fit over the disc brake pads. If new pads are being installed, chances are that the caliper will not fit easily over them due to their thicker linings. If this is the case, the piston in the caliper will have to be forced back, allowing more room. When the piston is forced back, fluid will also be forced back through the system which may cause an overflow at the master cylinder. Check the fluid level at the master cylinder and if you are in doubt attach a vinyl tube to the bleeder screw on the cylinder with the other end of the tube submerged in a jar of clean brake fluid. Loosen the bleeder screw to allow fluid to enter the jar without overflowing the master cylinder, then force the piston back using an expanding tool or carpenter's C-clamp.

13 After it has been determined that the caliper will fit over the pads, apply a light coat of lithium-based grease to the recessed areas of the caliper where the stopper plates touch the caliper (photo). Also apply a little grease to the stopper plates themselves, the edges of the caliper mounting plates and the edges of the caliper mounting bracket which contact the caliper. This is to prevent any squeaks or rattles in the braking system (photos).

14 When installing the caliper it is easiest to tilt the caliper slightly to lock it into position under the top tension spring and then push the other end into position under the remaining tension springs. As the caliper is slipped into place check that the anti-rattle spring is properly seated against the inside radius of the caliper and not hanging down below where damage can occur (photo).

15 Install the bottom stopper plate first, forcing the caliper upwards to allow room for the plate. Tap lightly with a hammer to force the plate in.

16 Install the top stopper plate using a screwdriver to carefully pry the caliper downward for clearance (photo).

17 Install the four locking clips into their respective holes in the stopper plates (photo).

18 As a final step, bleed the brakes (Section 17) to remove all air which has entered the system. Install the wheels and lower the vehicle to the ground.

19 Take a short test drive to confirm that the brakes are functioning properly and that there are no leaks in the system.

4 Front brake caliper – removal and installation

1 Raise the front end of the vehicle and support firmly with stands.
2 Remove the front wheel(s).
3 Temporarily loosen the flexible fluid line at the caliper. This is easier to break loose now, while the caliper is still solidly mounted (photo).
4 Remove the four locking clips which secure the stopper plates to the caliper. Remove the two stopper plates.
5 The caliper can now be lifted away from the rotor and the flexible hose completely disconnected. Have rags or newspaper handy to collect the excess fluid which will drip from the hose as this is done. Plug the end of the hose to prevent dirt from entering the system and to prevent further leaking.
6 When installing, apply a thin coat of lithium-based grease to all points where the caliper contacts other metal parts (at the recesses for stopper plates, inside edges of caliper mounting bracket).
7 Install the flexible hose loosely.
8 Tilt the caliper slightly and install the top lip under the tension spring in the caliper bracket. Then reach inside with your finger to make sure that the anti-rattle spring is seated properly against the inside radius of the caliper. Finally, push the caliper into position under the lower tension spring.
9 Push the stopper plates into position using a hammer to lightly tap them into place, or pry the caliper against the tension springs for clearance.
10 Install the four locking clips into the stopper plates.
11 Tighten the flexible fluid hose completely.
12 Install the wheel(s).
13 Bleed the brakes as described in Section 17 of this Chapter to remove all air which has entered the system.
14 Lower the vehicle to the ground and check for proper brake operation and for leaks.

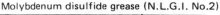
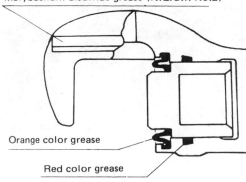

Molybdenum disulfide grease (N.L.G.I. No.2)

Orange color grease

Red color grease

Fig. 9.2 Areas on the caliper to which grease is applied during overhaul (Sec 5)

5 Front brake caliper – disassembly and inspection

1 Purchase a caliper overhaul kit which contains new seals which must be used.
2 Clean the outside of the caliper with soap and water. Do not use gasoline or kerosene as this may harm the caliper components.
3 Use a screwdriver to carefully pry the dust boot retainer from the bore. This is a thin wire retainer running around the outside of the bore.
4 The dust boot can now be pried out of the caliper.
5 Remove the piston from its bore in the caliper. If this proves difficult, as it may, apply compressed air to the fluid hole to force the piston out. Use a piece of wood inside the caliper recess to cushion the piston when it is forced out, as it may come out with considerable force depending on the amount of air pressure applied. Lightly tapping the area around the piston while air is applied will also help to remove the piston.
6 Use a seal remover or screwdriver to pry out the rubber seal behind the piston.
7 Remove the bleeder cap screw.
8 Clean all the disassembled parts in clean brake fluid or alcohol. Never use gasoline, kerosene or petroleum based cleaning solvent. Dry with compressed air if available.
9 Inspect the caliper bore and piston for scoring, scratches or rust. If any of these conditions are found, replace with new piston or calipers as required. Minor damage can be eliminated by polishing with crocus cloth.
10 Check that the fluid hole is clear of obstructions and that the threads for the flexible fluid hose and bleeder screw are clean.
11 Lubricate the cylinder bore with clean brake fluid. Install a new piston seal into the bore, making sure that it does not become twisted and that it is seated fully in the groove.
12 Lubricate the outside of the piston with clean brake fluid and slide it into position in the caliper bore.
13 Two small packets of grease are included in the caliper overhaul kit and should be applied to the areas shown in Fig. 9.2.
14 Install the new dust boot into position and lock it with the circular retainer.
15 Install the bleeder screw tightly and reinstall the rubber bleeder cap.

6 Front wheel hub and bearings – removal and installation

1 Raise the front end of the vehicle and support it with stands.
2 Remove the front wheel(s).
3 Referring to the appropriate Sections in this Chapter remove the four locking clips, stopper plates, caliper, anti-rattle spring and disc brake pads. Do not allow the caliper assembly to hang freely from the flexible hose as damage may occur.
4 Remove the caliper mounting bracket. This is attached with two bolts on the inner side. The top bolt is easily accessible. The lower bolt is rather hard to get to because of the drag link for the steering. The best way to get this bolt out is to use the box end of a suitable wrench, prying gently with a screwdriver for access. Once the bolt is broken

6.4a Gaining access to the caliper mounting attaching bolt by prying with a screwdriver

6.4b Removing the caliper mounting bracket

6.6 Removing the dust cap, nut lock, cotter key and adjusting nut from the end of the spindle

6.7 The washer and outer bearing removed from the spindle

6.9 The grease seal and inner bearing on the inboard side of the hub

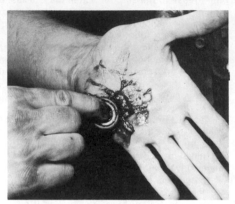

6.11 Packing the bearings with grease

6.16 Installing the nut lock and new cotter pin

8.4 Removing the brake drum

8.6 Inspect the inside of the brake drum for scoring, scratching or heat damage

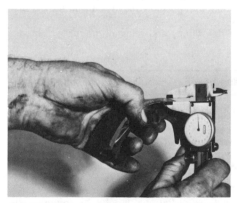

8.7 Measuring the thickness of the brake linings

9.6a Removing the top return spring

9.6b Removing the parking brake strut rod (with return spring) and the lower return spring

loose, remove the screwdriver and wrench and then loosen the bolt the rest of the way with the open end of the wrench, working the bolt a little at a time (photos).

5   From the end of the spindle remove the dust cap by prying it off with a screwdriver.

6   Remove the split pin, nut lock and adjusting nut now visible on the end of the spindle (photo).

7   Carefully pull the hub assembly outward slightly to force the washer and outer bearing to the end of the spindle. Push the hub assembly back into place and remove the washer and bearing (photo).

8   Pull the hub assembly off the spindle.

9   Remove the grease seal and inner bearing from the inboard side of the hub assembly (photo).

10 If the bearing outer race still inside the hub assembly appears pitted or deeply scratched, it can be removed by using a hammer and a drift in the slots provided. Do not remove the outer bearing race unless it is necessary to replace it.

11 Repack the bearings thoroughly with lithium based grease. Work the grease into the bearings from the larger diameter side of the bearing (photo).

12 Press the inner bearing into place and install a new grease seal.

13 Fill the hub cavity within lithium grease.

14 Install the hub onto the spindle and slide the outer bearing and washer into place.

15 Thread the adjusting nut onto the spindle and tighten the nut until the hub binds and will not move freely. Then loosen the nut one-sixth of a turn, making sure that the hub rotates freely. Spin the hub assembly a few times to seat the bearings. Grab the hub on either side and check for any sideways movement. If there is, tighten the adjusting nut slightly to eliminate the sideways movement, making sure that the hub still rotates freely.

16 Install the nut lock and new split pin (photo).

17 Tap the grease cap into place with a hammer.

18 Install the caliper mounting bracket, again using a screwdriver for access to bolts.

19 Install the disc brake pads, anti-rattle spring, caliper, stopper plates and locking clips as described in Section 3.

20 Install the front wheel(s).

21 Bleed the brakes as outlined in Section 17.

22 Lower the vehicle to the ground; test for proper operation and for leaks in the system.

7   Front wheel hub and bearings – inspecting

1   Clean the grease off the hub assembly and outer bearing races with cleaning solvent.

2   Thoroughly clean the bearings with cleaning solvent and dry thoroughly. Do not spin the bearings with compressed air.

3   Inspect the inner and outer bearings for scratches, pitting or excessive wear. Closely inspect the inside surface of the bearings for galling which indicates that the hub was installed too loose and was moving in a sideways direction, thus damaging the inside of the bearings.

4   Inspect the rotor surfaces for pitting, scratches or hot spots. If the rotor shows signs of wear it is advisable to have a machine shop turn the rotor on a lathe to remove any imperfections. If wear is severe the rotor must be replaced.

8   Rear brakes – checking

1   Raise the rear end of the car and place solidly on stands.

2   Release the parking brake from inside the car

3   Remove the rear wheel(s).

4   Remove the two brake drum attaching screws and pull the drum off. If the drum proves difficult to remove, check again that the parking brake is fully released and tap the drum with a rubber mallet. In extreme cases where the drum cannot be removed, local application of heat from a blowtorch may have to be used, but great care should be taken if this method is adopted (photo).

5   Blow all the dirt and dust from the inside of the brake drums, linings and related components. Try not to breathe this dust or get it on your clothes as it can be hazardous to your health.

6   Inspect the brake drum for wear, damage or deformation. Check the inside surfaces for scoring, scratching or heat damage indicating a failure of the linings. If any of these conditions exist, the linings should be replaced (Section 9) and the drum should be turned by a professional machine shop (photo).

7   Inspect the linings themselves for wear, damage, deformation or delamination (the linings coming loose from the metal shoe portion). The thickness of the lining material should be at least 0.04 in (1.0 mm). This is measured with micrometers, without including the thickness of the metal shoe portion (photo).

8   Check that the wheel cylinder does not show signs of leakage. This will be indicated by fluid on the rubber boot of the wheel cylinder. If this is the case, the wheel cylinder should be overhauled (Section 12).

9   Check that no grease or oil is leaking from the axle, indicating that the axle oil seal has failed and is in need of replacement (see Chapter 8).

10 Check all brake lines for leakage. Check that all brake pipes, hoses and connections are tight and show no signs of chafing, deterioration or other damage.

11 Replace the brake drum and the attaching screws.

12 Install the rear wheel(s).

13 Adjust the rear brakes (Section 10).

14 Lower the vehicle to the ground and test drive for proper operation.

9   Rear brake shoes – removal and installation

1   Raise the rear end of the vehicle and support firmly with jack stands under the rear axle housing.

2   Release the parking brake from inside the car.

3   Remove the rear wheel.

4   Remove the two brake drum attaching screws.

5   Pull off the brake drum. If the drum proves difficult to remove, check again that the parking brake is fully released and tap the drum with a rubber mallet. In extreme cases where the drum cannot be removed, local application of heat from a blowtorch may have to be used, but great care should be taken if this method is adopted.

6   Using pliers, unclip the return springs located at the top and bottom of the brake shoes. The parking brake strut rod is also connected at the top of the brake shoes and will come off with the top return spring. Carefully note the position of the parking brake strut rod before it is fully removed (photos).

7   Remove the brake shoe retaining springs and guide pins with pliers. Do this by grabbing the end of the retaining pin with a pair of pliers and then compressing the spring and at the same time turning the guide pin to align with the slot in the spring (photo).

8   Completely remove the forward brake shoe.

9   Release the rear brake shoe from the parking brake lever by grabbing the end of the parking brake cable with pliers and pulling the cable end to a point where the lever can be slipped out of the cable (photo).

10 If the brake shoes are being replaced, all of the shoes should be replaced with new ones at the same time in order to prevent uneven braking.

11 When replacing the rear brake shoes with new ones it is advisable to have the drums turned by a machine shop at the same time, even if wear on the drums is slight. This will speed the break-in time of the new linings. Most auto parts stores and machine shops will do this for a small fee if new brake shoes are purchased at the same time.

12 To eliminate squeaks in the braking system apply a small amount of multi-purpose grease to the following points where the brake shoes contact metal; where the shoes meet the cylinder pistons; on the anchor pins at the lower end of the brake shoes; at the six locations on the backing plate where the raised portions of the shoes contact the backing plate. The peviously mentioned contact area on the backing plate can be identified by small, shiny wear marks on the backing plate. Do not allow grease to get on the brake lining surfaces (photo).

13 Place a drop of oil on the anchor pin eccentrics which are used to adjust the brakes. This will allow the adjusters to move more freely (photo).

14 Note that the brake shoe with the parking brake lever attached has an indentation at the top of it for the parking brake strut rod. Match the new brake shoe with the old and then transfer the parking brake lever to the new brake shoe. The lever is attached with a C-clip.

15 Use a pair of pliers to force the parking brake cable spring upwards and slide the cable onto the parking brake lever (photo).

16 Place the shoes into position noting that the anchor pins have two

9.7 Removing the brake shoe guide pins

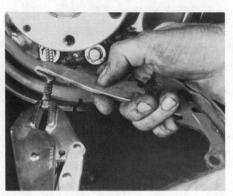
9.9 Slipping the parking brake lever out of the cable

9.12 Place some grease on wheel cylinder pins

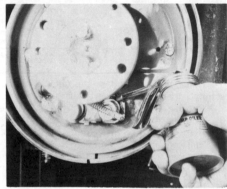
9.13 A little oil on the anchor pin eccentrics will allow free movement for adjusting the brakes

9.15 The spring on the parking brake cable must be forced upwards to allow the lever to be attached

flat spots on them which the bottom of the shoes must ride on.

17　Secure the shoes with the guide pins and retainer springs. Use a pair of pliers to compress the spring slightly as the guide pin is rotated into the lock position.

18　When replacing the parking brake strut at the top of the shoes, note that the strut has a cutout area at each end. The cutout which is exactly in the center of the strut goes towards the front of the vehicle. The cutout which is slightly offset to one side of the strut goes towards the rear brake shoe. Install the parking brake strut, engaging it at the top of each brake shoe.

19　Install the upper and lower return springs.

20　Check that all springs are located properly and that no grease has gotten onto the brake linings. If grease is on the linings it should be removed, as it may cause damage to the inside surface of the drum and will prevent the linings from bedding into the drum properly during operation. Remove the grease with a clean cloth and use sandpaper very lightly to remove the grease spots.

21　Install the brake drum with its two attaching screws.

22　Install the wheel.

23　Bleed the brake system as described as described in Section 17.

24　Adjust the rear brakes referring to Section 10.

10　Rear brakes – adjusting

1　Each of the four brake shoes has its own adjuster. These are located on the rear of the brake backing plate, near the bottom of the plate.

2　Raise the rear end of the vehicle and support firmly with jack stands under the axle housing.

3　Release the parking brake fully.

4　Start with the forward brake shoe and turn the lock nut towards the rear, in a counter-clockwise direction.

5　Hold the loosened lock nut and turn the anchor pin towards the rear, in a counter-clockwise direction until the wheel cannot be turned.

6　Back off the anchor pin until the wheel just turns freely.

7　Hold the anchor pin tightly in position and tighten the lock nut.

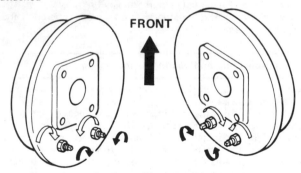

TURNING DIRECTION

↺ — Anchor pin (to expand brake shoe)

↻ — Lock nut (to tighten)

Fig. 9.3 Turning direction for adjusting each rear brake shoe (Sec 10)

Check that the wheel still turns freely (photo).

8　The other brake shoes are adjusted in the same way, except that it should be noted that the lock nut and anchor pin turns in the opposite direction on the rear mounted brake shoes.

9　After all brake shoes are adjusted lower the vehicle to the ground and test drive for proper operation.

11　Rear wheel cylinders – removal and installation

1　Raise the rear end of the vehicle and support firmly with jack stands under the axle housing.

2　Release the parking brake fully.

3　Remove the rear wheel.

10.7 One wrench is used to turn the adjuster while another wrench holds the locknut

11.7 Disconnecting the fluid pipes at the rear of the wheel cylinder

11.10 Removing the wheel cylinder

4   Remove the brake drum attaching screws and brake drum.
5   Remove the rear brake shoes as described in Section 9.
6   Have rags or newspaper ready to catch fluid which will leak from the fluid lines at the rear of the backing plate.
7   Loosen, but do not remove, the brake fluid lines where they enter the wheel cylinder at the inboard side of the backing plate (photo).
8   Remove the two wheel cylinder securing bolts from the inner side of the backing plate.
9   Now fully disconnect the two fluid pipes from the cylinder and plug the ends of the pipes to prevent dirt from entering the system and undue leakage of fluid.
10 Remove the wheel cylinder (photo).
11 To re-install, place the wheel cylinder into position on the backing plate and loosely install the two attaching bolts. Do not tighten at this time.
12 Thread the fluid pipes into the wheel cylinder until they are fingertight. Make sure that the connectors are not cross threaded in the cylinder.
13 With the fluid pipes started into the cylinder, fully tighten the two attaching bolts for the wheel cylinder.
14 Fully tighten the fluid pipe connections.
15 Installation of the brake shoes and related components are described in Section 9.
16 Install the brake drum with its two attaching bolts.
17 Install the rear wheel.
18 Bleed the brake system as outlined in Section 17.
19 Adjust the brakes as described in Section 10.
20 Lower the rear end of the car and test drive, checking for proper operation of the brakes and for leaks in the system.

12 Rear wheel cylinders – overhaul and inspection

1   Purchase a wheel cylinder kit which will contain all the parts it is necessary to replce whenever a wheel cylinder is disassembled.
2   Remove the dust boots at either end of the wheel cylinder by prying them off with your fingers.
3   Invert the wheel cylinder to each side and remove the two pistons.
4   Following the pistons from the bore of the wheel cylinder will be two piston cups, filling blocks and a spring. It may be necessary to pry these components out of the bore.
5   Remove the bleeder cap and screw from the rearside of the wheel cylinder being careful not to lose the steel check ball directly behind the bleeder screw.
6   Wash all parts in clean alcohol or brake fluid. Never use gasoline or kerosene.
7   Examine the cylinder bore and piston for wear, roughness or scoring. Replace as necessary. If damage to the cylinder bore is slight, it can be honed smooth using a honing device available at most auto supply stores.
8   Check the clearance between the piston and the cylinder bore walls. This can be done by placing the piston into the cylinder and inserting feeler gauges between the two, or by using calipers to measure the inside diameter of the cylinder and the outside diameter of the piston. The difference between these two measurements will give the clearance. The clearance limit is 0.006 in (0.15 mm). If

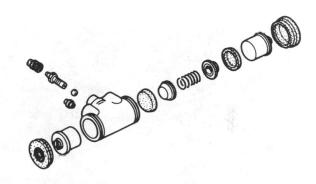
Fig. 9.4 Exploded view of a rear wheel cylinder (Sec 12)

clearance is greater than this replace the piston or cylinder as required.
9   Before reassembling the wheel cylinder components, lubricate the cylinder bore and pistons with new brake fluid.
10 Install the steel check ball, bleeder screw and cap into the cylinder.
11 Into the cylinder bore, place the spring followed by the filling blocks which should be pushed into the recessed area of the piston cups.
12 Push the lubricated pistons into the bore with the flange outward. Rotate the pistons so that the brake shoe slot on the outside is in the vertical position.
13 Push the dust boots over the end of each piston. Make sure the boots are fully seated.

13 Brake master cylinder – removal and installation

1   The master cylinder can be serviced by either installing a rebuilt unit or by overhauling the original one. This Section will describe the processes of removing the stock cylinder and replacing with a rebuilt unit. Section 14 outlines overhauling the original cylinder.
2   The master cylinder is located in the engine compartment at the front of the circular power brake assist unit.
3   Completely cover the front fenders and cowling area of the car, as brake fluid will ruin the painted surfaces of the car if spilled.
4   Disconnect the quick-disconnect coupler for the fluid level sensor. This connector is located just to the left of the master cylinder (photo).
5   Place rags or newspaper under the master cylinder to soak up excess fluid which will drain as the fluid pipes are disconnected.
6   Using a flare nut wrench, if available, disconnect the three fluid pipes leading to the master cylinder. There is one pipe at the forward

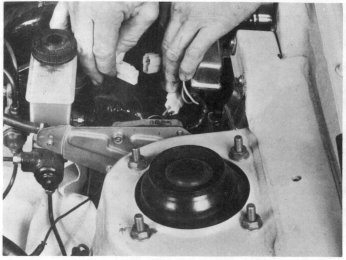

13.4 Disconnect the electrical coupler to the fluid level sensor

13.6 Disconnect each of the fluid lines leading to the master cylinder

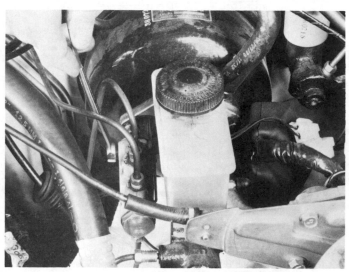

13.7 One bolt attaches the proportioning by-pass valve to the master cylinder

13.9 Removing the master cylinder

part of the cylinder, on the right side, and two pipes on the bottom side of the master cylinder. Plug the end of each fluid pipe as it is disconnected to prevent dirt from entering the system and to stop undue leakage from the pipes (photo).

7   Remove the bolt which attaches the proportioning by-pass valve to the right side of the master cylinder (photo).

8   Remove the three nuts and lockwashers securing the brake master cylinder to the power brake unit.

9   Remove the master cylinder, being careful not to drip any fluid on the painted surfaces of the car (photo).

10 To reinstall the master cylinder, place it into position against the power unit and install the three nuts with lockwashers loosely. Do not tighten at this time.

11 Thread each of the three fluid pipes into their appropriate bores in the master cylinder, moving the cylinder slightly if necessary to get the connections threaded properly. Tighten these fluid pipe connections only finger tight at this time.

12 Now fully tighten the three attaching nuts on the power brake unit.

13 Fully tighten the three fluid pipe connections.

14 Reinstall the bolt which attaches the proportioning bypass valve to the right side of the master cylinder.

15 Connect the wires to the fluid reservoir.

16 Fill the brake fluid reservoir with fluid and bleed the system as described in Section 17.

17 Road test the vehicle and check for proper operation and for leaks around the three fluid pipe connectors.

14 Brake master cylinder – overhaul

1   A master cylinder overhaul kit should be purchased before disassembling. This kit will include all parts which are necessary to replace if the cylinder is disassembled.

2   Drain all excess fluid from the master cylinder and the reservoir.

3   From the fluid reservoir, remove the fluid level sensor by pinching the tab on the right side of the reservoir and then pulling it out of the reservoir. Also remove the cap and float.

4   Remove the reservoir from the top of the master cylinder with its two bushings where it mounts to the top of the cylinder.

5   From the bottom of the master cylinder remove the joint bolt, check valve and spring. Note how the check valve is located for reassembly.

6   The remainder of the components will come out of the master cylinder bore.

7   Remove the stop ring with a screwdriver.

8   Following the stop ring out of the cylinder bore is a stop washer.

9   Invert the cylinder and remove the primary piston assembly and spring behind it.

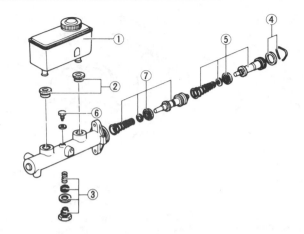

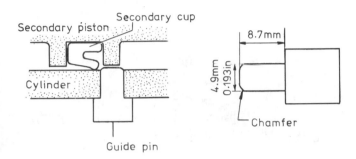

15.6 Pulling the power brake unit away from the firewall

Fig. 9.5 Exploded view of brake master cylinder with cross-section view of guide pin (Sec 14)

1 Reservoir	5 Primary piston assembly and
2 Bushings	spring
3 Joint bolt, check valve and	6 Secondary piston stop bolt
spring	and washer
4 Stop ring and stop washer	7 Secondary piston assembly
	and spring

10 To remove the secondary piston assembly, push in the secondary piston with a screwdriver and then remove the stop bolt and washer located at the top of the cylinder. Insert the guide pin (usually included with the overhaul kit) into the stop bolt hole and release the pressure forced on the secondary piston with the screwdriver. The piston assembly should then come out the end of the cylinder without damage to the piston cup. If necessary, use compressed air to force the piston assembly out of the cylinder.

11 Remove the secondary piston spring.

12 Wash all the parts in clean alcohol or brake fluid. Do not use gasoline or kerosene. Blow the parts dry with compressed air if available.

13 Examine the cylinder bore and pistons for wear, roughness or scoring. Slight imperfections in the cylinder bore can be corrected using a hone available at most auto supply stores.

14 Check the clearance between the cylinder bore and pistons. This can be done by placing the pistons, one at a time, into the bore and checking the clearance between the cylinder wall and piston with a feeler gauge. Another method is to measure the inside diameter of the cylinder and the outside diameter of the pistons with micrometers. The difference between the two measurements will give you clearance. There must be no more than 0.006 in (0.15 mm) of space between the piston and the walls of the cylinder bore.

15 Ensure that the ports are open and not clogged, which would impair the flow of fluid.

16 Wash all parts clean and free of any dirt, coat the inside of the cylinder with fresh brake fluid.

17 Dip the pistons and cups in clean brake fluid, and install the secondary and primary cups onto the pistons.

18 Fit the guide pin into the stop bolt hole and then push the spring and secondary piston assembly into the cylinder as far as they will go. Still applying pressure, remove the guide pin and install the stop bolt

and washer.

19 Install the lubricated primary piston assembly and spring into the cylinder bore.

20 Install the stop washer and stop ring.

21 Install the spring and check valve into the cylinder in their original positions. Tighten the joint bolt behind the check valve to a torque of 43 to 51 ft-lb (6.0 to 7.0 m-kg).

22 Before installing the reservoir assembly make sure that the piston cups do not cover the compensating ports.

23 Install the reservoir bushings and reservoir assembly.

15 Power brake unit – removal and installation

1 The power brake unit is located in the engine compartment on the firewall. The brake master cylinder is attached to the front of the power brake unit.

2 Remove the brake master cylinder as described in Section 13.

3 Disconnect the vacuum hose on the power brake unit by loosening the clamp and removing the hose from the metal nipple.

4 Move to the inside of the car and disconnect the push rod fork from the top of the brake pedal. You will need to remove the cotter pin and then relieve some of the pressure on the retaining pin to slide the pin out of the fork.

5 Still inside the car, remove the four nuts which secure the power brake unit to the firewall. These attaching nuts are in a square pattern, around the push rod fork previously disconnected.

6 Move back to the engine compartment and pull the power brake unit away from the firewall until the studs clear and then remove the power brake unit from the engine compartment (photo).

7 Before reinstalling the power brake unit, the push rod which fits into the master cylinder must be adjusted to arrive at a clearance of 0.004 to 0.020 in (0.1 to 0.5 mm). This can be done away from the car by putting the master cylinder up to the power brake unit and measuring the distance that the push rod enters the master cylinder bore (Fig. 9.6).

8 Apply a little silicone sealer to the firewall where the power brake unit fits against the firewall for an air-tight fit.

9 Push the unit through the firewall and move to the inside of the car and secure with the four nuts and lockwashers.

10 Align the push rod fork with the hole in the brake pedal and insert the retainer pin and split pin.

11 Connect the vacuum hose to the nipple on the shell of the unit. Tighten the hose clamp.

12 Install the brake master cylinder referring to Section 13.

13 Bleed the brake system as described in Section 17.

14 Check for proper operation of the power brake unit with the engine running.

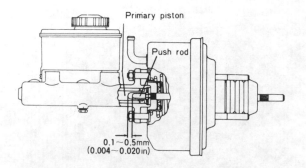

Fig. 9.6 Measuring clearance at power unit piston rod (Sec 15)

16 Power brake unit – overhaul and inspection

1   Overhauling the power brake unit is a somewhat difficult task, requiring special tools to be made or purchased. Also, replacement seals and inner components may not be readily available. Because of this, it may be advisable to merely purchase a rebuilt power brake unit and install it following the steps outlined in Section 15.
2   If it is decided to overhaul the power brake unit, first purchase an overhaul kit which will include all parts necessary if the unit is disassembled.
3   Scribe an identifying mark across the front and rear shell to enable you to reassemble the unit exactly as it was disassembled.
4   In order for the free travel of the brake pedal to be the same when the power unit is reassembled and reinstalled, measure the distance between the lock nut and the end of the fork. Then remove the lock nut and the fork end.
5   Remove the dust boot.
6   Place the power brake unit in a vise with the brake pedal push rod end up. Cushion the jaws of the vise and use the mounting flange for the master cylinder as the clamping spot.
7   The rear shell is attached to the front shell by a locking system on the outer edge of the shells themselves. To release the rear shell, it must be pushed downward and then rotated clockwise. A pair of long levers which will attach to the mounting studs are required. Loosen the shell carefully as it is spring-loaded and may come loose with considerable force.
8   Remove the spring.
9   Remove the air silencer retainer.
10 Remove the power piston, valve rod and plunger assembly from the rear shell. Note that the valve rod and plunger are serviced as an assembly only.
11 Remove the diaphragm.
12 Press in the valve rod and remove the valve retainer key.
13 Remove the valve rod and plunger assembly.
14 Remove the air silencer and filter.
15 Remove the reaction disc.
16 From the rear shell remove the serrated retainer and bearing.
17 Inspect the rear seal and if it is defective remove it as well.
18 From the front shell remove the push rod, flange, retainer, and support plate.
19 Inspect the front seal and remove only if it is in need of replacing.
20 Check the power piston for cracks, distortion, chipping and damaged seats.
21 Check the valve rod plunger to ensure that all seats are smooth and free of nicks and dents. Replace with a new one if defective.
22 Inspect the front and rear shells for scratches, scores, pits, dents or other damage.
23 Reassemble the power unit in the reverse order of disassembly, first assembling the components in the front shell and then those in the rear shell.
24 Use the new pieces which come in the overhaul kit and apply the silicone grease in the overhaul kit to the following areas:
25 Apply grease to the surfaces of the valve rod and plunger assembly.
26 Grease the whole surface of the reaction disc.
27 Grease the outer bead of the diaphragm.
28 Grease the front and rear seal lips.
29 When installing the valve retainer key, press down the valve rod

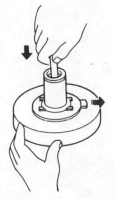

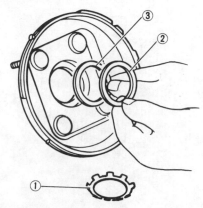

Fig. 9.7 Removing the valve retainer key (Sec 16)

Fig. 9.8 Removing the serrated retainer (1), bearing (2) and seal (3) from the rear shell (Sec 16)

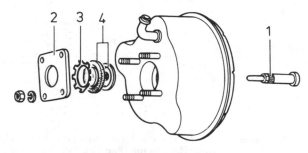

Fig. 9.9 Exploded view of front shell components (Sec 16)

| 1 | Pushrod | 3 | Retainer |
| 2 | Flange | 4 | Front seal and support plate |

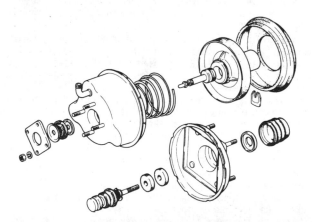

Fig. 9.10 Exploded view of power brake unit (Sec 16)

and align the groove on the valve rod with the slot of the power piston.
30 Install the rear shell assembly onto the front shell by using the long levers to push down on the shell and then rotate it counter-clockwise until your alignment marks mate.
31 Install the power brake unit as described in Section 15.

17 Bleeding the braking system

1   If the hydraulic system has air in it, operation will be spongy and imprecise. Air will get in whenever any part of the system is dismantled or if the fluid level runs low. Air can leak into the system, sometimes through a fault too slight to allow fluid to leak out. In this

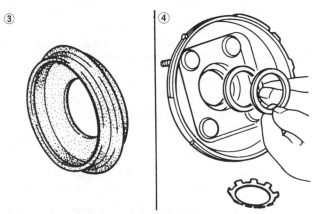

Fig. 9.11 Specific areas which require grease on reassembly (Sec 16)

1   Areas on valve rod and
    plunger
2   Reaction disc

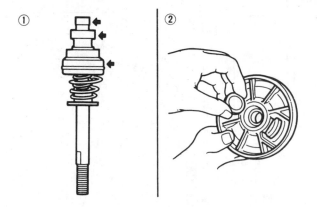

Fig. 9.12 Areas on the rear shell which receive grease on reassembly (Sec 16)

3   Outer bead of the diaphragm
4   Front and rear seal lips

Fig. 9.13 Installing the valve retainer key and aligning the groove with the power piston slot (Sec 16)

case it indicates that a general overhaul of the system is needed.

2   To bleed the brakes you will need an assistant to pump the pedal, a good supply of new brake fluid, an empty glass jar, a plastic or vinyl tube which will fit over the bleeder nipple and a wrench for the bleeder nipple.

3   There are four locations at which the braking system is bled of air; at the master cylinder, each of the front brakes and at the right rear wheel which bleeds both rear brakes.

4   The operation is the same for all four of the bleeding locations. The proper bleed sequence is the master cylinder first, the rear brakes, the right front wheel and finally the left front wheel.

5   Raise the vehicle and support with stands.

6   Remove the rubber cap from the bleeder scew and attach a vinyl or plastic tube to the bleeder screw.

7   Place the other end of the tube in a clear glass or plastic jar, submerged in a small amount of fresh brake fluid.

8   Check that the master cylinder is to the full mark before beginning and check the fluid level often during the process. The reservoir on the master cylinder must be kept at $\frac{3}{4}$ full to prevent air from entering the system through the master cylinder. Clean the cap and surrounding areas before removing to prevent dirt from entering the system (photo).

9   Loosen the bleeder screw slightly to break it loose, then tighten it to a point where it is snug but still can be loosened quickly and easily.

10 Have an assistant inside the car pump the brake pedal a few times to get pressure in the system. Then have the assistant hold the pedal firmly depressed.

11 With the brake pedal firmly depressed, open the bleeder nipple about $\frac{1}{2}$ to 1 turn and watch the flow of air or fluid through the tube and into the jar. As soon as fluid or air stops coming through the tube, shut the bleeder screw to prevent backflow. The assistant may then raise the brake pedal (photos).

12 Repeat this pumping and holding of the pedal and opening and closing the bleeder until no air comes through the tube and into the jar. Check the fluid level of the master cylinder frequently during the process.

13 Keep the hydraulic fluid away from the car's paint as it will ruin it.

14 Do not re-use any of the brake fluid as it attracts moisture which will deteriorate the brake system components.

18 Brake pedal – adjusting

1   There must be some free play between the pedal push rod and the master cylinder and servo pistons so that the master cylinder piston can return to the end of the cylinder. Unless it can do this the hydraulic

17.8 While bleeding the brakes make sure the reservoir remains at least $\frac{3}{4}$ full

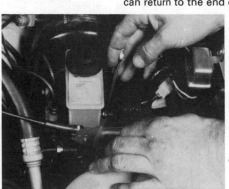

17.11a The master cylinder has a bleed screw on the left side

17.11b Open the bleed screw to allow the fluid and any air to escape the system

fluid in the pipes cannot escape back to the reservoir. Also, the reservoir cannot feed the system.

2   There are two adjustments which can be made to the brake pedal: brake pedal height and pedal free play. The height of the pedal, or the amount it is returned after depressing, should only need adjusting if the stop lamp switch is failing to make a good contact. Whenever the brake pedal height is changed the free play should also be checked and adjusted as necessary.

3   To adjust the height of the pedal, first disconnect the two wires from the stop lamp switch located at the top of the pedal arm.

4   Loosen the lock nut and turn the stop light switch until the specified pedal height is obtained. Measured at the center of the pedal foot pad this should be approximately 7.5 inches (190 mm) from the firewall.

5   Tighten the lock nut and connect the stop light wires. Check that the stop lights at the rear of the car operate properly.

6   The free play is adjusted at the fork coming out of the power brake unit and attached to the top of the brake pedal lever. Free travel should be 0.28 to 0.35 in (7 to 9 mm) from the point where the pedal is at its highest point to where the pedal just starts to operate the piston in the power brake unit.

7   Loosen the lock nut of the fork and turn the push rod coming out of the power brake unit until the proper free play is obtained.

8   Tighten the lock nut and test for proper operation.

19 Parking brake – adjusting

1   The parking brake should not need routine maintenance but after a time the cable may stretch, preventing the parking brake from functioning to its full potential.

2   Raise the rear end of the car until the rear wheels are free to turn. Then support firmly with stands.

3   Pull open the padded cover over the brake lever to gain access to the adjuster located on the right side of the lever.

4   Turn the adjusting screw until the rear brakes are locked and will not turn when the parking brake lever is pulled up 3 to 7 notches.

5   Release the parking brake lever and check that the rear wheels turn freely with no bind.

6   Lower the vehicle.

7   Adjust the parking brake warning light switch so that the light comes on with the parking brake lever pulled out 1 notch and turns off when the lever is fully released.

20 Brake fluid level sensor – removing, checking, replacing

1   The brake fluid level sensor is located on the brake master cylinder and warns the driver of low fluid level which can cause air to enter the hydraulic system.

2   To check for proper operation of the sensor, disconnect the electrical coupler located just to the left of the master cylinder.

3   To the half of the coupler coming from the master cylinder connect a circuit tester and check the continuity by moving the float inside the reservoir up and down. When the float is below the 'MIN' mark, the tester should show a continuity, while the tester should now show a continuity when the float is above the 'MIN' mark on the reservoir. If

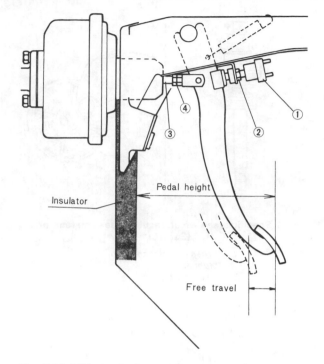

Fig. 9.14 Adjusting brake pedal height and freeplay (Sec 18)

1 Stop-light switch	3 Pushrod
2 Stop-light switch locknut	4 Pushrod locknut

this is not the case, replace the fluid level sensor (photo).

4   To remove the sensor in the fluid reservoir, simply push the flared end of the sensor to the right side of the reservoir and then pull it straight out of the reservoir from the left side (photos).

5   Push the new sensor block through the reservoir from the left side until it exits the reservoir on the right side and its flared end snaps into place.

6   Connect the electrical coupler.

21 Proportioning bypass valve – removal and installation

1   The proportioning bypass valve limits the proportion of brake effort that can be applied to the rear brakes. This is to prevent the rear brakes from locking and skidding during hard braking.

2   The bypass valve can be checked by braking hard on a dry hard road. The front wheels should lock up and skid, but not the rear ones.

3   The proportioning valve cannot be serviced or rebuilt, so must be replaced as a unit.

4   Cover the front fenders and cowling area of the vehicle to prevent brake fluid from harming the painted surfaces. Get a can or rags and

20.3 The fluid level sensor can be checked by using a circuit tester and moving the float up and down with a screwdriver

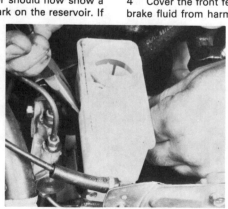

20.4a The level sensor is held in place on the right side by a flared end. Pinch the end of the sensor with pliers to remove

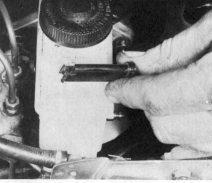

20.4b The level sensor removed from the master cylinder

newspapers ready to catch excess fluid which will come out of the pipes as they are disconnected.

5   Note the position of each fluid pipe and apply an identifying mark to them if necessary for proper re-installation.

6   Disconnect the fluid pipes from the proportioning bypass valve and plug the ends to prevent dirt from entering the system

7   Remove the bolt which secures the valve to the master cylinder mounting bracket.

8   Remove the proportioning bypass valve from the engine compartment, making sure that no fluid is dripped on painted surfaces.

9   Place the new valve into position and loosely install the mounting bolt. Do not tighten at this time.

10   Connect each of the fluid pipes to their original positions. Make sure that the connections are not cross-threaded. With the valve still loose on its bracket it can be moved slightly to make it easier to thread the pipe connections.

11   Tighten the mounting bolt securely.

12   Tighten each of the fluid pipes.

13   Bleed the brake system referring to Section 17, and check for leaks at the fluid pipes.

Chapter 10 Electrical system

Refer to Chapter 13 for specifications and information related to 1981 through 1985 models

Contents

Specifications

Battery

Type

California G60-5, Y60-5, N50-S, K60-5

Except for California:

    Manual transmission G60-5, Y60-5, N50-S, K60-5

    Automatic transmission NS70S

Capacity (20 hour rate) .... 55 amp. NS70S

     45 amp. G60-5, Y60-5, N50-S, K60-5

Voltage .... 12 volt

Terminal ground .... Negative

Specific gravity at 20°C (68°F) ....

	G60-5, Y60-5, N50-S, K60-5	**NS70S**
Fully charged	1.260	1.280
Recharged at	1.200	1.220

Alternator

Ground .... Negative

Rated output 12V 55A

Number of poles 12

No load test

    Voltage 14V

    Current .... 0 amp.

    Revolution .... Less than 1,100 rpm

Load test

    Voltage 14V

    Current .... 40 amp.

    Revolution .... Less than 2,500 rpm

Number of brushes 2

Brush length .... 18 mm (0.71 in)

    Wear limit .... 8 mm (0.31 in)

Brush spring pressure .... 370 gr (13 oz) ± 15%

Pulley ratio of eccentric shaft and alternator .... 1 : 1.82

Regulator

Constant voltage relay	
Air gap	0.7 to 1.3 mm (0.028 to 0.051 in)
Point gap	0.3 to 0.45 mm (0.012 to 0.018 in)
Back gap	0.7 to 1.5 mm (0.028 to 0.059 in)
Regulated voltage without load at 4,000 rpm of alternator	14.5 ± 0.5V
Pilot lamp relay	
Air gap	0.9 to 1.4 mm (0.035 to 0.055 in)
Point gap	0.7 to 1.1 mm (0.028 to 0.043 in)
Back gap	0.7 to 1.5 mm (0.028 to 0.059 in)
Pilot lamp light on	0.5 to 3.0V
Pilot lamp light out	4.5 to 5.5V

Starting motor

	Manual transmission	Automatic transmission
Capacity	1.2KW	2.0KW
Lock test		
Voltage	5.0 volt	5.0 volt
Current	Less than 600 amp	Less than 1,050 amp.
Torque	0.96 m-kg (6.9 ft-lb)	2.2 m-kg (15.9 ft-lb)
Free running test		
Voltage	11.5 volt	11.5 volt
Current	Less than 50 amp.	Less than 100 amp.
Speed	More than 5,600 rpm	More than 6,600 rpm
Number of brushes	4	4
Brush length	18.5 mm (0.73 in)	18.5 mm (0.73 in)
Wear limit	11.5 mm (0.45 in)	11.5 mm (0.45 in)
Brush spring pressure	1.4 to 1.8 kg (49 to 63 oz)	1.4 to 1.8 kg (49 to 63 oz)
Control switch	Solenoid	Solenoid
Voltage required to close solenoid contacts	Less than 8 volt	Less than 8 volt
Undercutting mica	0.5 to 0.8 mm (0.020 to 0.031 in)	0.5 to 0.8 mm (0.020 to 0.031 in)
	Less than 0.2 mm (0.008 in)	Less than 0.2 mm (0.008 in)
Clearance between armature shaft and bush	0.1 to 0.4 mm (0.004 to 0.016 in)	0.1 to 0.4 mm (0.004 to 0.016 in)
Armature shaft end play	0.5 to 2.0 mm (0.020 to 0.079 in)	0.5 to 2.0 mm (0.020 to 0.079 in)
Clearance between pinion and stop collar		

Bulb specifications (Wattage : W) 12V

Headlight	50/40
Front parking and turn signal light	27/8
Side marker light	3.8
Interior light	10
Glovebox light	3.4
Instrument panel illumination light	3.4
Warning light on instrument panel	1.4, 3.4
Map light	27
Rear turn signal light	27
Tail and stop light	27/8
Back-up light	27
License plate light	8

1 General description

1 The electrical system is 12 volt, negative ground. The charging is by an alternator, and the starter is of the pre-engaged type.
2 The emission control system incorporates many electric sensing and solenoid operations which are dealt with in Chapter 3.

2 Battery – checking

1 A relatively high amperage battery is fitted to the RX-7. This is because Wankel engines can call for much cranking to start, there being a lot of initial friction from the seals. Then the engine may not fire for some time because compression is poor until the engine is running, as there is no gas pressure behind the apex seals.
2 There are certain precautions which should be followed when checking or servicing the battery. Hydrogen, which is a highly combustible gas, is always present in the cells. Due to this, keep lighted tobacco or any other open flame away from the battery. The electrolyte fluid inside the battery case is actually sulfuric acid which can be hazardous to your skin or cause damage if splashed in the eyes. It will also ruin clothes or painted surfaces.

3 To check the electrolyte level in the battery, first remove all vent caps. If low, add distilled water as required to keep the level approximately 0.4 to 0.8 in (10 to 21 mm) over the cell plates. There is an upper level line marked on the battery to help judge this distance. Do not overfill.
4 Periodically check the specific gravity of the electrolyte with a hydrometer (Fig. 10.1). This is especially important during cold weather. If the reading is below the specification, the battery requires recharging.
5 Check the tightness of the battery terminals to ensure good electrical connections. The terminals can be cleaned with a stiff wire brush. Corrosion can be kept to a minimum by applying petroleum jelly or terminal grease to the terminal and cable connectors.
6 Inspect the cables for corrosion, cracking, or frayed wires. Check the cables their entire length.
7 Check that the rubber protector over the positive terminal is not ripped or missing. It should completely cover the terminal on the top of the battery.
8 Check that the battery is securely mounted (photo).
9 If the vehicle is not being used for an extended time, disconnect the cables and have the battery charged about every six weeks.
10 The battery case and caps should be clean and dry. There should be no evidence of corrosion. Refer to Section 4 for cleaning the battery.

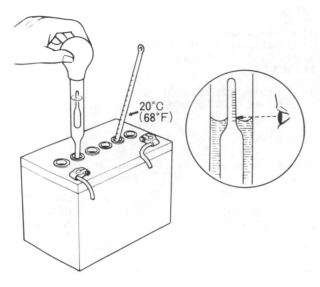

Fig. 10.1 Using a hydrometer to check the specific gravity of the electrolyte (Sec 2)

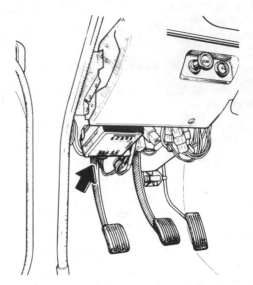

Fig. 10.2 Location of fuse box (Sec 5)

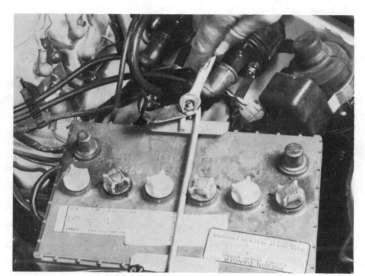

2.8 Periodically check that the battery hold-down strap is tight

3 Battery charging

1   If the car is used frequently, on relatively long journeys, the alternator will keep the battery fully charged.
2   Batteries, after a time, will not hold a full charge.
3   Short, around town journeys will not fully charge the battery due to extended periods of time with the engine idling.
4   If the battery is not fully charged, its plates will deteriorate more quickly, leading to battery failure.
5   When necessary, an outside battery charger with a rate not exceeding $3\frac{1}{2}$ amps should be used to charge the battery. A so-called 'boost charge', which takes only about 1 to 2 hours, will shorten the life of the battery.
6   Always disconnect the battery cables and vent caps when charging. Again, do not allow lighted cigarettes or open flames around the battery during charging.

4 Battery leaks and corrosion

1   If the battery develops a leak, remove it immediately before the acid can do further damage.

2   If the casing is cracked, take it to an expert for repair, or replace the battery with a new one.
3   Leakage on the battery hold-down components or inner fender panels should be washed thoroughly with clear water and baking soda.
4   Corrosion on the battery case and terminals can be cleaned with a solution of water and baking soda, using a stiff wire brush. Be careful that none of the solution is splashed into your eyes or onto your skin. Wear protective gloves.
5   Metal parts of the car which have come into contact with spilled battery fluid should be painted with a zinc based rust preventer and normal paint. Do this only after the area has been thoroughly cleaned and dried.

5 Fuses

1   The fuse box is location just under the lower lip of the dashboard. It is covered by a plastic lid and is easily accessible without removing additional components.
2   If an electrical accessory fails to operate properly, your first check should be at the fuse box. A blown fuse can be readily identified by the thin wire inside the glass fuse being broken or burnt. Replace the fuse only with one of the specified amperage. Do not be tempted to replace the fuse with one of a higher rating, as extensive damage to the electrical system – or even fire – can result. If a fuse blows consistently, this indicates a further problem in the system which should be traced and rectified as soon as possible.
3   Do not use a screwdriver or any other metal object to remove fuses, as an electrical short may occur and damage the system. Plastic fuse pullers are commonly available for this purpose. Also, do not install a wire, foil or any other object than the correct fuse, even for a temporary repair.
4   In addition to the main fuse box there are fusible links built into the system. The fusible links protect the ignition coils, starter, sub-zero assist motor, hot start assist motor and headlight switch and motors. The fusible links act much like the common fuses in protecting the circuit. However, the fusible links will allow an initial peak power load (as when the headlight motors are first activated) while still protecting the accessory once the peak has subsided. If one of the components covered by a fusible link fails, first check all the fuses in the fuse box, then use an ohmmeter to check for continuity at the appropriate fusible link. A fusible link will not ordinarily fail, but when it does the entire link must be replaced as a unit.

6 Alternator – general description and precautions

1   The alternator develops its current in the stationary windings and the rotor carries the field. The brushes, therefore, carry only a small

FUSE BLOCK

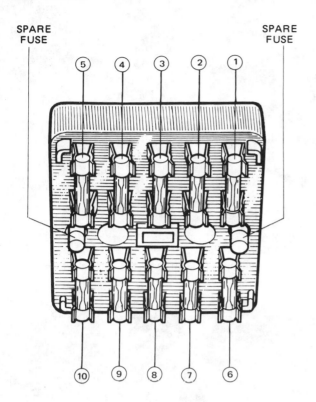

SPARE FUSE

SPARE FUSE

FUSE BLOCK		
①	10A	Hazard warning lights
②	10A	Illumination, tail, side marker & license lights
③	15A	Cigar lighter, interior light, 1g. key reminder buzzer & glass hatch release
④	15A	Horn & stop lights
⑤	20A	Rear window defroster & air conditioner (comp.)
⑥	10A	Wiper & screen washer
⑦	20A	Heater, stereo & radio
⑧	10A	Meter, back-up light, seat belt warn, turn signal & defroster light
⑨	15A	Kick-down & regulator
⑩	20A	Ignition, emission & fuel pump

Fig. 10.3 Electrical fuses and corresponding functions (Sec 5)

Fig. 10.4 Location of fusible links in steering column (b) and on front shock absorber tower (c)

current and should last a long time.

2   The most important adjustment and inspection process involving the alternator is the drve belt. It should be checked for proper tension and inspected for wear or damage at regular intervals. Further information on the drive belt can be found in the Routine Maintenance Section at the front of this book.

3   When servicing the charging system do not short across or ground any of the terminals on the alternator.

4   Never reverse the battery cables, even for an instant, as the reverse polarity current flow will damage the diodes of the alternator.

5   To prevent damage to the diodes, the alternator loads should be disconnected whenever electric welding is being carried out on the car.

6   Fault-finding is more a matter of confirming the fault is in the alternator than correcting the problem with replacement components. Overhaul of the alternator requires experience with a soldering iron and the need for replacement parts which are sometimes difficult to obtain. Due to this, it may be in the best interest of the home mechanic to replace the entire alternator with a new or rebuilt unit.

7   Alternator – testing on car (1979 models with external regulator)

1   If the charging system is not charging properly, indicated by the alternator warning light staying on or the battery continually being discharged, it is advisable to determine whether the trouble is in the alternator or regulator.

2   The alternator can be initially tested on the car, as it will need to be run up to speed by the engine. Later models with an integral regulator need special equipment for testing.

3   Disconnect the wire from the 'B' terminal at the rear of the alternator and connect an ammeter between the alternator terminal and the wire.

4   Disconnect the electrical coupler from the regulator and run jumper wires between the male and female spades as shown in Fig. 10.5.

5   Start the engine and take a reading of the ammeter while holding the engine speed at 2000 rpm.

6   Disconnect the wire from the 'F' terminal of the coupler and short-circuit the wire to the 'A' terminal for a moment. If the meter reading increases significantly, the trouble is in the regulator and if there is no change in the current, it is in the alternator.

8   Alternator – removal and installation

1   Disconnect the negative battery cable at the battery.

2   Remove the air cleaner assembly with its various hoses. See Chapter 3 for the proper positioning of the hoses.

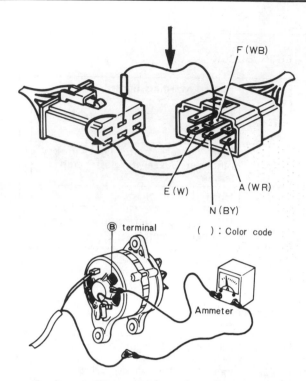

8.3 Disconnecting the single wire from terminal 'B' of the alternator

Fig. 10.5 Testing alternator on car (1979 models with external voltage regulator) (Sec 7)

3   Disconnect the wire from the wiring harness which leads to the terminal on the rear of the alternator marked 'B'. To do this, slide back the rubber protective boot and hold the wire as the nut and lockwasher are removed (photo).
4   Pull the multiple connector out from the rear of the alternator (photo).
5   Remove the main engine wiring harness from its clips at the alternator pivot bolt and air cleaner mounting bracket. Move the wiring harness aside.
6   Loosen the alternator strap bolt which fits through the adjusting bracket. Loosen the long pivot bolt by holding the nut on the rear side of the bolt. Push the alternator through the adjusting bracket to relieve tension on the drive belt. Slip the drive belt off the alternator pulley (photo).
7   Completely remove the adjusting bolt and long pivot bolt. Note that there is a spacer and adjusting shim used with the pivot bolt. Take note of their positions for reassembly.
8   The alternator can now be lifted off the engine (photo).
9   To install, place the alternator in position and install the long pivot bolt through the mounting flanges of the alternator and through the mounting bracket of the water housing. Be sure the metal spacer is installed.
10 Before tightening the pivot bolt, or installing the small adjustment strap bolt, measure the clearance between the alternator and bracket. If this distance is more than 0.0059 in (0.15 mm), install adjusting shims as necessary. This is to prevent the pivot bolt from pinching the mounting flanges of the alternator, thus affecting its operation.
11 Tighten the pivot bolt and adjusting strap bolt only finger-tight, allowing the alternator to be moved freely to adjust the belt tension.
12 Pull the drive belt over the alternator pulley and force the alternator against the drive belt until the tension of the belt is approximately 0.59 in (16 mm) when pressed with a finger half-way between the alternator pulley and eccentric shaft pulley.
13 Tighten the adjusting bolt and pivot bolt with the nut.
14 Place the wiring harness back into position in its retaining clips and check that none of the couplers or connections, other than the alternator ones, have been accidentally disconnected.
15 Plug the multiple connector back into the alternator. It will only go in one way.
16 Connect the wire to the 'B' terminal on the rear of the alternator. Tighten the nut with the lockwasher and then cover the connection

8.4 Removing the multiple connector at the rear of the alternator

8.6 Removing the long pivot bolt at the front of the alternator

8.8 Lifting the alternator off the engine

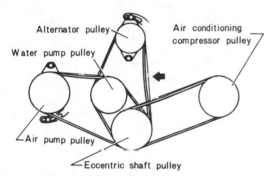

Fig. 10.6 Pressure point for checking alternator drive belt
deflection (Sec 8)

with the rubber boot.

17 Install the air cleaner assembly.

18 Connect the negative battery cable. Start the engine and check for proper operation.

9 Alternator – overhaul and testing

1 As previously mentioned, it may be advisable to simply replace the alternator with a new or rebuilt one should a failure occur. The alternator, however, can be disassembled and rebuilt if replacement parts are available.

2 Read through the entire overhaul process in this Section to ascertain the tools required and the parts which will probably need replacing. It should be noted that the 1980 models feature a built-in voltage regulator. Overhaul, however, follows the same basic principles.

3 Remove the radio noise suppression condensor from the outside of the alternator.

4 Remove the through bolts which hold the sections of the alternator together.

5 Separate the front housing assembly by prying it apart with a screwdriver at the slots provided for this on the front housing.

6 Remove the lock nut and insulator from the 'B' terminal at the rear side of the alternator.

7 Place the front housing and rotor assembly in a vise and remove the nut and washer. Cushion the jaws of the vise with blocks of wood to prevent damaging the housing.

8 Remove the pulley, fan, spacer and front slinger from the shaft. Make a note of their relative positions on the shaft.

9 The front housing and rear slinger can now be removed.

10 Inside the rear housing, in alignment with the mounting flange is a Phillips head screw which attaches the rectifier to the rear housing. Remove it.

11 Also inside the rear housing, remove the two screws which secure the brush holder.

12 With these three screws removed from the inside of the rear housing, the stator, rectifier and brush holder can be carefully lifted free as an assembly.

13 With a hot soldering iron, unsolder the stator leads from the rectifier and brush holder. This must be done quickly (less than twenty seconds) as the excessive heat may damage the rectifier.

14 Remove the rectifier and brush holder assembly from the stator.

15 If the bearings on the rotor shaft feel dry or rough, they should be replaced. The rear bearing is removed with a common bearing puller. To replace the front bearing, remove the bearing retainer and then press out the bearing from the front housing with a press.

16 There are two checks for the stator. To test for ground, hook up an ohmmeter and check for continuity between the stator core and each stator coil lead. If there is continuity, replace the stator. To check for open-circuit, check the continuity between the stator coil leads with an ohmmeter. If there is no continuity, replace the stator.

17 The rotor is also checked for ground and open-circuit. With an ohmmeter, check for lack of continuity between the rotor and each of the three slip rings on the shaft. If there is continuity, replace the rotor. Check the continuity between the slip rings with an ohmmeter. If the reading is within 5 to 6 ohms, the rotor is all right.

18 The rectifier has a positive and a negative side to it. Each side is checked separately. The negative side of the rectifier is the side with the wire leads.

19 For the positive side, connect an ohmmeter positive lead to the rectifier holder, and the minus lead to the rectifier terminal. If there is no continuity, replace the rectifier assembly. Reverse the polarity of the leads and check again. If there is continuity, replace the rectifier assembly.

20 The negative side is basically the same. The ohmmeter plug lead is connected to the rectifier terminal and the minus lead to the holder. Lack of continuity requires replacement. With the leads reversed, continuity again indicates replacement is necessary.

21 The brushes should be replaced when one-third of the original length is worn away. This is indicated by a wear limit line on the side face of each brush.

22 Before reassembling, all parts should be cleaned; however, they should not be dipped in any liquid.

23 If the bearings are in need of replacement, they should be pressed into position on the shaft and into the front housing. The bearings are pre-lubed and sealed at the factory.

24 Install the brush holder and rectifier assemblies in the stator and solder the leads into position. The soldering operation must take less than twenty seconds to prevent damage to the rectifier.

25 Carefully install the brush holder assembly, rectifier and stator into the rear housing. Install and tighten each of the attaching screws.

26 When installing the rotor assembly to the rear housing and stator assembly, hold the brushes in position by inserting a piece of stiff wire into the hole of the brush through the rear housing.

27 Install the front housing and rear slinger.

28 Install the front slinger, spacer, fan and pulley to the shaft.

29 Install the washer and nut and tighten the nut securely.

30 Install the insulator and nut to the 'B' terminal at the rear of the alternator.

31 Press the front housing into position and secure with the through bolts.

32 Refit the radio suppression condensor and install the alternator, referring to Section 8.

10 Voltage regulator – testing and adjustment (1979 models)

1 The voltage regulator is located on the inner fender panel, on the left side of the engine compartment, it is a controlling device incorporated to monitor the current and voltage output of the alternator in relation to battery condition and electrical load being drawn (photo).

2 The correct function of the regulator is shown by the use of an ammeter. Whenever the battery is less than fully charged, the charging rate shown on the ammeter is relatively high – extremely so immediately after starting up. As the battery becomes fully charged, the rate drops back to a trickle. If an electric charge is drawn, such as turning on the headlights, the regulator responds and keeps the battery charge much as it was before.

3 If the voltage regulator is not functioning properly and limiting

10.1 The voltage regulator is located on the left fender panel and is easily removed by disconnecting the couplers and removing the two attaching screws

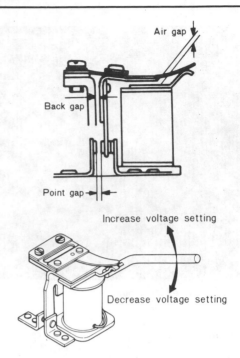

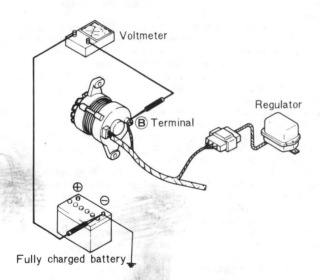

Fig. 10.7 Using a voltmeter to check the constant voltage relay (Sec 10)

	Constant voltage relay	Pilot lamp relay
Air gap	0.7 ~ 1.3 mm (0.028 ~ 0.051 in)	0.9 ~ 1.4 mm (0.035 ~ 0.055 in)
Point gap	0.3 ~ 0.45 mm (0.012 ~ 0.018 in)	0.7 ~ 1.1 mm (0.028 ~ 0.043 in)
Back gap	0.7 ~ 1.5 mm (0.028 ~ 0.059 in)	

Fig. 10.8 Checking various gaps of voltage regulator (Sec 10)

11 Starter motor – removal and installation

1   Disconnect the negative battery cable at the battery.
2   Raise the vehicle and support firmly with jack stands to gain access to the starter.
3   The starter motor is located on the left side of the engine, just above the oil pan (photo).

voltage too much, the battery will be kept just off full charge and will deteriorate. If the setting is too high, on long journeys the battery will be overcharged. In the short run this means frequent adding of water to the battery and, in the long run, this will eventually wear out the battery.
4   A voltmeter will be necessary to check the constant voltage relay. Connect a voltmeter between the fully charged battery (negative side) and the 'B' terminal at the rear of the alternator. Start the engine and allow the regulator to warm up to normal operating temperature (about ten minutes of running). With the engine speed set at 2000 rpm, the voltmeter reading should be 14 to 15 volts. If not, adjust the regulator.
5   Adjusting the regulator is a delicate process of adjusting three gaps by bending internal components. Depending on price and availability, it may be wise to simply replace the regulator with a new one if a fault is found.
6   Use Fig. 10.8 to check the air gap, back gap and point gap using a wire gauge. If they are not within specifications, adjust by holding the stationary contact bracket until the proper gap is achieved. After the correct gaps are obtained, adjust the voltage by bending the adjusting arm. The voltmeter is used to monitor this procedure.

11.3 The starter is located on the left side of the engine, with its wiring covered with rubber caps .

4   Disconnect the battery cable at the 'B' terminal of the solenoid. This is the large cable held in place with a lock nut.
5   Adjacent to the battery cable is an ignition wire leading to the solenoid terminal marked 'S'. This is also held in place with a lock nut.
6   On vehicles equipped with manual transmissions, remve the two attaching bolts. One long bolt runs through the engine, transmission bellhousing and into the starter flange. The other bolt is smaller and goes through the flange and into the bellhousing.
7   Remove the starter by pulling it straight out of the transmission.
8   If equipped with an automatic transmission, remove the starter bracket by removing the three attaching bolts and then remove the two attaching bolts and finally the starter.
9   To install, lift the starter into position and secure with the two attaching bolts. The small bolt will be towards the bottom of the starter, the longer bolt at the top of the starter.
10 On cars with automatic transmission, install the bracket and its three bolts.
11 Connect the ignition switch wire to the 'S' terminal on the solenoid.
12 Clean the end of the cable leading from the battery and connect it to the 'B' terminal on the solenoid. Tighten the lock nut securely.
13 Lower the vehicle to the ground and connect the negative battery cable at the battery.

12 Starter motor – overhaul

1   As with the alternator, the starter can either be disassembled and overhauled, or the unit can be simply replaced with a new or rebuilt one. Prices and parts availability can be your guides in deciding which course of action is taken.
2   Disconnect the field strap and remove the solenoid (magnetic switch) from the body of the starter.
3   Remove the spring, plunger and washer from the nose of the solenoid.
4   The rear cover is removed by taking out the through-bolts and the two screws securing the brush holder.
5   With the rear cover off, remove the insulator and washers from the rear end of the armature shaft.
6   The yoke and brush holder assembly can then be separated from the forward driving housing.
7   Remaining inside the driving housing is the armature, driving lever and over-running clutch assembly. These components can be lifted free of the front driving housing.
8   Place the armature assembly in a vise, using wood blocks on the vise jaws to prevent damage to the armature.
9   The stop ring at the end of the shaft must be removed. It may be necessary first to drive the pinion stop collar towards the armature for clearance.
10 With the stop ring removed, the stop collar and over-running clutch can be slid off the armature shaft.
11 To check the armature, use an ohmmeter to check the continuity between the armature coil core and each commutator. The commutators are located at the rear position of the armature, around the shaft. If there is continuity at any of the commutators, replace the armature with a new one.
12 Check the continuity between the commutators with an ohmmeter. If there is no continuity at any test point, replace the armature with a new one.
13 If the commutator is dirty, discolored or worn, clean it with emery paper. Undercut the mica between the commutators to the depth of 0.020 to 0.031 in (0.5 to 0.8 mm) as shown in Fig. 10.9.
14 The middle portion of the starter housing is the yoke. Attached to the yoke is the field terminal. Check the continuity between the yoke and terminal and if any exists, replace the field coil and yoke assembly with a new one.
15 Check the continuity between the field terminal and each field coil brush with an ohmmeter. If there is no continuity, replace the field coil and yoke assembly.
16 Check the continuity between each brush holder and brush holder frame. If there is any continuity, replace the brush holder assembly.
17 Check the brushes and replace if they are worn down more than one-third of their original length. To replace the brush, remove the brush from its holder and then smash the old brush with a small hammer or pliers. Clean the brush lead and insert the lead to the small chamfer side of the new brush. Solder the lead and brush together,

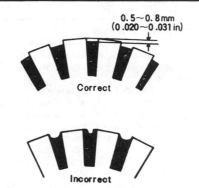

Fig. 10.9 Undercutting the mica between commutators of starter motor (Sec 12)

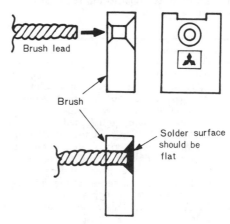

Fig. 10.10 Soldering new brushes in place (Sec 12)

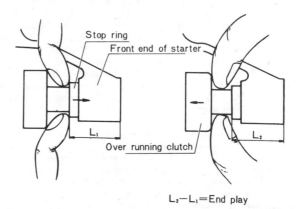

$L_2 - L_1 = $ End play

Fig. 10.11 Checking endplay of armature shaft (Sec 12)

using rosin core solder.
18 Check the clearance between the armature shaft and front and rear bushings. The clearance limit is 0.008 in (0.2 mm). If the clearance exceeds the limit, replace the bushings.
18 Assemble the starter motor in the reverse order of disassembly. Once assembled there are two clearance checks to be made and adjusted if necessary.
20 The end play of the armature shaft could be 0.004 to 0.016 in (0.1 to 0.4 mm). This is measured just before the armature assembly is installed into the driving housing. A thrust washer installed on the rear end of the shaft can be used to adjust this play.
21 When the solenoid is engaged the clearance between the pinion and stop collar should be 0.02 to 0.08 in (0.5 to 2.0 mm) measured through the cutout portion of the driving housing. This clearance is adjusted by inserting an adjusting washer between the solenoid body and the driving housing to space the solenoid away from the starter motor body.

13 Solenoid – testing and overhaul

1   There are three tests which can be carried out on the solenoid (magnetic switch). Each test is performed on the bench, with a fully-charged 12 volt battery.

2   To test the pull-in coil, apply 12 volts between the 'S' terminal and the 'M' terminal on the solenoid. This is done with jumper wires connected directly to the battery; the plus side to the 'M' terminal, negative to the 'S' terminal. If the magnetic switch is forcefully attracted, the pull-in switch is in good condition.

3   The holding coil is tested by grounding the 'M' terminal to the solenoid body with a lead and then attaching a jumper wire from the positive battery to the 'S' terminal of the solenoid. This should pull in the plunger. If the plunger remains attracted after disconnecting the 'M' terminal lead, the holding coil is all right.

4   To test for return, push in the plunger by hand and apply a jumper from the negative battery terminal to the 'M' terminal and a jumper from the positive battery terminal to the solenoid body. The plunger should not be attracted.

14 Headlights – adjusting

1   The proper way to adjust the headlights' beam is to take the vehicle to a Mazda dealer or reputable repair shop which has the delicate equipment necessary for the job. A professional can adjust the headlights to meet local or country-wide regulations.

2   The headlights can, however, be adjusted at home sufficiently to get you to a proper repair shop to have the job done professionally.

3   There are two adjustment screws on the headlight assembly. Facing the headlight, one is on a horizontal plane directly through the center of the light, towards the center of the car. The other is on a vertical plane directly through the center of the light, at the bottom.

4   The horizontal (side-to-side) adjustment is made by tightening or loosening the adjustment screw located along the edge of the light, towards the middle of the car. It is spring-loaded, meaning that tightening the screw will draw the illumination towards the center of the car and loosening will aim the lights more to the outside of the car (photo).

5   The vertical (up-and-down) adjustment is made in the same manner using the spring-loaded adjustment screw at the bottom of the headlight. Tightening the screw will pull the illumination towards the ground, loosening will raise the light beam.

6   As mentioned previously, adjusting the headlights yourself calls for patience and trial-and-error. The headlights can be aimed against a large surface, like a garage door or the side of a house or adjusted on a dark, seldom-used road.

15 Headlights – manual operation

1   Should the retractor not operate automatically after the retractor switch on the dashboard is pressed, the headlights can be operated manually from inside the engine compartment.

2   Disconnect the negative cable on the battery.

3   Pull apart the two quick-connect electrical couplers adjacent to the headlight motors at the front of the engine compartment. On each motor there is a three-pin connector and a one-pin connector.

4   Pry back the rubber cover on the top of the motor and turn the manual control knob on the retractor shaft until the headlight is fully raised or lowered (photo).

5   Connect the negative battery cable to the battery terminal.

6   Test the headlights for illumination by operating their control on the inside of the vehicle.

7   Leave the wiring couplers disconnected and the headlights in the 'up' position until the problem can be traced and rectified.

16 Headlights – removal and installation

1   Turn on the headlight retractor switch to raise the headlight in position.

2   As long as the two adjustment screws are not altered, the aim of the headlights should not change by merely replacing the headlight unit. See Section 14 for the location of these two adjustment screws

which should not be touched during the headlight replacement procedure.

3   Disconnect the negative battery cable from the battery.

4   Remove the six screws retaining the headlight bezel which wraps around the headlight (photos).

5   Loosen, but do not remove, the headlight retaining ring screws. Hold the front of the headlight to keep it from turning, while the retaining ring is rotated counterclockwise until it is free of the loosened screws (photos).

6   Pull out the headlight slightly and disconnect the electrical connector at the rear of the headlight (photo).

7   Remove the headlight.

8   Place the new headlight into position close to the mounting ring and plug in the electrical connector. Make sure it is fully seated against the light.

9   Push the headlight into the mounting ring making sure that the raised lugs on the light fit into the headlight and rotate it into position so that it fits over the loosened retaining screws.

10 Push the retaining ring over the headlight and rotate it into position so that it fits over the loosened retaining screws.

11 Tighten the retaining ring screws securely.

12 Install the headlight bezel around the headlight and tighten the six attaching screws.

13 Connect the negative battery cable and test the headlights for proper operation.

14 Check that the headlight aim has not been altered. Adjust as necessary referring to Section 14.

17 Headlight retractor assembly – removal and installation

1   Remove the headlight referring to Section 16.

2   Four screws hold the headlight lid in place. These are on tangs, with the screws going into the headlight mounting ring. Before removing these screws use a scribe or pen to mark around their locations for reassembly into the original position. Remove the screws and the headlight lid (photo).

3   Near the top of the headlight mounting ring is a spring. Disconnect this spring and then pull the mounting ring off the adjusting screws (photo).

4   Using a screwdriver disconnect the spring which runs from the body to the headlight ball pivot (photo).

5   Disconnect the link from the hinge assembly. This is located under the headlight assembly.

6   Remove the wires from their securing clips and lay the wires aside, out of the way.

7   Remove the hinge mounting nut and take out the hinge assembly. This nut is at the rear of the mounting ring assembly (photo).

8   To re-install, place the assembly into position and secure with the lock nut.

9   Place the wiring back into the securing clips.

10 Connect the link to the hinge assembly by pressing with your fingers until an audible click is heard. A small amount of multi-purpose grease should be applied to the pivot.

11 Connect the spring from the hinge to the body mounting point.

12 Install the headlight mounting ring and connect the spring at the top of the ring.

13 Install the headlight lid using the four screws and align the lid with the marks made upon disassembly.

14 Install the headlight referring to Section 16.

15 Connect the battery and check for proper operation of the mechanism. Adjust the headlight aim and headlight lid, referring to Sections 14 and 19.

18 Headlight retractor motors – removal and installation

1   Open the hood and raise the headlight to the 'up' position.

2   Disconnect the negative battery cable.

3   Remove the six screws securing the headlight bezel which wraps around the headlight. Remove the bezel.

4   Disconnect the electrical couplers leading to the headlight retractor motor.

5   Under the headlights, disconnect the link from the hinge assembly at its ball pivot location. The link is merely pried off the ball pivot.

6   Remove the four bolts which secure the motor assembly to the

14.4 Position of one of the spring-loaded headlight adjusting screws

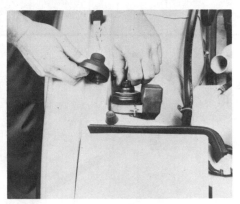

15.4 Raising the headlights manually

16.4a Six screws secure the headlight bezel

16.4b With the screws removed, the bezel can be lifted away from the headlight assembly

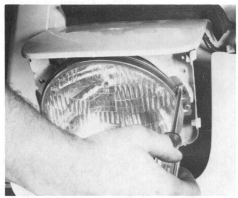

16.5a Loosening one of the retaining ring screws

16.5b The retaining ring should be rotated counterclockwise and then removed

16.6 Pull the headlight out slightly and disconnect the electrical connector at the rear

17.2 The headlight lid is held in place with four screws

17.3 Disconnecting the spring from the mounting ring

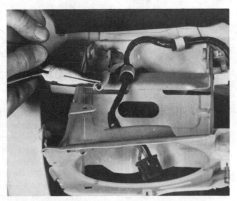

17.4 Disconnecting the spring from the ball pivot

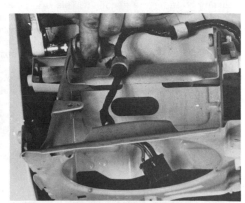

17.7 Removing the hinge mounting nut

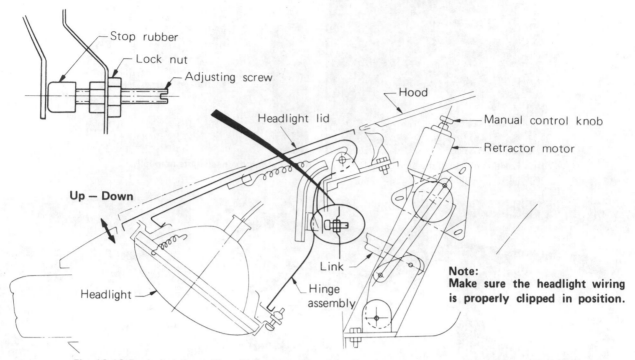

Fig. 10.12 Exploded view of headlight assembly with adjusting mechanism for headlight lid (Sec 19)

inner fender panel and remove the motor with the linkage as a unit.

7   If necessary, remove the linkage assembly from the motor.

8   To re-install, place the motor and linkage into position and loosely install the four securing bolts to the fender panel.

9   Connect a link which runs up the hinge assembly ball pivot. Apply a little multi-purpose grease to the pivot first.

10   Tighten the four attaching bolts securely.

11   Connect the electrical couplers.

12   Install the headlight bezel with the six screws.

13   Connect a negative battery cable and test the operation of the motor.

14   Adjust the headlight lid as detailed in Section 19.

19 Headlight lid – adjustment

1   The up-and-down adjustment of the headlight lid may be necessary whenever the headlight components are disassembled or replaced. This adjustment determines how far the headlight assembly is raised and lowered into the body.

2   Open the hood and raise the headlights to the 'up' position.

3   Disconnect the negative battery cable.

4   Disconnect the link which runs from the motor to the hinge assembly under the headlight. This is a 'pinch' connection over a ball pivot. Hold the front of the lid, then lower the lid.

5   Loosen the lock nut of the adjusting screw located inside the engine compartment. Turn the adjusting screw in or out to properly position the headlight lid. Tighten the lock nut after the lid is properly positioned.

6   Turn the manual control knob on the top of the motor (under the rubber cover) until the motor link comes to the lowest position, which is the automatic stop.

7   Loosen the retractor motor mounting bolts on the inner fender panel.

8   Connect the link to the hinge assembly ball pivot by pressing it into position with your fingers.

9   Move the motor forward or rearward until the desired position is obtained. Then tighten the mounting bolts.

20 Windshield wiper blade – replacement

1   After a time the rubber portion of the windshield wiper will need replacement due to wear and deterioration. Replacement blades, or 'refills' as they are commonly called, are easy to install. The rubber blades should be inspected periodically and not allowed to wear excessively as damage to the glass windshield may result.

2   Pivot the arm away from the windshield glass.

3   To remove the old rubber portion, pinch the tangs located on one end of the blade. Use your fingers for this, not pliers. This will release the securing mechanism and allow the rubber to be slid off the arm. Keep the tangs pinched closed while the rubber is removed.

4   Take the old rubber blade with you to an auto parts store, Mazda dealer or service station to match it with a new refill.

5   Pinch the tangs and slide the new blade onto the arm. After it is centered on the arm, release the tangs.

6   Pivot the windshield arm back into position against the windshield glass.

21 Windshield wiper motor – removal and installation

1   The motor which controls both windshield wipers is located under the metal cowling at the base of the windshield.

2   Loosen, but do not remove, the negative battery cable at the battery.

3   Have an assistant operate the windshield wiper control from inside the car, and then remove the negative battery cable when the wiper blades are in the straight up position.

4   Place some rags or a cover of some sort between the wiper blades and the glass windshield to prevent any accidental damage to the glass.

5   Pull back the protective cover where the wiper arms meet the body cowling.

6   Remove the lock nut, cup washer and outer bushing from each of the wiper arms (photo).

7   Before removing the wiper arms from their respective shafts, note and mark their locations for reassembly. This can be done by using tape on the windshield along the edge of the arms where they contact the glass.

8   Pull the wiper arm assemblies off the shafts and remove the shaft lock nut (photo).

9   Remove the four screws retaining the cowl plate to the body. Lift the cowl slightly and disconnect the washer hose at the washer nozzle on the cowl. Remove the cowl plate (photos).

10   Disconnect the two wiring couplers at the wiper motor.

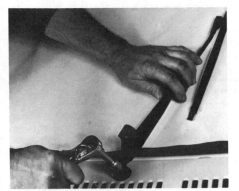

21.6 Pry back the protective cover and remove the locknut, cup washer and outer bushing

21.8 Removing the shaft locknut

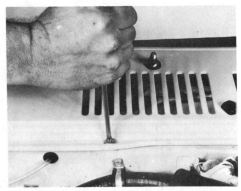

21.9a Removing one of the four cowl plate retaining screws

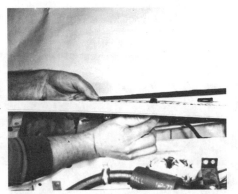

21.9b Lift the cowl plate up slightly and disconnect the windshield washer hose

21.12a Removing one of the motor retaining bolts on the linkage

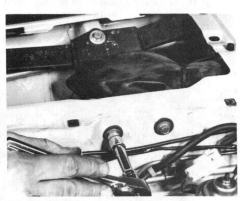

21.12b Removing one of the two motor retaining bolts located on the firewall

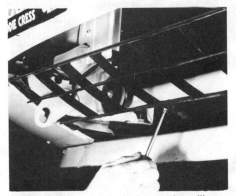

22.2 To gain access to the horns, the grille must be removed

22.3 Disconnect the two bullet electrical connectors behind the horn

22.4 One bolt secures the horn to the body

11 Unhook the wires from their clips and push aside for access for removing the motor and linkage assembly.

12 Remove the four bolts securing the motor assembly. There are two bolts side-by-side at the top of the firewall and two bolts on either side of the linkage arm (photos).

13 Pull the motor and linkage assembly out of the cowling recess.

14 To re-install, place the motor and linkage assembly into position and install each of the four securing bolts. Do not tighten the bolts until all the bolts are started in their threads. Tighten the four bolts.

15 Hook the wires into their clips, making sure the wires will not interfere with the motor operation.

16 Connect the two wiring couplers to the motor.

17 Lift the cowling piece into position and connect the washer hose to the nozzle.

18 Place the cowling into position and tighten the four attaching screws.

19 Push the wiper arms onto the splined shafts using your alignment marks on the windshield to get them into their original positions.

20 Install the outer bushing, cup washer and lock nut to each shaft. Tighten the nut securely.

21 Put the protective cover back into position over the lock nut.

22 Connect the negative battery cable and operate the wipers to check that they stop in the proper 'down' position and do not move onto the body cowling. Adjust the arms on the shaft as necessary.

22 Horn – removal and adjustment

1 The dial horns are located just in front of the radiator and are accessible through the grille under the nosepiece of the car.

2 To remove the horn, first remove the radiator grille under the front bumper. This is attached with sheet metal screws (photo).

3 Disconnect the two bullet wiring connectors at the horn, noting their color-coding (photo).

4 Remove the single bolt which secures the horn to the radiator support metal. Remove the horn (photo).

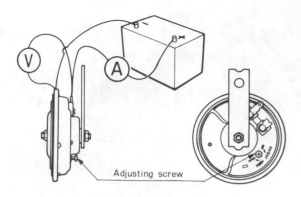

Fig. 10.13 Testing operation of horn using a voltmeter (V) and ammeter (A) (Sec 22)

5   The horn is adjusted by measuring the amperage at 12 volts. This requires that an ammeter and voltmeter be wired into the system, with power being applied from a battery source. Connect the ammeter and voltmeter as shown in Fig. 10.13. Turn the adjusting screw on the

back of the horn until the current flow reaches 3.0 plus-or-minus 0.5 amperes at 12 volts. Tighten the lock nut on the adjusting screw securely after adjustment.
6   After adjusting each horn separately, check for tone by operating as a pair.

23 Rear window defroster – checking and repairing

1   The rear window defroster incorporates a number of fine filaments running across the inside of the window. These filaments carry a specified degree of voltage which heats the window and thus defrosts the glass.
2   To check the defroster for proper operation, first switch on the defroster switch from the driver's seat.
3   Using a voltmeter, ground the negative probe to the body and touch the positive probe to each of the filaments, one at a time, at the center of the window. Measure the voltage of each filament. A normal filament should read approximately 6 volts at the center. The filament(s) not achieving this reading should be replaced (photo).
4   A small brush or ink pen and some conductive silver paint will be needed to repair a faulty filament.
5   Make sure the defrost switch is in the 'off' position.
6   Start by cleaning the broken portion with solvent to remove all traces of dirt, grease or adhesive.

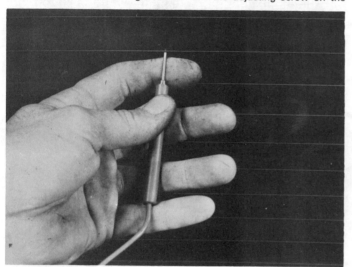

23.3 Using the probe of a voltmeter to check the rear window defroster

24.5 Pulling the light switch knob off the shaft

24.7 Two screws secure a cover at the top of the instrument cluster

24.8 Pull the instrument cluster out to gain access to the connector pin at the rear

7   Apply strips of adhesive tape to either side of the broken filament in need of repair. Get the edge of the tape as close as possible to the filament. Press the tape down tight against the window glass.
8   Using the small brush or ink pen, coat the broken portion of the filament with conductive silver paint (Mazda part number 2835 77 600, or Dupont number 4817).
9   Allow the painted portion to dry thoroughly for at least 24 hours at 68 degrees Fahrenheit (20 degrees Centigrade).
10 Never operate the heatable window before the paint has dried.
11 Remove the adhesive tape and check for proper operation with a voltmeter as described above.
12 Do not use any alkaline chemical cleanser to clean the repaired filament portion.

24 Main instrument panel – removal and installation

1   The main instrument cluster is located in the dashboard, straight in front of the driver. It will be necessary to remove this panel should any of the gauges or warning lights need servicing.
2   Disconnect the negative battery cable.
3   Disconnect the speedometer cable by reaching up under the dash. The cable is held to the rear of the gauge by a plastic clip, similar to the snap-lock connectors used for basic wiring. Push the plastic tang, then pull straight out from the gauge.
4   Remove the steering wheel.
5   Pull the light switch knob off the shaft. It has no retaining set screws (photo).
6   Remove the steering column cover under the steering column.

Note the type and length of the screws used, as they are different. To get the column cover over the combination switch it is necessary to remove a small hole cover which is secured by tangs to the inside of the main column cover. With this hole cover popped out of place, the main cover will come over the combination switch.
7   At the top of the instrument panel there is a cover held in place with two screws. Remove these two screws and then gently pry the cover piece out at the bottom, disengaging the clips near the bottom. Be careful not to bend or distort this cover trim piece (photo).
8   With the trim cover removed, the two attaching screws for the instrument panel are visible. Remove these two screws at the top of the panel plus the two screws on either side of the steering column, and draw the assembly out slightly (photo).
9   Disconnect the two keyed multiple connectors at the rear of the instrument panel and remove the panel from the car.
10 To install the instrument panel, place the assembly close enough to the dashboard so that the two connectors can be plugged into place. Install the connectors, noting that they are keyed and will only go in one way.
11 Push the unit fully into place and loosely install all four attaching screws before tightening. Tighten all screws.
12 Snap the bottom clips of the trim cover into place and then install the two top attaching screws. The trim cover is rather flimsy and may bow in the middle after disassembly. It may be necessary to use glue or double-faced tape to hold the center of the cover tightly against the dashboard.
13 Slide the column cover over the combination switch handle and then install the small hole cover by snapping it into place on the main column cover. Tighten the attaching screws for the column cover.

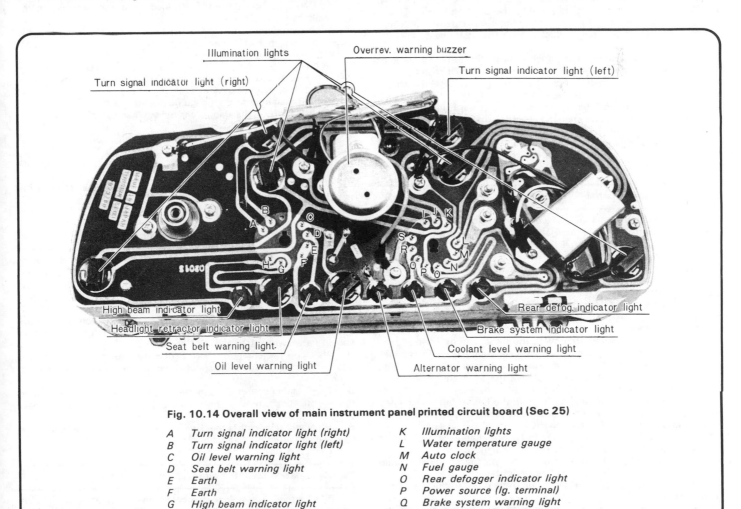

Fig. 10.14 Overall view of main instrument panel printed circuit board (Sec 25)

A   Turn signal indicator light (right)
B   Turn signal indicator light (left)
C   Oil level warning light
D   Seat belt warning light
E   Earth
F   Earth
G   High beam indicator light
H   Headlight retractor indicator light
I   Tachometer
j   Illumination lights

K   Illumination lights
L   Water temperature gauge
M   Auto clock
N   Fuel gauge
O   Rear defogger indicator light
P   Power source (Ig. terminal)
Q   Brake system warning light
R   Coolant level warning light
S   Alternator warning lights

14   Push the light switch knob fully onto the shaft.
15   Install the steering wheel and cap. Be sure to use a new nylon-insert lock nut on the steering wheel.
16   Reach under the dash and connect the speedometer cable. Hold the locking tab in while the cable is pushed into the receptacle at the rear of the gauge.
17   Connect the negative battery cable at the battery.

25   Main instrument panel – disassembly

1   Visually inspect the printed panel for any damage or rust.
2   Check the continuity between the connector pins and indicator lights, one at a time, using an ohmmeter. The continuity between each gauge and its appropriate connector pin should also be checked.
3   Before disassembling the instrument panel it may be advisable to draw your own rough sketch of the rear side of the panel noting the relative position of the wires and external components. Some of the wires and circuits are color-coded, some are not.
4   Remove all the illumination bulbs by turning the plastic connectors counter-clockwise and then pulling straight out. Note that there are different sizes used (photo).
5   Remove the four machine screws and seven sheet metal screws on the rear of the panel. Where wires are removed with screws note their position.
6   Remove the eight nuts and lockwashers on the studs protruding through the circuit board.
7   Disconnect the two bullet connectors for the rpm warning buzzer located at the center of the panel.
8   Remove the rubber plug adjacent to the warning buzzer.
9   Lift the printed circuit panel off the instrument panel (photos).
10   Remove the four screws which attach the instrument cluster to the hood.
11   From the front side of the panel, remove the trip indicator knob and clock reset knob. These are unscrewed from their shafts.
12   Remove the clear plastic hood from the gauge panel. Be careful that it is not scratched or damaged (photo).
13   The gauges can now be pulled out through the front.
14   When replacing the gauges and reassembling the unit, make sure that the wires to the gauges are properly routed through the back panel and that the gauges are centered in the front trim panel cutouts.
15   Do not overtighten the screws and lock nuts.

26   Center console panel – removal and installation

1   The center console panel is of a one-piece design which goes from the heater control unit to just above the shifter boot. It will be necessary to remove this panel to service the heater controls, radio, switches or cigarette lighter.
2   Disconnect the negative battery cable at the battery.
3   Unscrew the gearshift lever knob (gear selector knob on automatic transmissions).
4   Pull out the cigarette lighter.
5   Remove the two attaching screws for the shifter boot panel located just below the three switches and cigarette lighter receptacle.
6   With these two screws removed, the panel can be lifted slightly and then pried out at the rear. Spring clips secure the rear of this panel.
7   Remove the two screws securing the center panel set plate located above the heater control. Remove the set plate.
8   Position the heater control lever to the center.
9   Remove the heater control knobs and the heater fan switch knob by removing the small set screws at the bottom of each knob. Then pull the knobs straight off their shafts.
10   If equipped with a radio, remove the control knobs, attaching nuts and decorative bezel from the radio control shafts.
11   Draw out the center panel and disconnect the illumination bulb and wires to the switches and cigarette lighter.
12   The switches are removed by pushing them out through the front of the panel.
13   When reinstalling the panel, make sure the wiring connectors are fully pushed into place and the panel is centered on the control shafts and around the panel.
14   Do not overtighten the attaching screws as damage may occur to the panel.

27   Fuel gauge – checking

1   If there is reason to suspect that the fuel gauge is not functioning properly, the fault may lie in the sender unit at the fuel tank, the wiring leading to the gauge, or the gauge itself.
2   Raise the rear end of the vehicle and support firmly with jack stands.
3   Remove the left rear tire.
4   Remove the fuel tank cover on the left side of the tank. This cover is held in place by two bolts and one nut. A socket with a long extension will be needed to remove these (photo).
5   Disconnect the electrical connector on the gauge unit located at the top of the tank, on the left side (photo).
6   Scribe a mark across the gauge unit and tank for proper reassembly.
7   Remove the gauge unit from the tank, being careful not to bend the float rod as it is removed. Keep sparks, cigarettes and open flames away from the gas tank when the gauge unit is removed (photo).
8   Connect an ohmmeter to the fuel tank gauge unit terminals.
9   Slowly move the float arm until the arm contacts with the stopper on the unit body. With the float arm in the full position the resistance on the meter should be approximately 3 ohms. With the float arm in the empty position, the reading should be 110 ohms approximately.
10   If the readings are only slightly off from standard, correct by carefully bending the unit arm.
11   If the readings are way off from standard, replace the gauge unit with a new one.
12   To further check the system, place the gauge unit near enough to the fuel tank so that the wiring connector can be installed on the terminals of the gauge unit.
13   With the wiring connected to the gauge unit, manually move the float from the full to the empty positions and check for a proper reading on the gauge inside the car (the ignition switch must be turned to the one position, with the battery cable re-connected).
14   If the reading on the gauge is inconsistent with the movement of the float arm, it must be assumed that either the gauge itself is at fault or the wiring leading to the gauge holds the problem.
15   Fault-finding of the gauge and wiring harness can be found in Section 25.
16   Replace the gauge unit by using your identification marks to place the unit in its original position.
17   Install the fuel tank cover by working it into position, starting with the front end.
18   Install the tire, lower the vehicle to the ground and connect the negative battery cable if still disconnected.

28   Water temperature gauge – checking

1   Like the fuel gauge, troubleshooting problems with the water temperature gauge are basically a process of elimination. The sensor, wiring and the gauge itself must be checked out.
2   Disconnect the electrical coupler at the water temperature sensor located on the left side of the engine, by the oil filler neck.
3   Connect an ohmmeter to the coupler connection coming from the sensor and check the ohm reading. With the engine cold, the reading should be between 105 and 233 ohms.
4   Warm up the engine to normal operating temperature and take another reading. The reading should be in the neighbourhood of 20 to 50 ohms.
5   If the readings with the ohmmeter are significantly different than the specifications, replace the sensor unit in the engine with a new one.
6   If this test proves that the sensor is operating normally, check the gauge itself, referring to Section 25.

29   Combination switch – removal and installation

1   The combination switch is located on the steering column. It operates the headlights, turn signals, hazard lights, windshield wipers and windshield washers.
2   Disconnect the negative battery cable at the battery.
3   Remove the steering wheel.
4   Remove the steering column covers (Sec 24).

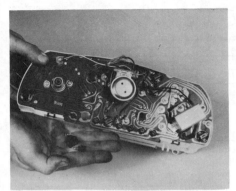

25.4 Removing the many illumination bulbs

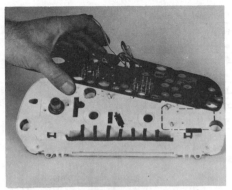

25.9a Lifting off the printed circuit board

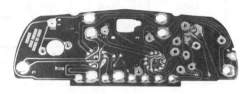

25.9b The painted circuit with its various electrical patterns

25.12 Removing the front hood from the gauge assembly

27.4 Removing the gas tank cover on the left side

27.5 Disconnecting the electrical connector on the gauge body

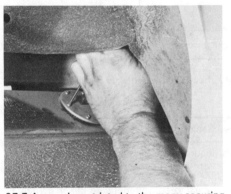

27.7 Access is restricted to the many securing screws on the gauge body

29.5 The many electrical connectors for the combination switch

29.8 The combination switch is slid off the end of the column as a unit

5   Disconnect the wire connectors located about half-way down the steering column. Remove the wires from the tie-straps and hold-down clamps as necessary (photo).

6   Disconnect the clamp at the rear of the combination switch. Note that there is a lug for alignment in the clamp.

7   Remove the stop ring, cancel cam and spring from the end of the shaft.

8   Remove the combination switch (photo).

9   The installation of the combination switch is basically the reverse procedure from removal. Make sure that the wiring is clamped into its original positions and the steering wheel is aligned to its original position. A new lock nut should be used for the steering wheel.

30 Combination switch – checking

1   To check the functions of the combination switch, an ohmmeter will be required. This will be used to check continuity between certain terminals on the electrical couplers, indicating a fault inside the switch. If a fault of the switch is diagnosed, the combination switch must be replaced as an entire unit.

2   Use the interconnection diagram to check the continuity of the terminals for the light, dimmer and passing switches (Fig. 10.15). The couplers being checked can be identified by the color-coding of the wire terminals indicated on the diagram. Two of the terminals on the passing switch coupler (the one with four terminals) are not used. The light coupler has twin-colored wires leading into it and has one of the six terminals not used.

3   The coupler for the turn signals and hazard warning lights can be identified by the fact that it has a total of eight terminals to it. One of the terminals is not used at all, and one of the terminals is not used for testing purposes.

4   The coupler for the wiper and washer can be identified by its six terminals with all the wires being of one solid color. All six of these terminals are used for testing, as the interconnection diagram indicates (Fig. 10.17).

Light switch	Passing switch	Dimmer switch	WR	LR	RL	RG	LY	RW	RB
OFF	OFF								
	ON			●	●—●—●				
Parking, Marker lights	OFF				●—●—●				
	ON			●	●—●—●				
Head light		LOW		●	●	●		●	
		HIGH			●	●		●	

Fig. 10.15 Continuity checks for light, dimmer and passing switches of combination switch (Sec 30)

Hazard switch	Turn signal switch	GY	WL	WG	GR	GW	GB
OFF	Left turn	●—●—●			●—●		
	Neutral	●—●					
	Right turn	●—●			●—●		
ON	Left, right turn or neutral		●—●		●—●		

Fig. 10.16 Continuity checks for turn signal and hazard light switch (Sec 30)

Switch	Switch position	Y	W	R	G	L	B
Wiper	INTERMITTENT	●—●			●—●—●		
	OFF	●—●					
	LOW			●—●—●			
	HIGH				●—●—●		
Washer	OFF						
	ON			●—●—●			

Fig. 10.17 Continuity checks for wiper and washer switch (Sec 30)

Key position	WR	BW	BW	L	YB	RB	YB	B
ACC	●—●							
ON	●—●—●				●—●			
START	●—●—●—●				●—●—●—●			

Fig. 10.18 Continuity checks for ignition switch and lock (Sec 31)

Switch position	LY	LR	LW	B
High	●———————————●			
Medium		●———●		
Low			●—●	

Fig. 10.19 Continuity checks for heater fan switch (Sec 32)

Switch position	GY	RY	BR	BW
P			●—●	
R	●—●			
N				●

Fig. 10.20 Continuity checks for automatic transmission inhibitor switch (Sec 33)

Switch position	WG	RW	RY	R
ON	●———————————●			
OFF		●—●		

Fig. 10.21 Continuity checks for retractable headlight switch (Sec 34)

5　If, by using an ohmmeter to check continuity, it is found that the combination switch is not at fault, the specific component system should be checked by following the wiring diagrams given elsewhere in this Chapter.

31 Ignition switch and steering lock – checking

1　Due to the method of attachment to the steering column, the ignition switch and steering lock should be checked for electrical faults while still attached to the column. Like the combination switch, continuity between specified terminals is checked using an ohmmeter. Refer to the interconnection diagram for the proper continuity check.

32 Heater fan switch – checking

1　The electrical operation of the heater fan switch is checked by the use of an ohmmeter. The ohmmeter will check for continuity between specified terminals of the electrical coupler leading from the heater switch and the single round connector identified as a solid black wire. Refer to the interconnection diagram to find out which of the terminals should have continuity with the black, round-headed connector (Fig. 10.19).

33 Inhibitor switch – checking

1　The inhibitor switch, incorporated only on cars with automatic transmission, is designed to prevent the car from being started when the selector is at any position besides 'Park' or 'Neutral'. Its electrical function can be checked by using an ohmmeter to check continuity between certain terminals of the four-pronged coupler and the single-wire connector. Refer to the interconnection diagram to ascertain which terminals should show continuity on the ohmmeter.

34 Retractable headlight switch – checking

1　To test the retractable headlight switch for proper electrical function an ohmmeter should be used to check the continuity between certain terminals of the four-pronged coupler. It will be necessary to remove the center panel (Section 26) to gain access to this coupler. Refer to the interconnection diagram for the terminals which should show continuity (Fig. 10.21).

35 Rear combination lights

1　To replace a bulb which has failed in the rear combination light system, first remove the six screws retaining the lens. Remove the lens (photos).

2　Ascertain which of the three bulbs has failed. This can be done by

35.1a There are six screws retaining the light lens

35.1b The lens can then be removed

35.3 To replace a bulb, push it in and then turn to release the mounting tangs

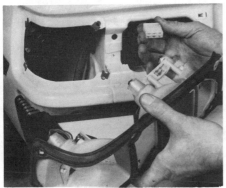

35.4 To remove the entire bucket assembly, pull it slightly outward and disconnect the electrical coupler

36.1 Removing the license plate illumination assembly from the rear body panel

36.7 Plastic inserts and a metal shield must be removed before the bulb can be taken out

operating the systems with the lens removed, or by simply examining the bulbs in place. A blown bulb can be identified by broken or burnt wires inside the glass bulb, or damage to the bulb or its metal connector.

3 To remove a bulb, push the bulb in and turn it counterclockwise. This is true for all three bulbs (back-up light, turn signal and tail/stop light) inside the combination unit (photo).

4 The entire bucket of the combination light should be replaced with a new one if it shows signs of damage or extreme corrosion. To remove it, pull out through the lens opening and then disconnect each of the connectors, noting their color coding and placement for reassembly (photo).

36 License plate lights

1 Access to the illumination lamps for the license plate is through the luggage compartment.

2 Pry back the carpet and remove the two nuts which secure the illumination brackets to the rear panel.

3 Disconnect the bullet wiring connector.

4 Remove the lamp assembly from the rear body panel (photo).

5 Unscrew the plastic inserts off the studs of the light assembly.

6 Pull the metal shield off the studs of the lamp assembly.

7 Push the bulb inward and twist it counterclockwise to remove (photo).

8 Install a new bulb in the socket by pushing and turning clockwise.

9 Install the metal shield and plastic inserts on the studs.

10 Install the lamp housing. Tighten the securing nuts and connect wiring.

11 Test for proper operation by turning on the headlights.

37 Front and side lights

1 At the front of the car, there is one bulb which functions as the parking lamp and as the turn signal lamp. At each front fender there is

also a side marker lamp. All of these are replaced in the same manner.

2 Remove the two screws securing the lens.

3 Gently remove the lens.

4 Push the bulb inward and turn it clockwise. Remove the bulb.

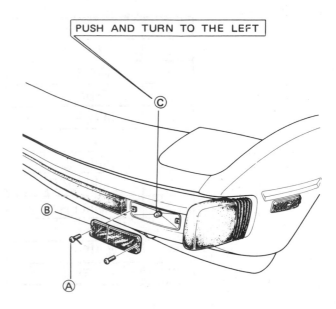

PUSH AND TURN TO THE LEFT

A. TWO SCREWS
B. LIGHT LENS
C. LIGHT BULB

Fig. 10.22 Exploded view of front parking and turn signal lights (Sec 37)

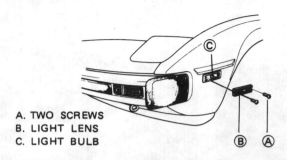

A. TWO SCREWS
B. LIGHT LENS
C. LIGHT BULB

Fig. 10.23 Exploded view of front side marker lights (Sec 37)

5   Inspect the bucket for damage or corrosion. The bucket can be removed by pulling it through the lens operating and then disconnecting the electrical connector.

6   Push the new bulb into the socket and turn clockwise to seat properly.
7   Install the lens and the two attaching screws.

38 Dome light activator switches

1   At the rear of each door frame there is a plunger-type switch which activates the interior dome light whenever the door is opened.
2   Remove the two screws from the switch housing.
3   Pull the plunger assembly away from the door frame being careful not to damage the gasket behind it.
4   On the rear of the switch, check that the wire has not broken. Check that it is fully tightened to the back of the switch. Check for corrosion of the wire or switch.
5   Install the assembly using the original gasket if in a useable state, or a new gasket. Tighten the screws securely and check for proper operation.

CODE	
B	BLACK
Br	BROWN
G	GREEN
Gy	GRAY
L	BLUE
Lb	LIGHT BLUE
Lg	LIGHT GREEN
O	ORANGE
R	RED
W	WHITE
Y	YELLOW

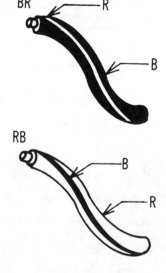

Fig. 10.24 Wiring code: the first letter indicates the basic wire color, the second letter the stripe color

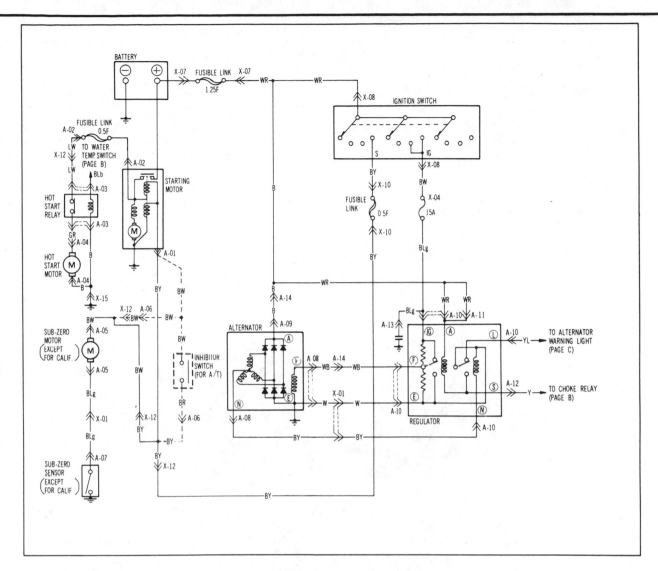

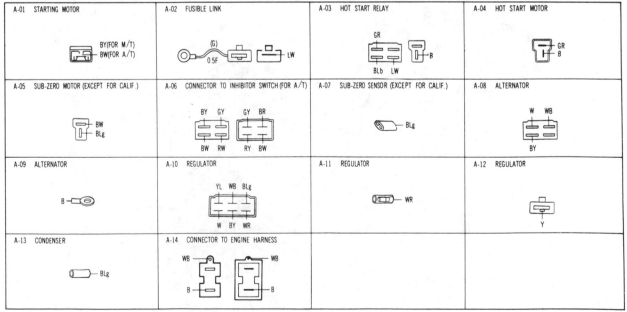

Fig. 10.25 System A: charging and starting systems (USA models) — schematic diagram

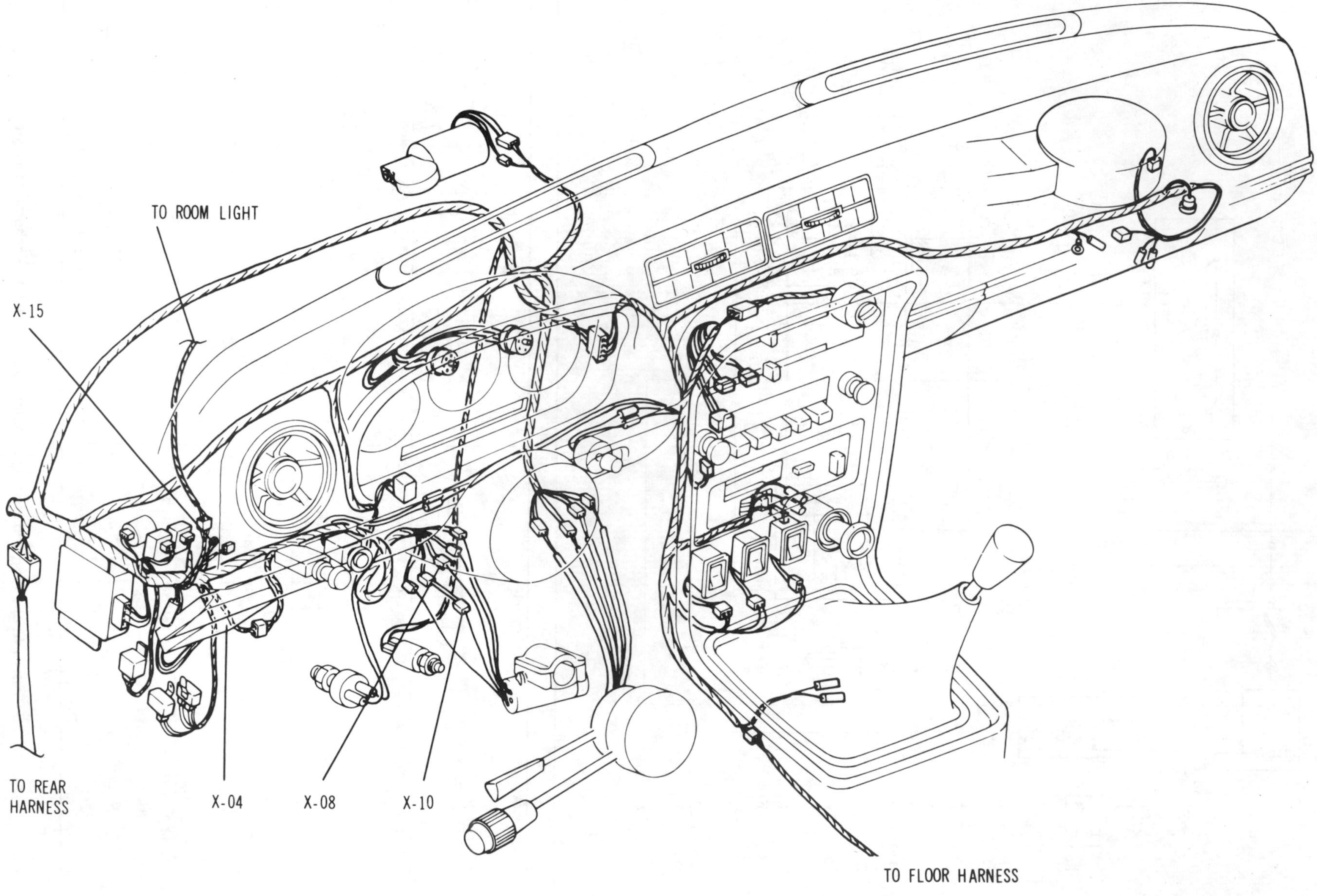

TO FLOOR HARNESS

Fig. 10.26A System A: charging and starting systems (USA models) — loom diagram

X-10

X-08

X-04

TO ROOM LIGHT

X-15

TO REAR
HARNESS

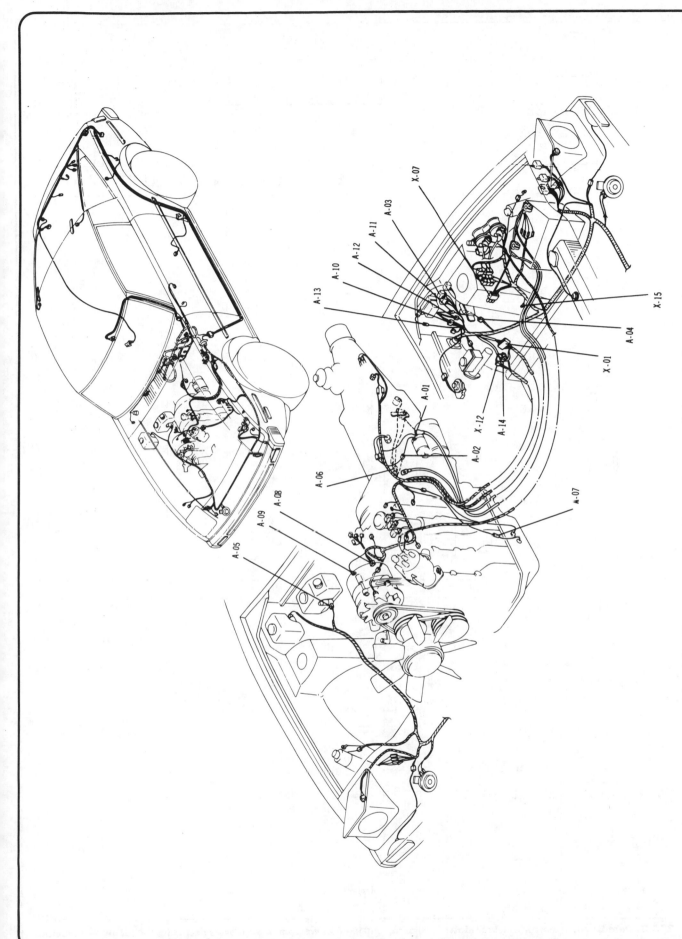

Fig. 10.26B System A: charging and starting systems (USA models) — loom diagram

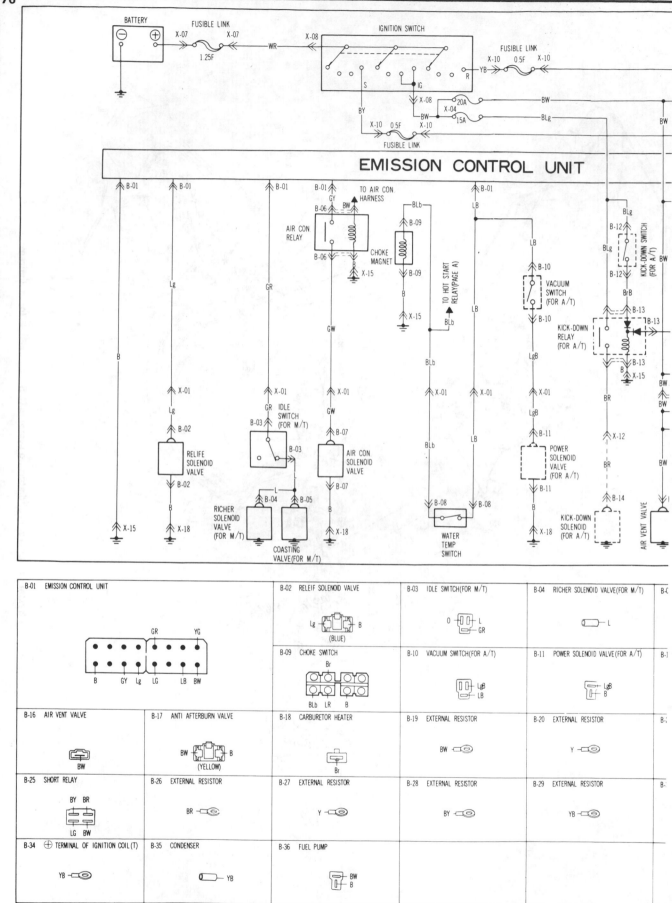

Fig. 10.27A System B: emission control, kick-down, fuel pump and ignition systems (USA models excluding California) — schematic diagram

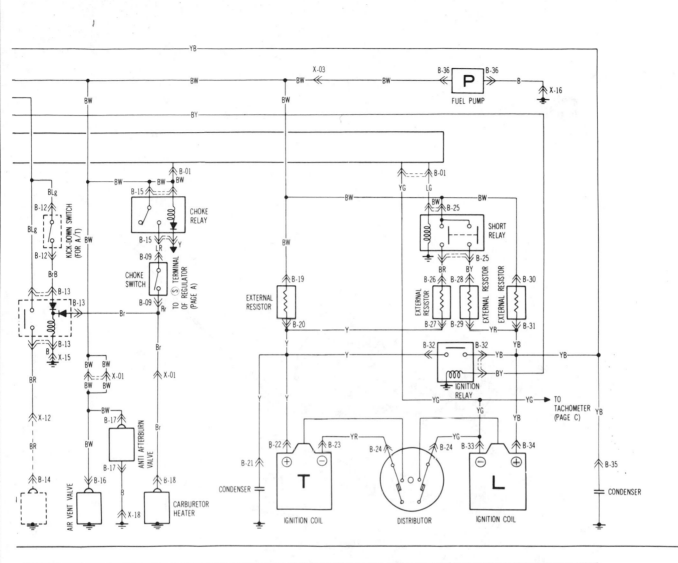

Fig. 10.27B System B: emission control, kick-down, fuel pump and ignition systems (USA models excluding California) — schematic diagram

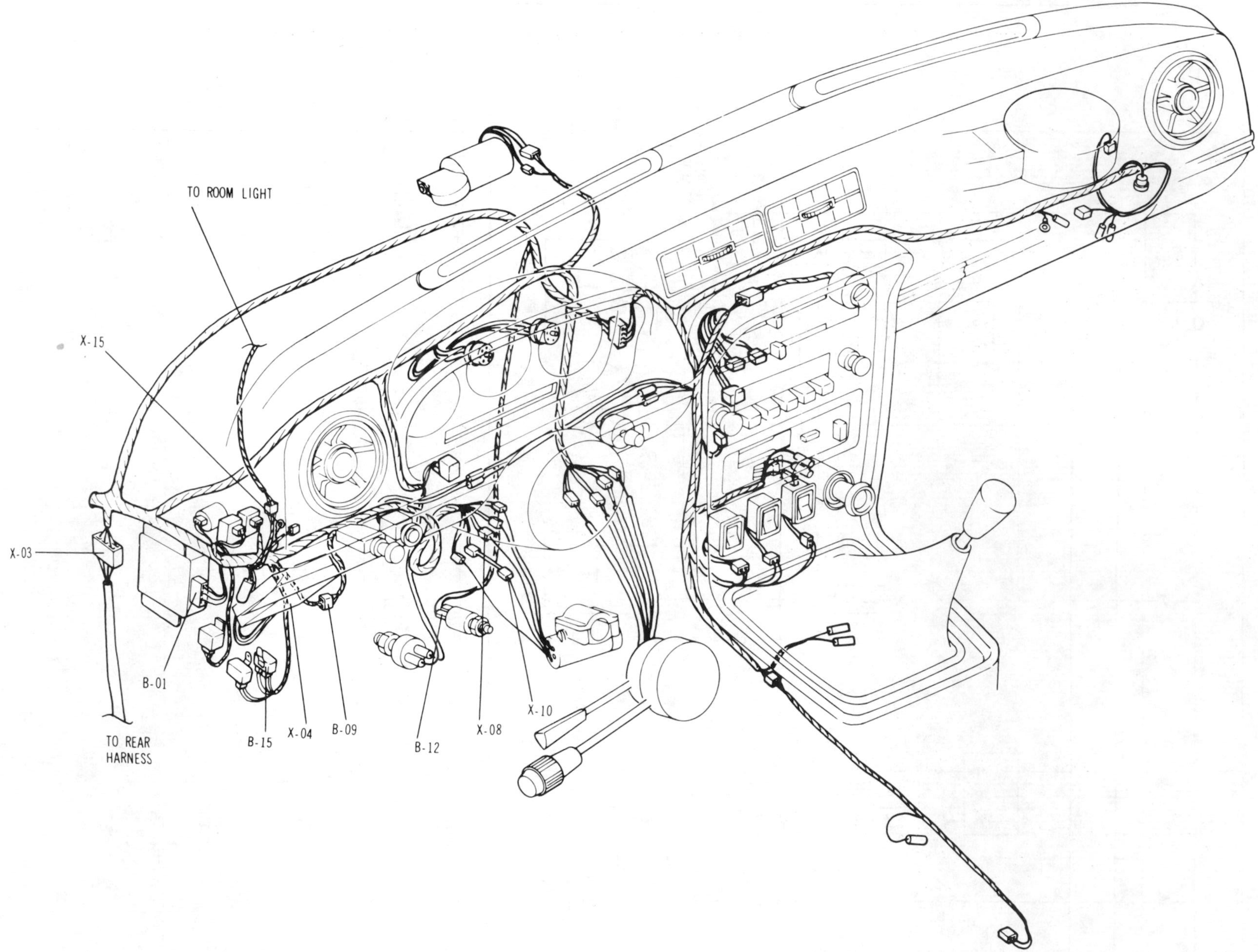

TO ROOM LIGHT

X-15

TO REAR HARNESS

B-01

X-03

B-15

X-04

B-09

B-12

X-08

X-10

Fig. 10.28A System B: emission control, kick-down, fuel pump and ignition systems (USA models excluding California) — loom diagram

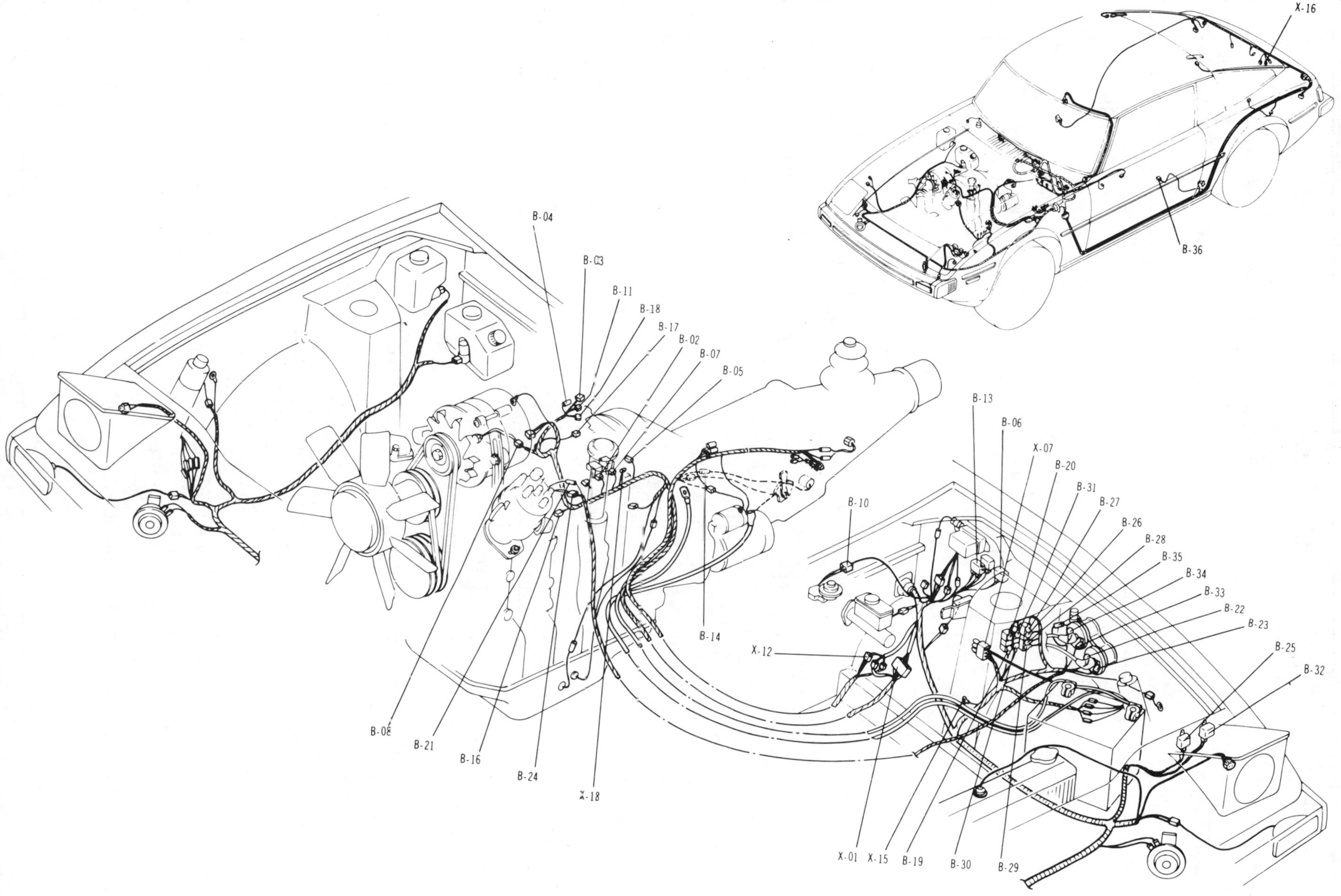

Fig. 10.28B System B: emission control, kick-down, fuel pump and ignition systems (USA models excluding California) — loom diagram

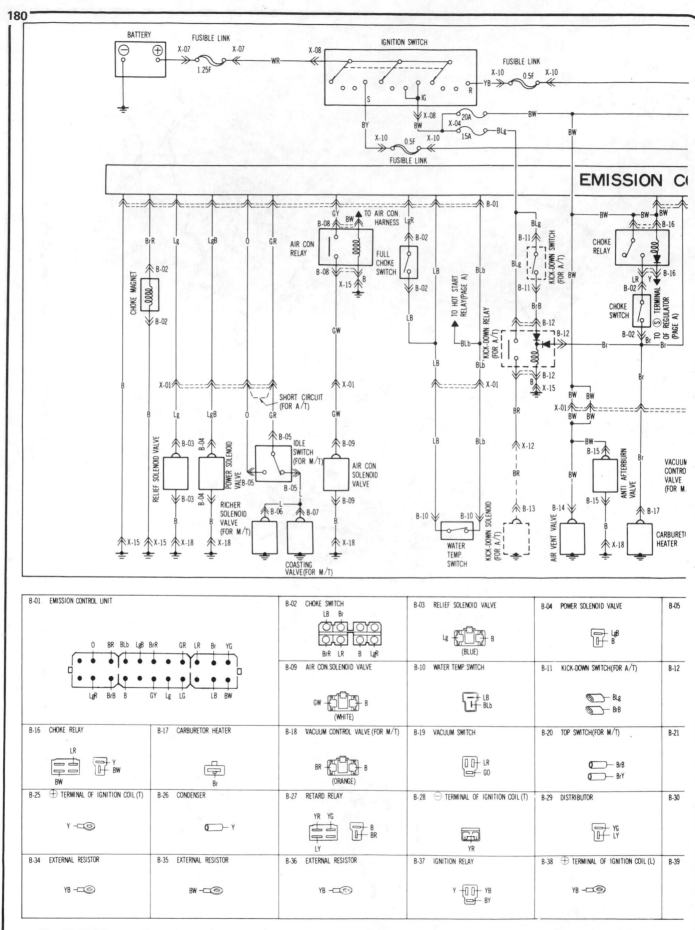

Fig. 10.29A System B: emission control, kick-down, fuel pump and ignition systems (California only) — schematic diagram

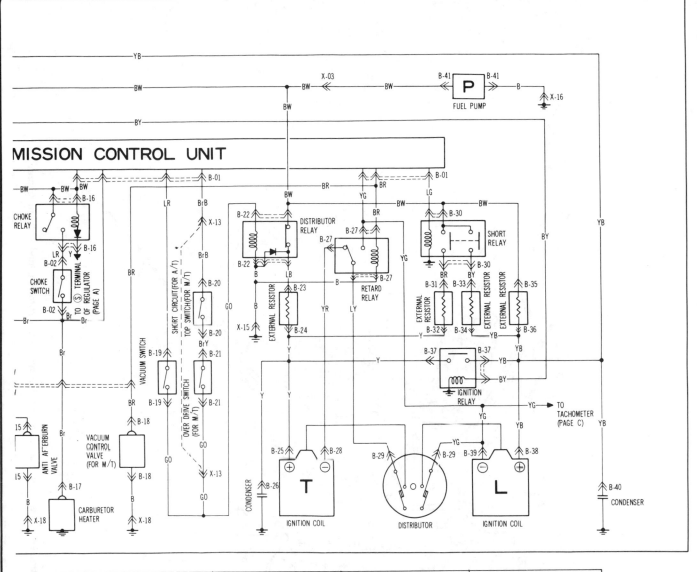

Fig. 10.29B System B: emission control, kick-down, fuel pump and ignition systems (California only) — schematic diagram

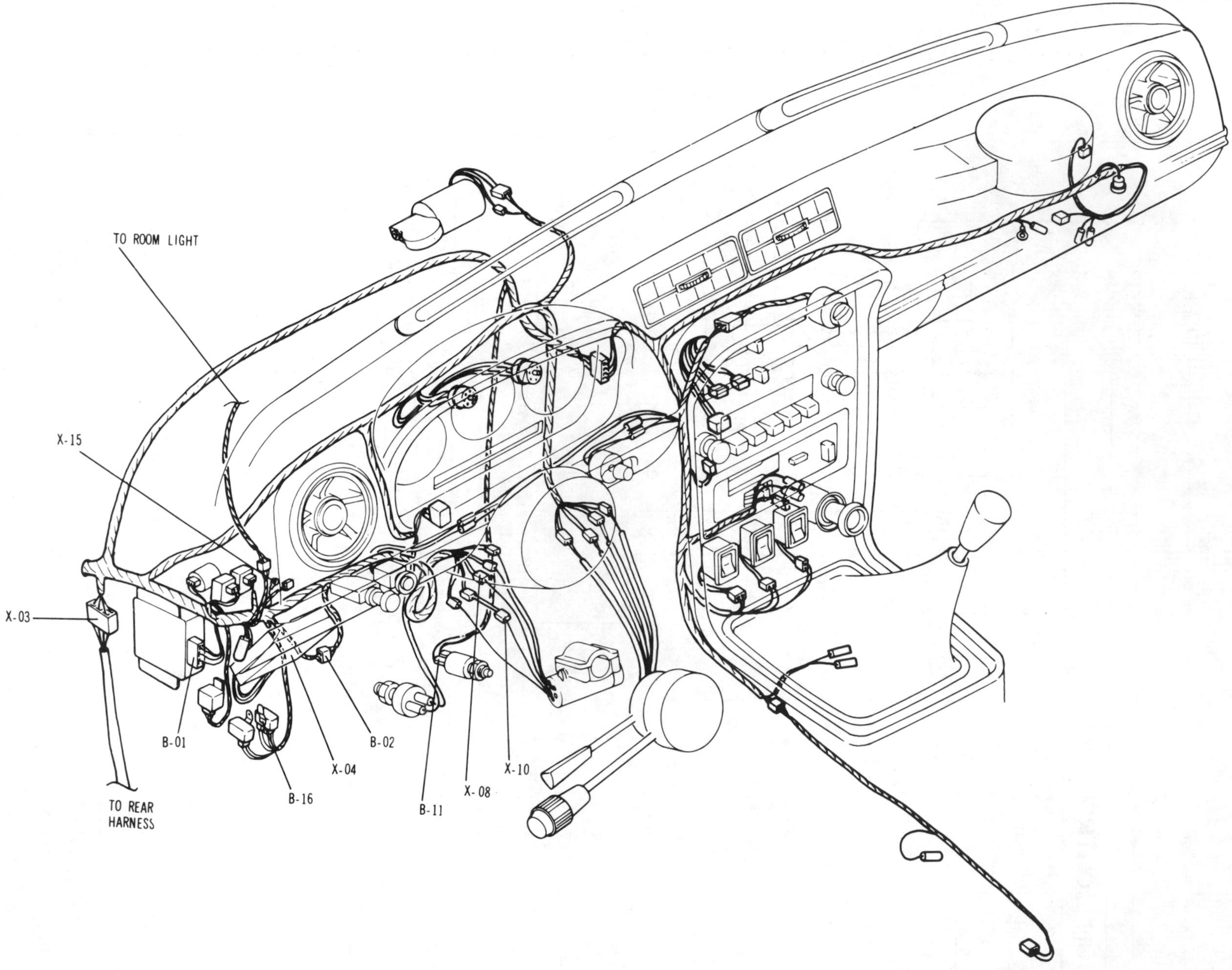

TO ROOM LIGHT

TO REAR HARNESS

X-15

X-03

B-01

B-16

X-04

B-02

B-11

X-08

X-10

Fig. 10.30A System B: emission control, kick-down, fuel pump and ignition systems (California only) — loom diagram

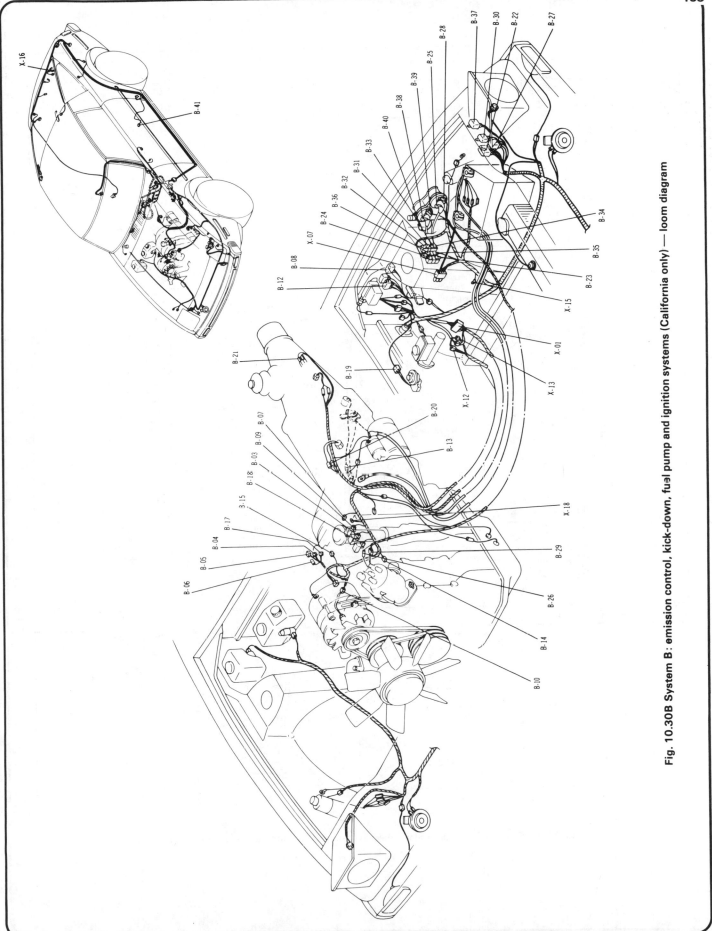

Fig. 10.30B System B: emission control, kick-down, fuel pump and ignition systems (California only) — loom diagram

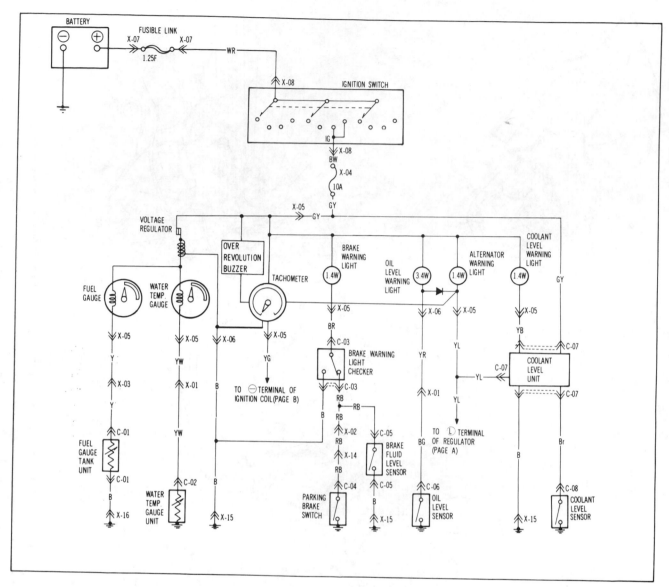

C-01	FUEL GAUGE TANK UNIT	C-02	WATER TEMP. GAUGE UNIT	C-03	BRAKE WARNING LIGHT CHECKER	C-04	PARKING BRAKE SWITCH
	B Y		YW		B — RB — BR		— RB
C-05	BRAKE FLUID LEVEL SENSOR	C-06	OIL LEVEL SENSOR	C-07	COOLANT LEVEL UNIT	C-08	COOLANT LEVEL SENSOR
	RB B		BG		YB YL GY Br B		— Br

Fig. 10.31 System C: meter and warning systems (USA models) — schematic diagram

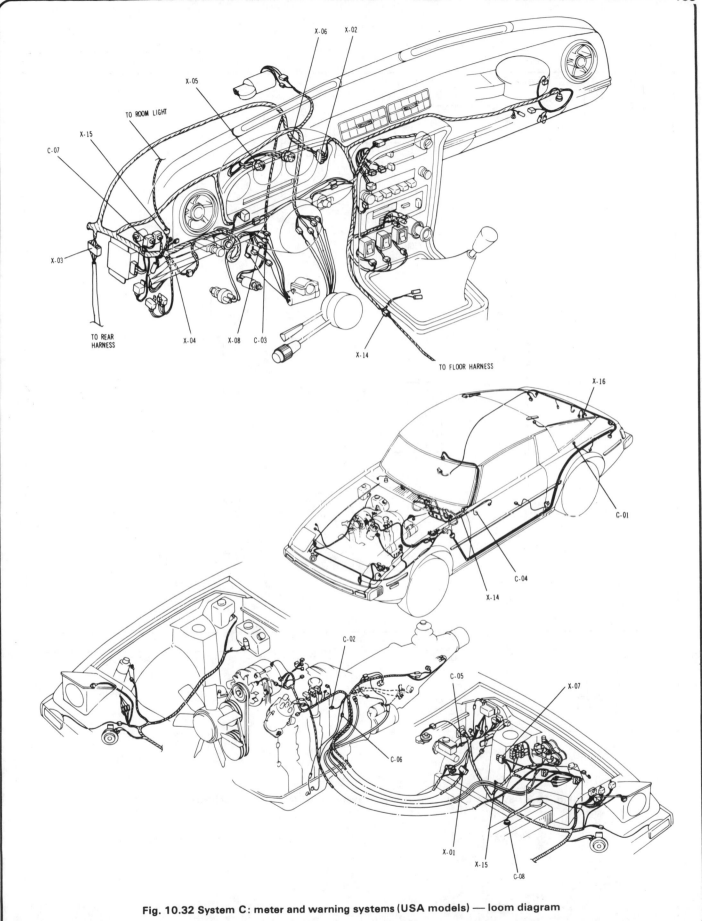

Fig. 10.32 System C: meter and warning systems (USA models) — loom diagram

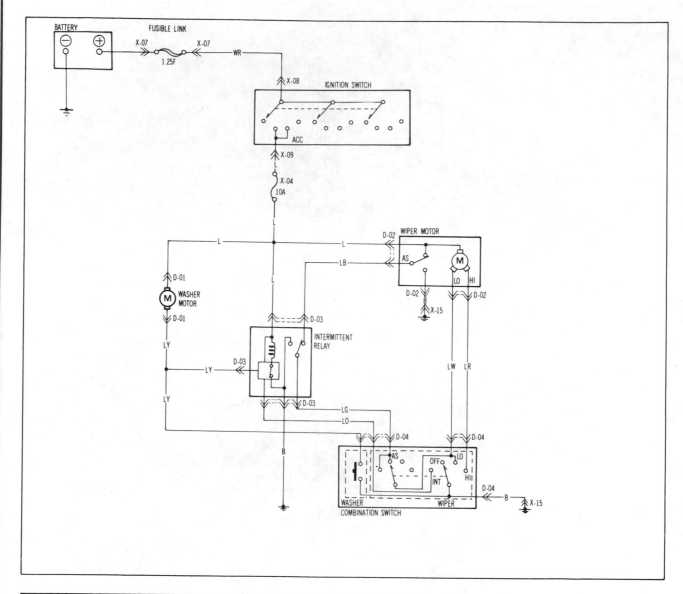

Fig. 10.33 System D: wiper and washer systems (USA models) — schematic diagram

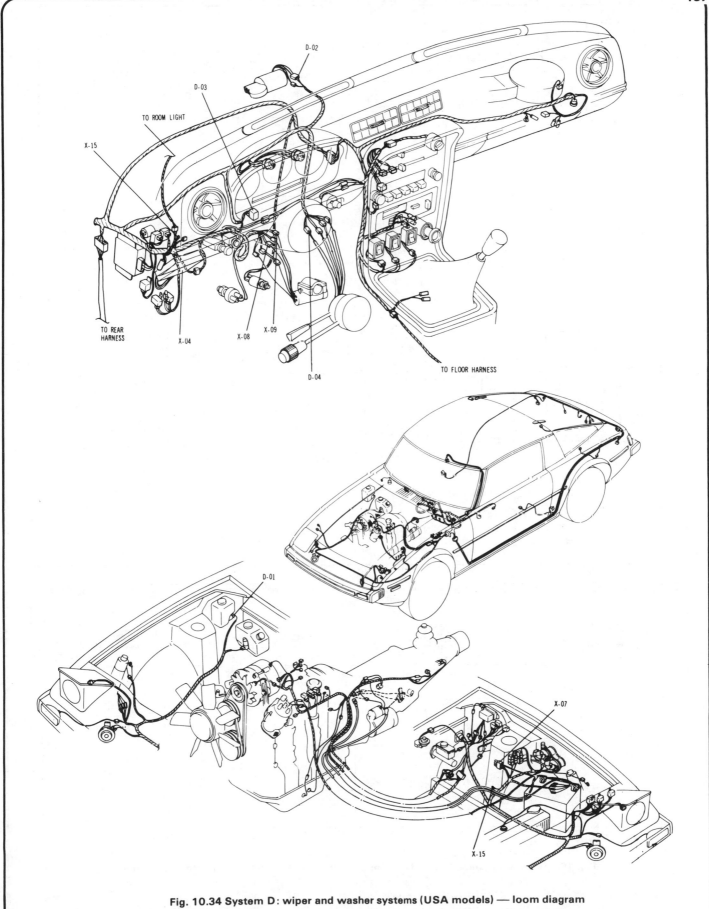

Fig. 10.34 System D: wiper and washer systems (USA models) — loom diagram

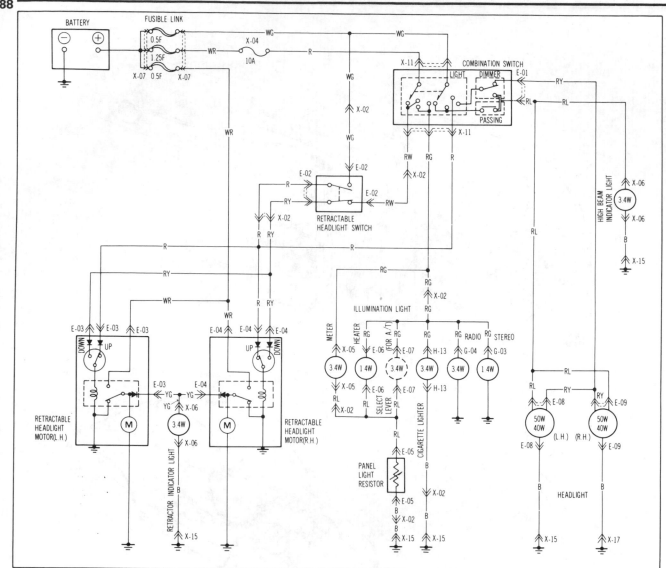

Fig. 10.35 System E: headlight and illumination system (USA models) — schematic diagram

E-01 COMBINATION SWITCH	E-02 RETRACTABLE HEADLIGHT SWITCH	E-03 RETRACTABLE HEADLIGHT MOTOR(L.H.)	E-04 RETRACTABLE HEADLIGHT MOTOR(R.H.)
RY ... RL	RY WG ... R RW	WR R RY YG	WR R RY YG
E-05 PANEL LIGHT RESISTOR	E-06 HEATER ILLUMINATION LIGHT	E-07 SELECT LEVER ILLUMINATION LIGHT (FOR A/T)	E-08 HEADLIGHT(L.H.)
RL ... B	RG RL	RG RL	RY RL B
E-09 HEADLIGHT(R.H.)			
RL RY B			

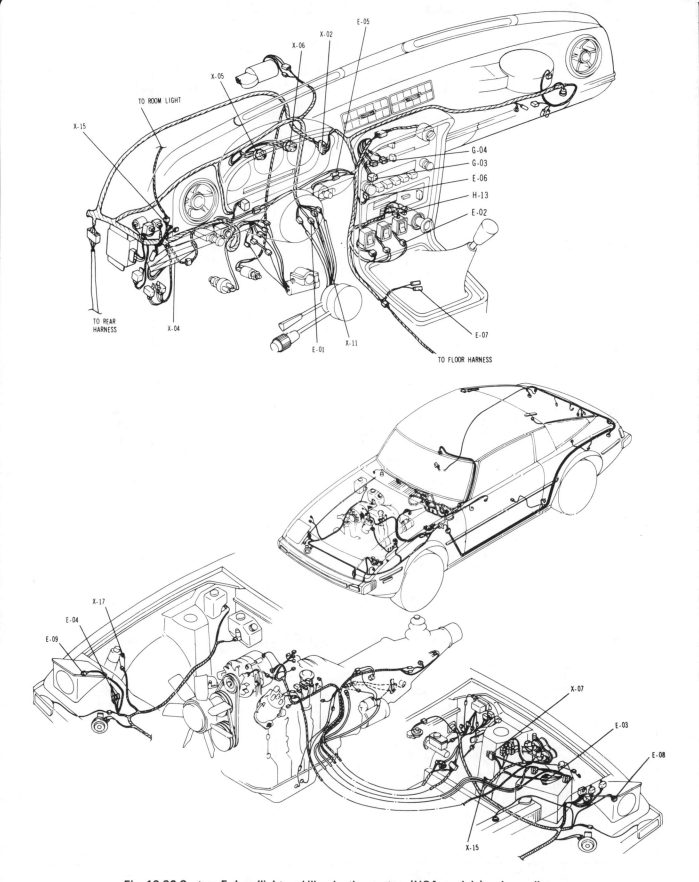

Fig. 10.36 System E: headlight and illumination system (USA models) — loom diagram

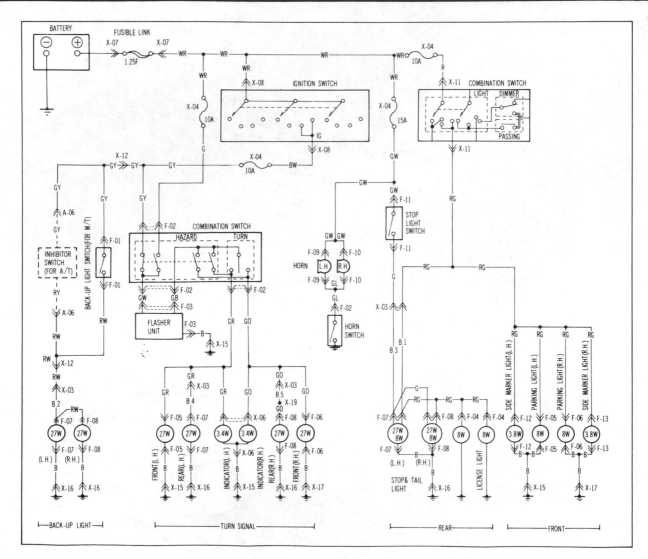

Fig. 10.37 System F: signal light and horn systems (USA models) — schematic diagram

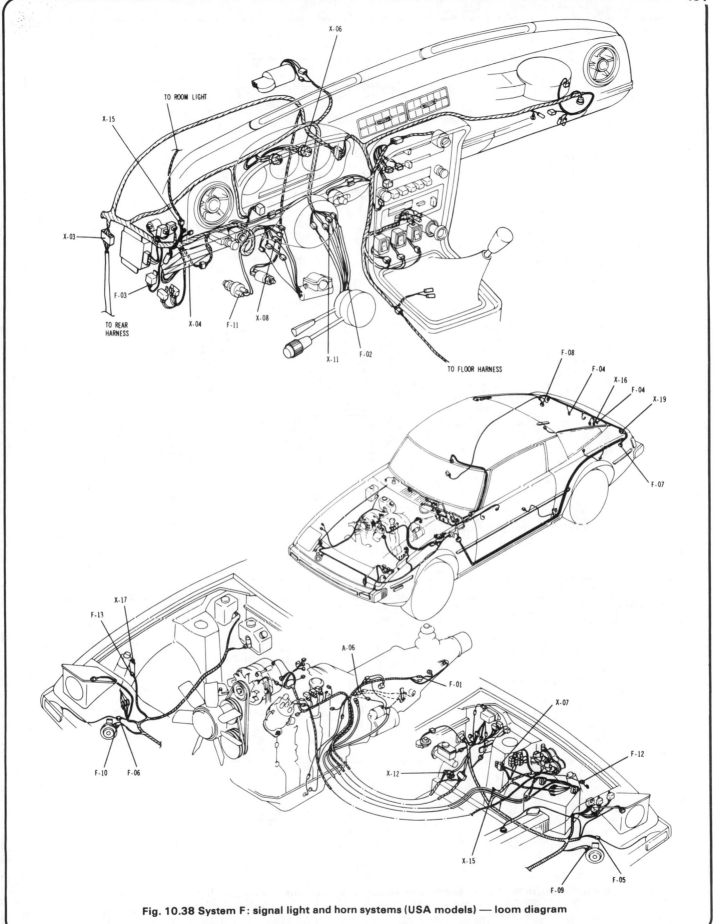

Fig. 10.38 System F: signal light and horn systems (USA models) — loom diagram

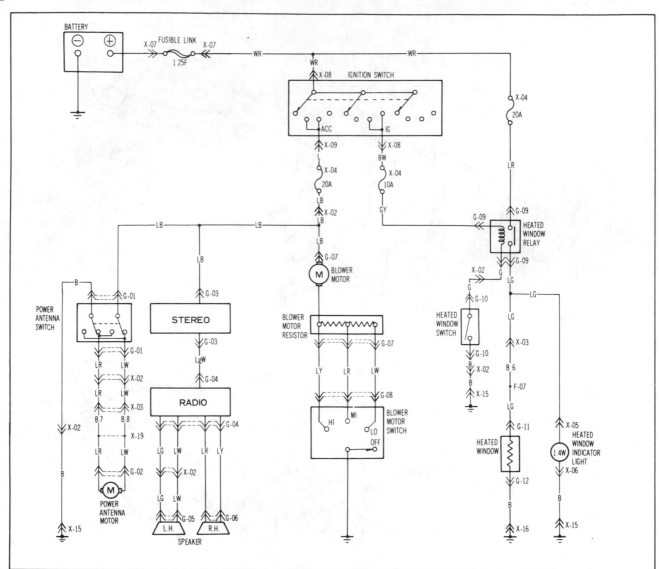

Fig. 10.39 System G: heater, radio, stereo, heated rear window and power antenna systems (USA models) — schematic diagram

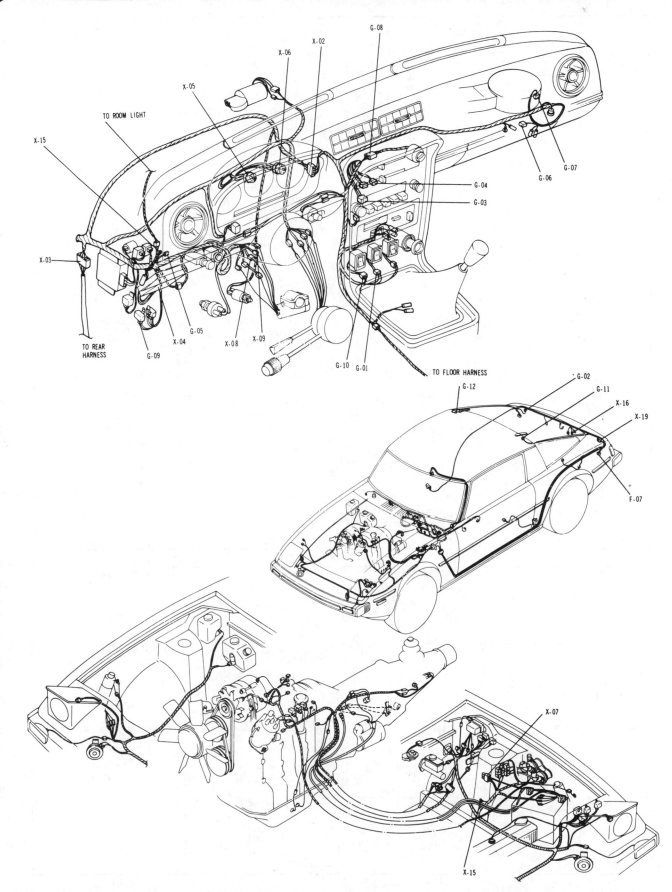

Fig. 10.40 System G: heater, radio, stereo, heated rear window and power antenna systems (USA models) — loom diagram

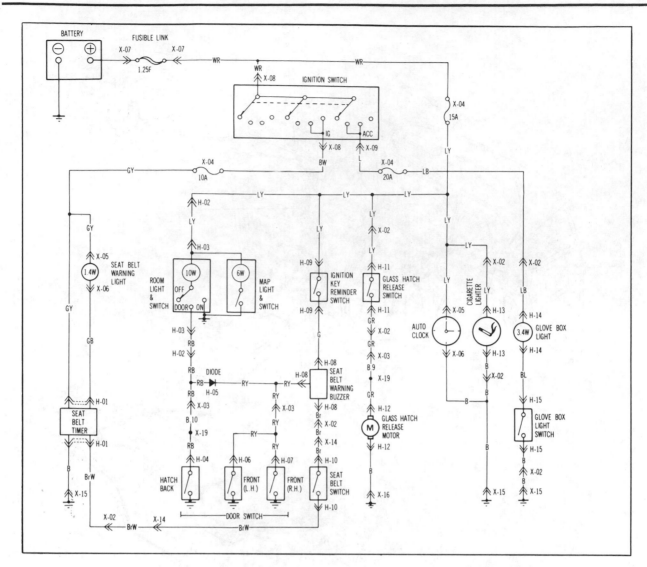

H-01 SEAT BELT TIMER	H-02 CONNECTOR TO ROOM LIGHT	H-03 ROOM LIGHT	H-04 DOOR SWITCH (GLASS HATCH)
GY BrW / GB B	RB — LY / RB — LY	LY / RB	RB
H-05 DIODE	H-06 DOOR SWITCH (L.H.)	H-07 DOOR SWITCH (R.H.)	H-08 SEAT BELT WARNING BUZZER
RB / RY	RY	RY	G — RY / Br
H-09 IGNITION KEY REMINDER SWITCH	H-10 SEAT BELT SWITCH	H-11 GLASS HATCH RELEASE SWITCH	H-12 GLASS HATCH RELEASE MOTOR
LY / G	Br / BrW	LY / GR	GR / B
H-13 CIGARETTE LIGHTER	H-14 GLOVE BOX LIGHT	H-15 GLOVE BOX LIGHT SWITCH	
LY / RG / B	LB / BL	BL / B	

Fig. 10.41 System H: seat belt warning, room and map light, auto clock, cigarette lighter, glove box light and glass hatch release systems (USA models) — schematic diagram

195

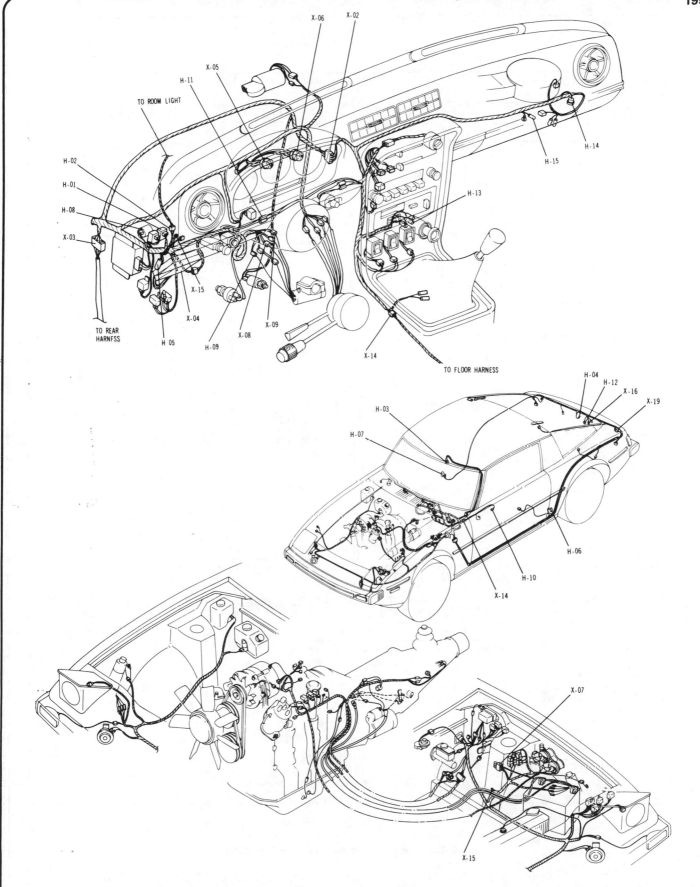

Fig. 10.42 System H: seat belt warning, room and map light, auto clock, cigarette lighter, glove box light and glass hatch release systems (USA models) — loom diagram

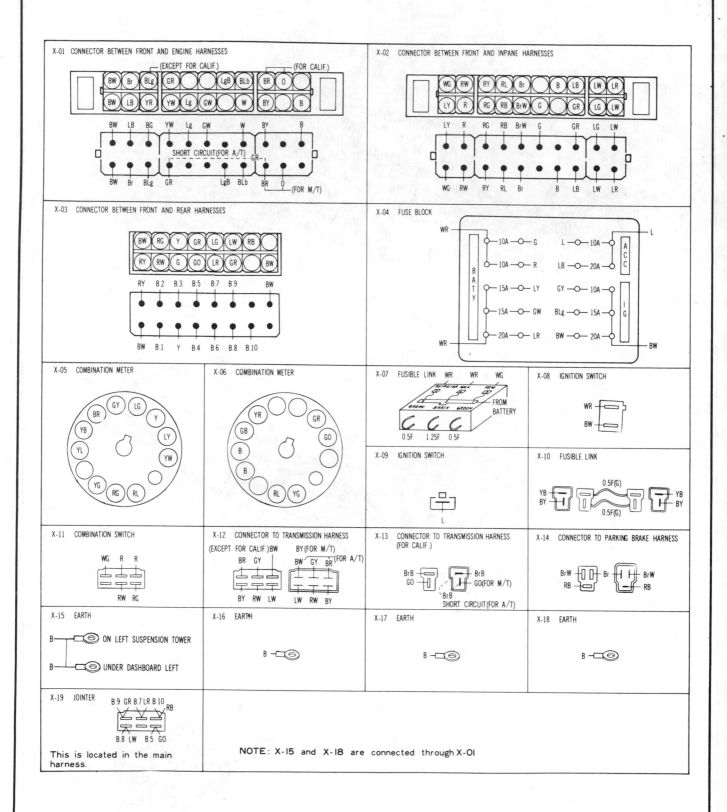

Fig. 10.43 Common connector chart (USA models)

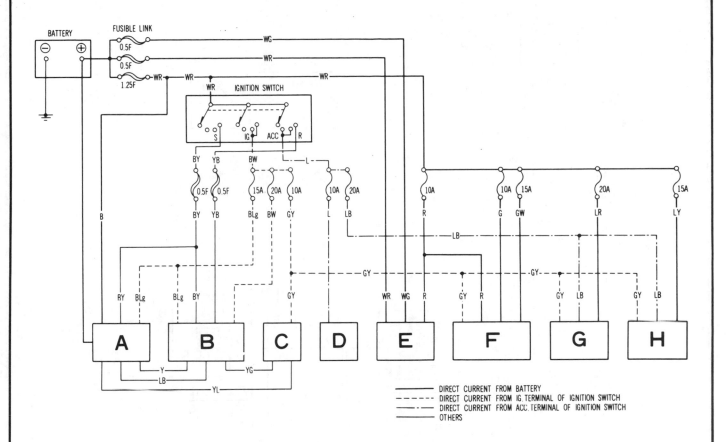

Fig. 10.44 Schematic diagram showing how the various electrical systems are connected (USA models)

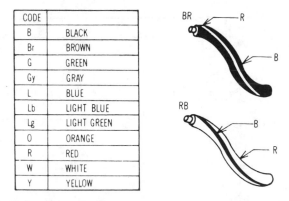

CODE	
B	BLACK
Br	BROWN
G	GREEN
Gy	GRAY
L	BLUE
Lb	LIGHT BLUE
Lg	LIGHT GREEN
O	ORANGE
R	RED
W	WHITE
Y	YELLOW

Fig. 10.45 Wiring code: the first letter indicates the basic wire color, the second letter the stripe color

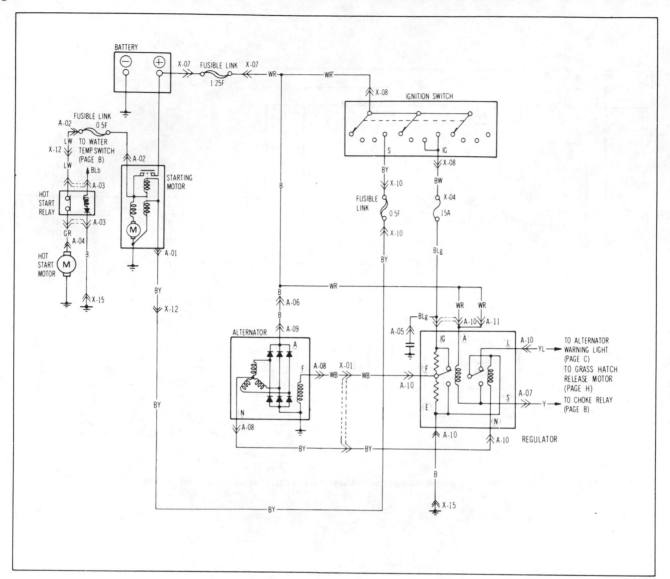

A-01	STARTING MOTOR	A-02	FUSIBLE LINK	A-03	HOT START RELAY	A-04	HOT START MOTOR
	BY		(G) 0 5F — LW		GR / B / BLb / LW		GR
A-05	CONDENSER	A-06	CONNECTOR TO ENGINE HARNESS	A-07	REGULATOR	A-08	ALTERNATOR
	BLg		B B		Y		WB / BY
A-09	ALTERNATOR	A-10	REGULATOR	A-11	REGULATOR		
	B		YL WB BLg / B BY WR		WR		

Fig. 10.46 System J: charging and starting systems (UK models) — schematic diagram

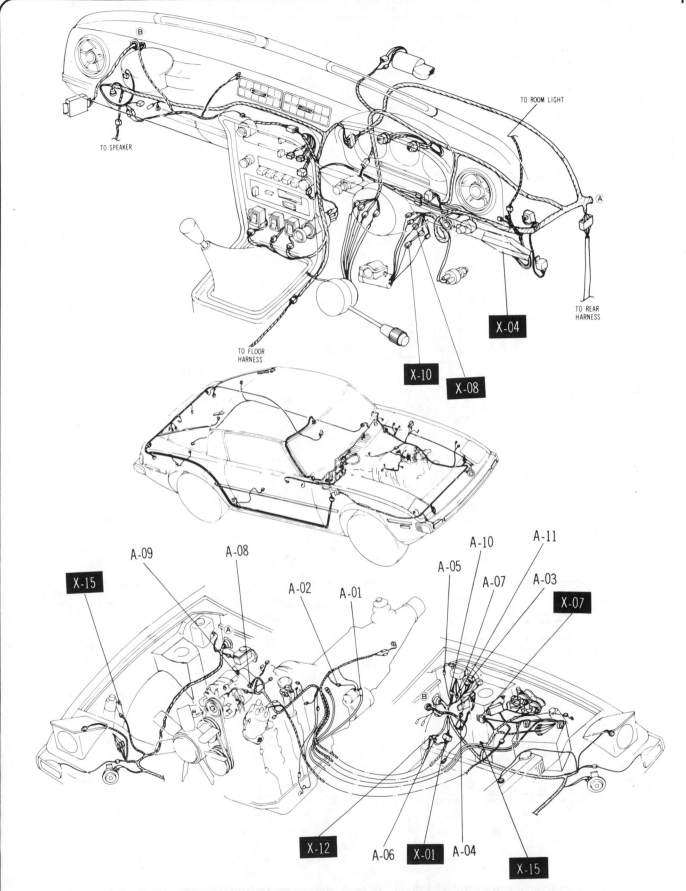

Fig. 10.47 System J: charging and starting systems (UK models) — loom diagram

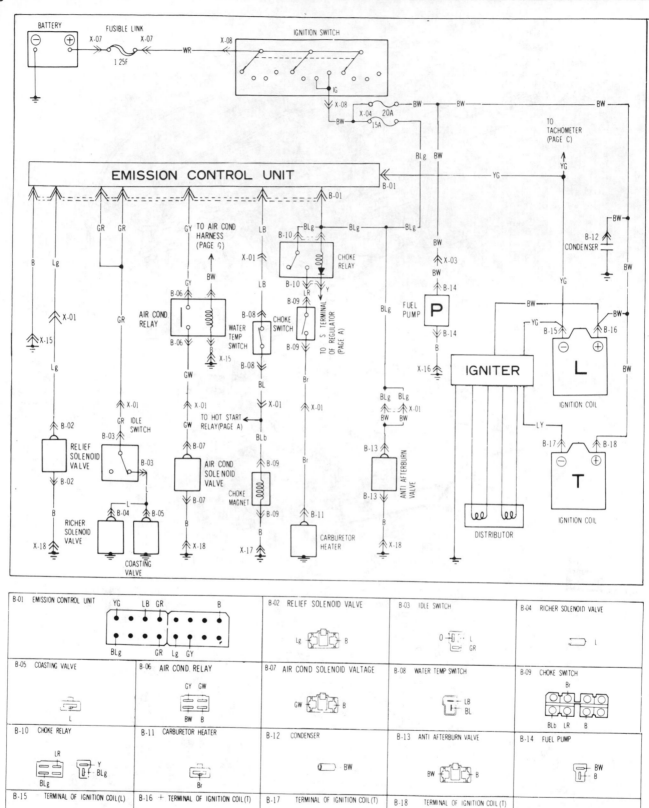

Fig. 10.48 System K: emission control, kick-down, fuel pump and ignition systems (UK models) — schematic diagram

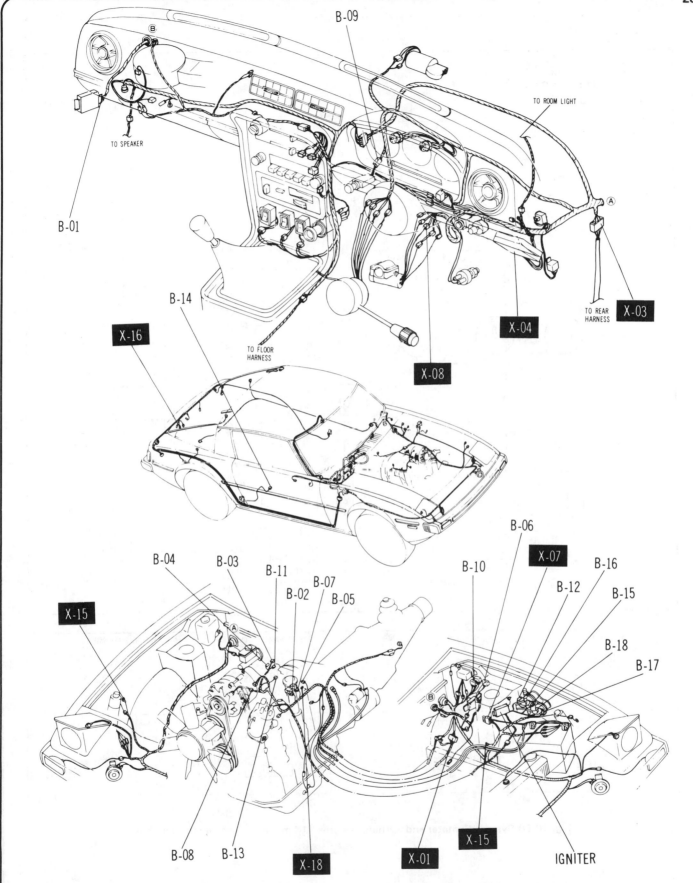

B-09

TO ROOM LIGHT

TO SPEAKER

B-01

A

X-03

TO REAR HARNESS

B-14

X-16

TO FLOOR HARNESS

X-04

X-08

B-06

X-07

B-10 B-12 B-16

B-15

B-18

B-17

B-04 B-03 B-11 B-07

B-02 B-05

X-15

A

B

B-08 B-13 X-18 X-01 X-15 IGNITER

Fig. 10.49 System K: emission control, kick-down, fuel pump and ignition systems (UK models) — loom diagram

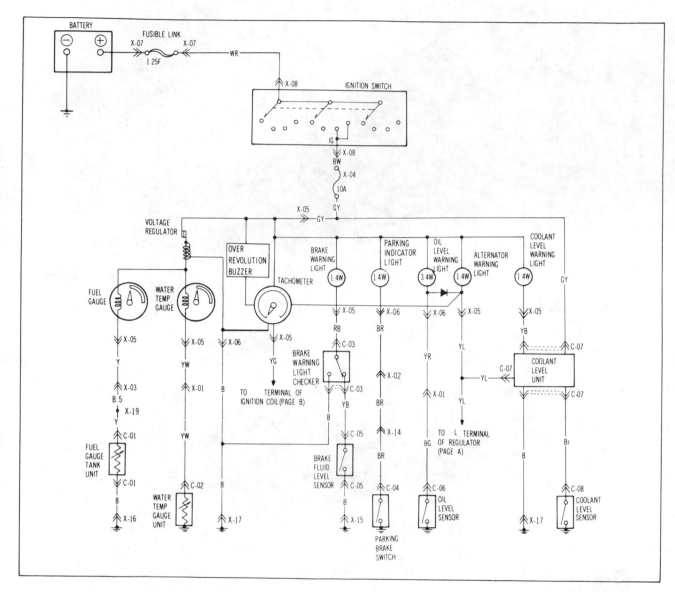

Fig. 10.50 System L: meter and warning systems (UK models) — schematic diagram

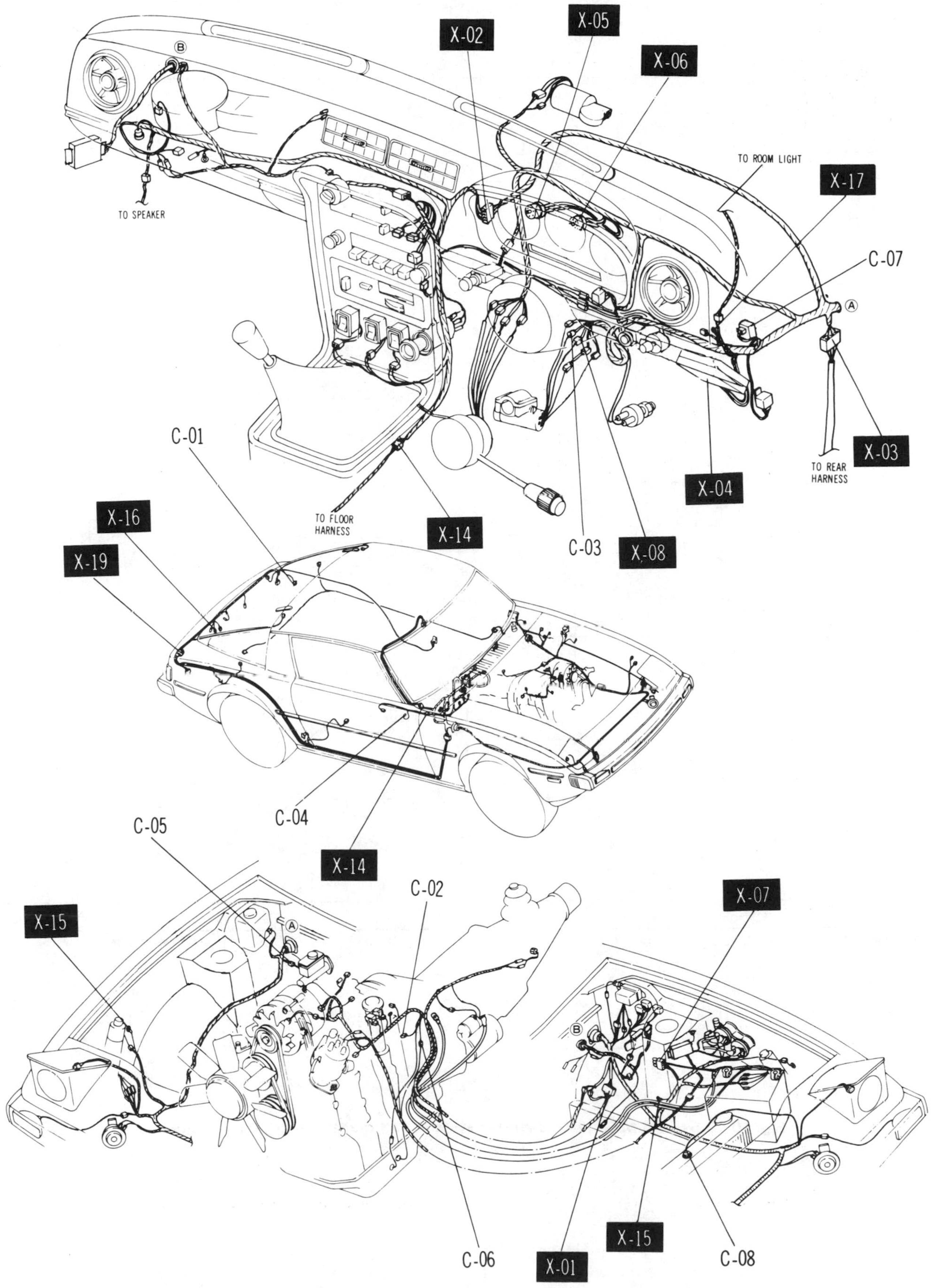

TO SPEAKER

X-02

X-05

X-06

TO ROOM LIGHT

X-17

C-07

A

X-03

TO REAR HARNESS

X-04

C-01

C-03

X-08

X-14

TO FLOOR HARNESS

X-16

X-19

C-04

C-05

X-14

C-02

X-07

X-15

C-06

X-01

X-15

C-08

Fig. 10.51 System L: meter and warning systems (UK models) — loom diagram

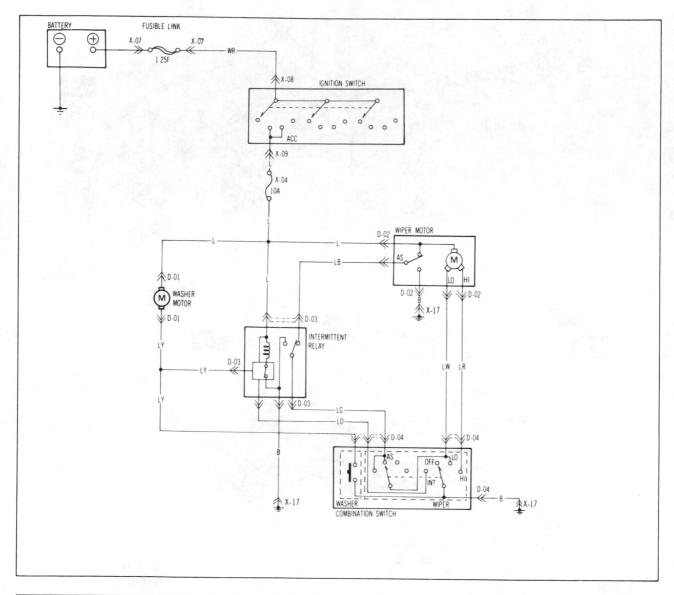

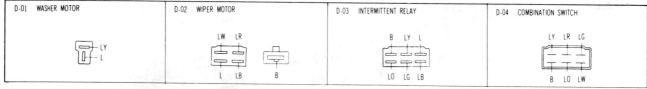

Fig. 10.52 System M: wiper and washer systems (UK models) — schematic diagram

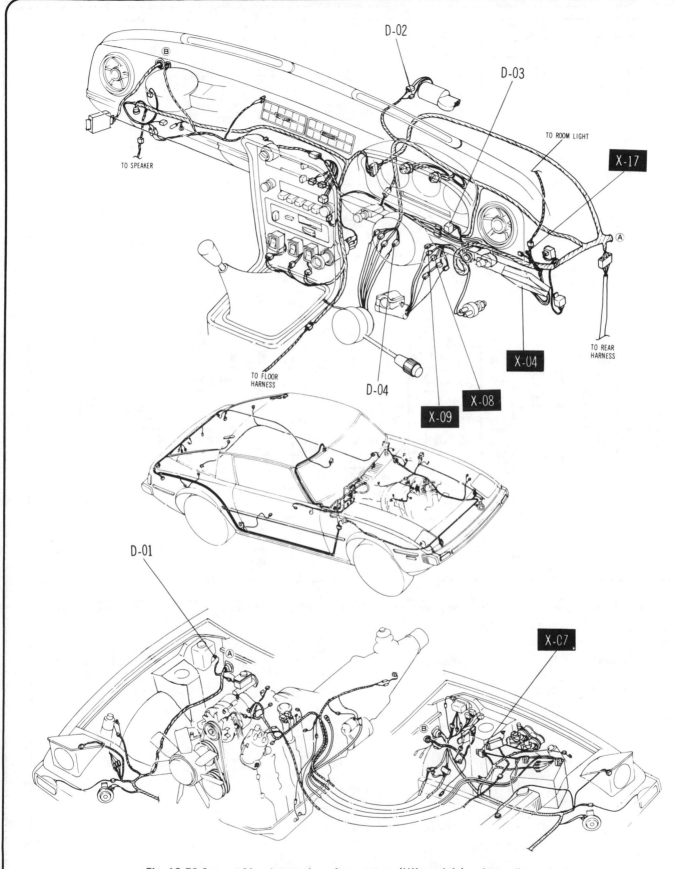

Fig. 10.53 System M: wiper and washer systems (UK models) — loom diagram

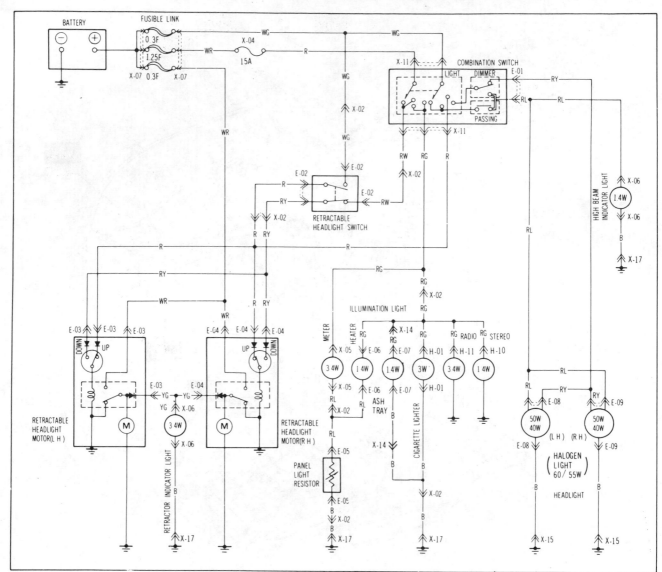

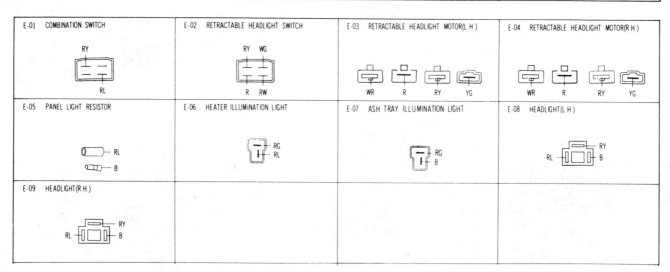

E-01	COMBINATION SWITCH	E-02	RETRACTABLE HEADLIGHT SWITCH	E-03	RETRACTABLE HEADLIGHT MOTOR(L H)	E-04	RETRACTABLE HEADLIGHT MOTOR(R H)
	RY ... RL		RY WG ... R RW		WR R RY YG		WR R RY YG
E-05	PANEL LIGHT RESISTOR	E-06	HEATER ILLUMINATION LIGHT	E-07	ASH TRAY ILLUMINATION LIGHT	E-08	HEADLIGHT(L H)
	RL ... B		RG RL		RG B		RL ... RY B
E-09	HEADLIGHT(R H.)						
	RL ... RY B						

Fig. 10.54 System N: headlight and illumination system (UK models) — schematic diagram

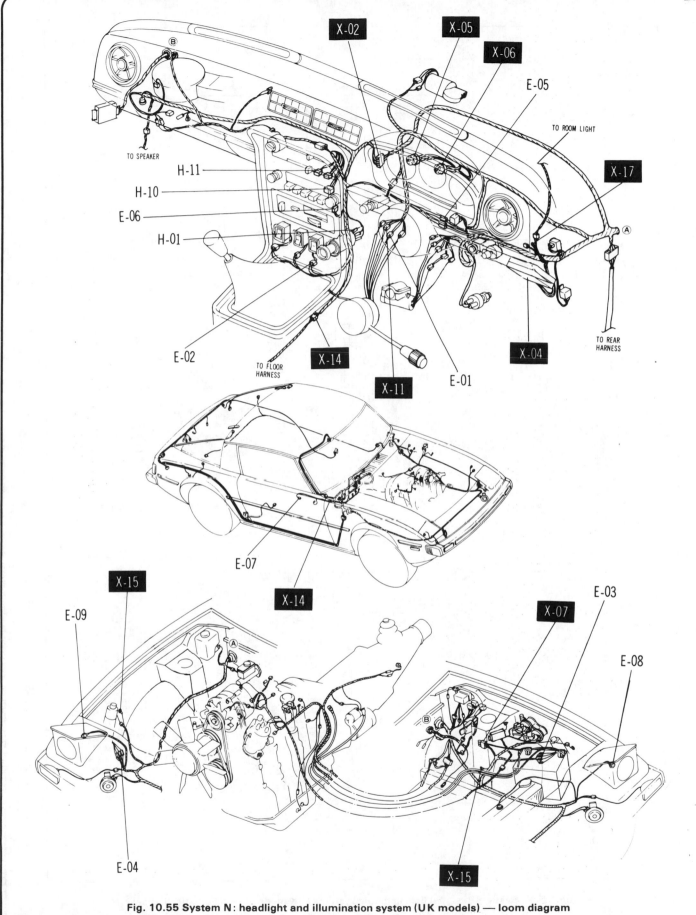

Fig. 10.55 System N: headlight and illumination system (UK models) — loom diagram

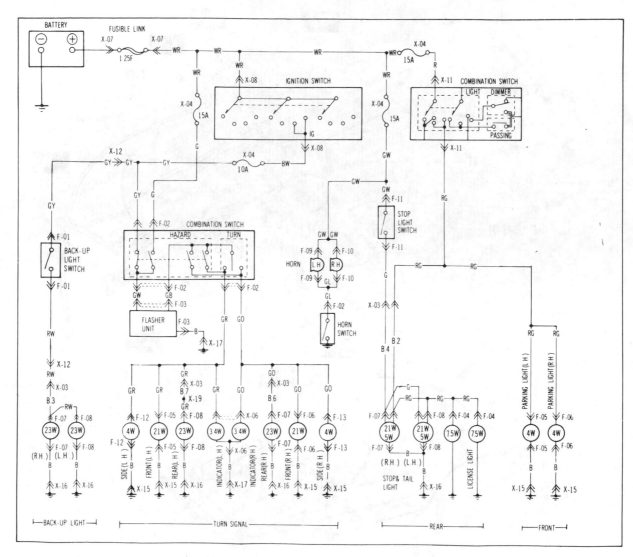

Fig. 10.56 System P: signal light and horn systems (UK models) — schematic diagram

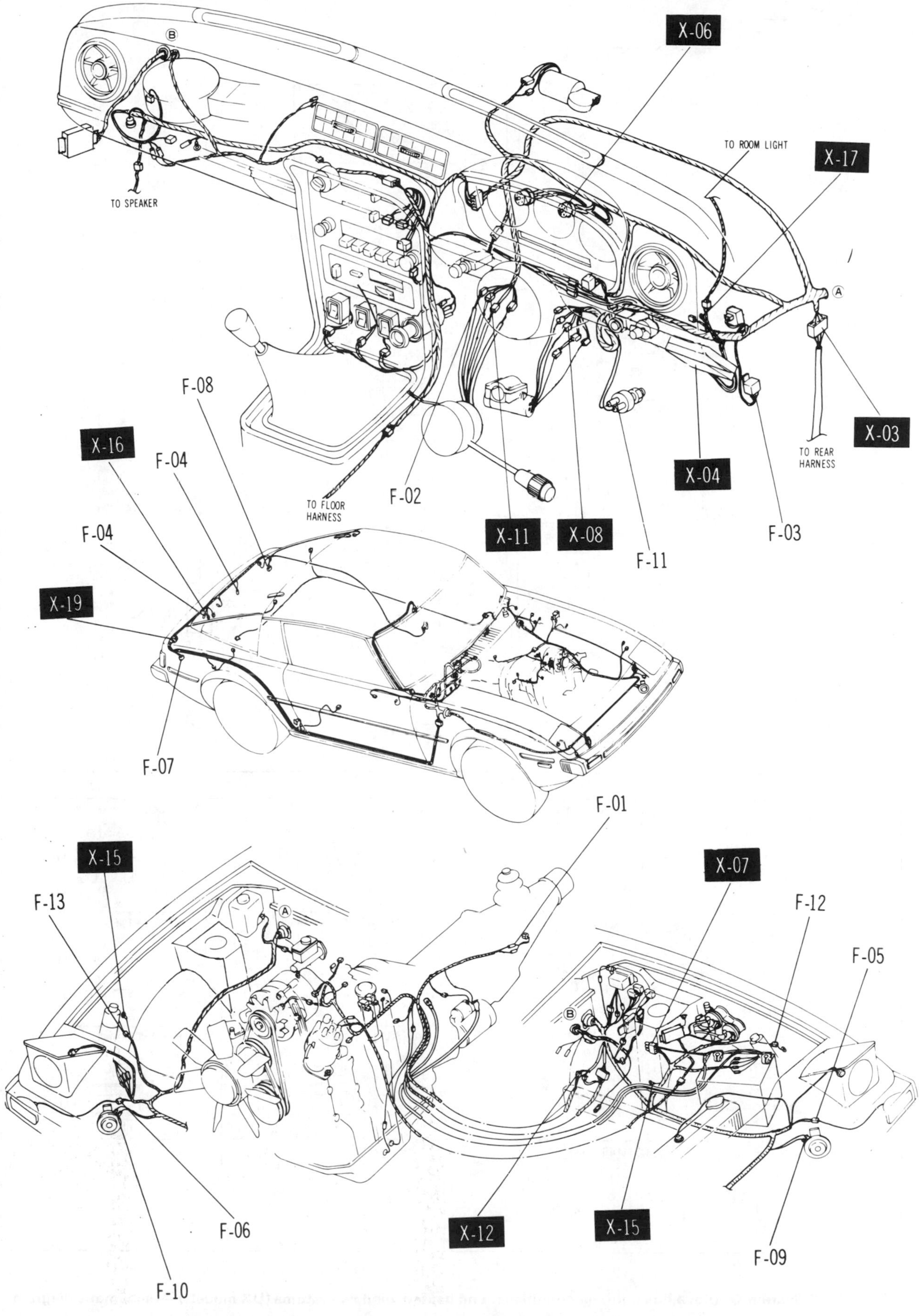

X-06

TO ROOM LIGHT

X-17

TO SPEAKER

A

X-03

TO REAR HARNESS

F-08

X-16

F-04

F-04

X-19

F-07

F-02

TO FLOOR HARNESS

X-11

X-08

F-11

X-04

F-03

F-01

X-15

X-07

F-13

F-12

F-05

A

B

F-06

X-12

X-15

F-09

F-10

Fig. 10.57 System P: signal light and horn systems (UK models) — loom diagram

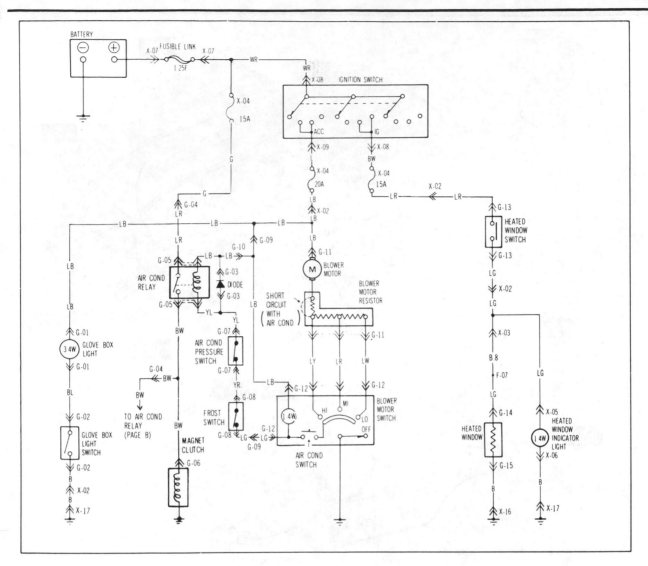

Fig. 10.58 System Q: glove box light, air conditioner and heated window systems (UK models) — schematic diagram

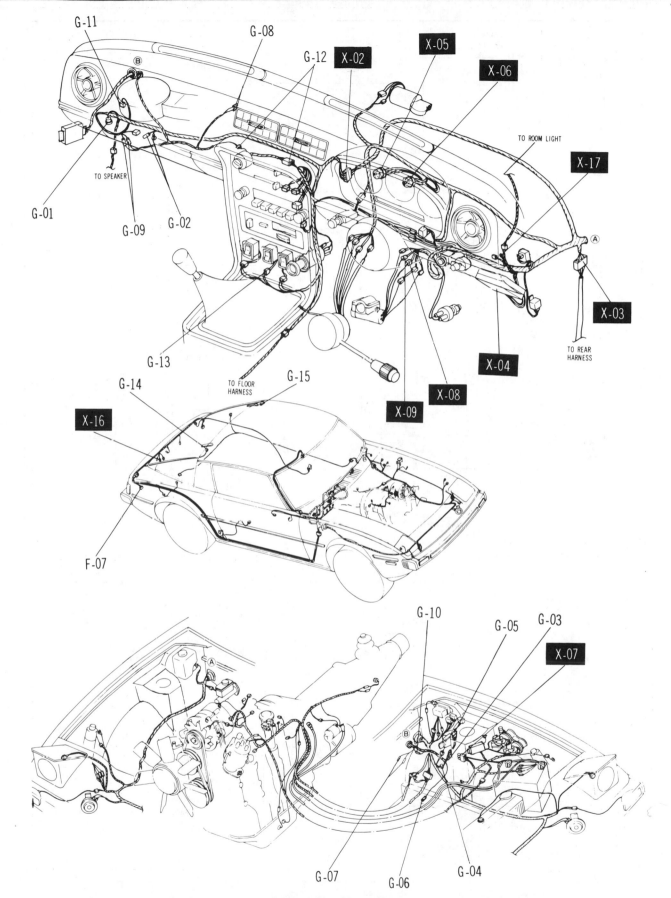

Fig. 10.59 System Q: glove box light, air conditioner and heated window systems (UK models) — loom diagram

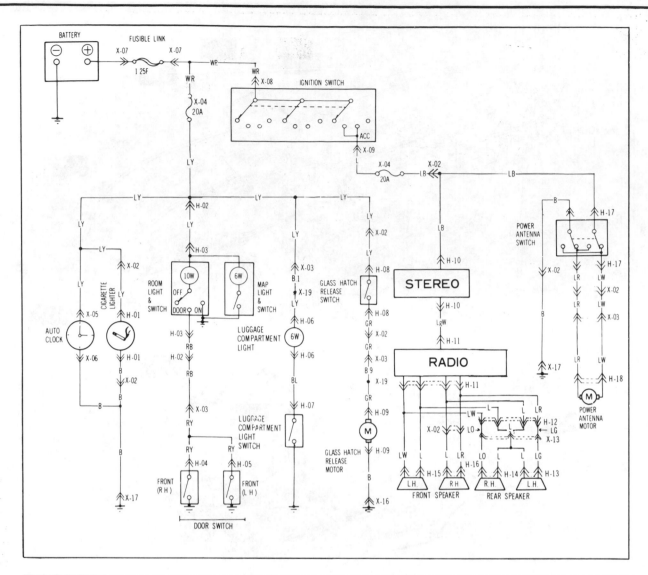

Fig. 10.60 System R: auto clock, cigarette lighter, room and map light, luggage compartment light, glass hatch release system, stereo, radio and power antenna systems (UK models) — schematic diagram

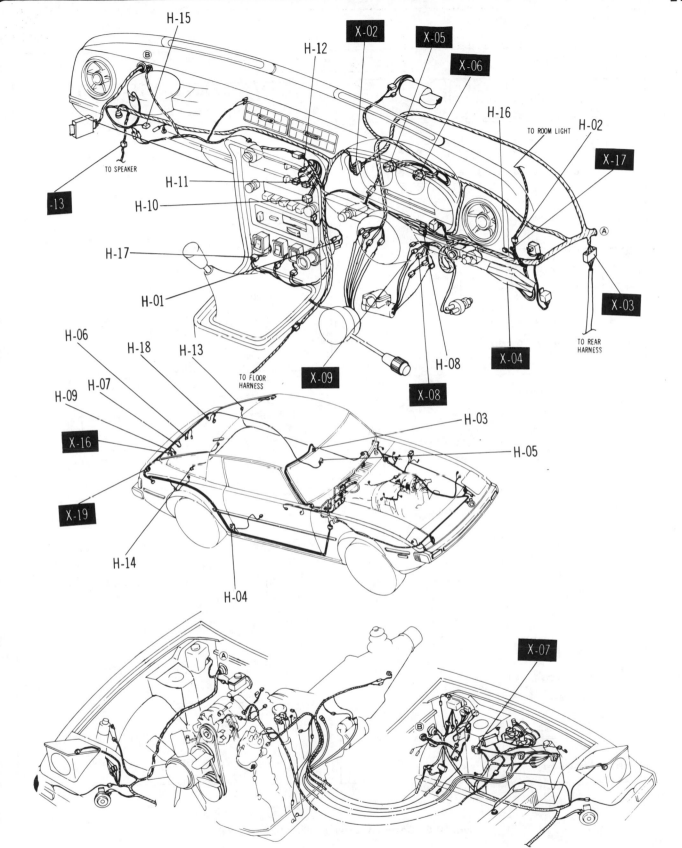

Fig. 10.61 System R: auto clock, cigarette lighter, room and map light, luggage compartment light, glass hatch release system, stereo, radio and power antenna systems (UK models) — loom diagram

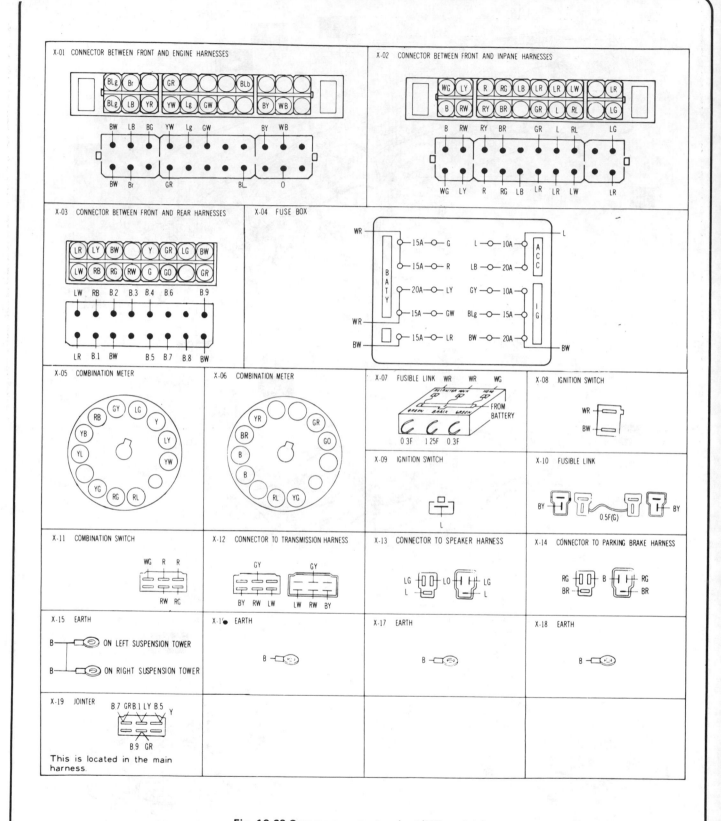

Fig. 10.62 Common connector chart (UK models)

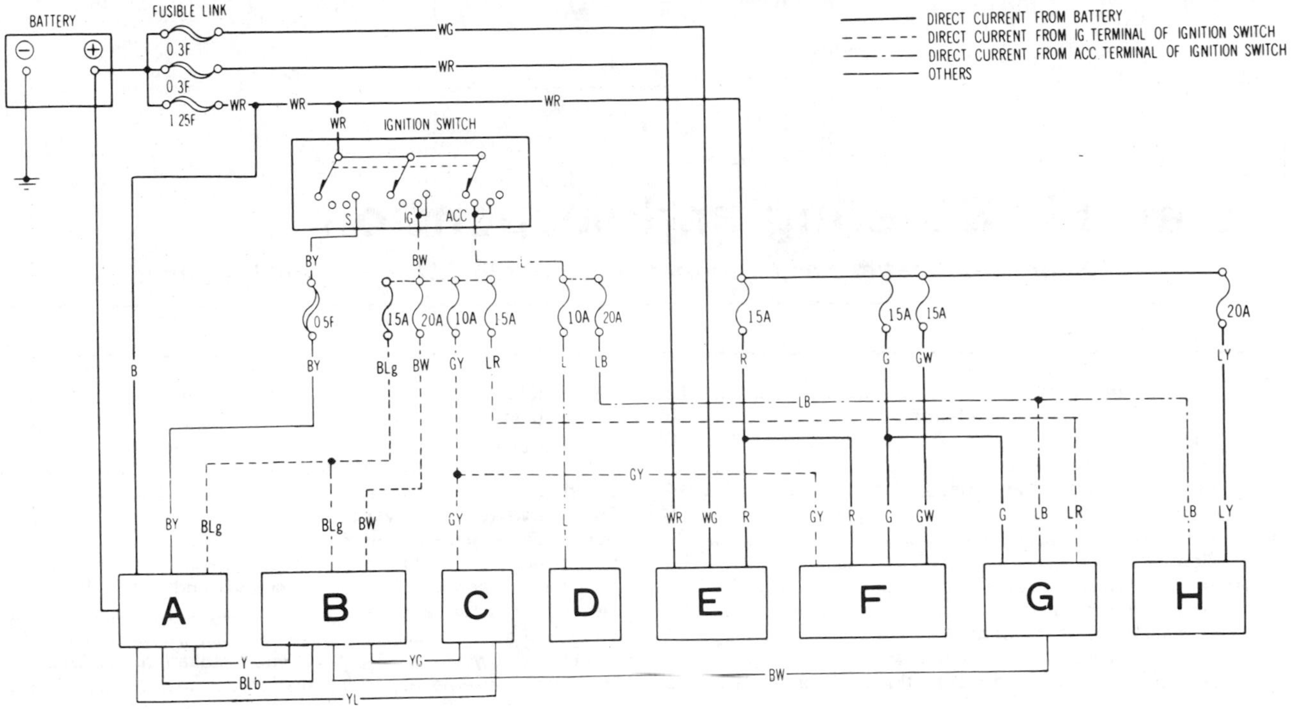

BATTERY

FUSIBLE LINK

0 3F

0 3F

1 25F

WG

WR

WR

WR

WR

WR

IGNITION SWITCH

S

IG

ACC

L

BY

BW

DIRECT CURRENT FROM BATTERY
DIRECT CURRENT FROM IG TERMINAL OF IGNITION SWITCH
DIRECT CURRENT FROM ACC TERMINAL OF IGNITION SWITCH
OTHERS

0 5F

15A 20A 10A 15A

10A 20A

15A

15A 15A

20A

BY

BLg BW GY LR

L LB

R

G GW

LY

B

BY

BLg

BLg BW

GY

LB

GY

LB

BY BLg BLg BW GY L WR WG R GY R G GW G LB LR LB LY

| A | B | C | D | E | F | G | H |

Y

YG

BLb

YL

BW

Fig. 10.63 Schematic diagram showing how the various electrical systems are connected (UK models)

Chapter 11 Steering and suspension

Refer to Chapter 13 for specifications and information related to 1981 through 1985 models

Contents

Specifications

Front coil spring
Spring constant.. 2.16 + 0.15 kg/mm
Free length
   Standard:
      Left... 334.5 mm (13.17 in)
      Right.. 325 mm (12.80 in)

Front shock absorber
Fluid capacity... $225 \begin{smallmatrix} +5 \\ -0 \end{smallmatrix}$ cc $(0.23 \begin{smallmatrix} +0.05 \\ -0 \end{smallmatrix}$ U.S. quarts)

Rear coil spring
Spring constant.. 1.8 ± 0.13 kg/mm
Free length
   Standard.. 323.5 mm (12.74 in)

Steering
Reduction ratio... 17.0 to 20.0:1
Free play of steering wheel (turning direction)
   Limit.. 40 mm (1.57 in)
Backlash between rack and sector gear............... Adjust to 0 mm
Worm bearing preload
   Without sector shaft and column bush........ 2 to 5 cm-kg (1.7 to 4.3 in-lb)
   With sector shaft and column bush.............. 6 to 12 cm-kg (5.2 to 10.4 in-lb)
Clearance between sector shaft and housing bush
Wear limit.. 0.1 mm (0.004 in)
End clearance of adjusting screw and sector shaft.... 0 to 0.1 mm (0 to 0.004 in)
Lubricant... A.P.I. Service (GL-4 SAE 90
Oil capacity... 290 cc (0.31 U.S. quarts, 0.26 Imp quarts)
Max. Wheel angle on full lock
   Wheel on inside of curve............................ 39° 40' ± 2°
   Wheel on outside of curve.......................... 32° 14' ± 2°
Idler arm revolving torque.................................... 2 to 6 kg/135 mm (4.4 to 13.2 lb/5.315 in)
Knuckle arm ball stud revolving torque............... 5 to 12 cm-kg (4.3 to 10.4 in-lb)
Steering geometry
   King pin inclination..................................... 10° 44'
   Camber... 1° 10' ± 30'
   Max. permissible difference in camber between sides.... ± 30'
   Camber offset... 38 mm (1.50 in)
   Caster... 4° 00' ± 45'
   Max. permissible difference in caster between sides.... ± 45'
   Caster trail... 20 mm (0.80 in)
   Toe-in... 0 to 6 mm (0 to 0.24 in)

Wheels
Front	5-J x 13WDC 5½-JJ x 13WDC (Aluminum)
Rear	5-J x 13WDC 5½-JJ x 13WDC (Aluminum)
Run-out limit	
Radial	1.0 mm (0.04 in) 0.5 mm (0.020 in) Aluminum
Lateral	1.0 mm (0.04 in) 0.5 mm (0.020 in) Aluminum

Tires
Front	185/70 HR 13 165 HR 13
Rear	185/70 HR 13 165 HR 13
Inflation pressure	
Front	1.8 kg/cm² (26 psi)
Rear	1.8 kg/cm² (26 psi)
Run-out limit (with wheel disc)	
Radial	2.5 mm (0.098 in)
Lateral	3.0 mm (0.118 in)
Front wheel bearing preload (at wheel set bolt)	0.45 to 0.65 kg (0.99 to 1.43 lb)

Torque wrench settings
	m-kg	ft-lb
Suspension arm to cross member	4.0 to 5.5	29 to 40
Knuckle arm to shock absorber	6.4 to 9.5	46 to 69
Suspension arm balljoint to knuckle arm	6 to 8	43 to 58
Front shock absorber		
Piston rod to mounting block	6.5 to 8.2	47 to 59
Seal cap nut	5 to 6	36 to 43
Piston rod nut	1.35 to 1.65	9.8 to 11.9
Tension rod to lower suspension arm	5.5 to 6.9	40 to 50
Tension rod to bracket	11 to 15	80 to 108
Tension rod bracket to frame	7.6 to 9.5	55 to 69
Stabilizer bar to suspension lower arm	2.4 to 3.5	17 to 25
Front stabilizer support plate	3.8 to 4.7	27 to 34
Shock absorber to axle housing	6.5 to 8.2	47 to 59
Upper link to axle housing	7.7 to 10.5	56 to 76
Upper link to frame	7.7 to 10.5	56 to 76
Lower link to axle housing	7.7 to 10.5	56 to 76
Lower link to frame	7.7 to 10.5	56 to 76
Shock absorber upper	1.3 to 2.5	9 to 18
Steering wheel nut	3.0 to 4.0	22 to 29
Steering gear housing to frame	4.4 to 5.5	32 to 40
Pitman arm to sector shaft	13 to 17	94 to 123
Idler arm bracket to frame	4.4 to 5.5	32 to 40
Idler arm to center link	2.5 to 3.5	18 to 25
Pitman arm to center link	3.0 to 4.5	22 to 33
Tie rod to center link	3.0 to 4.5	22 to 33
Tie rod to knuckle arm	3.0 to 4.5	22 to 33
Tie rod lock nut	7.0 to 8.0	51 to 58
Steering gear box end cover lock nut	23 to 26	166 to 188
Watt link bracket	7.7 to 10.5	56 to 76
Watt link to axle housing	6.5 to 8.2	47 to 59
Watt link to bracket	6.5 to 8.2	47 to 59
Rear stabilizer support plate	3.2 to 4.7	23 to 34
Stabilizer lock nut	1.0 to 1.6	7 to 12
Wheel bolts	9 to 11	65 to 80

1 General description

1 The RX-7 has an independent front suspension of the MacPherson strut type. The front also features coil springs, an anti-roll bar and tension rods. At the rear, a live axle is located by four trailing arms and Watts linkage. Also incorporated at the rear are coil springs and telescopic shock absorbers with a stabilizer bar offered as optional equipment.

2 A four-spoke, leather grip steering wheel gives the driver first contact with the recirculating ball and nut variable ratio steering box. Hooked to this is a steering linkage system consisting of a Pitman arm, idler arms and a three-piece tie-rod. Although fairly conventional in design, the steering system for the RX-7 carries numerous minor modifications.

3 The front hubs are conventional, using taper roller bearings. The rear hubs are of the semi-floating type, on the half-shaft. These are dealt with in Chapter 8.

2 Suspension – general checks

1 The suspension components should normally last a long time, except in cases where damage has occurred due to an accident. The suspension parts, however, should be checked from time to time for signs of wear which will result in a loss of precision handling and riding comfort.

2 Check that the suspension components have not sagged due to wear. Do this by parking the car on a level surface and visually checking that the car sits level. Compare with the photographs to see

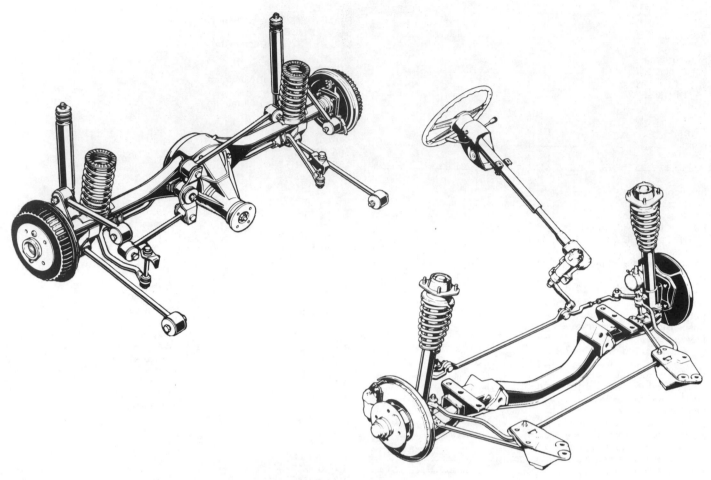

Fig. 11.1 Overall view of the RX-7 suspension and steering systems (Sec 1)

whether the car has markedly sagged. This will normally occur only after many miles and will usually appear more on the driver's side of the vehicle.

3   Put the car in gear and take off the handbrake. Grip the steering wheel at the top with both hands and rock it back and forth. Listen for any squeaks or metallic noises. Feel for free play. If any of these conditions is found, have an assistant do the rocking while the source of the trouble is located.

4   Check the shock absorbers, as these are the parts of the suspension system likely to wear out first. If there is any evidence of fluid leakage, they will definitely need replacing. Bounce the car up and down vigorously. It should feel stiff, and well damped by the shock absorbers. As soon as the bouncing is stopped. the car should return to its normal position without excessive up and down movement. Do not replace the shock absorbers as single units, but rather in pairs unless a failure has occurred at low mileage.

5   Check all rubber bushings for signs of deterioration and cracking. If necessary, replace the rubber portions of the suspension arm.

3   Front hub – removal, inspection and installation

1   Because the front hub assembly and bearings also acts as the rotor for the front brakes, servicing is covered in Chapter 9.

2   Refer to these Sections when the front hub assembly requires removal for checking the suspension components.

4   Front shock absorber – removal and installation

1   Raise the front of the vehicle and support firmly with stands.

2   Remove the front wheel.

3   Remove the front wheel hub as described in Chapter 9.

4   Remove the four bolts which secure the brake backing plate and inner caliper mounting bracket to the spindle (photos).

5   Disengage the flexible hose from the inboard side of the shock absorber by pulling the metal clip out of the bracket with pliers.

6   At the lower portion of the shock, remove the two bolts attaching the knuckle arm to the shock absorber assembly. Access is obtained by turning the steering (photo).

7   Inside the engine compartment, make note of the small triangular mark at the top of the shock absorber. Scribe a mark on the inner fender panel which aligns with this triangle. Upon reassembly, the shock absorber must be placed in this same location (photo).

8   Still inside the engine compartment, remove the four attaching nuts surrounding the top of the shock absorber (photo).

9   Lower the shock absorber assembly from out of its mounting position on the fender panel. Remove the shock absorber assembly through the wheel well (photo).

10   When installing the assembled shock absorber, be sure to line up the triangle with the locating mark you placed on the inner fender panel. If the mounting block is replaced the wheel alignment should be adjusted (Section 26).

11   Place the shock absorber into position at the inner fender and loosely install the four attaching nuts.

12   Install the two bolts at the lower end of the shock absorber into the knuckle arm. The short bolt goes into the front, the longer one at the rear. Turn the steering wheel as necessary for access. Torque these two bolts to 46 to 69 ft-lb (6.4 to 9.5 m-kg) (photo).

13   Torque the four attaching bolts on the inner fender panel to 17 to 22 ft-lb (2.3 to 3.0 m-kg).

14   Attach the flexible hose to the inboard side of the shock absorber with the metal clip. Make sure that the metal clip is fully engaged in the bracket.

15   When installing the backing plate and caliper bracket, make sure the lower mounting bolt is already installed through the bracket from

4.4a Removing the four backing plate attaching bolts ...

4.4b ... and then lifting off the backing plate

4.6 Two bolts secure the lower end of the shock absorber to the steering knuckle arm

4.7 A small locating triangle is at the top of the shock absorber. Make an alignment mark on the fender panel corresponding to this triangle

4.8 Removing the four attaching nuts of the shock absorber

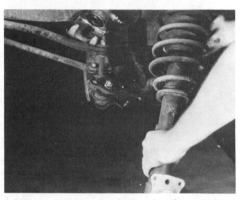

4.9 Removing the shock absorber from the vehicle

4.12 Tightening the knuckle joint bolts

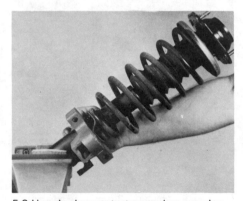

5.3 Use vise jaw protectors such as wooden blocks, while securing the shock absorbers

5.4 A good strong spring compressor should be used to compress the spring

the back side, as accessibility is difficult.

16 Install and tighten the four backing plate attaching bolts.

17 Install the front hub assembly, referring to Chapter 9.

5 Front spring – removal and installation

1 The spring on the front shock absorber is under considerable pressure, requiring a special spring compressor to be used to safely compress the spring and disengage its components. Do not attempt to disassemble the spring without the proper compressor, as serious injury can occur.

2 A strut spring compressor can either be purchased through Mazda dealers or through most auto parts stores. Compressors can also be rented on a daily basis from rental agencies and some auto parts stores.

3 Hold the shock in a vise using wood blocks to cushion the jaws to prevent damage to the shock (photo).

4 Following the manufacturer's instructions for the particular spring compressor being used, slightly compress the spring, making sure that the jaws of the compressor are firmly seated around the coils and cannot slip off (photo).

5 Tighten the compressor from side to side, a little at a time, until the spring seat is clear of the uppermost coil (photo).

6 With the spring firmly compressed and clear of its seat, remove the top lock nut and washer.

7 Pull the mounting block and adjusting plate off the top of the shock absorber (photo).

8 Remove the seat, thrust bearing, spring seat, rubber dust boot and bound bumper above the dust boot (photo).

9 It is wise at this time to relieve all tension on the spring and remove it from the shock absorber. Loosen the compressor, a little at a time, until it is free to be lifted off the shock absorber body. Although some compressors would allow you to lift the spring off the shock absorber in its compressed state, this could prove dangerous should the compressor and spring be jostled and accidentally disengaged

5.5 Tighten the spring compressor until the uppermost coil is clear of the spring seat

5.7 With the locknut removed, the mounting block and adjusting plate can be taken off the end of the shock

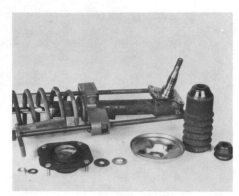

5.8 The components of the shock absorber assembly with the spring still in place

5.17 Tightening the locknut at the top to the proper torque

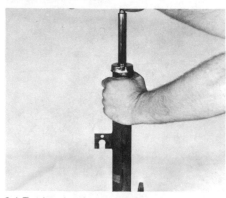

6.1 Testing the shock absorber

9.3 There are two attaching nuts which secure the tension rod to the suspension arm

9.6 Removing the locknut at the forward end of the torsion rod

9.8 The stabilizer bar is connected to the control links which run through the suspension arm

9.9 Unbolting the stabilizer bar, with the brackets still attached, from under the car

from each other.

10 The spring should be checked for cracking or deformation of any kind. If the vehicle was sagging in the front, this is an indication that the springs are in need of replacement.

11 Using the spring compressor, compress the spring approximately 2 in (50.8 mm).

12 With the shock absorber main body mounted in a vise with protective wood blocks, install the spring over the shock absorber body. Make sure the lower coil conforms to the spring seat.

13 Install the dust boot and bound bumper to the shock body.

14 Install the spring seat.

15 Apply a thin coat of rubber grease on both sides of the thrust washer and then install it on the shaft above the spring seat.

16 Install the seat, mounting block and adjusting plate.

17 Install the lock washer and lock nut to the top of the piston rod. Tighten this nut to a torque of 47 to 59 ft-lb (6.5 to 8.2 m-kg) (photo).

18 Carefully relieve tension on the coil spring by loosening the compressor from side to side, a little at a time. Check to be sure the top of the spring is raised properly into its seat.

6 Front shock absorbers – testing

1 To test the shock absorber, hold it in an upright position and work the piston rod up and down its full length of travel, four or five times. If you can feel a strong resistance because of hydraulic pressure, the shock absorber is functioning properly. If you feel no marked resistance or there is a sudden free movement in travel, the shock absorber should be repaired or replaced (photo).

2 If there are excessive amounts of fluid evident on the outside of the shock absorber, the shock absorber should be repaired or replaced.

7 Front shock absorber

1 Although it is possible to strip the shock and fit new parts the work is very intricate and demands extreme cleanliness. Numerous small parts will also be necessary. Because of this, it may be wise for the home mechanic to read over the disassembly process completely

before attempting the job. It may be decided that a Mazda dealer or repair shop specializing in MacPherson strut shock absorbers is better suited to install a replacement cartridge at this point.

2   Push the piston rod into the shock absorber body as far as possible.

3   Hold the shock absorber body in a vise, cushioned from the jaws with wood blocks.

4   .Remove the cap at the top of the shock absorber.

5   Using a wrench which will fit over the piston rod and go into the shock absorber body, remove the cap nut. Mazda has such a wrench available under part number (49 0259 700A) or a suitable wrench can be made from some steel water pipe.

6   .Pull the rubber O-ring from inside the shock absorber body.

7   Pull the piston rod and pressure tube assembly from the shock absorber body. Do not disassemble this assembly as it is available as a complete unit only. This is what is referred to as a replacement cartridge, and must be purchased as such.

8   Front shock absorber – assembly

1   Clean and·inspect all the disassembled parts for wear or fatigue. Replace parts as necessary.

2   Install the piston rod and pressure tube assembly into the shock absorber body.

3   Install a new O ring on the piston rod guide.

4   Fill the shock absorber body with 13.7 cu-in (225 cc) of shock absorber fluid.

5   Install a pilot over the threads of the piston rod to center it in the shock body. This pilot is available through Mazda dealers under part number 49 0370 590.

6   Apply grease to the lip of the seal, and insert the cap nut carefully through the pilot and onto the piston rod.

7   With the piston rod extended to its maximum length, tighten the cap nut temporarily with the wrench which will fit over the piston rod and into the shock absorber body.

8   Fully lower the piston rod and tighten the cap nut to a torque of 36 to 43 ft-lb (5.0 to 6.0 m-kg).

9   Install the spring and its related components referring to Section 5. Install the shock absorber to the car.

9   Tension rod and stabilizer bar – removal and installation

1   Raise the front end of the vehicle and support firmly with stands.

2   Remove the engine under-cover pan. This is done by removing the five forward bolts and single bolts on either side, and then lowering the pan out of the crossmember.

3   Remove the tension rod attaching nuts on the lower side of the suspension arm. There are two nuts to each tension rod (photo).

4   In order to retain the original front end geometry, measure the distance from the end of the tension rod to the support block before removing the large lock nut on the end of the tension rod. Also, do not change the position of the lock nut on the rear side of the support bracket, as this will help to position the bar in its original position.

5   Remove the cotter key going through the large lock nut.

6   Remove the large lock nut on the end of the tension rod (photo).

7   Push the rod through the mounting bracket and remove it from under the car. If both rods are removed at the same time, apply an identifying mark to each one designating it as either left or right.

8   Remove the lock nut and jamb nut from the end of the stabilizer bar where it mounts to the small control link. Due to the tension at this point it will probably be easier to completely remove the control link from the stabilizer bar and the suspension arm. Do this on both sides of the car (photo).

9   Directly behind the point from which the tension rods lock nut was removed, there is a bracket and rubber bushing for the stabilizer bar. Remove the bolt which secures this bracket and bushing (photo).

10 Remove the three bolts and one nut which secure each of the mounting brackets to the frame. The mounting brackets, left and right, will have to be removed with the stabilizer bar (photo).

11 Lower the stabilizer bar, along with the two front brackets, from the vehicle as a unit (photo).

12 Inspect the removed parts for cracks, deformation, damage or weakness. Replace as necessary.

9.11 Lowering the stabilizer bar support bracket from the body

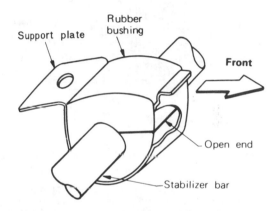

Fig. 11.2 Proper positioning of the rubber bushing on the front stabilizer bar (Sec 9)

13 It is advisable whenever these components are removed to install new rubber bushings.

14 The flat side of the rubber bushings on the tension rods go towards the bracket.

15 If the rubber bushings on the stabilizer bar are replaced or removed during the inspection process, the slit or opening in the rubber bushing should be rotated towards the front of the vehicle. The hole in the accompanying support plate should be towards the rear of the car.

16 Lift the stabilizer bar with the mounting brackets into position and install the bracket attaching bolts and nuts. Tighten these securely.

17 Install the bolts for the support plate loosely, but do not tighten at this time to ease movement of the stabilizer bar.

18 Install the short control links through the suspension arm and then install the stabilizer bar ends to the control links. Tighten the lock nut at the top of the control links until 0.512 in (13 mm) of threaded stock is above the nut. Install and tighten the jamb nuts on top of these lock nuts (Fig. 10.3).

19 Install the front end of the tension rod through the bracket, but do not tighten the large lock nut at this time.

20 Install the attaching nuts at the rear end of the tension rods. Torque to 40-50 ft-lb (5.5 to 6.9 m-kg).

21 Install and tighten the front lock nut at the tension rod until the same amount of threaded rod appears at the end of the rod. This will get the tension rod to its original position. Install the cotter pin through the lock nut.

22 It should be noted that the above procedure should be used only if the original components are retained. If new bushings or tension rods are used, there is an alternative method to arrive at proper rod tension.

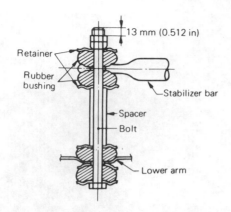

Fig. 11.3 Tightening measurements of control link lock and jam nuts (Sec 9)

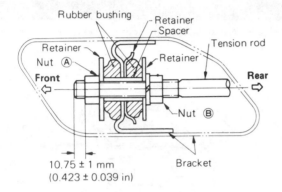

Fig. 11.4 Tightening measurement of tension rod locknut (Sec 9)

23 Install the tension rod lock until 0.423 plus or minus 0.039 in (10.75 plus or minus 1 mm) of rod is shown in front of the nut. Then tighten the rear lock to a torque of 80 to 108 ft-lb (11 to 15 m-kg) with an open-end torque wrench. Install the cotter pin.
24 Lower the vehicle to the ground and bounce it a few times to allow the components to settle in the proper position.
25 Tighten the support plates to the stabilizer bar to a torque of 40 to 50 ft-lb (5.5 to 6.9 m-kg).
26 Install the engine under-cover pan.
27 It is advisable to have the front suspension properly aligned after this work (Section 26).

10 Suspension arm – removal and installation

1 Raise the front end of the vehicle and support firmly with stands.
2 Remove the front wheel.
3 Remove the two knuckle arm attaching bolts at the lower end of the shock absorber. Gain access to these bolts by moving the steering wheel first to the right and then to the left. Note the length and positions of the bolts.
4 Disconnect the tie-rod end using a suitable puller. In the absence of a tie-rod puller, a common gear puller can be used. First remove the cotter pin, then loosen the lock nut to the top of the threads. Pry down the rubber bushing slightly to allow the jaws of the puller to be seated, and then use the puller to force the joint out of its mooring.
5 Disconnect the tension rod from the suspension arm by removing the attaching nuts on the lower side of the arm.
6 Disconnect the stabilizer bar from the suspension arm by removing the control link. Remove the lock nut and jamb nut at the top of the control link, then remove the top of the stabilizer bar and the control link. The tension rod and stabilizer bar do not need disconnecting at any other position.
7 Remove the suspension arm attaching bolt on the inboard end of the suspension arm. You will need two wrenches for this, one for the bolt and one for the lock nut on the other side of the arm (photo).

8 Remove the suspension arm with the knuckle arm attached to it.
9 Separate the knuckle arm from the suspension arm by using the puller in the same manner as used for the tie-rod end. Before disassembling note the relation of the knuckle arm to the suspension arm for reassembly (photo).
10 Inspect the suspension arm and knuckle arm for damage or deformation.
11 Check the balljoint for looseness or damage.
12 Check the balljoint dust cover for damage.
13 Check the arm bushing for damage or deterioration.
14 Replace parts as necessary. The suspension arm and balljoint cannot be disassembled from each other easily. If either is defective Mazda recommends that they be replaced as a unit.
15 The bushing in the suspension arm can be pressed out and a new one pressed in quite easily. Use a socket of the proper width to press the bushing out towards the front of the arm. A new bushing is pressed in from the front. A press or a vise can be used for this procedure. Do not use lubricant on the bushing or suspension arm bore.
16 Mount the knuckle arm to the suspension arm so that the threaded stop bolt is towards the front of the suspension arm, in its original position.
17 Tighten the lock nut on the knuckle arm to a torque of approximately 46 ft-lb (6.4 m-kg) and then tighten the nut until the cotter pin can be pushed through the rod and nut (photo).
18 Bend the cotter pin back over the nut and cut if necessary so as not to interfere with adjoining suspension or steering components.
19 Place the suspension arm into position and install the attaching bolt and nut. Do not tighten at this time.
20 Hinge the suspension arm into position and loosely install the two balljoint-to-knuckle arm bolts. The short bolt goes in the front, the longer bolt in the rear. Move the steering back and forth for access.
21 Move the tension rod into position and install the two attaching bolts. Torque these bolts to 40 to 50 ft-lb (5.5 to 6.9 m-kg).
22 Install the control link through the suspension arm and connect the end of the stabilizer bar to the top of the control link. Tighten the lock nut on the control link as illustrated (Fig. 11.3). Install the jam nut to prevent the link from becoming loose.
23 Install the tie-rod to the knuckle arm and tighten the locking nut to approximately 22 ft-lb (3.0 m-kg). Tighten the nut until the cotter pin can be forced through the stud and locking nut. Bend back the cotter pin and cut if necessary (photo).
24 Now fully tighten the two attaching bolts previously installed loosely at the knuckle arm. Torque should be 43 to 58 ft-lb (6.0 to 8.0 m-kg).
25 Install the wheel and lower the car to the ground.
26 Bounce the car a few times to allow the suspension to settle.
27 Tighten the suspension arm attaching bolt to 29 to 40 ft-lb (4.0 to 5.5 m-kg) (photo).
28 Install the engine under cover pan.
29 Road test the vehicle and check for noise or excessive movement.
30 It is recommended that the front end be aligned after performing these operations, as alignment may be changed slightly.

11 Tie-rod – removal and installation

1 Raise the front end of the vehicle and support firmly with stands.
2 Remove the front wheel.
3 Disconnect the tie-rod from the knuckle arm using a puller. A common gear puller will work. Remove the cotter pin and loosen the lock nut until it is at the top of the stud, covering the threads. Pry the rubber bushing down so the jaws of the puller can be forced between the rubber and the knuckle arm. Tighten the puller bolt at the top of the stud until the tie-rod breaks loose from the knuckle arm – assist by tapping the end of the puller bolt with a hammer (photos).
4 Perform these same steps to disconnect the tie-rod where it meets the center link (photos).
5 Remove the tie-rod from the vehicle (photo).
6 If the tie-rod ends are being replaced, carefully measure the distance between the two lock nuts on the tie-rod. Also measure the total distance of the complete tie-rod assembly. Note the relative position of the ends to the bar (photos).
7 To remove the tie-rod ends, loosen the lock nuts at the center, threaded portion of the rod and then unscrew the ends (photo).
8 Install the new tie-rod ends until the distances measured before disassembly are achieved. Turn the rod ends until they are turned in

10.7 Two wrenches must be used to loosen the suspension arm attaching bolt

10.9 Using a gear puller to separate the knuckle arm from the suspension arm

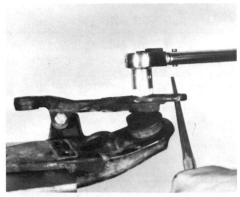

10.17 Tightening the knuckle arm locknut to the proper torque

11.3a Use pliers to straighten and then remove the cotter pin from the locknut

11.3b The locknut can then be removed from the tie-rod end

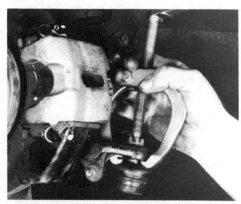

11.3c A gear puller can be used to loosen the connection where the tie-rod meets the knuckle arm

11.4a Removing the cotter pin from the tie-rod connection at the center link

11.4b The gear puller is again used to separate the tie-rod from the center link

11.5 The tie-rod can then be lifted clear from under the car

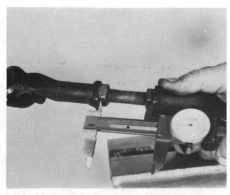

11.6a Measuring the distance between the locknuts before the tie-rod ends are removed

11.6b Applying marks on the center tie-rod portion and the ends in order to reassemble the components correctly

11.7 Two wrenches are needed to remove the tie-rod ends from the center threaded portion

the same direction as the original ones.

9   Install the tie-rod assembly to the center link and the knuckle arm. Tighten the lock nuts to a torque of 22 to 33 ft-lb (3.0 to 4.5 m-kg). Align the cotter pin hole with one of the grooves in the castellated nut and install new split pins to the lock nuts.

10 Install the wheel(s).

11 Lower the vehicle to the ground.

12 Whenever the tie-rod or balljoint is replaced, it is recommended that the toe-in for the front alignment be reset to achieve the proper geometry (Section 26).

12 Center link – removal and installation

1   Raise the vehicle and support firmly with stands.

2   Disconnect the center link from both tie-rods, and the Pitman arm and the idler arm using a puller. To do this remove the cotter pin and loosen the lock nut until it is at the top of the stud, covering the threads of the stud. Then pry down the rubber boot and install the fork of the puller (a common gear puller will work fine). Tighten the bolt of the puller until it is tight against the stud. Tap the head of the puller bolt with a hammer to break the connection. If this doesn't work, tighten the puller bolt one-quarter turn and strike with the hammer again (photo).

3   Remove the center link from under the vehicle (photo).

4   Check the center link for deformation, cracks or damage or any kind, and replace if necessary.

5   If the holes in the center link for the tie-rod ends or idler arm have been reamed and enlarged due to wear, the center link should be replaced.

6   Position the center link and loosely install each of the four connections. Do not tighten any of the castellated lock nuts until all joints are in place.

7   Tighten the idler-arm-to-center-link lock nut to 18 to 25 ft-lb (2.5 to 3.5 m-kg), aligning the cotter pin hole with one of the grooves in the nut. Install a new cotter pin.

8   Tighten all other ball joint locknuts to 22 to 33 ft-lb (3.0 to 4.5 m-kg), aligning the hole for the cotter pin with one of the grooves in the lock nut. Install new cotter pins.

9   Lower the vehicle and test drive.

13 Idler arm – removal and installation

1   Raise the vehicle and support firmly with jack stands.

2   Disconnect the idler arm from the center link. To do this, remove the cotter pin and loosen the lock nut until it is at the top of the stud, covering the threads of the stud. Then pry down the rubber boot and install the fork of the puller (a common gear puller will work fine). Tighten the bolt of the puller until it is tight against the stud. Tap the head of the puller bolt with a hammer to break the connection. If this doesn't work, tighten the puller bolt one-quarter turn and strike with the hammer again (photo).

3   Remove the two nuts attaching the idler arm to the inside frame rail (photo).

4   Remove the idler arm assembly from under the vehicle (photo).

5   To disassemble the idler arm, place the assembly in a vise and

remove the cotter pin, lock nut and washer (photo).

6   Before removing the idler arm from the bracket, make a mark across the arm and bracket for reinstallation in the same location (photo).

7   Separate the idler arm from the bracket and remove the two plastic bushings from the ends of the bracket (photo).

8   Check the bushings and replace if they show signs of wear (photo).

9   If the balljoint at the end of the idler arm is loose or shows signs of wear or damage, the idler arm should be replaced as a unit.

10 If a new idler arm is purchased, make sure that your alignment mark is transferred to a new arm in the same location.

11 Apply lithium based grease to the bushings and install them in the bracket (photos).

12 Liberally pack the idler arm shaft with grease where it runs through the bracket (photo).

13 Install the greased idler arm in the bracket, aligning the marks made upon disassembly (photo).

14 Install the washer and lock nut. Tighten the lock nut until snug. If a spring scale is available, check the revolving torque of the idler arm and adjust the lock nut until a reading of 4.4 to 13.2 lb (2 to 6 kg) is obtained on the scale.

15 Install a new cotter pin.

16 Install the idler arm assembly to the inside of the frame rail and tighten the attaching nuts to 32 to 40 ft-lb (4.4 to 5.5 m-kg).

17 Connect the idler arm to the center link and tighten the lock nut to a torque of 18 to 25 ft-lb (2.5 to 3.5 m-kg).

18 Install a new cotter pin.

19 Lower the vehicle and test drive.

14 Pitman arm – removal and installation

1   Raise the front end of the vehicle and support firmly with jack stands.

2   Disconnect the Pitman arm from the center link with the puller (a common gear puller will work fine). Remove the cotter pin and loosen the lock nut until it is at the top of the stud. Pry down the rubber boot and install the fork of the puller. Tighten the puller bolt on the top of the stud and then tap the puller bolt with a hammer, until the connection breaks free (photos).

3   From the other end of the Pitman arm, loosen the large lock nut from the sector shaft untl it is at the end of the shaft, covering the threads (photo).

4   As this large lock nut is installed with considerable torque, it may be necessary to use a large puller to remove the Pitman arm from the sector shaft. The small gear puller suitable for all other steering and suspension joints may not have enough force to break this connection.

5   With a suitable puller installed with the fork on top of the Pitman arm and the bolt tightened against the end of the sector shaft, strike the end of the puller bolt to break the connection It may be necessary to continue tightening the bolt and striking the bolt to free the Pitman arm (photo).

6   Remove the Pitman arm from the shaft, and check for deformation or damage.

7   Install the Pitman arm onto the sector shaft, aligning the serrations of the arm and shaft. The serrations will allow the installation in only one position. If the Pitman arm does not freely slide up the sector

12.2 Removing the cotter pin at the locknut where the center link meets the tie-rod

12.3 The disconnected center link can then be removed from under the vehicle

13.2 Removing the locknut where the idler arm meets the center link

13.3 Two nuts secure the idler arm to the inside of the frame rail

13.4 Disconnected from the center link and the frame, the idler arm can be removed from under the car

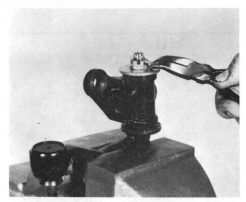

13.5a With the idler arm assembly placed in a vise, remove the cotter pin

13.5b After the cotter pin has been removed, the locknut and washer can follow

13.6 For reassembly purposes, make an identifying mark across the idler arm and bracket

13.7 Lifting the idler arm bracket off the idler arm

13.8 All parts should be cleaned and checked for signs of wear or damage

13.11 Lithium-based grease should be liberally applied to the bushings

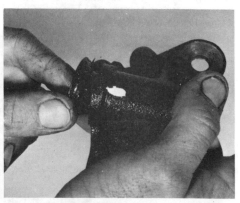

13.11b The greased bushings should then be placed inside the bracket

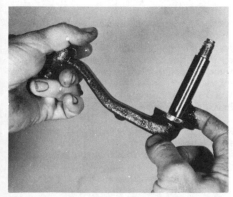

13.12 The idler arm shaft should also receive a generous portion of grease before it is installed into the bracket

13.13 Grease can also be packed into the bracket with the idler arm installed

14.2a Following the removal of the cotter pin, the locknut can be loosened until it is at the end of the threaded portion

14.2b With the locknut protecting the threads, a gear puller is used to break the connection

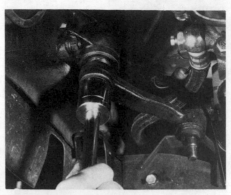

14.3 Loosening the large locknut where the Pitman arm meets the steering box sector shaft

14.5 A larger gear puller may be necessary to loosen this connection as the Pitman arm is installed with considerable force

15.2 The luggage compartment side covers must be removed for access to the top of the rear shock absorbers

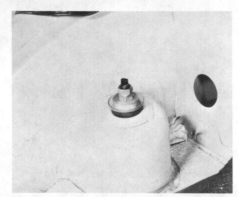

15.3 The top of the shock absorber with its lock and jam nuts

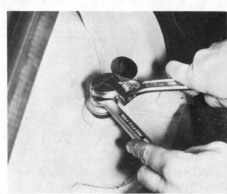

15.4 Two wrenches are needed to remove the lock and jam nuts from the shock absorber stud

15.6 Removing the bolt which travels through the lower 'eye' end of the shock absorber

15.7 The shock absorber can then be removed from under the vehicle

shaft, check that the serrations are matched.
8   Tighten the lock nut to a torque of 94 to 123 ft-lb (13 to 17 m-kg).
9   Connect the Pitman arm to the center link and tighten the lock nut to 22 to 33 ft-lb (3.0 to 4.5 m-kg). Install a new cotter pin.
10   Lower the vehicle and test drive.

15 Rear shock absorber – removal and installation

1   Raise the rear end of the vehicle and support firmly with jack stands positioned under the rear axle housings.
2   The side covers in the luggage compartment must be removed to gain access to the top of the shock absorber. There are four screws across the top of this trim panel, two of these screws being hidden with plastic plugs which must be pried out with a screwdriver. There are also two screws at the bottom of the trim panel which go into the floorboard, under the carpet. With all attaching screws removed, the trim panel can be lifted out from the vehicle (photo).

3   The upper end of the shock absorber is now visible at the top of its raised tower (photo).
4   While holding the top shock stud with a small wrench or vise grips, remove the lock nut and jamb nut on the shock absorber shaft (photo).
5   Also from the top of the shock absorber, remove the large washer and rubber bushing.
6   From under the vehicle, remove the nut and bolt at the lower 'eye' end of the shock absorber (photo).
7   Remove the shock absorber from under the vehicle. It may be necessary to use a screwdriver or bar to pry the lower end of the shock out of its mounting bracket (photo).
8   Measure the overall length of the shock absorber for easier reinstallation.
9   Inspect the shock absorber for noise, fluid leakage, function and bushing wear. Replace if any of these conditions is found.
10   The shock absorber should be compressed and then extended its full length a few times to check for any free movement. Replace if free movement is found.

11 To refit the shock absorber, install one cup washer (with the cupped portion towards the top) and one rubber bushing onto the top of the shock absorber shaft.

12 Extend the shock absorber until the overall length is approximately the same as when removed. It will be difficult to compress or extend the shock absorber once in position.

13 Push the top of the shock absorber through the hole in the floorboard and then install the bolt and lock nut through the lower bracket and 'eye' end of the shock absorber.

14 After checking that the upper end of the shock absorber shaft extends sufficiently through the hole in the floorboard, tighten the lower lock nut to 47 to 59 ft-lb (6.5 to 8.2 m-kg).

15 Push a rubber bushing and cup washer onto the top of the shaft.

16 Tighten the lock nut (the larger of the two nuts) until there is 0.323 in (8.2 mm) of threaded shaft visible on top of the lock nut and jamb nut. This means that both nuts must be in place on the shaft for

an accurate measurement.

17 Install the side trim panel in the luggage compartment.

18 Lower the vehicle to the ground.

16 Rear coil spring – removal and installation

1 As there may be slight tension on the rear suspension components as they are disconnected, do not use your fingers to push the connecting bolts through the brackets. Use a hammer and drift to follow the bolts through.

2 To aid in matching the correct connecting bolts and nuts to the suspension component, temporarily install each nut and bolt to the disconnected component.

3 Information on disconnecting or completely removing the various rear suspension components can be found elsewhere in this Chapter.

4 Raise the vehicle and support with jack stands at the forward brackets at the lower links on either side of the car (photo).

5 Support the rear axle casing with a jack which can be adjusted up or down.

6 Remove the rear wheel(s).

7 From the axle housing, remove the lower end of the shock absorber from its bracket.

8 Disconnect the lower link where it meets the axle housing adjacent to the shock absorber mounting. Use one wrench to loosen the nut and another wrench to hold the bolt head (photo).

9 Disconnect the upper link where it meets the axle housing near the top of the wheel. Again, use two wrenches to disconnect (photo).

10 If the car is equipped with a rear stabilizer bar, this should be disconnected at the front ends of the bar.

11 Disconnect the right and left Watts links from their brackets on the axle housing. It is advisable to completely remove the center pivoting bell crank for these links (photos).

12 Carefully lower the axle housing with the jack. Do this very slowly and watch for interference with brake lines, parking brake cables and other components.

13 Before removing the coil spring, place some identifying marks on it

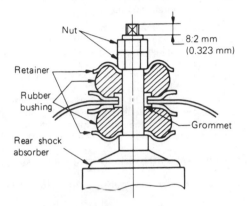

Fig. 11.5 Tightening measurement of rear shock absorber lock and jam nuts (Sec 15)

16.4 This is the correct location for the jack stands while rear suspension work is being done

16.8 Disconnecting the lower link using two wrenches

16.9 Disconnecting the upper link

16.11a Disconnecting the Watts link from its bracket

16.11b The Watts links can be completely disconnected at the pivot point on the differential

16.14 With the rear axle lowered, the coil springs can be lifted out of their seats

16.15 Remove the upper coil spring seat if it did not come out with the spring

16.16 The rubber limiter should be checked for wear or damage

to show which end is the top and also how the coils are positioned in the seats at the top and bottom.

14 Remove the coil springs by lifting them out of their seats (photo).

15 Check the rubber seat at the top of the coil spring for deterioration, cracking or damage and replace as necessary. This seat may or may not come down with the coil spring (photo).

16 Check the rubber limiter and replace as necessary (photo).

17 Check the coil spring itself for cracks or any damage. If the vehicle has been sagging in the rear, this is an indication that the coil springs are in need of replacement.

18 Coil springs should always be replaced in pairs.

19 Install the coil spring in the bottom seat using your reference marks for proper positioning.

20 Carefully raise the rear axle housing, again watching for interference with rear end components. As the axle housing is raised check to make sure the coil springs are properly seating themselves at the top.

21 Raise the rear axle housing until the weight of the vehicle is transferred from the jack stands on the sides of the car to the adjustable jack under the axle housing. Then lower the adjustable jack until the weight is transferred back to the jack stands.

22 Carefully check again that the springs are properly seated but do not jostle them as at this point they are under tension and could cause injury if dislodged from their seats.

23 Connect all the links and shock absorbers to their original positions on the axle housings but do not tighten any of the lock nuts at this time. When installing the upper links, the bolt head should be towards the inboard side of the vehicle with the nut on the outboard side of the bracket. To help in aligning the holes in the components and brackets, use a drift or alignment tool to move the component slightly to thread the bolt through the bracket and component.

24 With all bolts and lock nuts in place but not fully tightened, lower the vehicle to the ground to settle all the rear end components. Then tighten to specifications:

a) Watts links to bracket – 47 to 59 ft-lb (6.5 to 8.2 m-kg).

b) Upper and lower links to bracket – 56 to 76 ft-lb (7.7 to 10.5 m-kg).

c) Rear shock absorber lower end to bracket – 47 to 59 ft-lb (6.5 to 8.2 m-kg).

17 Watts links – removal and installation

1 Raise the rear end of the vehicle and support firmly on jack stands positioned at the forward side of the lower link brackets.

2 Support the rear axle housing with a jack in the center.

3 Disconnect the right Watts link from its mounting bracket on the frame. Do this by removing the lock nut, holding the bolt head with another wrench, and then forcing the bolt through the link and bracket with a hammer and drift.

4 Disconnect the left Watts link from its mounting bracket on the frame in the same manner.

5 Remove the lock nut on the center pivoting bell crank where the two Watts links meet.

6 Before removing the Watts links as an assembly, make an identifying mark on each of the links to indicate which is the outside end of the links and which is the rear of the links.

7 Pry the center bracket from the axle housing and remove the

bracket with the two links as an assembly.

8 Inspect the parts for damage, cracks or deformation.

9 Check the rubber bushings and, if defective, the link must be replaced as an assembly.

10 Install the Watts link, using your identifying marks for proper positioning.

11 Install the bolts and lock nuts temporarily at this time.

12 Lower the rear end of the vehicle and, with the full weight of the car on the suspension, tighten the nuts to the following specifications:

a) Watts link to bracket on body frame – 47 to 59 ft-lb (6.5 to 8.2 m-kg).

b) Watts link to bracket on rear axle housing – 47 to 59 ft-lb (6.5 to 8.2 m-kg).

c) Watts link bracket to rear axle housing – 56 to 76 ft-lb (7.7 to 10.5 m-kg).

18 Rear stabilizer bar – removal and installation

1 Raise the rear end of the vehicle and support with jack stands positioned at the front side of the lower link brackets.

2 Disconnect both ends of the stabilizer bar by removing the lock nut at the bottom of the control link. If necessary, remove the mounting bracket attached to the frame rail.

3 The stabilizer bar is now held in place by two support plates on the axle housing. Remove the bolts securing the support plates to the housing and remove the stabilizer bar and support plates from under the vehicle.

4 Inspect the bar for cracks, deformation and damage. Replace as necessary.

5 Inspect the rubber bushings used on the control links and on the support plates. If cracked, deteriorated or damaged, replace with new bushings.

6 If the support plate bushings were removed or replaced with new ones, turn the bushings so that the open end is towards the rear of the support plate and vehicle. The hole for the support plate mounting bolt

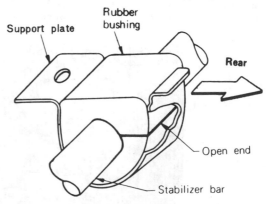

Fig. 11.6 Proper positioning of the rubber bushing on the rear stabilizer bar (Sec 18)

should be towards the front.

7   Place the stabilizer bar with the support plates attached into position and loosely install the support plate mounting bolts. Do not tighten at this time.

8   If removed, install the mounting brackets to the frame rails and tighten the nuts to a torque of 27 to 38 ft-lb (3.8 to 5.3 m-kg).

9   Install the control links and stabilizer bar ends using the four rubber bushings on each side. Thread the lock nut and jam nut onto the control link bolt and tighten until there is 0.169 in (4.3 mm) of threaded rod protruding through the tightened jam nut.

10   Lower the vehicle to the ground, and with the full weight of the car on the suspension, torque the support plate bolts to 23 to 34 ft-lb (3.2 to 4.7 m-kg).

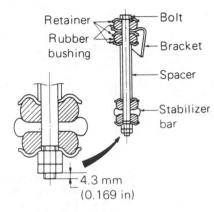

Fig. 11.7 Proper tightening measurement of the rear control link (Sec 18)

19 Upper and lower links – removal and installation

1   Raise the rear end of the vehicle and support firmly with jack stands at the front side of the lower link brackets.

2   Support the rear axle housing with a jack.

3   Remove the rear wheel(s).

4   Using one wrench to loosen the lock nut and one wrench to hold the bolt head, remove the lock nut at each end of the link. Force the bolt through the link and brackets using a hammer and drift. Be careful at the front mount due to the close proximity of the jack stands.

5   Make an identifying mark on the links for reassembly.

6   Remove the upper and lower links.

7   Inspect the links for cracks, deformation or damage. Replace as necessary.

8   Inspect the rubber bushings for damage or deterioration. If any is found, the links must be replaced as an entire unit.

9   Connect the links to their original positions, using the identifying marks made upon removal. Do not tighten the attaching lock nuts fully at this time. When connecting the rear side of the upper link, the bolt head goes towards the inside of the vehicle.

10   With the links loosely attached, lower the vehicle to the ground.

11   With the full weight of the car on the suspension, torque the lock nuts to specifications.

20 Steering wheel – removal and installation

1   Disconnect the negative cable at the battery.

2   Pull the horn cap off the steering wheel. It may be necessary to gently pry the cap off with a screwdriver (photo).

3   Apply identification marks to the steering wheel and to the steering column to enable the wheel to be replaced in the same location.

4   Remove the lock nut in the center of the steering wheel (photo).

5   Pull the wheel straight off the shaft. In most cases, a steering wheel puller will not be necessary.

6   Install the wheel by positioning it on the shaft, using the identification marks made upon disassembly.

7   Use a new lock nut with a nylon insert to secure the steering wheel to the shaft.

8   Push the horn cap into position, making sure it is fully seated all round.

9   Connect the negative battery cable and test the horn for correct operation.

20.2 The horn cap being removed from the steering wheel

20.4 There is a locknut at the center of the steering wheel

21 Steering gear – removal and installation

1   The steering gear assembly is a one-piece arrangement incorporating the steering box under the vehicle and a continuous steering shaft running through the steering column all the way to the steering wheel. Removal is a tedious and somewhat difficult procedure. Fortunately, overhaul of the steering gear should only be necessary after many, many miles or to correct damage from a frontal collision.

2   Disconnect the battery negative cable.

3   Move to the inside of the car and remove the horn cap.

4   Before removing the steering wheel (Section 20), apply identification marks on the steering column shaft and steering wheel for installation in the same location. Do not strike the steering column shaft end with a hammer as damage to the bearing and collapsible shaft may occur.

5   With the steering wheel removed, remove the steering column covers.

6   Remove the air duct under the dashboard and disconnect the electrical couplers.

7   At the end of the steering column remove the stop ring, cancel

cam and spring.

8   The combination switch assembly can now be slipped off the column and placed aside.

9   Remove the steering lock assembly referring to Section 23.

10   Wrap the steering lock hole on the column shaft with tape to prevent lubrication from leaking.

11   Remove the four bolts at the column jacket fixing brackets on the underside of the column.

12   Mark the hinge locations for the hood hinges and remove the hood (see Chapter 12).

13   Raise the front end of the car and support firmly with jack stands to complete the work under the car.

14   Disconnect the center link from the Pitman arm using a gear puller (Section 14).

15   Remove the Pitman arm from the sector shaft (Section 14).

16   Remove the steering gear housing attaching bolts which secure the steering box to the frame rail (photo).

17   Remove the steering gear assembly through the engine compartment, and make note of the positions of any shims located between steering box and frame.

18   To install, place the steering box in its proper location with any adjusting shims between it and the frame.

19   Tighten the attaching bolts to the frame.

20   Install the Pitman arm onto the sector shaft, aligning the identical serrations of the Pitman arm and sector shaft. The arm will only go on one way, so don't force it. Tighten the lock nut to the Pitman arm to 94 to 123 ft-lb (13 to 17 m-kg).

21   Adjust the backlash between the sector gear and the rack by first moving the Pitman arm back and forth to ensure that it turns smoothly. Stop the arm at the center of its travel. Mount a dial indicator and adjust the backlash at the center position of Pitman arm by turning the adjusting screw on the steering box in or out so that the movement of the arm is 0. to 0.004 in (0 to 0.1 mm). Tighten the adjusting screw lock nut securely.

22   Connect the center link to the Pitman arm and tighten the lock nut to a torque of 22 to 33 ft-lb (3.0 to 4.5 m-kg). Install a new cotter pin.

23   Lower the vehicle and install the hood, using your marked hinge locations to properly position the hood.

24   Install all the components on the steering column and remove the tape covering the steering lock hole. Refer to Section 23 for installation of the steering lock, and Section 20 for information on installing the steering wheel. Be sure to use your identification marks when installing the steering wheel.

25   Connect the negative battery cable.

26   Fill the gear housing with SAE 90 gear lubricant.

22   Steering gear – overhaul

1   Purchase a steering gear overhaul kit, which will contain all the small parts necessary to replace when disassembling the steering gear.

2   Allow the lubricant to drain from the steering box.

3   Place the steering gear housing in a vise with the adjustment screw pointed up. Use blocks of wood to cushion the jaws of the vise.

4   Slide the column jacket off the column shaft.

5   Loosen the adjusting screw lock nut and remove the three side cover attachment bolts.

6   Remove the side cover by rotating the adjustment screw clockwise through the side cover.

7   Lift the sector shaft from the gear housing noting its relative position to the related components. Be careful not to damage the shaft.

8   At the base of the worm shaft, unscrew the large lock nut. A large box wrench may be required to do this.

9   Loosen the end cover and remove the worm shaft and ball nut assembly. Do not dissassemble the worm shaft and ball nut assembly at this time.

10   Inspect the oil seal and remove the seal only if necessary to replace.

11   Check the operation of the ball nut assembly on the worm shaft. The ball nut should travel smoothly and freely on the shaft. If not, replace the entire steering gear assembly.

12   Check the worm bearings and cups for wear or damage. If any is found, replace the gear assembly.

13   Check the end clearance between the sector shaft and adjusting screw with a feeler gauge. If the clearance exceeds 0.004 in (0.1 mm),

replace the steering gear assembly.

14   Check the clearance between the sector shaft and the housing bore. If the clearance exceeds 0.004 in (0.1 mm), replace the steering gear assembly.

15   Check the oil seal in the steering box for damage or wear. If there appears to be any possibility of leakage, replace the seal. Pry the old seal out and tap a new seal into the bore. Use a wood block or seal installer but do not tap the seal directly with a hammer.

16   Install the worm shaft and ball nut assembly into their original position inside the housing.

17   Screw in the end cover until the preload of the worm shaft is 0.44 to 1.1lb (0.2 to 0.5 kg). Measure this preload by installing an attachment (Mazda part number 49 0180 510A) to the end of the worm shaft and then connecting a spring scale to this attachment. Take a reading when the shaft just starts to turn. Once adjusted, tighten the end cover lock nut and recheck the preload.

18   Turn the worm shaft and place the rack in the exact center of the worm.

19   Install the adjusting screw and shim into the slot at the end of the sector shaft and install them into the gear housing. Be careful not to damage the oil seal when fitting into the housing. Make sure the center of the sector gear is in alignment with the exact center of the worm shaft rack.

20   Apply a light coat of silicone sealer to the side cover and place the cover onto the adjusting screw. Turn the adjusting screw counter-clockwise until it is properly positioned.

21   Tighten the side cover mounting bolts.

22   Temporarily tighten the adjusting screw lock nut.

23   Install the column jacket over the column shaft.

24   Install and adjust the steering gear referring to Section 21.

23   Steering lock – removal and installation

1   Completely read through this Section before beginning work, as the steering lock is designed in such a way as to deter theft and its installation is somewhat permanent.

2   Disconnect the negative battery cable.

3   Remove the steering wheel as described in Section 20.

4   Remove the steering column covers.

5   Remove the air duct at the base of the steering column and disconnect the electrical couplers to the combination switch.

6   At the end of the steering column shaft, remove the stop ring, cancel cam and spring.

7   The combination switch assembly on the left side of the steering column can now be lifted free of the column.

8   The electrical operation of the switch and lock can now be checked (see Chapter 10).

9   There are two bolts which secure the steering lock body to the column jacket. Using a hammer and chisel, make a groove across the head of each bolt to enable you to use a standard screwdriver to loosen and remove the bolts (photo).

10   With these two bolts removed, the steering lock assembly can be separated from the column.

11   The steering lock must be replaced as an entire assembly.

12   Position a new steering lock assembly onto the steering column jacket and tighten the two attaching bolts until the head of each bolt snaps off.

13   Install the combination switch assembly to the steering column.

14   To the end of the shaft install the spring, cancel cam and stop ring.

15   Connect the couplers to the combination switch. They are keyed for easy installation.

16   Install the air duct to the underside of the dashboard.

17   Install the steering column covers onto the column.

18   Install the steering wheel referring to Section 20. Make sure the alignment marks made on the steering wheel and column match up.

19   Connect the negative battery cable and test the operation of the steering lock and horn.

24   Road wheels

1   Road wheels can become dangerous if impacted against a curb or similar solid object. In extreme cases, the wheels can be bent causing a hazardous condition. Dial indicators mounted on the side of the tire and at either the front or rear of the tire will show the run-out of the

21.16 Removing the steering box attaching bolts

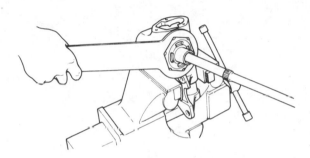

Fig. 11.8 Removing the large locknut on the steering box (Sec 22)

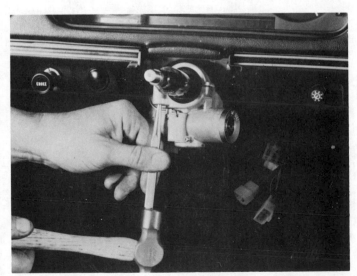

23.9 A chisel must be used to make a groove on the head of the bolt in order to remove it

tire and wheel. If the wheel has been bent, this test will reveal it. Measured on the tread of the tire, the radial run-out should not exceed 0.08 in (2.0 mm). With a dial indicator on the side of the tire, the lateral run-out limit is 0.10 in (2.5 mm).

2   Tire and wheel balance is also important in the overall handling, braking and performance of a car. Whenever a tire is disassembled for repair or replacement, the tire and wheel assembly should be statically

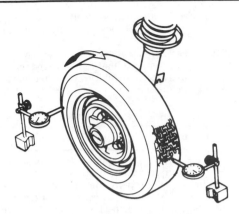

Fig. 11.9 Using dial indicators to check tire and wheel run-out (Sec 24)

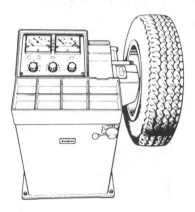

Fig. 11.10 Using a dynamic balance machine to check proper tire and wheel balance (Sec 24)

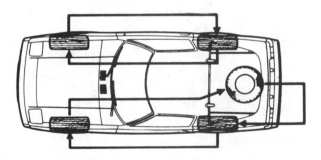

Fig. 11.11 Proper tire rotation for maximum tread life (Sec 25)

and dynamically balanced with a wheel balancer in accordance with the manufacturer's instructions. The allowable unbalance at the rim is less than 0.70 oz (20 gr).

3   Wheels should be periodically cleaned, especially on the inside where mud and road salts can eventually cause rust and, ultimately, wheel failure.

25 Tires

1   The tires are very important from the safety aspect. The tread should not be allowed to wear down to the legal limit. Not only is there fear of legal action, but it may be dangerous, particularly in wet weather conditions.

2   To equalize wear and add longevity to a set of tires it is recommended that the tires be rotated periodically, as shown in Fig. 11.11. When rotating, check for signs of abnormal wear and foreign objects in the rubber tread.

3   Proper tire inflation is essential for maximum wear of the tread and

for handling, braking and performance. Read through the appropriate Section in the beginning of this book for more information on tire inflation.

4   Tires which are wearing in an abnormal way are an indication that either their inflation is not correct or that the front-end components are not adjusted properly. Take the vehicle to a reputable front-end specialist to correct the situation.

26 Front wheel alignment

1   Getting the proper front wheel alignment is a very tedious exacting process and one in which complicated and expensive machines are necessary to perform the job properly. Because of this, it is advisable to have a specialist with the proper equipment perform these tasks.

2   We will, however, use this space to give you a basic idea of what is involved with front end alignment so you can better understand the process and deal intelligently with shops which do this work.

3   Toe-in, in basic terms, is the amount by which the front wheels diverge from the parallel when the steering is set straight ahead. In a car with zero toe-in the distance measured between the front edges of the wheels will be the same as the distance measured between the rear edges of the wheels. In the Mazda RX-7, which has a static toe-in of 0.24 in (6 mm), the distance between the front edges of the wheels should be 0.48 in (12 mm) less than the distance between the rear edges of the wheels – ie. 0.24 in (6 mm) for each wheel. Incorrect toe-in will cause the tires to wear improperly by making them 'scrub' against the road surface. Toe-in is adjusted by altering the length of the suspension tie rods.

4   Camber and caster are the angles at which the wheel and suspension upright are inclined to the vertical. Camber is the angle of the wheel in the lateral (side-to-side) plane, caster is the angle of the wheel and upright in the longitudinal (fore-aft) plane. Camber angle affects the amount of tire tread which contacts the road and compensates for changes in the suspension geometry when the car is travelling round bends or over an undulating surface. Caster angle affects the self-centering action of the steering, which aids stability when the car is travelling in a straight line.

5   Camber and caster are adjusted by removing the four attaching nuts around the top of the suspension strut and then moving the strut mounting block until the proper positions are attained. The correct camber angle for the RX-7 is 1° 10' plus or minus 30'; the correct caster angle is 4° 00' plus or minus 45'.

Chapter 12 Bodywork and fittings

Contents

1 General description

1 The body is fabricated from steel pressings welded together. At the front there is a crossmember between the front suspension arms to take the inner mountings of these and support the front of the engine. At the rear, the basic body shell is reinforced by boxed sections, but these too are welded on and are not detachable.

2 Maintenance – bodywork and frame

1 The condition of your vehicle's bodywork is of considerable importance as it is on this that the second hand value will mainly depend. It is much more difficult to repair neglected bodywork than to replace mechanical assemblies. The hidden portions of the body, such as the fenderwells, the underframe and the engine compartment are equally important, although obviously not requiring such frequent attention as the immediately visible paintwork.

2 Once a year or every 12 000 miles it is a sound scheme to visit your local dealer and have the underside of the body steam cleaned. All traces of dirt and oil will be removed and the underside can then be inspected carefully for rust, damaged hydraulic pipes, frayed electrical wiring and similar maladies. The front suspension should be greased on completion of this job.

3 At the same time, clean the engine and the engine compartment using either a steam cleaner or a water-soluble grease solvent.

4 The fenderwells should be given particular attention as undersealing can easily come away here and stones and dirt thrown up from the roadwheels can soon cause the paint to chip and flake, and so allow rust to set in. If rust is found, clean down to the bare metal and apply an anti-rust paint.

5 The bodywork should be washed once a week or when dirty. Thoroughly wet the vehicle to soften the dirt and then wash down with a soft sponge and plenty of clean water. If the surplus dirt is not washed off very gently, in time it will wear down paint.

6 Spots of tar or bitumen coating thrown up from the road surface are best removed with a cloth soaked in gasoline.

7 Once every six months, give the bodywork and chromium trim a thoroughly good wax polish. If a chromium cleaner is used to remove rust on any of the vehicle's plated parts remember that the cleaner also removes part of the chromium, so use it sparingly.

3 Maintenance – upholstery and carpets

1 Remove the carpets or mats and thoroughly clean the interior of the vehicle every three months or more frequently if necessary.

2 Beat out the carpets and vacuum clean them if they are very dirty. If the upholstery is soiled apply an upholstery cleaner with a damp sponge and wipe off with a clean dry cloth.

4 Bodywork repairs – minor damage

See photo sequence on pages 242 and 243.

Repair of minor scratches in the vehicle's bodywork

If the scratch is very superficial, and does not penetrate to the metal of the bodywork, repair is very simple. Lightly rub the area of the scratch with a paintwork renovator, or a very fine cutting paste, to remove loose paint from the scratch and to clear the surrounding bodywork of wax polish. Rinse the area with clean water.

Apply touch-up paint to the scratch using a thin paint brush; continue to apply thin layers of paint until the surface of the paint in the scratch is level with the surrounding paintwork. Allow the new paint at least two weeks to harden: then blend it into the surrounding paintwork by rubbing the paintwork, in the scratch area, with a paintwork renovator or a very fine cutting paste. Finally, apply wax polish.

An alternative to painting over the scratch is to use a paint transfer. Use the same preparation for the affected area, then simply pick a patch of a suitable size to cover the scratch completely. Hold the patch against the scratch and burnish its backing paper; the paper will adhere to the paintwork, freeing itself from the backing paper at the same time. Polish the affected area to blend the patch into the surrounding paintwork.

Where the scratch has penetrated right through to the metal of the bodywork, causing the metal to rust, a different repair technique is required. Remove any loose rust from the bottom of the scratch with a penknife, then apply rust inhibiting paint to prevent the formation of rust in the future. Using a rubber or nylon applicator fill the scratch with bodystopper paste. If required, this paste can be mixed with cellulose thinners to provide a very thin paste which is ideal for filling narrow scratches. Before the stopper-paste in the scratch hardens, wrap a piece of smooth cotton rag around the top of a finger. Dip the finger in cellulose thinners and then quickly sweep it across the surface of the stopper-paste in the scratch; this will ensure that the surface of the stopper-paste is slightly hollowed. The scratch can now be painted over as described earlier in this Section.

Repair of dents in the vehicle's bodywork

When deep denting of the vehicle's bodywork has taken place, the first task is to pull the dent out, until the affected bodywork almost attains its original shape. There is little point in trying to restore the original shape completely, as the metal in the damaged area will have stretched on impact and cannot be reshaped fully to its original contour. It is better to bring the level of the dent up to a point which is about $\frac{1}{8}$ in below the level of the surrounding bodywork. In cases where the dent is very shallow anyway, it is not worth trying to pull it out at all.

If the underside of the dent is accessible, it can be hammered out gently from behind, using a mallet with a wooden or plastic head. Whilst doing this, hold a suitable block of wood firmly against the inpact from the hammer blows and thus prevent a large area of the bodywork from being 'belled-out'.

Should the dent be in a section of the bodywork which has double skin or some other factor making it inaccessible from behind, a different technique is called for. Drill several small holes through the metal inside the area — particularly in the deeper sections. Then screw long self-tapping screws into the holes just sufficiently for them to gain a good purchase in the metal. Now the dent can be pulled out by pulling on the protruding heads of the screws with a pair of pliers.

The next stage of the repair is the removal of the paint from the damaged area, and from an inch or so of the surrounding 'sound' bodywork. This is accomplished most easily by using a wire brush or abrasive pad on a power drill, although it can be done just as effectively by hand using sheets of sandpaper. To complete the preparation for filling, score the surface of the bare metal with a screwdriver or the tang of a file, ar alternatively, drill small holes in the affected area. This will provide a really good 'key' for the filler paste.

To complete the repair see the Section on filling and re-spraying.

Repair of rust holes or gashes in the vehicle's bodywork

Remove all paint from the affected area and from an inch or so of the surrounding 'sound' bodywork, using an abrasive pad or a wire brush on a power drill. If these are not available a few sheets of sandpaper will do the job just as effectively. With the paint removed you will be able to gauge the severity of the corrosion and therefore decide whether to renew the whole panel (if this is possible) or to repair the affected area. New body panels are not as expensive as most people think and it is often quicker and more satisfactory to fit a new panel than to attempt to repair large areas of corrosion.

Remove all fittings from the affected area except those which will act as a guide to the original shape of the damaged bodywork (eg headlamp shells etc). Then, using tin snips or a hacksaw blade, remove all loose metal and any other metal badly affected by corrosion. Hammer the edges of the hole inwards in order to create a slight depression for the filler paste.

Wire brush the affected area to remove the powdery rust from the surface of the remaining metal. Paint the affected area with rust inhibiting paint; if the back of the rusted area is accessible treat this also.

Before filling can take place it will be necessary to block the hole in some way. This can be achieved by the use of Zinc gauze or Aluminum tape.

Zinc gauze is probably the best material to use for a large hole. Cut a piece to the approximate size and shape of the hole to be filled, then position it in the hole so that its edges are below the level of the surrounding bodywork. It can be retained in position by several blobs of filler paste around its periphery.

Aluminum tape should be used for small or very narrow holes. Pull a piece off the roll and trim it to the approximate size and shape required, then pull off the backing paper (if used) and stick the tape over the hole; it can be overlapped if the thickness of one piece is insufficient. Burnish down the edges of the tape with the handle of a screwdriver or similar, to ensure that the tape is securely attached to the metal underneath.

Having blocked off the hole the affected area must now be filled and sprayed — see Section on bodywork fitting and re-spraying.

Bodywork repairs — filling and re-spraying

Before using this Section, see the Sections on dent, deep scratch, rust holes and gash repairs.

Many types of bodyfiller are available, but generally speaking those proprietary kits which contain a tin of filler paste and a tube of resin hardener are best for this type of repair. A wide, flexible plastic or nylon applicator will be found invaluable for imparting a smooth and well contoured finish to the surface of the filler.

Mix up a little filler on a clean piece of card or board — use the hardener sparingly (follow the maker's instructions on the pack) otherwise the filler will set too rapidly or too slowly.

Using the applicator apply the filler paste to the prepared area; draw the applicator across the surface of the filler to achieve the correct contour and to level the filler surface. As soon as a contour that approximates the correct one is achieved, stop working the paste — if you carry on too long the paste will become sticky and begin to 'pick up' on the applicator. Continue to add thin layers of filler paste at twenty-minute intervals until the level of the filler is just proud of the surrounding bodywork.

Once the filler has hardened, excess can be removed using a metal plane or file. From then on, progressively finer grades of sandpaper should be used, starting with a 40 grade production paper and finishing with 400 grade wet-and-dry paper. Always wrap the sandpaper around a flat rubber, cork or wooden block — otherwise the surface of the filler will not be completely flat. During the smoothing of the filler surface the wet-and-dry paper should be periodically rinsed in water. This will ensure that a very smooth finish is imparted to the filler at the final stage.

At this stage the 'repair area' should be surrounded by a ring of bare metal, which in turn should be encircled by the finely 'feathered' edge of the good paintwork. Rinse the repair area with clean water, until all of the dust produced by the rubbing-down operation has gone.

Spray the whole repair area with a light coat of primer — this will show up any imperfections in the surface of the filler. Repair these inperfections with fresh filler paste or bodystopper, and once more smooth the surface with abrasive paper. If bodystopper is used, it can be mixed with cellulose thinners to form a really thin paste which is ideal for filling small holes. Repeat this spray and repair procedure until you are satisfied that the surface of the filler, and the feathered edge of the paintwork are perfect. Clean the repair area with clean water and allow to dry fully.

The repair area is now ready for final spraying. Paint spraying must be carried out in warm, dry, windless and dust free atmosphere. This condition can be created artificially if you have access to a large indoor working area, but if you are forced to work in the open, you will have to pick your day very carefully. If you are working indoors, dousing the floor in the work area with water will help to settle the dust which would otherwise be in the atmosphere. If the repair area is confined to one body panel, mask off the surrounding panels; this will help to minimise the effects of a slight mis-match in paint colours. Bodywork fittings (eg chrome strips, door handles etc) will also need to be masked off. Use genuine masking tape and several thicknesses of newspaper for the masking operations.

Before commencing to spray, agitate the aerosol can thoroughly, then spray a test area (an old tin, or similar) until the technique is mastered. Cover the repair area with a thick coat of primer; the thickness should be built up using several thin layers of paint rather than one thick one. Using 400 grade wet-and-dry paper, rub down the surface of the primer until it is really smooth. While doing this, the work area should be thoroughly doused with water, and the wet-and-dry paper periodically rinsed in water. Allow to dry before spraying on more paint.

Spray on the top coat, again building up the thickness by using several thin layers of paint. Start spraying in the center of the repair area and then using a circular motion, work outwards until the whole repair area and about 2 inches of the surrounding original paintwork is covered. Remove all masking material 10 to 15 minutes after spraying on the final coat of paint. Allow the new paint at least two weeks to harden, then, using a paintwork renovator or a very fine cutting paste, blend the edges of the paint into the existing paintwork. Finally, apply wax polish.

---

5 Bodywork and frame repairs — major damage

1   Major damage must be repaired by competent mechanics with the

necessary welding and hydraulic straightening equipment.

2 If the damage has been serious it is vital that the frame is checked for correct alignment as otherwise the handling of the vehicle will suffer and many other faults – such as excessive tire wear, and wear in the transmission and steering – may occur.

3 There is a special body jig which most body repair shops have and to ensure that all is correct it is important that this jig be used for all major repair work.

6 Maintenance – hinges and locks

Once every 3000 miles or 3 months the door and hood hinges and locks should be given a few drops of oil from an oil can. The door striker plates can be given a thin smear of grease to reduce wear and to ensure free movement.

7 Door rattles – tracing and rectification

1 Door rattles are due either to loose hinges, worn or maladjusted catches, or loose components inside the door.

2 Loose hinges can be detached by opening the door and trying to lift it. Any play will be felt. If this is the case, check that all the hinge bolts are tight or replace the hinges.

3 Worn or badly adjusted catches can be found by pushing and pulling on the outside handle when the door is closed. Once again play will be felt. Refer to Section 8 for adjusting the door lock striker.

4 Rattles emanating from inside the door itself are sometimes more difficult to trace. With the doors open, shake the door and listen for rattles. Do this with the window in the up and in the down positions. Refer to Section 11 for adjusting the door glass regulator, which will more than likely be the cause of the noise.

8 Adjusting the door lock striker

1 The striker located on the rear door jamb can be adjusted in all directions by loosening the two attaching screws (photo).

2 Before making any adjustment scribe around the striker with a pencil or felt pen to enable you to return it to its original position and also to check the amount the striker is moved.

3 Move the striker in small amounts only as a little makes a big difference.

4 Pull and push on the door with it closed to ensure that it is a good fit.

9 Door trim panel – removal and installation

1 Raise the window glass to the full up position.

2 Note the position of the window crank handle. Chalk or a strip of tape on the trim panel may be useful for this.

3 Remove the window crank handle. Do this by prying the cover off the front of the handle and then removing the bolt which goes through the base of the handle and into the shaft.

4 Pull the inside handle out slightly and remove the inner handle cover (photo).

5 Carefully pry out the three plug-type covers on the arm rest, then remove the three screws behind these plugs. Remove the arm rest from the door (photos).

6 The trim panel is held to the door with 11 metal clips located about one inch inward from the outside edge of the panel. Wrap some tape around the end of a screwdriver to prevent any sharp edges from damaging the panel. Use this padded screwdriver to carefully pry the trim clips out of their holes in the metal door. Pry close to the clips, and work around the left, right and bottom edges of the trim panel until all the clips are free (photo).

7 There are three locking tabs at the top of the trim panel. Once all the clips are out of their holes, lift up on the panel until it is clear of the inside lock button. Remove the panel from the door (photo).

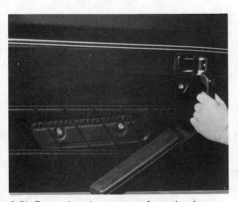
8.1 Adjusting the door lock striker

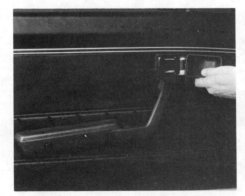
9.4 Removing the inner handle cover

9.5a The arm rest attaching screws are located behind decorative plugs

9.5b Removing the arm rest from the door panel

9.6 Prying the door panel away from the door

9.7 Lifting the door panel up and off the door

8   To install the trim panel, lower it over the inside lock button and push until the three locking tabs are seated.

9   Visually check around the edges of the panel to see if all the metal clips are in alignment with the holes in the metal door.

10 Push the panel directly over each clip with the palm of your hand to seat the clip.

11 Install the arm rest, securing with the three screws. Cover the screws with the decorative plugs.

12 Pull the inner handle slightly away from the door and install the cover behind it.

13 Install the window crank handle to its original position on the shaft and tighten with the bolt into the shaft. Push the cap over the securing bolt.

10 Door glass and regulator – removal and installation

1   Remove the door trim panel as described in Section 8.

2   Remove the inner handle assembly. This is held in place with two bolts and a lock tab (photo).

3   Gently peel the plastic water shield away from the door metal. This is held in place with glue all the way around the door. The shield can remain glued to the door along the bottom.

4   Temporarily install the window winder handle onto the crank so that the window can be raised or lowered. The top edge of the glass should be about two inches above the bottom window frame, lowered as far as possible, yet still raised enough to grab the top of the glass with your fingers.

5   On the inside of the door at the bottom, you will see two attaching screws which go through the window glass and into the regulator. Support the top of the window glass and remove these two screws and screw grommets (photo).

6   The glass is now free from the regulator and can be lifted up and out of the channel (photo).

7   Across the middle of the door panel are six bolts which attach the regulator to the door panel. Remove these bolts and then remove the regulator through the large access hole at the bottom of the door.

8   To install the glass and regulator, lift the regulator inside the door panel until the holes line up. Install all six regulator bolts and tighten.

9   Gently push the window glass through the door frame until the holes in the glass line up with the holes in the regulator. Install the two attaching bolts and grommets.

10 Temporarily install window winder crank and check for operation. Adjust as necessary.

11 Stick the water shield back onto the door panel, using new weatherstrip adhesive if necessary.

12 Install the inner handle assembly and trim panel as described in Section 8.

11 Adjusting door glass regulator

1   To make a vertical adjustment in the window, raise the window to the fully up position and loosen the two regulator attaching bolts toward the rear side of the door (photo).

2   With these two bolts loose the regulator guide can be moved up or down.

3   Tighten the bolts and make sure that the glass moves slowly.

4   To make a front-to-rear adjustment of the door glass, loosen the adjusting bolt located at the front of the door (photo).

5   With this bolt loosened the glass guide can be moved as required.

6   Tighten the bolt and check that the glass moves freely up and down as the window is operated.

12 Door exterior handle – removal and installation

1   Raise the window fully and remove the trim panel and its related equipment, referring to Section 8.

2   Carefully pry the plastic water shield away from the top left corner of the door.

3   Stuff rags or pieces of newspaper into the door cavity under the door handle assembly to prevent parts or tools from falling all the way to the bottom of the door if accidentally dropped.

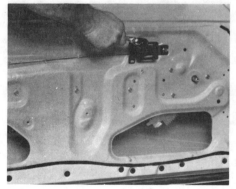

10.2 Removing the inner handle assembly

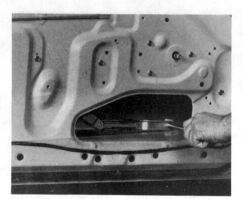

10.5 Two screws secure the window glass to the regulator

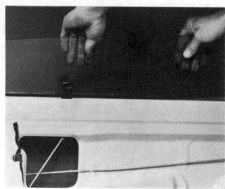

10.6 Lifting the window glass up and out of the door channel

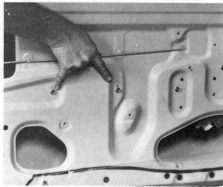

11.1 The two regulator attaching bolts which are used to adjust the vertical travel of the window glass

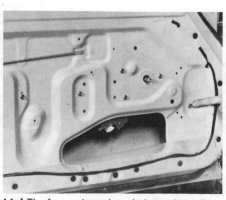

11.4 The forward regulator bolt used to adjust the front-to-rear movement of the glass

4   Disconnect the push rod at the outer handle assembly. This is held in place with a plastic locking clip which must be pried away from the rod.
5   Remove the two outer handle attaching nuts while supporting the handle on the outside of the door. Remove the handle from the outside of the door.
6   To install, push the studs on the outer handle through the holes in the door and secure with the two attaching nuts.
7   Connect the push rod with the locking clip.
8   Remove the protective rags or newspaper from the inside of the door and press the water shield back into position.
9   Check for proper operation of the outside handle.
10   Install the trim panel and its related components.

13 Door key cylinder – removal and installation

1   Raise the glass fully and remove the trim panel and its related components as described in Section 8.
2   Carefully pry the plastic water shield away from the door. This need only be done at the top left side of the door to uncover the access hole for the key cylinder.
3   Stuff rags into the door cavity under the key cylinder to prevent parts or tools from falling to the bottom of the door if dropped.
4   Disconnect the push rod end at the key cylinder. This is held in place by a plastic clip which is prised away from the rod.
5   Using a pair of pliers, carefully pull out the locking clip on the rear of the key cylinder. Do not damage the outside sheet metal while doing this.
6   Push the key cylinder out towards the outside of the door.
7   To install, push the key cylinder into the hole from the outside as far as it will go. Hold the cylinder tightly against the door as the locking clip is pushed into place against the inside of the cylinder. Make sure it is firmly seated.
8   Push the connecting rod into the hole in the swing arm and lock with the plastic clip.
9   Remove the protective rags from inside of the door and press the water shield back into position.
10   Close the door and check for proper operation.
11   Install the trim panel.

14 Door lock – removal and installation

1   Raise the glass fully and remove the interior trim panel and its related components as described in Section 8.
2   Carefully pry the plastic water shield away from the door. This is held in place with adhesive all around. The shield can remain intact along the bottom of the door.
3   The door lock mechanism is located on the inside of the door, at the rear jam. Look through the access hole and carefully note the position of each push rod where it meets the lock assembly. A hand-drawn sketch or identification marks applied to the push rod on the adhesive tape may help you keep track of which push rods are attached to which locations.
4   All of the push rods are held in place with plastic clips. To remove the push rods from the clips, rotate the locking arm of the clip counter-clockwise off the rod and then pull the rod out of the clip.
5   Disconnect the push rod which leads to the key cylinder at the lock.
6   Disconnect the push rod which leads to the outside handle.
7   Disconnect the push rod which leads to the inside handle.
8   Disconnect the push rod which leads to the lock button.
9   Remove the three door lock attaching screws on the outside of the door frame and remove the lock through the service hole.
10   Before installing the door lock assembly, the outer nylon bushing should be changed with a new one.
11   Connect all the push rods to their original position on the lock.
12   Check the operation of the lock assembly by operating the outside handle, the key cylinder, the inside lock button and the inner handle.
13   If everything functions properly, press the water shield back into position (using new weatherstripping adhesive if necessary) and install the trim panel.

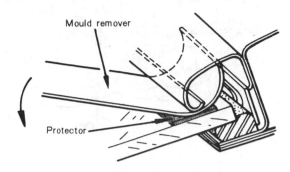

Fig. 12.1 Prying the molding from the windshield glass (Sec 15).

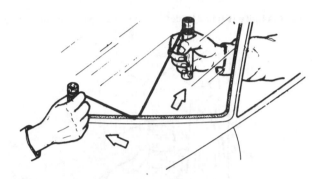

Fig. 12.2 Using piano wire to cut through the glass sealant around the windshield (Sec 15)

15 Windshield glass – removal

1   The windshield and side window are bonded in place, requiring special tools and sealant for removal and installation. This is also a messy job which, if not done carefully, can harm the glass and adjoining paint. For these reasons it may be to your best advantage to have a factory dealer or competent auto glass shop do the work for you.
2   Remove the wiper arms, interior mirror and all trims and garnishes surrounding the windshield.
3   Make sure the paint surrounding the windshield has been recently waxed with a good quality polish or wax.
4   Apply adhesive tape for protection of the paint surfaces. It is advisable to use a double thickness of tape immediately adjoining the windshield molding.
5   Using a piece of plastic or similar material as a protector, pry the molding from the glass with a curved instrument like the one illustrated.
6   Drill a small hole in the sealant and pass a length of piano wire through it. Wrap the ends of the wire around handles and use a long sawing action to saw through the sealant around the glass.
7   Support the glass and be careful that it does not harm any paint as it is removed from the car.

16 Windshield glass – installation

1   A sealant layer approximately 0.08 in (2 mm) thick must cover the entire circumference of the frame. Use a sharp knife to cut away the old sealant to this thickness, or use new sealant after applying primer to the area (Fig. 12.3).
2   Bond a new dam to the glass with bonding agent. This dam should be 0.3 in (7 mm) from the edge of the glass (Fig. 12.4).
3   Apply a thin coat of primer to the bonding area and allow it to dry for 30 minutes (Fig. 12.5). Do not touch the surface, and if any of the primer gets on your hands wash it off immediately.
4   Bond the spacers to the body in their upper and lower positions (Fig. 12.6). Insert the molding clips into position, replacing any found defective.
5   A cartridge-type gun with sealant should be prepared at this time.

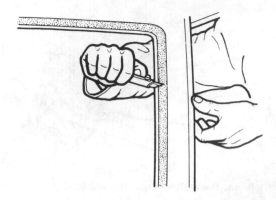

Fig. 12.3 A knife is used to cut away the old sealant (Sec 16)

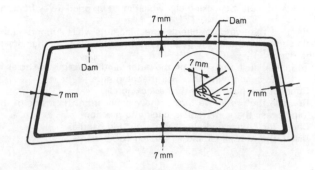

Fig. 12.4 Bonding a new dam of sealant to the windshield glass (Sec 16)

Fig. 12.5 A thin coat of primer is applied to the bonding area (Sec 16)

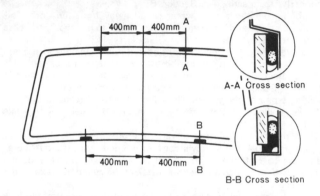

Fig. 12.6 Bonding new spacers to the windshield frame (Sec 16)

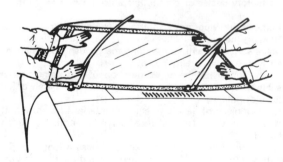

Fig. 12.7 Press the windshield into place and squeeze out sealing agent (Sec 16)

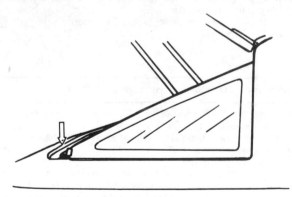

Fig. 12.8 Location of single glass plate attaching screw on side window (Sec 17)

Cut the nozzle in such a fashion as to allow the nozzle to run along the edge of the glass and apply the sealant to the area between the dam and the glass edge. The bead of sealant should be continuous at a height of approximately 0.3 in (8 mm). Reshape with a spatula where necessary.

6   Open an interior window to relieve pressure inside the car.

7   Lift the windshield into place and press lightly to squeeze the sealant and form a bond.

8   Wipe away any excess sealant which oozes out and check for proper contact all the way around. Add more sealant in poor contact areas.

9   Allow the sealant time to harden without disturbing it. This will take 5 hours at 68°F (20°C) and 24 hours at 41°F (5°C).

10   Recheck for any points that might allow a leak, and add extra sealant as necessary.

11   Clip the molding into place. Refit the interior mirror and all trims and garnishes.

17 Side window glass – removal

1   As the side windows are bonded in the same fashion as the windshield, it may once again be better to have a professional do the work on these.

2   Apply adhesive tape to the painted areas surrounding the side windows to protect the paint.

3   Remove the decorative garnish and the single glass plate attaching screw at the rear of each window.

4   Open the rear glasshatch and disconnect the electrical connector from the rear pillar.

5   Remove the rear pillar trims and the glass attaching nut.

6   Brace the rear of the glass hatch with a piece of wood at the hatch. This will keep the hatch in the up position as the damper stay end is disconnected at the rear pillar.

7   Drill a hole in the sealant and pass a length of piano wire through

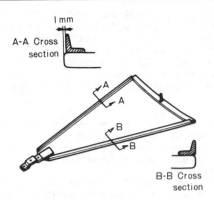

Fig. 12.9 Bonding a new sealant dam along the edges of the side window glass (Sec 18)

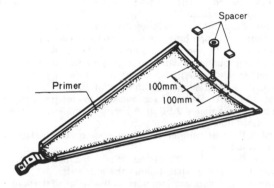

Fig. 12.10 New spacers attached to the side window glass (Sec 18)

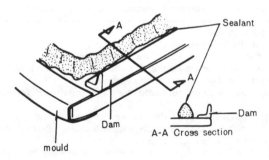

Fig. 12.11 Apply a bead of sealant around the side window glass (Sec 18)

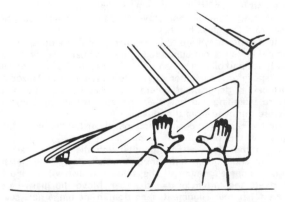

Fig. 12.12 Press the side window into place and secure with the rear attaching screw and front attaching nut (Sec 18)

it. Wrap the ends of the wire around handles and use a long sawing action to saw through the sealant around the glass.

8   Support the glass and be careful that it does not harm the paint as the window is removed from the car.

18 Side window glass – installation

1   Build up a layer of sealant which is 0.08 in (2 mm) thick around the circumference of the frame. See Section 15 for details of this.

2   Bond the new dam to the glass positioning it along the edge of the glass as shown in the Figure 12.9.

3   Apply a thin coat of primer to the bonding area of the body and glass.

4   Bond the spacers to the glass. These should be positioned 100 mm from the glass attaching bolt.

5   Apply a bead of sealant around the whole circumference of the glass, just inside the dam.

6   Press the window into place, securing it with the glass attaching nut at the front and attaching screw at the rear.

7   Wipe away any excess sealant and fill in any gaps which could cause leaks.

8   Install the pillar trim pieces and the damper stay for the rear hatch.

9   Allow the sealant to thoroughly harden and then replace the garnish molding.

19 Hood – removal

1   Removing the hood is a two-man job, with one supporting the hood while the other removes the attaching bolts.

2   Scribe identifying marks completely around the hood hinges where they meet the hood. Use a pencil, felt pen or paint, but make sure they are clearly marked before proceeding (photo).

3   Place some foam rubber padding or rags between the front of the hood and the body. This is to protect the paint and enable the front edge to take the weight when the hinges are slackened.

4   Remove the hood stay rod.

5   With an assistant supporting the hood, remove the four hinge bolts and lift the hood clear of the car. Place it on padding and cover it to protect from damage (photo).

20 Hood – adjusting and installation

1   Lift the hood onto padding placed on the front nose of the car.

2   While an assistant lifts the hood into position, install the four securing bolts through the hinges.

3   While the bolts are still somewhat loose, move the hood until the hinges line up with the scribing marks previously drawn on the hood.

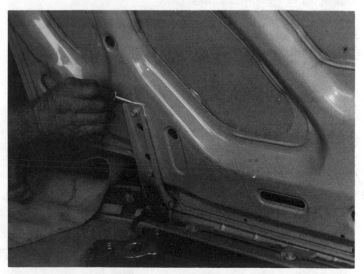

19.2 Scribe the outline of each hood hinge on the hood to ensure same location on reinstallation

19.5 With the help of an assistant, remove the four securing bolts and lift the hood away from the car

All side-to-side and up-and-down adjustments are made in this manner.

4   If the hood is returned to its exact original position, the striker and lock will be in proper alignment without further adjustment.

5   Re-install the stay rod.

6   If adjustments are made to the hood, it is advisable to slacken the bolts securing the hood catch located on the firewall. With these bolts loosened, the catch will realign itself in the new position of the hood striker. If this is not done, the hood may jam shut, leading to major problems. Reopen the hood and tighten the catch in the new position.

7   Should the hood ever fail to open due to catch failure or misalignment, do not be tempted to pry it up at the rear edge of the hood. Take the car to a dealer where, as a last resort, an access hole will have to be cut in the firewall or hood to free the catch.

8   Oil the catch and cable regularly to lessen the risk of jamming or breaking.

21 Front bumper – removal and installation

1   Disconnect the two battery cables and remove the battery from its mounting plate. Be careful not to damage the front fender in the process. Set the battery aside in a safe place.

2   For access, remove the coolant recovery tank located on the right side of the engine compartment. This is held in place with an integral clip to the side of the radiator support.

3   Disconnect the wire connectors from the front turn signal lights and feed the wires through the hole in the front body panel to a point in front of the radiator.

4   Working through the access hole under the hood hinge, remove the two nuts attaching the piston rod end of the shock absorber.

5   Raise the front end of the vehicle for better access to the remaining components which are under the car. Support firmly with jack stands.

6   Remove the five screws which secure the front radiator grille to the body (photo).

7   Unclip all wires in this area from their support clips.

8   Use a scribe or pen to outline the bracket location on the frame.

9   Remove the two bolts attaching the bumper shock absorber bracket to the frame. Support the bumper as this is being done. With the four bracket bolts removed (two on each side), the bumper, shock absorber bracket and shock absorber can be lifted away from the car (photos).

10 Measure the length of the shock absorber spring. It should be approximately 2.50 in (64 mm) in total length. If not within specifications, the shock absorber should be replaced with a new one (photo).

11 The shock absorber is easily removed from the bumper by removing the attaching bolts.

12 To install the bumper, first assemble the shock absorber and bracket to the bumper.

13 Lift the bumper assembly into position and install the four attaching bolts loosely. Line up the bracket to the frame using the identification marks made upon disassembly. Then tighten the forward bolts first. Tighten the rearward bolts.

14 Feed the turn signal light wires through the body panel to the inside of the engine compartment.

15 Install the remaining components in the reverse order of disassembly.

22 Rear bumper – removal and installation

1   Open the rear glass hatch and peel back the floorcovering at the rear of the luggage compartment.

2   On each side of the floor is a service hole covered by a plate. Remove the two securing screws and then lift off the service hole cover.

3   Remove the lock nut and jam nut of the shock absorber piston which are now accessible inside the service holes (photo).

4   Raise the rear end of the vehicle and support firmly with stands for the remaining procedures.

5   Looking under the bottom lip of the bumper, you will notice the shock absorber mounting brackets and attaching nuts. Use a scribe or pen to mark around these brackets on the body panel.

6   Remove the four nuts (two on each side bracket) while supporting the bumper assembly. With the four nuts removed, the bumper assembly can be lifted away from the car (photos).

7   Inspect the shock absorber and measure the length of the spring. It should be approximately 2.50 in (64 mm). If not, replace the shock absorber with a new one.

8   To install the rear bumper, lift it into position and install the four securing bolts loosely.

9   Move the bumper until it matches up with the identification marks made upon disassembly. Then tighten the four nuts.

10 Tighten the lock nuts and jam nuts on the inside of the vehicle and install the access hole covers.

11 Place the floorcovering in its original position.

23 Rear glass hatch – removal, installation and adjustment

1   Open the hatch fully.

2   Disconnect the negative battery cable at the battry.

3   Remove the forward portion of the rear window trim.

4   Pull the weatherstripping off the rear end of the roof and lower the headliner slightly to gain access to the hatch hinges.

5   Disconnect the electrical connector for the rear defroster from the rear pillar.

6   While an assistant supports the rear end of the hatch, disconnect the dampr stay nut where the damper meets the side pillar (photo).

7   Carefully close the rear glass hatch.

8   Move to the inside of the car and scribe around the hinge attaching nuts with a pen or metal scribe. This will locate the glass in its original position.

9   Remove the hinge attaching nuts.

10 Release the hatch lock and, with an assistant, lift the hatch, dampers and hinges off the car as a unit (photo).

11 If necessary, the damper stays, hinges and hatch lock can be removed from the glass hatch.

12 If the damper stays are to be replaced with new ones, be careful that the old units are not punctured or placed in an open fire. They are filled with gas and oil and are under high pressure. The best and safest way to dispose of the damper stays is to take them to a Mazda dealer or your local fire department, where they will be disposed of properly.

13 Before installing the hatch to the car, install any components which were removed from the glass.

14 Place the hatch into position and loosely install the hinge nuts. Do not tighten at this time.

15 Line up the hinge attaching nuts with the marks made upon disassembly and tighten until snug. Carefully lower the hatch and check for proper alignment at the sides and also where the hatch striker meets the hatch lock at the rear. Move the glass hatch as necessary for proper alignment, then tighten the hinge nuts securely.

16 Connect the damper stays to their mountings on the rear pillar.

17 Connect the electrical connectors for the defroster.

18 Wrap the material headliner around the metal lip of the hatch until

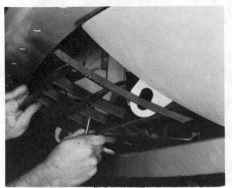

21.6 Removing the grille attaching screws

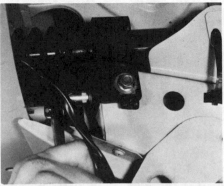

21.9a Removing the bumper shock absorber bracket from the frame

21.9b Lifting the bumper away from the car

21.10 Measuring the length of the shock absorber spring

22.3 The rear bumper lock and jam nuts are located inside a service hole in the luggage compartment

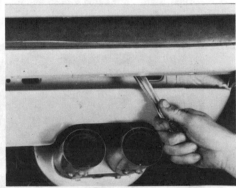

22.6a The bumper attaching nuts are located under the lower lip of the bumper

22.6b The bumper is then lifted away from the vehicle

23.6 Removing the locknut where the hydraulic damper meets the body side pillar

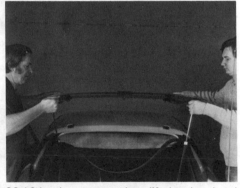

23.10 It takes two people to lift the glass hatch free of the car

19 Install the rear window trim piece.
20 Connect the negative battery cable and check for proper operation of the defroster.

24 Seat belts and retractor assembly – removal and installation

1   Remove the rear floor mat behind the front seats.
2   Remove the screws attaching the floor plate. Lift out the floor plate.
3   At the anchoring point on the side body pillar, pry back the cover and remove the anchor bolt.
4   At the bottom of the assembly, remove the anchor bolt for the retractor.
5   Remove the assembly.
6   The installation is basically the reverse procedure; however, sealant should be applied where the floor plate attaches to the floorboard to prevent leakage.

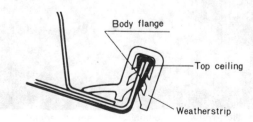

Fig. 12.13 Wrapping the headliner material around body flange and securing with the weatherstripping (Sec 23)

tight and then press the weatherstripping over the material and metal lip. It may take some time to work out all the wrinkles in the material headliner.

This photo sequence illustrates the repair of a dent and damaged paintwork. The procedure for the repair of a hole is similar. Refer to the text for more complete instructions

After removing any adjacent body trim, hammer the dent out. The damaged area should then be made slightly concave

Use coarse sandpaper or a sanding disc on a drill motor to remove all paint from the damaged area. Feather the sanded area into the edges of the surrounding paint, using progressively finer grades of sandpaper

The damaged area should be treated with rust remover prior to application of the body filler. In the case of a rust hole, all rusted sheet metal should be cut away

Carefully follow manufacturer's instructions when mixing the body filler so as to have the longest possible working time during application. Rust holes should be covered with fiberglass screen held in place with dabs of body filler prior to repair

Apply the filler with a flexible applicator in thin layers at 20 minute intervals. Use an applicator such as a wood spatula for confined areas. The filler should protrude slightly above the surrounding area

Shape the filler with a surform-type plane. Then, use water and progressively finer grades of sandpaper and a sanding block to wet-sand the area until it is smooth. Feather the edges of the repair area into the surrounding paint.

Use spray or brush applied primer to cover the entire repair area so that slight imperfections in the surface will be filled in. Prime at least one inch into the area surrounding the repair. Be careful of over-spray when using spray-type primer

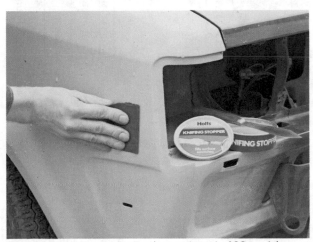

Wet-sand the primer with fine (approximately 400 grade) sandpaper until the area is smooth to the touch and blended into the surrounding paint. Use filler paste on minor imperfections

After the filler paste has dried, use rubbing compound to ensure that the surface of the primer is smooth. Prior to painting, the surface should be wiped down with a tack rag or lint-free cloth soaked in lacquer thinner

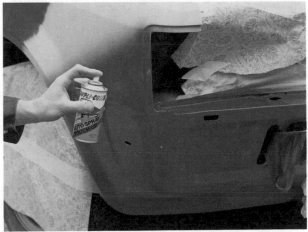

Choose a dry, warm, breeze-free area in which to paint and make sure that adjacent areas are protected from over-spray. Shake the spray paint can thoroughly and apply the top coat to the repair area, building it up by applying several coats, working from the center

After allowing at least two weeks for the paint to harden, use fine rubbing compound to blend the area into the original paint. Wax can now be applied

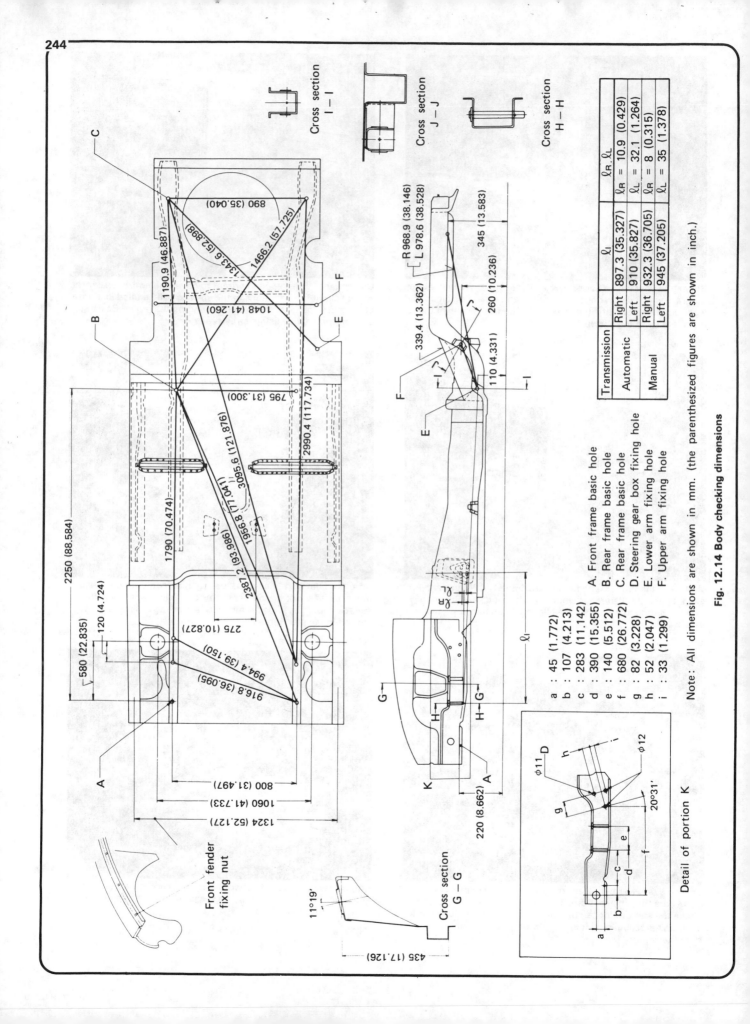

Cross section I–I

Cross section J–J

Cross section H–H

Transmission		ℓ_l	ℓ_R, ℓ_L
Automatic	Right	897.3 (35.327)	ℓ_R = 10.9 (0.429)
	Left	910 (35.827)	ℓ_L = 32.1 (1.264)
Manual	Right	932.3 (36.705)	ℓ_R = 8 (0.315)
	Left	945 (37.205)	ℓ_L = 35 (1.378)

A. Front frame basic hole
B. Rear frame basic hole
C. Rear frame basic hole
D. Steering gear box fixing hole
E. Lower arm fixing hole
F. Upper arm fixing hole

a : 45 (1.772)
b : 107 (4.213)
c : 283 (11.142)
d : 390 (15.355)
e : 140 (5.512)
f : 680 (26.772)
g : 82 (3.228)
h : 52 (2.047)
i : 33 (1.299)

Note: All dimensions are shown in mm. (the parenthesized figures are shown in inch.)

Fig. 12.14 Body checking dimensions

Front fender fixing nut

Detail of portion K

Cross section G–G

Chapter 13 Supplement:
Revisions and information on later models

Contents

1 Introduction

This Supplement contains specifications and information that applies to Mazda RX-7s produced from 1981 through 1985. Also included is information related to previous models that was not available at the time of original printing of this manual.

Where no differences (or very minor differences) exist between 1981 through 1985 models and earlier models, no information is given here. In those cases, the original material included in Chapters 1 through 12 should be used.

2 Specifications

Note: *The Specifications listed here include only those items which differ from those listed in Chapters 1 through 12. For information not specifically listed here, refer to the appropriate Chapter.*

General dimensions and capacities
Fuel tank .... 16.4 US gal (13.9 Imp. gal, 63 liters)
Engine oil (1983 on — with filter change)
  12A engine .... 4.9 US qts (4.0 Imp. qts, 4.6 liters)
  13B engine .... 6.1 US qts (5.1 Imp. qts, 5.8 liters)
Manual transmission oil (1982 on) .... 2.1 US qts (1.8 Imp. qts, 2.0 liters)

Recommended lubricants and fluids
Limited slip differential .... SAE 90 gear oil specially formulated for limited slip differentials
Power steering fluid .... ATF type F

Engine

Rotor width
  12A engine . . . .   2.7481 in (69.8 mm)
  13B engine . . . .   3.1438 in (79.85 mm)
Rotor housing width (13B engine) . . . .   3.1497 in (80 mm)
Standard side housing-to-rotor clearance
  12A engine (1983 on) . . . .   0.0047 to 0.0075 in (0.12 to 0.19 mm)
  13B engine . . . .   0.0047 to 0.0083 in (0.012 to 0.21 mm)
Apex seal length
  12A engine . . . .   2.7481 in (69.8 mm)
  13B engine . . . .   3.1418 in (79.8 mm)
Apex seal spring height (13B engine)
  Standard . . . .   0.2244 in (5.7 mm)
  Limit . . . .   0.1496 in (3.8 mm)

Torque specifications	M-kg	Ft-lbs
Oil pump sprocket bolt	3.2 to 4.7	23 to 34
Oil pan bolts	0.8 to 1.1	6 to 8
Exhaust manifold bolts	4.4 to 4.7	23 to 34
Spark plugs	1.3 to 1.5	9 to 11
Tension bolts (13B engine)	3.2 to 3.8	23 to 27
Oil line-to-cooler banjo bolt	6.0 to 8.5	43 to 61

Cooling and lubrication

Oil pump output at 1000 engine rpm
  (1983 on — US only) . . . .   7.0 liters (7.4 US qts, 6.2 Imp. qts) per minute
Pressure control valve spring free length (US only)
  12A engine (1983 on) . . . .   2.74 in (69.6 mm)
  13B engine . . . .   2.87 in (73.0 mm)
Oil cooler by-pass valve opening pressure (1983 on — US
  only) . . . .   300 kpa at 60 °C (42.7 psi at 140 °F)
Oil metering pump capacity (1984 on)
  12A engine . . . .   1.8 to 2.2 cc/6 min
  13B engine . . . .   0.8 to 1.2 cc/6 min

Fuel, exhaust and emissions control systems

Fuel pressure
  Carburetor . . . .   2.84 to 3.55 psi (.19 to .24 bars)
  Fuel injection . . . .   49.8 to 71.1 psi (3.43 to 4.90 bars)
Feed capacity
  Carburetor . . . .   1.48 US qts (1.23 Imp. qts, 1400 cc) per minute
  Fuel injection . . . .   1.80 US qts (1.49 Imp. qts, 1700 cc) per minute

Ignition system

Air gap
  1980 . . . .   0.008 to 0.024 in (0.2 to 0.6 mm)
  1981 thru 1985 . . . .   0.020 to 0.035 in (0.5 to 0.9 mm)
Maximum centrifugal advance (UK only) . . . .   12.5° at 1750 rpm
Leading ignition timing (UK only) . . . .   5° ± 1° ATDC
Leading ignition timing (13B engine only) . . . .   5° ATDC
Spark plug type
  US (1981 thru 1985) . . . .   NGK BR7EQ14, BR8EQ14, BR9EQ14
  UK (early models) . . . .   NGK BR7ET, BR8ET, BR9ET
  UK (later models) . . . .   NGK L4071K
Spark plug gap
  US (1981 thru 1985) . . . .   0.055 in ± 0.002 in (1.4 mm ± 0.05 mm)
  UK (later models) . . . .   0.014 in ± 0.006 in (0.35 mm ± 0.15 mm)

Manual transmission

Torque specifications	M-kg	Ft-lbs
Shift fork bolts	1.5	9 to 12

Braking system

Rear disc brake disc thickness
  Standard . . . .   0.3937 in (10 mm)
  Limit . . . .   0.3543 in (9 mm)
Maximum allowable lateral runout . . . .   0.0039 in (0.1 mm)
Rear brake pad lining thickness
  Standard . . . .   0.2362 in (6 mm)
  Limit . . . .   0.040 in (1 mm)

Torque specifications	M-kg	Ft-lbs
Rear caliper mounting bolt	3.0 to 4.2	22 to 30

Steering and suspension

Front coil spring free length (UK only)

Left .... 327.2 mm (12.88 in)
Right .... 336.5 mm (13.25 in)
Power steering pump drivebelt tension .... 10 to 12 mm (0.390 to 0.470 in)

Torque specifications	M-kg	Ft-lbs
Stabilizer bar-to-suspension lower arm	1.3 to 1.6	9 to 13
Steering wheel nut	4.0 to 5.0	29 to 36
Power steering pump mounting bolts	3.2 to 4.7	23 to 34
Power steering pump pulley nut	5.0 to 6.0	36 to 43
Power steering gear mounting bolts	4.5 to 5.7	33 to 41
Power steering shaft coupling bolt	4.4 to 5.5	32 to 40

---

3 Routine maintenance

Weekly and/or whenever you refuel

Check the power steering fluid level (it should be between the L and F marks on the dipstick)

Every 15 months or 15,000 miles (24,000 Km)

Check the automatic choke (except for vehicles with fuel injection and all California vehicles)

Every 30 months or 30,000 miles (48,000 Km)

Replace the fuel filter (except for California vehicles)

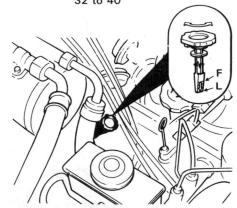

Fig. 13.1 The power steering fluid level can be checked with the dipstick attached to the reservoir cap

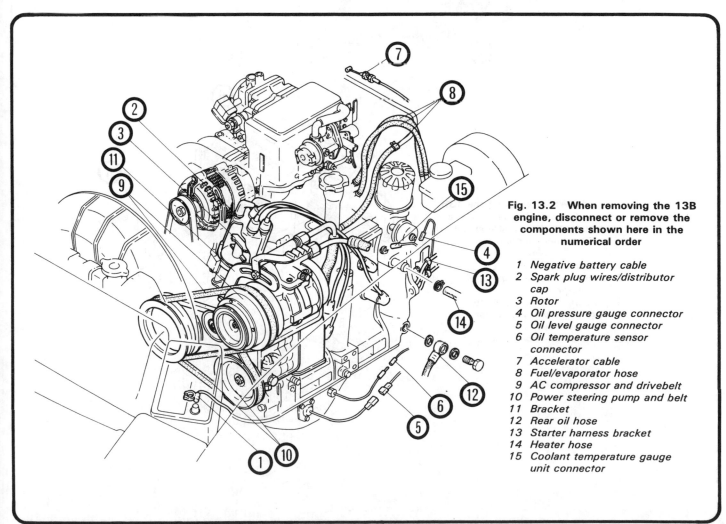

Fig. 13.2 When removing the 13B engine, disconnect or remove the components shown here in the numerical order

1 Negative battery cable
2 Spark plug wires/distributor cap
3 Rotor
4 Oil pressure gauge connector
5 Oil level gauge connector
6 Oil temperature sensor connector
7 Accelerator cable
8 Fuel/evaporator hose
9 AC compressor and drivebelt
10 Power steering pump and belt
11 Bracket
12 Rear oil hose
13 Starter harness bracket
14 Heater hose
15 Coolant temperature gauge unit connector

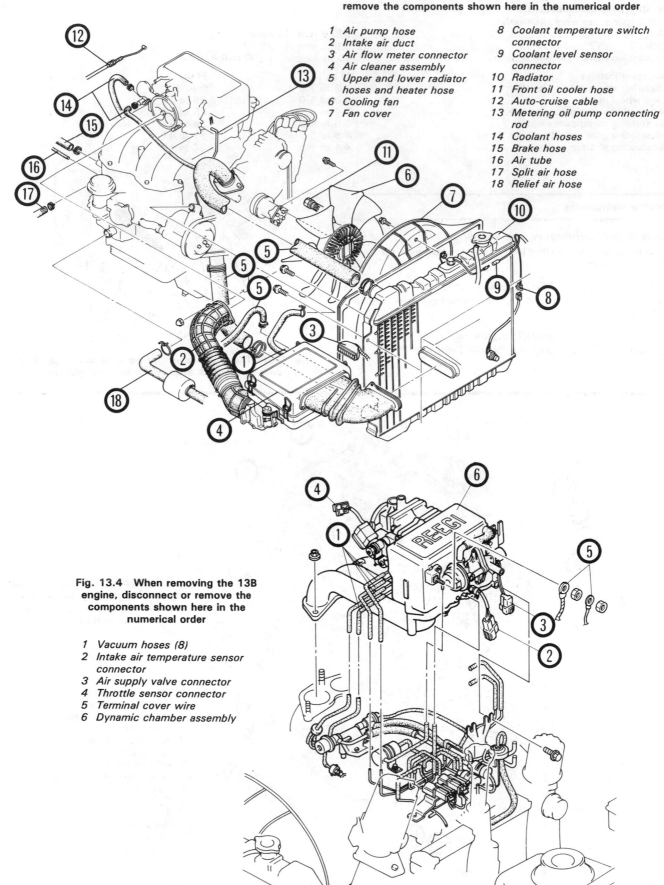

Fig. 13.3 When removing the 13B engine, disconnect or remove the components shown here in the numerical order

1 Air pump hose
2 Intake air duct
3 Air flow meter connector
4 Air cleaner assembly
5 Upper and lower radiator hoses and heater hose
6 Cooling fan
7 Fan cover
8 Coolant temperature switch connector
9 Coolant level sensor connector
10 Radiator
11 Front oil cooler hose
12 Auto-cruise cable
13 Metering oil pump connecting rod
14 Coolant hoses
15 Brake hose
16 Air tube
17 Split air hose
18 Relief air hose

Fig. 13.4 When removing the 13B engine, disconnect or remove the components shown here in the numerical order

1 Vacuum hoses (8)
2 Intake air temperature sensor connector
3 Air supply valve connector
4 Throttle sensor connector
5 Terminal cover wire
6 Dynamic chamber assembly

4 Engine

General information

Beginning with 1984 models, a larger engine, designated the 13B, was made available in the RX-7. Unless otherwise noted, the service procedures outlined in Chapter 1 are also applicable to the new engine. Be sure to refer to the Specifications Section in this Supplement for 13B engine specifications that differ from the 12A engine.

Engine — removal and installation (13B only)

1 The removal and installation procedures for the 13B engine are very similar to the procedures described in Chapter 1 (without transmission), so refer to them for general instructions. To ensure that nothing is overlooked, refer to the accompanying illustrations and disconnect/remove the components shown, in the numerical order indicated in each illustration, before lifting the engine out of the vehicle. Installation is the reverse of removal.

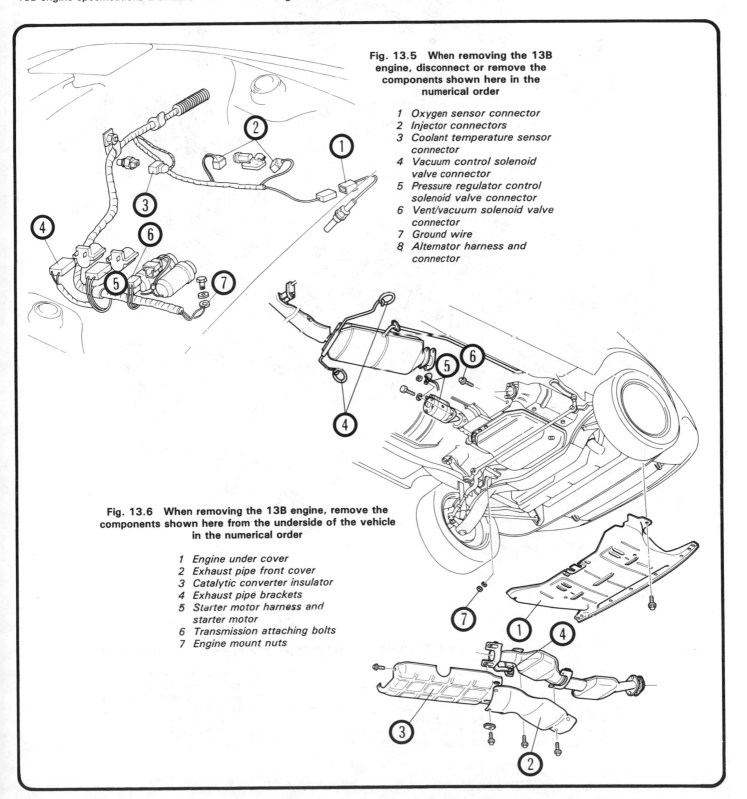

Fig. 13.5 When removing the 13B engine, disconnect or remove the components shown here in the numerical order

1 Oxygen sensor connector
2 Injector connectors
3 Coolant temperature sensor connector
4 Vacuum control solenoid valve connector
5 Pressure regulator control solenoid valve connector
6 Vent/vacuum solenoid valve connector
7 Ground wire
8 Alternator harness and connector

Fig. 13.6 When removing the 13B engine, remove the components shown here from the underside of the vehicle in the numerical order

1 Engine under cover
2 Exhaust pipe front cover
3 Catalytic converter insulator
4 Exhaust pipe brackets
5 Starter motor harness and starter motor
6 Transmission attaching bolts
7 Engine mount nuts

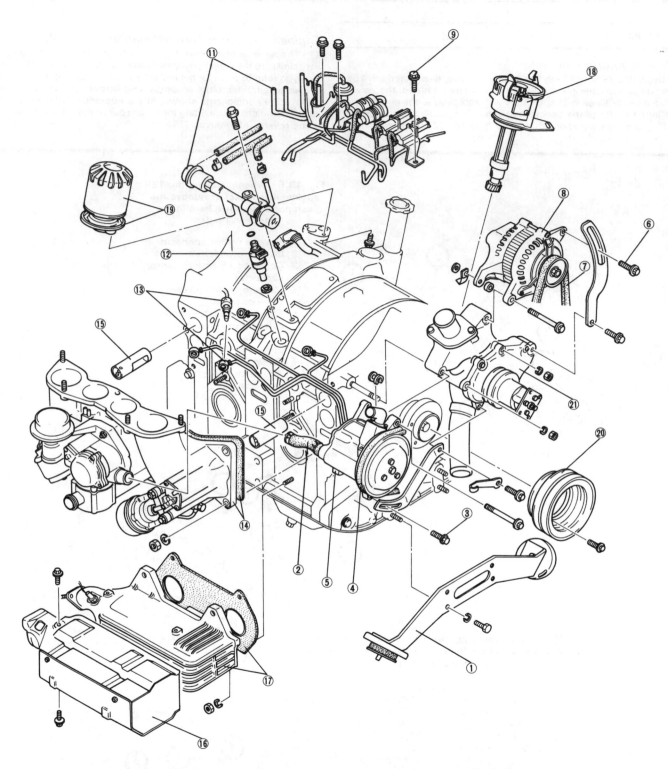

Fig. 13.7 When disassembling the 13B engine, remove the components shown in the numerical order

1 Engine mount	8 Alternator	15 Auxiliary port valves
2 Air hose	9 Emission device bolts	16 Exhaust manifold covers
3 Bolt	10 Pipe bolts	17 Exhaust manifold and gasket
4 Drivebelt	11 Emission device/pipe assembly	18 Distributor
5 Air pump	12 FI nozzles	19 Oil filter and body
6 Bolt	13 Metering oil pump hoses	20 Eccentric shaft pulley
7 Drivebelt	14 Intake manifold/gasket	21 Water pump

Removing components from the outside of the engine (13B only)

2   Refer to the accompanying illustration and remove the components in the numerical order that they are assigned. Reverse the order when reinstalling them.

Cleaning

3   When cleaning the rotors, be careful not to damage the soft material coating the side surfaces of each rotor.

Inspection

4   During inspection of the rotor components, be aware that a new "soft seal" has been added to the rotor corner seal assembly. This new seal fits inside the corner seal and should be carefully checked for evidence of excessive heat, wear and damage whenever major engine work is done.
5   On 13B engines, the auxiliary port valves must be checked for abnormal wear, damage and cracks. Slight wear and abrasion is not a problem. Insert the valves into the side housing and make sure they turn smoothly.

Engine — reassembly

6   On 1984 models only, apply a light coat of moly-based grease to the trochoid surfaces of the front and rear housings (from the direct oil port to the exhaust port) before reassembly (see the accompanying illustration).

Minor engine components — installation

12A engine

7   When reinstalling the oil cooler, be sure to tighten the front oil pipe fitting before tightening the banjo fitting bolt on the cooler body. If this is not done, the front fitting may leak.

13B engine

8   When installing the water pump, note that shims are used under the pump on the bolts in positions 2 and 4 in the accompanying illustration. If the shims are not installed, coolant leaks will develop.
9   The auxiliary ports must be installed before the intake manifold gasket is positioned on the engine. Make sure the larger sides of the auxiliary port valve shafts are aligned with the marks on the gasket.

***

5   Cooling and lubrication

Water pump — removal and installation (13B engine only)

1   When installing the water pump, note that shims are used under the pump on the bolts in positions 2 and 4 (see the illustration in Section 3). If the shims are not installed, coolant leaks will develop.

Water pump — overhaul and inspection

2   The water pump used on 1984 and 1985 models must be disassembled and reassembled following a slightly different procedure

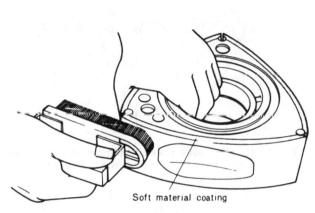

Fig. 13.8   When cleaning the rotors, be careful not to scratch or damage the soft material coating along the edges

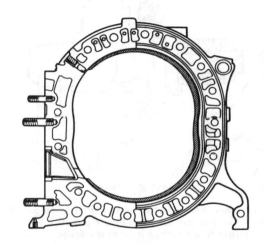

Fig. 13.9   Apply moly-based grease to the shaded area when reassembling the engine (1984 only)

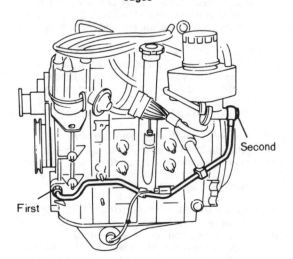

Fig. 13.10   Tighten the front oil line fitting first or oil leaks could result

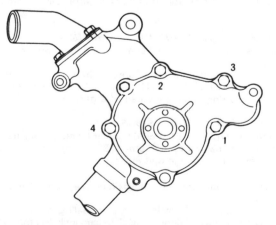

Fig. 13.11   Shims are installed behind bolts numbered 2 and 4 when installing the water pump on 13B engines

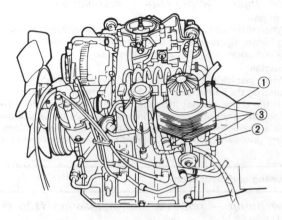

Fig. 13.12   The oil cooler on 12A engines is directly below the oil filter

1 *Coolant hoses*
2 *Oil line banjo fitting bolt*
3 *Cooler assembly*

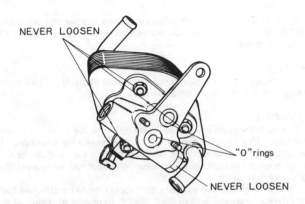

Fig. 13.13   Be sure to use new O-rings when reinstalling the oil cooler

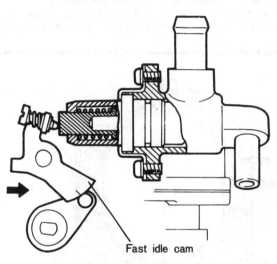

Fast idle cam

Fig. 13.14   When adjusting the metering oil pump on 13B engines, move the fast idle cam in the direction of the arrow to disengage it from the lever

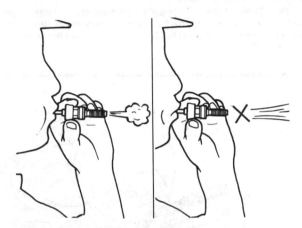

Fig. 13.15   The check valve should pass air when blowing into the fitting and close when applying suction

than the one described in Chapter 2. If the pump fails, a new or factory reconditioned unit should be installed (rather than attempting to rebuild the original).

Oil level sensor — removal and installation

3   The oil level sensor unit has been changed from a thermistor-type to a float-type.
4   The removal and installation procedures are basically the same as for the older type found in Chapter 2. Note that bolts secure the sensor to the pan and an O-ring is used instead of a gasket.

Oil cooler — removal and installation

5   Later models incorporate a finned oil cooler located under the oil filter (12A engine) or behind the radiator (13B engine). It should be periodically checked for damage and leaks.

12A engine
6   Disconnect and remove the water hoses (one inlet, one outlet) from the cooler.
7   Remove the oil pipe banjo fitting bolt and sealing washer.
8   Remove the fasteners and detach the oil cooler, including the filter.
9   Remove the O-rings.
10   Be sure to use new O-rings and sealing washers during installation and follow the recommended torque specifications when tightening the oil pipe fitting(s). Check for water and oil leaks when finished.

13B engine
11   Disconnect the oil cooler hoses from the engine, then plug the fittings to prevent contamination by dirt.
12   Carefully detach the oil cooler and remove it from the vehicle.
13   Installation is the reverse of removal. Be sure to use new sealing washers on the banjo fitting and bolt and check for leaks when finished.

Oil pressure control valve — checking

14   Note that the free length of the control valve spring is different, depending on model year and engine type. If new parts are needed, be sure to obtain the correct ones. The cap bolt and valve spring for all 12A engines, 1983 on, are painted yellow to aid in identification, but note that the spring length was changed on 12A engines in 1983.

Oil filter — removal and installation

15   Note that on 1983 through 1985 12A engines, the oil filter must be tightened an additional 1/8-turn from hand tight with a band-type filter wrench. On 13B engines the filter is tightened hand tight only (as described in Chapter 2).

Metering oil pump — adjusting (13B engine only)

16   Follow the procedure in Chapter 2, but note that the fast idle cam must be disengaged from the lever before the metering pump lever-to-washer clearance is checked (make sure that the lever contacts the stopper on the pump body when the clearance is checked).
17   Also, 13B engines are equipped with check valves in the rotor housing and intake manifold. To check their operation, unscrew them and blow into the fitting end; air should pass through. Apply a vacuum to the fitting and make sure the valve is closed (does not pass air).

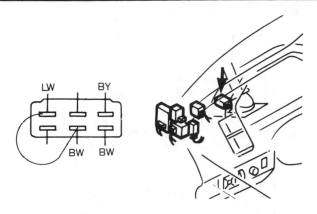

Fig. 13.16 Connect a jumper wire across the terminals in the fuel pump cut relay connector before checking the fuel pump pressure

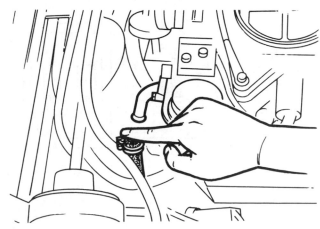

Fig. 13.17 Checking the air injection system check valve

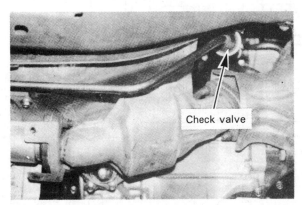

Fig. 13.18 Air injection system check valve location

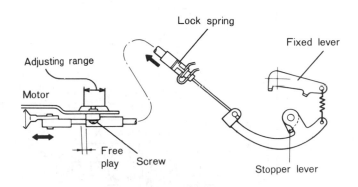

Fig. 13.19 Hot start assist cable adjustment details

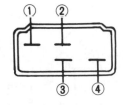

Fig. 13.20 Hot start assist relay terminal locations

6 Fuel, exhaust and emissions control systems

Fuel filter — replacement

1   A slightly different fuel filter has been installed on some later models. Although the appearance and type of mount (bolt and bracket rather than a clip) may be somewhat changed, the procedure in Chapter 3 still applies.

Fuel pump — testing

2   Follow the procedure in Chapter 3, but note that the fuel pump cut relay connector must be unplugged and a jumper wire connected between the terminals shown in the illustration before checking the fuel pressure on 1984 and 1985 models. The fuel pressure and volume for later models, both carbureted and fuel injected are listed in the Specifications at the beginning of this Chapter.

Fuel tank — removal and installation

3   The fuel tank on 1983 and later models incorporates a drain plug, which greatly simplifies the task of removing the tank. After draining the fuel, follow the procedure in Chapter 3.

Air injection system and catalytic converters

4   On later models the air injection system has been changed in an effort to better control exhaust emissions. Basically, two small pre-monolith converters and a main monolith converter have been located in the exhaust system near the front of the vehicle. The converters and associated heat shields should be inspected for damage whenever the vehicle is raised. Replacement should be done by a dealer service department or exhaust system specialist. In addition to the converters, 1983 through 1985 models also are equipped with a second check valve between the intake manifold and the catalytic converter. To test the valve, disconnect the intake manifold-to-converter air hose (at the rear of the manifold), start the engine and run it at 1500 rpm while checking for exhaust gas leakage at the open end of the hose. If leakage is evident, the valve is faulty and should be replaced with a new one.

Heat hazard warning sensor — general description

5   A sensor has been positioned under the floor to detect abnormally high temperatures in the exhaust system components and catalytic converters. A dashboard lamp alerts the driver to excessive heat. If overheating of the exhaust system persists, see your dealer service department for corrective action.

Hot start assist system — checking and adjusting

6   The cable free play check and adjustment is different on 1984 and 1985 models. Pull out on the inner cable until the stopper lever touches the start lever, then check the free play as shown in the accompanying illustration. If the free play is not 0.04 to 0.08-inch (1 to 2 mm), loosen the clamp screw and move the cable until it is correct.

7   The relay check is also different. Refer to the accompanying illustration and connect the leads of an ohmmeter or self-powered test light to terminals 1 and 4 of the relay connector. Continuity should be indicated. Use jumper leads to connect terminal 2 to the positive battery post and terminal 3 to the negative battery post. When the relay is energized, no continuity should exist between terminals 1 and 4.

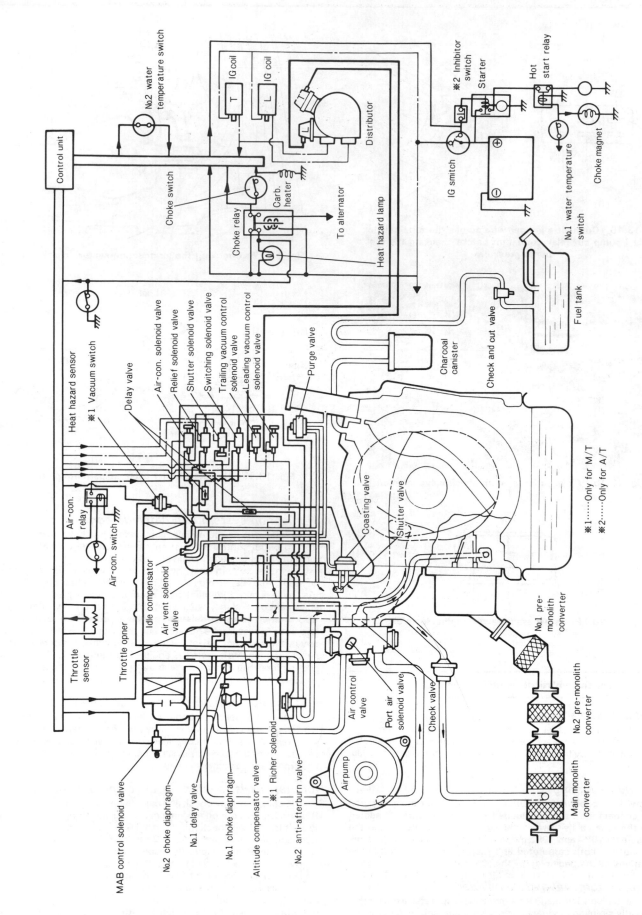

Fig. 13.21 Later model emission control systems schematic diagram

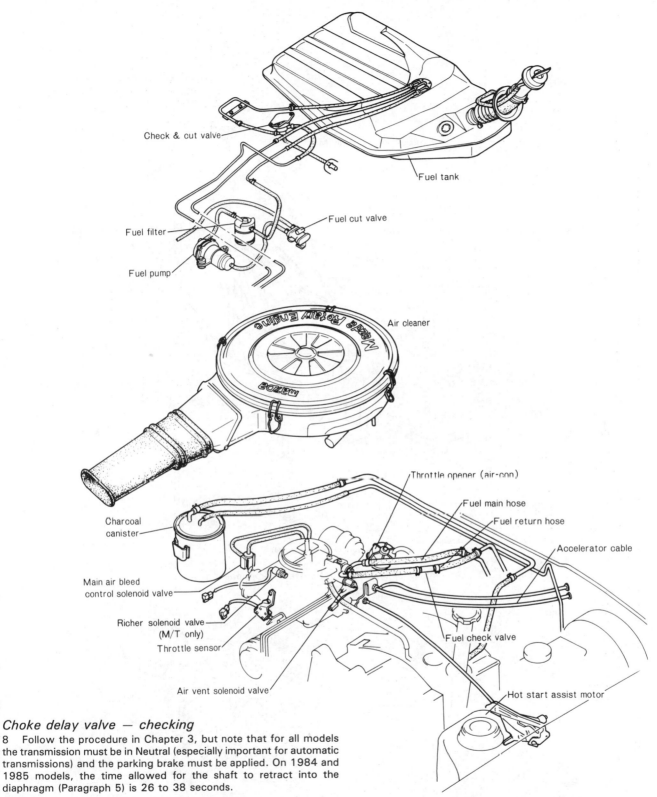

Check & cut valve

Fuel tank

Fuel filter

Fuel cut valve

Fuel pump

Air cleaner

Throttle opener (air-con)

Fuel main hose

Fuel return hose

Charcoal canister

Accelerator cable

Main air bleed control solenoid valve

Richer solenoid valve (M/T only)

Throttle sensor

Fuel check valve

Air vent solenoid valve

Hot start assist motor

Choke delay valve — checking

8   Follow the procedure in Chapter 3, but note that for all models the transmission must be in Neutral (especially important for automatic transmissions) and the parking brake must be applied. On 1984 and 1985 models, the time allowed for the shaft to retract into the diaphragm (Paragraph 5) is 26 to 38 seconds.

Secondary air control system

9   This system has been changed slightly and additional components have been used on 1984 and 1985 model vehicles, which affects the checking procedures somewhat. Note also that the system used on 1985 models is slighlty different than the system used on 1984 models.

Relief solenoid valve signal check

10   To check the signal for the relief solenoid valve on later models, warm up the engine and run it at idle, then connect a tachometer to the engine (follow the instrument manufacturer's instructions).

Fig. 13.22   Later model evaporative emission control system component layout

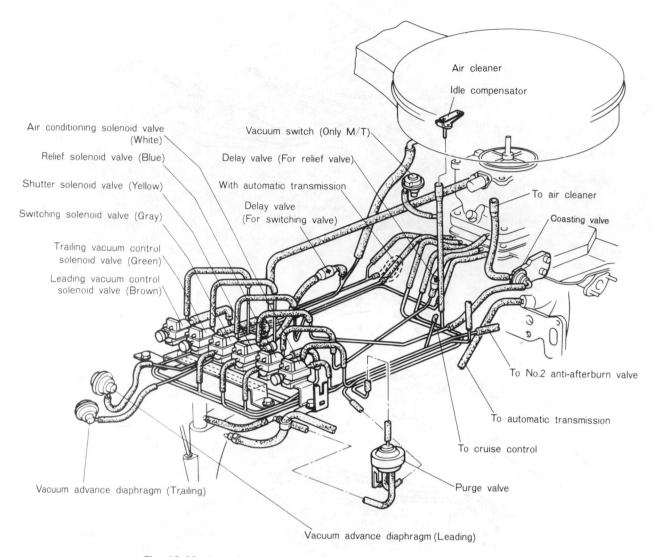

Air conditioning solenoid valve (White)

Relief solenoid valve (Blue)

Shutter solenoid valve (Yellow)

Switching solenoid valve (Gray)

Trailing vacuum control solenoid valve (Green)

Leading vacuum control solenoid valve (Brown)

Vacuum switch (Only M/T)

Delay valve (For relief valve)

With automatic transmission

Delay valve (For switching valve)

Air cleaner

Idle compensator

To air cleaner

Coasting valve

To No.2 anti-afterburn valve

To automatic transmission

To cruise control

Purge valve

Vacuum advance diaphragm (Trailing)

Vacuum advance diaphragm (Leading)

Fig. 13.23   Later model emission control systems component locations

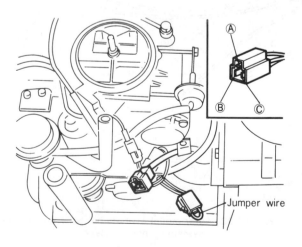

Jumper wire

Fig. 13.24   Throttle sensor terminal locations

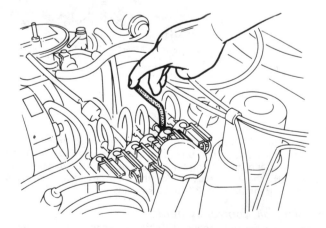

Fig. 13.25   Checking for relief solenoid valve vacuum signal

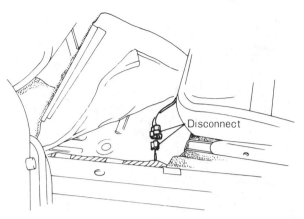

Fig. 13.26   Catalytic converter thermo sensor connector location

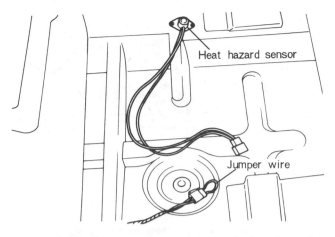

Fig. 13.27   Connect a jumper wire to the heat hazard sensor wire terminals

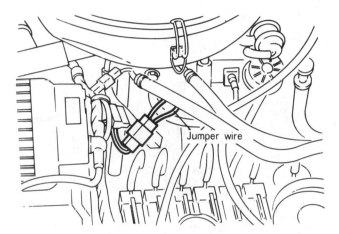

Fig. 13.28   Connect a jumper wire to the number 1 water temperature switch terminals

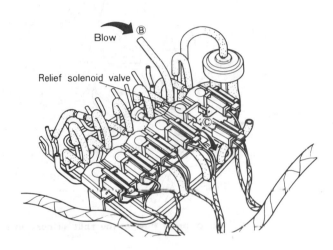

Fig. 13.29   Relief solenoid valve vacuum hose and port locations

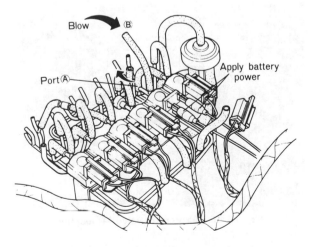

Fig. 13.30   Relief solenoid valve terminal and port locations

11 Unplug the throttle sensor connector and attach a jumper wire to terminals A and C in the connector (see the accompanying illustration).
12 Disconnect the vacuum line (relief solenoid valve-to-pipe) at the pipe and place your finger over the vacuum line open end. Suction should be felt.
13 Increase the engine speed to 3600 to 4400 rpm and make sure the suction stops.
14 Unplug the catalytic converter thermo sensor connector, then gradually increase the engine speed and make sure the suction is not present at 1000 to 1200 rpm and higher.
15 Rejoin the thermo sensor connector sections, then disconnect the jumper wire and rejoin the throttle sensor connector sections.
16 Unplug the heat hazard sensor connector and attach a jumper wire between the wire harness terminals. No suction should be felt at the vacuum line, regardless of engine speed.
17 Disconnect the jumper wire and rejoin the heat hazard sensor connector sections.
18 Stop the engine and unplug the number 2 water temperature switch connector at the radiator. Unplug the number 1 water temperature switch connector and attach a jumper wire between the connector terminals.
19 Pull the choke knob out about 0.60-inch (15 mm) and start the engine. Gradually increase the engine speed and make sure no suction is felt at the vacuum line at 1000 to 1200 rpm and higher. Stop the engine and reattach the vacuum line to the pipe. Remove the jumper wire and rejoin the water temperature switch connectors.

Relief solenoid valve check
20 Follow the procedure in Chapter 3, but note that the air should exit port C when the solenoid is not energized and port A when it is energized (see new illustrations).

Air control valve check
21 Start the engine and allow it to reach normal operating temperature, then connect a tachometer.
22 Disconnect the air cleaner-to-air control valve hose at the air cleaner

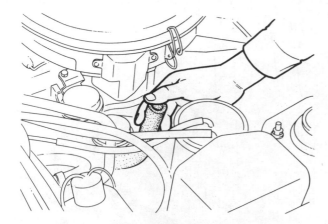

Fig. 13.31   Checking air control valve

Fig. 13.32   Relief solenoid valve-to-pipe hose location

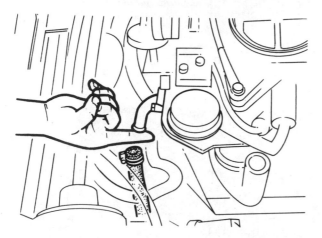

Fig. 13.33   Checking for air flow at the split air hose port

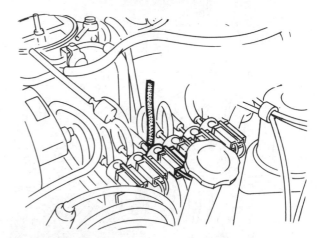

Fig. 13.34   Switching solenoid valve-to-pipe hose location

and place your finger over the hose opening. Increase the engine speed and make sure that air flows out of the hose when engine speed reaches 1500 to 2500 rpm or more.

23 Allow the engine to idle, then disconnect the relief solenoid valve vacuum line at the pipe. Air should now flow out of the air control valve hose.

24 Reconnect the vacuum line and the air control valve hose, then disconnect the split air hose (check valve-to-intake manifold) at the manifold and place your finger over the port opening.

25 Disconnect the switching solenoid valve vacuum line at the pipe and make sure air flows out of the split air hose port. If it doesn't, replace the air control valve with a new one.

26 Reconnect the vacuum line and split air hose.

Air control valve removal and installation

27 To replace the air control valve, remove the hot air duct, disconnect the air hose, unplug the port air solenoid connector and remove the air control valve. Installation is the reverse of removal.

Switching solenoid valve signal check

28 Warm up the engine and run it at idle, then connect a tachometer to the engine (follow the instrument manufacturer's instructions).

29 Unplug the throttle sensor connector and attach a jumper wire to terminals A and C in the connector (see Fig. 13.24 on page 256).

30 Disconnect the vacuum line (switching solenoid valve-to-pipe) at the pipe and place your finger over the vacuum line open end. Suction should be felt.

31 Increase the engine speed to 1000 to 1200 rpm and make sure the suction stops.

32 Unplug the number 1 water temperature switch connector and attach a jumper wire between the connector terminals.

33 Pull the choke knob out about 0.60-inch (15 mm), gradually in-

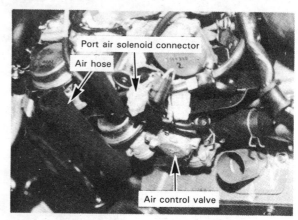

Port air solenoid connector

Air hose

Air control valve

Fig. 13.35   Air control valve (4) location

crease the engine speed and make sure that suction is felt at the vacuum line at all engine speeds.

34 Remove the jumper wire and rejoin the water temperature switch connectors.

35 Disconnect the jumper wire and rejoin the throttle sensor connector sections.

36 Gradually increase the engine speed and make sure that suction is felt at all engine speeds. **Note:** *If the engine is accelerated quickly, the suction will stop.*

37 Reconnect the vacuum line to the pipe.

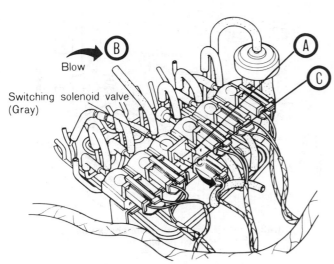

Fig. 13.36 Switching solenoid valve vacuum hose and port locations

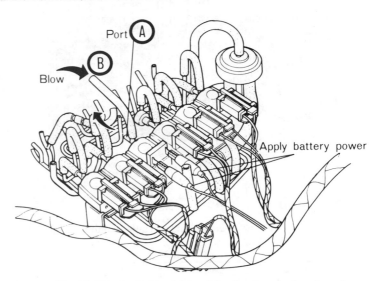

Fig. 13.37 Switching solenoid valve terminal and port locations

Fig. 13.38 Port air solenoid valve location

Engine speed (rpm)	Voltage (V)
Idling speed ~ 3,000	below 2
3,000 ~ 4,000	approx. 12
more than 4,000	below 2

Fig. 13.40 Port air solenoid valve voltage readings

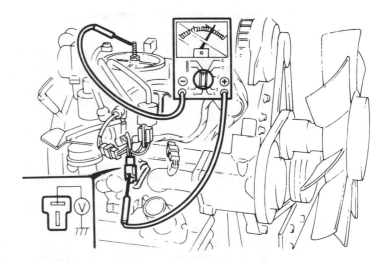

Fig. 13.39 Port air solenoid valve check voltmeter hookup details

Switching solenoid valve check
38 Disconnect the vacuum lines from the switching solenoid valve and pipes, then blow into the open end of vacuum line B (see accompanying illustration). Air should pass through the valve and exit port C.
39 Unplug the connector from the switching solenoid valve and use jumper wires to apply battery power to the valve terminals (be careful not to short the jumper wires together).
40 Blow into the open end of vacuum line B and make sure air passes through the valve and exits port A.

Port air solenoid valve check
41 Warm up the engine and run it at idle, then connect a tachometer to the engine (follow the instrument manufacturer's instructions).
42 Unplug the throttle sensor connector and attach a jumper wire to terminals A and C in the connector (see the accompanying illustration).

43 The port air solenoid valve is located adjacent to the air control valve. Connect a voltmeter to the port air solenoid connector terminal (green wire with black stripe) and a good ground, then increase the engine speed and note the voltmeter readings at the rpm indicated in the accompanying table.
44 Disconnect the jumper wire and rejoin the throttle sensor connector sections. Position the voltmeter inside the vehicle and secure the leads so the vehicle can be driven and the voltmeter can be read from the driver's seat.
45 At speeds below 50 mph, the voltmeter should read less than two volts. At speeds greater than 50 mph, the voltmeter should indicate approximately 12 volts.

Port air solenoid valve removal and installation
46 The port air solenoid valve can be unscrewed after unplugging the wiring connector. Installation is the reverse of removal.

Port air switching valve check (1985 models only)
47 Warm up the engine and run it at idle, then connect a tachometer to the engine (follow the instrument manufacturer's instructions).
48 Unplug the throttle sensor connector and attach a jumper wire to terminals A and C in the connector (see the accompanying illustration).

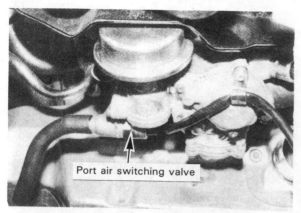

Fig. 13.41   Port air switching valve location

Engine speed (rpm)	Voltage (V)
Idling speed ~ 3,000	approx. 12
3,000 ~ 4,000	below 2
more than 4,000	approx. 12

Fig. 13.43   Port air switching valve voltage readings

49 The port air switching valve is located adjacent to the air control valve. Connect a voltmeter to the port air switching valve connector terminal (red wire) and a good ground, then increase the engine speed and note the voltmeter readings at the rpm indicated in the accompanying table.

50 Disconnect the jumper wire and rejoin the throttle sensor connector sections. Position the voltmeter inside the vehicle and secure the leads so the vehicle can be driven and the voltmeter can be read from the driver's seat.

51 At speeds below 50 mph, the voltmeter should read approximately 12 volts. At speeds greater than 50 mph, the voltmeter should read less than two volts.

Port air switching valve removal and installation (1985 models only)

52 The port air switching valve can be unscrewed after unplugging the wiring connector. Installation is the reverse of removal.

Catalytic converter thermo sensor check

53 Raise the vehicle and support it securely with jackstands, then crawl under it and unplug the thermo sensor wire connector.

54 Check for continuity between the thermo sensor wire terminals with an ohmmeter or self-powered test light. If there is no continuity, replace the sensor with a new one.

Catalytic converter thermo sensor removal and installation

55 The thermo sensor is attached to the converter with two nuts, which must be removed to separate the sensor from the converter. Don't forget to rejoin the connector sections when the installation is complete.

Ignition control system

56 The ignition control system used on 1984 and 1985 models is slightly different than the system described in Chapter 3. There is no longer any distinction between the system used in California vehicles and non-California vehicles.

Leading vacuum control solenoid valve signal check

57 Warm up the engine and run it at idle, then connect a tachometer to the engine (follow the instrument manufacturer's instructions).

58 Disconnect the vacuum line (leading vacuum advance diaphragm-to-pipe) at the pipe and place your finger over the pipe opening. No suction should be felt.

59 Gradually increase the engine speed to 1000 to 1200 rpm. Suction should be felt as the engine speed goes above this range.

60 Quickly increase the engine speed to more than 4000 rpm, allow it to decrease rapidly and make sure that no suction is felt as the engine decelerates.

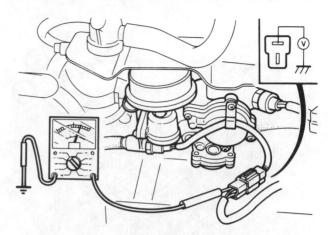

Fig. 13.42   Port air switching valve check voltmeter hookup details

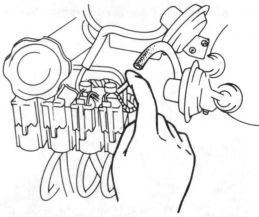

Fig. 13.44   Checking vacuum signal for leading vacuum control solenoid valve

61 On vehicles equipped with an automatic transmission, allow the engine to idle and make sure suction is felt with the shift lever in Reverse, Drive, Drive 1 and Drive 2. Shut off the engine.

62 Unplug the number 1 water temperature switch connector and attach a jumper wire between the terminals in the wire harness connector section. Pull the choke knob out about 0.60-inch (15 mm) and start the engine. Gradually increase the engine speed and make sure no suction is felt at the vacuum pipe at any engine speed.

63 Stop the engine and unplug the number 2 water temperature switch connector at the radiator. Start the engine and make sure suction is felt at engine speeds greater than 1200 rpm. Rejoin the water temperature switch connectors and reattach the vacuum line to the pipe.

Trailing vacuum control solenoid valve signal check

64 Warm up the engine and run it at idle, then connect a tachometer to the engine (follow the instrument manufacturer's instructions).

65 Disconnect the vacuum line (trailing vacuum advance diaphragm-to-pipe) at the pipe and place your finger over the pipe opening. No suction should be felt.

66 Gradually increase the engine speed to 2900 to 3100 rpm. Suction should be felt as the engine speed goes above this range.

67 Repeat the checks outlined in Paragraphs 60 through 63 above.

Leading vacuum control solenoid valve check

68 Disconnect the vacuum lines from the solenoid valve and pipe, then blow into the open end of vacuum line B (see accompanying illustration). Air should pass through the valve and exit filter C.

69 Unplug the connector from the leading solenoid valve and use jumper wires to apply battery power to the valve terminals (be careful not to short the jumper wires together).

70 Blow into the open end of vacuum line B and make sure air passes through the valve and exits port A.

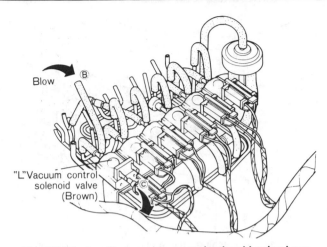

Fig. 13.45 Leading vacuum control solenoid valve hose
and port locations

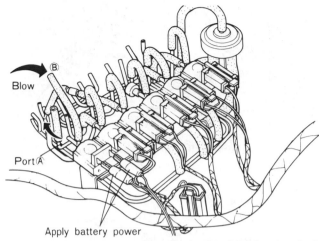

Fig. 13.46 Leading vacuum control solenoid valve terminal
and port locations

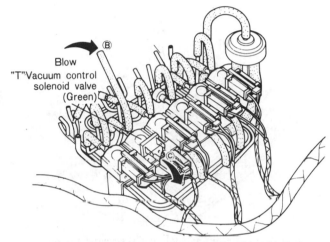

Fig. 13.47 Trailing vacuum control solenoid valve hose
and port locations

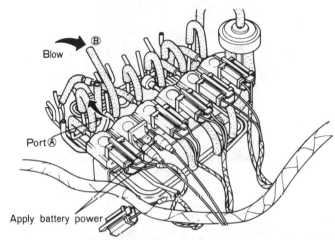

Fig. 13.48 Trailing vacuum control solenoid valve terminal
and port locations

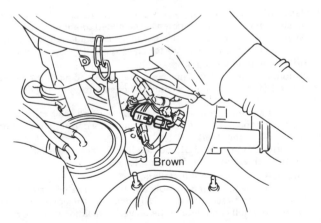

Fig. 13.49 Throttle sensor (brown) connector location

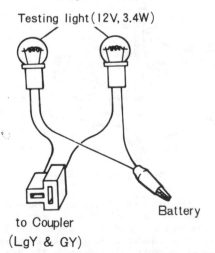

Fig. 13.50 Throttle sensor test light details

Trailing vacuum control solenoid valve check

71 Disconnect the vacuum lines from the solenoid valve and pipe, then blow into the open end of vacuum line B (see accompanying illustration). Air should pass through the valve and exit filter C.

72 Repeat the procedure described in Paragraphs 69 and 70 above, but refer to the illustrations for the trailing vacuum control solenoid valve.

Deceleration control system

73 The deceleration control system used on 1984 and 1985 models is slightly different than the one described in Chapter 3. It has additional components and requires revised checking procedures.

Throttle sensor check and adjustment

74 Warm up the engine, then connect a tachometer to the engine (follow the instrument manufacturer's instructions).

75 Unplug the sensor connector and attach the special test lamp shown in the accompanying illustration to the sensor side of the connector and the positive battery post.

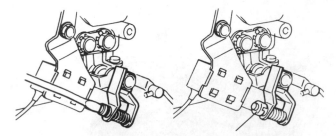

Fig. 13.51   Turning the throttle sensor adjusting screw

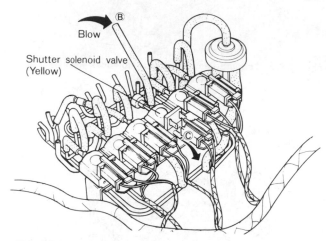

Fig. 13.53   Shutter solenoid valve vacuum hose and port locations

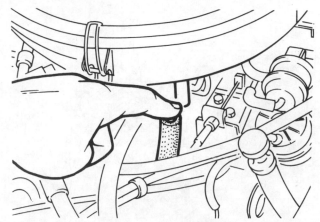

Fig. 13.52   Checking for the shutter solenoid vacuum signal

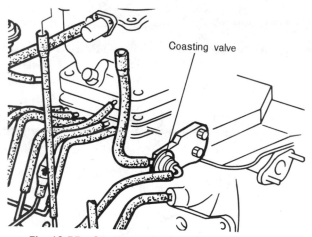

Fig. 13.55   Coasting valve location (later models)

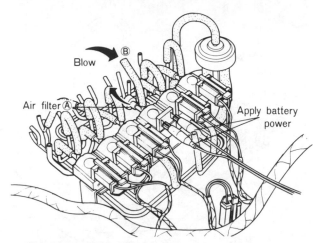

Fig. 13.54   Shutter solenoid valve terminal and port locations

79   Place your finger over the open end of the hose and make sure that no suction is felt at idle. Increase the speed to above 3000 rpm, then allow it to decelerate rapidly and make sure suction is felt until the engine speed slows to 1000 to 1200 rpm.

Shutter solenoid valve check
80   Disconnect the vacuum lines from the valve and pipe, then blow into the end of vacuum line B. Air should pass through the valve and exit port C.
81   Unplug the connector from the solenoid valve and use jumper wires to apply battery power to the valve terminals (be careful not to short the jumper wires together).
82   Blow into the open end of vacuum line B; make sure air passes through the valve and exits through filter A.

Coasting valve removal and installation
83   Remove the air cleaner assembly and the carburetor (Chapter 3), then disconnect the vacuum line and air hose from the coasting valve.
84   Remove the bolts and detach the valve. Installation is the reverse of removal.

Number 1 anti-afterburn valve check
85   Warm up the engine and allow it to idle, then disconnect the air control valve-to-air pump hose at the pump.
86   Place your finger over the hose and make sure that there is no suction felt with the engine idling. Increase the engine speed to more than 3000 rpm, then allow it to decelerate rapidly. Suction should be felt as the engine speed drops. If it isn't, the anti-afterburn valve is defective and the air control valve assembly must be replaced with a new one.

Number 2 anti-afterburn valve check
87   Warm up the engine and allow it to idle, then disconnect the air cleaner-to-number 2 anti-afterburn valve hose at the air cleaner.
88   Place your finger over the hose and make sure that there is no suc-

76   Start the engine and increase the speed to above 3000 rpm, then allow it to decelerate rapidly and make sure the lamps light simultaneously when the engine speed is 1000 to 1200 rpm.
77   If the lamps light at different times, remove the cap from the throttle sensor adjusting screw and turn the screw until the lamps light at the same time when the check is repeated. Turning the screw will change the timing of the current flowing through the light green wire with the yellow stripe (when the screw is turned in, current will flow earlier; when it is turned out, current will flow later). Be sure to reinstall the adjusting screw cap when finished.

Shutter solenoid valve signal check
78   Warm up the engine, then connect a tachometer to it (follow the instrument manufacturer's instructions). Unplug the throttle sensor connector (brown) and disconnect the coasting air valve-to-air cleaner hose at the air cleaner.

Fig. 13.56 Checking the number 1 anti-afterburn valve

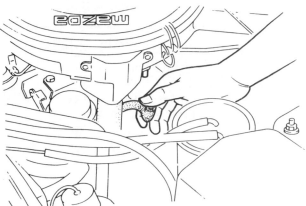

Fig. 13.57 Checking the number 2 anti-afterburn valve

Fig. 13.58 Dashpot adjustment details

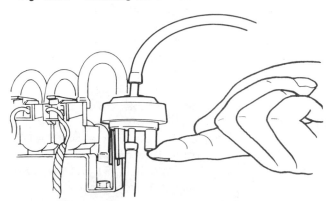

Fig. 13.59 Checking purge valve

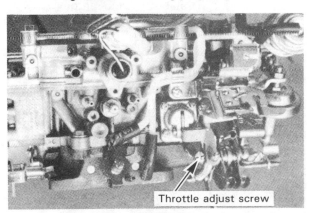

Fig. 13.60 Throttle adjust screw location

tion felt with the engine idling. Increase the engine speed to more than 3000 rpm, then allow it to decelerate rapidly. Suction should be felt as the engine speed drops. If it isn't, the number 2 anti-afterburn valve is defective and must be replaced with a new one.

Dashpot check and adjustment
89 Remove the air cleaner assembly and make sure the dashpot rod doesn't prevent the throttle lever from returning to the idle stop position.
90 Open the throttle quickly and see if the dashpot rod extends without hesitation. Release the throttle and make sure it returns to the idle stop position slowly after it contacts the dashpot rod.
91 Connect a tachometer to the engine, start it and allow it to reach normal operating temperature, then verify that the idle speed is correct.
92 Operate the throttle until the lever moves away from the dashpot rod, then slowly decrease the engine speed and note the rpm at which the throttle lever just contacts the dashpot rod. It should be 3800 to 4200 rpm. If it isn't, loosen the locknut and turn the dashpot diaphragm until it is within the specified range.

Auxiliary emission control devices
Control unit
93 When checking the control unit on 1984 and 1985 models, attach the negative meter lead to a good ground, turn the ignition switch on and probe each of the remaining terminals with the positive lead. Refer to illustration on next page for the terminal locations and desired voltage readings. **Note:** *The engine must be at normal operating temperature, but do not start the engine with the voltmeter leads hooked to the connector terminals.*

Number 1 and number 2 water temperature switches
94 1984 and 1985 models have two water temperature switches; one in the water pump housing (number 1) and one in the lower radiator tank (number 2). The checking procedure in Chapter 3 is valid for both switches, but note that the number 1 switch is checked for the

temperature at which continuity ceases to exist (above 158 ± 11.7 °F) and the number 2 switch is checked for the temperature at which continuity exists (above 59 ± 7 °F).

Crankcase and evaporative emission control system
95 A purge valve is used on 1984 and 1985 models in place of the ventilation and check valve mentioned in Chapter 3. To check the purge valve, disconnect the oil filler pipe-to-valve hose at the valve, start the engine and run it at idle.
96 Place your finger over the valve port and make sure no suction is felt. Increase the engine speed to 2000 rpm and verify that suction is present at the valve port.

Idle speed — adjusting
97 Follow the procedure in Chapter 3, but note that on 1984 and 1985 models the richer solenoid valve connector must be unplugged before checking the idle speed. Also, the idle speed is adjusted by turning the throttle adjust screw, not an air adjust screw (see accompanying illustration). After adjusting the idle speed the throttle sensor must also be adjusted.

Terminal	Connection to	Voltage with ignition ON (When functioning properly)
A	Ignition coil ⊖ terminal	approx. 12V
B	Ignition switch	approx. 12V
C	Choke switch	below 1.5V
D	Ignition coil ⊖ terminal	approx. 12V
E	Throttle sensor	approx. 8V
F	Switching solenoid valve	approx. 12V
G	Throttle sensor	1 ~ 2V
H	Ignition switch "START" terminal	below 1.5V (above 8V at "START")
I	Throttle sensor	0V
J	No. 2 water temperature switch	below 1.5V
L	Air-con. solenoid valve	approx. 12V
M	Main air bleed solenoid valve	approx. 12V
N	Relief solenoid valve	below 2V
O	Heat hazard sensor	below 2V
P	Ground	0V
Q	Shutter solenoid valve	below 1.5V
R	Idle richer solenoid valve	0V
S	Vacuum control solenoid valve (L)	approx. 12V (in neutral)
T	Vacuum control solenoid valve (T)	approx. 12V (in neutral)
U	Port air solenoid valve	below 1.5V
V	Ignition switch "START" terminal	below 1.5V (above 8V at "START")
a	Catalyst thermo sensor	below 1.5V
b		
c	Catalyst thermo sensor	below 1.5V
d		
e		
f		
h	Vehicle speed sensor	0V: Reed switch (speedometer) . . . closed 6 ~ 12V: Reed switch (speedometer) . . . open
i	Air-con. cut relay	below 1.5V . . . air con. switch OFF
j		
k	Neutral switch	0V . . . in gear approx. 12V . . . in neutral
l	Clutch switch	0V . . . pedal released approx. 12V . . . pedal depressed
m		
n	Fuel pump cut relay	below 1.5V

Control unit connector

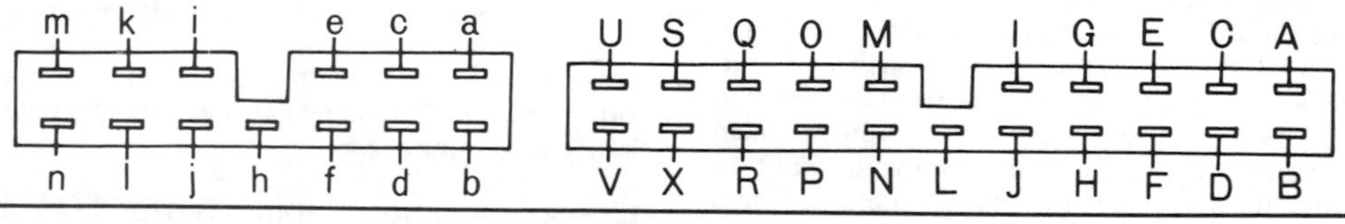

Fig. 13.61   Control unit terminal locations and voltage readings (12A engine only)

Idle mixture — adjusting

98   The idle mixture should be adjusted by a dealer service department to ensure compliance with emissions regulations.

Choke magnet — checking

99   The procedure and illustration (Fig 3.13 — except for California) in Chapter 3 can be used for 1984 and 1985 models, but note that when the choke knob is pulled out 0.40 ± 0.080-inch (10 ± 2 mm),

continuity should also exist between terminals 3 and 7. When the choke knob is in any position, continuity should exist between terminals 6 and 8.

Throttle opener (air conditioner equipped vehicles only)
Signal check
100 Start and run the engine until it is warm, then shut it off and connect a tachometer.

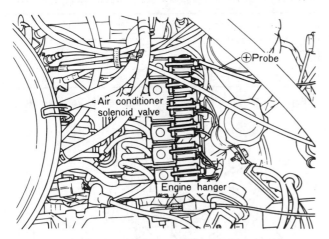

Fig. 13.62   Air conditioner solenoid valve location

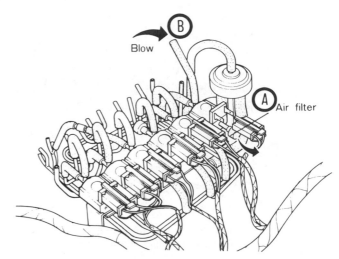

Fig. 13.63   Air conditioner solenoid valve vacuum hose and port locations

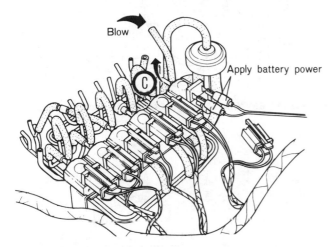

Fig. 13.64   Air conditioner solenoid valve terminal and port locations

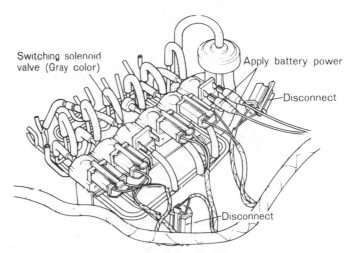

Fig. 13.65   Switching solenoid valve location

Fig. 13.66   Throttle opener adjusting screw location

101 Connect the positive lead of a voltmeter to the white wire in the air conditioner solenoid valve connector and ground the negative voltmeter lead.

102 Start the engine and turn on the air conditioner. Increase the engine speed to 2000 rpm, then slowly close the throttle and see if the voltmeter indicates zero volts at 1000 to 1200 rpm.

Air conditioner solenoid valve check

103 Disconnect the vacuum lines from the valve and pipe, then blow into the end of vacuum line B. Air should pass through the valve and exit filter A (see accompanying illustration).

104 Unplug the connector from the solenoid valve and use jumper wires to apply battery power to the valve terminals (be careful not to short the jumper wires together).

105 Blow into the open end of vacuum line B; make sure air passes through the valve and exits through port C.

Throttle opener check and adjustment

106 Make sure all accessories are off and remove the fuel filler cap, then disconnect and plug the idle compensator vacuum line in the air cleaner.

107 Connect a tachometer, then start and run the engine until operating temperature is reached.

108 Unplug the connector from the switching solenoid valve (gray mark) and disconnect the vacuum lines from the vacuum advance units on the distributor (plug the vacuum lines).

109 Turn the air conditioner off and unplug the connector from the air conditioner solenoid valve. Apply battery power to the valve terminals and make sure the throttle opener operates. Engine speed should increase to 1200 ± 50 rpm with the transmission in Neutral. If it doesn't, turn the adjusting screw on the throttle opener.

Mixture control system (1984 and 1985 models only)

Main air bleed control solenoid valve signal check

110 Warm up the engine and run it at idle, then connect a tachometer to the engine (follow the instrument manufacturer's instructions).

111 Unplug the throttle sensor connector and attach a jumper wire to terminals A and C in the connector (see the illustration in the *Secondary air control system* sub-Section).

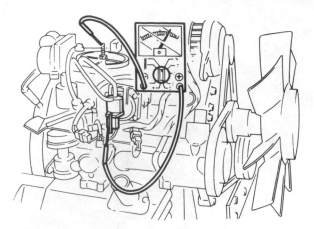

Fig. 13.67   Voltmeter connected to main air bleed control solenoid valve terminal and ground

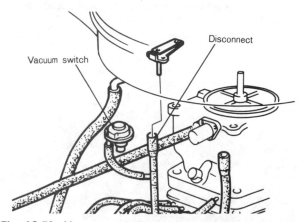

Fig. 13.70   Vacuum switch and idle compensator locations

Engine speed (rpm)	Voltage (V)
Idling speed ～ 3,000	approx. 12
3,000 ～ 4,000	below 2
more than 4,000	approx. 12

Fig. 13.68   Main air bleed control solenoid valve voltage readings

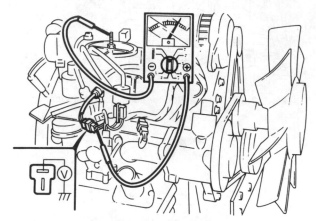

Fig. 13.69   Checking signal for richer solenoid valve

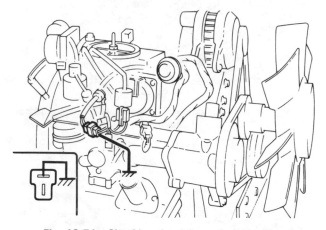

Fig. 13.71   Checking the richer solenoid valve

112 Connect a voltmeter to the main air bleed control solenoid terminal (brown wire) and a good ground, then increase the engine speed and note the voltmeter readings at the rpm indicated in the accompanying table.

113 Disconnect the jumper wire and rejoin the throttle sensor connector sections. Position the voltmeter inside the vehicle and secure the leads so the vehicle can be driven and the voltmeter can be read from the driver's seat.

114 At speeds below 50 mph, the voltmeter should read approximately 12 volts. At speeds greater than 50 mph, the voltmeter should read less than two volts.

Richer solenoid valve signal check (manual transmission only)

115 With the engine running at idle, connect a voltmeter to the richer solenoid valve terminal (white wire with red stripe) and a good ground. The voltmeter should indicate 12 volts.

116 Increase the engine speed to more than 1500 rpm, then allow it to decelerate while watching the voltmeter. It should indicate less than two volts for 30 seconds when the engine speed drops below 1100 rpm.

117 Disconnect the vacuum line from the idle compensator vacuum switch and see if the voltmeter indicates zero volts. Reconnect the vacuum line.

118 Unplug the clutch switch wiring connector, depress the clutch pedal and shift from 1st through 5th gear. Increase the engine speed to more than 1500 rpm in each gear, then allow it to decelerate while watching the voltmeter. It should indicate 12 volts each time.

Richer solenoid valve check

119 With the engine idling, ground the valve terminal (white wire with red stripe) and listen for a clicking sound, which indicates that the valve is operating.

Vacuum switch check

120 Remove the switch, connect an ohmmeter or self-powered test light to the switch terminals, apply a vacuum to the switch port and

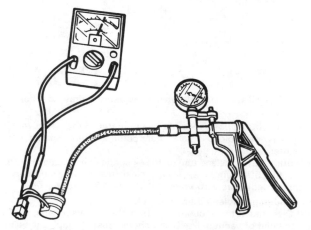

Fig. 13.72   Checking the vacuum switch

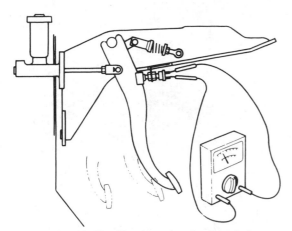

Fig. 13.73 Checking the clutch switch

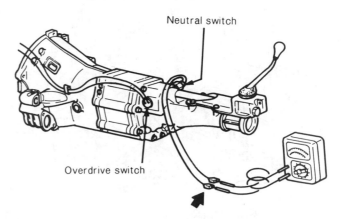

Fig. 13.74 Checking the Neutral switch

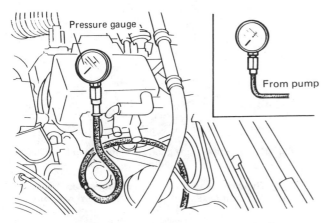

Fig. 13.75 Fuel injection fuel pump pressure check gauge hookup

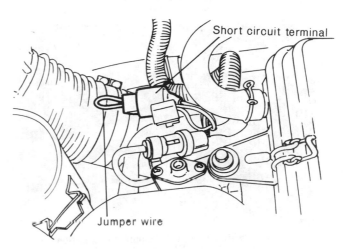

Fig. 13.76 Connect a jumper wire across the fuel pump short circuit connector terminals

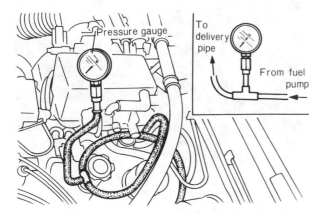

Fig. 13.77 Checking the pressure regulator

watch the ohmmeter or test light. At zero to 4.7 in-Hg of vacuum, no continuity should exist. At 4.7 in-Hg or more vacuum, continuity should exist.

Clutch switch check

121 Unplug the clutch switch wiring connector and attach an ohmmeter or self-powered test light to the switch terminals. With the clutch pedal depressed, continuity should be indicated. With the clutch pedal released (all the way up), no continuity should exist.

Neutral switch check

122 Raise the vehicle and support it securely on jackstands, then crawl under it and disconnect the neutral switch wiring connectors (the switch is located on the right-hand side of the transmission).

123 Connect an ohmmeter or self-powered test light to the switch terminal wires. With the transmission in Neutral, continuity should exist. With the transmission in any gear, no continuity should be indicated.

Fuel injection system (13B engine only)

Warning: *Gasoline may spray or drip from the connections as the fuel hoses are removed during the following operations, so be sure to perform the procedures in an area that is away from sparks, open flames, bare light bulbs and appliance pilot lights. Also, wrap a cloth around each connection as the hose is disconnected to contain any spilled fuel.*

Fuel pump — testing

124 Disconnect the negative battery cable from the battery, then wrap a cloth loosely around the main fuel hose where it connects to the metal pipe. Carefully loosen and slide back the hose clamp, then detach the hose from the pipe.

125 Attach a fuel pressure gauge to the open end of the fuel hose.

126 Reconnect the negative battery cable, then attach a jumper wire between the fuel pump short circuit connector terminals and turn on the ignition switch. The pump should start to run and fuel pressure will be indicated on the gauge. It should be 49.8 to 71.1 psi. If it isn't, the pump is defective and should be replaced with a new one.

Pressure regulator — checking

127 Disconnect the negative battery cable from the battery, then wrap a cloth loosely around the main fuel hose where it connects to the metal pipe. Carefully loosen and slide back the hose clamp, then detach the hose from the pipe.

128 Attach a fuel pressure gauge to the hose and pipe with a short section of fuel hose and a T-fitting.

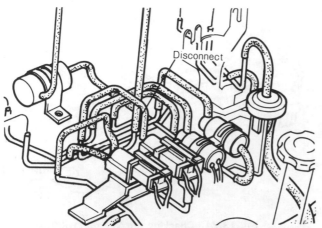

Fig. 13.78   **Disconnect the vacuum hose at the pressure regulator control valve**

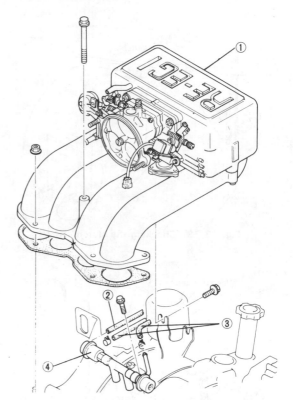

Fig. 13.79   **Pressure regulator removal and installation details**

1 Dynamic chamber   *3 Fuel hoses*
2 Vacuum hose   *4 Pressure regulator*

Fig. 13.80   **EGI main fusible link location**

Fig. 13.81   **Main relay location**

Main relay

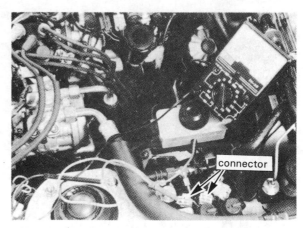

Fig. 13.82   **Checking for voltage at the main relay connector number 2 terminal wire**

connector

129 Reconnect the negative battery cable and start the engine, then disconnect the vacuum hose from the pressure regulator control valve.
130 The fuel pressure at idle should now be approximately 36.97 psi.
131 Reconnect the vacuum hose and make sure the pressure is now 28.44 psi. Replace the pressure regulator if it fails the checks.

Pressure regulator — removal and installation
132 Cover the starter motor with a cloth to keep gasoline out of it.
133 Detach the air cleaner-to-throttle chamber duct, then refer to *Emissions control systems (13B engine only)* in this Section and separate the dynamic chamber, throttle chamber and intake manifold from the engine as an assembly.
134 Detach the vacuum and fuel return hoses from the pressure regulator, then unscrew the regulator from the delivery pipe.

135 Installation is the reverse of removal. Before installing the dynamic chamber, operate the fuel pump as described in Paragraph 126 above and check for leaks at the pressure regulator and fuel hose.

Injectors — checking
136 Use a stethescope, or hold the handle of a long screwdriver to your ear and touch its tip against the base of the injector. Listen for operating noises from each injector with the engine idling and accelerating. **Warning:** *Do not place the tip of the screwdriver near any moving parts inside the engine compartment.*
137 If no operating sounds are heard, check for continuity in the wire from the trailing ignition coil terminal to terminal U in the control unit connector.
138 Check the EGI main fusible link to make sure it has not blown.
139 Turn the ignition switch on and verify that the main relay clicks when power is applied to it.

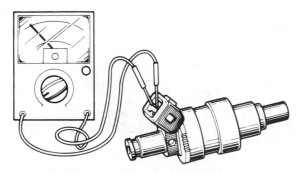

Fig. 13.83 Checking the injector resistance

140 If no click is heard, check for battery voltage (12 volts) at the main relay connector number 2 terminal (black wire with white stripe).
141 After the injectors are removed, measure the resistance by attaching the leads from an ohmmeter to the injector terminals. The resistance should be 1.5 to 3 ohms. Injector leakage and volume checks should be done by a dealer service department.

Injectors — removal and installation

142 Detach the air cleaner-to-throttle chamber duct, then refer to *Emissions control systems (13B engine only)* in this Section and separate the dynamic chamber, throttle chamber and intake manifold from the engine as an assembly.
143 Detach the vacuum and fuel hoses from the pressure regulator and fuel delivery pipe, then detach the wiring harness connector from each injector.
144 Unbolt and remove the delivery pipe, then lift out the injectors.
145 Installation is the reverse of removal. Be sure to use new insulators,

grommets and O-rings. Apply a small amount of gasoline to the O-rings to act as a lubricant and be very careful not to damage them as the injectors are installed.

Pulsation damper — checking

146 With the engine idling, place your finger over the pulsation damper and check for a pulsating motion.

Atmospheric pressure sensor — checking

147 Attach one voltmeter lead to terminal D in the atmospheric pressure sensor wiring harness connector and ground the other lead.
148 Turn the ignition switch on and note the voltage reading. It should be 4 ± 0.5 volts at sea level and 3 ± 0.5 volts at altitudes above 6500 feet.

Idle speed — adjusting

149 Before adjusting the idle speed, make sure all accessories are off, remove the fuel tank cap and connect a tachometer to the engine (follow the instrument manufacturer's instructions).
150 Start and run the engine until it reaches normal operating temperature.
151 Refer to the *Emissions control systems (13B engine only)* Section and perform the throttle sensor check and adjustment procedure.
152 Unplug the vent and vacuum solenoid valve connector, then remove the blind cap from the air adjust screw.
153 Turn the air adjust screw until the idle speed is 800 rpm, then install the blind cap on the screw.

Idle mixture — adjusting

154 Idle mixture adjustment is not normally necessary unless the variable resistor is replaced with a new one. At any rate, have the mixture adjustment done by a dealer service department to ensure compliance with emissions regulations.

Emissions control systems (13B engine only)

155 The emissions control systems used on 13B engines are very similar to the systems used on 12A engines. Many of the checks and

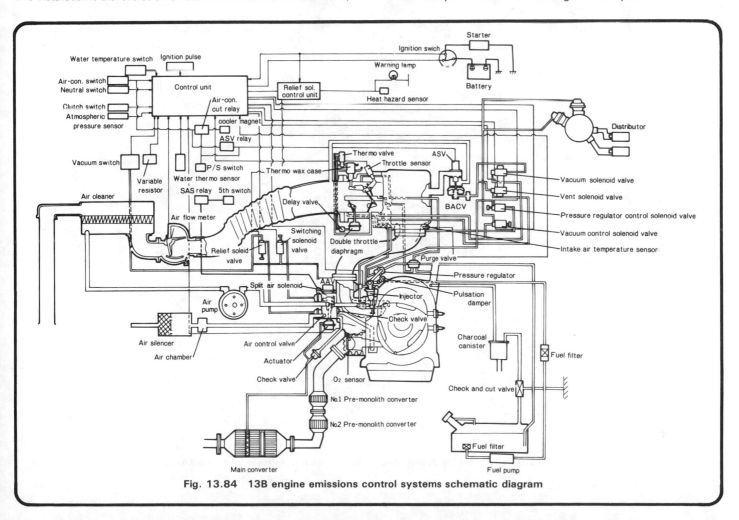

Fig. 13.84 13B engine emissions control systems schematic diagram

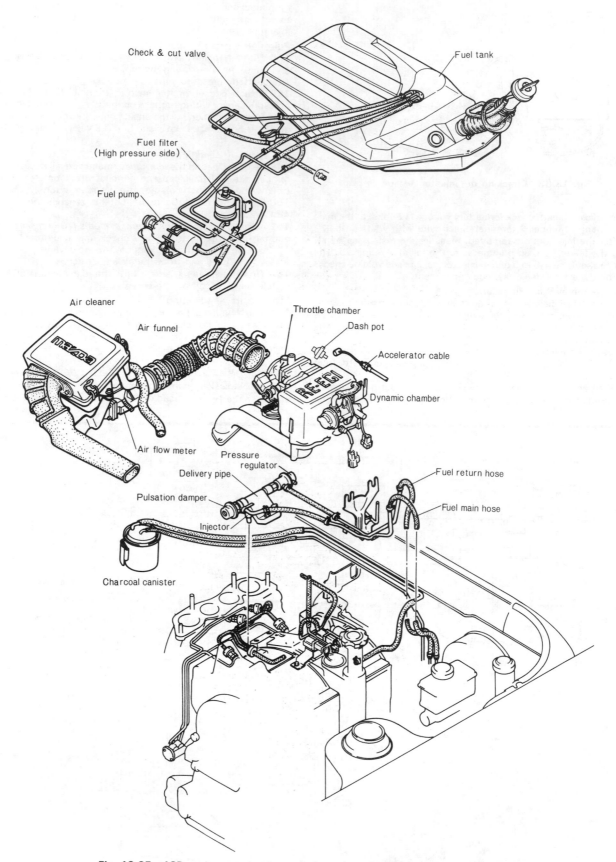

Check & cut valve

Fuel tank

Fuel filter
(High pressure side)

Fuel pump

Air cleaner

Air funnel

Throttle chamber

Dash pot

Accelerator cable

Dynamic chamber

RE-EGI

Air flow meter

Pressure regulator

Delivery pipe

Fuel return hose

Fuel main hose

Pulsation damper

Injector

Charcoal canister

Fig. 13.85   13B engine evaporative emissions control system component layout

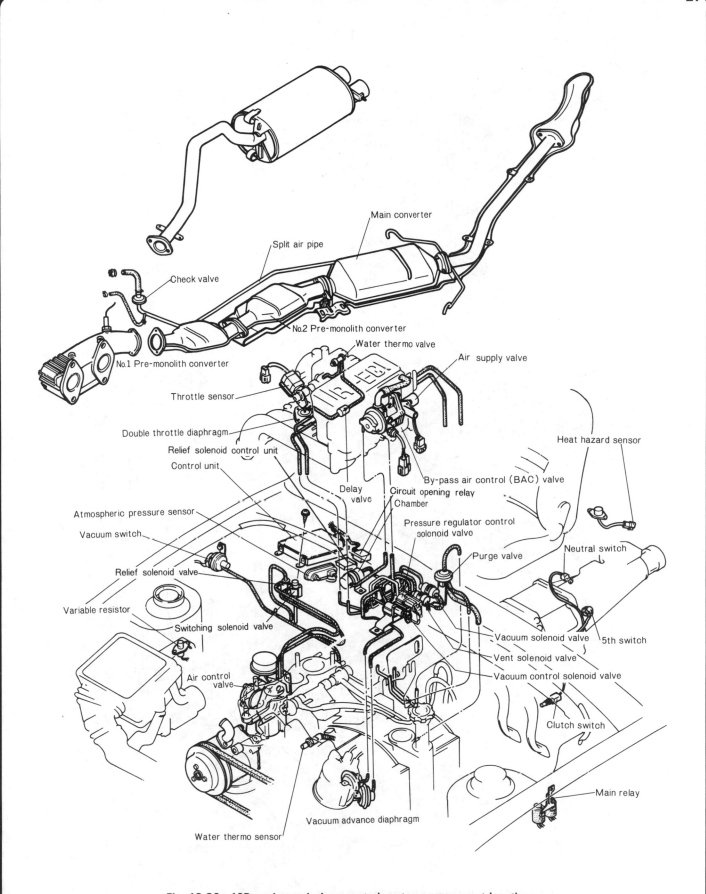

Fig. 13.86   13B engine emissions control systems component locations

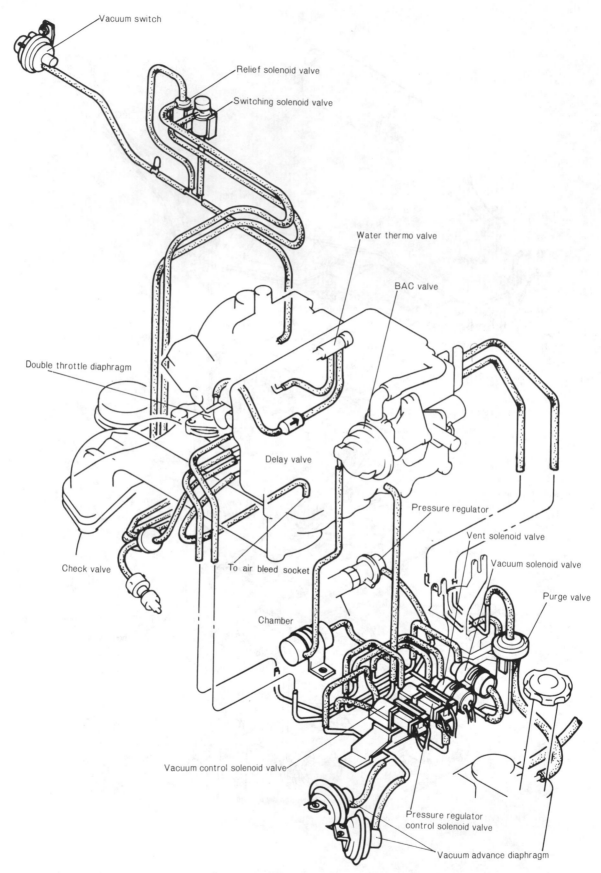

Vacuum switch

Relief solenoid valve

Switching solenoid valve

Water thermo valve

BAC valve

Double throttle diaphragm

Delay valve

Pressure regulator

Vent solenoid valve

Vacuum solenoid valve

Purge valve

Check valve

To air bleed socket

Chamber

Vacuum control solenoid valve

Pressure regulator control solenoid valve

Vacuum advance diaphragm

Fig. 13.87   13B engine emissions control systems vacuum hose routing diagram

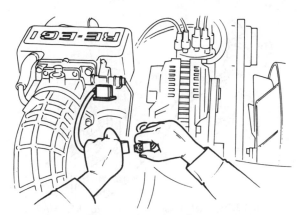

Fig. 13.88 Unplugging the throttle sensor connector

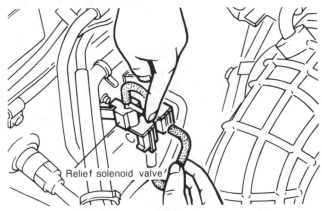

Fig. 13.89 Checking vacuum signal for relief solenoid valve

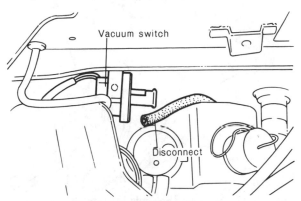

Fig. 13.90 Vacuum switch hose disconnected

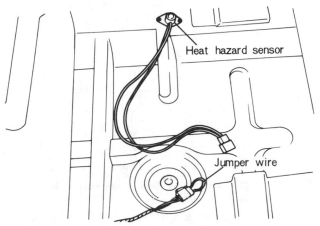

Fig. 13.91 Heat hazard sensor connector location (note the jumper wire connected across the terminals)

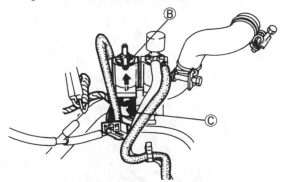

Fig. 13.92 Relief solenoid valve port locations

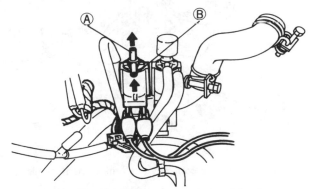

Fig. 13.93 Relief solenoid valve port location

component replacement procedures are identical, which means that some of the material in Chapter 2 and at the beginning of this Section pertaining to 12A engines is also valid for 13B engines. Included here are the procedures which are different or that apply only to emissions systems on 13B engines.

Secondary air control system

Relief solenoid valve signal check

156 To check the signal for the relief solenoid valve, warm up the engine and run it at idle, then connect a tachometer to the engine (follow the instrument manufacturer's instructions).

157 Unplug the throttle sensor connector and disconnect the vacuum line (relief solenoid valve-to-air control valve) at the relief solenoid valve. Place your finger over the port opening; suction should be felt.

158 Increase the engine speed to 3500 to 3700 rpm and make sure the suction stops.

159 Disconnect the vacuum hose from the vacuum switch, then make sure no suction is felt at any engine speed. Reconnect the hose to the switch.

160 Rejoin the throttle sensor connector momentarily, then unplug it again and increse the engine speed to 1500 rpm. Suction should be felt for 120 seconds, then it should cease.

161 Rejoin the throttle sensor connector, then unplug the heat hazard sensor connector and attach a jumper wire between the wire harness terminals. No suction should be felt at the vacuum line, regardless of engine speed.

162 Disconnect the jumper wire and rejoin the heat hazard connector sections.

163 Stop the engine and unplug the radiator water temperature switch connector. Start the engine, gradually increase the engine speed and make sure no suction is felt at the vacuum line at 1000 to 1200 rpm and higher. Stop the engine and rejoin the water temperature switch connector.

Relief solenoid valve check

164 Follow the procedure in Chapter 3, but note that the air should exit filter C when the solenoid is not energized and port A when it is energized (see new illustrations). Blow into port B, not the vacuum hose.

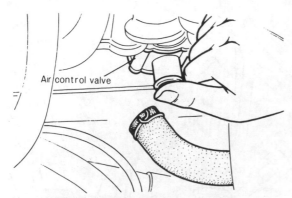

Fig. 13.94   Checking air control valve

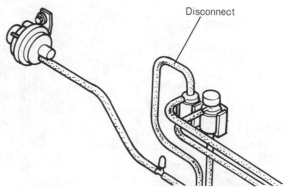

Fig. 13.95   Relief solenoid valve-to-air control valve
vacuum hose location

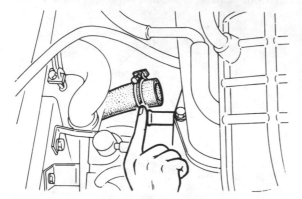

Fig. 13.96   Checking for air flow at the split air hose port

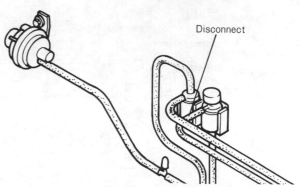

Fig. 13.97   Switching solenoid valve-to-air control valve
vacuum hose location

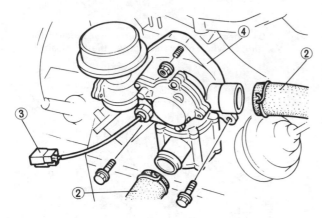

Fig. 13.98   Air control valve replacement details

   2   *Air hoses*   4   *Air control valve*
   3   *Connector*

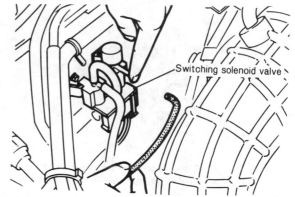

Fig. 13.99   Checking signal for switching solenoid valve

Air control valve check

165 Start the engine and allow it to reach normal operating
temperature, then connect a tachometer.
166 Disconnect the silencer-to-air control valve hose at the air control
valve and place your finger over the control valve port. Increase the
engine speed and make sure that air flows out of the port when engine
speed reaches 1500 to 2500 rpm or more.
167 Allow the engine to idle, then disconnect the relief solenoid valve-
to-air control valve vacuum hose at the relief solenoid valve. Air should
now flow out of the air control valve port.
168 Reconnect the vacuum hose and the air control valve hose, then
disconnect the split air hose (check valve-to-intake manifold) at the
manifold and place your finger over the port opening.
169 Disconnect the switching solenoid valve-to-air control valve
vacuum line at the switching solenoid valve and make sure air flows
out of the split air hose port. If it doesn't, replace the air control valve

with a new one.
170 Reconnect the vacuum line and split air hose.

Air control valve removal and installation

171 To replace the air control valve, remove the air funnel from the
throttle chamber, disconnect the air hoses, unplug the air control valve
solenoid connector and remove the air control valve. Installation is the
reverse of removal.

Switching solenoid valve signal check

172 Warm up the engine and run it at idle, then connect a tachometer
to the engine (follow the instrument manufacturer's instructions).
173 Disconnect the vacuum line (switching solenoid valve-to-air control
valve) at the switching solenoid valve and place your finger over the
port opening. Suction should be felt regardless of engine speed.
174 Unplug the throttle sensor connector, increase the engine speed
to 1000 to 1200 rpm and make sure the suction stops.
175 Decrease the engine speed to idle again and make sure that suction
is felt for eight seconds.
176 Rejoin the throttle sensor connector sections and reattach the
vacuum line.

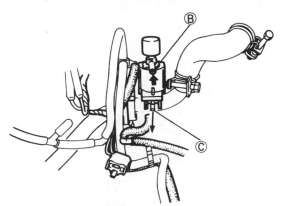

Fig. 13.100   Switching solenoid valve port locations

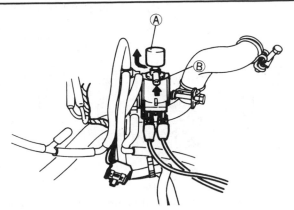

Fig. 13.101   Switching solenoid valve filter location

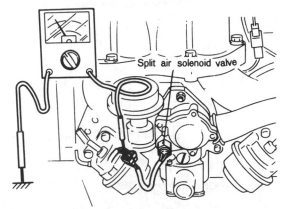

Split air solenoid valve

Fig. 13.102   Checking split air solenoid valve

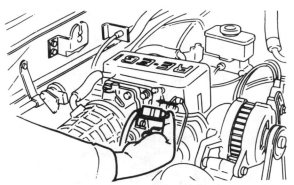

Fig. 13.103   Checking fuel cut operation by pushing on throttle sensor rod

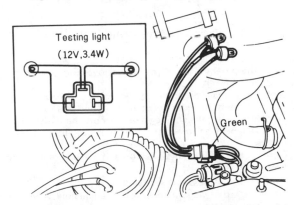

Testing light
(12V, 3.4W)

Green

Fig. 13.104   Throttle sensor test light details

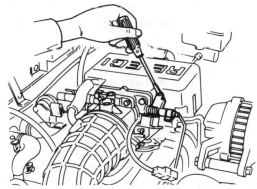

Fig. 13.105   Adjusting the throttle sensor

Switching solenoid valve check
177 Disconnect the vacuum lines from the switching solenoid valve, then blow into port B (see accompanying illustration). Air should pass through the valve and exit port C.
178 Unplug the connector from the switching solenoid valve and use jumper wires to apply battery power to the valve terminals (be careful not to short the jumper wires together).
179 Blow into port B and make sure air passes through the valve and exits filter A.

Split air solenoid valve check
180 Attach the leads from a voltmeter to the split air solenoid valve terminal (blue wire with red stripe) and a good ground, then turn the ignition switch on and shift the transmission into 5th gear. The voltmeter should indicate zero volts when the transmission is in 5th gear and 12 volts when it is in any other gear.

Water temperature switch check
181 Refer to Paragraph 94 above and follow the procedure described there (for the number 2 switch).

Vacuum switch check
182 Refer to Paragraph 120 above and follow the procedure described there, but note that the vacuum required to close this switch is 3.9 in-Hg, rather than 4.7 in-Hg.

Water thermo sensor check
183 With the engine cold, unplug the wiring harness connector (the thermo sensor is threaded into the water pump) and attach the leads from an ohmmeter to the sensor terminals. With the engine coolant at a temperature of 68°F, the resistance should be 2.45 ± 0.24K ohms. Start the engine and allow it to reach operating temperature (the coolant must be approximately 176°F), then check the resistance again. It should now be 0.32 ± 0.032K ohms.

Deceleration control system
Fuel cut operation check
184 Attach a tachometer so the engine speed can be monitored. Hold the engine speed at 2000 rpm and push in on the throttle sensor rod; the engine speed should change.

Throttle sensor check and adjustment
185 Warm up the engine, then shut it off. Locate the green check connector and attach two 12 volt/3.4 watt light bulbs to the connector terminals as shown in the illustration. Turn the ignition switch on and

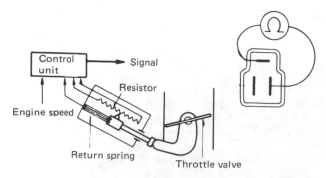

Fig. 13.106 Throttle sensor ohmmeter hookup details

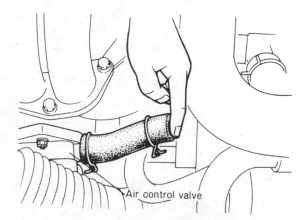

Fig. 13.107 Checking the anti-afterburn valve

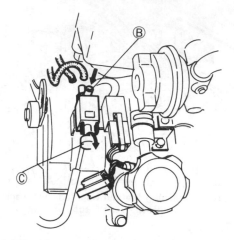

Fig. 13.108 Vacuum control solenoid valve port locations

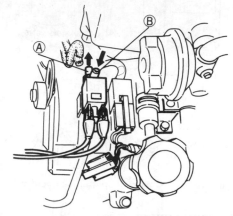

Fig. 13.109 Vacuum control solenoid valve port locations

make sure only one of the bulbs lights. If both bulbs light or if neither one lights, turn the throttle sensor adjusting screw until only one of the lights comes on (if both of them do, turn the screw counterclockwise; if neither one does, turn the screw clockwise).
186 Unplug the sensor connector and check the resistance between the terminals in the sensor as shown in the accompanying illustration. At idle the resistance should be about 1K ohm. At wide open throttle the resistance should be about 5K ohms.

Anti-afterburn valve check
187 Warm up the engine and allow it to idle, then disconnect the air control valve-to-air pump hose at the pump.
188 Place your finger over the hose and make sure that there is no suction felt with the engine idling.
189 Increase the engine speed to more than 3000 rpm, then allow it to decelerate rapidly. Suction should be felt for a few seconds as the engine speed drops. If it isn't, the anti-afterburn valve is defective and the air control valve assembly must be replaced with a new one.

Dashpot check and adjustment
190 Make sure the dashpot rod doesn't prevent the throttle lever from returning to the idle stop position.
191 Open the throttle quickly and see if the dashpot rod extends without hesitation. Release the throttle and make sure it returns to the idle stop position slowly after it contacts the dashpot rod.
192 Connect a tachometer to the engine, start it and allow it to reach normal operating temperature, then verify that the idle speed is correct.
193 Operate the throttle until the lever moves away from the dashpot rod, then slowly decrease the engine speed and note the rpm at which the throttle lever just contacts the dashpot rod. It should be 2350 to 2650 rpm. If it isn't, loosen the locknut and turn the dashpot diaphragm until it is within the specified range.

Ignition control system
Vacuum control solenoid valve signal check
194 Warm up the engine and run it at idle, then connect a tachometer to the engine (follow the instrument manufacturer's instructions).
195 Disconnect the vacuum line (leading vacuum advance diaphragm-

to-pipe) at the pipe and place your finger over the pipe opening. No suction should be felt.
196 Gradually increase the engine speed to 1000 to 1200 rpm. Suction should be felt as the engine speed goes above this range.
197 Quickly increase the engine speed to more than 4000 rpm, allow it to decrease rapidly and make sure that no suction is felt as the engine decelerates.
198 Turn the air conditioner switch on and make sure that suction is felt at idle.

Vacuum control solenoid valve check
199 Disconnect the vacuum lines from the solenoid valve and pipe, then blow into port B of the valve (see accompanying illustration). Air should pass through the valve and exit filter C.
200 Unplug the connector from the solenoid valve and use jumper wires to apply battery power to the valve terminals (be careful not to short the jumper wires together).
201 Blow into port B and make sure air passes through the valve and exits port A.

Air induction system
Fast idle operation check
202 The underhood temperature must be approximately 77 °F for this check. See if the matching mark on the fast idle cam is aligned with the center of the cam roller. If it isn't, turn the cam adjusting screw until it is.
203 With the marks aligned, check the primary throttle valve-to-throttle chamber clearance with a feeler gauge (the intake air duct must be removed to gain access to the throttle valve). It should be 0.016 to 0.020-inch (0.4 to 0.5 mm).
204 If it isn't, turn the fast idle adjusting screw until the clearance is as specified.
205 Start the engine and allow it to reach normal operating temperature. Make sure the thermo wax rod extends outward and separates the idle cam from the roller.

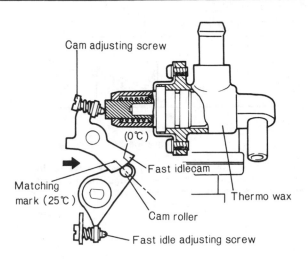

Fig. 13.110 **Checking fast idle operation**

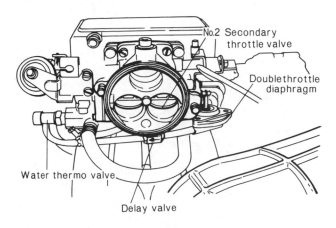

Fig. 13.111 **Number 2 secondary throttle valve location**

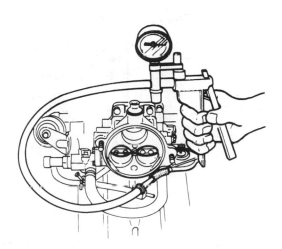

Fig. 13.112 **Apply a vacuum to the double throttle diaphragm, then allow it to decrease and note the vacuum reading when the number 2 secondary throttle valve starts to open as well as the reading when it is fully open**

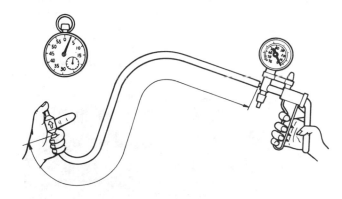

Fig. 13.113 **Checking the delay valve operation (note the direction of the arrow on the valve)**

Number 2 secondary throttle valve check
206 Detach the intake air duct from the throttle chamber and make sure the number 2 secondary throttle valve is wide open.

Double throttle vacuum check
207 Disconnect the vacuum hose from the double throttle vacuum valve and apply a vacuum to the valve port with a hand pump (at least 7.87 in-Hg).
208 Make sure the number 2 secondary throttle valve moves to the closed position. Slowly lower the vacuum applied to the valve and make sure the secondary throttle valve starts to open at 4.7 in-Hg and is fully open at zero to 1.8 in-Hg.

Delay valve check
209 Disconnect the delay valve and attach a 3-foot (1.0 meter) long section of hose to a hand vacuum pump and the delay valve (see accompanying illustration).
210 Cover the open end of the valve with your thumb, then apply a 19.7 in-Hg vacuum with the hand pump.
211 Release your thumb from the valve and measure the time required for the vacuum to fall to 3.9 in-Hg. It should take 9 to 15 seconds. If not, replace the valve with a new one (make sure the hose connections were not leaking first).

Water thermo valve check
212 Disconnect the water thermo valve and attach a short section of vacuum hose to each port. Place it in a Pyrex container filled with water. Immerse a cooking thermometer in the water.
213 Heat the water temperature to just below 140°F, blow into hose A. Air should pass through the valve and exit port B.
214 Heat the water to above 140°F. Air should now pass through the valve and exit port C.
215 Reconnect the vacuum hoses when the check is complete.

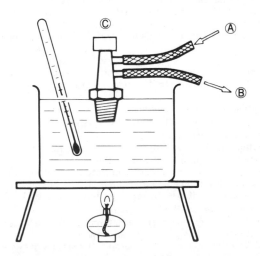

Fig. 13.114 **Water thermo valve port locations**

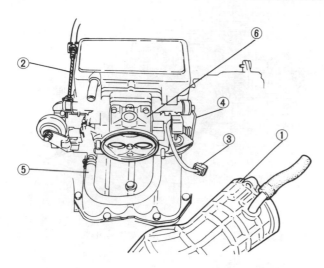

Fig. 13.115   Throttle chamber removal and installation details

1   Intake air duct
2   Throttle cable
3   Throttle sensor connector
4   Metering oil pump connecting rod
5   Coolant hose(s)
6   Throttle chamber

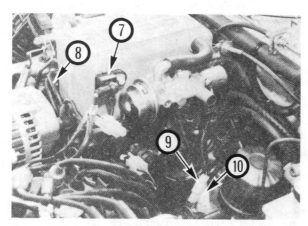

Fig. 13.118   Dynamic chamber removal and installation details

7   Terminal cover
8   Vacuum hoses
9   Air supply valve connector
10 Intake air temperature sensor connector

Throttle chamber removal and installation
216 Detach the intake air duct and the throttle cable from the throttle chamber.
217 Unplug the throttle sensor connector and disconnect the metering oil pump connecting rod.
218 Slide back the hose clamps and remove the coolant hose(s).
219 Loosen the bolts in a criss-cross pattern, then remove them and carefully separate the throttle chamber from the dynamic chamber.
220 Installation is the reverse of removal. Be sure to tighten the bolts a little at a time, following a criss-cross pattern to avoid warping the chamber.

Number 1 secondary throttle valve check
221 This procedure may be easier to perform if the throttle chamber is removed first.
222 The number 1 secondary throttle valve should start to open when the primary throttle valve is open 15 degrees and should be fully open at the same time as the primary throttle valve.
223 Using a feeler gauge, check the primary throttle valve-to-throttle chamber clearance at the moment the number 1
secondary throttle valve starts to open. It should be 0.043 to

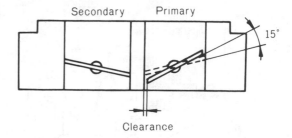

Fig. 13.116   Check the primary throttle valve-to-throttle chamber clearance with a feeler gauge and make sure the number 1 secondary throttle valve starts to open when the clearance is as specified

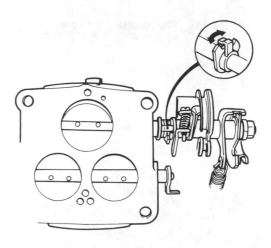

Fig. 13.117   The clearance can be changed by bending the tab on the shaft

0.067-inch (1.1 to 1.7 mm). If it isn't, bend the tab on the throttle shaft until it is as specified.

Dynamic chamber removal and installation
224 Refer to Paragraphs 216 through 218 above and disconnect the components mentioned there, but don't remove the throttle chamber-to-dynamic chamber bolts.
225 Disconnect the negative battery cable at the battery and position it so the clamp cannot contact the battery post.
226 Remove the bolt and separate the terminal cover from the dynamic chamber.
227 Detach the vacuum hoses from the chamber ports and unplug the air supply valve connector and the intake air temperature sensor connector.
228 Remove the bolts and separate the chamber from the intake manifold (cover the manifold opening to prevent the entry of dirt and foreign objects).
229 Installation is the reverse of removal. Be sure to use a new gasket/O-ring at the manifold-to-chamber joint.

Auxiliary port valve actuator check
230 Detach the air hose from the valve pipe and connect a pressure gauge with a T-fitting as shown in the accompanying illustration.
231 Apply low pressure compressed air to the T-fitting port and make sure the actuator rod begins to move at 1.8 psi. It should be fully extended at 2.7 psi. If it isn't, replace the actuator with a new one.

Air flow meter removal and installation
232 Remove the air cleaner element, then remove the bolts and detach the air cleaner housing from the air flow meter.
233 Loosen the intake air duct clamp and separate the air flow meter from the duct.
234 Installation is the reverse of removal.

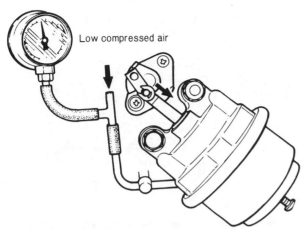

Fig. 13.119   Apply low pressure air as shown to check the operation of the auxiliary port valve actuator

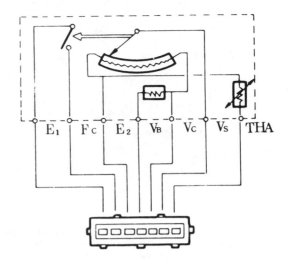

Fig. 13.120   Air flow meter terminal locations

Terminal	Resistance (Ω)	
$E_2 \leftrightarrow V_S$	20 ~ 400	
$E_2 \leftrightarrow V_C$	100 ~ 300	
$E_2 \leftrightarrow V_B$	200 ~ 400	
$E_2 \leftrightarrow$ THA (Intake air temperature sensor)	-20°C (-4°F) 0°C (32°F) 20°C (68°F) 40°C (104°F) 60°C (140°F)	10,000 ~ 20,000 4,000 ~ 7,000 2,000 ~ 3,000 900 ~ 1,300 400 ~ 700
$E_1 \leftrightarrow$ Fc	∞	

Fig. 13.121   Air flow meter terminal-to-terminal resistance values

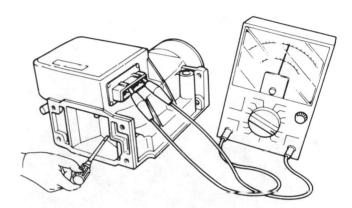

Fig. 13.122   Push down on the plate with the ohmmeter hooked to the specified terminals and note the resistance readings

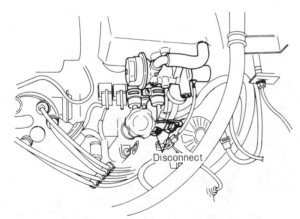

Fig. 13.123   Vent/vacuum solenoid valve connector location

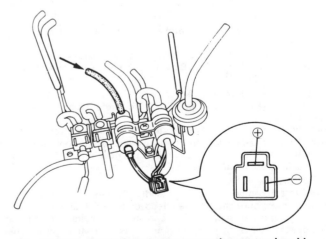

Fig. 13.124   Apply battery power to the vent solenoid valve terminals as shown when checking to see if the valve is open

Air flow meter check
235 Check the meter body for cracks. Using an ohmeter, check the resistance between the various meter terminals by referring to the accompanying table.
236 Connect the ohmmeter leads to terminals E1 and Fc. With the air flow meter measuring plate closed all the way, the resistance should be infinite. With the plate open all the way it should be zero.
237 Connect the ohmmeter leads to terminals E2 and Vs. With the plate closed the resistance should be 20 to 400 ohms. With it open all the way it should be 20 to 1000 ohms.

By-pass air control system
System check
238 With the engine at normal operating temperature and running at

idle, turn the headlight switch on and disconnect the vent and vacuum solenoid valve connector. The engine speed should decrease.
239 Rejoin the connector and make sure the engine speed increases to 800 rpm.
Vent solenoid valve check
240 Disconnect the vacuum hose from the pipe and unplug the connector.

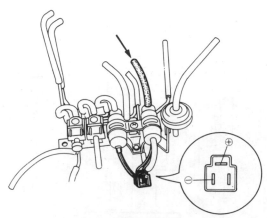

Fig. 13.125 Apply battery power to the vacuum solenoid valve terminals as shown when checking to see if the valve is closed

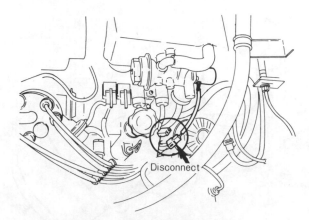

Fig. 13.126 Air supply valve connector location

Fig. 13.127 Remove the blind cap and use a small screwdriver to adjust the air supply valve

Fig. 13.128 Power steering switch connector location

241 Blow into the hose and make sure air does not pass through the valve.

242 Using jumper leads, apply battery power to the connector terminals as shown in the illustration. Blow into the hose and make sure air will now pass through the valve.

Vacuum solenoid valve check

243 Disconnect the vacuum hose from the pipe and unplug the connector.

244 Blow into the hose and make sure air passes through the valve.

245 Using jumper leads, apply battery power to the connector terminals as shown in the illustration. Blow into the hose and make sure air does not pass through the valve.

Air supply valve check

246 Start the engine and allow it to idle. Turn the air conditioner switch on and make sure the engine speed does not decrease.

247 Unplug the air supply valve connector and make sure engine speed decreases. Rejoin the connector and make sure the engine speed increases to idle (800 rpm).

248 Turn the steering wheel in either direction and make sure the compressor switches off.

Air supply valve adjustment

249 With the engine at normal operating temperature and idling, connect a tachometer to monitor engine speed.

250 Unplug the vent and vacuum solenoid valve connector, then check and adjust the idle speed (if necessary).

251 Unplug the air supply valve connector and apply battery power to the valve terminals with jumper wires. The engine speed must be between 1000 and 1070 rpm.

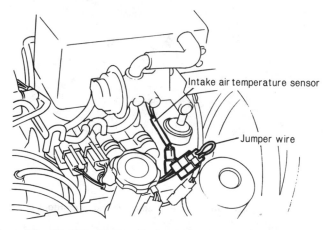

Fig. 13.129 Unplug the intake air temperature sensor connector and attach a jumper wire to the terminals as shown

252 If it isn't, remove the blind cap and turn the adjusting screw until it is. Be sure to reinstall the blind cap.

Power steering switch check

253 Start the engine and run it at idle, then unplug the power steering switch connector.

254 Attach the ohmmeter leads (or a self-powered test light) to the switch terminals, then turn the steering wheel in either direction. As the wheel is turned and pressure is built up in the pump, the ohmmeter should indicate continuity. As the steering wheel is centered, the ohmmeter should indicate no continuity.

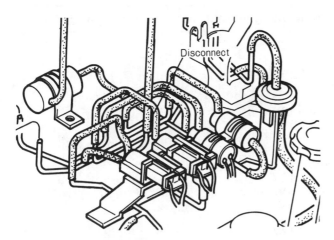

Fig. 13.130   Disconnect the vacuum hose from the pressure regulator control solenoid valve

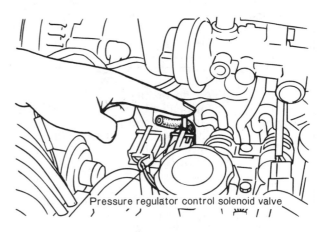

Fig. 13.131   Checking for suction at the pressure regulator control solenoid valve port

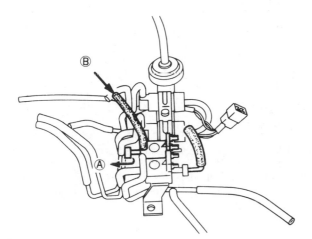

Fig. 13.132   Pressure regulator control solenoid valve port locations

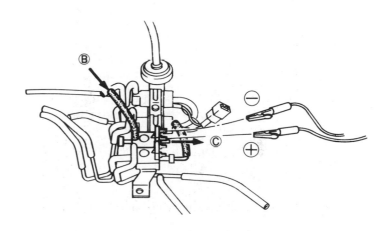

Fig. 13.133   Pressure regulator control solenoid valve terminal and port locations

Clutch switch check

255 Unplug the clutch switch connector and connect the ohmmeter leads (or a self-powered test light) to the switch terminals.

256 When the clutch pedal is depressed continuity should exist. When it is released (all the way up), no continuity should be indicated.

Neutral switch check

257 Raise the vehicle and support it securely on jackstands. Crawl under it and unplug the neutral switch connectors (the switch is located on the right-hand side of the transmission).

258 Connect the ohmmeter leads (or a self-powered test light) to the switch terminal wires, then make sure continuity is indicated with the transmission in neutral. No continuity should exist with the transmission in any gear.

Hot start assist system

System check

259 Unplug the intake air temperature sensor connector and connect a jumper wire between the terminals of the wire harness.

260 Disconnect the vacuum hose from the pressure regulator control solenoid valve.

261 Connect a tachometer to monitor engine speed, then start the engine. After starting, engine speed should be about 850 rpm for 60 seconds. After 60 seconds the engine speed should be 800 rpm.

262 For 60 seconds after the engine is started, make sure no suction can be felt at the pressure regulator control solenoid valve. After 60 seconds, suction should be felt at the valve.

Intake air temperature sensor check

263 Remove the sensor from the dynamic chamber and connect an ohmmeter to the sensor terminals. At 68°F the resistance should be 41.5 ± 4.15K ohms.

264 Warm the sensor with a heat lamp and monitor the temperature. At 122°F the resistance should be 11.85 ± 1.19K ohms. At 185°F the resistance should be 3.5 ± 0.35K ohms.

Pressure regulator control solenoid valve check

265 Disconnect the vacuum hoses from the valve and pipe, then blow into hose B. Air should pass through the valve and exit filter A.

266 Unplug the valve connector and apply battery power to the valve terminals with jumper wires.

267 Blow into hose B again. Air should now pass through the valve and exit port C.

Sub-zero starting assist device

268 The checking procedure in Chapter 3 is correct for these models, but note that the dynamic chamber must be removed and the starting assist valve separated from the intake manifold. The starting fluid should be ejected from the valve (rather than the carburetor nozzle) when the key is turned to Start (direct the valve orifice into a metal container as the key is turned on). Also, the air bleed button on the starting fluid tank must be depressed during the check.

Control unit

269 When checking the control unit on models with 13B engines, attach the negative meter lead to a good ground, turn the ignition switch on and probe each of the remaining terminals with the positive lead. Refer to the accompanying illustration for the terminal locations and desired voltage readings. **Note:** *The engine must be at normal operating temperature, but do not start the engine with the voltmeter leads hooked to the connector terminals.*

Terminal	Connection to	Voltage with ignition ON (when functioning properly)
A	Main relay	approx. 12V
B	Ground	0V
C	Water thermo sensor	1 ~ 2V (warm engine)
D	Ground	0V
E	Air flow meter	4 ~ 6V . . . at 20°C 1.5 ~ 3.5V . . . at 50°C
F	Injector (#20)	approx. 12V
G	Throttle sensor & Atmospheric pressure sensor	4.5 ~ 5.5V
H	Injector (#10)	approx. 12V
I	Throttle sensor	approx. 1V
J	Vacuum switch	approx. 12V
L	Variable resistor (V/R)	0 ~ 12V (Varies according to the V/R adjustment)
M	Ignition switch "START" terminal	below 1.5V
N	O₂ sensor	0V
O	Air flow meter	approx. 12V
P	Atmospheric pressure sensor	approx. 4V
Q	Air flow meter	approx. 2V
R	Air flow meter	approx. 7.5V
S	Ground	0V
T	Ground	0V
U	Ignition coil (T) – terminal	approx. 12V
V	Main relay	approx. 12V
a	Switching solenoid valve	approx. 12V
b	Relief solenoid valve control unit	approx. 12V
c	Checking connector	0V
d	Vacuum control solenoid valve (T/L)	approx. 12V
e	Pressure regulator control valve	below 1.5V
f	Checking connector	0V
h	Vent solenoid valve	below 1.5V (throttle sensor is adjusted properly)
i	Clutch switch	below 1.5V . . . pedal released approx. 12V . . . pedal depressed
j	Neutral switch	below 1.5V . . . in neutral approx. 12V . . . in gear
k	Water temperature switch	below 1.5V . . . above 15°C
l	Intake air temperature sensor	8.5 ~ 10.5V . . . at 20°C 5 ~ 7V . . . at 50°C
m	Air-con. switch	below 1.5V . . . air-con. switch OFF
n	Vacuum control valve	approx. 12V (throttle sensor is adjusted properly)

Control unit connector

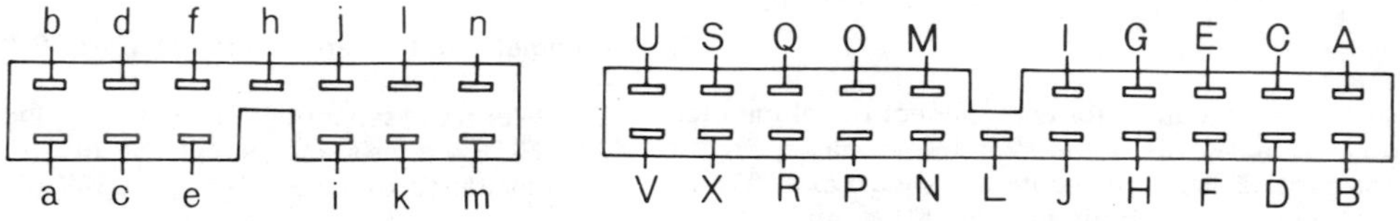

Fig. 13.134   Control unit terminal locations and voltage readings (13B engine only)

7   Ignition system

Distributor — overhaul

1   The distributors used on later models may differ slightly in certain details from the ones used on earlier models, so the overhaul procedure in Chapter 4 may have to be modified slightly for later model distributors. For example, note that the igniters have been positioned on the side of the distributor on later models. They are held in place with screws and are easily removed during disassembly.

Air gap — checking

2   Whenever the distributor is overhauled or an ignition problem is suspected, an air gap check should be done.
3   Remove the distributor cap and rotor to expose the pick-up coils and the signal rotor. Turn the distributor shaft until two of the four signal rotor protrusions are opposite the core of each pick-up coil. If

the distributor is in place on the engine, have an assistant turn the ignition switch to Start in short bursts while you watch the movement of the distributor shaft.
4   Using a feeler gauge, check the gap between the signal rotor protrusions and the pick-up coils. If the gap is not as specified, replace the pick-up coil/bearing assemblies or the distributor shaft with new parts.

Igniter — checking

5   The igniters (one leading and one trailing) on later models require a different checking procedure than the one outlined in Chapter 4.
6   Detach the igniter from the distributor and connect a test light to the igniter terminals as shown in the accompanying illustration (the light bulb must be less than 10 watts).
7   Turn the switch on and off quickly and make sure the test light flashes. If it doesn't, replace the igniter with a new one. The check can be used for both igniters.

Fig. 13.135   The air gap can be measured with a feeler gauge

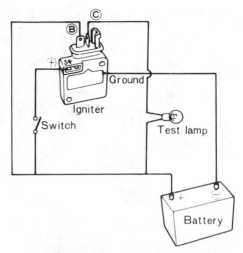

Fig. 13.136   Igniter test light hookup details

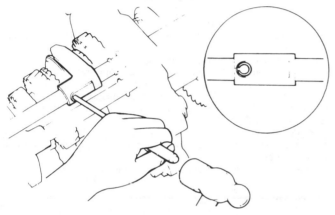

Fig. 13.137   When removing and installing the shift forks, the spring pins can be removed/installed with a hammer and pin punch (note the position of the spring pin slit in relationship to the shift rod centerline)

Fig. 13.138   When checking the rear brake disc, the thickness should be measured at several points around its circumference with a micrometer

Fig. 13.139   A dial indicator should be used to check for excessive runout (spin the disc slowly and check around its entire circumference)

8   Manual transmission

Disassembly/reassembly

1   It should be noted that the shift forks in later model transmissions are attached to the shift rods with spring pins (roll pins) instead of bolts as in previous models.

2   When disassembling the transmission, follow the instructions in Chapter 6, Part 1, up to shift fork removal. Use a small pin punch to drive the spring pins out so the shift forks can be removed from the rods. Be sure to use new spring pins when reassembling the transmission.

3   When installing the shift forks, make sure the spring pin slit in each fork is positioned as shown in the accompanying illustration before the pin is driven into place.

9   Rear axle

Axle shaft — removal and installation

1   The procedure in Chapter 8 is valid for later models, but note that on vehicles with rear disc brakes, the brake caliper, brake disc and dust shield must be removed instead of the drum brake components.

10   Braking system

General information

1   Beginning with 1981 models, rear disc brakes were offered as an option.

Rear disc brake pads — checking

2   Raise the rear of the vehicle and support it securely on jackstands, then remove the rear wheels.

3   Visually check the thickness of the brake pad lining material by looking through the opening in the caliper.

4   At least 0.040-inch (1 mm) of lining material must be visible on each pad. If not, replace them with new ones (on both rear wheels).

5   At the same time, check the rotor (disc) surface for signs of wear and damage. Look for score marks and discolored areas, as well as cracks. The rotor thickness and runout should be checked with a micrometer and dial indicator (if the special tools are not available, have

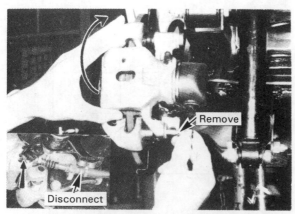

Fig. 13.140   To gain access to the rear brake pads, remove the lower bolt and pivot the caliper up carefully (do not detach the brake hose from the caliper)

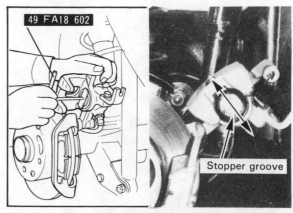

Fig. 13.141   A special tool is required when installing the new pads (after the piston is seated, make sure the stopper groove is aligned as shown)

it done by a repair shop). If damage or wear is evident, replace the pads with new ones, remove the rotor and have it resurfaced at an automotive machine shop or replace it with a new one.

Rear disc brake pads — removal and installation

6   Raise the rear of the vehicle and support it securely with jackstands, then remove the rear wheels.
7   Disconnect the parking brake cable from the top of the caliper.
8   Remove the lower caliper mounting bolt and pivot the caliper upward to expose the brake pads.
9   Note how it is installed, then remove the anti-rattle spring from the caliper mount.
10   Lift out the pads and shims, noting how they are installed.

11   Using the special brake piston wrench (number 49 FA18 602), turn the piston in a clockwise direction until it is completely seated in the caliper. The stopper groove should be in line with the caliper cutout as shown in the accompanying illustration.
12   Install the new pads in the reverse order of removal. Be sure the dowel pin on the pad is seated properly in the piston stopper groove.
13   Apply the grease provided with the new pads to the caliper mounting pin and bolt. Pivot the caliper down over the pads, install the bolt and tighten it to 22 to 30 ft-lbs.
14   Repeat the procedure for the remaining rear brake. Never replace the pads on only one wheel; always replace the pads on both rear wheels as a set.
15   Check the brake operation before driving the vehicle.

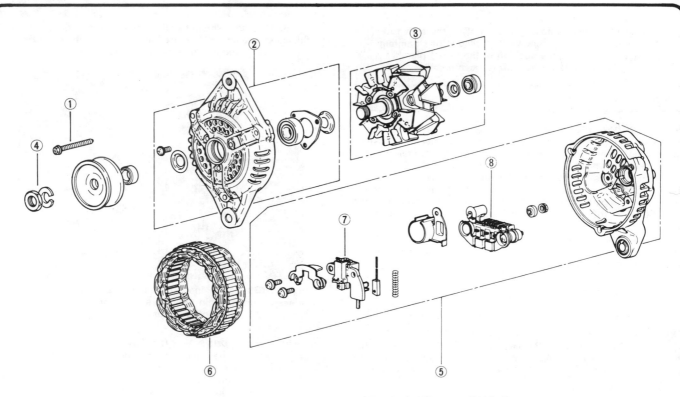

Fig. 13.142   Later model alternator components — exploded view

1 Through bolt	3 Rotor and fan assembly	5 Rear bracket assembly	7 Brush holder assembly
2 Front bracket assembly	4 Pulley locknut	6 Stator	8 Rectifier

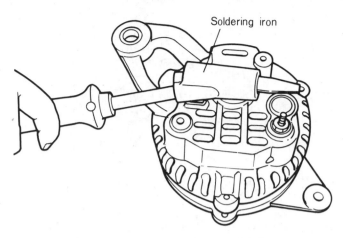

Fig. 13.143   The bearing box on later model alternators must be heated before the alternator is disassembled

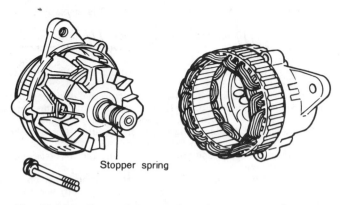

Fig. 13.144   Be careful not to lose the stopper spring on the rear bearing race as the alternator is separated into the major components

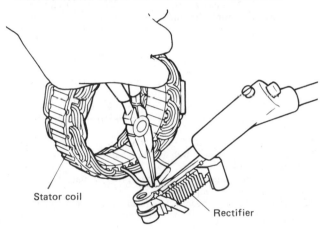

Fig. 13.145   The rectifier must be unsoldered from the stator coil lead

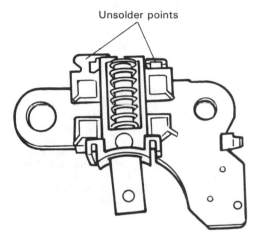

Fig. 13.146   The brush leads must be unsoldered if new brushes are required

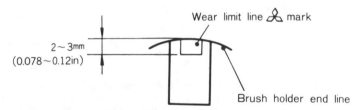

Fig. 13.147   When installing the new brushes, make sure the wear limit line is the specified distance from the brush holder before soldering the leads in place

Rear disc brake caliper — removal, overhaul and installation

Removal

16 Refer to Paragraphs 6 through 10 above to remove the brake pads from the caliper.

17 Loosen the brake hose fitting at the caliper. Slide the caliper towards the inside of the vehicle, then disconnect and plug the flexible brake hose.

Overhaul

18 Due to the need for special tools, the rear brake caliper should be rebuilt by a dealer service department. As an alternative, new or rebuilt calipers can be purchased and installed.

Installation

19 Installation is the reverse of removal. Be sure to bleed the brakes before driving the vehicle.

Rear brake disc — removal and installation

20 The rear brake disc is attached to the axle hub with screws, which must be removed to allow the disc to be pulled off.

11 Electrical system

Alternator — overhaul and testing

1 The alternators used on later models are different than the one described in Chapter 10 and require different overhaul procedures.

2 Use a 200 watt soldering iron to heat the bearing box at the rear of the alternator for 3 or 4 minutes (122 to 144°F). **Note:** *If the bearing box is not heated, the alternator will not come apart.*

3 Remove the three bolts and separate the alternator components.

Insert a screwdriver between the stator core and front bracket and pry carefully. Be careful not to lose the stopper spring that fits around the outer race of the rear bearing.

4 When the pulley nut is removed, the pulley, rotor and front bracket can be separated.

5 The front bearing can be pressed out of the bracket with a vise and a socket that bears against the outer race of the bearing.

6 The rear bearing can be removed with a bearing puller. When the new one is pressed into place, make sure the groove is against the slip rings, not the end of the shaft.

7 Remove the nut and insulation bushing from terminal B on the rear bracket. Remove the rectifier mounting screws and the brush holder screw and separate the rear bracket and stator.

8 Detach the IC regulator.

9 Use a soldering iron to melt the solder joint and separate the rectifier from the stator coil lead.

10 The brushes can be removed by unsoldering the leads. When installing the new brushes, make sure the wear limit line is 0.079 to 0.118-inch (2 to 3 mm) from the end of the brush holder, then resolder the leads.

11 The rotor and stator check in Chapter 10 is also valid for these models.
12 The rectifier/IC regulator can be checked by referring to Chapter 10 as well. If the checks are inconclusive, have them checked by a dealer service department.
13 Reassembly is basically the reverse of disassembly, but note the following points.
14 Fit the stopper spring into the eccentric groove of the rear bearing race. The protruding part of the spring should fit into the deepest part of the groove (the edge of the deepest portion is chamfered).
15 Before assembly, use a finger to push the brushes into the holder and insert a large paper clip through the hole in the bracket to hold them in the retracted position. When the alternator is reassembled, pull the paper clip out.
16 Heat the rear bearing box before reassembling the components.
17 After reassembly, turn the rotor and make sure it moves smoothly, without binding or hanging up.

Starter motor — overhaul
18 The starter motors used on later model vehicles may differ slightly in some details from those used on earlier models, but the procedure in Chapter 10 can be used regardless.

Rear fog lamp — removal and installation (UK models only)
19 Unplug the connectors leading to the fog lamp switch and the main switch.
20 Remove the bolt retaining the fog lamp bracket to the bumper.
21 Separate the lamp from the bracket.
22 Installation is the reverse of removal. Make sure the replacement lamp is equipped with the same type of connectors as the original.

Rear wiper motor — removal and installation
23 Remove the wiper arm, then remove the cover and unplug the connector.
24 Remove the nut and bolt and detach the motor from the hatch.
25 Installation is the reverse of removal.

Wiring diagrams
26 Note that wiring diagrams for later models have been included at the end of this Chapter. Due to space limitations, we are not able to provide every diagram for each year; however, a representative sampling is included.

---

12 Steering and suspension

Steering wheel/steering lock — removal and installation
1 The steering column shaft and the inner steering wheel fitting were changed to a serration and taper type on some 1980 and all later models.
2 Use of a steering wheel puller is recommended when removing the steering wheel. It is applied to the center of the shaft and the back of the steering wheel hub after the steering wheel locknut has been removed. Other procedures involving removal of the steering wheel and column are similar to those in Chapter 11.
3 The method of securing the steering lock body to the column jacket was changed so that the bolts are removed from above the column, rather than from underneath. This requires the installation of a prop between the lock assembly and the floor of the vehicle to keep the steering column from being moved or damaged while cutting grooves in the bolt heads with a hammer and chisel (necessary for their removal). Other procedures related to steering lock replacement are similar to those in Chapter 11.

Power steering pump — removal and installation
4 Place a container or rags under the pump to catch any fluid that may leak out of the hoses, then detach both hoses from the pump.
5 Push on the drivebelt to keep the pulley from turning and loosen the pulley mounting nut.
6 Loosen the drivebelt adjusting bolt, then remove the belt and pulley.
7 Remove the air conditioner compressor mounting bolts and secure the compressor out of the way with the hoses still attached (do not disconnect the hoses or loosen the fittings for any reason).

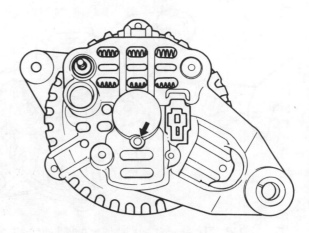

Fig. 13.148 Pass a large paper clip (or other large section of wire) through the hole (arrow) to retain the brushes in the retracted position (reassembly will be much easier)

8 Remove the mounting bolts and separate the power steering pump from the bracket.
9 Installation is the reverse of removal. Be sure to tighten the fasteners to the specified torque and bleed the system when finished.

Power steering gear — removal and installation
10 Disconnect the negative battery cable from the battery, then remove the steering column lower cover and the heater duct.
11 Remove the column fixing bracket, the set plate, the steering gear clamp bolt and the coupling bolt.
12 Raise the front of the vehicle and support it securely on jackstands, then separate the center link from the Pitman arm with a special puller-type tool.
13 Remove the steering gear bolts.
14 Disconnect the fluid lines from the steering gear, remove the nuts and detach the steering gear.
15 Installation is the reverse of removal. Be sure to tighten the fasteners to the specified torque and bleed the system when finished.

Control valve — removal and installation
16 Place a container or rags under the valve to catch any fluid that may leak out when the lines are disconnected, then loosen the fittings and detach the lines.
17 Remove the mounting bolts, detach the valve and unplug the wire harness connector.
18 Installation is the reverse of removal. Be sure to thread the fittings into the valve body before installing the mounting bolts. Bleed the system when finished with the installation.

Power steering fluid — replacement
19 Raise the front of the vehicle and support it securely with jackstands.
20 Place a container under the fitting and remove the pressure hose from the pump. Keep the container under the fitting and leave the hose end in the container as well, then have an assistant operate the starter motor several times, without starting the engine, to empty the pump. Do not let the engine start and do not run the starter motor for more than 10 seconds at a time (if necessary, disconnect the ignition coil secondary wires and ground them to the engine with jumper leads to keep the engine from starting).
21 Turn the steering wheel from lock-to-lock several times to empty the hose, then reconnect it to the pump.
22 Refill the pump reservoir with ATF type F and bleed the system.

Power steering system — bleeding
23 Raise the front of the vehicle and support it securely on jackstands.
24 Make sure the fluid level in the pump reservoir is correct, then turn the steering wheel fully clockwise and have an assistant operate the

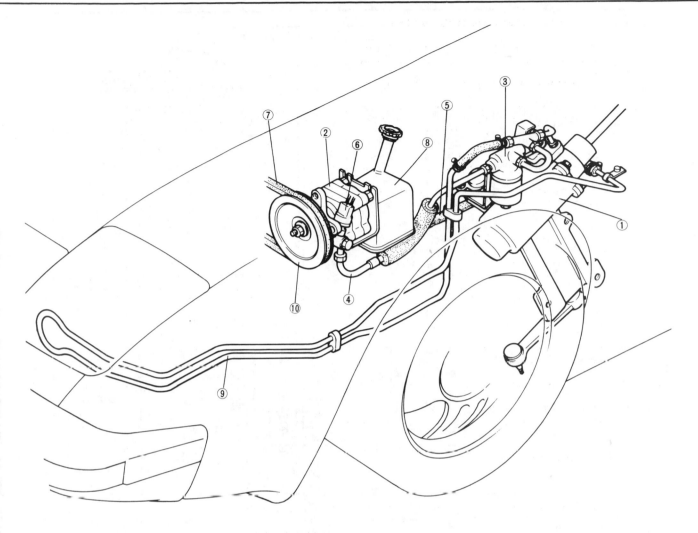

Fig. 13.149 Power steering system components

1 Steering gear
2 Pump
3 Control valve
4 Pressure hose

5 Return hose
6 Pressure switch
7 Drivebelt

8 Fluid reservoir
9 Fluid cooler pipe
10 Pump pulley

starter motor, without starting the engine (see Paragraph 20 above). Watch the fluid level while the starter is running.

25 Turn the wheel fully counterclockwise and repeat the procedure. If the oil level remains correct, start the engine and turn the wheel from lock-to-lock.

26 Lower the vehicle and turn the steering wheel from lock-to-lock two or three times with the engine running. Keep an eye on the fluid level as this is done. If noise is heard in the line, the air bleeding procedure is incomplete.

27 Place the steering wheel in the straight ahead position and shut off the engine while observing the fluid level in the reservoir. If the level rises, turn the steering wheel from lock-to-lock several times, stop the engine, then repeat the procedure in Paragraph 26 after waiting five to ten minutes.

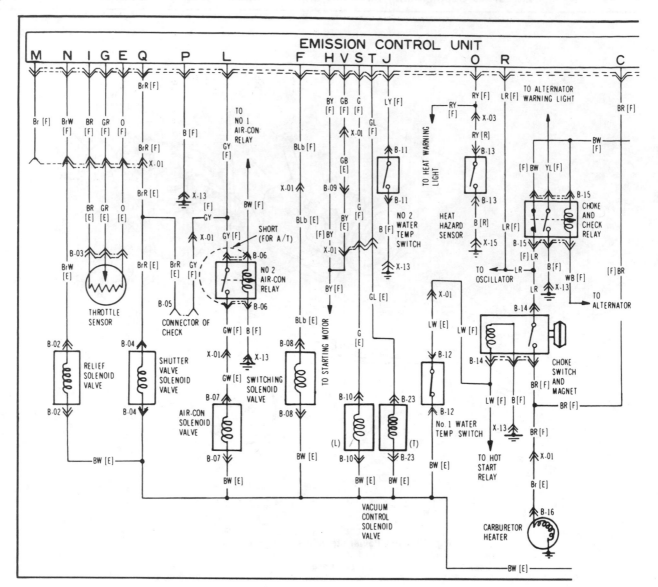

Wiring diagram and connectors — emission controls, ignition, cruise control and kick-down system (1981 thru 1983 models)

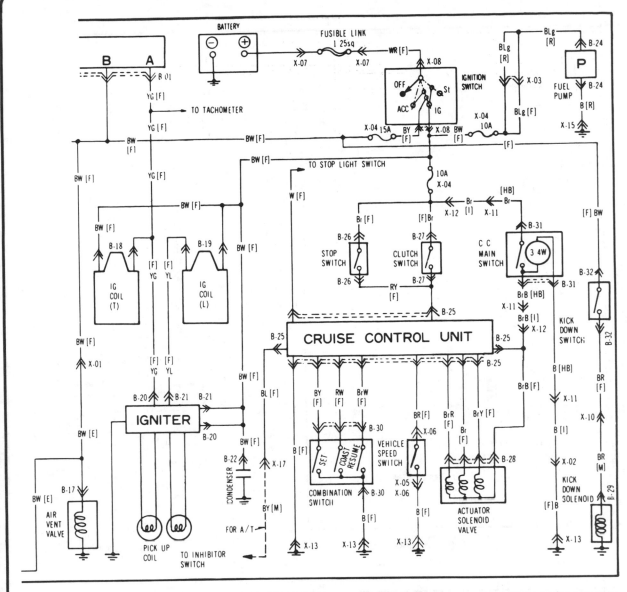

Wiring diagram and connectors — emission controls, ignition, cruise control and kick-down system
(1981 thru 1983 models — continued)

B-05 CONNECTOR OF CHECK [E]	B-06 NO 2 AIR-CON RELAY [F]	B-07 AIR-CON SOLENOID VALVE [E]	B-08 SWITCHING SOLENOID VALVE [E]
BrR / GY	GY BW GW / B	GW — BW (White)	BLb — BW (Gray)
B-12 NO 1 WATER TEMP SWITCH (Eng) [E]	B-13 HEAT HAZARD SENSOR [R]	B-14 CHOKE SWITCH AND MAGNET [F]	B-15 CHOKE AND CHECK RELAY [F]
LW / BW	RY / B	BR / LW LR B	LR B / BW YL — WB BW
B-21 IGNITER (L) [F]	B-22 CONDENSER [F]	B-23 VACUUM CONTROL SOLENOID VALVE [E]	B-24 FUEL PUMP [R]
YL / BW	— BW	GL — BW (Green)	BLg / B
B-29 KICK DOWN SOLENOID [M]	B-30 COMBINATION SWITCH [F]	B-31 C C MAIN SWITCH [HB]	B-32 KICK DOWN SWITCH [F]
— BR	BrW BY / B RW	B — BrB / Br	BW BR

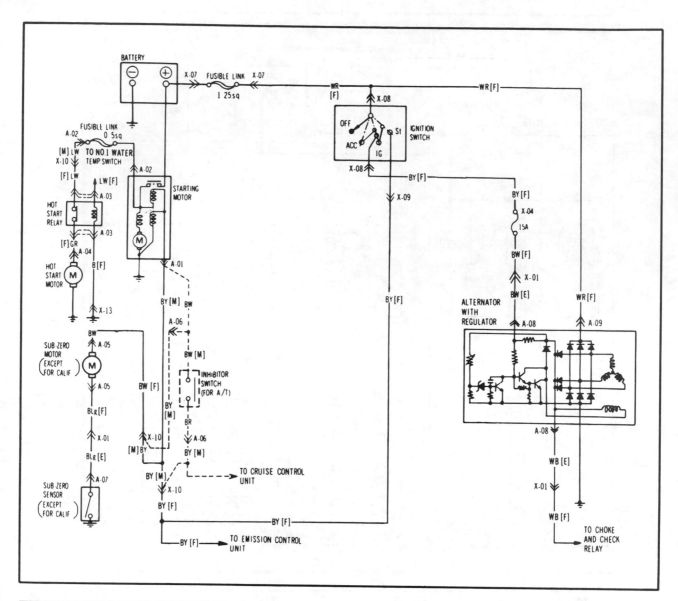

A.01 STARTING MOTOR [M]	A.02 FUSIBLE LINK [M]	A.03 HOT START RELAY [F]	A.04 HOT START MOTOR [F]
BY(FOR M/T) BW(FOR A/T)	(G) 0 5sq LW	LW GR LW B	GR
A.05 SUB ZERO MOTOR (EXCEPT FOR CALIF) [F]	A.06 INHIBITOR SWITCH (FOR A/T) [M]	A.07 SUB-ZERO SENSOR (EXCEPT FOR CALIF) [E]	A.08 ALTERNATOR WITH REGULATOR [E]
BW BLg	BY GY BW RW	BLg	BW WB
A.09 ALTERNATOR WITH REGULATOR [F]			
WR			

Wiring diagram and connectors — instrument panel and gauges (1981 thru 1983 models)

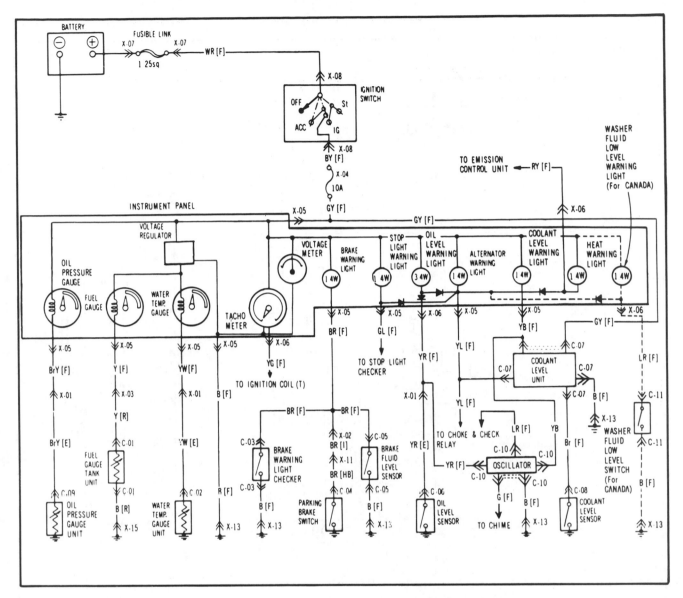

Wiring diagram and connectors — instrument panel and gauges (1981 thru 1983 models)

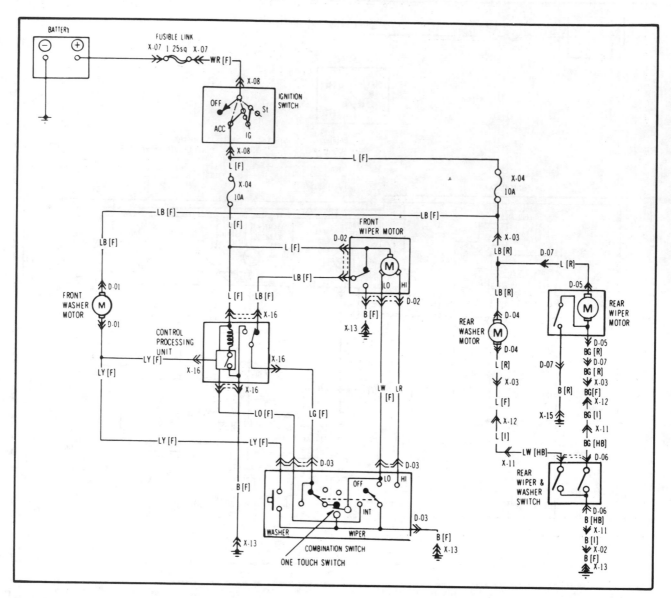

Wiring diagram and connectors — windshield wipers/washers (1981 thru 1983 models)

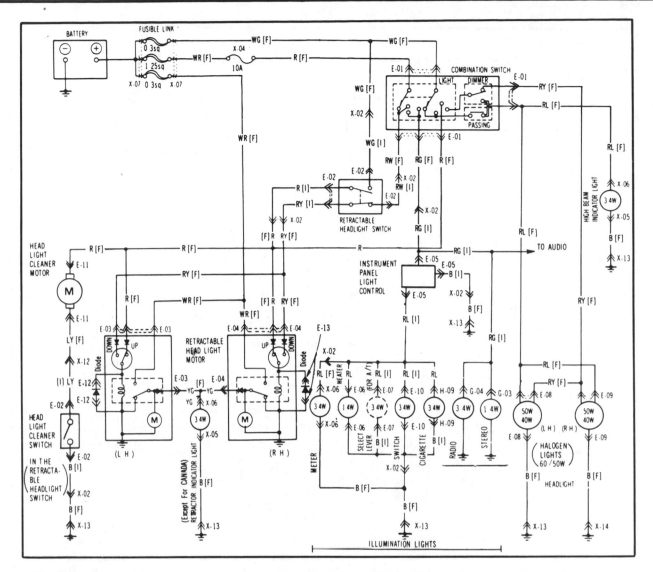

Wiring diagram and connectors — headlights and interior lights (1981 thru 1983 models)

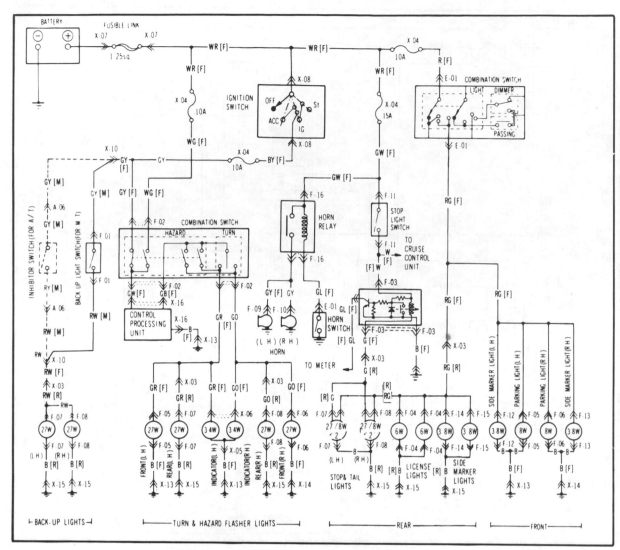

Wiring diagram and connectors — exterior lights (1981 thru 1983 models)

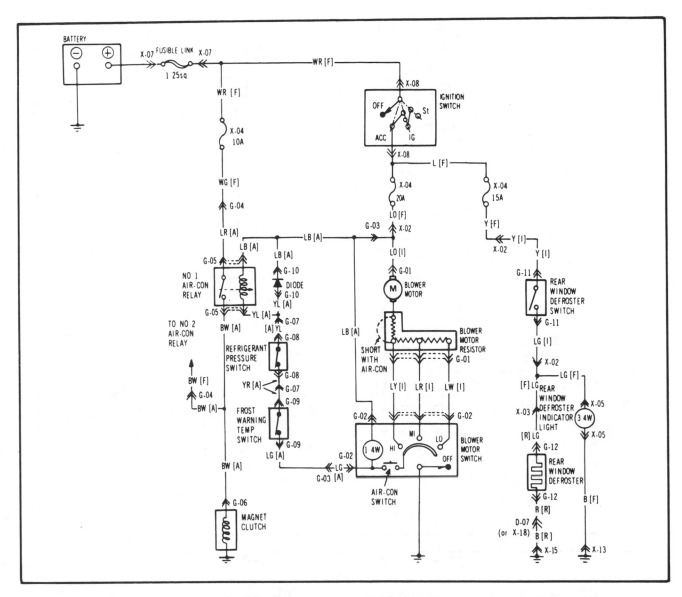

G-01 BLOWER MOTOR & RESISTOR [I]	G-02 BLOWER MOTOR SWITCH [I]	G-03 CONNECTOR BETWEEN INPANE AND AIR-CON. HARNESS [I] [A]	G-04 CONNECTOR BETWEEN FRONT AND AIR-CON. HARNESS [F] [A]
LO LR / LY LW	LW LY / LG LR [A] LB	LG — LG / LO — LB	BW WG — BW LR
G-05 No. 1 AIR-CON. RELAY [A]	G-06 MAGNET CLUTCH [A]	G-07 CONNECTOR TO REFRIGERANT PRESSURE SWITCH [A]	G-08 REFRIGERANT PRESSURE SWITCH [A]
LB LR / YL BW	— BW	YR — YR / YL — YL	YL YR
G-09 FROST WARNING TEMP SWITCH [A]	G-10 DIODE [A]	G-11 REAR WINDOW DEFROSTER SWITCH [I]	G-12 REAR WINDOW DEFROSTER [R]
— LG / — YR	LB — YL (IN THE AIR-CON. HARNESS)	Y / LG	LG — B

Wiring diagram and connectors — heater/air conditioner and rear window defogger (1981 thru 1983 models)

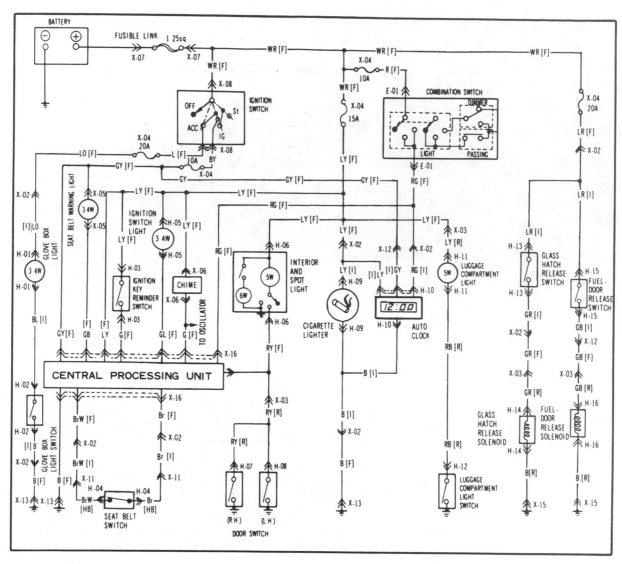

H-01 GLOVE BOX LIGHT [I]	H-02 GLOVE BOX LIGHT SWITCH [I]	H-03 IGNITION KEY REMINDER SWITCH [F]	H-04 SEAT BELT SWITCH [HB]
LO / BL	BL / B	G / LY	Br / BrW
H-05 IGNITION SWITCH LIGHT [F]	H-06 INTERIOR & SPOT LIGHT [F]	H-07 DOOR SWITCH(FRONT R H) [R]	H-08 DOOR SWITCH(REAR L H) [R]
LY / GL	LY / RY	RY	RY
H-09 CIGARETTE LIGHTER [I]	H-10 AUTO CLOCK [I]	H-11 LUGGAGE COMPARTMENT LIGHT [R]	H-12 LUGGAGE COMPARTMENT LIGHT SWITCH [R]
LY / RL / B	B RG / LY GY	LY / RB	RB
H-13 GLASS HATCH RELEASE SWITCH [I]	H-14 GLASS HATCH RELEASE SOLENOID [R]	H-15 FUEL-DOOR RELEASE SWITCH [I]	H-16 FUEL-DOOR RELEASE SOLENOID [R]
LR / GR	GR / B	LR ✕ / ✕ GB	GB / B

Wiring diagram and connectors — miscellaneous interior lights and optional equipment (1981 thru 1983 models)

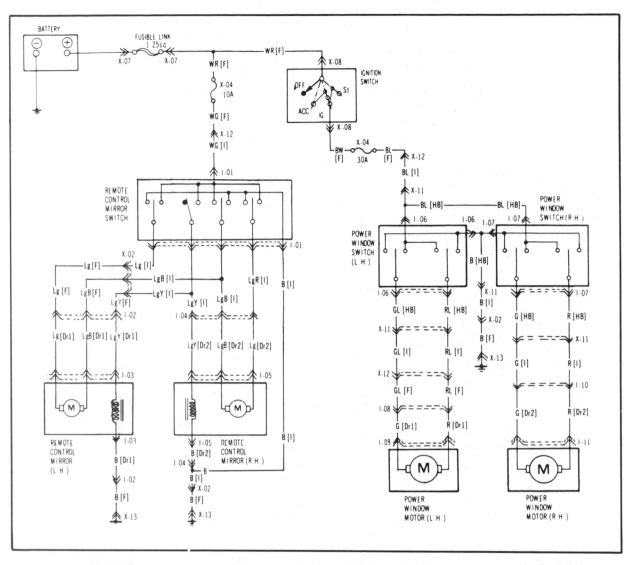

Wiring diagram and connectors — remote-controlled mirrors/power windows (1981 thru 1983 models)

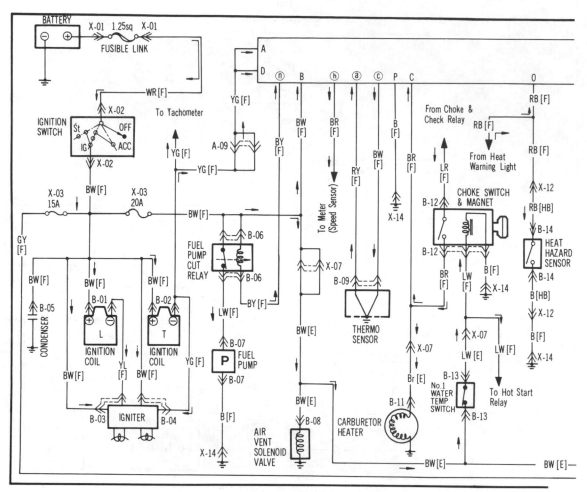

Wiring diagram and connectors — 12A engine emissions control systems, ignition and fuel pump (1984 and 1985 models)

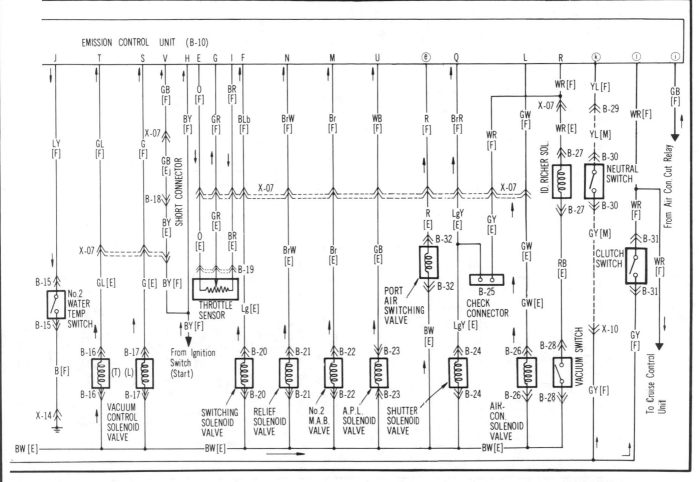

Wiring diagram and connectors — 12A engine emissions control systems, ignition and fuel pump (1984 and 1985 models — continued)

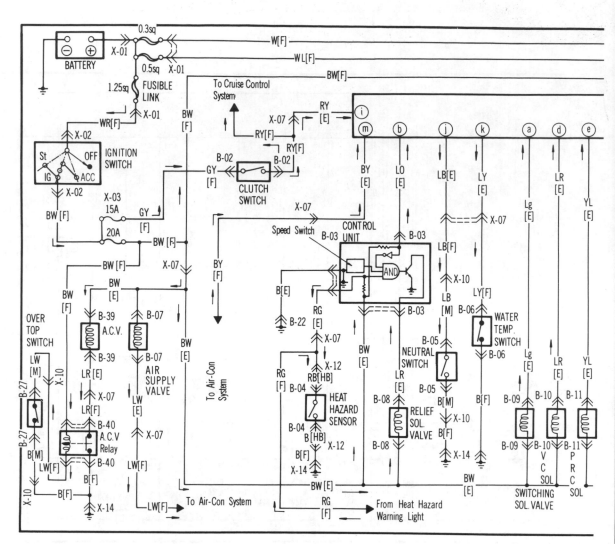

B-01 E.G.I.& Emission Control Unit [E]		B-02 Clutch Switch [F]

B-01 E.G.I.& Emission Control Unit [E]

Gy	B	LgB	RW	BR		Br	GB	GW	GL	BY
U	S	Q	O	M		I	G	E	C	A
V	T	R	P	N		L	J	H	F	D	B
RW	GR	LgR	LgY	Gy		L	YW	BrY	YR	B	B

BY	LY	RY			YL	G	Lg
m	k	i			e	c	a
n	l	j		h	f	d	b
WG	LW	LB	WB	R	LR	LO

B-02 Clutch Switch [F]
GY
RY

B-10 Vacuum Control Solenoid Valve [E] (Green)	B-11 P.R.C.V. [E] (Orange)	B-12 V.S.V. [E]	B-13 Setting Connector [E]
BW LR	BW YL	WB—⊏⊐—WG / —BW	WB—⊏⊐—WG / —BW

B-21 Ground [E]	B-22 Ground [E]	B-23 O₂ Sensor Check Connector [E]	B-24 O₂ Sensor [E]
B—⊚	B—⊚	Gy ✕ ✕ / RW ✕ ✕ B	Gy

B-31 Injector No.2 [E]	B-32 Connector Between Front[F] and Engine Halness[E]	B-33 Main Relay [F]	B-34 Igniton Coil (T) [F]
BY YR	BY ✕ Gy / Gy ✕ BY / BY ✕ YG / YG ✕ BY	WL B / W B / RW BW / BY BW	BY—⊚ / YG

Note: ✕···Not Used

Wiring diagram and connectors — 13B engine fuel injection/emissions control systems, ignition and fuel pump (1984 and 1985 models)

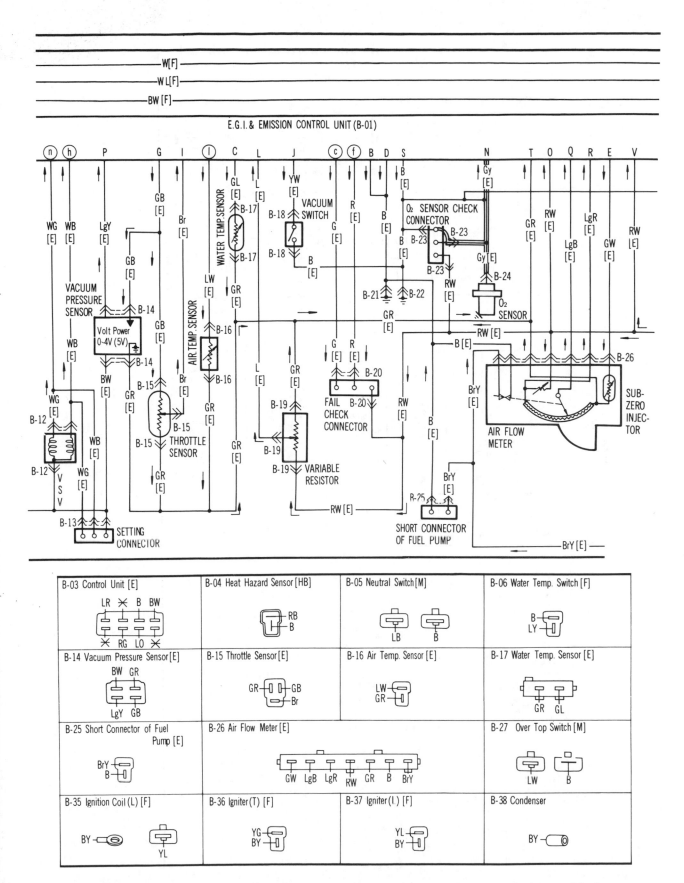

Wiring diagram and connectors — 13B engine fuel injection/emissions control systems, ignition and fuel pump (1984 and 1985 models — continued)

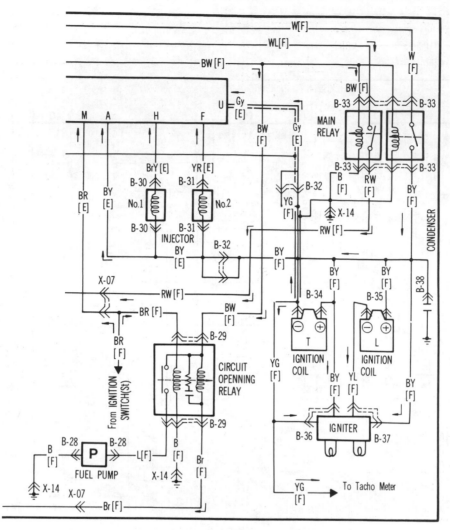

B-07 Air Supply Valve [E]	B-08 Relief Solenoid Valve [E] (Blue)	B-09 Switching Solenoid Valve [E] (Gray)
LW BW	BW LR	BW Lg
B-18 Vacuum Switch [E]	B-19 Variable Resistor [E]	B-20 Fail check Connector [E]
YW B	RW GR L	RW R G
B-28 Fuel Pump [F]	B-29 Circuit Openning Relay [F]	B-30 Injector No.1 [E]
L B	BR BW L B Br	BY BrY
B-39 A.C.V. [E]	B-40 A.C.V. Relay [F]	
LR BW	BW LR LW B	

Wiring diagram and connectors — 13B engine fuel injection/emissions control systems, ignition and fuel pump (1984 and 1985 models — continued)

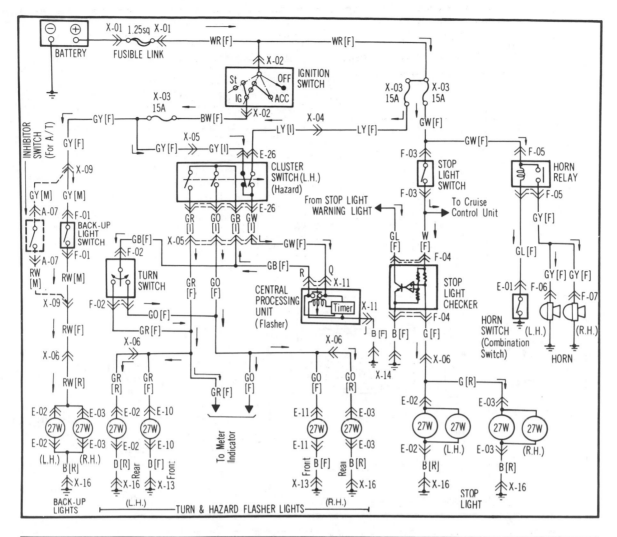

F-01 Back-Up Light Switch [M]	F-02 Turn Switch [F]	F-03 Stop Light Switch [F]	F-04 Stop Light Checker [F]
GY—⊙ RW—⊙	GR ✕ ✕ ✕ GB GO ✕ ✕	GW W	GL W G B
F-05 Horn Relay [F]	F-06 Horn (L.H.) [F]	F-07 Horn (R.H.) [F]	A-07 Inhibitor Switch [M] (For A/T)
GW—□ □—GY —GL	GY—▭	GY—▭	GY BY RW BW
E-01 Combination Switch [F]	E-02 Rear Combination Light (L.H.) [R]	E-03 Rear Combination Light (R.H.) [R]	E-10 Front Combination Light (L.H.) [F]
GL R RW RG RY RL	✕ RW GR B RG G	✕ RW GO B RG G	B—□ □—RG —GR
E-11 Front Combination Light (R.H.) [F]	E-26 Cluster Switch (L.H.) [I]		
B—□ □—RG —GO	GR GW LY LG WG RW M K I E C A N L J H F D B GO GB GY RL B R RY		

Note: ✕ ⋯Not Used

Wiring diagram and connectors — turn signal/hazard flasher/back-up/brake lights and horn (1984 and 1985 models)

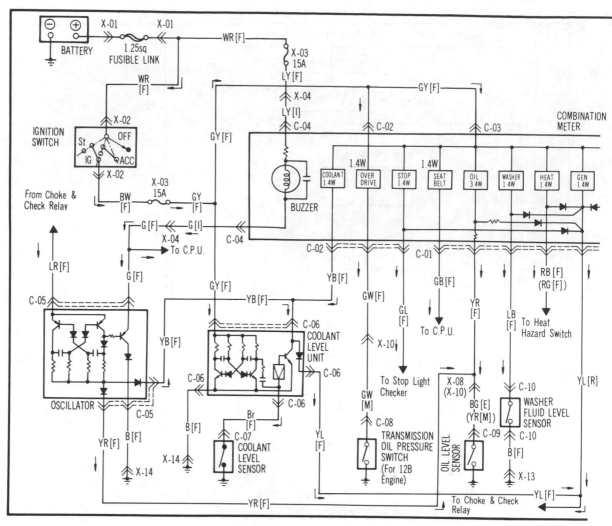

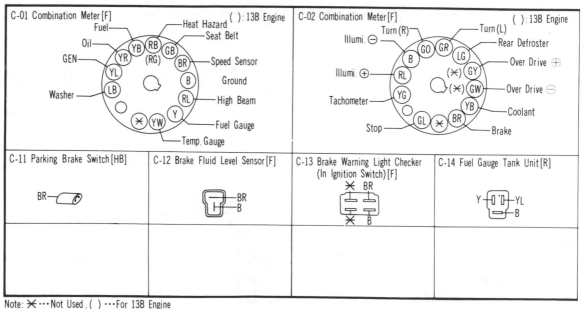

Note: ✳ ···Not Used , ( ) ···For 13B Engine

Wiring diagram and connectors — meters and warning lights (1984 and 1985 models)

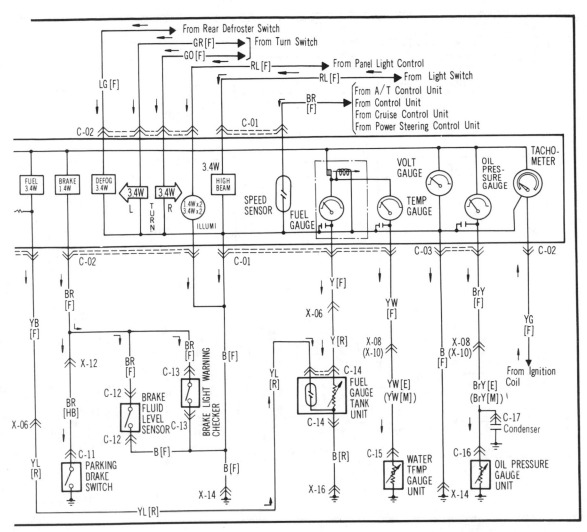

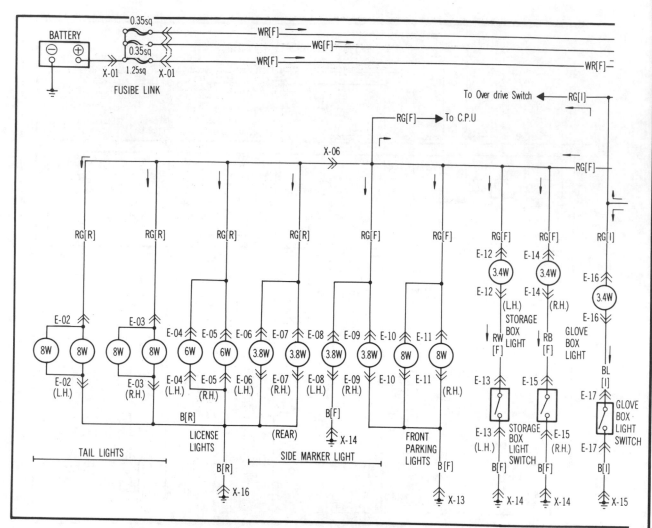

Wiring diagram and connectors — exterior lights and miscellaneous interior lights (1984 and 1985 models)

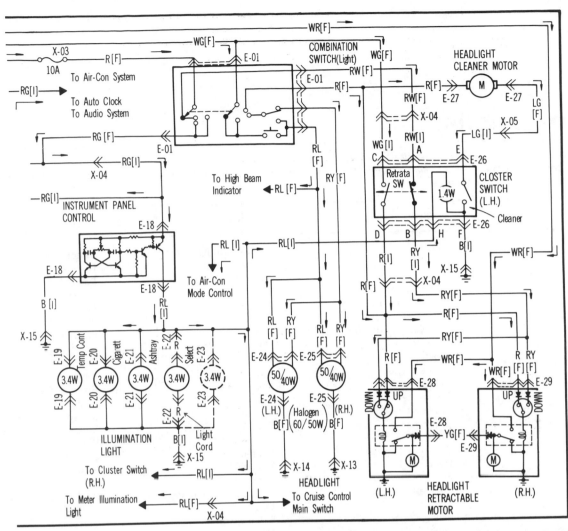

E-05 License Light(R.H.)[R]	E-06 Rear side marker Light(L.H.)[R]	E-07 Rear side marker Light(R.H.)[R]	E-08 Front side marker Light(L.H.)[F]
RG B	B RG	B RG	B RG
E-13 Storage Box Light Swight(L.H.)[F]	E-14 Storage Box Light(R.H.)[F]	E-15 Storage Box Light Switch(R.H.)[F]	E-16 Glove Box Light[I]
RW B	RG RB	RB B	RG BL
E-21 Cigarette Lighter Illumination Light [I]	E-22 Ashtray Illumination Light[I] [I]	E-23 Select Lever Illumination Light[I] (For A/T)	E-24 HeadLight(L.H.)[F]
RL B	R R RL B Light Cord	RL B	B RY RL
E-28 Retractable HeadLight Motor(L.H.)[F]	E-29 Retractable Headlight Motor(R.H.) [F]		
YG RY WR R	RY YG WR R		

Wiring diagram and connectors — exterior lights and miscellaneous interior lights (1984 and 1985 models — continued)

Use of English

As this book has been written in America, it uses the appropriate American component names, phrases, and spelling. Some of these differ from those used in the U.K. Normally, these cause no difficulty, but to make sure, a glossary is printed below. In ordering replacement parts remember the parts list may use some of these words:

American	English	American	English
Antenna	Aerial	Freeway, turnpike etc	Motorway
Gas pedal	Accelerator	License plate	Number plate
Stabilizer or sway bar	Anti-roll bar	Kerosene	Paraffin
Hood	Bonnet (engine cover)	Gasoline (gas)	Petrol
Trunk	Boot (luggage compartment)	Gas tank	Petrol tank
Firewall	Bulkhead	'Pinging'	'Pinking'
Valve lifter or tappet	Cam follower or tappet	Driveshaft	Propeller shaft
Carburetor	Carburettor	Quarter window	Quarter light
Latch	Catch	Recap	Retread
Barrel	Choke/venturi	Back-up	Reverse
Snap-ring	Circlip	Valve cover	Rocker cover
Lash	Clearance	Sedan	Saloon
Ring gear (of differential)	Crownwheel	Frozen	Seized
Rotor/disc	Disc (brake)	Side marker lights	Side indicator lights
Pitman arm	Drop arm	Parking light	Side light
Convertible	Drop head coupe	Muffler	Silencer
Generator (DC)	Dynamo	Wrench	Spanner
Ground	Earth (electrical)	Rocker panel	Sill panel (beneath doors)
Prussian blue	Engineer's blue	Lock (for valve spring retainer)	Split cotter (for valve spring cap)
Station wagon	Estate car	Cotter pin	Split pin
Header	Exhaust manifold	Spindle arm	Steering arm
Troubleshooting	Fault finding/diagnosis	Oil pan	Sump
Float bowl	Float chamber	Tang; lock	Tab washer
Lash	Free-play	Valve lifter	Tappet
Coast	Freewheel	Throw-out bearing	Thrust bearing
Piston pin or wrist pin	Gudgeon pin	High	Top gear
Shift	Gearchange	Tie rod (or connecting rod)	Trackrod (of steering)
Transmission	Gearbox	Secondary shoe	Trailing shoe (of brake)
Axleshaft	Halfshaft	Whole drive line	Transmission
Parking brake	Handbrake	Tire	Tyre
Soft top	Hood	Panel wagon/van	Van
Heat riser	Hot spot	Vise	Vice
Turn signal	Indicator	Lug nut	Wheel nut
Dome lamp	Interior light	Windshield	Windscreen
Countershaft	Layshaft (of gearbox)	Fender	Wing/mudguard
Primary shoe	Leading shoe (of brake)		
Latches	Locks		

Miscellaneous points

An 'oil seal', is also fitted to components lubricated by grease!

A 'shock absorber' is a 'damper', it damps out bouncing and absorbs shocks of bump impact. Both names are correct, and both are used haphazardly.

Note that British drum brakes are different from the Bendix type that is common in America, so different descriptive names result. The shoe end farthest from the hydraulic wheel cylinder is on a pivot; interconnection between the shoes, as on Bendix brakes, is most uncommon. Therefore the phrase 'Primary' or 'Secondary' shoe does not apply. A shoe is said to be 'Leading' or 'Trailing'. A 'Leading' shoe is one on which a point on the drum, as it rotates forward, reaches the shoe at the end worked by the hydraulic cylinder before the anchor end. The opposite is a 'Trailing' shoe and this one has no self servo from the wrapping effect of the rotating drum.

Conversion factors

Length (distance)
Inches (in)	X	25.4	= Millimetres (mm)	X	0.0394	= Inches (in)
Feet (ft)	X	0.305	= Metres (m)	X	3.281	= Feet (ft)
Miles	X	1.609	= Kilometres (km)	X	0.621	= Miles

Inches (in)　X 25.4 = Millimetres (mm)　　X 0.0394 = Inches (in)
Feet (ft)　X 0.305 = Metres (m)　　X 3.281 = Feet (ft)
Miles　X 1.609 = Kilometres (km)　　X 0.621 = Miles

Volume (capacity)
Cubic inches (cu in; in³)　X 16.387 = Cubic centimetres (cc; cm³)　　X 0.061 = Cubic inches (cu in; in³)
Imperial pints (Imp pt)　X 0.568 = Litres (l)　　X 1.76 = Imperial pints (Imp pt)
Imperial quarts (Imp qt)　X 1.137 = Litres (l)　　X 0.88 = Imperial quarts (Imp qt)
Imperial quarts (Imp qt)　X 1.201 = US quarts (US qt)　　X 0.833 = Imperial quarts (Imp qt)
US quarts (US qt)　X 0.946 = Litres (l)　　X 1.057 = US quarts (US qt)
Imperial gallons (Imp gal)　X 4.546 = Litres (l)　　X 0.22 = Imperial gallons (Imp gal)
Imperial gallons (Imp gal)　X 1.201 = US gallons (US gal)　　X 0.833 = Imperial gallons (Imp gal)
US gallons (US gal)　X 3.785 = Litres (l)　　X 0.264 = US gallons (US gal)

Mass (weight)
Ounces (oz)　X 28.35 = Grams (g)　　X 0.035 = Ounces (oz)
Pounds (lb)　X 0.454 = Kilograms (kg)　　X 2.205 = Pounds (lb)

Force
Ounces-force (ozf; oz)　X 0.278 = Newtons (N)　　X 3.6 = Ounces-force (ozf; oz)
Pounds-force (lbf; lb)　X 4.448 = Newtons (N)　　X 0.225 = Pounds-force (lbf; lb)
Newtons (N)　X 0.1 = Kilograms-force (kgf; kg)　　X 9.81 = Newtons (N)

Pressure
Pounds-force per square inch (psi; lbf/in²; lb/in²)　X 0.070 = Kilograms-force per square centimetre (kgf/cm²; kg/cm²)　　X 14.223 = Pounds-force per square inch (psi; lbf/in²; lb/in²)
Pounds-force per square inch (psi; lbf/in²; lb/in²)　X 0.068 = Atmospheres (atm)　　X 14.696 = Pounds-force per square inch (psi; lbf/in²; lb/in²)
Pounds-force per square inch (psi; lbf/in²; lb/in²)　X 0.069 = Bars　　X 14.5 = Pounds-force per square inch (psi; lbf/in²; lb/in²)
Pounds-force per square inch (psi; lbf/in²; lb/in²)　X 6.895 = Kilopascals (kPa)　　X 0.145 = Pounds-force per square inch (psi; lbf/in²; lb/in²)
Kilopascals (kPa)　X 0.01 = Kilograms-force per square centimetre (kgf/cm²; kg/cm²)　　X 98.1 = Kilopascals (kPa)

Torque (moment of force)
Pounds-force inches (lbf in; lb in)　X 1.152 = Kilograms-force centimetre (kgf cm; kg cm)　　X 0.868 = Pounds-force inches (lbf in; lb in)
Pounds-force inches (lbf in; lb in)　X 0.113 = Newton metres (Nm)　　X 8.85 = Pounds-force inches (lbf in; lb in)
Pounds-force inches (lbf in; lb in)　X 0.083 = Pounds-force feet (lbf ft; lb ft)　　X 12 = Pounds-force inches (lbf in; lb in)
Pounds-force feet (lbf ft; lb ft)　X 0.138 = Kilograms-force metres (kgf m; kg m)　　X 7.233 = Pounds-force feet (lbf ft; lb ft)
Pounds-force feet (lbf ft; lb ft)　X 1.356 = Newton metres (Nm)　　X 0.738 = Pounds-force feet (lbf ft; lb ft)
Newton metres (Nm)　X 0.102 = Kilograms-force metres (kgf m; kg m)　　X 9.804 = Newton metres (Nm)

Power
Horsepower (hp)　X 745.7 = Watts (W)　　X 0.0013 = Horsepower (hp)

Velocity (speed)
Miles per hour (miles/hr; mph)　X 1.609 = Kilometres per hour (km/hr; kph)　X 0.621 = Miles per hour (miles/hr; mph)

Fuel consumption*
Miles per gallon, Imperial (mpg)　X 0.354 = Kilometres per litre (km/l)　　X 2.825 = Miles per gallon, Imperial (mpg)
Miles per gallon, US (mpg)　X 0.425 = Kilometres per litre (km/l)　　X 2.352 = Miles per gallon, US (mpg)

Temperature
Degrees Fahrenheit = (°C x 1.8) + 32　　　Degrees Celsius (Degrees Centigrade; °C) = (°F - 32) x 0.56

It is common practice to convert from miles per gallon (mpg) to litres/100 kilometres (l/100km), where mpg (Imperial) x l/100 km = 282 and mpg (US) x l/100 km = 235

Index

Printed by
J H Haynes & Co Ltd
Sparkford Nr Yeovil
Somerset BA22 7JJ England